LIVERPOOL   POLYTECHNIC

Department   of

TOWN   AND   COUNTRY   PLANNING

The Rôle of Public Transport

in New Towns.

A Bibliography and Research Guide with special reference to Runcorn, Skelmersdale and Telford.

by   Mary Alpert
        Lewis Lesley

53, Victoria Street,   February 1979
Liverpool. L1 6EY   ISBN 0 906442 00 1
051 709 0571

ABSTRACT

This bibliography covers literature
relating to a study of the role of public
transport in the new towns of Runcorn,
Skelmersdale and Telford.
Entries are classified under eight main
headings according to subject matter, with
an additional section on sources of
information.   Annotations are presented
for a number of the references and an
authors' index is also included.

Contents

INTRODUCTION.

(a)   The Research Project

The bibliography presented in this report is the result of
an investigation to discover literature and statistical
data relevant to a comparative study of the rôle of public
transport in the three new towns of Runcorn, Skelmersdale
and Telford. This research project, which is expected to
continue for two years from September 1977, is being
conducted within the Department of Town and Country
Planning at Liverpool Polytechnic. The literature survey
which forms the basis of the bibliography represents part
of the initial phase of the study.

The overall objective of the research is to gain a better
understanding of the decision-making process used by
residents in making local journeys in these new towns. To
this end travel needs of residents in the three new towns
will be examined in relation to existing levels of public
transport provision and to the use made of these. A
comparison will be made between existing public transport
provision and use in the three towns and the official goals
for the rôle of public transport as set out initially in
their Master Plans and as expanded or modified in subsequent documents. Later stages of the project will involve
an assessment of residents' perceptions of the quality of
local public transport services in Runcorn, Skelmersdale
and Telford, and an attempt to establish the influence of
consumer perception on choice of travel mode.

The research programme outlined above is clearly closely
concerned with transport and mobility problems in the three
new towns under study and it is hoped that useful practical
findings and recommendations will emerge from the study.
These should include the identification of cost-effective
methods of improving the quality of existing public trans-
prot facilities and of consumer perception of these, which
should benefit both the operators in terms of increased
patronage and enhanced image and the consumer in terms of
better local public transport services.

(b)   The Literature Survey

The literature survey was initiated to provide a theoretical
framework to the practical examination of transport problems
in the three new towns as an aid to their clearer understanding. It has also generated an awareness of research
already done and currently in progress in this and related
fields, of available statistical and other information
sources, and of the relative advantages and disadvantages
of the various research techniques and methodologies which
could be applied in approaching the subject.

A research programme as broad in scope as that outlined above
has necessarily involved, even in the preliminary stages, the
examination of a wide range of published and unpublished

material relating both to transportation and to new towns.
It has touched on the literature of the social sciences
and of psychology in addition to that of urban and transport planning. It was decided at an early stage to
formalise this literature survey into a classified annotated bibliography which would serve as a basis for
subsequent phases of the current research project. The
bibliography should also be a useful preliminary guide to
relevant reading and information sources for other
researchers investigating aspects of transport in new
towns and for practising urban and transport planners and
transport operators working in this and associated fields.
It could also be of use to researchers and practitioners
in related disciplines, such as geographers, architects
or sociologists, who may be examining non-transport
aspects of new or expanded towns and their development.

The amount of formal published material relating to
public transport in British new towns is not abundant,
and what is available tends to be widely dispersed. Much
of it is concerned with specific new towns and very little
comparative assessment has been carried out. In the
course of the current research project it will undoubtedly
be necessary to examine many other aspects of new towns
than those specifically connected with transport, and also
to draw on a broad span of current technical literature in
the fields of transport studies and related disciplines.
Material concerned with research techniques and methodologies will also be examined.

The literature survey has therefore, covered a wide
variety of reports, books, research papers, journal
articles, statistical data and other material considered
to be relevant to a study of public transport in new towns.
The references have been assembled from a number of
sources by several methods. Starting from a small
initial nucleus of books, reports and official Development Corporation material relating to Runcorn, Skelmersdale
and Telford an attempt was made to work outwards from
references contained therein, using the citation analysis
technique. Briefly, this involved assembling citations
from books, papers and journal articles within the given
subject field and making a quantitative analysis of these
in order to identify further relevant literature, to which
the same process was in turn applied. This approach
proved useful in determining a number of key references,
authors and source journals. However, several disadvantages are inherent in the citation analysis method and it
was found not to be entirely suitable for discovering all
the literature relevant to the current research project.
For instance, the method is more appropriate when applied
to fairly narrowly defined areas of study. The broad
scope of this research programme meant that a meticulous
application of citation analysis would have been an
extremely lengthy and laborious task, involving the
danger of the literature search becoming an end in itself
rather than a research tool. Another disadvantage is that
the most recent material is excluded, and owing to the time-
lag before an item enters the citation network and becomes

widely cited there can be an over-emphasis on older
material which may have been superseded by more recent
studies. The results of citation analysis are also
subject to a number of other distortions, including the
not uncommon tendency for researchers to cite works
orginating from within their own research establishment
or sponsoring body. For these and other reasons it was
found that some of the more commonly cited references
were unlikely to be particularly helpful, while certain
more relevant and potentially useful specialised items
were not identified. The citation analysis technique
was therefore supplemented by several other methods of
collecting literature and references. These included
contacts, in many cases involving visits, with the
Development Corporations and with public transport
operators in the three new towns, and with planning and
transportation consultants, researchers and Government
departments actively concerned with areas of study
related to this project. These contacts have provided
much primary data, including reports and results of
a number of relevant surveys. They also gave pointers
to further material likely to be pertinent to the
studies. A number of libraries has also been visited,
and use has been made of several abstracting services.
Searches have been made of appropriate journals, bibliographies, research registers, conference proceedings and
lists of publications produced by various research
establishments and other organisations. Through these
approaches references to a substantial body of additional
literature have been assembled. Details of these various
sources of information are given in Section 9 of this report.

(c)   The Bibliography

An attempt has been made to categorize the references
according to the main focus of their subject matter. The
bibliography is arranged in eight main sections according
to subject matter, several of these being further subdivided. A ninth section lists sources of information,
giving addresses where appropriate, and statistical
sources. A three-point decimal numbering system has been
used for identifying the references, with the first
number denoting the main section, the second the subsection, and the third a unique serial number of each
entry in sequence. The material is arranged as follows:

  1. New Towns (General)

       1.1 Transport and Mobility
       1.2 Non-Transport Aspects

  2. New Towns (Specific)

       2.1 Runcorn
       2.2 Skelmersdale
       2.3 Telford
       2.4 Other New Towns

3. Transport and Mobility (General)

    3.1 Studies of Modal Choice Behaviour and
           Value of Travel Time
    3.2 Social Aspects of Mobility
    3.3 Interaction between Land Use and Travel
    3.4 General and Miscellaneous

4. Public Transport

    4.1 Operational Aspects
    4.2 Marketing Approach
    4.3 Ergonomic Aspects
    4.4 Demonstration Projects and Innovatory Systems
    4.5 General and Miscellaneous

5. Private Motor Transport

6. Non-Motorised Travel

7. Transport Policy

8. Research Techniques and Methodology

    8.1 Survey Techniques: Behavioural and Attitudinal
    8.2 Economic Evaluation
    8.3 General and Miscellaneous

9. Information Sources

    9.1 Journals
    9.2 Bibliographies
    9.3 Abstracting and Indexing Services
    9.4 Research Registers
    9.5 Statistical Sources
    9.6 Other Sources

Each section or subsection is preceded by a brief introduction describing the subject matter covered, explaining the arrangement of the entries where appropriate, and identifying certain key references. These are referred to in the introductory passages by author and/or title, underlined, followed by the reference number in brackets. An alphabetical index of authors follows the bibliography, and this includes second and additional authors of multi-author works.

Within each section or subsection the bibliographic entries are normally arranged alphabetically by title, according to the first word of the key phrase contained therein. Variations from this arrangement have been adopted in the subsections relating to individual new towns (2.1 to 2.4), to transport policy (Section 7) and to information sources (Section 9), and explanatory details are given in the relevant introductory passages. Publications by the Department of the Environment's two specialised research establishments, the Transport and Road Research Laboratory (TRRL) and Building Research Station, are included in the main lists. Other Government reports and publications are listed separately within the subsections, following the main entries. Where it has been necessary to rearrange a title so that the key phrase appears first, the original opening phrase has been bracketed and marked by an asterisk on the left-hand side. For example:-

        A Study in Supplementary Licensing. (1974)
               would read:-
      Supplementary Licensing. [*A Study in] (1974)

This procedure necessarily involves making subjective decisions as to the most significant phrase in the title, but it has the advantage of bringing together (as much as possible) material relating to specific topics within each subsection.

Each title is preceded by the decimal reference number and followed by the date of publication in brackets. The name of the author/s and/or publishing organisation as appropriate is given on the line below. For books, papers and reports this is followed by further details of the publisher and relevant organisation, research establishment or conference, as appropriate. In the case of journal articles the name of the journal is given below that of the author, followed by the volume and issue numbers and further details of the date of publication. Page numbers (preceded by pp....) or number of pages (followed by ...pp.) are given where this information is available. and bracketed. Annotations or abstracts are presented for approximately one-third of the entries. The inclusion of and amount of space given to an annotation does not necessarily reflect the importance that should be attached to the item to which it relates.

It was found when categorizing the references that the subject matter covered by many of them fell into more than one subsection of the classification. In these cases the main entry is recorded in the subsection considered to be most appropriate to the subject matter and subsidiary cross-references are given in other subsections as appropriate. The list of subsidiary references is presented as an appendage to the main entries in each subsection.

The references contained in the bibliography are substantially to British material. However, a number of foreign items, mainly of United States origin, are also included particularly in the sections on Transport and Mobility, Public Transport, and Research Techniques and Methodology.

A degree of subjectivity has had to be exercised in the final selection of items to be included in the bibliography. The main criterion has been relevance to studies of the provision and use of public transport in British new towns with particular reference to Runcorn, Telford and Skelmersdale, either through subject matter or by method of approach. Fresh material is continually becoming available or being discovered and further items will undoubtedly be added to the present list during the course of the research programme. In particular the material relating to perception of transport modes is likely to be expanded substantially as the research proceeds in this direction and could form both the subject matter of a subsequent supplementary bibliography and a separate section in a later version of the current list.

1. New Towns (General).

1.1 Transport and Mobility.

Section 1 of the bibliography provides references to literature relating to new towns in general, to works which include coverage of a number of new towns, and to comparative assessments of two or more new towns. Individual British new towns are covered in Section 2.

Subsection 1.1 covers general and comparative studies of transport and mobility in new towns. The subsidiary references at the end of the subsection list relevant literature relating to specific British new towns from subsections 2.1 - 2.4; items from the general new town literature (subsection 1.2) referring to aspects of transport or mobility; and items from the transport literature (sections 3-7) and information sources sections (9.1-9.6) which have particular relevance to transport in new towns.

The emphasis in subsection 1.1 is on British new towns, but a number of international references have also been included, principally relating to the United States where a substantial body of experience in the planning and functioning of private new communities is accumulating. Much of this experience has relevance to new town studies in this country, despite the considerable differences in concept and reality between British and North American new towns - for instance, in the level of car ownership and usage, amount of employment provided and degree of outward commuting, as well as in the general social and ideological background to their existence.

The following are the more important subject areas covered by the literature listed in this subsection:-

- The historical background and development of transport planning in British new towns.

- Studies of the interrelationship between transport and patterns of land use in the new town context. These include several theoretical analyses and a number of policy-oriented studies.

- Reports of operational experience with public transport in new towns, including studies of the planning and operation of experimental services and innovatory systems.

- Behavioural material on travel patterns and modal choice in new towns, including examinations of journey to work movements in relation to the concept of 'self containment'.

The early background to transport planning in British new towns is documented by POTTER in Volume One of Transport in New Towns (1.1.16) which describes the transport and land use principles of Ebenezer Howard's theoretical Garden City, and those included

in the design of Letchworth and Welwyn Garden Cities. Volume
Two of the trilogy (1.1.17) presents a chronological examination of the transport planning principles underlying the design
of British new towns from 1946, tracing changing emphases
reflecting developments in the wider contexts of urban and
transport planning,and national socio-economic trends generally.

The NEW TOWNS TECHNICAL OFFICERS' COMMITTEE'S Review of Public
Transport in New Towns (1.1.13) includes a brief historical
examination of the rôle of public transport in British new
town planning, taking as its starting point the principles set
out in the Final Report of the New Towns Committee, 1946 (the
'Reith Report'). The review attempts to demonstrate a changing
attitude towards, and increasing emphasis on, public transport
in a number of new towns from about 1964 onwards, although it
also reveals marked differences between new towns in their
approach to public transport provision. The changing trends in
transport provision in British new town master plans are also
discussed by MEADS (1.1.14) in his examination of bus transport
provision in the context of new town configurations.

Several valuable primary sources of historical material are
contained in section 1.2 of the bibliography and are listed
as subsidiary references at the end of this subsection. These
include HOWARD'S Garden Cities of Tomorrow (1.2.13), the Final
Report of the New Towns Committee, 1946 (1.2.55), and the Annual
Reports of the Development Corporations in England and Wales,
from 1947. (1.2.51)

A number of studies have focussed on the relationship between
movement systems and urban form in new towns, both in Britain
and abroad. HILLMAN's thesis Mobility in New Towns - 1970
(1.1.7) determined criteria for an optimal urban structure based
primarily on the relationship between accessibility and population density, in order to assess the efficiency of movement
systems in new towns. A postal survey of individual mobility
in Stevenage indicated that although basic essential and
leisure travel needs were relatively constant, the actual
mobility of individuals in the new town varied substantially
according to their age and household car ownership. Hillman
established that a movement system designed principally for the
needs of pedestrians and public transport (but without restr-
icting car usage) would satisfy the mobility requirements of
individuals of all ages more equitably than systems based on
the requirements of car owning households for motorised movement. Proposals for a new community environment based on this
finding are outlined in the thesis. Other theoretical analyses
of optimal land use/transport configurations in new towns are
presented by POTTER in Volume Three of Transport and New Towns
(1.1.19) and in several North American studies, notably those
relating to Columbia, Maryland, recorded by STEVENS and SMITH
(1.1.6) and STEVENS and BACALIS (1.1.21). STONE's book, The
Structure, Size and Costs of Urban Settlements (3.3.49) reports
a study on the economics of urban form which examined the

Suburb (now withdrawn), and Milton Keynes. The reports by
STEVENS and SMITH (1.1.6), STEVENS and BACALIS (1.1.21) and
BAUMANN et al (1.1.22) describe innovative transit systems in
North American new communities, and that by the U.S. DEPARTMENT
OF HOUSING AND URBAN DEVELOPMENT (1.1.23) presents a review of
international developments which includes a description of
experimental bus services in selected British new towns.

Descriptive data on travel patterns and modal choice behaviour
in British new towns is largely confined to specific new towns:
relatively little systematic comparative investigation has
been carried out to date, but an important exception is the
study of the three County Durham new towns - Aycliffe, Peterlee
and Washington - reported by HUDSON and JOHNSON (1.1.16) in
which the comparative framework was considered by the researchers
to be essential to the evaluation of mobility in particular
new town environments.

Relatively few British researchers have attempted systematic
comparisons of travel behaviour in new towns with that in
older established urban areas. Again, the study by HUDSON and
JOHNSON (1.1.16) is useful in incorporating systematic comparisons of travel behaviour and attitudes between 'New' and 'Old'
Washington. The article by WILLIAMS (1.1.28) includes a more
general comparison between the problems of movement in older
urban areas with those in new towns. The travel surveys
carried out in 1971 by Political and Economic Planning in five
areas, including a ward of a new town, are also of value in the
area of comparative studies although the new town was not
identified in the presentations of the research results by
HILLMAN, HENDERSON and WHALLEY in Personal Mobility and Transport
Policy (3.2.37) and Transport Realities and Planning Policy
(3.2.63). In the United States research conducted by The
University of North Carolina comparing patterns of travel
behaviour and transport provision in planned new communities
with those in conventional suburbs has been reported by ZEHNER
(1.1.2); and MORGAN and DICKEY (1.1.4) have described the
results of a comparative study of travel patterns in a new town
and a suburban development, both on the outskirts of Washington
D.C.

Detailed information on travel patterns in individual new towns
is provided by the Telford Transportation Study (2.3.6), and
the Runcorn Travel Survey and Busway Study (2.1.10 and 2.1.6).
The Glenrothes (2.4.11) and Harlow (2.4.15) Public Transport
Studies also offer relevant and comparatively up-to-date
information on travel patterns. The latter two studies together
with the Telford Transportation Study, (2.3.6), the Telford
Short Term Bus Study (2.3.1) and the Runcorn Busway Study
(2.1.6) are also useful sources of information on transport
provision in these respective new towns.

Less comprehensively, the various household surveys listed in
subsections 2.1 and 2.4 - for instance, those conducted in
Runcorn (2.1.20), Skelmersdale (2.2.8), Harlow (2.4.13), and
Stevenage (2.4.56) - provide data from sample interview surveys
on usual mode of transport to work, school and shops. Several

studies have examined journey to work patterns in and from new
towns, particularly in relation to the London new towns and in
the context of the 'self-containment' concept. These include
the studies by THOMAS (1.1.5 and 1.2.16), the research on
Stevenage reported by CRESSWELL (2.4.53), and that carried out
by the Building Research Station and described by OGILVY
(1.2.11 and 1.2.41). Statistical data on mode of travel to work
in relation to new towns in England and Wales and on the extent
of inward and outward commuting is contained in the 1971
Census volume: England and Wales: Economic Activity New Towns.
(9.5.16)

It is perhaps surprising that relatively little systematic
evaluation of the social impacts of decisions and policies
relating to access and mobility in British new towns has been
carried out to date. HUDSON and JOHNSON have pointed out in
Transport and Mobility in Durham New Towns (1.1.16) that
because new town environments have evolved from what is
essentially a 'land use blueprint' (the master plan) which is
more a reflection of planners' ideologies than a response to
the needs of the people who live there, it is even more
important than in established towns that the effects of the
planners' decisions on residents' lifestyles and quality of
life should be monitored and assessed. Their research is a
useful contribution which relates attitudinal with behavioural
travel data on a comparative basis for Aycliffe, Peterlee,
and both 'New' and 'Old' Washington, and discusses the policy
implications of the findings. Information on other attempts
to link attitudinal with behavioural travel data in new
towns is much more fragmentary, but some material on attitudes
to bus services is included in reports of surveys carried out
in Telford (2.3.1 and 2.3.4), Glenrothes (2.4.11), Harlow
(2.4.15), Runcorn (2.1.6), and Skelmersdale (2.2.8). LICHFIELD's
cost benefit analysis of the effects of alternative future
transport systems in Stevenage (2.4.57) and the Summary Report
of the Stevenage Superbus Experiment (2.4.59) also contain
some relevant material.

1.1. Transport and Mobility

1.1.1. Access and Mobility in New Towns. (1976)
HILLMAN, M. and POTTER, S.
'Perspectives on New Town Development'. Proceedings
of a conference organised by the New Towns Study
Unit and the Regional Studies Association at the
Open University. Nov.1975. (pp.133-156)

This paper examines the assumptions and planning
philosophies underlying the transport goals for the
three new towns of Cumbernauld, Runcorn and Milton
Keynes, and their associated urban forms. The way in
which both urban form and planning philosophies have
been modified in practice are discussed, and the
inherent conflicts between the optimal urban forms
required for the three major transport modes are
examined. The authors recommend a 'balanced' movement system which adequately caters for the travel
needs of all sectors of the population, and point to
the need to interpret such a system in a suitable
urban form.

1.1.2 Access, Travel and Transportation in New Communities. (1977)
ZEHNER, R.B.
Ballinger Publishing Co., Cambridge, Mass., U.S.A.
1977.

The book forms part of a series presenting the
findings of a large scale study and evaluation of
new community development in the United States
carried out by the Center for Urban and Regional
Studies at the University of North Carolina. This
volume summarises the results of the transportation
aspects of the study, which compared patterns of
travel behaviour and transport provision in the
planned new communities with those in conventional
suburban areas in the U.S.A.

1.1.3 Bus Transport in New Towns. (1959)
CHURCHILL, J.D.C.
Town and Country Planning. Vol.27. No.1. January
1959. (pp.41-44).

The article argues that new towns were not planned
in such a way as to help passenger transport
operation, and discusses how planning could help
to make public transport pay.

1.1.4   Characteristics of New Town Travel [*The] :
         A case study of Reston, Virginia.(1974)
         MORGAN, K.R. and DICKEY, J.W.
         Report No. VITSG - 7412, Virginia InterUniversity
         Transportation Study Group. Blacksburg, Virginia, U.S.A.
         May 1974. (81pp.)

         New towns have often been proposed as a significant
         factor in alleviating transportation problems in urban
         areas.   To test this hypothesis a comparative study
         was made between Reston and Vienna, Virginia.   Both
         towns are located on the outskirts of Washington D.C.,
         the former being a new town and the latter a typical
         suburb.   The results of the study refer to automobile
         ownership levels, average total mileage driven,
         average distance for journey to work, average number
         of person trips, the number of walk trips, and the
         roadspace required and noise levels.

1.1.5.   Commuting Flows and the Growth of London's New Towns,
         1951-1971. (1977)
         THOMAS, R.
         The Open University, New Towns Study Unit. April 1977.

1.1.6.   Demand Bus for a New Town.(1971)
         STEVENS, R.D. and SMITH, R.L.
         Highway Research Board Special Report, No. 124.
         Highway Research Board, Washington D.C. 1971. (pp.6-13)
         (see also ref. 1.1.21 below).

         Columbia, Maryland, is a planned cummunity situated
         between Baltimore and Washington D.C. whose 1971
         population of 10,000 is expected to increase tenfold
         by 1982.   An exclusive bus right-of-way is being
         integrated into the land-use plan so that 40% of the
         ultimate population will be within a 3-minute walk.
         A study and demonstration programme are being under-
         taken to determine the optimum transit configuration
         for Columbia and for new towns generally.   The approach
         has been to formulate postulates about transit and
         then to test them through opinion surveys, mathematical
         analysis and experimentation.   Both fixed route and
         demand-actuated systems have been tested as part of
         the experimentation.   The operating characteristics
         of the planned system are described.   A demand analysis
         for 1985 using modal split has also been made for
         various forms of service.   Ridership varied from
         1,300 per day for a low-frequency scheduled bus to
         over 40,000 for a computer-scheduled, demand-
         actuated system.   However, the latter could not
         survive a financial analysis.   On a town-wide basis
         it required too many miles of operation and too many
         vehicles, while on a feeder basis it could not provide
         an acceptable frequency of service without requiring
         a considerable increase in the number of vehicles
         over a scheduled service.

1.1.7   Mobility in New Towns. (1970)
         HILLMAN, M.
         Unpublished Ph.D. Thesis. University of Edinburgh.
                                                       1970.
         (For details see Introduction to this subsection)

1.1.8.   New Towns in Britain (their transport plans).(1973)
         HAWKES, J.E.Y.
         Paper read at Session 7 of: 'Transportation and
         Environment: Policies, Plans and Practice'.
         Proceedings of a Symposium held at the University of
         Southampton, Department of Civil Engineering. April 1973.

1.1.9.   New Towns in the London Transport Area and their
         Passenger Transport. [*The] (1959)
         FERNYHOUGH, G.
         Omnibus Society. November 1959.(11pp.)

1.1.10. Project for a Linear New Town.(1957)   ,
         HILLMAN, M. and LEHRMAN, J.B.
         Architects' Journal. 4th April 1957.(pp.503-507)

1.1.11   Public Transport in a New City (1967)
         BERRETT, B.
         Paper read at Hornsey College of Art Conference, 1967.

1.1.12. Public Transport in its Exclusive Right
         of Way in Evry.(1973)
         FERRAGU, H.
         Equipement, Logement, Transports. Paris, France.
         No. 81/82. September 1973 (pp.41-49)
         (Le Transport en Commun en Site Propre à Evry)

         All major public and private activities in the new
         town of Evry are concentrated in the town centre,
         necessitating an efficient internal public transport
         service.   Details are given of the exclusive right
         of way and services, together with the financial,
         administrative and political problems which arose
         during its setting up.

1.1.13. Public Transport in New Towns [*A Review of](1974)
         NEW TOWNS TECHNICAL OFFICERS' COMMITTEE
         Sub-Committee on Public Transport in New Towns.
         May 1974 (30pp.)

         The report gives a comparative assessment of the aims
         and progress of the British new towns in relation to
         public transport provision up to 1974, based largely
         on the results of a questionnaire distributed to the
         Development Corporations.   It reveals a substantial
         change in attitudes to public transport in new towns
         designated after 1964, but wide variations between
         these towns in the type of approach adopted.   There
         are also separate detailed reports on public transport
         developments in Redditch, Runcorn, Stevenage, Harlow
         and Bracknell and on the results of public transport
         studies carried out in Basildon and Greater Peter-
         borough.

1.1.14.   Public Transport in New Towns in Great Britain.(1971)
MEADS, R.H.
UITP Revue. Vol.20. No.3.1971.(pp.279-285)

This article discusses the provision made for public
transport services in the planning of British new towns,
with the emphasis on bus transport.   Local bus services
in the Mark I new towns faced many problems arising
from the emphasis in their Master Plans on land use
considerations rather than on mobility requirements.
In the planning of more recent new towns, such as
Runcorn and Redditch, public transport
has been treated as an integral part both of the
transport system and of the new town structure itself.

1.1.15.   Public Transportation and the Needs of New Communities.
(1972)
SALLEY, M.A.
Traffic Quarterly.
Vol. 26.No. 1. January 1972. (pp. 33-51)

An attempt is made to determine the general characteristics of transportation systems to meet the social,
economic and human requirements of new cities.   Basic
transportation needs (social, environmental, access
and economic) are identified.   The necessity for some
form of public transport to meet these needs is
established.   Individual and community criteria for
transit systems are developed, and a public transport
system which satisfies all criteria,for example the
dial-a-bus system, is suggested.

1.1.16.   Transport and Mobility in Durham New Towns.(1974-5)
HUDSON, R. and JOHNSON, M.R.D.
Working Paper No.16. Durham University North East
Area Study. 1974-75.

1.1.17.   Transport and New Towns. Volume One.
The Historical Perspective - The development of
Transportation planning for new communities,
1898-1939. (1976)
POTTER, S.
The Open University, New Towns Study Unit.
July 1976. (63 pp.)

The original conception of Ebenezer Howard's
theoretical Garden City is described.   A model of
this theoretical city was tested using the results of
the 1901 Census.   Details are given of the principles
of Howard's "Social City", consisting of six pedestrianised Garden Cities surrounding a larger Central
City (population 58,000).   All would be linked by
major roads and an 'Inter-Municipal Railway'.   The
first two Garden Cities, Letchworth and Welwyn Garden
Cities, are described together with the land use and
road network principles utilised.   Some smaller-scale
'Garden City' developments in the United States are
discussed, including Radburn, New Jersey.

1.1.18. Transport and New Towns. Volume Two.
The Transport Assumptions Underlying the Design of
Britain's New Towns. 1946-1976 (1976).
POTTER, S.
The Open University, New Towns Study Unit.
December 1976. (208 pp.)

This volume describes the first new towns built in
the United Kingdom between 1946-1950 : Stevenage,
Crawley, Cwmbran, Harlow and Aycliffe. From 1950
onwards the concept of compact new towns was evolved
and examples of this are given in Cumbernauld, Boston
Manor, Hook, Skelmersdale and Andover Expanded Town.
The influence of the Buchanan Report : 'Traffic in
Towns' on transport planning in new towns since 1963
is discussed. The term "mobility" and its definition
in a planning context were introduced in the latter
half of the 1960's. The Runcorn Experiment is cited
as an example of the application of this concept, and
details are given of the plan drawn up for Milton
Keynes and of its implementation from 1973. The
development of public transport priority in new towns
and the importance given to pedestrians and cyclists in
the planning of new towns are examined. In conclusion
the principles of design and the application of those
principles after eighty years' experience are discussed.

(Part of Transport and New Towns has now been
updated by the author into: The Rôle of Segregation
Planning and the Pedestrian/Vehicle Conflict in
Britain's New Towns. New Towns Study Unit.
                                              April 1978.)

1.1.19. Transport and New Towns. Volume Three.
Conflicts and Externalities in New Town Transport
Plans. (1977)
POTTER, S.
The Open University, New Towns Study Unit.
February 1977. (158 pp.)

The author examines the nature and inter-relation-
ship of the major external costs and benefits arising under different transport policies in the
planning of a new town. The conflicting optimal
requirements of the three major forms of transport
(car, public transport, and walking/cycle) are
discussed. The major intangible externalities
are examined under the general headings of health
and safety considerations and environmental
factors. Several studies which have attempted to
quantify transport infrastructure costs in alternative urban designs are critically discussed.
Finally, an example of three possible alternative
land use/transport designs for a theoretical new
town of 100,000 people is used to illustrate the
overall effects of the externalities previously
examined. An analysis of the major quantifiable
and non-quantifiable costs and benefits indicates
clear financial and socio-environmental gains in
public transport and pedestrian/public transport-
oriented designs as compared with a car-oriented
design. However, cost benefit analysis was not

23

able to show a clear advantage between the two
non-car-oriented designs and the author concludes
that a subjective value judgement would be needed
finally to decide the balance of relative advantages between these two designs in any particular
case.

1.1.20   Transport Planning. (1968)
PROUDLOVE, J.A.
Town Planning Review. Vol.39. No.2. July 1968.
(pp. 85-98)
A review of transport planning in British new towns
based on the illustrated inaugural lecture given by
Professor Proudlove in February 1968 at the University
of Liverpool, entitled : 'New Towns - or transport
test-beds?'

1.1.21.   Transportation for a New Town. (1971)
STEVENS, R.D. and BACALIS, G.J.
Highway Research Record No.367.
Highway Research Board. Washington D.C. 1971.
(pp. 9 - 16).
(see also ref. 1.1.6. above)

Columbia, Maryland, is a new town currently under
construction in the Baltimore-Washington corridor.
The transportation system for the town includes a
street network, a pathway network and a proposed
innovative transit system. The transit system design
evolved from a systematic study of Columbia's needs
in the context of available technology. This paper
describes the methods and results of forecasts of
public transport ridership made for several alternative
transit configurations. The recommended system would
consist of 300 six-passenger vehicles operating au-
tomatically on 17 miles of two-way exclusive right-of-
way, and ten 25-passenger buses operating as a feeder
service to the automatic system. A majority of the
trip origins and destinations would be within a
3-minute walk of one of the 46 stations on the exclusive right-of-way. It was estimated that the
system would attract around 17% of total trips and
that it would be financially feasible.

1.1.22.   Transportation for New Towns and Communities.
[*Workshop on] (1969)
BAUMANN, D. et al.
Institute of Public Administration. New York.
December 1969. (310 pp.)
Several papers on transport systems in new town
developments are included.

1.1.23. Transportation Innovations in New Communities Abroad. (1973)
U.S.DEPARTMENT OF HOUSING AND URBAN DEVELOPMENT
Washington D.C., U.S.A. No.19. December 1973 (15 pp.)

The private car, while the most popular form of transportation, has more than its share of negative effects, especially in an urban area. One of these has been to discourage people from using public transport. Technology in improving old systems and creating viable new ones is being implemented to help solve urban transport problems. Developments in Germany, France, Japan, Sweden and Britain are reviewed and the British new town concepts and experimental bus services for some of these new towns are described. The general conclusion is that car ownership will remain high but that efficient public transport will satisfy demand from those without cars available and divert some car owners to using public transport.

1.1.24. Transportation Inputs in New Town Planning. (1969)
ABEND, N.A.
Traffic Quarterly. Vol.23. No.2. April 1969. (pp.243-261).

The author discusses the importance of land use considerations, public transportation and road network planning in the preliminary design of roadway systems in new communities. Mention is made of the rôle of electronic computation, trip distribution and traffic assignment models. The necessity for integrating economic and social factors from the conceptual stage of transport planning is stressed.

1.1.25. Transportation Planning for New Towns. (1969)
MORRIS, R.L.
Highway Research Record No.293. Highway Research Board. Washington D.C. 1969. (pp.104-116)

New towns offer transportation planners an opportunity to build on the basic research that has been carried out in urban areas in recent years. Employment opportunities juxtaposed with residential development can reduce trip lengths. Good-quality public transport operation can be feasible and exclusive rights-of-way can ensure good public transport services at relatively low cost.

1.1.26. Urban Cluster Villages. (1976)
KOSCHADE, J.B.
Australian Road Research. Nunawading, Victoria, Australia. Vol.6. No.4. December 1976. (pp.35-38).

This discussion paper suggests that the form of urban extensions to our cities and new towns should be reassessed and designed to ensure that public transport

25

systems can offer more effective competition with private transport in a suburban context. This is relevant to energy considerations and it proposes one form of integrated land use and transport planning. The paper also suggests that social integration and amenity may be improved by a 'residential village' formation within the suburban context.

1.1.27. Urban Public Transport.(1971)
        GLENROTHES DEVELOPMENT CORPORATION.
        Department of Architecture, Planning and Quantity
        Surveying. Glenrothes, Scotland. May 1971.(101 pp.)

        This report outlines the advantages and disadvantages of public and private transport and discusses the relation between public transport and land use planning. Details are given of various methods of improving bus operation and three public transport case studies are described, viz: Stevenage, Milton Keynes and Runcorn new towns.

1.1.28. Urban Transportation: Problems and Progess.(1972)
        WILLIAMS, T.E.H.
        The Highway Engineer. Vol. XIX. No. 5. May 1972.
        (pp. 9-22)

        The general inter-relation of urban form, land use, and traffic movements is considered in relation to environment. Comparisons are made between the problems of older urban areas and new towns. Some of the current research and development projects in the field of advanced urban transportation systems are described, with particular reference to dial-a-bus and cabtrack.

GOVERNMENT REPORTS AND PUBLICATIONS.

1.1.29   Financing of New Town Transport Requirements. (1976)
        DEPARTMENT OF THE ENVIRONMENT.
        H.M.S.O. 1976.

1.1 Subsidiary References.

1.2 New Towns - Non-Transport Aspects.

1.2.11   *Employment Expansion and the Development of New Town Hinterlands.*
                                                1961-1966. (1971)
1.2.13   *Garden Cities of Tomorrow. (1965 edition)*
1.2.41   *The Self-Contained New Town: employment and population. (1968)*
1.2.50   *Commission for the New Towns: Annual Reports.*
1.2.51   *Annual Reports of the Development Corporations.*
1.2.55   *Final Report of the New Towns Committee. (1946)*

2.1 Runcorn.

2.1.1-11

2.2 Skelmersdale

_2.2.1-2_

2.3 Telford.

2.3.1-8,2.3.14 and 2.3.21

2.4 Other New Towns.

_2.4.6_   Traffic and Transport in Crawley. (1971)
_2.4.11_   Glenrothes Area Public Transport Study: Final Report. (1977)
_2.4.13-23_ [Harlow]
_2.4.26-27_ [Irvine]
2.4.31-34,2.4.36-39 and 2.4.42 [Milton Keynes]
_2.4.45_   Cycleways for Greater Peterborough. (1973)
_2.4.47_   Transport in Peterlee. (1961)
2.4.53-62 and 2.4.64 [Stevenage]

3.2 Social Aspects of Mobility.

_3.2.8_   Planning for Disabled People in the Urban Environment. (1969)
_3.2.11_   Bus Passes and the Elderly: A Need for More Informed Policy
                   Making? (1976)
_3.2.12_   An Examination of the Extent and Welfare Implications of Bus
                   Use by the Elderly in Harlow. (1977)
_3.2.37_   Personal Mobility and Transport Policy. (1973)
_3.2.49_   Some Social Aspects of Public Passenger Transport. (1977)
_3.2.63_   Transport Realities and Planning Policy. (1976)

3.3 Interaction between Land Use and Travel.

_3.3.21_   Passenger Transport as an Urban Element. (1976)
_3.3.49_   The Structure, Size and Cost of Urban Settlements. (1973)

4.1 Public Transport - Operational Aspects.

_4.1.89_   Planning for Public Transport. (1976)
             [Includes a brief description of transport planning in British
                   new towns - pp.94-96.]

4.4 Public Transport - Demonstration Projects and Innovatory Systems.

_4.4.16_   Dial-a-Ride in Britain: Experience to mid-1974 and Research
                   Programme. (1974)
_4.4.41_   Promotion of Urban Public Transport. (1973)

6.1 Non-Motorised Travel.

_6.1.4_   Planning for the Cyclist in Urban Areas. (1968)
             [Includes reference to cycleways in British new towns.]
_6.1.6_   The Peachtree City Path Experience. (1974)
_6.1.9_   People First in Transport Planning: did they get it wrong at
             Radburn and will it be right at Cumbernauld? (1977)

9.4 Research Registers.

*9.4.6   1977 Summary of Research being Undertaken in New Towns. (1977)
          [Includes a number of projects investigating various aspects
                                     of transport in new towns.]*

9.5 Statistical Sources.

*9.5.16   Census of Population. [The volume: Census 1971: England and
          Wales: Economic Activity New Towns (10% Sample) gives figures
          of method of transport to work for individual new towns.
          Statistics on car availability in new towns are given in:
          Census 1971: England and Wales: Availability of Cars.]*

9.6 Other Sources of Information.

*9.6.2   National Index of Traffic and Transportation Surveys. (1975)
          [Includes details of traffic and transportation surveys in
                                     several new towns.]*

9.6.14   New Towns in the U.K. (1977)

1.2   Non-Transport Aspects.

This subsection includes literature on new communities
which, although not relating primarily to transport, provides
a broader basis for the understanding of transport/mobility
patterns and problems in new towns.   Those general works
which contain specific reference to transport or mobility
are cross-referenced at the end of subsection 1.1, and those
which include substantial reference to individual new towns
are cross-referenced under the relevant subsection in
Section 2.   The material included is not restricted to the
28 British new towns designated under the 1946 and 1965 New
Towns Acts: some items have been incorporated which relate
to other new community developments, including town expansion
schemes arising from the 1952 Town Development Act (1957 in
Scotland), and new housing estates in other urban areas.
The references are drawn predominantly from British experience,
but some international material has also been included.

A substantial and growing volume of literature on new towns
is available.   The selected items included in this subsection
relate particularly to the following dimensions:-

- The general philosophical and legislative background
  to the development of new towns in Britain.

- The social and economic functioning of new communities.

- The spatial aspects of the planning and design of new
  towns.

The British new towns movement is widely considered to have
had its main impetus in the general ideas and detailed
proposals set out in EBENEZER HOWARD'S Tomorrow: a Peaceful
Path to Real Reform - 1898, which was revised and reissued
in 1902 as Garden Cities of Tomorrow (1.2.13).   In these
books Howard presented and developed the concept of creating
complete new social and functional structures (the 'Garden
City' and the 'Social City')as a solution to the urban problems
associated with Nineteenth Century industrial development.
Although not all Howard's ideas were original the 'Social
City' was a fundamental advance over most other more piecemeal
contemporary attempts to design and build pleasanter urban
environments,   such as those at Port Sunlight and Bourneville
Village.   The development of the British new towns movement
through the first half of the Twentieth Century has been
described by a number of authors.   Outlines are presented
by SCHAFFER both in The New Town Story (1.1.27), and in
Chapter Two of New Towns: the British Experience, edited by
EVANS (1.2.33).   F.J. OSBORNE and A. WHITTICK in The New Towns:
the Answer to Megalopolis (1.2.32) describe the work of
Howard, the planning of Letchworth and Welwyn Garden City,
the evolution of new town policy and the development of the
first towns designated under the 1946 New Towns Act.

Other historial accounts are provided in Social Development
Work in the New Communities, by HORROCKS (1.2.43) and in VEAL'S
New Communities in the U.K: A Classified Bibliography (9.2.20),
and Recreation Planning in New Communities (1.2.39), which
examines the particular aspect of recreation planning in the
context of new community development from the Nineteenth
Century.

The Reports of the New Towns Committee - 1946 (1.2.55) and the
New Towns Acts (1.2.54) are the principal primary sources of
background material concerning the legislation, administration
and planning of new towns in the U.K. During the early 1940's
the building of new towns became an important component of
Government policy for post-war reconstruction and national
planning. During the inter-war years the Town and Country
Planning Association (formerly the Garden Cities Association)
had played an influential rôle in promoting the idea of garden
cities generally, and in particular in lobbying for political
support for the building of new towns as part of a national
planning policy. The report of the Royal Commission on the
Distribution of the Industrial Population (the 'Barlow Report')
in 1939 had recommended a policy of developing and expanding
towns to prevent unrestrained urban and industrial sprawl.
The Scott Report on the Utilization of Land in Rural Areas (1942)
also recommended the development of garden cities and satellite
towns, and Abercrombie's Greater London Plan of 1944 included
proposals for syphoning off population and industry from the
capital to a series of satellite new towns. In the context of
the growing body of opinion in favour of developing planned
new communities around London the New Towns Committee was set
up under the chairmanship of Lord Reith in 1945 to consider all
aspects arising from the establishment of new towns and to
suggest the principles on which these towns should be developed
as 'self-contained and balanced communities for work and living'.
The First and Second Interim Reports of the Reith Committee dealt
with the questions of the agency by which the new towns should
be developed and the legislation needed; the Final Report set
out detailed planning principles. Together the three reports
constituted a blueprint for the development of new towns which
became the basis of the first post-war Government's new towns
policy as set out in the 1946 New Towns Act. The 1965 New Towns
Act consolidates a number of modifications made to the 1946 Act
during the 1950's and early 1060's, and other minor amendments
are set out in subsequent Acts. Since 1976 Government policy
has been seen to shift away from further expansion of the new
towns programme and towards greater concern with inner city renewal. Town and Country Planning magazine records and discusses
all important policy developments affecting new towns, and the
article by STRANZ in the June 1977 issue (1.2.10) traces these
changes as expressed in statements made by the Secretary of State
for theEnvironment between August 1976 and April 1977. Hansard
(9.6.11) is also a valuable and detailed source of background
material to official policy on new towns. For instance, the
Secretary of State for the Environment's statement on the Reappraisal of the New Towns Programme on 5th April 1977 was reported
in Vol.929, C.1110-25. This was the first comprehensive Government reappraisal of the programme since the mid-1960's, and
included the announcement of reduced population targets for
several new towns, including Telford. The NEW TOWNS ASSOCIATION'S
monthly New Towns Bulletin presents summaries of Parliamentary
references to new towns.

The British new towns movement originally developed out of concern
with social problems and the amount of attention that has subsequently been given to the social aspects of new town planning
and development is reflected in the large volume of literature on
the subject. The Needs of New Communities - the report of the
CENTRAL HOUSING ADVISORY COMMITTEE, chaired by Professor
CULLINGWORTH (1.2.53) - is a basic text on social provision in new
and expanding communities. Following the publication of this
report in 1967 a research programme on Social Planning in New
Communities was initiated at Birmingham University's Centre for
Urban and Regional Studies from wich a number of reports has resulted.
The study by HORROCKS (1.2.43) considers the social aspects of new
town legislation and describes the results of an examination of the
work of Social Development staff in new communities. VEAL'S report
on Recreation Planning in New Communities (1.2.39) considers the
recreation content of plans for new communities in Britain and
examines problems in recreation provision. These and other papers
produced as a result of this research programme contain summaries
of all previous publications arising from the project. NICHOLSON'S
New Communities in Britain: Achievements and Problems (1.2.23)
examines social problems arising from new housing, and Community
Organisation in Britain (1.2.7)edited by KUENSTLER and published in
the same year (1961) includes contributions on social problems in
new towns and on housing estates. More recently, WIRZ'S book,
Social Aspects of Planning in New Towns (1.2.42) presents a detailed
examination of social development in new towns, with specific reference to East Kilbride, Glenrothes and Livingston. The chapter
on'Planning for People' (Ch.13) in PORTEOUS'S Environment and
Behavior (3.4.1) also includes a concise discussion of attempts to
plan for social balance within new towns, paricularly in relation
to the neighbourhood unit concept, and points to more detailed
studies in this field. On a more specific level, ARMEN'S two
articles on the Programming of Social Development in New Towns
(1.2.46) discuss the problems of assessing and predicting demand
for social facilities in new communities and of developing a
theoretical framework as a basis for comparative assessments.
G.BROOKE TAYLOR has written a number of papers and articles on
social development in new towns, including the chapter on Social
Development in New Towns: the British Experience (1.2.33) and the
article in Built Environment which identifies some problems of
social provision in new towns and suggests   remedial policy
measures. (1.2.47)

Residents' attitudes towards and reactions to new towns in which
they live can provide important 'feedback' on the success or
otherwise of various aspects of planning and policy. A useful
general bibliographical reference, based largely on experience
in the United States, is provided by the annotated bibliography
compiled by GLANCE AND FREUND (9.2.30). Material of this
type relating to British new towns is relatively scattered and
little is available on a general comparative level. The chapter
entitled A Consumer's View by PITT in New Towns: the British
Experience (1.2.33) discusses the contribution made by various
facets of the new town environment to the quality of life
experienced by and expected by the residents, making particular
reference to the London new towns.

The paper by CRESSWELL (1.2.15) also discusses residents'
and prospective residents' attitudes and expectations. The
University of Durham has carried out a study of attitudes to
and perceptions of new towns in County Durham as part of its
North East Area Study, part of which is reported in the paper
by HUDSON and JOHNSON (1.2.1). Most other work in this field
is restricted to studies of individual new towns, several of
which are listed in the subsidiary references at the end of
this subsection. A number of new town household surveys have
attempted to measure residents' levels of satisfaction with
specific aspects of the town (such as housing, shopping and
health facilities) or with the town in general. Quantitative
assessments are included, for instance, in the annual Skelmersdale New Town Population and Social Surveys (2.2.8), the
Harlow 1976 Household Survey (2.4.13) and the social and
economic survey carried out by STRATHCLYDE UNIVERSITY at
East Kilbride in 1970 (2.4.9). More detailed qualitative
information is contained in the reports of the major social
studies carried out by Social and Community Planning Research
in Runcorn in 1972 and 1974, reported by BERTHOUD and JOWELL
(2.1.24) and PRESCOTT-CLARKE and STOWELL (2.1.25), and on a
smaller scale in TELFORD DEVELOPMENT CORPORATION'S pilot study
of new residents' initial reactions to Telford and to their
move in general, reported in: To Me-This is Telford.(2.3.24)

Economic activities in new towns have been the subject of a
substantial amount of research. Studies of daily work
movements into and out of the London ring of new towns by
OGILVY (1.2.11 and 1.2.41), CRESSWELL (2.4.53) and THOMAS
(1.1.5 and 1.2.16) have been mentioned in the introduction
to subsection 1.1. A recent publication based on research
carried out at the University of Newcastle Upon Tyne * presents
net commuting flows in diagrammatic form for each new town
in England, Scotland and Wales together with statistical
profiles based on 1971 Census data and a brief discussion of
the salient socio-economic characteristics of each town. The
book also contains a general discussion of economic activities
and commuting characteristics of British new towns and a more
detailed examination of the economic activities of the new
towns within their regional contexts. On a less comprehensive
scale REASON'S unpublished thesis examines the employment and
industrial structure of five British new towns including Runcorn,
Skelmersdale and Telford (1.2.12), and the specific topic of
office employment in new towns is considered in the article
by DANIELS (1.2.36).

---

* Facts About the New Towns: a socio-economic digest. (1977)

  CHAMPION, A.G., CLEGG, K. and DAVIES, R.L. (University of
  Newcastle Upon Tyne.)

  Retailing and Planning Associates. (268 pp.)

The distinction between the social and spatial aspects of planning and development is of course arbitrary. It is however a convenient one to use in discussing literature on the earlier (Mark I and II) British new towns, which were developed according to 'blueprints' which preceded the build-up of incoming population and which would substantially affect the lifestyles of both new and original residents. The physical plans have therefore been the subject of considerable attention and discussion. Much of this commentary however has focussed on the master plan proposals for individual new towns (see subsections 2.1 - 2.4) or on specific spatial aspects such as net residential densities and the distribution of land uses. GOLANY'S book: New Town Planning: principles and practice (1.2.26) presents a comprehensive analysis of the processes, principles and practice of the planning and development of new towns based on worldwide experience, but there has been relatively little theo-retical research into the general principles underlying new town design in Britain. The chapter by GIBBERD in New Towns: the British Experience (1.2.33) discusses specific design aspects of some of the British new towns, concentrating particularly on the Mark I towns. Plans for later (Mark III) new towns, such as those for Telford, Milton Keynes and Warrington have attempted to incorporate a greater degree of flexibility, freedom of individual choice and public participation. LLEWELYN DAVIES in the same book (1.2.33 and 2.4.39) outlines the effect on new town rôles of social and economic changes which took place between 1950 and 1970, and considers the implications of these on design objectives for the Mark III new towns, referring particul-arly to Milton Keynes.

Largely in an attempt to investigate the basis of criticisms that the early new towns were planned at densities which were excessively wasteful of land, detailed research into their quantitative land use structures was carried out in the early 1960's and has been fully reported by BEST. An outline of the results of this research, based on data for the first fifteen new towns, and of similar research on nine subsequently designated new towns is presented by BEST in New Towns: the British Experience (1.2.33 -Chapter 3). The later study is also described by CHAMPION in the article Recent Trends in New Town Densities - 1970 (1.2.25). Both investigations found that overall new town densities were reasonably typical of those in existing towns with similar populations, although there were considerable variations in the space standards adopted both in total provision of land and in net housing densities. Land use and densities of develop-ment for both new and established settlements were considered in some detail in the research project on the economics of urban form carried out by the National Institute of Economic and Social Research in the late 1960's. The results of this examination of the effects of size, shape and form on costs of construction for various theoretical model settlements are set out by STONE in The Structure, Size and Costs of Urban Settlements. (3.3.49). In the early 1970's a series of comparative studies of specific spatial aspects of new town master plans, including densities and land uses, was carried out at the Centre for Land Use and Built Form Studies at Cambridge University (now the Martin Centre for Architectural and Urban Studies).

Some results of this research programme, together with methodological background information, are presented in the Working Papers by COOPER, LINDSAY, CHEESMAN, TAYLOR and DE PORZECANSKI (1.2.28, 1.2.30, 1.2.31, 1.2.34, 1.2.35).

The distribution of local shopping facilities is an aspect of both land use planning and social provision which has particular relevance to studies of personal accessibility and mobility. The articles by GUY (1.2.21) and GOSS (1.2.22) both examine the provision of and need for local shopping in new towns.

The principal bibliographies on new towns are listed in subsection 9.2 (refs. 9.2.19 - 30). Some other bibliographies are provided as appendages to books or reports which are listed in this subsection. GOLANY'S New Town Planning and Development : A Worldwide Bibliography is a major source of international references on new towns, containing over 4,500 items. The most comprehensive British bibliography (which also includes some references on new towns abroad) is the list of over 2,600 items compiled by the Headquarters Library of the DEPARTMENTS OF THE ENVIRONMENT AND TRANSPORT, which is updated approximately every three years (9.2.27). The NEW TOWNS ASSOCIATION regularly produces a much smaller but up-to-date list of current references on British new towns (9.2.25), and fresh additions to the literature are listed each year in the February edition of TOWN AND COUNTRY PLANNING magazine (1.2.48). Other bibliographies are contained in several of the basic general texts on British new towns, including New Towns: the British Experience edited by EVANS (1.2.33) and The New Town Story by SCHAFFER (1.2.27). The Catalogues of the U.K. Department of the Environment Library produced by G.K.HALL & CO.(9.2.40) also contain numerous references on the history, planning and development of new towns; the subject index includes entries on various aspects of new towns as well as on individual towns. Several of the bibliographies available are concerned with specific aspects of new towns. These include those published as a result of Birmingham University CENTRE FOR URBAN AND REGIONAL STUDIES' research on new communities: the lists compiled by VEAL draw together material on the social aspects of new communities (9.2.20 -21) and on recreation in new communities (1.2.39); and that by HORROCKS relates to writings by and about Social Development Officers (1.2.43).

The main sources of statistical data on British new towns are listed under the heading: 'Statistical Sources' at the end of this subsection. The 1971 Census (9.5.16) provides the most detailed published information on population, households and economic activities for all new towns, and further unpublished Census data can be obtained from the

Census Office. The recently published book : Facts About The New Towns presents summaries of socio-economic statistics for individual new towns, based on 1971 Census data. However, the 1971 Census data is at the time of writing some seven years old, although some of it has only recently been published, and a time lapse of this order can be particularly significant in new towns. More up-to-date - although less detailed - figures on population, housing and other aspects of development are presented quarterly in the NEW TOWNS DIRECTORATE'S 'Publicity Sheet'(9.5.21); and annually in the February issue of Town and Country Planning magazine(1.2.48), the Annual Reports of the Development Corporations in England and Wales (1.2.51) and of the Commission for the New Towns (1.2.50), and in Local Government Trends, published by the CHARTERED INSTITUTE OF PUBLIC FINANCE AND ACCOUNTANCY (9.5.19). Detailed household surveys provide another source of statistical data on individual new towns which can be particularly useful when carried out at regular intervals, such as SKELMERSDALE DEVELOPMENT CORPORATION'S Annual Population and Social Surveys (2.2.8). However, care must be exercised in using household survey data comparatively for different new towns since no standard methodological base has been adopted.

Among other sources of information, the Reports of the House of Commons Expenditure Committee on New Towns - 1974 (1.2.52) contain much general and detailed material; and information on current developments is included in The NEW TOWNS ASSOCIATION'S monthly publication, the New Towns Bulletin (9.1.32); in HANSARD (9.6.11); and in Town and Country Planning magazine (1.2.48). New Towns in the U.K.(9.6.14) compiled by the Headquarters Library of the DEPARTMENTS OF THE ENVIRONMENT AND TRANSPORT is a valuable preliminary guide to sources of information which draws together details of organisations and publications covering many aspects of new towns in this country.

Abstracting and Indexing services which can be used for identifying source material on new towns are listed in the subsidiary references at the end of this subsection, under the sub-heading 9.3. Information on current research relating to British new towns is presented in the NEW TOWNS ASSOCIATION's regular summaries of Research Being Undertaken in New Towns (9.4.6) and in the Environmental Planning subsection of the DEPARTMENT OF THE ENVIRONMENT'S annual Register of Research (9.4.1). Details of publications arising from specific research programmes on new communities are available from the Open University NEW TOWNS STUDY UNIT (9.4.17) and Birmingham University's CENTRE FOR URBAN AND REGIONAL STUDIES (9.4.20).

International experience in the planning and development of new communities is drawn together in the books by GOLANY (1.2.26), by BURBY III and WEISS (1.2.24), and in New Perspectives on Community Development edited by APGAR IV(1.2.6). OSBORN and WHITTICK'S The New Towns: the Answer to Megalopolis (1.2.32) also incorporates a survey of new town development throughout the world.

1.2   Non-Transport Aspects

1.2.1   Attitudes to New Towns in County Durham.
[*Survey of] (1975)
HUDSON, R. and JOHNSON, M.R.D.
Working Paper No. 15.   Durham University North
East Area Study.   1974-1975.   (36pp.)

1.2.2   Aycliffe to Cumbernauld : a study of seven new towns
in their regions. (1969)
THOMAS, R.
P.E.P.   Broadsheet 516.   1969. (162pp.)

The basic aims of the new town planners are
compared with the outcome some 20 years later.

1.2.3   Britain's New Towns and Cities. (1972)
THOMAS, W.
Paper read at the Second Meeting of the Urban
Environment Sector Group, O.E.C.D., Paris. April   1972.

1.2.4   Britain's New Towns : an experiment   in living. (1961).
DUFF, A.C.
Pall Mall Press. 1961.   (108pp.)

1.2.5   British Townscapes. (1965)
JOHNS, E.
Edward Arnold. 1965. (210pp.)

See especially Ch.11.   'The Modern Town'.(pp.161-179)

1.2.6   Community Development.   [*New Perspectives on] (1976)
APGAR IV, M. (ed.)
McGraw Hill. 1976.   (363pp.)

Includes a chapter on the British new towns.
(pp.23-37).

1.2.7   Community Organisation in Britain. (1961)
KUENSTLER, P.   (ed.)
Faber. 1961. (164pp.)

This book contains papers by nine authors on the
social problems in new towns, on housing estates
and in central areas of large cities.

1.2.8   Community.   [*The Quest for] (1976).
THORNS, D.C.
Allen and Unwin. 1976.   (164pp.)

1.2.9   Criteria for Evaluating New Towns. (1975).
CRESSWELL, P.A.
Paper read at the Centre for Environmental Studies'
Seminar on New Towns, October   1975.(6pp.)
Available from the Open University. New Towns Study
Unit.

1.2.10   Education of a Secretary of State. [*The](1977)
         STRANZ, W.
         Town and Country Planning. Vol.45. No.6. June 1977.
         (pp.292-295).

         This article traces perceived changes in the
         Secretary of State's attitude to new towns between
         his statements on their future in August 1976,
         indicating a shift in emphasis towards inner city
         policy, and 5th April 1977.   These changing
         attitudes are considered in the context of four main
         criticisms commonly levelled at new towns: that
         there is direct conflict for financial resources
         between new towns and inner cities; that new towns
         are required to absorb population growth only; that
         new town employment growth 'drains blood' from inner
         city industry; and that new towns have attracted
         the economically most active and left the socially
         disadvantaged in the inner cities. These arguments
         are examined and shown to be invalid.

1.2.11   Employment Expansion and the Development of New Town
         Hinterlands.1961 -1966 (1971)
         OGILVY. A.A.
         Town Planning Review. Vol. 42. No. 2. April 1971. (pp113-129)
         (also published by the Building Research Station
         as BRS Current Paper 10/71, March 1971 - 13pp.)

         This paper follows up an earlier study of the eight
         London new towns.(see ref. 1.2.41 below). Using
         Census data it shows that these new towns had
         undergone an employment expansion compared with the
         earlier period and that the self-sufficiency of all
         except one had declined. Each had become more
         closely linked by work journeys with the surround-
         ing districts, and the paper describes the develop-
         ment of the new town hinterlands and their 'displace-
         ment' away from London.

1.2.12   Employment and Industrial Structure of Five British
         New Towns. [*An Analysis of the] (1971).
         REASON, L.
         Unpublished Diploma in Town and Country Planning
         thesis, Liverpool Polytechnic.1971.

         The new towns studied in the thesis include Runcorn,
         Skelmersdale and Telford. Analyses are made of past
         economic trends, locational advantages, industrial
         and employment growth, industrial and employment
         structure, commuting, unemployment and female
         labour requirements.

1.2.13   Garden Cities of Tomorrow. (1965 edition).
         HOWARD, EBENEZER.
         Faber and Faber, 1965. (168 pp.) reprinted as a
         paperback in 1970.)

         This edition has a preface by F.J. Osborn and contains
         an introductory essay by Lewis Mumford. The work was
         first published in 1898 as:"Tomorrow: a Peaceful Path

to Real Reform." The 1902 revised reissue was given
the title: "Garden Cities of Tomorrow." Howard's
classic text presents his general philosophy for the
creation of complete new urban units, and sets out
planning guidelines for their development. Within
individual Garden Cities (covering a circular area up
to 1.4 miles in diameter and containing a population of
some 30,000) land uses were to be arranged so as to
provide maximum accessibility by foot to work and other
facilities. Particular stress was laid on keeping work
journeys short and simple through the dispersal of
industrial employment towards the peripheries of the
Garden City, and of commercial and service employment
towards the centre. Electric tram services along the main
radial highways would cater for internal public transport
requirements. Within the 'Social City', comprising a series
of Garden Cities clustered around a larger Central City,
a system of rapid rail transit links were to fulfil the
requirements of easy access and short journey times.

1.2.14   General Medical Care in New Towns.[*The Provision of] (1966)
OFFICE OF HEALTH ECONOMICS (ed.FRY,J. and McKENZIE, J.)
Paper read at a Symposium held at the College of
General Practitioners, London. April 1966.

1.2.15   Justifying New Towns: an analysis of the attitudes
of actual and prospective residents. (1975)
CRESSWELL, P.A.
Paper read at the Centre for Environmental Studies'
Seminar on New Towns, October 1975. (26 pp.)
Available from the Open University, New Towns Study Unit.

1.2.16   London's New Towns: A Study of Self-Contained and
Balanced Communities. (1969)
THOMAS, R.
P.E.P. Broadsheet 510. 1969. (105 pp.).

1.2.17   London Town Expansion Programme.[*The Future of the] (1974)
HUDSON, D.M.
Paper read at the Regional Studies Association's East
Anglia Branch Conference, University of Essex. 12th December
1973. Regional Studies Association, March 1974.

1.2.18   Master Plans. [Progress in] (1967)
PEAK, J.
Paper read at a Conference held at Hornsey College
of Art. 1967

1.2.19   Mental Health and Environment. (1964)
TAYLOR, LORD and CHAVE, S.P.W.
Longmans. 1964. (239 pp.)

The report of a detailed survey of all forms of
psychiatric illness in a new town (Harlow), a housing
estate and a London Borough over a period of one year.

1.2.20   Mental Health on a New Housing Estate:a comparative
study of health in two districts of Croydon.(1965)
HARE, E.H. and SHAW, G.K.
Oxford University Press. 1965. (144 pp.)

1.2.21 Neighbourhood Shops in New Towns. (1976)
        GUY,C.
        Town and Country Planning Vol.44No.4 April 1976.
        (pp.221-224)

        Trends affecting the supply and demand for local shops
        in new towns, and problems arising from these, are
        discussed. Examples are given showing that Runcorn's
        local shopping provision is inferior to that of Bracknell.
        Some possibilities for improving deteriorating local
        shopping opportunities are discussed. These include
        maximising the commercial potential of new shopping
        developments by more careful choice of location by
        planners; increased provision of mobile shops; and
        building smaller and simpler premises with lower over-
        heads to the retailer. Failing these methods, improved
        public transport to town centre shops should be provided.
        The author concludes by pointing to the need for more
        flexible attitudes to local shopping provision,
        involving a willingness to research into customers'
        requirements and to consider new forms of shopping
        provision.

1.2.22 Neighbourhood Units in British New Towns.(1961)
        GOSS, A.
        Town Planning Review. Vol.32. No.1. 1961.

1.2.23 New Communities in Britain: Achievements and Problems.
                                                    (1961)
        NICHOLSON, J.H.
        National Council of Social Service. 1961. (191pp.)

1.2.24 New Communities U.S.A. (1976)
        BURBY III, R., and WEISS, S.F.
        Lexington Books/D.C. Heath Ltd., 1976

1.2.25 New Town Densities.[*Recent Trends in](1970)
        CHAMPION,A.G.
        Town and Country Planning. Vol.38.No.5. May 1970.
                                                (pp.252-255)

1.2.26 New-Town Planning: principles and practice.(1976)
        GOLANY, G.
        John Wiley & Sons, Inc. New York. 1976.(388pp.).

        This book gives a broad-based analysis of the principles
        and practice of new town planning. A bibliography
        of international references is included.

.2.27   New Town Story. [*The] (1970)
        SCHAFFER, F. (Foreward by the Rt.Hon.Lord Silkin)
        MacGibbon and Kee . London.1970 . (342pp.)

        This book reviews the whole of Britain's post-war new
        town movement up to 1970, and discusses likely
        developments by the year 2000AD. and beyond. An
        Appendix gives statistical and other factual details
        of individual new towns, and a bibliography is included.

.2.28   New Towns: A Comparative Atlas.(1972)
        LINDSAY,W., CHEESMAN, R., de PORZECANSKI, M.
        Working Paper No.62. Centre for Land Use and Built
        Form Studies, University of Cambridge. 1972. (24pp.)

1.2.29 New Towns: Als Mittel der Regionalen Industrialisier-
        ungspolitik in Unterentwickelten Regionen Grossbritan-
        niens. (1976).
        CASPER, U.
        Wissenschaftszentrum. Berlin. 1976.
        (New Towns as instruments of regional industrial
        development policy in Great Britain).

1.2.30 New Towns: analysis of activities and their densities
                                                    (1972)
        COOPER. P. , LINDSAY,W. and TAYLOR, E.
        Working Paper No.73. Centre for Land Use and Built
        Form Studies, University of Cambridge. 1972. (86pp.)

1.2.31 New Towns : analysis of land uses.(1972)
        COOPER, P. , LINDSAY W. and TAYLOR, E.
        Working Paper No.72. Centre for Land Use and Built
        Form Studies, University of Cambridge. 1972.   (80pp.)

1.2.32 New Towns [*The]: The Answer to Megalopolis.(1969)
        OSBORN, Sir F.J. and WHITTICK, A. (Introduction by
        Lewis Mumford).Leonard Hill, London.1969 (456pp.)

1.2.33 New Towns: the British Experience.(1972)
        EVANS, H. (ed.)
        published for the Town & Country Planning Association
        by Charles Knight. London.1972. (207pp.)

        This volume contains a collection of fifteen essays
        about British new towns with an Introduction by
        Peter Self. The essays are arranged in four main
        sections under the headings : Administrative Framework;
        Regional and Economic Planning; The Planning of New
        Towns; and New Towns to Live in. Individual chapters
        include:-

            Land Needs of New and Old Towns - R. Best.
            Shops and Shopping - Sir Frank Price.
            Social Development - G. Brooke Taylor
            Changing Goals in Design : the Milton Keynes example -
            Lord Llewelyn Davies. (see ref. 2.4.39 below)

        A selected annotated bibliography is provided, listing
        both general items and studies of individual new towns.
        There is also a new town directory and an appendix
        containing statistics relating to the progress of new
        towns, Town Development Act schemes and Scottish
        'overspill' figures.

1.2.34 New Towns : the data bank, its construction and
        organisation (1972)
        CHEESMAN, R., LINDSAY, W. and de PORZECANSKI, M.
        Working Paper No.63.Centre for Land Use and Built
        Form Studies. University of Cambridge.1972. (96pp.)

1.2.35 New Towns : the Evolution of Planning Criteria.(1972)
        de PORZECANSKI, M., CHEESMAN, R., LINDSAY, W.
        Working Paper No.64.Centre for Land Use and Built
        Form Studies. University of Cambridge. 1972. (42pp.)

1.2.36 Office Employment in New Towns. (1976)
DANIELS, P.W.
Town Planning Review. Vol.47.No.3,July 1976(pp.209-224)

1.2.37 Perspectives on New Town Development. (1975)
THOMAS, R. (ed.)
Proceedings of a Conference organised by the New
Towns Study Unit & the Regional Studies Association
at the Open University, November 1975. (157pp.)

1.2.38 Prairie Planning in the New Towns. (1953)
CULLEN, G.
Architectural Review, Vol.114. No.679. July 1953. (pp.33-36)

1.2.39 Recreational Planning in New Communities: A Review of
British Experience. (1975)
VEAL A.J.
Research Memorandum No.46.Centre for Urban and
Regional Studies, University of Birmingham. June 1975(110pp).

This document draws together information and sources on
recreation and leisure planning and provision in new
communities in Britain,   covering housing estates and
expanded towns in addition to new towns . It traces back
the importance of recreation provision in the new
community tradition to the 19th. Century, and reviews
ways in which this ideal has been expressed and the
extent to which it has been realised.

In Chapter 1 the rôle of recreation and leisure in the
early new towns movement is examined. In the second
chapter the legal and administrative background to
recreation provision in new communities is outlined.
Chapter III analyses and compares the recreation content
of published new community plans, distinguishing between
Mark I, II and III New Town Master Plans; and a number
of plans dealing exclusively with recreation are
reviewed in Chapter IV. Chapter V assesses the
problems and achievements of the new communities in
implementing the ideals set out in the plans. A
review of research carried out on recreation in new
communities is presented in Chapter VI , and in Chapter
VII the rôle of Social Development Departments in
recreation is examined. The Report includes a bibliography on recreation in new communities and an annotated
list of publications and reports related to the
'Social Development in New Communities' research
programme conducted by Birmingham University's Centre
for Urban and Regional Studies.

1.2.40 Regions of Tomorrow : Towards the Open City. (1969)
ASH, M.
Evelyn Adams and Mackay. 1969. (106pp.)

Self-contained New Town : [The]. employment and
population. (1968)
OGILVY, A.A.
Town Planning Review. Vol.39. No.1 April 1968.
(pp. 38-54) (also published by the Building Research
Station as BRS Current Paper 56/68.)

This paper examines the growth of population and employment in the eight London new towns during an early ten
years of their development (1951-1961), with particular
reference to the extent to which they had achieved their
objective of being 'self-contained communities'. It
shows that although the numbers of jobs and employed
residents were roughly equally balanced there was a
substantial amount of work travel between each new town
and the surrounding towns, and concludes that whether
any of the new towns could be called 'self-contained'
was questionable.
(see also ref. 1.2.11 for report of a follow-up study,
covering the period 1961-1966).

1.2.42   Social Aspects of Planning in New Towns. (1975)
WIRZ, H.M.
Saxon House Studies. D.C. Heath Ltd., 1975 (244 pp.)
The book presents a detailed study of social development
in new towns, with specific reference to East Kilbride,
Glenrothes and Livingston.   It examines in particular
the assumptions underlying the Reith Report's recommendations as to the kind of social life and recreational
opportunities which should be available to new town
residents. Chapter 4 discusses the concept of social
balance in relation to the Reith Report's goal that the
British new towns should be "self-contained and balanced
communities" and reviews earlier literature on this
subject.

1.2.43   Social Development Work in the New Communities.(1974)
HORROCKS, M.
University of Birmingham Centre for Urban and Regional
Studies. Occasional Paper No. 27. 1974 (72 pp.)

The history of the new town movement is outlined and the
social aspects of new town legislation examined. A
description is given of the work of Social Development
staff in new communities, based mainly on information
obtained from a series of unstructured depth interviews
with Social Development Officers in the new towns and
some expanded and other towns. A bibliography of writings
by and about Social Development Officers is appended.

1.2.44   Social Factors Involved in the Planning and Development
of New Towns. (1964)
WHITE, L.E.
Harlow Development Corporation, 1964.Paper read at United
Nations Symposium on New Towns in Moscow. 1964.
(see ref. 1.2.49 below)

1.2.45   Social Planning in New Communties. (1971)
NORTH WEST ECONOMIC PLANNING COUNCIL. 1971. (28 pp.)
A report by a Working Party with particular reference to
the North West, containing a number of recommendations
to the Secretary of State for the Environment and to local
authorities involved in the planning of new communities .

1.2.46   Social Provision in New Communities.[*The Programming of]
ARMEN. G.   (1976)
Part I: Basic Problems and General Theories.
Town Planning Review.Vol.47.No.2.April 1976 (pp.105-126)

Part II : Some Case Studies and Conclusions.
Town Planning Review. Vol. 47. No.3.July 1976(pp.269-288)

Part I of the article is related to the more general
problems of assessing and predicting demand for social
facilities and of developing a theoretical framework
for measuring the performance of new communities both
in Britain and in other countries with different
political and legal systems. Part II discusses some of
these examples and attempts to draw conclusions for
future practise.

1.2.47 A Success Story with some Exceptions.(1973)
BROOKE TAYLOR, G.
Built Environment. Vol. 2. No.3. (Expanded Towns special
issue). March 1973. (pp.148-150).

In this article some of the weaknesses apparent in the
growth of the new and expanded towns up to 1973 are
identified, and suggestions made as to means of overcoming these. The main problems are seen as delays in
the provision of the social, welfare and recreational
facilities needed for adequate community development,
largely resulting from the complexity of administrative
authorities - often with conflicting interests and
commitments - controlling their provision; and the
failure of the new towns to accommodate the socially
disadvantaged elements of the inner cities' population.
Possible remedies include more grants from development
corporations to local authorities to raise the standard
of provision of social services; undertakings for
investment from central government in social and welfare
infrastructure at the time of approval of major new
town or expansion shemes; and a programme for selecting
and transferring groups of disadvantaged families from
the central parts of cities to new or expanded towns.

1.2.48 Town and Country Planning. (1978)
Vol. 46. No.2. February 1978.(pp. 51-135)

The February issue of Town and Country Planning each
year (January issue before 1975) is concerned almost
wholly with new towns and includes a selection of
topical articles and a factual record of the progress
of individual new towns during the previous year. An
annual bibliography and a new town directory are also
included. Statistical summaries of the progress of
each new town give details of population, employment,
schools, annual capital expenditure, housing, industry,
commercial premises and financial results. Details
are also given of Scottish Overspill agreements and
progress under the Town Development Act.
(see also ref. 9.1.37 below).

1.2.49 United Nations Symposium on the Planning and Development
of New Towns, held in Moscow, USSR. (Aug-Sept. 1964)

UNITED NATIONS, New York. 1966.

1.2.50   Commission for the New Towns: Annual Reports.
                              (Annually from 1963)
          (Crawley, Hatfield, Hemel Hempstead, Welwyn Garden
          City.) H.M.S.O. (House of Commons Command Papers.)

          Summaries of progress during the year in each of the
          Commission's new towns are included. These contain
          statistics on employment, industry, commerce, housing,
          educational facilities, social and community buildings,
          and roads and sewers.

1.2.51   Annual Reports of the Development Corporations in
          England and Wales. (Annually from 1947)
          H.M.S.O.   (House of Commons Command Papers.)

          The Annual Reports of the Development Corporations
          comprise progress reports of developments which have
          taken place under each Corporation during the
          previous year, accompanied by statistical summaries.
          There is no standard format as between the different
          new towns, but progress in housing, industry, roads
          and social and community facilities is normally
          covered in all reports. The reports also contain
          official statements on policy matters which may
          expand and update those contained in the Master
          Plans and related documents. For instance, the 1976
          Chairman's Report for Skelmersdale expresses increas-
          ing official concern over the future of the bus services
          in the town. It emphasises the need for special
          consideration to be given to the public transport
          needs of Skelmersdale as a developing new town, in
          particular stressing the importance of services to
          newly developed areas distant from the town centre
          to meet the needs of early residents.
          [Reports included in the 1977 volume are for:
           Aycliffe, Basildon, Bracknell, Central Lancashire,
           Corby, Harlow, Milton Keynes, Northampton,
           Peterborough, Peterlee, Redditch, Runcorn,
           Skelmersdale, Stevenage, Telford, Warrington,
           Washington.]

1.2.52   Expenditure Committee on New Towns (1974): Reports
          from the House of Commons Expenditure Committee
          inquiry into new towns. 1974-5. 3 volumes, covering
          Minutes of Evidence, Appendices and an Index.

1.2.53   Needs of New Communities [*The] ; a report on social
          provision in new and expanding communities. (1967)
          MINISTRY OF HOUSING AND LOCAL GOVERNMENT.
          Prepared by a sub-committee of the Central Housing
          Advisory Committee (Chairman: J.B. Cullingworth).
          H.M.S.O. 1967. (123pp.)

1.2.54   New Towns Acts: 1946, 1952, 1953, 1955, 1958, 1964
(No.2), 1965, 1966, 1975, 1977, and
New Towns (Amendment) Act 1976.

1.2.55   New Towns Committee. [*Final Report of the]. July
1946.
MINISTRY OF TOWN AND COUNTRY PLANNING and DEPARTMENT
OF HEALTH FOR SCOTLAND (Chairman: Lord Reith of
Stonehaven) Cmnd. 6876 (Reprinted in 1963.) H.M.S.O.
1946.(83pp.)

This report (the 'Reith Report'), which was preceded
by the Interim and Second Interim Reports (Cmnd.6759
and 6794), summarises the findings of the Committee
set up to consider matters arising from the establishment of new towns, and to suggest guiding principles for their development. The findings are arranged
in three main sections, covering principles in
planning, factors affecting the preparation of the
plan (including a subsection on communications) and
execution of the plan. Regarding public transport
it states that a frequent internal bus service is
indispensable, and that in default of the local
transport undertakings providing it, the new town
agency should provide it. Specially designed bus
stations with facilities including waiting rooms,
enquiry offices and refreshment services should be
built adjoining shopping centres and should also allow
for easy interchange with main railway stations. The
railway stations should be an outstanding feature of
the new towns, with high-quality facilities and
situated as near as possible to the main shopping
centres. Ample provision of car parks is also seen
as necessary, and these should be well-distributed
and should also accommodate cycles.

1.2.56   New Towns in England and Wales: a consultation document.
DEPARTMENT OF THE ENVIRONMENT. 1975.   (1975)

1.2.57   New Towns: United Nations Seminar on New Towns.(1973)
DEPARTMENT OF THE ENVIRONMENT.

Contains: Planning - by J.R. James
Architecture - by O. Cox
Social Development - by G.Brooke Taylor
Finance - G.R. Rawes and K. Wren
Management - by Sir W. Hart et al.
H.M.S.O. London. 1973 (156pp.).

1.2.58   Planning in the United Kingdom: The Rôle of
Government in New Urban Developments in the United
Kingdom. (1976)
DEPARTMENT OF THE ENVIRONMENT
Prepared for Habitat, United Nations Conference
on Human Settlements. 1976. (8pp.)

1.2 *Subsidiary References.*

3.2 *Social Aspects of Mobility.*

3.2.66   *Common Sense and Vandalism.   (1977)*
3.2.73   *Planning for Leisure.   (1969)*

3.3 *Interaction between Land Use and Travel.*

3.3.46   *A Theory of the Urban Land Market. (1960)*
3.3.49   *The Structure, Size and Cost of Urban Settlements. (1973)*

3.4 *Transport and Mobility – General and Miscellaneous.*

3.4.1   *Environment and Behavior: planning and everyday life. (1977)*
         [Includes a consideration of social aspects of new town planning.]

8.1 *Survey Techniques: Behavioural and Attitudinal.*

8.1.63   *Monitoring in Practice. A household survey: its use and*
         potential for local authorities and new towns.   (1976)
8.1.102 *Social Research and New Communities. (1968)*

9.1 *Journals.*

9.1.32   *New Towns Bulletin.*

9.2 *Bibliographies.*

9.2.19-30 and 9.2.33 *[New town bibliographies.]*

9.3 *Abstracting and Indexing Services.*

9.3.6   *Departments of the Environment and Transport Library Bulletin.*
         [Includes a subsection on new and expanded towns.]
9.3.9   *Geo Abstracts.*
         [Includes items on new towns.]
9.3.21   *Urban Abstracts.*
         [Includes a subsection on new towns and town development.]

9.4 *Research Registers.*

9.4.1   *Register of Research, 1977. Part II: Environmental Planning.*
                                                               (1977)
         [Includes a section on new towns.]
9.4.6   *1977 Summary of Research being Undertaken in New Towns.(1977)*
9.4.9   *Building Research Establishment – Annual Report.*
         [Includes details of the B.R.E's research relating to new towns.]
9.4.15   *The Martin Centre for Architectural and Urban Studies, University*
                                          of Cambridge – Annual Report.
9.4.17   *Open University: New Towns Study Unit – list of publications.*
9.4.20   *University of Birmingham: Centre for Urban and Regional Studies –*
                                                   Annual Report.
         [Gives details of the Centre's research into the social develop-
                                          ment of new communities.]

9.5 Statistical Sources.

9.5.16   Census of Population.
9.5.19   Local Government Trends. (Annually)
          [Includes statistics on British new towns.]
9.5.21   Progress on Land Sold or Leased by Development Corporations/
          Commission for the New Towns. ["The Publicity Sheet".]
                                                    (Quarterly).
          [Includes statistics for each new town in England, Wales and
                                                           Scotland.]

9.6 Other Sources of Information.

9.6.10   Guide to Official Statistics. (1976 and 1978)
9.6.11   Hansard. (Daily, Weekly and Sessional)
9.6.14   New Towns in the U.K. (1977)
9.6.16   Sourcebook of Planning Information. (1971)

2. New Towns (Specific).

2.1 Runcorn.

The bibliographic entries on Runcorn are arranged in the following order:-

1. Items relating specifically to transport. (2.1.1 - 2.1.11)

2. Other Development Corporation and planning consultants' reports, beginning with the Master Plan and related documents, which are listed chronologically. (2.1.12 - 2.1.22)

3. Other reports. (2.1.23 - 2.1.25)

The subsidiary references listed at the end of the subsection include a number of general studies on aspects of new towns or of transport which make specific reference to Runcorn.

The planning and operation of the Runcorn Busway system have received a substantial amount of attention both in Britain and abroad. Descriptive accounts are provided in the DEVELOPMENT CORPORATION's booklet: RUNCORN BUSWAY (2.1.3), in several articles by MERCER (for example, 2.1.2, 2.1.7 and 2.1.9), in the NEW TOWNS TECHNICAL OFFICERS' COMMITTEE's Review of Public Transport in New Towns (1.1.13) and in the report on Urban Public Transport by GLENROTHES DEVELOPMENT CORPORATION. (1.1.27)

The planning philosophy which gave rise to the concept of the Busway is revealed in LING's Draft Plan (2.1.12) and Master Plan (2.1.14). POTTER, in Volume Two of Transport and New Towns (1.1.18) has examined the Runcorn approach to transport planning in some detail, pointing out the significance of Ling's Master Plan in recognising the social and economic importance of mobility in the creation of a new community, in treating transport as a means rather than as an end in itself, and in posing the questions of what constitutes mobility and of how best to cater for it in terms of urban form. Potter also examines in some detail the "balanced transport" solution attempted at Runcorn, in which priority has been given to public transport in the urban form, pointing out comparisons and some contrasts with that at Redditch which was designated at the same time (April 1964). Comparative assessments of Runcorn's approach to transport/land use planning are also reported in the paper by HILLMAN and POTTER (1.1.1), which contrasts Runcorn with Cumbernauld and Milton Keynes, and in that by LEMBERG (3.3.21) which compares the transport goals and achievements of Runcorn with those of Milton Keynes.

The Transport and Road Research Laboratory carried out a series of surveys in Runcorn in 1973 in an attempt to monitor the progress of the then partially - constructed Busway. The results of these studies of the operation of buses on the Busway and of residents' travel behaviour are summarised in the report by VINCENT, LAYFIELD and BARDSLEY (2.1.6). The results of an attitude survey carried out in conjunction with a household travel survey by Social and Community Planning Research are presented in an appendix to the main report.

Methodological details of the household travel survey are recorded in the report by BERTHOUD (2.1.10). Some more recent data on travel patterns and car ownership levels in Runcorn New Town are contained in RUNCORN DEVELOPMENT CORPORATION's report on their 1976 Household Census (2.1.20). Additional (non-quantitative) data on residents' attitudes to the part-finished Busway, derived from a series of tape-recorded group discussions carried out by Social and Community Planning Research in 1974, is presented in the report: Runcorn: A Second Look, by PRESCOTT - CLARKE and STOWELL. (2.1.25).

A substantial body of background data which makes an important contribution to the understanding and evaluation of Runcorn's social development at an earlier stage of the new town's progress is provided in the report of Social and Community Planning Research's major community study carried out in Runcorn in 1972 - Creating a Community, by BERTHOUD and JOWELL (2.1.24). This report is also a useful methodological source, notably with regard to the exposition and application of priority evaluation methodology in a new town situation. The qualitative studies carried out two years later and reported by PRESCOTT - CLARKE and STOWELL in: Runcorn: A Second Look provide some follow - up data (2.1.25).

Useful statistical information on Runcorn is contained in the reports of the DEVELOPMENT CORPORATION's biennial Household Censuses (2.1.20 and 2.1.22) and in the Annual Reports of the Development Corporation (1.2.51). Further statistical and other sources of information are listed in the subsidiary references at the end of this subsection.

2.1 Runcorn

Transport - related items

2.1.1 Highway Hierarchy - or please don't bring your car
into the living room. (1975)
JENKINS, E.
The Highway Engineer. Vol. XXII. No.11. November 1975.
(pp.17-22).

2.1.2 People and Transportation-Runcorn New Town. (1974)
MERCER, J.
The Highway Engineer. Vol. XXI. No. 1. January 1974.
(pp.22-28).

2.1.3 Runcorn Busway. (undated)
RUNCORN DEVELOPMENT CORPORATION. (16 pp.)

This short booklet outlines the planning rationale
behind the conception and development of the Runcorn
Busway and gives technical details on operational and
engineering aspects of the system.

2.1.4 Runcorn Busway Experiment.(1971)
ANON.
Highways Design and Construction. Vol. 39. Sept.1971.
(pp.54-55)

2.1.5 Runcorn Busway. [*Progress with the] (1973)
ANON.
Motor Transport. 6th April 1973.

2.1.6 Runcorn Busway Study (1976)
VINCENT, R.A., LAYFIELD, R.E. and BARDSLEY, M.
TRRL   Report LR 697. 1976

In 1973 surveys were carried out to determine the
travel behaviour of residents living in Runcorn's
new estates and to observe the operation of buses on
the partially completed Busway (see reference 2.1.10
for an account of the methodology of the surveys).
Information was also collected on pedestrian walking
speeds,journey times by car, and car parking; and an
attitude survey was also conducted.   This report
presents and comments on the results obtained, with
particular reference to the planning objectives stated
in the Runcorn Master Plan. A forecast is given
relating the future modal split for internal journeys
to work to increases in car ownership. The effects
of road congestion, fuel prices, bus subsidies and
parking charges on the generalised costs of travel by
bus and car are also examined.   Car ownership and
parking charges are the factors most likely to
influence modal choice.   A simple cost benefit

analysis showed that construction and land costs of
about £6 millions for the Busway are justified by a
reduction of about £7 millions in expenditure on
other transport infrastructure and by benefits to the
bus operator and bus users.

2.1.7   Runcorn and its Busways.(1974)
         MERCER, J.
         Institution of Civil Engineers Transportation
         Engineering Group Informal Discussion. April 1974.
         (Includes diagram).

2.1.8   Runcorn New Town.(1973)
         CROSVILLE MOTOR SERVICES.
         Paper read at a conference on : "Moving People in
         Cities" held at the Transport and Road Research
         Laboratory, Crowthorne, Berkshire, April 1973.
         TRRL   Supplementary Report SR 6UC. (pp.142-144).

2.1.9   Runcorn Plan for a Rapid Transit Bus Service.
         [*The] (1971)
         MERCER,J.
         Paper read at a symposium on : "Public Transport for
         Policy Makers" held at Newcastle Upon Tyne School of
         Advanced Studies in Applied Science. Department of
         Civil Engineering. March 1971. (pp.38-54 of
         Proceedings and Discussion pp.55-58).

         The planning principles underlying the design of
         Runcorn New Town are described and the civil
         engineering design features of the Busway track are
         outlined in this paper.   A discussion follows.

2.1.10   Runcorn Travel Survey.(1973)
         BERTHOUD, R.
         Social and Community Planning Research. Report P.276.
         October 1973. (16pp. plus appendices).

         This methodological report describes a household
         survey conducted in Runcorn New Town in 1973 to
         establish details of the pattern of travel there.
         It outlines the methods used in data collection and
         data preparation.   It also describes innovatory
         departures from the standard transportation study
         questionnaire format, including attitude questions
         asked to supplement the information on travel
         behaviour provided by the basic household travel
         survey.   A preliminary analysis of the global
         response to the attitude questions is presented.
         Copies of the main questionnaire, Interviewers'
         Manual, and Editing and Coding Instructions are
         appended to the report. (see also reference 2.1.6 above
         for results of the survey.)

2.1.11 <u>Transportation Problems in Runcorn New Town</u>. (1973)
HARRISON, R.
Urbanisme, Paris, France. No. 134. (pp.76-79).
(Les Problemes de Transports a Runcorn, Ville
Nouvelle Anglaise).

This article outlines the Master Plan for Runcorn
New Town, the originality of which lies in the
public transport system based on the Busway. The
planning and development of the Busway and its
integration into the design for the new town are
described.

See also Master Plan Documents - refs. 2.1.12-16 below.

<u>Development Corporation and Planning Consultants' Reports.</u>

2.1.12 <u>Runcorn New Town Draft Plan.</u>(1965)
LING, ARTHUR and ASSOCIATES and RUNCORN
DEVELOPMENT CORPORATION.
Runcorn Development Corporation.1965.

2.1.13 <u>Runcorn New Town Draft Plan Proposals</u> [*<u>The</u>] ;
<u>Consultants' Report on</u>. (1966)
GODDARD and SMITH, SIR FREDERICK SNOW and PARTNERS,
R. SEIFERT and PARTNERS.
Runcorn U.D.C. 1966.(2 vols.)

2.1.14 <u>Runcorn New Town Master Plan</u>.(1967)
LING, ARTHUR and ASSOCIATES and RUNCORN DEVELOPMENT
CORPORATION. (1967).
Runcorn Development Corporation. 1967.

2.1.15 <u>Master Plan Amendment No. 1 - Runcorn New Town Urban</u>
<u>Renewal</u>.(1971)
RUNCORN DEVELOPMENT CORPORATION.1971.

2.1.16 <u>Master Plan Amendment No. 2</u>.(1975)
RUNCORN DEVELOPMENT CORPORATION.1975.

2.1.17 <u>Home Interview Social Survey</u>.(1966)
RUNCORN DEVELOPMENT CORPORATION.1966.

2.1.18 <u>The Leisure Activities of Young Children : A Prelim-</u>
<u>inary Report</u>.(1971)
RUNCORN DEVELOPMENT CORPORATION - SOCIAL DEVELOPMENT
DEPARTMENT.

This report concerns a pilot study of 7 to 11 year
olds involving a questionnaire survey of children and
parents. Recommendations are made for swimming
lessons, a children's council, a mobile library, a
pony club, and club premises for 7 to 8 year olds.

2.1.19 <u>Meeting Places in Runcorn</u>.(1971)
RUNCORN DEVELOPMENT CORPORATION - SOCIAL DEVELOPMENT
DEPARTMENT.

2.1.20 1976 Runcorn Household Census.(1976).
RUNCORN DEVELOPMENT CORPORATION. 1976 (101 pp.)

The basis of this report is the 1976 Biennial Census
of the new town, which included questions on shopping
and leisure activities and on means of travel to these,
in addition to the demographic, socio-economic and
vehicle ownership questions covered in the 1974
Census.   A distinction is generally made between the
rented and private sectors, and the final chapter
records variations between the individual estates.
The report is illustrated with graphs and sketch maps;
and appendices provide technical details of the survey
methods and response rates, detailed tabulations, and
copies of the self-completion questionnaires used.

2.1.21 1969 Social Survey : the First 500 Families. (1969).
RUNCORN DEVELOPMENT CORPORATION - SOCIAL DEVELOPMENT
DEPARTMENT.   1969

2.1.22 Statistical Profile of Runcorn New Town. (1974).
RUNCORN DEVELOPMENT CORPORATION. June   1974.(28 pp.)

The report presents a selection of statistical data
derived from the Development Corporation's 1974
Biennial Census, together with information from the
annual Employment Survey and the Household Record
System to give a profile of the new town at June 1974.
Most analyses differentiate between individual
estates, and some comparisons are made with statistics
for other new towns (including Skelmersdale) and with
national averages.   The data is presented in four
main sections, covering demographic aspects (age
structure, household size, marital composition);
employment levels, structure, groupings and location;
an analysis of movers to the new town by place of
origin, previous accommodation, housing qualifications
and religion;   and car ownership.   A copy of the
Census form is included.

See also ref. 2.1.3 : Runcorn Busway (RUNCORN
DEVELOPMENT CORPORATION).

Other Reports, Papers and Articles

2.1.23 Birth Control in Runcorn and Coalville : a study of
the F.P.A. Campaign. (1974).
ALLEN, I.
P.E.P. 1974.

2.1.24 Creating a Community : A Study of Runcorn New Town. (1973)

BERTHOUD, R. and JOWELL, R.
Social and Community Planning Research. Report P.217,
Dec. 1973.(90 pp. plus appendices).

This report covers the first of three phases of a
research study of Runcorn New Town, the aim of which
was to examine the effects of largescale developments
on both the incoming and receiving populations and to
use research methods as a means of communication and
participation within these developments. The first
phase was concerned with establishing a 'baseline'
situation against which changes could be measured in
the later phases of the research programme. The
report begins by describing the physical and social
characteristics of the study area and then gives
details of the broad research strategy and methods
before presenting the principal findings and conclusions from this phase of the study. Appendices give
details of the survey methodology. Briefly,this
consisted of a preliminary programme of depth interviews and group discussions, and a main survey in
which nearly 2,000 fully structured interviews were
conducted with random samples of householders in
Runcorn Old Town and Runcorn New Town and with new
town applicants living in the Liverpool area.
Copies of the questionnaires are included. The
priority evaluator technique was used as an attempt
to measure "trade-offs" in public preferences and
to assign weights to these so that some idea of
community priorities could be obtained. A description of the technique is given and copies of the
pictures used in its implementation are included.
A bibliography is also appended.

2.1.25 Runcorn : A Second Look. (1975)
PRESCOTT-CLARKE, P. and STOWELL, R.
Social and Community Planning Research. Report 339.
July 1975. (45 pp.).

This report describes the findings of two surveys
carried out in Runcorn in 1974 as a follow-up to a
major social survey conducted there in 1972 which
examined the views of residents on Runcorn New
Town and its facilities. The 1974 surveys consisted
of a qualitative study based on group discussions
with selected residents of the old and new towns, and
a quantitive questionnaire study of 61 residents
planning to move house either within or out of
Runcorn. (see ref.2.1.24 above)

The quantitative survey indicated that although some
aspects of Runcorn were unsatisfactory, changes were
taking place which were likely to be for the better.
The two main problems concerned employment (limited
local job opportunities and poor wage rates) and a
deterioration in the quality of the transport services.
In particular, the poor reliability and high bus fares
of the Busway were criticized. Inadequate local
social, recreation and welfare facilities also gave
rise to complaints.

The quantitative study of prospective movers showed
that most were moving primarily to buy their own
homes, usually because of the investment value as
compared with rented accommodation. These people
had been generally satisfied with the quality of
their housing and with Runcorn itself, but the limited
supply of houses for sale locally meant that most of
them had to look elsewhere. Their main complaints
were noise in the flats, inadequate recreation facilities and the poor bus service.

Copies of the Movers' Questionnaire and an outline of
group discussion subjects are appended to the report.

2.1 Subsidiary References.

1.1 New Towns - Transport and Mobility.

1.1.1	Access and Mobility in New Towns. (1976)
1.1.13	A Review of Public Transport in New Towns. (1974)
1.1.14	Public Transport in New Towns in Great Britain. (1971)
1.1.18	Transport and New Towns. Volume Two. (1976)
1.1.27	Urban Public Transport. (1971)

1.2 New Towns - Non-Transport Aspects.

1.2.12	An Analysis of the Employment and Industrial Structure of Five British New Towns. (1971)
1.2.21	Neighbourhood Shops in New Towns. (1976)
1.2.48	Town and Country Planning. (February 1978)
1.2.51	Annual Reports of the Development Corporations.

3.3 Interaction between Land Use and Travel.

3.3.21	Passenger Transport as an Urban Element. (1976)

9.2 Bibliographies.

9.2.25	New Towns Bibliography. 1977. (1977)
9.2.27	New Towns. (1976)

9.4 Research Registers.

9.4.6	1977 Summary of Research being Undertaken in New Towns. (1977)

9.5 Statistical Sources.

9.5.16	Census of Population.
9.5.19	Local Government Trends. (Annually.)
9.5.21	Progress on Land Sold or Leased by Development Corporations/ Commission for the New Towns. ['The Publicity Sheet'.] (Quarterly)

9.6 Other Sources of Information.

9.6.2	National Index of Traffic and Transportation Surveys. (1975)
9.6.16	Sourcebook of Planning Information. (1971) [pp.198-9]

2.2   Skelmersdale.

Material relating to Skelmersdale is arranged as follows:

1. Items concerned specifically with transport (2.2.1)
2. Development Corporation and planning consultants' reports, beginning with the Basic Plan and related documents which are arranged chronologically (2.2.2-8)
3. Other reports, papers and articles (2.2.9-14)

More general reports and documents which include specific reference to Skelmersdale are listed in the subsidiary references at the end of this subsection.

Comparatively little published material is available which relates directly to transport in Skelmersdale. The background to transport planning in the new town is set out in WILSON and WOMERSLEY'S Skelmersdale New Town Planning Proposals (2.2.2) which give priority to catering for a high level of car ownership and usage in the new town, while also stressing the importance of facilitating pedestrian movement. The latter was to be attained through the provision of a segregated footpath system within a relatively compact urban form in which land uses would be arranged in such a way that a large proportion of the population would live within easy access by foot of the town centre, local shops, the main industrial sites and recreation areas. An examination of the transport goals and proposals as set out in the Skelmersdale Basic Plan is included in POTTER'S review of transport planning in the Second Generation new towns (Volume Two of Transport and New Towns - 1.1.18). Potter has also examined the influence on the Skelmersdale Basic Plan of the L.C.C.'s plan (later abandoned) for a new town of 100,000 people at Hook in Hampshire*, drawing comparisons between the seven 'Fundamental Requirements' of the Skelmersdale Basic Plan and the 'Main Aims' set out in the Hook report. Like Cumbernauld both Hook and Skelmersdale were planned as compact, high density new towns giving emphasis to pedestrian access to facilities but also incorporating road networks designed to cater for 'full motorisation'. The neighbourhood principle, which had been a major element in the design of the Mark I new towns, was dropped and services were to be more strongly concentrated in the town centre. SKELMERSDALE DEVELOPMENT CORPORATION's Annual Population and Social Surveys (2.2.8) contain data on residents' mode of transport to work, school, shops and other facilities, and in certain years the surveys have included questions on residents' opinions of the local bus services. The survey reports also include up-to-date information on car ownership, and on usage of and opinions about the footpath system. POTTER has included a graphical presentation of the proportion of work journeys made by foot in Skelmersdale, based on data from the Population and Social Surveys from 1969 to 1975, as an Appendix to Volume Two of Transport and New Towns (1.1.18). The Appendix also shows diagrammatically the

---

* The Planning of a New Town. LONDON COUNTY COUNCIL. 1961.

opinions of Skelmersdale residents on the town's public
transport (bus) services, footpath system and road system for
1973 and 1975, revealing an overall favourable opinion on
the road and footpath system and unfavourable opinion on
public transport. Background information on the official
Development Corporation view of the rôle of public transport
in the new town is contained in the reports for Skelmersdale
included in the Annual Reports of the Development Corporations,
(1.2.51) especially for 1976 and 1977, and these reports also
provide a detailed yearly record of proposed and actual
developments concerning the new town's road and transport
infrastructure.

Much press comment in relation to Skelmersdale over the past
few years has focussed on the new town's employment situation
and general economic development. A recent review is provided
by the article in the ESTATES GAZETTE, April 1978 (2.2.12).
The Annual Reports of the Development Corporation (1.2.51)
and SKELMERSDALE DEVELOPMENT CORPORATION'S Annual Population and
Social Survey reports are both valuable sources of other
background material on the progress of the new town and the
demographic structure, activities and opinions of its residents.
Other relevant statistical sources are listed in the subsidiary
references appended to this subsection.

2.2   Skelmersdale.

Transport - related items

2.2.1   Transportation in New Towns with Particular
         Reference to Skelmersdale.(1968)
         RADCLIFFE, D.R.
         Surveyor. Vol. 131. April 20th. 1968. (pp.20-24).

         [See also Consultants' planning proposals - ref.
         2.2.2 below]

Development Corporation and Planning Consultants' Reports

2.2.2   Skelmersdale New Town Planning Proposals.(1964)
         (Vols. 1 and 2).
         WILSON,L.HUGH.   and WOMERSLEY, LEWIS.
         Skelmersdale Development Corporation. December 1964.

         The Consultants use the term 'Basic Plan' in
         preference to 'Master Plan' in an attempt to indicate
         that it is a flexible basic framework for guiding
         development rather than a finite set of proposals.
         Alternative plans are given for ultimate populations
         of 80,000 and 90,000 and the Preamble sets out
         several fundamental principles on which the develop-
         ment proposals are based.   The first of these is
         that the plan should provide for a high level of car
         ownership and "full use" of the motor car, together
         with maximum separation of vehicles and pedestrians.
         A footpath system would enable people to walk to
         various parts of the town without coming into contact
         with main traffic.   The neighbourhood system is
         abandoned, the town being seen as a compact urban
         centre with surrounding recreation areas, a large
         proportion of the population living within easy
         access by foot of both the central area and areas of
         open space.   Local shopping facilities would be
         provided only where residential areas were more than
         10 minutes walking distance from the town centre,
         corner shops distributed throughout the housing
         areas meeting day-to-day shopping needs.   Industrial
         sites should be located in a dispersed manner to ease
         traffic problems.   Public transport is not given
         emphasis in the proposals, but regarding siting of
         bus stops it recommends that these be provided on
         secondary roads only, in relation to the footpath
         crossing points, and within "easy walking distance
         of all houses."

2.2.3   Digmoor Planning Proposals.(1964).
         SKELMERSDALE DEVELOPMENT CORPORATION. 1964.

2.2.4   Little Digmoor, Skelmersdale.(1964).
         SKELMERSDALE DEVELOPMENT CORPORATION. 1964.

2.2.5   Hillside Planning Proposals. (1965)
        SKELMERSDALE DEVELOPMENT CORPORATION. 1965

2.2.6   New Town Progress. (1973)
        SKELMERSDALE DEVELOPMENT CORPORATION. January 1973.

        The report summarises progress made in the new
        town's development from the date of designation
        (October 1961) to January 1973. It covers population
        housing, industry, employment, roads, sewers, the
        town centre, central and local shops, schools,
        religious and medical facilities, landscaping and
        open spaces, and gives details of weekly rents and
        rates.

2.2.7   Recreation and Leisure Facilities in Skelmersdale
        New Town. [Report on] (1969)
        SKELMERSDALE DEVELOPMENT CORPORATION. March 1969.
                                                (32pp.)

        Various factors which affect the planning and development
        of leisure and recreation facilities are discussed,
        and the main problems are identified as the complexity
        of powers and responsibilities involved in their
        provision, and financial limitations on Development
        Corporation spending in this area. The existing and
        projected leisure and recreation needs and provision
        in Skelmersdale are discussed under four main heads
        according to the body responsible (Outside Bodies;
        Public Authorities; Joint Provision; and others). A
        general short-term programme is presented for each of
        the four categories, and the financial implications
        are outlined. In conclusion the report stresses
        that the popularity and growth of the new town's
        leisure and recreation facilities will depend upon the
        encouragement of full participation in their develop-
        ment and management by the residents.

        Tabulated appendices give details of existing (March
        1969) recreation and leisure facilities in Skelmersdale,
        and of services or facilities which may be provided
        by local authorities under various statutory powers.
        Sketch maps show existing (March 1969) and proposed
        (1969-1972) facilities in the new town.

2.2.8   Skelmersdale New Town Population and Social Surveys
                                        (Annually from 1964).
        SKELMERSDALE DEVELOPMENT CORPORATION

        This series of reports summarises the results of
        annual sample population and social surveys carried
        out in Skelmersdale new town since 1964 to provide
        information for planning and management. Over the
        period the surveys and analysis have become increas-
        ingly detailed and refined. The Introduction to the
        1977 report includes an outline of the statistical
        basis of the survey and a summary of the results.
        This is followed by the findings from a supplementary
        survey of school-leavers carried out in 1977.

The main part of the report comprises detailed tabulations which, in addition to demographic and employment
data, present information on car ownership; the use
of shopping, health and leisure facilities; means of
travel to work, shops and school; and use of the footpath system. Information is also provided on the
opinions and attitudes of the inhabitants towards
various aspects of the new town, thus providing valuable
'feedback' on the relevance of the Development Corporation's policies and relative success of their
implementation

Other Reports, Papers and Articles

2.2.9   Environmental Recovery at Skelmersdale: report on an
environmental recovery project carried out in
Skelmersdale from June 1966 to June 1969. (1969)
CIVIC TRUST FOR THE NORTH-WEST. 1969.

2.2.10 Environmental Recovery at Skelmersdale. (1970)
ASHWORTH, G.
R.I.B.A. Journal. May 1970. (p.216)
Town Planning Review. Vol.41. No.3· July 1970.
                                    (pp.263-292)

The articles describe a scheme carried out by the
Civic Trust for the North-West for rehabilitation
and total environmental improvement in the centre
of Old Skelmersdale.

2.2.11 Environmental Recovery - the Skelmersdale Project.(1968--9)
ANON.
Surveyor. 31st, August 1968 (pp.22-26)
and "   17th. October 1969 (pp.36-37)

2.2.12 Skelmersdale New Town. (1978)
ANON.
Estates Gazette. Vol. 246. April 29th. 1978. (pp. 389-
                                                 393)

The article reviews the new town's industrial and
commercial development and assesses future employment
prospects as being on the whole favourable.

2.2.13 Skelmersdale: Review of the New Town after Ten Years.
PHELPS, R.   (1972)
Town and Country Planning Vol.40. No.1. January 1972.
                                          (pp.70-72)

2.2.14 Skelmersdale's Community Programme. (1966)
PRITCHARD, N.
Town and Country Planning. Vol.34. No.1. January 1966.
                                              (p.70)

2.2 Subsidiary References.

1.1 New Towns - Transport and Mobility.

1.1.18   *Transport and New Towns. Volume Two.* (1976)

1.2 New Towns - Non-Transport Aspects.

1.2.12   *An Analysis of the Employment and Industrial Structure of Five British New Towns.* (1971)
1.2.48   *Town and Country Planning.* (February 1978.)
1.2.51   *Annual Reports of the Development Corporations.*

9.2 Bibliographies.

9.2.25   *New Towns Bibliography. 1977.* (1977)
9.2.27   *New Towns.* (1976)

9.4 Research Registers.

9.4.6   *1977 Summary of Research being Undertaken in New Towns.* (1977)

9.5 Statistical Sources.

9.5.16   *Census of Population.*
9.5.19   *Local Government Trends.* (Annually.)
9.5.21   *Progress on Land Sold or Leased by Development Corporations/ Commission for the New Towns.* ['The Publicity Sheet'.] (Quarterly.)

9.6 Other Sources of Information.

9.6.2   *National Index of Traffic and Transportation Surveys.* (1975)
9.6.16   *Sourcebook of Planning Information.* (1971) [pp.197-8]

2.3   Telford.

Material on Telford is set out in the following order, following
the arrangements used for references relating to Runcorn and
Skelmersdale:-

1. Items relating specifically to transport (including
   a number of Development Corporation and transport
   planning consultants' reports)   (2.3.1 - 2.3.8).
2. Other Development Corporation and planning consultants'
   reports, beginning with the Master Plan and related
   documents which are listed chronologically (2.3.9 -
   2.3.24). The Consultants' Proposals for the development of Dawley, Wellington and Oakengates, which
   preceded the designation of Telford, are included
   (2.3.9).
3. Other, miscellaneous articles   (2.3.25 - 2.3.26).

Most of the available data on Telford has resulted
from feasibility studies of travel behaviour and demand in
relation to land use, and the development of public transport
and highway strategies based on these. This contrasts with
Runcorn where most of the published material consists of
descriptive comment or assessments of the transport planning
carried out as a result of the Master Plan proposals. A
considerable volume of detailed information on transport and
mobility in Telford is embodied in the various documents arising from the Telford Transportation Study and Short Term Bus
Study (2.3.1 and 2.3.4 to 2.3.7). These studies include
material on the following aspects:-

- The present provision of facilities for private
  road transport, public transport, and pedestrian and
  cycle movements.
- Bus transport operation.
- Existing travel patterns, for all modes of transport.
- Car ownership and availability.
- Attitudes of Telford residents to the bus services.
- Present and likely future demand for different
  modes of transport.
- The development of alternative future highway and
  public transport strategies.
- Policy recommendations based on the findings and
  conclusions of the studies.

Earlier data on travel patterns in Telford and on car ownership and availability are included in Volume Two of TELFORD
DEVELOPMENT CORPORATION'S Social Survey (2.3.21), which also
includes some information on attitudes towards public and
private transport provision. Attitudinal material is also
contained in the Facility Survey of Telford Development
Corporation Industrial Estates (2.3.14) which was based on
a study of local firms' opinions on the public transport and
other service facilities provided on Development Corporation-
owned industrial estates in 1974.

The subject of rail travel in Telford is examined in the
study by KIMBERLEY, which assesses future rail travel demand
and makes detailed recommendations as to how British Rail
could open up its full market potential in the area.

The early background to transport planning in Telford is
provided by the Development and Basic Plan Proposals set out
by the JOHN MADIN DESIGN GROUP and TELFORD DEVELOPMENT
CORPORATION (2.3.10 and 2.3.11), and in the DEVELOPMENT
CORPORATION's Master Plan Policy: Public Transport. However,
many of the original recommendations for the future transport
network have been superseded by subsequent proposals based on
the findings of the Telford Transportation and Short Term Bus
Studies.

TELFORD DEVELOPMENT CORPORATION's Progress Reports for 1974
and 1976 (2.3.18 and 2.3.19) together with the yearly summaries
contained in the Annual Reports of the Development Corporations
in England and Wales (1.2.51) provide a factual record of the
main facets of the new town's development. The social aspects
have been examined in a number of surveys carried out by the
Development Corporation's Social Development and Planning
Departments, the results of which have been well-documented.
The summary reports arising from the 1973 Social Survey (2.3.21)
contain detailed information on various socio-economic aspects
of Telford residents and their activities. Reports of the
studies of leisure and recreation activities and provision
(2.3.16, 2.3.17), elderly people (2.3.15), and shopping patterns
and provision (2.3.20 and 2.3.22) also provide valuable background material for the examination of Telford residents' travel
patterns and transport needs. Further information on shopping
patterns is contained in Volume 1 of the Social Survey report
(2.3.21), and reference to shopping provision in Telford is
made in the chapter on 'Shops and Shopping' by Sir FRANK PRICE
in New Towns: the British Experience (1.2.33). In the same book,
G. BROOKE TAYLOR, discussing social development in new towns,
draws illustrative examples from Telford's experience (among
other new towns). The DEVELOPMENT CORPORATION's report: To Me -
This is Telford (2.3.24), based on qualitative social research
through in-depth family interviews, provides interesting in-
sights into new residents' early reactions to Telford.

Transport-related items

2.3.1 Bus Services for Telford: Report of the short term
       bus study.(1976)
       COLIN BUCHANAN & PARTNERS
       Colin Buchanan & Partners, Salop County Council,
       Telford Development Corporation, Midland Red Omnibus
       Company, District of the Wrekin Council, The Indepen-
       dent Operators. April 1976.(140pp.)

       This report presents the findings and conclusions
       from the Telford Short Term Public Transport Study,
       the main objective of which was to define and recom-
       mend a public transport service restructuring plan
       for Telford which would be capable of short-term
       implementation. In the first part of the report the
       present bus system is described in terms of operators,
       services operated, the levels of accessibility
       provided, fares systems and staffing. The costs of
       the present bus system are examined, and passenger
       use of and attitudes towards the bus system are
       considered. Part 2 presents options for new bus net-
       works and fares systems, and considers different
       organisational structures through which these could
       be provided. Costing and passenger/revenue estimation
       methods are developed and used to compare the different
       route and fares options, and the most promising options
       are identified.

2.3.2 Master Plan Policy : Public Transport Study, Bulletin 3.
                                                        (1970)
       TELFORD DEVELOPMENT CORPORATION. December 1970.(30pp.)

       This report presents the results of a study of existing
       public transport within the new town as at 1970, and
       of the proposed future public transport network up to
       1981. The future proposals have now been superseded
       by those contained in the Short Term Bus Study (1976)—see
       ref. 2.3.1 above.

2.3.3. Roads in Urban Areas : Brookside 4. (Undated)
        TELFORD DEVELOPMENT CORPORATION.(10pp.)

        The design principles underlying the planning of the
        layout for the Development Corporation's Brookside 4
        estate are described in this report. The context for
        the development of these principles is outlined and
        some design details are set out. The experimental lay-
        out, partially influenced by the planning of The Brow
        estate at Runcorn, represents a compromise between
        Radburn principles and a more traditional housing lay-
        out. The informal estate layout provides for a mix of
        vehicles and pedestrians, giving pedestrians priority
        by positive restrictions to the speed of vehicles and
        by providing footpaths in some places. The estate was
        planned for 100% garaging and 100% parking, close road
        access being made available to every dwelling. This
        reflects both the Master Plan's goal for providing

the optimum conditions for the use of private motor
transport in the new town, and the possibility of
the eventual sale of individual houses.

2.3.4   Telford Bus Use Attitude Survey : An investigation
         of citizen attitudes towards public transportation
         in Telford. (1976).
         TELFORD DEVELOPMENT CORPORATION and COLIN BUCHANAN
         & PARTNERS. (28pp. plus appendices).

         The report presents an analysis of the findings from
         two attitude surveys carried out as part of the
         Telford Transportation Study. The aims of the surveys
         were to identify deficiencies in the existing bus
         services in the new town and to obtain an indication
         of residents' evaluation of priorities in bus service
         improvements and of alternative future financial
         strategies for the bus operators. Self-completion
         interviews were conducted among a sample of all
         Telford residents (648 home interviews) and a sample
         of bus users (461 bus stop interviews), the latter
         being a shortened version of the home interviews.

         The survey found that about 70% of the respondents
         regarded public spending on public transport as import-
         ant or very important, when considered in the context
         of other major areas of public spending, and that the
         main priority in improving bus services was to keep
         the fares down. Respondents were also asked about
         their awareness and use of bus service information
         and it was found that although over three-quarters
         normally planned to catch specific buses, less than
         20% possessed a timetable. Copies of the questionnaires
         are included as appendices.

2.3.5   Telford Short Term Bus Study. [*The](1976)
         BUCHANAN, C.M., et al.
         Paper read at PTRC Summer Annual Meeting. Seminar
         M: Public Transport. July 1976. (pp. 1-13 of Proceedings)
         (see ref. 2.3.1. above).

2.3.6   Telford Transportation Study. (1976/7)
         COLIN BUCHANAN & PARTNERS.

         The objectives of the Study, commissioned in August
         1974 were:-

         (i)   To examine and report on the existing travel
                 and transport situation in Telford New Town.

         (ii)   To investigate alternative future strategies
                 for public transport and highway provision
                 relative to land-use distribution and the
                 phasing of development.

         (iii)   To enable the Development Corporation to
                 review the overall transportation strategy
                 of the New Town and to select a strategy for
                 future public transport and highway provision

appropriate for the foreseeable availability
of resources.

1. Report of Surveys. (June 1976)
   The Report describes the findings of the
   Transportation Study's examination of the existing
   travel and transportation situation in the Telford
   New Town area.

2. Summary Report and Revised Basic Transport Plan
   for Telford New Town. (May 1977)

3. Report and Recommended Revised Basic Transport
   Plan. (November 1977) 204pp.

   The Report examines the future transport situation
   in Telford, assuming a 1996 population of over
   210,000 and two alternative economic growth rates,
   the lower rate (2.5% per annum) being the value
   then recommended by the Department of Transport.
   The major factors likely to affect travel demand
   and mode choice are reviewed and alternative
   transport plans are developed to match the alternative economic growth rates assumed. The travel
   demands likely to result from these transport
   plans are assessed and the plans are compared
   from various aspects, including that of cost-
   effectiveness. The results of special sub-studies
   of the Town Centre and Severn Gorge are summarised.
   The preferred future highway and public transport
   networks are developed, and proposals made for
   the adoption of a revised Basic Transport Plan
   consisting of a completely new bus network and a
   reduced highway network which could be expanded
   to cope with the extra traffic volumes that
   would arise should the economic growth rate be
   higher than that forecast. Recommendations are
   made as to the implementation and phasing of the
   proposed Revised Basic Transport Plan.

4. Telford Transportation Study Review. (October 1977).
   67pp.

   The report reviews the planning and land use data
   changes expected to result from the Secretary of
   State for the Environment's revised population
   target for Telford (from 210,000 to 150,000 at
   1996) announced in April 1977 and confirmed in
   July 1977. It also reviews the economic growth
   rates assumed in the main Transportation Study
   for the period 1974-1996. A single (low) rate of
   growth in GDP is assumed. A likely 1996 highway
   plan and public transport network are defined.
   Travel demand estimates likely to result from the
   changed population and economic circumstances are
   described. These are used to test and evaluate
   possible alternatives within the transport plan,
   resulting in the development of a revised recommended Basic Transport Plan and recommendations as to
   the phasing of its construction.

2.3.7   Telford Transportation Study :
         1. An aid to the preliminary evaluation of long-term
            public transport options.(1976)
         PIKE, D.H., FULLER, P.I.and WHITE, M.T.
         Traffic Engineering and Control. Vol.17. No.2.
         February 1976. (pp.52-55)

The authors describe a simple accessibility model
devised to aid the preliminary evaluation of a large
number of bus options. The objective was to select
five bus networks to combine with complementary
highway networks to form comprehensive policy packages
for testing,using a conventional transportation model.
The accessibility function used to measure the performance of the bus options in meeting the requirements
of groups of potential users is described. Ten bus routeing
concepts were tested at four operating cost levels and
the results are reported and discussed.

         2.   New techniques in the modelling of trip
         generation and modal split.(1976)
         MULLEN, P., BURSEY, N.C. and WHITE, M.T.
         Traffic Engineering and Control.Vol. 17.No.3. March
                                   1976. (pp.106-109)

This paper describes the development and calibration
of a transportation study model based on the individual
trip-maker rather than the conventional household -
based approach. New forms of vehicle ownership and
trip-generation models were calibrated using
disaggregated data. The modal choice model for bus,
car and walk modes was calibrated for three vehicle
availability groups rather than the usual practice of
grouping all members of car owning households together.
The methods adopted for each of these models are
outlined and the results are presented.

2.3.8   Telford - Whose Opportunity? An Appraisal of Changes
         in the Rail Travel Market of the Telford Area.(1978.)
         KIMBERLEY, C.
         Wolverhampton Polytechnic. B.A. (Business Studies)
                               Dissertation. 1978. (94pp.)

An examination of developments in the travel market
in the area of Telford New Town, concentrating
particularly on rail services. Some conclusions are
drawn about likely future travel demand patterns and
recommendations are made as to the way in which
British Rail should develop its full market potential
in the area.

(See also Development Corporation documents - refs.
2.3.9, 2.3.10, 2.3.11, 2.3.13, 2.3.14, 2.3.18,
2.3.19, 2.3.21. below.)

2.3.9   Dawley, Wellington, Oakengates - Consultants'
          Proposals for Development. (1966)
          J.H.D. MADIN and PARTNERS.
          H.M.S.O. London. November 1966.

2.3.10   Telford: Development Proposals. Vols., 1 and 2.
                                                    (1969)
          JOHN MADIN DESIGN GROUP.
          Telford Development Corporation. June 1969.

          The structure proposed by the Consultants for the
          new town's development was based on the dispersal
          of key attraction points within the framework of a
          primary grid, so as to provide optimum conditions
          for the distribution of traffic volumes. Within this
          context freedom to use the motor car as far as
          practicable was taken as the main aim of the trans-
          portation proposals. The rôle of public transport
          would be to provide for the residual element of travel
          demand, although the plan should be sufficiently
          flexible for a change of emphasis to public transport
          if necessary. Buses are seen as the most economical
          and flexible form of public transport and where practi-
          cable should have their own right of way. The proposals
          for railways include a recommendation for an additional
          station at the new central area of Telford.

          Volume 2 is a Technical Supplement to the proposals
          set out in Volume 1.

2.3.11   Telford Basic Plan Proposals. (1973)
          TELFORD DEVELOPMENT CORPORATION. March 1973. (35pp.)

          This document sets out the basic framework for the
          development of Telford up to 1991. The plan is
          based substantially on the Consultants' proposals,
          but incorporates some subsequent amendments. The
          report discusses these changes and describes the
          proposals and constituent elements of the plan,
          finally outlining the phasing and processes of
          implementation. A copy of the Secretary of State's
          letter to the Development Corporation setting out
          his comments and observations on the plan and
          indicating his general acceptance of it, is appended.
          (Revised proposals in accordance with amended
          population targets [of 130,000 by 1986 rising to
          150,000 by 1996], as confirmed by the Secretary of
          State for the Environment in July 1977, are set out
          in: Telford Development Strategy. TELFORD DEVELOPMENT
          CORPORATION. 1978).

2.3.12   Children's Play. (1973)
          TELFORD DEVELOPMENT CORPORATION. 1973.

2.3.13   Executive Housing Survey: a study of attitudes
          in the medium to upper private housing market.
                                                    (1976)
          TELFORD DEVELOPMENT CORPORATION - PLANNING
          DEPARTMENT. March 1976. (26pp. plus appendices).

          Includes an examination of factors affecting choice
          of location and attitudes to areas within Telford.

2.3.14 A Facility Survey of Telford Development
Corporation Industrial Estates.(1974)
TELFORD DEVELOPMENT CORPORATION. 1974.(21pp.)

This report presents the findings of a survey
carried out on Corporation-owned industrial
estates in 1974 in order to quantify the opinions
held by resident firms with regard to the public
transport and service provisions made for the
estates.

2.3.15 "Help": A report on the needs of and services
for the elderly in Telford. (1975)
TELFORD DEVELOPMENT CORPORATION - DEPARTMENT OF
SOCIAL DEVELOPMENT. September 1975.(139 pp.)

A survey conducted among the elderly of Telford
is described in this report. The purpose of the
survey was to identify the characteristics of
elderly persons living in Telford, to estimate
their needs for specific services, to assess the
existing level of provision of services and to
estimate the extent of unmet needs for services
and support. The report shows that in 1973
approximately one-third (3,500) of Telford's
elderly people suffered some restriction in
mobility outdoors and that one-third of all those
interviewed had difficulties in climbing steps
outside. Of those aged 80 years and over, three-
quarters were restricted in mobility, the severity
of the restriction increasing with age. The
survey indicated that levels of support services
provided for the elderly in Telford in 1973 did not
meet needs (with the exception of Meals on Wheels)
and recommendations are made as to ways in which
support could be improved. Appendices include a
copy of the questionnaire and detailed statistical
analyses.

2.3.16 The Ironbridge Gorge Recreation Planning Report.
(1973).
TELFORD DEVELOPMENT CORPORATION - PLANNING
DEPARTMENT.(Unpublished report).1973.

2.3.17 Leisure and Recreation Study.(1972)
Part   I   : Background and Method.
Part   II : Home-based Activities and Rural Activities.
Part   III: Outdoor Urban Activities.
Part   IV : Indoor Urban Activities.
Part   V   : Provision of Recreation Facilities.
TELFORD DEVELOPMENT CORPORATION. 1972.(800 pp.)

2.3.18 Progress Report.(1974.)
TELFORD DEVELOPMENT CORPORATION. 1974 (20pp.)

Progress in the new town as at 1973-4 is summarised,
and information given on housing, manufacturing,

employment, service employment and population on Development Corporation estates. An outline of proposed development for the period 1974-9 is given.

2.3.19   Progress Report.(1976)
TELFORD DEVELOPMENT CORPORATION. 1976 (49pp.)

A broad review of progress in Telford up to 1975/6 is given and detailed information presented for housing and population; employment and industry; Development Corporation tenants; and social and community development. An assessment is made of the new town's development within the context of the West Midland Planning Authorities' Conference's Regional Strategy.

2.3.20   Shopping Patterns in a New Town - Madeley District
(undated).
TELFORD DEVELOPMENT CORPORATION.

Results of household and street interviews.

2.3.21   Social Survey.(1973).
TELFORD DEVELOPMENT CORPORATION - PLANNING DEPARTMENT and DEPARTMENT OF SOCIAL DEVELOPMENT.
1.   Shopping. 1974.
2.   Transport.(21 pp.) 1974.
3.   Housing and Households. (22 pp.) 1974.
4.   Social Activities. (18 pp.) 1974.
5.   Employment and Income.(22 pp.) 1974.

The aims of the social survey of Telford, carried out in May/June 1973, were:
(i)   to obtain and update basic data on nucleus and incoming population.
(ii)   to monitor existing and changing patterns of movement within the town.
(iii)   to enable testing of the overall concepts and policies of the new town.
The five separate topic reports each cover a section of the questionnaire. There are also a Preliminary Report, and Area Reports on Donnington; St. Georges/Priorslee; Trench and Severn Gorge.
The Transport Report presents information on ownership, availability and garaging of cars; method of journey to work, school and shop; and attitudes towards provision for public and private transport. The results of the survey were analysed by 16 areas based on traffic zones. Conclusions are drawn and recommendations made.

2.3.22   Telford Survey Report - Shopping Patterns in
New Towns.(undated)
TELFORD DEVELOPMENT CORPORATION.

2.3.23   Telford Tenants' Reports. (1974, 1975 and 1976-8)
          TELFORD DEVELOPMENT CORPORATION.

          These reports describe various characteristics of the
          Development Corporation's tenants, including age,
          household size, occupation, car ownership, workplace,
          place of origin, and - in the case of leavers - place
          of destination and reasons for leaving.

2.3.24   To Me - This is Telford. (1977)
          TELFORD DEVELOPMENT CORPORATION - DEPARTMENT OF
          SOCIAL DEVELOPMENT. June 1977. (33 pp. plus Appendices)

          A report on a series of pilot interviews carried out
          with 46 households in new areas of Telford in the
          spring of 1977.
          (See also refs: 2.3.1,   2.3.2,   2.3.3,   2.3.4,
          2.3.6 above.)

Other Reports, Papers and Articles.

2.3.25   Telford New Town: Concept and reality in West Midlands
          industrial overspill. (1972)
          TOLLEY, R.S.
          Town Planning Review. Vol.43. No.4. October 1972.
                                          (pp.343 - 360)

2.3.26   Telford: New Town with a Past. (1975)
          SPRING, M.
          Architectural Design. Vol.XLV. September 1975.
                                          (pp. 561-562)

2.3 Subsidiary References.

1.1 New Towns - Transport and Mobility.

1.1.18   Transport and New Towns. Volume Two. (1976)

1.2 New Towns - Non-Transport Aspects.

1.2.12   An Analysis of the Employment and Industrial Structure of Five
          British New Towns. (1971)
1.2.33   New Towns: the British Experience. (1972)
1.2.48   Town and Country Planning. (February 1978)
1.2.51   Annual Reports of the Development Corporations.

5.1 Private Motor Transport.

5.1.2   Forecasting Car Ownership: a new approach. (1977)
          [Refers to the Telford Transportation Study].

9.2 Bibliographies.

9.2.25   New Towns Bibliography. 1977. (1977)
9.2.27   New Towns. (1976)

9.4 Research Registers.

9.4.6   1977 Summary of Research being Undertaken in New Towns. (1977)

9.5 Statistical Sources.

9.5.16   Census of Population.
9.5.19   Local Government Trends. (Annually)
9.5.21   Progress on Land Sold or Leased by Development Corporations/
          Commission for the New Towns. ['The Publicity Sheet'.] (Quarterly.)

9.6 Other Sources of Information.

9.6.2   National Index of Traffic and Transportation Surveys. (1975)
9.6.16   Sourcebook of Planning Information. (1971) [pp. 194-6]

2.4   Other New Towns.

Selected material considered to contribute towards establishing
a comparative framework for the study of public transport in
Runcorn, Skelmersdale and Telford is drawn together in this
subsection. The references are presented under new town
headings, arranged in alphabetical order. Under the individual
new town headings master plans and other official Development
Corporation reports - where included - are listed first, in
chronological order. Other items are arranged alphabetically
by title. The list of subsidiary references contains items
entered elsewhere in the bibliography which incorporate
material relating to specific new towns listed in this subsection.

The references provide material covering a fairly wide spectrum
of new town development, and include the following:-

- Master plans and related official reports.
- Articles and papers describing and examining the
  transport goals and proposals set out in specific
  new town master plans.
- Studies of public transport provision and need.
- Reports and papers describing the planning of and
  operational experience with experimental or innovatory
  public transport services in specific new towns.
- Reports of Household Surveys and other studies relating
  to social aspects of individual new towns.

Comprehensive coverage of master plans has not been attempted,
but some selected plans which offer useful comparisons with
or contrasts to those of the three new towns under study have
been included. Comparisons in terms of designated acreage,
target population and scale of development can be drawn between
Milton Keynes and Telford, and the Milton Keynes Master Plan
(2.4.29) also reveals marked similarities with the Telford
Basic Plan Proposals (2.3.10-11) in respect of the broad planning goals laid down, particularly with reference to the
emphasis on freedom of choice and ease of movement and access.
In both plans this was interpreted as involving the provision
of optional conditions for the use of the private car, although
the detailed transport proposals set out in the two plans
differ in a number of respects. Several studies, notably those
by POTTER AND HILLMAN (1.1.1) and LEMBERG (3.3.21), have examine
the contrasts between the Milton Keynes and the Runcorn approac
to transport planning. On the other hand, there are similaritie
between the Redditch Master Plan (2.4.48) and that of Runcorn
in the degree of priority given to public transport, and the
means by which this was to be achieved:- a figure-of-eight
public transport spine linking a series of residential district
The Redditch Master Plan, although drawn up by the same consult
ants as that for Skelmersdale, reflects a substantially differe
approach to the plan produced for Skelmersdale which gave
primary emphasis to private car movement, although pedestrian
movements were also given considerable attention. In this
respect the Washington Master Plan (2.4.65) bears certain

similarities to the Skelmersdale proposals. Transport has
also been a major factor in the design of Irvine New Town
(2.4.24-28) which offers a different example of the inter-
gration of public transport provision into the new town
structure. The Master Plan for Stevenage (2.4.50/51), the
first new town to be designated under the New Towns Act 1946,
has been included for comparative purposes as an example of
a Mark I new town master plan. Although the original proposals
were modified in several ways as the town developed, the
master plan, which was not published until 1965/6 exhibits
a number of features usually considered to be typical of the
first generation new towns, including the emphasis on segregated pedestrian movement within relatively low-density
Radburn-type housing layouts in a series of neighbourhoods
arranged around the town centre, and a hierarchical road
network designed principally for private car usage rather
than public transport. The Stevenage Master Plan also provides
insight into the background to the planning and development
of the Stevenage Superbus Service.

Among studies of public transport provision and demand the
Glenrothes Area Public Transport Study (2.4.11) and Harlow
Bus Study (2.4.15) offer a basis for comparison with the
findings of the Telford Short Term Bus Study (and, to a lesser
extent, with TRRL's monitoring study of the Runcorn Busway).
The Glenrothes and Harlow reports both present data on trip-
making characteristics derived from household interview
surveys and some attitudinal data, as well as the results
of detailed investigations into current bus service provision and operation. The Glenrothes study also includes the
results of bus usage surveys and an assessment of future
demand for public transport in the town. Both reports make
recommendations on methods for improving both the bus services
and the public's perception of the services, in the respective new towns. LICHFIELD'S Stevenage Public Transport:
Cost Benefit Analysis (2.4.57) includes some less recent but
still relevant data on public transport provision and usage.

A substantial body of material is available concerning both
the planning stages and subsequent operation of experimental
bus services and innovatory demand-responsive transport
services in certain British new towns. The Stevenage Superbus Service, which was introduced following the recommendations of Lichfield's Cost Benefit Analysis study, has been
monitored in detail and well-documented in a series of reports
and papers (2.4.54-5 and 2.4.58-60). The Harlow Dial-a-Bus
service which connected Old Harlow with Harlow town centre
and other parts of the new town has also been the subject of
detailed monitoring studies. Reports of both the demand
modelling and preliminary planning procedures, and of studies
of the service in operation have been published by TRRL and the
Cranfield Institute of Technology Centre for Transport Studies.
A number of these reports and related material have been
included in the bibliography. (2.4.16-23 and 4.4.15-16).
The Milton Keynes dial-a-ride service is described and discussed in several reports and articles listed under the Milton
Keynes subheading, and passenger statistics on both this and

the Harlow Service are presented in MITCHELL'S report: <u>Some</u>
<u>Social Aspects of Public Passenger Transport</u> (3.2.49).

The Household Surveys and other socially-oriented reports
and articles included in this subsection offer a range of
comparative data on population, housing, employment, the
provision and use of leisure, recreation and shopping faciliti
and the needs of children and teenagers. Car ownership data i
normally also included in the reports of household interview
surveys, as is some information on residents' usual mode of
transport to various facilities and, in some cases, data on
residents' attitudes to various aspects of the new town. Repo
of general household surveys in <u>Basildon</u> (2.4.3), <u>Bracknell</u>
(2.4.4), <u>Cumbernauld</u> (2.4.7), <u>East Kilbride</u> (2.4.9), <u>Harlow</u>
(2.4.13), <u>Milton Keynes</u> (2.4.40) and <u>Stevenage</u> (2.4.56) have
been included.

Aycliffe

2.4.1   Aycliffe Housing Survey: A Study of Housing in a
         New Town. (1970)
         KARN, V.
         Occasional Paper No.9. University of Birmingham.
         Centre for Urban and Regional Studies. 1970. (68pp.)

2.4.2   Newton Aycliffe - doubled in size. (1967)
         WHITTICK, A.
         Town and Country Planning. Vol.35. No.10. Nov.1967.
                              (pp.503-506)

Basildon

2.4.3.   Basildon - Shopping; Work for Women; Leisure. (1967)
         BYRON, C.H.
         Basildon Development Corporation. 1967.

         This household survey was initiated by the Development
         Corporation to obtain data which would be useful in planning
         for the expansion of the new town beyond the original
         target population.   Over 200 households were interviewed
         in each of three neighbourhoods, differing from one an-
         other in average income levels, socio-economic structure
         and lifestyle.   It was found that there were substantial
         differences in shopping and leisure habits and requirements
         between people living in the three areas.   The survey also
         showed that, without much distinction by class, 34% to
         45% of the sample of housewives were working outside
         their homes, as many as half part-time.

Bracknell

2.4.4   Various reports on research carried out by the Social
         Development Department of the Development Corporation,
         for example:
         Youth in Bracknell. (1960)
         Size of Neighbourhood. (1962)
         Household Survey. (1966)
         Wildridings Social Study - Residents' Use of and
         Satisfaction with Pedestrian/Vehicle Segregation. (1969)

Crawley

2.4.5   Crawley: A Study of Amenities in a New Town. (1967)
         BROOKE TAYLOR, G.
         New Towns Commission. 1967.

2.4.6   Traffic and Transport in Crawley. (1971)
         CRAWLEY PLANNING GROUP. 1971.

Cumbernauld

2.4.7   Cumbernauld '67: A Household Survey and Report. (1968)
         CUMBERNAULD DEVELOPMENT CORPORATION. 1968.

         Research into attitudes of residents to the new town
         carried out by Strathclyde University in September 1967
         showed a generally favourable (87%) attitude. Only two-
         thirds of car owners had garages or car spaces.

East Kilbride

2.4.8   East Kilbride Housing Survey: A Study of Housing
        in a New Town.   (1970)
        KARN, V.

        Occasional Paper No. 8.   University of Birmingham.
        Centre for Urban and Regional Studies.   1970.   (77p.)

2.4.9   East Kilbride '70.   A Social and Economic Survey.   (197
        STRATHCLYDE UNIVERSITY.   1970.

        Research showed that 90.6% of residents were generally
        satisfied with the town.

2.4.10 Mental Health and Social Adjustment in a New Town:
        an exploratory study in East Kilbride.   (1965)
        COLEMAN, S.D.

        Glasgow University.   Department of Economic and
        Social Research.   1965.

Glenrothes

2.4.11 Glenrothes Area Public Transport Study: Final Report.
                                                        (1977)
        JAMIESON MACKAY & PARTNERS.
        Fife Regional Council.   July 1977.   (57pp. plus append

        The main purposes of the study were to establish the
        demand for additional public transport services in
        the new town and/or the need to rationalise existing
        services to provide an optimum bus network and service
        The report contains summaries of the results of all
        surveys undertaken, followed by conclusions and
        recommendations.   The surveys included a Bus Passenge
        Survey in which information was collected on trip orig
        and destination, boarding and alighting bus stops, tri
        purpose, mode of transport used to and from the bus,
        and ticket type.   Data relating to bus operations was
        also collected, including journey times, vehicle
        capacities and bus stop positions.   A household inter
        view survey was carried out to ascertain trip-making
        characteristics of residents in particular areas, and
        a journey to work survey was conducted among employees
        in Glenrothes.   A study was also made of existing use
        of rail services.   Investigations were made into
        residents' attitudes to bus services in Glenrothes wit
        a view to assessing latent demand for bus travel.
        Assessments of bus/rail and car/rail interchange
        facilities at two points were also made.

        The surveys showed that about four times as many trips
        are made by private car in Glenrothes as are made by
        bus, and that the demand for public transport arises
        almost entirely from persons with no car at their
        disposal.   A general level of dissatisfaction with

existing public transport services in the new town
was revealed. The report concludes that a policy
directed towards altering the present modal split
would not be feasible in Glenrothes. However, a
number of short-term proposals are made aimed at
improving the service, eliminating certain sources
of dissatisfaction, and saving costs so as to reduce
the subsidy to the bus operator. These include
phased introduction of one-man operation, the
provision of better information on bus services,
and some rationalisation of the route pattern.

Harlow

2.4.12   Harlow New Town.(1952)
         GIBBERD, F.
         Harlow Development Corporation. 2nd edition. 1952

2.4.13   Harlow 1976 Household Survey. (1977)
         HARLOW DEVELOPMENT CORPORATION. 1977.

         The series of reports present information derived
         from Harlow Development Corporation's tenth Household
         Survey. In addition to factual information the survey
         provides data on residents' opinions and comments on
         aspects of their housing, leisure and recreation
         facilities, and shopping provision. The sample covered
         2,713 households out of a town total of 25,500 house-
         holds.

         Vol.1: Harlow 1976 Household Survey. March 1977. (66pp.
                 plus Appendices).
                 This introductory report presents a broad
                 picture of Harlow, drawing data from both the
                 1977 Household Survey and other sources. The
                 main characteristics of the new town's
                 population, households and employment patterns
                 are outlined, significant trends are identified
                 and the data is related to the regional and
                 national contexts.

         Vol.2: Demographic Characteristics. July 1977. (40pp.
                 plus Appendices)

         Vol.3: Residents' Opinions and Comments on Shopping
                                 Provision. July 1977. (23pp.)

         Vol.4: Residents' Opinions on Leisure and Recreation
                         Facilities. December 1977. (26pp. plus Appendix)

         Vol.5: Vehicle Ownership. July 1977. (24pp. plus
                                                 Appendices)
                 Ownership of bicycles, motor cycles and caravans
                 is covered as well as that of cars.

         Vol.6: Statistical Basis: Technical Report. December
                                                 1977. (14pp.)

Vol.7: Journey to Work and Commuting. September 1977.
(24pp. plus Appendices)

Vol.8: Household Characteristics and Dwelling Sizes.
September 1977.(37pp. plus Appendic

Vol.9: Some Characteristics of Second Generation
Households and Leavers.(28pp. plus Appendix).

2.4.14 Attitudes to Transport Provision in Old Harlow.(1974)
MORTON-WILLIAMS, J. and BUTLER, J.
Social and Community Planning Research. Report P.315.
1974. (37pp. plus appendices)

The results of an in-depth qualitative study carried
out before the introduction of Dial-a-Ride in Old
Harlow are described and discussed. The main objectives were to investigate how decisions to make trips
and to use particular modes of transport are made;
to explore perceptions of and attitudes to the main
modes of transport; and to identify travel needs and
wants and formulate hypotheses about how they relate
to attitudes and to modes of transport. The data was
collected by means of tape-recorded semi-structured
depth interviews with a sample of 45 residents of
Old Harlow. A brief 7-day trip diary was used as a fr
work for more detailed enquiries into the decision-
making processes involved in planning trips and choosing modes of transport. The interview included a
brief section on awareness of and attitudes towards
the proposed Dial-a-Ride system, which enabled some
conclusions to be drawn as to the needs that the servic
could meet. Appendices provide details of the sample
and copies of the trip diary and depth interview guide

2.4.15 Harlow Bus Study. Final Report.(1976)
ALASTAIR DICK & ASSOCIATES. April 1976.
Volume 1: Main Report (93pp.)
Volume 2. Technical Appendices (49pp. plus hole count
printouts).

The report deals with a preliminary feasibility study
of bus services in Harlow. The objectives of the
study were to identify current problems in the use
of public transport in Harlow and to recommend proced
for more detailed studies. The Main Report (Vol.1)
describes the background to the study and gives detai
of existing bus operations in Harlow. The results of
a smallscale household attitude survey, which investigated trip-making characteristics as well as attitudes
towards the bus services, are presented. An evaluatic
of problem areas in bus operation is made, in which
the reality is compared with perceived attributes
derived from the attitudinal data.

A major conclusion is that much of the problem in

the future could be in the public's perception of the
bus service rather than in the service itself. A
marketing campaign is recommended which would be both
an informative public relations exercise and a sales
point for promoting an attractive public transport
service related to residents' travel needs. The
necessity for further data collection is also stressed,
and some suggestions are made for service alterations
and improved operating procedures.

Volume 2 contains details of the survey methodology,
selected verbatim quotations from the interviews,
and hole counts from the survey data.

2.4.16   A Category Analysis Approach to Estimating the
         Influence of Dial-a-Ride on the Community of Old
         Harlow. (1976)
         OCHOJNA, A.D.
         Cranfield Institute of Technology, Centre for Transport
         Studies. Report 10.   June 1976.

         This report analyses the results of household travel
         surveys carried out before the Old Harlow Dial-a-Ride
         service started operations in August 1974, and after
         it had 'settled down'.   The system provides a many-to-many
         service within the neighbourhood and a many-to-few link
         with Harlow Town Centre.   The main objective of the
         surveys was to identify those groups in Old Harlow
         which have been affected by the operations of the
         service.   Household surveys were conducted concurrently
         in the Latton Bush area of Harlow New Town in order to
         provide a control group so as to isolate the effects
         of Dial-a-Ride from 'externalities' which have influenced
         travel behaviour during the period between the 'before'
         and 'after' surveys.   Much of the report is concerned
         with setting up a valid methodological framework with-
         in which to effect this comparison.   The main conclusion
         was that in general the new mode had had a minimal
         effect on the travel patterns of people living in the
         service area-possibly reflecting the relative self-
         sufficiency of the district.   However, elderly people
         did seem to be relying to a considerable extent on the
         doorstep pick-up and set-down features of the Dial-a-
         Ride service.   Appendices provide examples of the
         questionnaires used and statistical analyses of trip rates.

2.4.17   Dial-a-Bus Demand Modelling and Evaluation:
         Predictions for the Harlow Experiment. (1975).
         MARTIN, P.H.
         TRRL Supplementary Report SR 154 UC. 1975.

2.4.18   Dial-a-Ride Planning Survey of Old Harlow. (1973)
         OCHOJNA, A.D. and WARD, V.
         Cranfield Institute of Technology, Centre for Transport
         Studies.   Memorandum No.128.   November 1973.

2.4.19 Harlow Dial-a-Bus Experiment [*The] : Comparison of
predicted and observed patronage. (1977)
MARTIN, P.H.
TRRL Supplementary Report SR 256 UC. 1977. (6pp.)

This report provides a preliminary validation of the dem
model used in the TRRL programme of research into dial-a
It compares the observed ridership of the experimental H
dial-a-bus system with predictions obtained from a modal
model. It is shown that the predicted patronage was abo
one-third too high but that the predicted distributions
age of the passengers, their journey purposes and the mo
foregone, were in reasonable agreement with the observati
These results indicate that the basic structure of the d
model is sound, but that in the modelling too low a
generalised cost had been assumed for dial-a-bus.

2.4.20 Harlow Dial-a-Bus Service[*The] : some operational statis
WATTS, P.F.   (1
TRRL Supplementary Report SR 225 UC. 1976.

2.4.21 Harlow Dial-a-Ride Experiment.[*The] (1975)
MITCHELL, C.G.B. and SPELLER, B.E.
TRRL Supplementary Report SR 127 UC. 1975.

2.4.22 How was the Harlow Dial-a-Ride Service Planned? (1974)
SPELLER, B.E. (TRRL.)
Paper read at the first British Dial-a-Ride Symposium.
Cranfield Institute of Technology, Centre for Transport
Studies. September 1974. (see ref. 4.4.14 below)

Details are given of the selection of Harlow as a servic
area, the vehicles used, the radio-telephone system, and
the design and implementation of the Dial-a-Ride system.
A breakdown of the operating costs is also given.

2.4.23 Some Preliminary Results of the Harlow Dial-a-Bus Experi
MITCHELL, C.G.B. and MARTIN, P.H.   (19
Paper read at the PTRC Summer Annual Meeting.
Seminar S-Public Transport. July 1975.
(Also published as TRRL Supplementary Report SR 214 UC.

The Harlow experimental Dial-a-Bus service commenced in
August 1974, connecting the residential neighbourhood of
Old Harlow to a number of destinations in the new town.
After 6 months the service was carrying over 4,000 passe
per week at an average load factor of 50%. Lack of a
telephone had not proved a significant deterrent to usin
the service. About 75% of passengers were booking jour
and/or receiving doorstep service. Survey results are
presented, indicating the purposes for which journeys we
made and the mode that would have been used had Dial-a-B
not been available. The experimental results were foun
to compare well with predictions made using a convention
modal choice model. The cost of the experimental servi
was £4.86 per bus hour, about 30% of which was covered b
the gross revenue. It was estimated that a non-experim
service could cost £3.09 per bus hour (1975 prices), of
which revenue should cover 60% to 70%.

2.4.24   Irvine New Town: final report on planning proposals.(1967)
HUGH WILSON AND LEWIS WOMERSLEY in association with
JAMIESON AND MACKAY and WILLIAM GILLESPIE AND ASSOCIATES.
A report to the Secretary of State for Scotland.
Scottish Development Department.
H.M.S.O. 1967. (240 pp.)

2.4.25   Irvine New Town Plan. (1971)
IRVINE DEVELOPMENT CORPORATION. 1971

2.4.26   The Best of Both Worlds: transportation planning
for Irvine New Town. (1971)
PRINCE, E.J.
Journal of the Institution of Municipal Engineers.
Vol. 98. No.5. May 1971. (pp. 118-129)

The development of the Transport Plan for Irvine New Town
is described and compared with plans proposed for other
new towns. Other points discussed include the use of
land for housing, industry and recreational purposes; the
location of community facilities such as schools and
health centres; and the planning and location of distrib-
utor roads, public transport routes and pedestrian areas.

2.4.27   Land Use and Transportation Integration in Irvine New Town.
(1975)
PRINCE, E.J. (1975)
The Highway Engineer. Vol XXII. No.10. October 1975.
(pp.14-21)

The paper describes the original planning proposals for
Irvine New Town and the need, arising from sub-regional
developments and additional information, to revise the plan.
This gave the opportunity to integrate land use and
transportation in conjunction with the public transport
operators. The financing method for the new town's infrastructure provision is outlined and its shortcomings
highlighted. Suggestions are made as to how this might be
improved following local government reorganisation in
Scotland (May 1975). The paper was presented at a
Conference arranged by the Scottish Association for Public
Transport in January, 1975, entitled: "Public Transport
and the New Regional Authorities".

2.4.28   The Plan for Irvine. (1967)
WHITTICK, A.
Town and Country Planning. Vol.35. No.9. October 1967.
(pp. 449-456)

Milton Keynes

2.4.29   The Plan for Milton Keynes. Vols. 1 & 2 (1970)
LLEWELYN-DAVIES, WEEKS, FORESTIER-WALKER & BOR.
Milton Keynes Development Corporation. 1970.
See Technical Supplement No.7. Transportation. Vols. 1 & 2.

2.4.30   New City: Milton Keynes 1974 and 1975.
MILTON KEYNES DEVELOPMENT CORPORATION. (1974 & 1975)

2.4.31   Dial-a-Bus News Letter No.1 (1975)
MILTON KEYNES DEVELOPMENT CORPORATION. December 1975.

2.4.32   Concern No.3: (Weekly news letter of the Milton Keynes
          Community Services Association).
          Conference Edition.(1975)
          MILTON KEYNES COMMUNITY SERVICES ASSOCIATION.
          Proceedings of a seminar on transport planning held in
          Milton Keynes, June 1975. (27 pp.) The following papers
          are included:-

          Who is Milton Keynes for? How can we assess?
          EVERSLEY, D. and DALE, P.
          New Town Goals - THOMAS, R.
          Careless Policies for Carless People - HILLMAN, M.
          Paratransit and Non-Motorised Transport - BENDIXSON, T.

          The Value of the Car and Transport Centres - FISHMAN, L.
          (Available only from the Open University New Towns
          Study Unit).

2.4.33   The Disadvantages of Milton Keynes. (1973)
          HILLMAN, M. and WHALLEY, A.
          Architectural Design. Vol. XLIII. August 1973.(pp.540-541

          The authors examine the likely social consequences of the
          proposals for the movement system of Milton Keynes
          contained in the Interim Report for the city.

2.4.34   Inertia Inside the Development Corporation. (1975)
          NANKIVELL, C. and COUSINS , S.
          Architectural Design. Vol. XLV. March 1975.(pp.172-173)
          An examination of the original goals set out in the
          Milton Keynes Master Plan in relation to subsequent
          developments, with particular reference to transport.

2.4.35   A New Policy for North Bucks: Submission on matters to be
          included in the County Structure Plan.(1974)
          CRESSWELL, P.A.
          The Open University. New Towns Study Unit. May 1974.(54 p

2.4.36   A Preliminary Analysis of the Transportation Plan for
          Milton Keynes. (1974)
          GREGERMAN, A.S.
          North Western University, Evanston, Illinois. August 1974
          (Available from the Open University New Towns Study Unit)

2.4.37   Public Transport in the City. (1975)
          MILTON KEYNES DEVELOPMENT CORPORATION INFORMATION UNIT.
          Press Release. 23rd April 1975.
          (Milton Keynes Development Corporation have published a
          number of other press releases on public transport - for
          example, press releases on buses were issued on 24/4/75,
          22/11/76, 11/1/76 and 15/8/77. Their Quarterly Progress
          Reports, issued as press releases, also contain informati
          on public transport).

2.4.38   Public Transport in Milton Keynes: Report of the Working
          Party. (1974)
          MILTON KEYNES DEVELOPMENT CORPORATION, NATIONAL BUS COMPA
          and DEPARTMENT OF THE ENVIRONMENT. Milton Keynes Develop-
          ment Corporation. January 1974.

2.4.39   Changing Goals in Design: the Milton Keynes example.(1972
          LLEWELYN-DAVIES, LORD.
          In: New Towns: the British Experience. 1972.
          Hazel Evans (ed.) (Chapter 11, pp.102-116).
          (see ref. 1.2.33 above).

The author traces the changing rôle of new towns in response to developments in social policy and general social and economic trends between 1950 and 1970. The overall effect of these trends has been a demand for freedom to choose between alternatives in housing, work and recreation. Providing for these freedoms has become a goal in new town planning and the implications on design objectives are examined, using Milton Keynes as a case study. Six design goals are set out and the questions of whether they can be met and of the effects on the functioning and physical form of a new town incorporating these goals are then discussed in relation to four particular aspects of the planning of Milton Keynes:-
Land use and transportation patterns; Public transport and roads; Nodes as activity centres; and Visual Character.

2.4.40   "Seven Years On..." Milton Keynes Household Survey.1976
                                                                (1977)
          MILTON KEYNES DEVELOPMENT CORPORATION.
          The results of an earlier household survey were
          published in 1974, in the report "Four Years On".

2.4.41   Milton Keynes: the Creation of a City. (1969)
          COWAN, P.
          New Society. 13th February 1969. (p. 237)

2.4.42   Milton Keynes - So Far So Good. (1977)
          MILNE, R.
          New Scientist. Vol. 74. No. 1049. April 1977.(pp.196-197)

          The article reviews briefly the development of the new
          town since designation in 1964, and includes an assessment
          of the transport system. The operation of the Milton
          Keynes Dial-a-Ride service is described. Seven vehicles
          are used carrying an average of 3,600 passengers a week
          but the service has been expensive to operate and requires
          a subsidy three or four times greater than a conventional
          operation.

2.4.43   Return to the Garden City - interim proposals for Milton
          Keynes. (1969)
          WHITTICK, A
          Town and Country Planning. Vol 37. No.4. April 1969.
                                              (pp. 151-155)

Peterborough

2.4.44   Expansion of Peterborough. Consultants'
          Proposal for Designation (1966)
          HANCOCK, TOM.
          H.M.S.O. 1966.

2.4.45   Cycleways for Greater Peterborough.(1973)
          PETERBOROUGH DEVELOPMENT CORPORATION.September 1973.

Peterlee

2.4.46   Some Aspects of the Growth and Development of Peterlee
                                                    New Town.   (
          ROBINSON, J.F.F.
          Durham University. North East Area Study Working Paper
          No.21. Part 2. (1960-70). November 1975. (81pp.)

2.4.47   Transport in Peterlee.(1961)
          DIXON, M.G.
          The Omnibus Magazine. September   1961.

Redditch

2.4.48   Redditch New Town. Report on Planning Proposals.
          REDDITCH DEVELOPMENT CORPORATION and HUGH WILSON &
          LEWIS WOMERSLEY.
          (Interim Report 1965; Final Report 1967)

2.4.49   Redditch Town Centre Plan.(1969)
          STRANZ, W.
          Town and Country Planning.Vol.37. No.4. April 1969.
          (pp.171-173)

Stevenage

2.4.50   Stevenage Master Plan.Vols 1-3.(1965 and 1966)
          STEVENAGE DEVELOPMENT CORPORATION. 1965/6.

2.4.51   Stevenage Master Plan.Vol 4. (1969)
          W.S.ATKINS & PARTNERS.
          Stevenage Development Corporation. 1969.

2.4.52   Needs of Youth in Stevenage [*The](1959)
          CALOUSTE GULBENKIAN FOUNDATION.1959.

2.4.53   New Town Goal of Self-Containment.[*The] (1974)
          CRESSWELL, P.A.
          The Open University. The New Towns Study Unit,
          January 1974. (240 pp.).

          The aims of the research reported in this volume
          were to investigate by means of case study (Stevenage
          the goal of self-containment for the London new towns
          to discover the reasons behind the decisions of
          individuals to commute or to work locally and the
          likely future trends in respect of self-containment
          in terms of journeys to work. The field methods
          used consisted of surveys of the workforce in
          Stevenage new town based on a stratified sample of
          employers; of samples of reverse commuters and of
          persons living in Stevenage and working in Stevenage
          or outside (residents and commuters). This report
          describes in detail the methods used and results from

interview surveys with reverse commuters and with
residents and commuters. Conclusions are drawn from
the findings in relation to the major objectives of
the research. Appendices contain copies of the
questionnaires, notes for the interviewers and an
outline of the sampling procedure and structure from
the residents' survey.

2.4.54   Promoting Public Transport in a New Town: the
Superbus Experiment in Stevenage. (1973)
(Promotion des Transports Collectifs dans une
Ville Nouvelle: L'Experience Superbus de Stevenage).
BUISSON,C.
Rev. Transp. Publics.Urb. Reg. No. 699. Paris, France.
July 1973. (pp.86-89)

Describes the background to the setting up of the
Stevenage Superbus Experiment and presents early
results in terms of increased passenger trips.

2.4.55   Some results from the Second Stevenage Superbus
Experiment. (1974)
BUCKLES, P.A.
Paper read at the   PTRC   Summer Annual Meeting.
July 1974. (pp.146-160 of Conference proceedings).

2.4.56   Stevenage Household Survey. March 1976   (1976).
STEVENAGE DEVELOPMENT CORPORATION. 1976.
            (22pp. of text plus 45 statistical Appendices)

The report presents and discusses the results of a
10% sample survey of the new town's households,
updating those carried out in 1966 and 1971.
Successful interviews were carried out with 2,285
households, giving an 87% response rate. The main
findings and conclusions were:-

(i)   The towns's population is growing 'older' and the
town is moving gradually towards a more typical
population with smaller households.

(ii)   A growing number of residents are working outside the town, but probably fewer go outside it
for education, shopping and entertainment.

(iii)   The greater affluence of the new town's
residents is indicated by higher incomes, more
cars and more home ownership.

(iv)   A very large increase in the numbers of school
leavers in the next ten years will result in a
substantial growth in demand for employment
during the period to 1986. At the same time
comparatively few job vacancies will be created
by people retiring during this period.

(v)   If the amount of commuting by car continues to
grow this will have wide-ranging implications

for Stevenage and the surrounding region. On
the other hand, the Survey indicated that the
Superbus services have made a useful contribution
to the mobility needs of those living and
working in the town.

2.4.57   Stevenage Public Transport: Cost Benefit Analysis.
                                         2 Vols. (1969)
         NATHANIEL LICHFIELD & ASSOCIATES.
         Stevenage Development Corporation. 1969.

         The method and results of a cost benefit analysis
         into the effects of alternative future transport modes
         in Stevenage are set out in this report. The study
         was carried out (1967-9) to discover whether a greater
         community benefit would be attained by encouraging
         the use of a high-quality bus service or by allowing
         unrestricted use of the private car, which would
         necessitate costly elevated roadworks after 1976.
         The main purpose of the enhanced bus service would
         be to attract passengers from cars during the peak
         flows to and from the industrial area and town centre.
         Three alternative schemes were analysed, two based on
         a high-quality bus service and the third on unrestrict
         use of private cars with a 'residual' bus service.
         The report sets out the modal split predictions for
         each scheme and outlines the methodology and results
         of the Planning Balance Sheet analysis (applying
         social cost benefit analysis techniques to both
         measured and unmeasured elements) and the closely
         interlinked Financial Operating Analysis. The
         Consultants concluded that the general community
         interest would be better served by encouraging
         travellers to use public transport rather than by
         facilitating the unrestricted use of cars. They
         recommended the implementation of a demonstration
         bus scheme to test the validity of the modal split
         hypotheses made in the study, to test public reaction
         and to prepare the way for future services.

2.4.58   Stevenage Superbus Experiment.(1973)
         BUCKLES, P.A.

         Paper read at a Symposium on Promoting Public
         Transport. University of Newcastle Upon Tyne.
         April 1973.

2.4.59   Stevenage Superbus Experiment: Summary Report.(1974)
         UNIVERSITY COLLEGE LONDON RESEARCH GROUP IN TRAFFIC
         STUDIES and DEPARTMENT OF THE ENVIRONMENT.
         Stevenage Development Corporation. 1974.

         The report outlines the results of an experiment
         conducted in Stevenage to test the conclusions of a
         cost benefit study (Lichfield, 1969 - see ref. 2.4.57)
         that a high-quality bus service could give greater
         net benefits to Stevenage than unrestricted car usage.
         The experiment was introduced in phases from March 19
         and the results were continuously monitored by passeng

surveys, analysis of bus revenues, household interview
and public opinion surveys, and traffic counts. Both
peak and off-peak bus usage increased substantially,
and total weekly passenger trips rose by 180% from
17,300 in 1971 to 48,200 by the end of 1974. Household
interviews showed a 10% reduction in the numbers of
people driving to work in areas directly served by
Superbus (there being no concurrent restraint on the
use of cars). Benefits to bus users consisted of
reduced waiting and travelling times, and lower fares.
In terms of generalised cost of travel these were
estimated at £2,000 per week at 1974 prices and values.
An operating deficit had been anticipated before the
experiment began and by summer 1973 amounted to
approximately £740 per week.

2.4.60   Stevenage Superbus Public Transport Demonstration.(1974)
LENTHALL, R.B. (Stevenage Development Corporation)
Paper read at the PTRC   Summer Annual Meeting.
July 1974. (pp.126-145 of Conference proceedings).

2.4.61   Stevenage Traffic Accident Survey 1957-1966. (1967)
STEVENAGE DEVELOPMENT CORPORATION. 1967.

2.4.62   Travel and Land Use in Stevenage. (1968)
BUNKER, R.C.
Department of Transportation and Environmental
Planning. University of Birmingham. 1968

2.4.63   Under Five in a New Town. (1970)
STEVENAGE DEVELOPMENT CORPORATION. 1970.

2.4.64   The Urban Transport Problem and Modal Choice. (1971)
LICHFIELD, N. and CHAPMAN, H.
Journal of Transport Economics and Policy. Vol. V. No.3.
                                      September 1971.

The article discusses the problem arising from the
imbalance between the supply of transport infrastructure and the increasing demand for its use, and
the wide-ranging impact on urban living as a whole
of the failure to resolve this. The authors pose the
question as to whether the community as a whole will
benefit if more people are persuaded to use public
transport in preference to private cars, as an efficient
'engineering' solution to the problem. A cost benefit
study of alternative modal splits in Stevenage is used
as a case study in an attempt to answer this question
(see ref. 2.4.57 above.) This indicated that the
general community interest would be better served by
investment in a fast, efficient and convenient bus
service than by planning for 'full motorisation'.
General conclusions are drawn, and the need for further
research into the determinants of modal choice behaviour
stressed.

Washington

2.4.65 Washington New Town Master Plan and Report. (1966)
LLEWELYN-DAVIES and PARTNERS.
Washington Development Corporation. December 1966.

2.4 Subsidiary References.

1.1 New Towns - Transport and Mobility.

1.1.1	*Access and Mobility in New Towns. (1976)*
	[Milton Keynes and Cumbernauld.]
1.1.7	*Mobility in New Towns. (1970)*
	[Stevenage.]
1.1.8	*New Towns in Britain (their transport plans.) (1973)*
1.1.13	*A Review of Public Transport in New Towns. (1974)*
1.1.14	*Public Transport in New Towns in Great Britain.(1971)*
1.1.16	*Transport and Mobility in Durham New Towns. (1974-5)*
	[Aycliffe,Peterlee and Washington.]
1.1.18	*Transport and New Towns. Volume Two. (1976)*
1.1.27	*Urban Public Transport. (1971)*

1.2 New Towns - Non-Transport Aspects.

1.2.1	*Survey of Attitudes to New Towns in County Durham. (1975)*
	[Aycliffe, Peterlee and Washington.]
1.2.2	*Aycliffe to Cumbernauld: a study of seven new towns in their regions.(1969)*
1.2.11	*Employment Expansion and the Development of New Town Hinterland 1961-1966 (1971*
	[The eight London new towns.]
1.2.12	*An Analysis of the Employment and Industrial Structure of Five British New Towns.(1971*
1.2.13	*Garden Cities of Tomorrow. (1965 edition.)*
1.2.16	*London's New Towns: A Study of Self-Contained and Balanced Communities. (19*
1.2.17	*The Future of the London Town Expansion Programme. (1974)*
1.2.19	*Mental Health and Environment. (1964)*
	[Harlow.]
1.2.21	*Neighbourhood Shops in New Towns. (1976)*
1.2.33	*New Towns: the British Experience. (1972)*
1.2.41	*The Self-Contained New Town: employment and population. (1968)*
	[The eight London new towns.]
1.2.42	*Social Aspects of Planning in New Towns. (1975)*
	[East Kilbride, Glenrothes, Livingston.]
1.2.44	*Social Factors Involved in the Planning and Development of New Towns. (1964)*
	[Harlow.]
1.2.48	*Town and Country Planning. (February 1978)*
1.2.50	*Commission for the New Towns: Annual Reports.*
1.2.51	*Annual Reports of the Development Corporations.*

3.2 Social Aspects of Mobility.

3.2.8	*Planning for Disabled People in the Urban Environment. (1969)*
	[Cumbernauld.]
3.2.11	*Bus Passes and the Edlerly: A Need for More Informed Policy Making? (1976)*
	[Harlow.]

3.2.12   *An Examination of the Extent and Welfare Implications of*
         Bus Use by the Elderly in Harlow. *(1977)*
3.2.35   *The Olney Residents' Survey.* *(1974 and 1975)*
         [*Milton Keynes.*]
3.2.49   *Some Social Aspects of Public Passenger Transport.* *(1977)*
         [*Milton Keynes, Harlow.*]

3.3 Interaction between Land Use and Travel.

3.3.21   *Passenger Transport as an Urban Element.* *(1976)*
         [*Milton Keynes.*]

4.4 Public Transport – Demonstration Projects and Innovatory Systems.

4.4.15   *How Does Dial-a-Bus Work?* *(1975)*
         [*Old Harlow.*]
4.4.16   *Dial-a-Ride in Britain: Experience to mid-1974 and Research*
                                        Programme. *(1974)*
         [*Harlow.*]
4.4.41   *Promotion of Urban Public Transport.* *(1973)*
         [*Stevenage.*]

6.1 Non-Motorised Travel.

6.1.4   *Planning for the Cyclist in Urban Areas.* *(1968)*
6.1.9   *People First in Transport Planning: did they get it wrong*
         at Radburn and will it be right at Cumbernauld? *(1977)*

8.1 Survey Techiques: Behavioural and Attitudinal.

8.1.63   *Monitoring in Practice.* *A household survey: its use and*
         potential for local authorities and new towns. *(1976)*
         [*Washington.*]

9.2 Bibliographies

9.2.25   *New Towns Bibliography 1977.* *(1977)*
9.2.27   *New Towns.* *(1976)*

9.4 Research Registers.

9.4.6   *1977 Summary of Research being Undertaken in New Towns.* *(1977)*

9.5 Statistical Sources.

9.5.16   *Census of Population.*
9.5.19   *Local Government Trends.* *(Annually)*
9.5.21   *Progress on Land Sold or Leased by Development Corporations/*
         Commission for the New Towns. [*'The Publicity Sheet'.*]
         (Quarterly.)

9.6 Other Sources of Information.

9.6.2   *National Index of Traffic and Transportation Surveys.* *(1975)*
9.6.14   *New Towns in the U.K.* *(1977)*
9.6.16   *Sourcebook of Planning Information.* *(1971)*

3. Transport and Mobility (General).

3.1 Studies of Modal Choice Behaviour and Value of Travel Time.

Section 3 of the bibliography is concerned with transport and mobility in general; sections 4, 5 and 6 refer to specific modes. Subsection 3.1 draws together material relating to modal choice behaviour and the valuation of travel time; the subsidiary references at the end of the subsection point to material listed elsewhere in the bibliography which has relevance to these topics, including a number of methodological studies from subsections 8.1 and 8.3. Items from this subsection which refer particularly to one or more modes of transport are cross-referenced at the end of the relevant subsections. Specific topics cover in this subsection include:-

- Research into factors influencing modal choice behaviour, including studies of modal choice for the work journey, travellers' perceptions of alternat transport modes, and behavioural and attitudinal travel demand forecasting.

- Research into valuation of travel time savings.

- Empirical studies of travel patterns and of journey times by different modes.

Transport policy and planning have over the past fifteen years increasingly recognised that since existing urban areas cannot reasonably accommodate predicted increases in traffic volumes, effective measures to restrain private car usage and promote the use of public transport are required. This applies also to some of the earlier British new towns, such as Stevenage, the road networks of which were not designed to accommodate the level of increase in car owners which has already taken place there. In the Mark II and III new towns high levels of car ownership were assumed from the design stage and the assumptions which were made of future modal split-both in the car-oriented and public transport-based plans (notably Runcorn) have had a significant effect on the physical layout of the town. Initial investment in road networks designed to accommodate full car usage at the final design year is high, and its inflexibility during the build-up period when car ownership is lower than that finally planned for can lead to problems of providing alternative means of transport for those witho the regular use of a car, and restricted mobility for this substantial group of people. In these contexts the import ance of a sound understanding of modal choice behaviour an of establishing a strong theoretical basis for travel dema forecasting is axiomatic, and has been reflected in the amount of research carried out in this field.

Up to the late 1960's research on modal split was closely linked to the macroscopic transportation study approach, using aggregated household data on a zonal level in models in which time and cost played a major part. Increasingly

however, modal choice research has recognised that factors
other than time and cost influence travel behaviour.
Stemming from the hypothesis that travel decisions are based
on perceived rather than actual mode attributes, various
attempts have been made to measure travellers' perceptions
of and satisfaction with mode attributes through psychological
research techniques. In the United States major empirical
studies were carried out by the University of Maryland
[reported in 1967 by PAINE, NASH, HILLE and BRUNNER (3.1.15-16] ,
and by the General Motors Research Laboratories [reported
in 1972 by GOLOB, CANTY and GUSTAFSON (3.1.18)] . More recent
work in the United States and Australia has attempted a
greater degree of refinement in the measurement of generalized
attributes such as 'comfort' and 'convenience', and the
development of attitudinal modelling as an aid to travel demand
forecasting. GOLOB's paper: Attitudinal Models (3.1.5) and
McFADGEN's: Transportation Mode Choice Research: Recent
Contributions from the Social Sciences (3.1.50) have summarised
the development of attitudinal modelling in transport research
up to 1975. SPEAR (3.1.3) has discussed the application of
attitudinal modelling to travel demand forecasting up to
1975 and points to specific areas needing further research.
The published proceedings of three major conferences held in
the United States summarise the results of research in this
field up to 1975. These are: the 1972 Conference on Urban
Travel Demand Forecasting held at Williamsburg, Virginia
(3.1.75), the Conference on Behavioral Demand Modeling and
Valuation of Travel Time, held at South Berwick, Maine, in
1973 (3.1.7), and the second Conference on Behavioral Travel
Demand Models held at Asheville, North Carolina, in 1975
(3.1.10). A summary of the third International Conference
on Behavioral Travel Modeling, 1977, is given   by HENSHER
and STOPHER in Traffic Engineering and Control, June 1977
(3.1.11). The published papers from these conferences draw
together a large number of further references to work in
this field. SHEPARD's Annotated Bibliography of the Application
of Behavior and Attitude Research to Transportation System
Planning and Design - 1976 (9.2.1) is also a useful source
of references to material published up to 1975.

The macroscopic approach can offer a satisfactory basis for
forecasting travel demand in a future assumed to have few
changes. But it fails to provide a rigorous tool for
explaining travel behaviour and predicting adaptive responses
to policy changes at a personal level. Some studies are
now being reported which have sought a greater depth of
understanding of personal travel behaviour. The European
Conference of Ministers of Transport (ECMT) report:
Psychological Determinants of User Behaviour - 1977 (3.1.98)
describes the results of recent research into transport users'
behaviour, based largely on studies carried out in West
Germany, and briefly reviews the development of techniques
in this research area, describing the movement from traffic
censuses and macroscopic models to disaggregate models and

behavioural approaches. The book: <u>Modal Choice and the</u> <u>Value of Travel Time</u> - 1976 (3.1.41) edited by <u>HEGGIE</u> presents the findings of a collection of empirical studies which cast doubt on the validity of a number of conventional assumptions on modal choice behaviour and the value of travel time. Research at Oxford University using unstructured depth interviews and time-budget diaries is described in the paper by <u>DIX</u> (8.1.42). More recent developments at Oxford using a combination of quantitative and qualitative techniques are summarised in the paper by <u>JONES</u> (8.3.12) and the article by <u>HEGGIE</u> (8.3.26). The approach described includes the use of a gaming technique entitled the Household Activity Travel Simulator (HATS) in an attempt to study and predict adaptive behaviour resulting from changes in transport provision.

During the 1960's much investment in transport improvements was directed towards reducing journey times by car. Knowledge of travellers' valuation of travel time was considered to be a potentially useful aid in evaluating alternative schemes and a substantial amount of research effort was directed towards identifying values of travel time. <u>BEESLEY</u> (1965) in Value of Time Spent Travelling: some new evidence (3.1.1) and <u>QUARMBY</u> (1967) in Choice of Travel Mode for the Journey to Work: some findings (3.1.31) reported studies which had a considerable influence on later research. A number of Government-commissioned studies were carried out during the late 1960's and early 1970's in both Britain and the United States, concentrating largely on the work journey. <u>THOMAS</u> and <u>THOMPSON</u>'s reports: <u>The Value of Time for Commuting</u> <u>Motorists as a Function of their Income Level and Amount</u> <u>of Time Saved</u> - 1970 (3.1.103) and <u>Value of Time Saved by</u> <u>Trip Purpose</u> 1970 (3.1.106) summarise the results of some of the U.S. research effort in this field. In this country major studies carried out by the Local Government Operational Research Unit (LGORU) have been reported by <u>ROGERS, TOWNSEND</u> and <u>METCALF</u> in Planning for the Work Journey: a generalised explanation of Modal Choice (3.1.30), and by <u>DAVIES and</u> <u>ROGERS</u> in Modal Choice and the Value of Time (3.1.40). In the latter study the value of travel time was defined as-- "the amount of money that an individual is prepared to spend (or save) in order to save (or forgo) one unit of journey time". A study of London commuters carried out by Social and Community Planning Research, also as part of the DOE research programme on value of travel time, used the Prior Evaluator technique to collect data on the importance of time savings in relation to other journey attributes. <u>HOINVILLE</u> and <u>JOHNSON</u> described the results of this research and the methodology used in <u>The Importance and Value Commuters</u> <u>Attach to Time Savings</u> - 1971 (3.1.63), and Commuter <u>Preferences: Summary Report</u> - 1972 (3.1.13). The <u>MINISTRY</u> <u>OF TRANSPORT</u>'s Technical Note <u>The Value of Time Savings in</u> <u>Transport</u> - 1969 (3.1.117) sets out the official values of travel time, which have been regularly revised since then.

An early review of value of time methodology is given by HARRISON and QUARMBY in The Value of Time in Transport Planning: A Review - 1969 (3.1.104), and more recent reviews and assessments of research in this field are presented in the reports by HENSHER (3.1.112) and GOODWIN (3.1.102), which both include substantial lists of references. GOODWIN's paper to the European Conference of Ministers of Transport identifies and discusses a number of the problems associated with attempts to evaluate travel time in money terms, and his article in the Journal of Transport Economics and Policy (3.1.108) discusses the effect of another major factor (effort) on travel behaviour. Other research has concentrated on inferring values of time from modal choice models, and papers by ROGERS and by SEARLE and CLARK at the Second International Conference on Behavioral Travel Demand in 1975 [published in Behavioral Travel-Demand Models (3.1.10)] discuss the use of modal choice models for deriving values of travel time.

This subsection also draws together the results of several studies of journey times and travel patterns.These include surveys of journey times by bus and car in London and Edinburgh (3.1.24 - 29, 3.1.37, 3.1.81-2), and of waiting times for buses in London and Manchester (3.1.113-115); the results of travel surveys carried out by the Transport and Road Research Laboratory in Gloucester, Northampton and Reading (3.1.83-84); and Social and Community Planning's Mid Glamorgan Transport Use and Attitude Survey, reported by SMITH and HOINVILLE, which attempted to link attitudes to travel behaviour and travel circumstances (3.1.67).

3. TRANSPORT AND MOBILITY (GENERAL)

3.1 Studies of Modal Choice Behaviour and Value of
      Travel Time.

3.1.1 Attitudes and Behavior. [*National Survey of
                    Transportation] (1968/9)
        McMILLAN, R.K. and ASSAEL, H.
        Highway Research Board. Washington D.C.
        Phase I: Summary Report. National Co-operative
                  Highway Research Program, Report No. 49.
                  1968. (71 pp.)
        Phase II: Analysis Report. National Co-operative
                  Highway Research Program, Report No. 82.
                  1969. (89 pp.)

        In Phase I the initial results of two independent
        nationwide surveys are presented and compared.
        In Phase II a multivariate analysis technique
        was used to determine the attitudes and behaviour
        of the public in relation to transportation and
        an attempt is made to identify the factors
        influencing these attitudes and behaviour.

3.1.2 Attitudinal Measures in Investigating the Choice
                    of Travel Mode. [*Usefulness of] (1975)
        HENSHER, D.A., McCLEOD, P.B. and STANLEY, J.K.
        International Journal of Transport Economics.
                              Vol. 2. No. 1. April 1975.

3.1.3 Attitudinal Modeling: Its Rôle in Travel-Demand
                              Forecasting.(1976)
        SPEAR, B.D.
        Chapter 4 in:'Behavioral Travel-Demand Models'.
        Edited by P.R. Stopher and A. H. Meyburg. 1976.
                              (pp. 89-98)

        This paper evaluates progress made with attitud-
        inal modelling as applied to travel demand fore-
        casting between 1972 and 1975, and in the light
        of this assessment gives guidelines for future
        research. Studies carried out by Hensher, McLeod
        and Stanley (1975), Spear (1974) and Nicolaidis
        (1974) in identifying and measuring attributes
        of transportation through attitudinal studies
        and incorporating them into disaggregate travel-
        demand forecasting models are examined and
        assessed. An assessment is also made of a study
        conducted by General Motors' Research Laboratories
        from 1972, which sought to ascertain user percep-
        tions and preferences for a new transportation
        concept, the Metro Guideway, through an attitude
        survey. The author concludes that attitudinal
        modelling of travel-demand behaviour has introduce
        a number of potentially useful methodologies to
        transportation planning, but that further research
        is needed into the specific problem areas identi-
        fied in his review if attitudinal work is to have
        useful practical applications in this field.
        (see ref. 3.1.10 below.)

3.1.4   Attitudinal Modeling.[*Uses and Limitations of]
                                                    (1976)
         DOBSON, R.
         Chapter 5 in: 'Behavioral Travel-Demand Models'.
         Edited by P.R. Stopher and A.H. Meyburg. 1976.
              (pp. 99-106) (see ref. 3.1.10 below)

3.1.5   Attitudinal Models.(1973)
         GOLOB, T.F.
         Transportation Research Board. Special Report
              No. 143. Washington D.C. 1973.(pp. 130-146)

3.1.6   Behavioral Approach to Modal Split Forecasting.
                                        [*A] (1970)
         LAVE, C.A.
         Transportation Research. Vol. 3. No. 4. December
                                 1970.(pp. 463-486)

3.1.7   Behavioral Demand Modeling and the Valuation of
                            Travel Time. (1974)
         TRANSPORTATION RESEARCH BOARD.
         Proceedings of a Conference held at South Berwick,
         Maine, July 1973.
         Transportation Research Board.Special Report No.149.
         Washington D.C.1974 . (234 pp.)

         [Includes paper read by T.F. Golob and R. Dobson:
         'Assessment of Preferences and Perceptions toward
         Attributes of Transportation Alternatives' - see
         ref. 3.1.59 below].

3.1.8   Behavioural Explanation of the Association Between
         Bus and Passenger Arrivals at a Bus Stop. [*A]
                                                    (1974)
         JOLLIFFE, J.K. and HUTCHINSON, T.P.
         Transportation Science. Vol. 9. No. 3. August 1975.
                                         (pp. 248-282).

3.1.9   Behavioral Modeling: An Evaluative Perspective.
                                                    (1977)
         STANLEY, J.K.
         Paper read at the Third International Conference
         on Behavioral Modeling, South Australia, 1977.

         The author describes recent attitudinal work in
         Australia which has sought to quantify certain
         less easily measurable modal attributes ('comfort'
         and 'convenience') so that their influence on modal
         choice decisions can be evaluated on a comparable
         basis with that of the more easily measurable
         attributes normally considered (time and cost).
         The data can also be used in predictive work, enabl-
         ing the assessment of the influence of a greater
         range of measurable variables than used in tradit-
         ional behavioural models. The paper outlines the
         stages used in the identification and measurement
         of the major component dimensions of 'comfort' and
         'convenience' through attitudinal surveys, and their
         use in extending traditional behavioural choice models.

3.1.10   Behavioral Travel-Demand Models.(1976)
STOPHER, P.R. and MEYBURG, A.H. (Eds.)
Lexington Books. D.C. Heath and Co., Lexington,
Mass. 1976. (336 pp.)
Proceedings of the Second International Conference
on Behavioral Travel Demand held at Asheville,
North Carolina, May 1975.

This book comprises the proceedings of the Second
International Conference on Behavioral Travel
Demand, held in Asheville, North Carolina, in May
1975. This Conference, jointly sponsored by the
U.S. Department of Transportation and the Engineer
ing Foundation, was the immediate successor to the
Conference in Travel Behavior and Values held in
South Berwick, Maine, in 1973.(see ref. 3.1.7 abov
The Conference took the form of a research forum
organised around a series of concurrent workshops
for the discussion of current research problems.
The book contains the position papers and a
summary of the discussions of each workshop and
of their recommendations for future research and
action. The topics covered by the eight workshops
were:
1.   The application of behavioral travel-demand
     models.
2.   Uses and limitations of attitudinal modeling.
3.   Development of disaggregate distribution mode
4.   Travel-demand theory: latent demand, the valu
     of travel, and impact on life style.
5.   Uses of behavioral models for deriving values
     of travel time.
6.   Development of travel-supply models.
7.   Use and application of market segmentation.
8.   Mathematical theory and demand models.
The final chapter, by the editors, summarises the
findings and recommendations of the eight workshop
and identifies some common themes and convergence
of thought emerging from them.
(see refs. 3.1.3 and 3.1.4 above and 3.1.69 and
3.1.77 below.)

3.1.11   Behavioral Travel Modeling.[*Report of the Third
                 International Conference on] (1977)
HENSHER, D.A. and STOPHER, P.R.
Traffic Engineering and Control. Vol. 18. No. 6.
                        June 1977 (pp. 319-322)

3.1.12   Behavioral Views of Transportation Attributes.
                  [*Disaggregated] (1974)
DOBSON, R. and KEHOE, J.F.
Transportation Research Record No. 527. Transportation Research Board. Washington D.C.1974. (pp. 1-
(see also refs. 3.1.69 - 3.1.71 below.)

3.1.13   Commuter Preferences: Summary Report.(1972)
          HOINVILLE, G. and JOHNSON, E.
          Social and Community Planning Research. Report
             P. 237. July 1972.(22 pp. plus appendix)

          This report describes work undertaken by SCPR
          as part of the Department of the Environment's
          research programme on the value of travel time
          savings. It summarises the methodology and
          findings of an interview survey of a sample of
          London commuters in 1971. Respondents' existing
          travel patterns, attitudes towards these journeys
          and preferences were examined in order to obtain
          information on the importance which they attached
          to journey times and on variations in the import-
          ance of time savings between different groups of
          commuters. The Priority Evaluator method was used
          to provide information about the importance of time
          savings in relation to other journey attributes.
          The main finding was that many commuters had little
          effective choice of mode of transport available to
          them. They were thus not in a position of being
          able to choose between a range of alternatives to
          obtain the optimum 'mix' of journey characteristics.
          Where a choice was available decisions were based
          mainly on considerations of speed and directness,
          and major speed differences were shown to be much
          more significant than marginal time savings.

3.1.14   Commuters Transferring to Bus Travel. [*A Theoret-
          ical Estimate of the effect of London Car] (1968)
          WEBSTER, F. V.
          RRL Report LR 165. 1968. (40 pp.)

3.1.15   Consumer Attitudes toward Auto versus Public
                         Transport Alternatives.(1969)
          PAINE, F.T., NASH, A.N., HILLE, S.J. and BRUNNER, G.A.
          Journal of Applied Psychology. Vol. 53. No. 6. 1969.
                                         (pp. 472-480)
          [This paper is partially based on: 'User Determined
          Attributes of Ideal Transportation Systems'. 1966,
          (177 pp.) by Brunner, Hille, Nash, Paine,
          Schellenberger and Smerk; and: 'Consumer Conceived
          Attributes of Transportation'. 1967, by Paine,
          Nash, Hille and Brunner - see ref. 3.1.16 below]

          This paper describes two pilot studies into consumer
          attitudes to cars versus public transport for work
          and non-work trips, carried out in Baltimore and
          Philadelphia. From self-completion questionnaires
          a hierarchy of key trip attributes was developed
          for each type of journey. The relative satisfaction
          with car and public transport modes to meet each of
          these was measured by satisfaction ratings on a 7-
          point Likert scale. The data was analysed by inner
          city and suburban location and by demographic
          characteristics to try and ascertain to what extent

these are related to the ranking of and satisfaction
with trip mode attributes. The results showed a
consistent preference for car for each trip attribut
but with marked differences in the magnitude of
preference between attributes. In choosing between
car and public transport perception of travel time,
susceptibility to the weather, avoidance of changing
vehicles, avoidance of waiting, avoiding the unfami1
iar, and feeling independent were more significant
than cost, reliability of destination achievement,
state of vehicle, congestion and diversions. The
most satisfied group were those who used cars most
and public transport least - middle and upper -
income suburbanites living more than 3 miles from
the central business district. The authors discuss
the implications of these findings for campaigns
to promote increased use of public transport amongst
such groups, and conclude that substantial ingenuity
and resources would be required to make public
transport an attractive alternative.

3.1.16   Consumer Conceived Attributes of Transportation:
                        An Attitude Study.(1967)
          PAINE, F.T., NASH, A.N. HILLE, S.J. and BRUNNER, G.
          Department of Business Administration, College Park
          University of Maryland. PB 176 485. June 1967.

          The report summarises the results of an urban trans
          portation consumer attitude study conducted in
          Philadelphia, Pennsylvania. The central objective
          of the study was to develop an evaluation of resear
          methodology which permits the efficient   accumula-
          tion of consumer transportation attitude informatio

3.1.17   Consumer Preferences.[*Measuring and Interpreting]
                                                    (1970)
          BRUNNING, S.M.
          Paper in: 'Urban Transportation Innovation', edited
                         by D.Brand. 1970. (18 pp.)

3.1.18   Consumer Preferences for a Public Transportation
          System.[*An Analysis of] (1972)
          GOLOB, T.F., CANTY, E.T. and GUSTAFSON, R.L.
          Transportation Research. Vol. 6.No. 1. March 1972.
                                            (pp. 81-102)

          This paper describes a methodology for analysing
          the importance which potential users of a new or
          modified transportation system place on various
          design characteristics of the system. The method-
          ology involves the selection and grouping of system
          characteristics, the adaptation and integration of
          psychological scaling techniques, the stratificatic
          of consumers and the design of an attitudinal surve
          as the basic data collection device.

3.1.19　　Consumer Preferences in Urban Trip-Making. (1974)
　　　　　HENSHER, D.A.
　　　　　Commonwealth Bureau of Roads, Melbourne, Australia,
　　　　　　　　　　　1974. (5 volumes).

3.1.20　　Consumer Response to Public Transport Improvements
　　　　　and Car Restraint: some practical findings. (1977)
　　　　　HEGGIE, I.G.
　　　　　Oxford University Transport Studies Unit. Working
　　　　　　　　　　　Paper No. 2. (revised). 1977.

3.1.21　　Generalised Cost Time and the Problem of Equity in
　　　　　　　　　　　　　　Transport Studies. (1973)
　　　　　GOODWIN, P.B.
　　　　　Transportation. Vol. 3. No. 1. April 1974.(pp. 1-21)

3.1.22　　Generalizing and Generalized Cost Function.(1974)
　　　　　HENSHER, D.A. and McLEOD, P.B.
　　　　　Melbourne,Australia. December 1974. (unpublished)

3.1.23　　Journey Series [*A Study of Individual]: an
　　　　　integrated interpretation of the transportation
　　　　　　　　　　　　　　process. (1972)
　　　　　VIDAKOVIC, V.
　　　　　In: G.F. Newell (ed.):- 'Traffic Flow and Transport-
　　　　　ation.' New York. American Elsevier. 1972.

3.1.24　　Journey Times by Bus and Car in Central London
　　　　　　　　　　　in 1972.(1973)
　　　　　BUCKLES, P.A.
　　　　　Traffic Engineering and Control. Vol. 15.No. 7,
　　　　　　　　　　　November 1973.(pp. 337-339)

　　　　　The results are described of a repetition in 1972
　　　　　of a survey made by Holroyd and Scraggs for the
　　　　　RRL in 1963 (ref. 3.1.25) which measured
　　　　　journey times by car and bus on 25 journeys between
　　　　　randomly selected points in Central London.   The
　　　　　1972 survey also measured motor-cycle journey times.
　　　　　The study showed the relationship between journey
　　　　　times and direct distance for the three modes,
　　　　　and the effect of changes since 1963 in the road
　　　　　and bus systems on car and bus journey times.   The
　　　　　main findings were:-
　　　　　(i)　　In 1972 the average bus journey took 2.5 times
　　　　　　　　as long as the average car journey (in 1963
　　　　　　　　it was twice as long).
　　　　　(ii)　The fastest mode in 1972 was motor cycle
　　　　　　　　(mean direct travel speed 13.2 m/h, compared
　　　　　　　　with 11.2 m/h for car and 4.4 m/h for bus)
　　　　　(iii)　Between 1963 and 1972 there was an increase
　　　　　　　　in direct car journey speed for 64% of journeys
　　　　　　　　and decrease in direct bus journey speed for
　　　　　　　　75% of journeys.

(iv) Total bus journey time rose by 12% between 1963 and 1972, and 80% of this increase was time spent 'in bus'. This indicates that traffic measures designed to increase flows generally may have caused delays to buses (one-way systems; linked traffic signals, etc

(v) The cost of bus fares over 20 of the journeys rose by 122.5% between 1963 and 1972. This was more than double the rate of increase in the retail price index (49%).

3.1.25   Journey Times by Car and Bus in Central London. (1964)
HOLROYD, E.M. and SCRAGGS, D.A.
Traffic Engineering and Control. Vol. 6. No. 3.
July 1964 (pp.169-173)
(see ref. 3.1.24 above for results of 1972 re-surve

3.1.26   Journey Times by Car and Bus in Central London: 1977 re-survey. (1977)
NICHOLL, J.P.
Traffic Engineering and Control. Vol. 18.No. 12.
December 1977.(pp. 581-582)

3.1.27   Journey Times by Car in Central London. (1969)
YATES, L.B. and HOWERD, T.J.
GLC. Research Memorandum 150.
Greater London Council. 1969.

3.1.28   Journey Times in London, 1970. [*Car] (1971)
LYNAM, D.A. and EVERALL, P.F.
RRL Report LR 413. 1971. (24 pp.)

3.1.29   Journey Times in London, 1970. [*Public Transport (1971)
LYNAM, D.A. and EVERALL, P.F.
RRL Report LR 416. 1971. (16 pp.)

3.1.30   Journey [*Planning for the Work] ; a generalised explanation of modal choice. (1970)
ROGERS, K.G., TOWNSEND, G.M. and METCALF, A.E.
Local Government Operational Research Unit (LGORU)
Report C.67. April 1970. (97 pp
Royal Institute of Public Administration.

3.1.31   Journey to Work [*Choice of Travel Mode for]: Some Findings. (1967)
QUARMBY, D.A.
Journal of Transport Economics and Policy. Vol. 1.
No. 3. September 1967. (pp.273-314)

3.1.32   Journey to Work: Modal Split. (1967)
WILSON, F.R.
MacLaren and Sons, London. 1967. (270 pp.)

This book reports on a research project carried out by the University of Birmingham to study

problems associated with the choice of travel mode
for journeys to work in urban areas. The principal
objective of the study was to produce a model
capable of forecasting the percentage of work trips
which will be made by public transport, and the
author indicates that the resulting model could be
used for new towns. A substantial proportion of
the book is concerned with examining factors
influencing the choice of mode of travel to work,
using base data provided by field surveys conducted
in Coventry and Greater London. The organisation
and control of the fieldwork are described in
detail. Statistical survey data and copies of
questionnaires used are included in the Appendices.
The book also contains a review of some of the
existing literature on modal choice, further works
being listed in a bibliography at the end.

3.1.33   Journey to Work [*Residential Location and the]:
                  an empirical analysis. (1977)
            McCARTHY, P.S.
            Journal of Transport Economics and Policy. Vol. XI.
                        No. 2. May 1977. (pp.169-184)

            The purpose of the study reported in this article
            was to formulate and test a behavioural model of
            transport modal choice which incorporates resident-
            ial location decision-making and specifically
            examines its impact upon modal choice for the work
            trip. The data needed for testing the model was
            obtained from a mail survey of 2,078 new residents
            in 36 San Francisco Bay Area communities. The
            analysis indicated that residential location is a
            significant factor in an individual's modal choice.
            Further areas for research are suggested.

3.1.34   Journey to Work Survey. [*Report on the] (1966)
            STOPHER, P.R.
            G.L.C. Department of Highways and Transportation.
            Research Memorandum. 48.
            Greater London Council. 1966.

3.1.35   Journey to Work. [*The] (1968)
            THOMAS, R.
            P.E.P. 1968.

3.1.36   Journeys and Activity Linkages. [*Intra-Urban]
                                                    (1977)
            BENTLEY, G.A., BRUCE, A. and JONES, D.R.
            Socio-Economic Planning Sciences. Vol. 11. No. 4.
                        1977. (pp. 213-220)
            (also published by the Building Research Establish-
                              ment as BRE CP 36/77).

            Data from a travel diary study of Watford residents
            are used to examine the linkages between successive

stages of multi-stage journeys. The linkage pattern
in the journeys made each day by housewives and by
other adults are described. A simple model of the
number of stages to which journeys are extended is
presented. The number of journeys made each week
by various population subgroups, including teenagers
and elderly people, are also described. Some implications for planning and transport prediction are
discussed. Some evidence is presented to support
the view that analysis of journey initiation and
continuation is more appropriate for studying
urban travel patterns than is analysis of individual trips. The authors conclude that further
investigation, especially of the individual's
conception of travel options and of the factors
determining the chosen behaviour, is required to
establish the case. There may be significant
implications for transportation modelling since
multi-stage journeys constitute an appreciable
proportion of all travel undertaken.

3.1.37   Journeys to and from Central London in Peak Hours.
                         [*Car and Bus] (1969)
           GOODWIN, P.B.
           Traffic Engineering and Control. Vol. 11. No. 8.
                         December 1969.(pp. 376-378)

3.1.38   Minibus Service W9: Bus/Minibus Modal Choice
              Analysis and Cost-Benefit Assessment. (1975).
           LINDSAY, J.F.
           London Transport Executive. Economic and Operational
           Research Report R 211. January 1975. (20 pp. plus
                                              appendices).

           The factors influencing individuals' choice between
           the W9 minibus route and conventional bus services
           are examined, and these factors are then used to
           estimate social costs and benefits resulting from
           the introduction of the W9 service. The results
           show that for the work journey walking time is the
           most important single factor governing the choice
           between minibus and bus, while for non-work journeys
           fares become more important. The presence of close
           substitute bus services in the W9 catchment area
           was found to make minibus demand highly sensitive
           to fares, and the estimated effects of possible
           fare manipulations are discussed. The social cost
           benefit analysis indicated that user benefits cover
           less than one-third of the net cost to London Trans-
           port of providing the service. Various policy
           implications of the findings are discussed, and the
           values of time obtained are compared with DOE
           recommended values.

3.1.39   Modal Choice and the Pedestrian.(1969)
          EYLES, D. and SPILLER, C.J.
          Traffic Engineering and Control. Vol. 11. No. 5.
                    September 1969. (pp. 228-232)

3.1.40   Modal Choice and the Value of Time.(1973)
          DAVIES, A.L. and ROGERS, K.G.
          Local Government Operational Research Unit. (LGORU)
                    Report C 143. 1973. (51 pp.)
          Royal Institute of Public Administration.

3.1.41   Modal Choice and the Value of Travel Time. (1976)
          HEGGIE, I.G. (ed.)
          Clarendon Press, Oxford, England. 1976. (190 pp.)

          The book brings together a number of recent research
          studies dealing with the topics of modal choice
          (by individuals) and the value of savings in travel
          time. An Introduction by Ian Heggie indicates ways
          in which the studies call into question accepted
          views and assumptions on modal choice behaviour
          and the value of travel time savings. Some general
          conclusions and suggestions for a new approach to
          transport planning are set out. The main conclusions
          emerging are that the modal choice process is not
          based on a mental comparison of the attributes of
          competing modes, so that attempts to 'attract' users
          onto public transport are probably doomed to failure;
          that changing modal attributes can interact with the
          decision of whether or not to make a journey; and,
          on a more general level, that current theories of
          modal choice and the accepted value of travel time
          are not based on models which reasonably represent
          the decision processes involved. A recommendation
          is made for the development of new behavioural models
          more closely related to intuitive notions of how
          people behave.
          The following studies are included in the book:
          1.   A Diagnostic Survey of Urban Journey-to-Work
               Behaviour. I. HEGGIE
          2.   Modal Choice Behaviour and the Value of Travel
               Time: Recent Empirical Evidence. J.H. EARP,
               R.D. HALL and M.McDONALD.
          3.   The Skyport Special: An Experimental Personal-
               ized Bus Service. M.J. HERATY.
          4.   Valuation of Commuter Travel Time Savings: An
               Alternative Procedure. D.A.HENSHER.
          5.   The Value of Travel Time Savings and Transport
               Investment Appraisal. A. JENNINGS and C.SHARP.
          6.   Resource Value of Business Air Travel Time.
               R.C. CARRUTHERS and D.A. HENSHER.
          Reference sections are included at the end of each
          chapter.

3.1.42   Modal Choice for Dual-Mode Transit, People Mover a
          Personal Rapid Transit Systems.[*An Investigation c
                                                          (197
          CONSTANTINO, D.P., DOBSON, R. and CANTY, E.T.
          Paper read at the First International Conference on
          Dual-Mode Transportation. Washington D.C.May 1974.

          The attitudes of individuals regarding dual-mode
          transit, personal rapid transit and people mover fc
          of urban transportation were collected through a hc
          interview survey. It was hypothesised that a more
          thorough understanding of mode choice could be obtai
          by stratifying the sample into homogeneous groups.

3.1.43   Modal Choice in Greater London.(1969)
          RESEARCH PROJECTS LTD. 1969.
          Presents data on feeder trips to London.

3.1.44   Modal Split.[*Demand and Choice Models of] (1970)
          McGILLIVRAY, R.G.
          Journal of Transport Economics and Policy. Vol. IV
                            No. 2. May 1970.(pp. 192-207).

3.1.45   Modal Split in the Journey to Work. [*Urban Structu
                                                     and] (1977)
          SAMMONS, R. and HALL, P.
          Urban Studies. Vol. 14. No. 1. February 1977.(pp.1-

          Relationships between modal split for the journey
          to work and patterns of social and economic activit
          in large urban areas are investigated in this pape
          Small zone data from six major land use transporta
          studies were used as a basis for a systematic comp
          ative analysis of these relationships. Three of t
          studies were British (London, West Midlands and
          SELNEC) and three American. Standard correlation
          and regression programmes were employed on a wide
          range of data, using three different models. The
          results reveal the overriding influence of car
          ownership on modal split, but also demonstrate the
          limitations imposed by urban structure in the form
          employment and population densities.

3.1.46   Modal Split. [*The Effects of Changes in Travel Cos
                          on Trip Distribution and] (1968)
          HYMAN, G.M. and WILSON,A.G.
          Centre for Environmental Studies. Working Paper 21
                                                  December 1968.

          This paper presents a generalised model of a trans-
          portation system, applicable to urban or inter-urba
          transportation, which overcomes some of the diffic
          ties associated with many conventional models. The
          elasticity implications of the model are examined
          and compared with a number of alternative assumpti
          A number of general results are given relating to
          the sensitivity of the model, particularly when
          components of travel costs are changed. In conclus

ion it is suggested that more tests of the models
are needed to see which hypotheses best fit the facts,
and that a study of elasticities is very important
to the policy maker because these represent a measure
of system response to policy changes.

3.1.47   Modal Trip Assignment. [*Factors Influencing] (1968)
          HIGHWAY RESEARCH BOARD.
          National Co-operative Highway Research Program
          Report. Pub. 1711. Highway Research Board.
                            Washington D.C. 1968.(78 pp.)

3.1.48   Mode Choice for the Work Journey. [*A Probability
                                   Model of Travel](1969)
          STOPHER, P.R.
          Highway Research Record No. 283. Highway Research
                     Board. Washington D.C. 1969.

3.1.49   Mode Choice in Dutch Cities. [*The Determinants
                             of Transport] (1971)
          DE DONNEA, F.
          University Press, Rotterdam. 1971.(238 pp.)

3.1.50   Mode Choice Research [*Transportation]: Recent
          Contributions from the Social Sciences. (1975)
          McFADGEN, D.G.
          Report 7502. Travel Demand Forecasting Project.
          University of California. Berkeley. 1975.

3.1.51   Mode in Urban Travel [*Stochastic Choice of]:A
                            Study in Binary Choice.(1962)
          WARNER, S.L.
          Northwestern University Press. Evanston, Illinois.
                                                      1962.

3.1.52   Mode of Transport. [*Choice of] (1969)
          a)   Psychological Motivation.
          b)   The Econometric Approach.
          MARCADAL, G.
          European Conference of Ministers of Transport.(ECMT)
          Report of the Third Round Table on Transport Economics.
          Economic Research Centre. Paris. 1969.

3.1.53   Motivation and Attitudes of Passengers and Potential
          Passengers of London Transport Buses.[*Report of a
          Study into the] (1968)
          WASEY, E.
          London Transport Executive. 1968.

3.1.54   Movement in London.(1969)
          GREATER LONDON COUNCIL. 1969.

3.1.55   Moyen de Transports par les Usagers. [*Choix du]
                                          (1963)
          INSTITUT D'AMENAGEMENT ET D'URBANISME DE LA REGION
                            PARISIENNE. October 1963.

3.1.56   Non-Work Travel. [*The Demand for] (1972)
VICKERMAN, R.
Journal of Transport Economics and Policy. Vol. VI.
No. 2. May 1972.(pp. 176-210)

From National Travel Survey data the author builds
generation models for shopping, recreational, social
and pleasure trips for each of four regions. Trip
making is found to be sensitive to factors such as
car ownership, accessibility of transport and types
of areas, but to different degrees for different
groups of people and in different regions.

3.1.57   Perception and Commuter Modal Choice - An
Hypothesis.(1975)
HENSHER, D.A.
Urban Studies. Vol. 12. No. 1. February 1975.
(pp. 101-104)

This article discusses modal choice for the
journey to work, focussing on the relationship
between information acquisition and perceived
travel mode attributes. The cost of information
gathering and the effect on this of individual
incomes are examined, and some conclusions drawn
as to the influence on travel mode decisions.

3.1.58   Perception of Public Transport by the User.(1970)
STARK, S.
Paper read at Lanchester Polytechnic Conference.
June 1970.

This paper examines attitudes which affect people's
behaviour with regard to public transport, and the
psychological factors which affect the perception
of public transport and so help to form these
attitudes. Much of the material relates to London
and is concerned particularly with perceptions by
bus users, but comparisons are also made with
attitudes to other modes and there is some discuss
of factors affecting modal choice. The effect of
availability and format of information is discusse
and bus users' images of the bus and attitudes to
bus reliability, routes and interchange are examin
and problems arising from these attitudes outlined
Main points emerging from the planning and operati
viewpoints are:-
  (i)   People do feel differently about and act diff
ently towards different modes of transport.
 (ii)   The development of public transport must go h
in-hand with restraints on the use of the pri
car.
(iii)   People need to believe that the operator unde
stands and cares about them. This involves t
successful projection of information.
 (iv)   New forms of transport will need very careful
projection and marketing if their potentials
are to be realised.

3.1.59   Preferences and Perceptions toward Attributes
          of Transportation Alternatives. [*Assessment of]
                                            (1974)
          GOLOB, T.F. and DOBSON, R.
          Transportation Research Board. Special Report
          No. 149. Washington D.C. 1974. (pp. 58-81)
          [The paper was read at the Conference on Behavio-
          ral Demand Modeling and Valuation of Travel Time,
          held at South Berwick, Maine, July 1973 - see ref.
                                        3.1.7   above].

          The authors use a combination of psychological
          measurement and economic utility theories to
          derive an approach for improving understanding
          of decision-making with respect to transportation
          alternatives. A bibliography is appended contain-
          ing over one hundred references to literature
          concerned with the methodology of attitudinal surveys,
          mostly published in the late 1960's and early 1970's.

3.1.60   Preferences for Transit Service by Homogeneous
                          Groups of Individuals. (1974)
          DOBSON, R. and NICOLAIDIS, G.
          Transportation Research Forum Proceedings. Vol.XV.
          No. 1. 1974. Published by Richard B. Cross. (pp.
                                               326-335).

          A major objective of the study was to demonstrate
          the value of aggregating a sample into groups of
          individuals which have homogeneous patterns of
          preferences for various attributes of transport
          services.

3.1.61   Relationships between Socio-Economic Factors,
          User Attitudes and Preferences and Urban Transport-
          ation System Attributes. [*A Pilot Study of]
                                         (1969)
          SMITH, R.W.
          Darnas and Smith Ltd. Toronto, Canada. April 1969.

3.1.62   Shopping Habits. [*The Influence of Car Ownership
                              on] (1964)
          KENT COUNTY PLANNING DEPARTMENT. 1964. (25 pp.)

          This report presents the results of investigations
          carried out to try and ascertain differences in
          shopping habits between households with and those
          without the use of a car. Households with a car
          were defined as those whose head of household or
          housewife owned or had the use of a car, van or
          motor-cycle with sidecar. They were classed as
          being without a car if another member of the house-
          hold had such a vehicle, unless the vehicle was
          clearly used for household shopping. The places
          visited for 'weekly' and 'luxury' (i.e. occasional
          trips to buy major consumer durable items) shopping

were analysed by car ownership and by status of the
head of household. The main general findings were
that, particularly for 'luxury' shopping, households with cars relied less on their local centres
and travelled over greater distances and to a
wider variety of centres than households without
cars. These differences were more pronounced in
the higher status groups, who also made more use
of their cars for shopping than did car owning
households in lower status groups. London was
used to a greater extent by households with cars
than those without, although most shopping trips
to London were made by train.

3.1.63   Time Savings. [*The Importance and Value Commuters
                                    Attach to] (1971
         HOINVILLE, G. and JOHNSON, E.
         Social and Community Planning Research. 1971.
                                    (73 pp.)

3.1.64   Time Savings in Transport Studies.(1968)
         TIPPING, D.G.
         Economic Journal. Vol. LXXVIII. No. 312. December
                                    1968.(pp. 843-854)

3.1.65   Transport Demand [*Report on a Market Research
         Survey into] : Waveney Valley Area. (1976)
         EASTERN COUNTIES OMNIBUS CO. LTD. June 1976.(18 p

         The report summarises the results of a question-
         naire survey of travel habits and needs carried ou
         in South East Norfolk and North East Suffolk in
         November 1975, the major aims being to establish t
         existing and potential patterns of travel in the
         area. The results showed that although car owner-
         ship was relatively high (60% of households survey
         some two-thirds of the respondents were without
         access to private transport for most of the week.
         A supplementary timetable test indicated that appr
         imately half of the persons tested were unable to
         read a conventional bus timetable, the main reason
         being difficulties in comprehending the 24-hour cl
         and the timetable layout. A copy of the questionn
         is included, and appendices present statistical
         analyses of the survey results and a catalogue of
         changes to bus and rail services thought necessary
         by respondents.

3.1.66   Transport Gaps. [*The] (1968)
         BOULADON, G.
         Science Journal. Vol. 3. No. 4. April 1967. (pp. 4
         46), and: Ekistiks. Vol.25.No.146.
                                    January 1968. (pp. 6-10)

3.1.67   Transport Use and Attitude Survey. [*Mid Glamorgan]
                                                            (1976)
           SMITH, D. and HOINVILLE, G.
           Social and Community Planning Research. Report
           P. 379. September 1976. (101 pp. plus appendices).

           This report presents the results and conclusions from
           a large-scale study carried out in Mid Glamorgan in
           1975 to examine the use of transport facilities and
           the public's attitudes towards them. Most of the
           topics covered centred on three main areas of inter-
           est, viz:-reactions of the public to existing trans-
           port facilities; attitudes towards constraints
           placed on the private motorist; and reactions to
           alternative transport policies and proposals. The
           study focussed on the relationship between behaviour,
           circumstances and attitudes. This was achieved by
           means of detailed questionnaires which linked respond-
           ents' attitudes with their use of transport facilities
           and their own travel circumstances relating to work,
           school and shopping journeys. A series of group
           discussions conducted before the main survey enabled
           the identification of various topics to be covered
           by the attitudinal investigation. Appendices provide
           copies of the questionnaires and details of the samp-
           ling, coding, questionnaire development and fieldwork
           processes.

3.1.68   Transportation Planning. [*Need as a Criterion for]
                                                        (1973)
           BURCKHARDT, J.E. and EBY, C.L.
           Highway Research Record No. 435. Highway Research
           Board. Washington D.C. 1973. (pp. 32-41)

3.1.69   Travel Adjustments and Life Styles - A Behavioral
                                                Approach. (1976)
           REICHMAN, S.
           Chapter 8 of: 'Behavioral Travel Demand Models'.
           Edited by P.R. Stopher and A.H. Meyburg. 1976.
                        (pp. 143-152) (see ref. 3.1.10 above.)

3.1.70   Travel Behavior. [*The Effect of Age on Urban]
                                                (1971)
           ASHFORD, N. and HOLLOWAY, F.N.
           Traffic Engineering. Vol. 41. No. 7. April 1971
                                            (pp. 46-49)

3.1.71   Travel Behaviour. [*The Structure of Movement and
                                  Household] (1969)
         ELIOT HURST, M.E.
         Urban Studies. Vol. 6. No. 1. February 1969. (pp.
                                                      70-82)

         Transportation studies have tended to take a
         macroscopic view of movement patterns. A more
         detailed study of travel motivation is suggested
         to fully understand these patterns and to increase
         the possiblity of predicting behaviour. Some explo
         atory conceptualisations, including that of 'movemen
         space' are examined. Travel motivation is broken do
         into goals and occurences, and further research is
         indicated to clarify household travel-decision maki
         In particular, the author proposes that a series
         of intensive case studies of families and other
         groups of individuals in varying social and spatial
         contexts be undertaken, to ascertain the actually
         significant elements of travel-decison situations.
         Guidelines for interviews are set out.
         (see also refs. 3.1.6-3.1.12 above)

3.1.72   Travel Characteristics with Age. [*Variations of
                                               Urban] (1972)
         ASHFORD, N. and HOLLOWAY, F.N.
         Transportation Engineering Journal of ASCE. (Procee
         ings of the American Society of Civil Engineers.)
         Vol. 98. No. T.E.3. August 1972. (pp. 691-704 and
                                                715-732)

         Using origin and destination data previously assemb
         led in urban transportation studies, analyses were
         carried out to determine the effect of the age of
         the tripmaker on urban travel behaviour. The stud
         examined variations with age in travel parameters
         in five medium-sized Georgia cities and in Milwauke
         Wisconsin. Large variations in demand were determi
         Additionally, regression analysis was conducted to
         relate travel parameters to the socio-economic
         characteristics of individual tripmakers. Age was
         found to be highly influential in thirteen of the
         fifteen travel parameters examined, and in ten
         parameters age was the most important contributory
         variable used in regression analysis. The study
         questions the validity of planning which concentrat
         on aggregate zonal averages for travel demand and
         neglects these wide variations in travel for differ
         ent age groups.

3.1.73   Travel Choice and Demand Modelling.[*Urban] (1974)
         HENSHER, D.A. (ed.)
         Australian Road Research Board Special Report No. 1
         Melbourne, Australia. 1974.

3.1.74   Travel Demand and Estimation: A New Prescription.
                                                        (1974)
          STOPHER, P.R. and MEYBURG, A.H.
          Traffic Engineering and Control. Vol. 15. No. 19.
                                          November 1974.(pp. 879-884)

          This article presents a new approach to travel demand
          estimation in which models are constructed at a dis-
          aggregate level, using theories of individual choice
          behaviour in addition to consumer choice theory.

3.1.75   Travel Demand Forecasting.[*Urban] (1973)
          HIGHWAY RESEARCH BOARD.
          Proceedings of a Conference held at Williamsburg,
          Virginia, December 1972.
          Highway Research Board.Special Report No. 143.
                                          Washington D.C. 1973.

3.1.76   Travel Demand. [*Qualitative Aspects of Urban
                                          Personal] (1968)
          ABT ASSOCIATES INC. August 1968.

3.1.77   Travel-Demand Theory: Latent Demand, The Value of
          Travel, and Impact on Life Style. (1976)
          CHESLOW, M.D.
          Chapter 9 in: 'Behavioral Travel-Demand Models'.
          Edited by P.R. Stopher and A.H. Meyburg. 1976.
                                          (pp. 153-163).
          (see ref. 3.1.10 above.)

3.1.78   Travel Demand [*Urban]: A Behavioral Analysis.(1975)
          DOMENCICH, T.A. and McFADDEN, D.
          A Charles River Associates Research Study.
          North-Holland Publishing Co. Amsterdam, Oxford.
          American Elsevier Publishing Co. Inc.   New York.
                                          1975. (215 pp.)

3.1.79   Travel Demands. [*An Analysis of Urban] (1962)
          OI, W. and SCHULDINER, P.
          Northwestern University Press, Evanston, Illinois.
                                          1962.(291 pp.)

          This book presents a statistical analysis of urban
          traffic generation in which household size, car
          ownership, distance from the CBD and residential
          density are examined as explanatory variables.

3.1.80   Travel in Britain. [*Road Talk:] (1978)
          BRITISH ROAD FEDERATION.
          Roadtalk No. 4. January 1978. (4 pp.)

          This report summarises information on choice of
          travel mode from the 1975/76 National Travel Survey
          and compares figures with those for 1972/73.

3.1.81   Travel in Central Edinburgh. [*Car and Bus] (1968
        JACKSON, P. and PALMER, R.W.
        Traffic Engineering and Control. Vol. 10.No. 7.
                November 1968.(pp. 354-357)

3.1.82   Travel in Central London. [*A Theoretical Study of
                      Bus and Car] (1972)
        WEBSTER, F.V. and OLDFIELD, R.H.
        TRRL Report LR 451. 1972. (13 pp.)

3.1.83   Travel in Gloucester, Northampton and Reading.
                      [*Studies of] (1968)
        TAYLOR, M.A.
        RRL Report LR 141. 1968. (243 pp.)

3.1.84   Travel in the Reading Area. [*1971 Repeat Survey
                      of] (1974)
        DOWNES, J.D. and WROOT, R.
        TRRL Supplementary Report SR 43 UC. 1974. (39 pp.)

3.1.85   Travel in Urban Areas. [*An Exploratory Comparison
        of the Advantages of Cars and Buses for] (1964)
        SMEED, R.J. and WARDROP, J.G.
        Institute of Transport Journal. Vol. 30. No. 9.
                March 1964. (pp.301-305)

3.1.86   Travel Study. [*Report on West Midlands] (1975)
        OPINION RESEARCH CENTRE.
        ORC Report 874 25. Cranfield Institute of Technolo
                1975.

3.1.87   Travel [*The Demand for] : Theory and Measurement.
                      (1970)
        QUANDT, R.E. (ed.)
        Heath Lexington Books. 1970.

3.1.88   Traveltime Budgets and Mobility in Urban Areas.
                      (1974)
        ZAHAVI, Y.
        Final Report, U.S. Department of Transportation,
        Federal Highway Administration. Washington D.C.
                1974.

3.1.89   T.T. Relationship [*The] : a Unified Approach to
                      Transportation Planning. (1973)
        ZAHAVI, Y.
        Traffic Engineering and Control. Vol.15. No. 4/5.
                Aug./Sept. 1973.(pp. 205-212)

3.1.90   Travel Times by Private and Public Transport in
        Greater London. [*A Study of] (1967)
         MUNT, P.W. and WOODHALL, R.
        Greater London Council Research Memorandum 44. 196

3.1.91   Traveller's Behaviour. [*Research into the Urban]
                                                    (1971)
          LE BOULANGER, H.
          Transportation Research. Vol. 5. No. 2. June 1971.
                                              (pp. 113-122)

          Current methodology in traffic forecasting has
          satisfied neither practitioners nor researchers, a
          possible reason being that travellers' behaviour
          is insufficiently understood and not always included
          in the models. In addition, the different kinds of
          urban problems treated by traffic models are not
          sufficiently distinguished. The main shortcomings
          of contemporary methodology are identified, and
          elements for a 'traveller's behaviour theory'
          suggested, based on recent statistical evidence
          and analysis of fifty depth interviews with urban
          residents of various French towns. The interviews
          throw light on the main factors and constraints
          which could explain the potential travel demand and
          choice processes of urban residents. The evidence
          suggests that psychological and sociological
          factors and constraints are more important than
          economic ones. Conclusions are drawn from this
          improved knowledge both in the approach to various
          traffic problems and as to improvements in recent
          operational models, and suggestions are made for
          further research.

3.1.92   Trip Generation. [*Activity-Accessibility Models of]
                                                    (1972)
          NAKKASH, T.Z. and GRECO, W.L.
          Highway Research Record No. 392. Highway Research
          Board. Washington D.C. 1972.

3.1.93   Trip Generation Models. [*Some Studies of the
                    Temporal Stability of Person] (1977)
          DOUBLEDAY, C.
          Transportation Research. Vol. 11. No. 4. August
                              1977.(pp. 255-263)
          (This is a later version of a paper read at the
          Annual Conference of the Universities' Transport
          Studies Group at the University of Aston, January
                                              1976).

3.1.94   Trip Generation Relations.[*Temporal Stability of]
                                                    (1973)
          KANNEL, E.J. and HEATHINGTON, K.W.
          Highway Research Record. No. 472. Highway Research
          Board. Washington D.C. 1973. (pp. 17-27)

3.1.95   Trip Modelling. [*An Alternative Approach to Person
                                                      (1974)
          JONES, P.M.
          Paper read at the PTRC Summer Annual Meeting.
          Seminar N: Urban Traffic Models. Vol. II. July 1974
                  (pp. 384-401 of Conference Proceedings)

3.1.96   Trip Production Models. [*Time Stability of Zonal]
                                                      (1972)
          ASHFORD, N. and HOLLOWAY, F.N.
          Transportation Engineering Journal of A.S.C.E.
          (Proceedings of the American Society of Civil
          Engineers). Vol. 98. No. TE4. November 1972.(pp.799
                                                          806

3.1.97   Urban Mobility. (1970)
          INTERNATIONAL ROAD FEDERATION, Washington D.C.
          Theme 2 of Proceedings of Sixth World Highway
                          Conference, Montreal. October 19

          See especially: McCallum, E.P. 'Factors Affecting
          Public Transport needs in Brisbane, Australia'.

3.1.98   User Behaviour. [*Psychological Determinants of]
                                                      (1977)
          EUROPEAN CONFERENCE OF MINISTERS OF TRANSPORT(ECMT)
          Report of the 34th Round Table on Transport
          Economics held in Paris, May 1976.   Economic
          Research Centre. Paris. 1977.

3.1.99   User Misperception of Costs. [*The Effects on
          Transport Benefit Evaluation of] (1974)
          BAMFORD, T.J.G. and WIGAN, M.R.
          TRRL Supplementary Report SR 23 UC. 1974.(18 pp.)

3.1.100   Value of Commuters' Travel Time - A Study in Urban
                                  Transportation. (1968)
          LISCO, T.E.
          Highway Research Record No. 245. Highway Research
                  Board. Washington D.C. 1968.

          This study was based on data collected by the
          Skokie Swift surveys (see ref. 4.4.45).   It
          concludes that the actual comfort provided by the
          transit vehicle can be very important in contribut-
          ing to commuter satisfaction.   It found that
          commuters make modal choice decisions rationally
          on the basis of alternatives available to them,
          placing a value of $2.50-$2.70 per hour on their
          commuting time and an extra value of $2.00 per
          day for the difference in 'comfort' between driving
          and using a rapid transit system.   It was concluded
          that the fare played a smaller part in commuters'
          modal choice decisions than either comfort or
          journey time.

3.1.101   Value of Journey Time, the Rate of Time Preference
           and the Valuation of Some Aspects of Environment
           in the London Metropolitan Region.[*A Study of
           House Prices as a Means of Establishing the] (1971)
           WABE, J.S.
           Applied Economics. Vol. 3. December 1971. (pp. 247-
                                                         255).

3.1.102   Value of Time.(1976)
           GOODWIN, P.B.
           European Conference of Ministers of Transport (ECMT).
           Report of the 30th. Round Table on Transport Economics.
                 Economic Research Centre, Paris. 1976 (71 pp.)

           The object of the report is to identify and discuss
           a number of the problems associated with putting a
           money value on time spent travelling. These include
           time spent travelling in working hours (including a
           discussion of the working time of housewives and of
           non-wage sources of income); behavioural aspects of
           the value of time (including a discussion of percep-
           tion of time and costs); and problems associated with
           equity values and the incidence of costs and benefits.
           The paper outlines the value of time procedures
           presently used by the United Kingdom Department of
           the Environment and recommends that these are broadly
           satisfactory and should be more widely applied, but
           with some modifications. Further research is recomm-
           ended into areas such as values of working time;
           disentangling the effects of the duration and the
           unpleasantness of travel activities; the perception
           of time spent travelling; the importance of the
           amount of 'spare' time people have at their disposal;
           and public transport mode choice. An appendix
           outlining recent themes in research on the value of
           time is followed by a substantial list of references
           on the subject. The report concludes with a summary
           of the discussion on the paper.

3.1.103   Value of Time for Commuting Motorists as a
           Function of their Income Level and Amount of Time
                                Saved. [*The] (1970)
           THOMAS, T.C. and THOMPSON, G.I.
           Highway Research Record. No. 314. Highway Research
                      Board.Washington D.C. 1970.

3.1.104   Value of Time in Transport Planning [*The]: A
                                Review.(1969)
           HARRISON, A.J. and QUARMBY, D.A.
           European Conference of Ministers of Transport (ECMT)
           Report of the 6th. Round Table on Transport Economics.
           Economic Research Centre, Paris. 1969.

This paper gives the background theory to subsequent
methodology on the value of travel time.

3.1.105   Value of Time on Short Urban Leisure Trips. [*The]
                                                           (1970)
           VEAL, A.J.
           Birmingham University. Centre for Urban and Regional
                                               Studies. 1970

3.1.106   Value of Time Saved by Trip Purpose. (1970)
           THOMAS, T.C. and THOMPSON, G.I.
           Highway Research Record.No. 314. Highway Research
           Board. Washington D.C. 1970.

3.1.107   Value of Time Spent Travelling: some new evidence.
                                                          (1965)
           BEESLEY, M.E.
           Economica. Vol. 32. May 1965.(pp. 174-185)

3.1.108   Value of Travel Time. [*Human Effort and the] (19
           GOODWIN, P.B.
           Journal of Transport Economics and Policy. Vol. X.
                               No. 1. January 1976. (pp. 3

           This paper reviews some aspects of the use of
           'generalised cost' as an aid to explaining travel
           behaviour and, arising from this, puts forward a
           hypothesis that not only time and money but also
           'effort' are thought to affect the demand for trave
           Various possible measures of 'effort' are considere
           including energy expenditure, heart rate and galva
           skin response. Finally, some problems are discuss
           and proposals made for further research to establis
           the effect of 'effort' on travellers' behaviour an
           to find methods of using the results in planning.
           A useful list of relevant references is given.

3.1.109   Value of Travel Time. [*Variations in the] (1969)
           LEE, N. and DALVI, M.Q.
           Manchester School of Economic and Social Studies.
                       Vol. 37. No. 3. 1969. (pp. 213-236)

3.1.110   Value of Travel Time [*Variations in the]:
                               Further Analysis.(1971)
           LEE, N. and DALVI, M.Q.
           Manchester School of Economic and Social Studies.
                       Vol. 39. No. 3. 1971. (pp. 187-204)

3.1.111   Value of Travel Time Savings [*The] - U.K.
           Studies, Transportation and Environment: Policies,
                                    Plans, Practice.(197
           BARBER, J. and SEARLE, G.
           University of Southampton. 1973.

3.1.112   Values of Travel Time. [*A Review of Studies
                    Leading to Existing] (1976)
           HENSHER, D.A.
           Transportation Research Record No.587
           Transportation Research Board. Washington D.C.
                    1976. (pp. 30-41).

3.1.113   Waiting Times for Buses in Central London. (1966)
           HOLROYD, E.M. and SCRAGGS, D.A.
           Traffic Engineering and Control. Vol. 8. No. 3.
                    July 1966. (pp. 158-160)

3.1.114   Waiting Times in Central Areas. [*Bus Passenger]
                                                    (1970)
           O'FLAHERTY, C.A. and MANGAN, D.O.
           Traffic Engineering and Control. Vol. 11. No. 9.
                    January 1970. (pp. 419-421)

3.1.115   Waiting Times in Greater Manchester. [*Bus
                    Passenger] (1974)
           SEDDON, P.A. and DAY, M.P.
           Traffic Engineering and Control. Vol. 15. No. 9.
                    January 1974.(pp. 442-445)

GOVERNMENT REPORTS AND PUBLICATIONS.

3.1.116   Time Budgets and Models of Urban Activity Patterns.
                                                    (1974)
           BULLOCK, N., DICKENS, P., SHAPCOTT, M. and
                                    STEADMAN, P.
           In: Social Trends No. 5. Central Statistical Office.
                    H.M.S.O. 1974. (pp. 45-63).

3.1.117   Value of Time Savings in Transport. [*The] (1969)
           MINISTRY OF TRANSPORT. Economic Planning Directorate.
           Technical Note 3. 1969.

3.1 Subsidiary References.

1.1 New Towns - Transport and Mobility.

1.1.16   Transport and Mobility in Durham New Towns.   (1974-5)

2.1 Runcorn.

2.1.6   Runcorn Busway Study.   (1976)
2.1.10   Runcorn Travel Survey. (1973)

2.2 Skelmersdale.

2.2.8   Skelmersdale New Town Population and Social Surveys. (Annually)

2.3 Telford.

2.3.6   *Telford Transportation Study. (1976-7)*
2.3.7   *Telford Transportation Study:*

        1. *An aid to the preliminary evaluation of long-term public*
                   transport options.
        2. *New techniques in the modelling of trip generation and*
                   modal split. (1976)

2.3.21   *Telford Social Survey. (1973)*

2.4 Other New Towns.

2.4.11   *Glenrothes Area Public Transport Study: Final Report. (1977)*
2.4.13   *Harlow 1976 Household Survey. (1977)*
2.4.14   *Attitudes to Transport Provision in Old Harlow. (1974)*
2.4.15   *Harlow Bus Study. Final Report. (1976)*
2.4.56   *Stevenage Household Survey. March 1976. (1976)*
2.4.57   *Stevenage Public Transport: Cost Benefit Analysis. (1969)*
2.4.59   *Stevenage Superbus Experiment: Summary Report. (1974)*
2.4.64   *The Urban Transport Problem and Modal Choice. (1971)*

3.2 Social Aspects of Mobility.

3.2.9   *A Study of Travel Behaviour of the Elderly. (1976)*
3.2.14   *Lifestyles and the Transportation Needs of the Elderly in*
                   Los Angeles. (1976)
3.2.16   *Travel Patterns of Elderly People Under a Concessionary Fares*
                   Scheme. (1977)
3.2.29   *Mobility and Accessibility in the Outer Metropolitan Area. (197*
3.2.37   *Personal Mobility and Transport Policy. (1973)*
3.2.39   *Transportation and Retirement. (1972)*
3.2.41   *Journeys to School: a survey of Secondary Schools in Berkshire*
                   and Surrey. (1977)
3.2.48   *Shopping in Watford. (1971)*
3.2.49   *Some Social Aspects of Public Passenger Transport. (1977)*
3.2.61   *The Effects of Differing Levels of Spatial Mobility: a*
                   discussion. (1976)
3.2.63   *Transport Realities and Planning Policy. (1976)*
3.2.64   *Travel Needs of Individuals. (1974)*
3.2.65   *Understanding Travel. (1978)*
3.2.69   *The Elderly at Home: a study of people aged sixty five and*
                   over living in the community in England in 1976. (1978)
3.2.73   *Planning for Leisure. (1969)*
3.2.77   *Shopping Habits and Attitudes to Shop Hours in Great Britain.*
                   (1975)

3.3 Interaction between Land Use and Travel.

3.3.2   *Accessibility and Choice as Quantifiable Variables in Land Use*
                   Planning. (1972)
3.3.3   *The Rôle of Accessibility in Basic Transportation Choice*
                   Behaviour. (1976)
3.3.4   *Accessibility of Various Social Groups to Different Activities.*
                   (1977)

4.5 Public Transport - General and Miscellaneous.

4.5.1	An Examination of Attitudes and Beliefs Underlying the Use of Local Bus Services. (1975)
4.5.8	Public Attitudes to Transport in the Eastbourne, Bexhill and Hastings Area. (1975)
4.5.9	Public Transport in Bedfordshire: Facts, Views, Issues, Option (1974)
4.5.16	Public Transport's Rôle in Urban Areas. (1968)
4.5.17	Use of Public Transport in Urban Areas. (1962)
4.5.18	Urban Passenger Transport: Some trends and prospects. (1977)
4.5.23	Study of Rural Transport in Devon. (1971)

5.1 Private Motor Transport.

5.1.1	Initial Study of Car Availability. (1974)
5.1.10	A Theory of Household Automobile Allocation Decisions. (1976)
5.1.11	Theory of Urban Household Automobile Ownership Decisions. (197
5.1.16	The Possible Effects of Petrol Rationing on Travel in London.(

7.1 Transport Policy.

7.1.3	Changing Directions. (1974)
7.1.10	Getting Nowhere Fast. (1976)
7.1.11	Distributional Aspects of Investment in Urban Transport. (1973
7.1.12	The Economic and Social Impact of Investments in Public Transi (1973
7.1.26	Effect of Traffic Engineering Methods on London. (1963)
7.1.27	An Evaluation of Two Proposals for Traffic Restraint in Centra London. (1967)
7.1.28	Study of Traffic Restraints in Singapore. (1975)

8.1 Survey Techniques: Behavioural and Attitudinal.

8.1.2	Attitude - Behavior Models for Public Systems Planning and Design. (1975)
8.1.4	The Use of Attitude Measurement in the Forecasting of Off-Peak Behaviour.(1977)
8.1.11	Application of Attitude Surveys in Transportation Planning and Impact Studies: A case study of Southwest Washington D.C. (197
8.1.19	Perceived Attribute Importance in Public and Private Transport ation. (1973)
8.1.24	A Pragmatic Application of Category Analysis to Smallscale Household Travel Surveys. (1976
8.1.42	Application of In-Depth Interviewing Techniques to the Study o Travel Behaviour: some preliminary results. (1975)
8.1.69	On the Application of Psychological Measurement Techniques to Travel Demand Estimation. (1977)
8.1.70	The Application of Psychological Research and Theory to Urban Transportation Planning. (1975)
8.1.77	Quantification of the Comfort Variable. (1975)
8.1.94	Multidimensional Scaling of Consumer Preferences for a Public Transportation System. (1974)
8.1.96	An Application of Multidimensional Scaling Techniques to the Quantification of the Comfort Variable for Use in Binary Disaggregate Mode Choice Models. (1974)

8.1.114   User Preferences for a Demand - Responsive Transportation
                        System: A case - study report. (1971)

8.2   Economic Evaluation.

8.2.17   Estimating the Social Benefit of Constructing an Underground
                        Railway in London. (1963)
8.2.18   Social Cost-Benefit Study of the Manchester-Glossop and
          Manchester-Marple/New Mills Suburban Railway Services.(1972)

8.3   Research Techniques and Methodology - General and Miscellaneous.

8.3.5   Modelling London Transport's Demand and Supply Markets. (1975)
8.3.6   Choice, Demand and User Cost. (1975)
8.3.7   Applications of Information-Processing Theory to the Analysis
                        of Urban Travel Demand. (1977)
8.3.8   Passenger Transport Demand in Urban Areas: Methodology for
                        analysing and forecasting. (1976)
8.3.9   Demand Responsive Diversions on a Rural Bus Service. (1975)
8.3.10   Determination of Functional Sub-Regions Within an Urban Area
                        for Transportation Planning. (1974)
8.3.12   A Gaming Approach to the Study of Travel Behaviour in Oxford.
                                                              (1976)
8.3.13   A Gravity Distribution Model. (1971-2).
8.3.14   Information Availability and Travel Characteristics in
                        Developing Cities. (1977)
8.3.18   A Model of Vehicle Comfort and a Method for its Assessment.
                                                              (1973)
8.3.23   Rural Public Transport - A Study in Bedfordshire. (1974)
8.3.26   Socio-Psychological Models of Travel Choice - the T.S.U.
                        approach.   (1977)
8.3.31   Report on Investigations of Household Travel Decision - Making
                        Behaviour.(1977)
8.3.32   Trip Generation Techniques. (1971)

9.2   Bibliographies.

9.2.1   Annotated bibliography of the application of behavior and
          attitude research to transportation system planning and design.
                                                              (1976)
9.2.18   Trip Generation. (1967)

9.5   Statistical Sources.

9.5.6-8   National Travel Survey 1972/3.
9.5.14   Transport Statistics. (Annually.)

3.2 Social Aspects of Mobility.

The references listed in this subsection include the
following types of material:-

- Items concerned with the social implications of transp
  and mobility.

- Socially-oriented planning studies not specifically
  relating to transport, but with implications for trans
  and mobility.

- Other more general social studies which contribute
  towards an awareness of and insight into current socia
  trends and problems which have an environmental dimens
  and some implications for transport planning and polic

Literature concerned with the social aspects of new towns
is included in sections 1 and 2 of the bibliography and
discussed in the introductions to these sections. The majo
Government policy documents are listed in section 7.
Relevant items from these and other parts of the bibliograp
are cross-referenced at the end of this subsection.

Material which is concerned with the social implications
of transport and mobility forms the greater part of this
subsection. This includes general studies such as the two
P.E.P. Broadsheets by HILLMAN, WHALLEY and HENDERSON (3.2.?
and 3.2.63) and HILLMAN's paper Social Goals for Transport
Policy (3.2.55), which relate various social considerations
to transport and planning policies; and studies of specifio
aspects such as the mobility problems and requirements of
the elderly and of people without cars, fare concession
schemes, and school transport. Many of these specific stud
incorporate policy recommendations.

British transport policy has shown an increasing concern
with social considerations since the early 1970's.
Personal Mobility and Transport Policy (3.2.37) by HILLMAN,
WHALLEY and HENDERSON published in 1973, and the influenti
report of the INDEPENDENT COMMISSION ON TRANSPORT, Changin
Directions (7.1.3) published in 1974, helped to focus atte
on the particular mobility problems of certain sectors of
population. These reports pointed to the need for transpo
policy to consider the differing transport requirements of
all sectors of the community, particularly those without a
car normally available, and including the elderly, the
handicapped, housewives and children. The Government's
Consultation Document on Transport Policy (7.1.77) publishe
in 1976 stated the need for a national transport policy to
take into account "the social objective of providing mobil
for the still large minority without access to a car," whi
would involve giving a higher priority to essential bus se

The Consultation Document recommended a reappraisal of
priorities within the total of public spending on transport
so as to emphasise the rôle of selective subsidies and
expenditure designed to achieve these social objectives.
The Government's 1977 White Paper on Transport Policy (7.1.76)
formalised these recommendations by listing as the second of
the three principal objectives of a national transport policy
that of meeting social needs by securing a reasonable level
of personal mobility, in particular by maintaining public
transport for the many people without the effective choice
of travelling by car. The White Paper gives recognition to
the special transport needs of elderly people and disabled
people and points out that many of these are sufficiently
mobile to benefit greatly from a reliable public transport
system if it is accessible and within their financial means.
The Transport Policy White Paper also points to the need for
research to identify and measure the transport requirements
of different sectors of the community.

A number of studies have investigated the travel behaviour
and needs of elderly people. The report by the NATIONAL OLD
PEOPLE'S WELFARE COUNCIL [AGE CONCERN] (3.2.1) presents the
results of a survey of transport problems encountered by
elderly people in urban and rural areas and sets out a policy
on transport for the elderly based on the survey findings.
A more recent study published by the National Corporation for
the Care of Old People: Transport and the Elderly:problems
and possible action,by NORMAN (3.2.19) also pinpoints barriers
which hinder the mobility of elderly people and suggests means
of overcoming or reducing them. Personal Mobility and Transport
Policy (3.2.37), Transport Realities and Planning Policy
(3.2.63), and Mobility and Accessibility in the Outer
Metropolitan Area (3.2.29), by HILLMAN, WHALLEY and HENDERSON,
all contain survey data on travel patterns and needs of
pensioners. The recent Government report The Elderly at Home
(3.2.69) includes an examination of elderly people's mobility
and travel patterns and of their access to certain essential
facilities. Articles by CARP (3.2.3 and 3.2.39), GILLAN and
WACHS (3.2.14), PAASWELL and EDELSTEIN (3.2.9), and ASHFORD
and HOLLOWAY (3.1.70 and 3.1.72) discuss travel behaviour and
mobility problems of the elderly in the United States. Studies
investigating the effects of concessionary fares schemes for
the elderly are described in the article and report by BENWELL
(3.2.11-12), based on a survey carried out in Harlow; in the
London Transport Executive report by FREEMAN (3.2.13); in the
TRRL report by SKELTON (3.2.16), and in the paper by JENKINS
and SKELTON (3.2.17). The results of a Government survey of
concessionary travel schemes in England and Wales have recently
been published by the DEPARTMENT OF TRANSPORT (4.1.101). Other
relevant material on fares policies is included in subsection
4.1 of the bibliography and listed in the subsidiary references
at the end of this subsection.

School transport is the subject of the LGORU report Cutting the Cost of School Buses (3.2.40), the two DEPARTMENT OF EDUCATION AND SCIENCE reports (3.2.75-76), and the Report to the D.E.S. Working Party on School Transport by the NATIONAL CONFEDERATION OF PARENT-TEACHER ASSOCIATIONS (3.2.42). A large-scale questionnaire survey of school children's journey to school in Berkshire and Surrey is described in the TRRL report by RIGBY and HYDE (3,2,41).

Socially-oriented planning studies which have been incorporat in this subsection include some general works, such as CULLINGWORTH'S The Social Framework of Planning (3.2.54) and the National Council of Social Service's publication on the social context of planning by BROADY (3.2.38); and studies wh examine specific topics including the location of schools, hospitals, hypermarkets and other shopping facilities. Such material is clearly relevant to considerations of personal accessibility and mobility. HILLMAN (3.2.51) and HILLMAN, HENDERSON and WHALLEY (3.2.28) have examined the social implications of large out-of-town or edge-of-town hypermarke developments, with particular reference to the difficulties of access by those without the use of a car, especially the elderly, the disabled, and housewives with small children. The Building Research Station has carried out a programme of research into the location of shopping facilities in towns a the reports by DAWS (3.2.46) and by DAWS and BRUCE (3.2.48) present some results and conclusions from this research.

More general material, not directly concerned with transport or other planning considerations but with implications for t include sociological studies of family organisation such as two books by YOUNG and WILLMOTT (3.2.21-22) and the P.E.P. Broadsheet by FOGARTY, RAPOPORT and RAPOPORT (3.2.45); and studies of the lifestyles of elderly people. The latter inc books by TUNSTALL (3.2.31), SHANAS, TOWNSEND et al (3.2.32), and TOWNSEND (3.2.34). The article in Urban Studies by WILL (3.2.58) reviews trends in social relationships and behaviou both within and outside the family, and examines likely tren in social structure and patterns of social life in Britain during the next twenty years or so.

3.2   Social Aspects of Mobility

3.2.1   Age Concern on Transport. (2nd Edition 1973)
        NATIONAL OLD PEOPLE'S WELFARE COUNCIL.
        (AGE CONCERN).1973 (36 pp.)

        Part 1 of the report presents the results of a
        questionnaire survey carried out among sixty old
        people's welfare organisations in 1971 to ascertain how
        the lives of old people were restricted by the then
        current transport policies. Appendix I outlines the
        survey methods and response rates. The survey
        concentrated on bus travel, this being the principle
        form of public transport used by old people in both
        urban and rural areas. The main problems identified in
        urban areas were (in order of priority): fare increases,
        design of vehicles, infrequent or inconvenient services,
        withdrawal of services, and driving standards. The main
        problems identified in rural areas were inconvenient or
        non-existent services, and high fares. Suggestions by
        the respondents for improvements are set out, most of
        these being related to fares and concessionary schemes.

        The survey results were used by Age Concern as a basis
        for drawing up a policy on transport for the elderly,
        and the fifteen policy points, with explanatory notes,
        form Part 2 of the report. Part 3 consists of summar-
        ies of discussions held with various groups following
        the first edition of the report, and of the various
        changes which have resulted from them. Conclusions are
        drawn, emphasising the extent of the hardships suffered
        by elderly people as a result of the decline in public
        bus transport. Recommendations are made for more
        comprehensive concessionary fares policies; greater
        attention to the requirements of old people in bus
        design; and service improvements.

3.2.2. Ageing [* Easing the Restrictions of] (1972)
        NATIONAL OLD PEOPLE'S WELFARE COUNCIL (AGE CONCERN).1972

3.2.3. Automobile and Public Transportation for Retired People.
                                                        (1971)
        CARP, F.M.
        Highway Research Record No. 348. Highway Research Board.
        Washington DC. 1971
        (see also ref. 3.2.39 below.)

3.2.4. Automobiles by Older People. [*On the Driving of](1964)
        McFARLAND, R.A. et al.
        Journal of Gerontology. Vol.19. 1964. (pp.190-197)
        (see also refs.3.2.7; 3.2.9-19; 3.2.23; 3.2.29-34;
          3.2.36-37; 3.2.39; 3.2.44; 3.2.63; 3.2.65, and 3.2.69)

3.2.5. Banding Poverty. (1972)
        BOSANQUET, N.
        New Society. 2nd March 1972.

3.2.6 Captive Wife [*The] : conflicts of housebound mothers
.   (1966)
GAVRON, H.
International Library of Sociology and Social Recon-
struction.
Routledge and Kegan Paul. 1966. (190pp.)

3.2.7. Carless in the U.K. and U.S.[* Problems of the](1973)
PAASWELL, R.E.
Transportation. Vol.2.No.4. December 1973.(pp.351-371

3.2.8. Disabled People in the Urban Environment.[*Planning fo
(1969)
UNIVERSITY OF EDINBURGH, DEPARTMENT OF URBAN DESIGN
AND REGIONAL PLANNING, PLANNING RESEARCH UNIT and
CENTRAL COUNCIL FOR THE DISABLED. 1969. (64 pp.)

This report discusses the effects of disability on
physical mobility and presents case studies to illustrate problems of mobility in three British town cent:
developments, at Cumbernauld, Coventry and the
Birmingham Bull Ring. Recommendations are put forwar
concerning planning with regard to the needs of disab
persons in private and public transport, pedestrian
routes and vertical circulation (ramps, steps, lifts,
escalators) as well as in the design of public places
and new buildings.

3.2.9. Elderly. [*A Study of Travel Behaviour of the] (1976)
PAASWELL, R.E. and EDELSTEIN, P.
Transportation Planning and Technology. Vol.3.No.3.197(

3.2.10 Elderly. [*Attitudes of the Retired and the](1974)
NATIONAL OLD PEOPLE'S WELFARE COUNCIL. (AGE CONCERN)1!

3.2.11 Elderly [*Bus Passes and the]: A Need for More Inform
Policy Making? (1976)
BENWELL, M.
Local Government Studies.Vol.6.No.3.October 1976.
(pp.51-57)

This article examines the issuing of free or reduced-
bus passes to the elderly by local authorities and hi
lights the absence of a common code of practice in the
allocation. The most usual practice has been to iss
passes on the same terms to all persons within the
qualifying age group, but the Government's Consultati(
Document on Transport Policy in 1976 emphasised the
principle of greater selectivity in subsidy, and with
likely financial constraints local authorities may in
future need to make decisions as to how best to maxim:
benefits to pensioners. This was done in Harlow in 1!
when a choice of alternative concessions was introduc(
and a £30 a week household income limit was imposed.
The author describes research carried out in Harlow t(
obtain information on the choice of pattern of conces:
and on pensioners' travel habits. Although restricted

130

scope this provided data which would assist future
policy decisions on concessionary fares. Such data
is not generally available to local authorities, and
the author points to the need for much more research
into elderly people's lifestyles and travel habits,
examining differences between them in order to identify
who are the concession-takers and users and which
sectors do not benefit from concessions; how much and
what kind of travel the passes are used for; and what
are pensioners' needs for and attitudes towards travel.

3.2.12 Elderly in Harlow. [*An Examination of the Extent and
        Welfare Implications of Bus Use by the] (1977)
        BENWELL, M.
        Cranfield Institute of Technology.Centre for Transport
        Studies. Memorandum No.22. June 1977.(70 pp.)

        This report describes research carried out for Harlow
        District Council to provide information on bus use and
        travel behaviour by its elderly citizens to facilitate
        policy decisions on fare concession allocation in
        particular, and on welfare generally. Interviews were
        conducted among over 500 concession applicants in March
        1977 and information was obtained about the pattern of
        concessions taken, frequency and purpose of bus and other
        forms of travel both within and outside Harlow, and about
        access to cars. The results are compared with those of
        a similar survey carried out in 1976. The findings
        showed that the bus pass generated a travel surplus of
        approximately 2½ trips per user per week on average,
        and that the replacement of a half fare by a free pass
        had had little effect on trip-making within Harlow but
        had increased the level of out-of-Harlow trip-making.
        Within these averages there were substantial differences
        in travel habits, and significant variations were
        identified in the use of and dependence on buses between
        different neighbourhoods. A £20 household income
        supplement was available as an alternative to the bus
        pass and was shown to benefit infrequent bus users,
        there being a fairly close match between type of
        concession chosen and frequency of bus travel.
        Appendices include copies of the questionnaires;
        analyses of shopping, health and social facilities in
        Harlow by neighbourhood; and a copy of the 1977
        concession application form and explanatory leaflet.

3.2.13 Elderly in London - 1974 Survey.[*Free Travel for the]
                                                       (1975)
        FREEMAN, J.D.
        London Transport Executive. Operational Research Report
        R.208. January 1975.

        The report presents the results and conclusions from
        an interview survey of the usage of pensioners' permits

carried out in May/June 1974. This showed that the
average number of trips per holder per week under the
free travel scheme was the same as that found in a
1973 survey of concessionary fare usage, before free
travel was introduced. (4.6 trips per holder per wee
Within this average, previous permit holders had
increased their usage by some 30%, and it was conclud
that the large number of new pass-holders who had app
for and received the free permits since the 1973
survey were making much less than average use of the
facility.

3.2.14. Elderly in Los Angeles. [*Lifestyles and the
Transportation Needs of the] (1976)
GILLAN, J. and WACHS, M.
Transportation. Vol. 5. No. 1. March 1976.
(pp. 45-62)

The major shortcoming of most research concerned with
the transportation needs of the elderly has been that
the aged have been treated as a homogeneous group
without recognizing the various lifestyles within
the group. This paper describes a study of trip-
making behaviour of persons over 65 years of age livi
in Los Angeles County, distinguishing between those
residing in the inner city and those in suburban
fringe areas. An analysis of modal choice, trip
purpose and frequency of travel exhibited many
similarities but some significant differences in the
travel behaviour and problems of these two groups.
An additional survey of taxi usage showed that
elderly persons represent a substantial proportion
of taxicab patrons, and this is one indication of
the change that occurs in mobility patterns on
reaching retirement.

3.2.15. Elderly.[*Lifeline Telephone Service for the] (1972)
GREGORY, P. and YOUNG, M.
National Innovations Centre. London 1972. (26pp.)

An account of a pilot project in Hull.

3.2.16. Elderly People Under a Concessionary Fares Scheme.
[*Travel Patterns of] (1977)
SKELTON, N.G.
TRRL Supplementary Report SR 280. 1977 (34pp.)

This report describes the methods and results of four
travel surveys of the movements of elderly people on
Tyneside, carried out between March 1973 and June
1974. The findings are compared with analogous data
from a sample of younger people. The study examined
the overall patterns of travel by different modes
and for various purposes; the effects of changing
from a half-fare to a zero-fare concession; and

seasonal differences in travel patterns. Walk trips
of less than half a mile were excluded. Of the
remaining trips (on average 10.8 per person per week)
56% were by bus, 23% by car and 18% on foot. It was
estimated that the change in concession generated a
34% increase in the number of bus trips made; and it
was found that 8% more trips were made in early summer
than in early spring, the difference being mainly in
recreational trips. Appendices provide methodological
details, including copies of the questionnaires and
travel diaries used and notes on the survey design,
fieldwork and statistical significance of the results.

3.2.17 Elderly. [*Some Implications of Fare Concessions for
the] (1975)
JENKINS, I.A. and SKELTON, N.G.
Paper read at the PTRC Summer Annual Meeting. Seminar
S. July 1975.

3.2.18 Elderly. [* The Organisation of Voluntary Service:
a study of domiciliary visiting of the] (1972).
SHENFIELD, B. and ALLEN, I.
P.E.P. Broadsheet No. 533. 1972.

3.2.19 Elderly [*Transport and the]: problems and possible
action. (1977)
NORMAN, A.
National Corporation for the Care of Old People.
London. 1977. (142 pp.)

This book identifies the barriers which hinder the
mobility of elderly people and discusses practical
ways of removing or reducing them. Suggestions
include both improvements involving policy changes
at government level, such as the rationalisation of
concessionary fare schemes, and practical initiatives
at local level.
(see also refs. 3.2.1-4; 3.2.7; 3.2.23; 3.2.29-34;
3.2.36-7; 3.2.39; 3.2.44; 3.2.63; 3.2. 65 ,and 3.2.69)

3.2.20 Employment, Mobility and Public Transportation. (1971)
WACHS, M.
Highway Research Record No.348. Highway Research Board.
Washington D.C. 1971.

3.2.21 Family and Kinship in East London. (1957)
YOUNG, M. and WILLMOTT, P.
Institute of Community Studies Report.
Routledge and Kegan Paul. London. 1957. (231 pp.)

3.2.22 Family [*The Symmetrical]: a study of work and
leisure in the London Region. (1973)
YOUNG, M. and WILLMOTT, P.
Institute of Community Studies Report.
Routledge and Kegan Paul. London. 1973. (398 pp.)

3.2.23   Free Bus Passes in Reading. [*Estimating the Use of]
         - survey of the number of trips by pass-holders. (197?
         DALY, A.J., ROGERS, K.G. and WHITBREAD, A.W.
         Local Government Operational Research Unit. (LGORU)
                              Report C174. 1973.(26 pp.)
         Royal Institute of Public Administration.
         (see also refs. 3.2.1-4; 3.2.7; 3.2.9-19; 3.2.29-34;
             3.2.36-7; 3.2.39; 3.2.44; 3.2.63; 3.2.65 and 3.2.69)

3.2.24   Hypermarket Survey. [*The Sunderland] (1971)
         SUNDERLAND CORPORATION. November 1971. (57 pp.)

         An investigation into the possible effects which a
         hypermarket on the south-western boundary could have
         on the central shopping area and district centres in
         Sunderland itself.

3.2.25   Leisure in the North West. (1972)
         NORTH WEST SPORTS COUNCIL. 1972. (270 pp.)

         The technical report of the Leisure Activities Survey
         carried out by the North West Sports Council.

3.2.26   Living Suburb [*The]: scheme for the redevelopment
                                        of Boston Manor. (1958)
         CHAMBERLIN, POWELL and BON; SHANKLAND, G. and JONES,
                                                          D.G.
         Architecture and Building. Special Issue. Vol.33. No.9
         September 1958.(pp. 321-356). Analysis and comments-
         October 1958.(pp. 364-373). Further comments - Novembe
         1958 pp.(418-421) and Vol.34. February 1959. (pp. 44-49

3.2.27   Loneliness: a new study. (1972)
         NATIONAL COUNCIL OF SOCIAL SERVICE.
         Women's Group on Public Welfare. Bedford Square Press.
                                             1972 (68 pp.)

3.2.28   Market Place [*In the]: the hypermarket debate. (1972
         HILLMAN, M., HENDERSON, I. and WHALLEY, A.
         New Society. 21st September 1972. (pp. 543-546)

3.2.29   Mobility and Accessibility in the Outer Metropolitan
                                                Area. (1974)
         HILLMAN, M., HENDERSON, I. and WHALLEY, A.
         P.E.P. Report to the Department of the Environment.
                              (unpublished).June 1974. (300 p
         (available from the Department of the Environment
              Library under the Inter-Library Loan Scheme).
         (see also refs. 3.2.37 and 3.2.63 below)

         The aims of the study were to investigate variations
         in personal and household access to a range of commonl
         used facilities and to examine two selected groups of
         the population with special mobility problems:-mothers
         of young children and elderly people. The report is
         divided into two parts, the first describing and
         analysing the findings of a large scale postal surve

of a sample of all households in the Outer
Metropolitan Area; and the second concerned with the
results of detailed personal interviews with mothers of
young children and with elderly people.

3.2.30   Old Age. (1968)
OFFICE OF HEALTH ECONOMICS. March 1968. (36 pp.)

3.2.31   Old and Alone: A sociological study of old people.
(1966)
TUNSTALL, J.
Routledge and Kegan Paul. 1966. (355 pp.)

3.2.32   Old People in Three Industrial Societies. (1968)
SHANAS, E., TOWNSEND, P. et al.
Routledge and Kegan Paul. 1968. (478 pp.)

This book presents information about old people in
Denmark, Britain and the U.S.A. and the data is used
to test various hypotheses about the place of old
people in industrial societies.

3.2.33   Old People [*Rehousing of]: some planning implications.
(1962)
HOLE, V. and ALLEN, P.G.
Building Research Station. Miscellaneous Paper.
C.P. Design Series 33. 1962

3.2.34   Old People [*The Family Life of]:an inquiry in East
London. (1957)
TOWNSEND, P.
Institute of Community Studies.
Routledge and Kegan Paul. London. 1957.(300 pp.)
(see also refs. 3.2.1-4; 3.2.7; 3.2.9-19; 3.2.23;
3.2.36-7; 3.2.39; 3.2.44; 3.2.63; 3.2.65,and 3.2.69)

3.2.35   Olney Residents' Survey. [*The] (1974 and 1975)
Vol. 1: Preliminary Report and Residents' Comments.
October 1974. (155 pp.)
Vol. 2: Final Report. July 1975. (38 pp.)
HUDSON, D.M.
The Open University. The New Towns Study Unit.

3.2.36   Pensioners' Jaunts. (1974)
DALY, A. J.
New Society. 29th August 1974.
(see also refs. 3.2.1-4; 3.2.7; 3.2.9-19; 3.2.23;
3.2.29-34; 3.2.37; 3.2.39; 3.2.44; 3.2.63; 3.2.65,
and 3.2.69)

3.2.37   Personal Mobility and Transport Policy. (1973)
         HILLMAN, M., HENDERSON, I. and WHALLEY, A.
         P.E.P. Broadsheet No.542. June 1973.(134 pp.)

         The book examines personal mobility in daily life
         from the individual and community viewpoints and
         relates these to physical urban and transport
         planning policies and to broader aspects of governmen
         policy. In Chapter 1 the travel needs and mobility
         levels and restraints of different age and other
         groups are considered, and the requirements and
         problems of children, teenagers, mothers of small
         children, elderly, and handicapped people are high-
         lighted. Chapter 2 presents a comparative examinatio
         of travel modes from both the individual and the
         community viewpoints. The conflict of interests
         between these two aspects is revealed, cars being the
         preferred mode by individuals for all but the shortes
         trips, but having the most disadvantages to the
         community as a whole. The extent of access to a car,
         and consequently the real degree of choice of transpo
         mode available to the individual, are shown to be mor
         limited than had hitherto often been assumed.

         The findings from the studies of personal mobility
         and of travel modes are synthesised in the third
         chapter, which presents a comparative analysis of
         travel and social surveys conducted in five different
         locations, including a new town. Level of access to
         car was found to be a highly significant influence on
         choice of travel mode and on mobility, and four level
         (related to household car ownership and personal
         licence-holding) were identified and used in the
         analysis.

         The final chapters relate the findings of the earlier
         studies to transport planning policies and to broader
         government policies. These are shown to have concent
         rated on car movements at the expense of both pedestr
         movements and public transport. At the same time the
         dispersal of facilities in urban areas and lowering
         of residential densities have encouraged increasing
         dependence on personal motorised movement. These
         trends have exacerbated the problems of sectors of th
         population without access to a car. Suggestions are
         made for future policies which would reflect an aware-
         ness of the problems identified in the study. Major
         requirements would be a clear national transport poli
         guaranteeing an adequate level of personal mobility t
         all sectors of the community, giving first priority t
         pedestrian movements, followed by public transport; a
         urban land use policies directed towards reducing the
         need for motorised movement.
         (see also refs. 3.2.29 above and 3.2.63 below).

3.2.38   Planning for People: essays on the social context of
                                 planning. (1968)
         BROADY, M.
         National Council of Social Service. Bedford Square
                                 Press. 1968 (119 pp.)

3.2.39   Retirement.[*Transportation and] (1972)
         CARP, F.M.
         Transportation Engineering Journal of the A.S.C.E.
         (Proceedings of the American Society of Civil
         Engineers) Vol. 98. No. TE 4. November 1972.(pp.787-
                                                        798).
         (see also refs. 3.2.1-4; 3.2.7; 3.2.9-19; 3.2.23;
           3.2.29-34; 3.2.36-7; 3.2.44; 3.2.63; 3.2.65,and 3.2.69)

3.2.40   School Buses. [*Cutting the Cost of] (1970)
         LOCAL GOVERNMENT OPERATIONAL RESEARCH UNIT (LGORU).
                                 Report C73.
         Royal Institute of Public Administration. 1970.

3.2.41   School [*Journeys to]: a survey of Secondary Schools
         in Berkshire and Surrey. (1977)
         RIGBY, J.P. and HYDE, P.J.
         TRRL Report LR 776. October 1977. (89 pp.)

         The report describes the background to the study and
         the design, implementation and findings of a question-
         naire survey conducted amongst 2,415 secondary school
         pupils to obtain information on the basic pattern of
         school journeys in terms of travel mode, time and
         distance. Interrelationships between these variables
         are examined; additional explanatory variables include
         school type, school location, respondent's family
         background, and service quality. Walk and bus were
         the most important modes used, and distance had the
         most significant effect on modal split. Differences
         in the quality of pupils' journeys were assessed and
         bus travel was rated lowest, largely because of poor
         service quality.

3.2.42   School Transport. [*Report to D.E.S. Working Party on]
                                                        (1972)
         NATIONAL CONFEDERATION OF PARENT-TEACHER ASSOCIATIONS.
                                                        1972.

3.2.43   Schools. [*The Location of Primary] (1968)
         LEVIN, P.H. and BRUCE, A.J.
         Journal of the Town Planning Institute. Vol. 54. No. 2.
                                 February 1968.(pp.55-66)

3.2.44   Seven Ages of Man [*The]: Beyond Sixty. (1969)
          WELFORD, A. T.
          New Science Publications. 1969.
          (see also 3.2.1-4; 3.2.7; 3.2.9-19; 3.2.23; 3.2.29-34
           3.2.36-7; 3.2.39; 3.2.63; 3.2.65, and 3.2.69)

3.2.45   Sex, Career and Family. (1971)
          FOGARTY, M., RAPOPORT, R. and RAPOPORT R.N.
          P.E.P.
          George Allen and Unwin. 1971. (581 pp.)

3.2.46   Shoppers' Requirements for the Location of Shops in
                                         Towns. [*On] (1974)
          DAWS, L.F.
          Building Research Establishment. CP. 23/74. 1974. (16 pp.)

3.2.47   Shopping for Food. (Undated.)
          NATIONAL OLD PEOPLE'S WELFARE COUNCIL. (AGE CONCERN.)

3.2.48   Shopping in Watford. (1971)
          DAWS, L. F. and BRUCE, A.J.
          Building Research Station. 1971. (143 pp.)

3.2.49   Social Aspects of Public Passenger Transport. [*Some
                                                        (1977)
          MITCHELL, C.G.B.
          TRRL Supplementary Report SR 278. 1977. (21 pp. plus
                                                      appendix)
          The paper reviews some of the existing data on the
          patronage of conventional stage bus services to identi
          the groups that comprise the market for bus travel.
          It is shown that about one-sixth of bus passengers are
          children, one-third men and one-half women. Nationally
          approximately 35% of bus trips are made for work, 10%
          for education, 21% for shopping and 16% for social
          purposes. The availability of a car is shown to be a
          major reason for not using a bus. A similar analysis
          is made of the patronage of five experimental dial-a-
          bus services: those at Old Harlow; Hampstead Garden
          Suburb; Sale; Woughton (Milton Keynes); and Dorridge
          and Knowle (Solihull). These have attracted considera
          numbers of passengers to public transport, but only
          slightly from private cars. A higher than normal
          proportion of dial-a-bus passengers are women and the
          analysis shows that the dial-a-bus services attract a
          more representative cross-section of the community
          than do conventional buses.

3.2.50   Social Choice and Individual Values. (1953 and 1970)
          ARROW, K.J.
          John Wiley. 1953. (2nd Edition: Yale University Press.
                                              1970. 135 pp.)

3.2.51 Social Costs of Hypermarket Developments. (1973)
HILLMAN, M.
Built Environment. Vol.2. No.2. February 1973. (pp. 88-
91)

This article presents the argument that while
hypermarkets answer the needs of the mobile majority,
the large non-car owning minority, especially the
elderly, the disabled and most women with small
children, may suffer from the concentration of retailing facilities in out-of-town or edge-of-town centres.
The shopping needs of this sector would best be met
by the improvement of existing high street or neighbourhood shopping centres.

3.2.52 Social Environment. [*The Transportation Analyst and
the] (1969)
SOMMERS, A.N.
High Speed Ground Transportation Journal. Vol.3. No.2.
May 1969.

3.2.53 Social Forecasting. [*Notes on] (1968)
DE JOUVENEL, B.
In: Forecasting and the Social Sciences, by M.Young (ed.)
Heinemann. London. 1968 (175 pp.)

A collection of papers commissioned by the Social
Science Research Council.

3.2.54 Social Framework of Planning. [*The] (1973)
CULLINGWORTH, J.B.
Vol.1. of: Problems of an Urban Society.
Birmingham University Centre for Urban and Regional
Studies.
Urban and Regional Studies No.4.
George Allen and Unwin. London. 1973. (174 pp.)

3.2.55 Social Goals for Transport Policy. (1975)
HILLMAN, M.
Paper read at the Conference on Transport for Society.
The Institution of Civil Engineers. November 1975.
(pp. 13-20 of Conference Proceedings, with discussion on
pp. 21-30.)

The paper suggests that social and ethical principles
should be introduced more widely into the transport
planning process and that it should become less
mechanistic. It sets out goals based on these principles
and draws on data from a variety of sources to question
the suitability of current policies in the light of
these goals. Alternative policies for the effective
pursuit of the goals are set out, and some of the
implications of adopting these are outlined.

3.2.56   Social Impact Study. [*Environment and] (1976)
         BRITISH RAIL.
         Strategic Planning Studies. 1976.

3.2.57   Social Processes, Spatial Form and the Redistribution
         of Real Income in an Urban System. (1971)
         HARVEY, D.
         In: Regional Forecasting. M. Chisholm et al. (eds.)
         Butterworth. London. 1971.

3.2.58   Social Trends. [*Some] (1969)
         WILLMOTT, P.
         Urban Studies. Vol.6. No.3. November 1969. (pp. 286-
                                                           308)

         This paper examines some of the ways in which the
         social structure of Britain and the patterns of socia
         life are likely to develop during the next two or thr
         decades. Past and present trends in occupational
         structure and social class are discussed. Some trend
         in social relationships and behaviour both within and
         outside the family are examined. Major questions are
         posed and some suggestions offered on research priori

3.2.59   Sociological Implications of Transport Planning.(1972
         AMOS, F.J.C.
         Transportation Planning and Technology. Vol.1. No.2.
                                        September 1972.(pp. 101

3.2.60   Spatial Mobility and an Analytical Approach. [*The
                                        Concept of] (1975)

         DOUBLEDAY, C.
         Paper read at Conference on Transportation and Urban
         Munich. September 1975. Reprinted in: "Transportation
         Planning for a Better Environment". ed. Stringer and
         Wenzel. New York. Plenum. 1975. (10 pp.)

         The individual's level of spatial mobility is describ
         in this paper in terms of the range of activity-space
         time options available to him in the context of a set
         of external (societal) restrictions and personal con-
         straints on his pattern of use of space and time. A
         special case of this broad concept, in which mobility
         is viewed in terms of car availability and accessibil
         is used in an empirical approach to assessing the eff
         of differing levels of mobility and to evaluating
         changes in the situation over a period of a decade or
         so. Some implications for transport modelling
         procedures are outlined.

3.2.61   Spatial Mobility [*The Effects of Differing Levels
                            of]: a discussion. (1976)
         DOUBLEDAY, C.
         Transactions of the Martin Centre for Achitectural
         and Urban Studies. University of Cambridge. Vol.1.
                            1976. (pp. 95-112)

         This paper reports the initial stages of a study of
         the impact of differing levels of spatial mobility
         upon various sections of the population and is based
         on a review of the literature relevant to the social
         dimension of the urban transport problem. A conceptual
         framework for studying mobility is outlined, but the
         difficulty of defining operational measures is
         emphasised. A summary follows of the principal results
         of empirical studies which have sought to describe
         variations in mobility in the population and their
         effects on both trip-making behaviour and activity
         patterns. Relevant social, economic and physical
         trends are discussed and conflicting views of the
         value to society of increasing mobility are presented.
         This leads to an assessment of the objectives and
         policies which might be pursued in approaching the
         social aspect of the urban transport problem and of
         the planning process necessary for devising suitable
         policies. Finally, areas for further research are
         identified.

3.2.62   Stress and Release in an Urban Estate: a study in
                            action research. (1964)
         SPENCER, J.
         Tavistock Publications. 1964.(369 pp.)

3.2.63   Transport Realities and Planning Policy. (1976)
         HILLMAN, M., HENDERSON, I. and WHALLEY, A.
         P.E.P. Broadsheet. No.567. December 1976 (196 pp.)

         The book presents analyses of surveys carried out
         between 1971 and 1973 as part of a programme of
         research into personal mobility and travel needs. The
         surveys were designed to overcome the inadequencies
         of methods previously used in transport planning, as
         outlined in the Introduction. Chapters I to III present
         detailed analyses of data derived from a series of self-
         administered questionnaire surveys conducted in five
         areas in 1971 to show the ways in which mobility and
         travel behaviour vary between different people living
         in areas with contrasting physical characteristics.
         The analyses relate to junior school-children and to
         teenagers as well as to adults' travel. The remainder
         of the book relates to two surveys carried out in the
         Outer Metropolitan Area (OMA) to discover the way in
         which accessibility varies for different facilities,
         people and travel methods. These consisted of a large-
         scale postal survey in 1972 with over 15,000 respondents,
         and a series of structured personal interviews in 1973
         with mothers of young children and persons over retire-
         ment age living within the OMA. The final chapter

summarises the findings of the surveys and points
out the implications of these for transport and land
use policies. Methodological details are given in the
appendices.
(see also refs. 3.2.29 and 3.2.37 above).

3.2.64   Travel Needs of Individuals.(1974)
          HILLMAN, M.
          Paper read at the Public Transport Fares Symposium.
          TRRL. November 1973.
          TRRL Supplementary Report SR 37 UC. 1974.
          (see ref. 4.1.52 below).

3.2.65   Travel.[*Understanding] (1978)
          SKELTON, N.G.
          Paper read at the   International Conference on
          Transport for Elderly and Handicapped Persons.
                              Cambridge. April 1978.(9 pp.)

          The paper discusses various points relating to a
          clearer understanding of the nature of travel, with
          particular reference to travel by elderly people.
          Definitions are suggested for various commonly used
          terms, with implications for both research and policy
          Three particular questions are discussed: the nature
          of constraints on mobility and their effects; the
          importance of understanding travel in the context of
          activity; and the definition of groups 'in need' of
          better opportunities for access and/or travel.
          (see also refs. 3.2.1-4; 3.2.7; 3.2.9-19; 3.2.23;
            3.2.29-34; 3.2.36-7; 3.2.39; 3.2.44; 3.2.63 and
                                                    3.2.69)
3.2.66   Vandalism. [*Common Sense and](1977)
          COUNCIL. June 1977. (pp. 22-23)

          An investigation into why the rate of vandalism is
          lower in new towns than in the old industrial centres.

3.2.67   Vandalism in Public Tansportation. [*Crime and] (197
          TRANSPORTATION RESEARCH BOARD (5 reports).
          Transportation Research Record No. 487. Transportation
          Research Board. Washington D.C. 1974. (55 pp.)

3.2.68   Women at Work. (1969)
          PINDER, P.
          P.E.P. Broadsheet No. 512. 1969.(130 pp.)

GOVERNMENT REPORTS AND PUBLICATIONS.

3.2.69   Elderly at Home [*The] : a study of people aged sixty
          five and over living in the community in England in
          1976. (1978)
          HUNT, A.
          Office of Population Censuses and Surveys. Social
          Survey Division. H,M,S.O. 1978. (177pp.)

          The study, carried out on behalf of the Department of

Health and Social Security, is based on personal interviews with 2,622 elderly persons at 1,975 households. Chapter 14, dealing with transport and accessibility, examines the availability of private cars for elderly people as individuals, the extent to which concessions are given on public transport, and the accessibility of certain essential facilities, such as the nearest public transport, chemist's shop,doctor's surgery and Post Office.
(see also refs. 3.2.1-4; 3.2.7; 3.2.9-19; 3.2.23; 3.2.29-34; 3.2.36-7; 3.2.39; 3.2.44; 3.2.63 and 3.2.65).

3.2.70 Handicapped and Impaired in Great Britain. (1971)
HARRIS, A.I., COX,E. and SMITH, C.R.W.
Office of Population Censuses and Surveys. Social
                                    Survey Division.
H.M.S.O. 1971.

3.2.71 Hospital Patients and Visitors. [*Travelling Expenses
                        and Transport for] (1973)
DEPARTMENT OF HEALTH AND SOCIAL SECURITY and WELSH
                                    OFFICE. 1973.

3.2.72 Hospital Plan for England and Wales. (1962)
MINISTRY OF HEALTH.
H.M.S.O. Cmnd 1604. 1962. (283 pp.)

Revision to 1972-3. April 1963. (7 pp.)
Revision to 1973-4. May   1964. (24 pp.)

3.2.73 Leisure. [*Planning for] (1969)
SILLITOE, K.K.
Government Social Survey.
H.M.S.O. 1969. (261 pp.)

This report presents the results of an interview survey undertaken on behalf of the Ministry of Education in 1965/6, based on a national sample with separate samples of inner London and eight new towns (Basildon, Crawley, Cwmbran, Harlow, Hemel Hempstead, Peterlee, Stevenage and Welwyn Garden City). The main aims of the inquiry were to investigate the current pattern of participation in outdoor and physical recreation and the frequency and manner of use of public open spaces; and to provide some measure of unsatisfied latent demands for these facilities. Information on the supply of facilities for sports and games is also given. The survey included questions on satisfaction with facilities and the report indicates the main improvements thought by respondents to be necessary.

The survey covered a wide range of leisure activities and a number of the tables present data for the eight new towns alongside the national and inner London data, revealing various differences between new town dwellers and others. Questions on mode of travel to

facilities used, and on journey times, fares and car
ownership were included in the questionnaire, and a
consideration of these factors in relation to the use
of each type of facility is given in the report.
Appendices include demographic data, a copy of the
questionnaire, and information on the sample design an
response rates.

3.2.74 Rate Fund Expenditure and Rate Calls in 1975-6. (1974)
        DEPARTMENT OF THE ENVIRONMENT. Circular 171/74. 1974.

3.2.75 School Transport. (1973)
        DEPARTMENT OF EDUCATION AND SCIENCE and WELSH OFFICE.
        Report of the Working Party on School Transport
                                     (Chairman:M.W. Hodges).
        H.M.S.O. 1973.(79 pp.)

3.2.76 School Travel [*Revised Arrangements for]:
                       Consultation Document. (1975)
        DEPARTMENT OF EDUCATION AND SCIENCE. August 1975.

3.2.77 Shopping Habits and Attitudes to Shop Hours in Great
                                          Britain. (1975)
        BRADLEY, M.and FENWICK, D.
        Office of Population Censuses and Surveys. Social
                                        Survey Division.
        H.M.S.O. 1975. (184 pp.)

        The results of a questionnaire survey conducted in
        1970 among a random (probability) sample of adults
        aged 18 years and over in Britain are described in
        this report. The purpose of the survey was to estab-
        lish general attitudes to the prevailing restrictions
        on shop hours and to deduce the amount of public
        pressure for change in the legislation. Details are
        given of present arrangements for shopping of various
        kinds, including division of responsibilities within
        the family, times when it is done, distance travelled
        to the shops, mode of travel, and usage of delivery
        services and mobile shops. Details of respondents'
        opinions about the relative convenience of their
        present shopping arrangements and their knowledge of
        and attitude towards present shop hours and legisla-
        tion are also presented. The data is analysed by a
        number of variables including, in many cases, working
        housewives, households containing children, distance
        from the nearest shops, and ownership of cars and
        refrigerators or deep freezes, in addition to age and
        sex. Details of the sample design and composition an
        a copy of the questionnaire are appended.

3.2.78 Shopping. [*The Future Pattern of] (1971)
        ECONOMIC DEVELOPMENT COMMITTEE FOR THE DISTRIBUTIVE
        TRADES: Report of the Shopping Capacity Sub-Committee
        National Economic Development Office.
        H.M.S.O. 1971. (121 pp.)

3.2.79   Women's Employment. [*A Survey of] (1968)
          HUNT, A.
          A survey carried out on behalf of the Ministry of
          Labour by the Government Social Survey in 1965.
          Vol. 1 - Report.
          Vol. 2 - Tables.
          H.M.S.O. 1968.

3.2.80   Working Hours. [*Changing Patterns of] (1975)
          SLOANE, P.J.
          Department of Employment. Manpower Paper No.13.
          H.M.S.O. 1975. (51 pp.)

          The Department of Employment's booklet describes the
          main methods of flexible working which are recommended
          to local authorities and to employers and unions in
          the public and private sectors.

3.2 Subsidiary References.

1.1 New Towns - Transport and Mobility.

1.1.7   Mobility in New Towns. (1970)
1.1.15   Public Transportation and the Needs of New Communities. (1972)

1.2 New Towns - Non-Transport Aspects.

1.2.4   Britain's New Towns: an experiment in living. (1961)
1.2.6   New Perspectives on Community Development. (1976)
1.2.7   Community Organisation in Britain. (1961)
1.2.8   The Quest for Community. (1976)
1.2.11   Employment Expansion and the Development of New Town Hinterlands.
*   1961-1966. (1971)*
1.2.14   The Provision of General Medical Care in New Towns. (1966)
1.2.15   Justifying New Towns: an analysis of the attitudes of actual and
*   prospective residents.(1975)*
1.2.16   London's New Towns: A Study of Self-Contained and Balanced
*   Communities. (1969)*
1.2.19   Mental Health and Environment. (1964)
1.2.20   Mental Health on a New Housing Estate: a comparative study of
*   health in two districts of Croydon. (1965)*
1.2.21   Neighbourhood Shops in New Towns. (1976)
1.2.22   Neighbourhood Units in British New Towns. (1961)
1.2.23   New Communities in Britain: Achievements and Problems. (1961)
1.2.24   New Communities U.S.A. (1976)
1.2.33   New Towns: the British Experience. (1972)
1.2.39   Recreational Planning in New Communities: A Review of British
*   Experience. (1975)*
1.2.41   The Self-Contained New Town: employment and population. (1968)
1.2.42   Social Aspects of Planning in New Towns. (1975)
1.2.43   Social Development Work in the New Communities. (1974)
1.2.44   Social Factors Involved in the Planning and Development of New
*   Towns. (1964)*
1.2.45   Social Planning in New Communities. (1971)
1.2.46   The Programming of Social Provision in New Communities. (1976)

2.4.32   Concern No.3. [Milton Keynes Transport planning seminar edition.]
                                                                    (1975)
2.4.33   The Disadvantaged of Milton Keynes. (1973)
2.4.39   Changing Goals in Design: the Milton Keynes example.   (1972)
2.4.40   Seven Years On---". Milton Keynes Household Survey.1976 (1977)
2.4.52   The Needs of Youth in Stevenage. (1959)
2.4.56   Stevenage Household Survey. March 1976. (1976)
2.4.63   Under Five in a New Town. (1970)

3.1 Studies of Modal Choice Behaviour and Value of Travel Time.

3.1.36   Intra - Urban Journeys and Activity Linkages. (1977)
3.1.38   Minibus Service W9: Bus/Minibus Modal Choice Analysis and Cost-
                                           Benefit Assessment (1975)
3.1.45   Urban Structure and Modal Split in the Journey to Work. (1977)
3.1.61   A Pilot Study of Relationships between Socio - Economic Factors,
          User Attitudes and Preferences and Urban Transportation System
                                                 Attributes. (1969)
3.1.62   The Influence of Car Ownership on Shopping Habits. (1964)
3.1.69   Travel Adjustments and Life Styles - A Behavioral Approach.
                                                              (1976)
3.1.70   The Effect of Age on Urban Travel Behavior. (1971)
3.1.71   The Structure of Movement and Household Travel Behaviour.(1969)
3.1.72   Variations of Urban Travel Characteristics with Age.   (1972)
3.1.76   Qualitative Aspects of Urban Personal Travel Demand.   (1968)
3.1.77   Travel - Demand Theory: Latent Demand, The Value of Travel, and
                                      Impact on Life Style. (1976)
3.1.88   Traveltime Budgets and Mobility in Urban Areas. (1974)
3.1.91   Research into the Urban Traveller's Behaviour.   (1971)
3.1.105   The Value of Time on Short Urban Leisure Trips. (1970)
3.1.116   Time Budgets and Models of Urban Activity Patterns. (1974)

3.3 Interaction between Land Use and Travel.

3.3.1   Access for All: Transportation and Urban Growth. (1975)
3.3.4   Accessibility of Various Social Groups to Different Activities.
                                                                  (1977)
3.3.9   Activity Patterns of Urban Residents. (1973)
3.3.14   Fair Play For All: a study of access to sport and informal
                                          recreation.(1977)
3.3.24   Centrism and the Provision of Services in Residential Areas.
                                                                (1975)
3.3.41   Transportation Implications of Employment Trends in Central
                                    Cities and Suburbs.   (1967)
3.3.43   Urban Developments in Britain: Standards, Costs and Resources.
          1964-2004. Vol.I. Population Trends and Housing. (1970)

3.4 Transport and Mobility - General and Miscellaneous.

3.4.1   Environment and Behavior: planning and everyday life.   (1977)
3.4.2   Environmental Psychology: Man and his Physical Setting. (1970)
3.4.4   The Citizen and Transportation. (1968)

4.1 Public Transport - Operational Aspects.

4.1.53   Low Fares and the Urban Transport Problem. (1969)
4.1.58   Urban Fares Policy. (1975)
4.1.62   Free Public Transport. (1973)
4.1.63   Some Data on the Effects of Free Public Transport. (1972)
4.1.64   Free Transit. (1970)
4.1.101   Report on the Survey of Concessionary Travel Schemes in Englan
                                              and Wales. (1977)

4.2 Public Transport - Marketing Approach.

4.2.4   Bus Promotion. (1975)
4.2.29   Towards a Description of L.T's Markets. (Undated)
4.2.41   An Opinion Survey of the Yorkshire Dales Rail Services in 197£
                                                          (197?

4.3 Public Transport - Ergonomic Aspects.

4.3.1   Biology of Ageing. (1957)
4.3.11   An Investigation of Factors Affecting the Use of Buses by Bot£
                Elderly and Ambulant Disabled Persons. (1974)
4.3.26   Human Factors in Engineering and Design. (1974)
4.3.46   Rides, Trips and Moves on a Bus. (1970)
4.3.48   Toward a Sociology of Public Transit. (1967)
4.3.56   Travel Barriers. (1970)

4.4 Public Transport - Demonstration Projects and Innovatory Systems.

4.4.35   Para-Transit: Neglected Options for Urban Mobility. (1976)
4.4.38   The Postbus - a new element in Britain's rural transport patte
                                                          (197
4.4.39   The Scottish Postbus Network. (1975)
4.4.42   The Ramblers' Bus: Service 417 to the Surrey Hills. (1977)
4.4.47   Zonal Taxi Systems: An Improvement in Local Mobility.(1976)
4.4.52   Symposium on Unconventional Bus Services: summaries of papers
                                              and discussions. (1977)

4.5 Public Transport - General and Miscellaneous.

4.5.3   Community Involvement Programme. Household Reviews. Report c
          Phases 1 and 2. (Sheffield and Rotherham Land Use/Transporta
                                                          Study.) (1977)
4.5.4   Summary of the Issues Raised by the Public through the Commun
                                  Involvement Programme. (1976)
4.5.9   Public Transport in Bedfordshire: Facts, Views, Issues, Optio
                                                          (1974)
4.5.12   Survey of Public Transport. (1972)
4.5.13   Public Transport for Rural Communities. (1977)
4.5.14   Some Aspects of the Rural Transport Problem among Norwich
                                  Commuter Villages. (1975)
4.5.15   Rural Transport: What Future Now? (1971)
4.5.18   Urban Passenger Transport: Some Trends and prospects. (1977)
4.5.19   Mobility Evaluation for Urban Public Transportation. (1976)

9.2.30	The Urban Environment and Residential Satisfaction with an Emphasis on New Towns: an annotated bibliography. (1973)
9.2.35	Bibliography on Methods of Social and Business Research. (1973)
9.2.36	Social Aspects of Planning: a select list of references. (1972)

9.3 Abstracting and Indexing Services.

9.3.15	Social Sciences Citation Index. (Annually)
9.3.16	Social Sciences Index. (Quarterly)
9.3.17	Sociological Abstracts. (Five times a year.)
9.3.21	Urban Abstracts. (Monthly)

9.4 Research Registers.

| 9.4.1 | Register of Research, 1977. Part II: Environmental Planning. (1977) |
| 9.4.20 | University of Birmingham: Centre for Urban and Regional Studie Annual Report. (Annual |

9.5 Statistical Sources.

9.5.15	Annual Abstract of Statistics. (Annually)
9.5.16	Census of Population.
9.5.17	Family Expenditure Survey. (Annually)
9.5.18	General Household Survey.
9.5.20	Monthly Digest of Statistics. (Monthly)
9.5.22	Regional Statistics. (Annually)
9.5.23	Social Trends. (Annually)

9.6 Other Sources of Information.

9.6.10	Guide to Official Statistics. (1976 and 1978)
9.6.15	Quality of Life in Urban Settlements. (1974)
9.6.16	Sourcebook of Planning Information. (1971)
9.6.17	Sources of Economic and Business Statistics. (1972)
9.6.18	Sources of Social Statistics. (1974)

3.3 Interaction between Land Use and Travel.

Literature relating to the interrelationships between travel and land use in planned new communities is included in sections 1 and 2 of the bibliography, and discussed in the introductions to subsections 1.1 and 1.2. This subsection contains more general background material concerning the relation between transport and land use. The following aspects in particular are included:-

- The influence of transport on land use and urban form, and other environmental impacts.

- The influence of urban form, density of development and patterns of land uses on personal mobility and accessibility.

- The effects of urban form and land use on transport provision (notably on public transport operation).

The subsidiary references at the end of the subsection point to material in other parts of the bibliography which have especial relevance to the relationship between movement and urban structure. These include items from subsection 3.2 relating to the distribution of shopping facilities and to personal mobility in general; some items from subsection 3.1 concerning the influence of urban structure on modal choice, particularly for work journeys; and relevant transport policy documents from section 7.

The book Town Planning and Road Traffic by H. ALKER TRIPP (3.3.32), published in 1942, presented a study of the relationship between traffic and urban structure which outlined design principles intended to minimise traffic accidents. The author discussed both detailed standards for the layout of road systems in residential areas and more general considerations of the shape which a town's layout and road pattern should have in order to maximise road safety.

This work had a significant effect on subsequent town and transport planning philosophies generally. The design principles which it established were closely followed by the Ministry of War Transport's manual: Design and Layout of Roads in Urban Areas, published in 1946 (later superseded by Roads in Urban Areas, 1966 - 3.3.54). From the late 1950's the effects of increasing traffic volumes in towns gave rise to growing concern and in 1961 a Steering Group and Working Group were appointed by the Ministry of Transport to "study the long term development of roads and traffic in urban areas and their influence on the urban environment". The findings and recommendations of the Working Group, as set out in Traffic in Towns (7.1.73) focussed contemporary attention on the potentially harmful environmental effects of traffic movements in towns. Both the detailed design recommendations and the general philosophies set out in Traffic in Towns had a profound influence on subsequent British planning thought and practice. Its effect on transport planning in new towns designated after its publication is discussed by POTTER in Volume Two of Transport and New Towns (1.1.18). The design principles recommended in some ways closely resemble those previously suggested by Tripp.

The need for a close integration of transport and land use planning is particularly stressed in Traffic in Towns. One of the basic underlying assumptions of the study was that traffic is generated by buildings and that rather than the two being treated separately they should be interrelated in an "overall concept of town planning". During the 1960's it became generally accepted that planners should recognise and plan for this interdependence of land use and transport. The initiation of the Structure Planning system under the Town and Country Planning Act 1968, and subsequently of the Transport Policies and Programmes system through which counties' transport programmes were to be related to county Structure Plans, gave statutory recognition to the close links between movement and land use at the strategic planning level. The amalgamation in 1970 of the former Ministries of Transport, Housing and Local Government, and Public Buildings and Works under the new Department of the Environment had also been partly aimed at facilitating this integration of planning functions at policy level. In 1976 part of these functions were removed from the Department of the Environment with the establishment of a new Department of Transport.

Recently HILLMAN et al (for example, in Transport Realities and Planning Policy - 3.2.63) and others, have drawn attention to the gap between concern with the transport/land use interdependency at strategic planning level and the failure of local plans effectively to integrate the two. In Transport Realities and Planning Policy and elsewhere Hillman recommends specific ways in which land use planning and development control could be used to "facilitate access to people and places, to provide for safe and convenient movement, and to minimise the conflicts and social costs of travel". Many of these recommendations point towards the benefits of a 'low movement policy' in improving personal accessibility. The INDEPENDENT COMMISSION ON TRANSPORT's report Changing Directions (7.1.3) and the Friends of the Earth publication Getting Nowhere Fast (7.1.10) have also drawn attention to the value of such measures, which would in addition have beneficial implications for energy consumption and for the reduction of the harmful environmental consequences of road traffic. These views have been given some recognition in the Government's White Paper on Transport Policy, 1977 (7.1.76) which refers to the need to decrease absolute dependence on transport and the number and length of some journeys (para.35), to ensure that transport "makes its contribution to the conservation of energy resources "and to" key transport into our wider policies for the environment and our views of how we want our communities to develop". (para.295)

The importance of quantifying the relationships between land uses, activities and traffic generation and of predicting movement demands between zones within towns was emphasised in Traffic in Towns. The report advocated the preparation of transportation plans to supplement statutory development plans in large urban areas to help to "enforce the much-needed integration of land use planning and traffic and transport planning". This, together with the availability from 1963 of grant aid and technical assistance from the Ministry of Transport, gave impetus to the carrying out of land use/transport studies in a number of large (and some medium-sized) urban areas which had already commenced in the early 1960's. Criticisms of the assumptions and techniques used in large scale transportation studies on grounds of modal split forecasting have already been mentioned in the introduction to subsection 3.1. A number of writers have also criticised conventional transport planning based on transportation studies for failing to deal adequately with the dynamics of the reciprocal relationships between movement and land use patterns. This aspect has been discussed, for instance, in the paper by LEMBERG (3.3.21). HILLMAN and his associates have also pinpointed a number of inadequacies in the methods and practices adopted in transport planning during the 1960's, including the tendency to relate a "narrow definition of personal mobility to an equally narrow definition of land use planning". (3.2.63 and 3.2.37)

During the 1970's a broader conception of urban transport planning in terms of facilitating personal accessibility to opportunities rather than ease of vehicular movement has developed. The work of HILLMAN and others has pointed to the need for a closer integration of transport and land use planning in order to reduce variations in personal accessibility. Accessibility has been defined by MITCHELL and TOWN (3.3.4) as a function of two distinct factors: "the spatial location of people relative to activities and destinations, and the mobility available to these people to reach the activities". The level of access offered by land use/transport configurations has a significant bearing on quality of life through its effect on the range of activity choices available to individuals for a given expenditure of time, cost and effort (or, alternatively, its effect on the expenditure of time, cost and effort required to reach a given activity location). A number of attempts have been made to develop measures which could be used to identify disparities in accessibility to various kinds of activity between different sectors of the population; to define catchment areas for shopping, education, recreational and other facilities; or to investigate the likely effects of alternative transport and land use policies on personal accessibility. Time, distance and cost have all been used as units of measurement, and generalised cost has been used in a number of land use/transport models. BAXTER and LENZI's paper The Measurement of Relative Accessibility (3.3.7) presents a technique based on distance measurements using an abstract network with a grid pattern of similar shape and size to the real network, and which also takes into account the basic geographical constraints of an urban environment. However, like some of the more complex and sophisticated measures (which are sometimes difficult to apply) it does not allow for disaggregation between sectors of the population with differing travel opportunities and needs. MITCHELL AND TOWN have presented evidence which indicates that door-to-door travel time by the quickest mode economically available to the individual traveller is a simpler and more effective measure than distance of the effort people are prepared to expend on travelling to a given activity. Their paper Accessibility of Various Social Groups to Different Activities (3.3.4) briefly reviews several simple objective measures of accessibility based on travel time. A different kind of approach to assessing accessibility requirements, using attitudinal survey data, is presented in the paper by PETERSON and WORRALL (3.3.8). A study is described which examined the locational preferences of a sample of Chicago residents with respect to eight selected neighbourhood services. A simple theory of accessibility preference is developed, based on individuals' perceived trade-offs between the desire for ready access to a service and the competing desire for insulation from 'irritation'.

Much of the large body of theory attempting to explain the spatial characteristics of urban areas which has developed since the 1930's is peripheral to the scope of this bibliography. However, several such studies, which have particular significance for the planning of transport systems in new towns, have been incorporated. These include works by STONE (3.3.43 and 3.3.49), HILLMAN (1.1.7) and POTTER (1.1.17 - 19) already referred to in the introductions to subsections 1.1 and 1.2, and by ALONSO (3.3.46) and JAMIESON, MACKAY and LATCHFORD (3.3.17).

The reciprocal relationships between transport and urban structure have been described by many authors. Access for All by SCHAEFFER and SCLAR (3.3.1) provides a useful historical outline of the effects of movement systems on urban form and of the influence of both movement systems and land use configurations on personal accessibility. The book focuses in particular on the effects on accessibility of the trends for urban sprawl and dispersal of facilities and employment from city centres which have accompanied the growth of private motor transport in cities.

Although the study relates principally to North American
cities the main arguments and the recommendations for
policy measures directed towards achieving a more equitable
distribution of accessibility and an economically more
efficient urban environment are of general relevance.
More detailed analyses of the relationship between transport
demands and land use in American cities have been made by
MEYER, KAHN and WOHL (3.4.6) and by OI and SCHULDINER
(3.1.79). The Management of Urban Public Transport by
HOVELL, JONES and MORAN (4.2.25) includes an examination
of the centrifugal forces behind the dispersal of cities
during the Twentieth Century as a background to a study
of the demand for public transport within towns.
LEMBERG's paper Passenger Transport as an Urban Element
(3.3.21) also considers the interdependency of land use
and transportation in towns, with particular reference to
public transport provision within the urban structure.

The relationship between public transport operation and
urban structure is examined in some detail by WHITE
in Chapter 5 of Planning for Public Transport (4.1.89).
The book includes a discussion of the implications of
different levels of residential density for public transport
demand and operation, and of ways in which land use can
be shaped to support public transport operations. The
paper Bus Operation in Alternative Urban Structures by
NEWBERRY (3.3.50) presents data from the 1972/3 National
Travel Survey which indicates that controlled land use
development, particularly since the Second World War, has
resulted in excessive land, time and energy being expended
on local travel and has increased the difficulties and
resource costs of providing local passenger transport
services. The paper discusses short-term constraint
measures designed to make optimum use of buildings and
transport infrastructure, and longer term measures directed
towards reducing the need for local private motor transport
and encouraging the efficient operation of public transport.
In new towns transport planning based on these principles
from the outset is seen by the author as more likely to
prove continously acceptable to residents than attempts
to superimpose public transport networks on layouts which
were not originally planned with sufficient consideration
for their provision.

Residential density has a significant effect on the demand
for and operation of public transport services, and on
modal split generally. Its effect in North American cities
has been examined by, among others, MEYER, KAHN and WOHL
(3.4.6). GOODWIN's paper (3.3.23) presents an analysis
of data from the 1972/3 National Travel Survey, linking
variations in numbers of journey stages and distance
travelled per day by different travel modes with gross
residential density of travellers' home areas. SAMMONS
and HALL's (3.1.45) analysis of small-zone data from six

major land use transportation studies indicates a relationship between patterns of social and economic activity and the demand for public and other forms of transport. The authors suggest that the relationships between the variables (population and employment density per square mile, car ownership and public transport usage) were sufficiently stable to be of potential use to planners in linking broad dispositions of land uses or urban activities with transportation patterns in Structure Plans for large urban areas. However, as car ownership levels rise, the possibility of using land use to influence modal split is recognised as being likely to diminish.

3.3   Interaction between Land Use and Travel.

3.3.1   Access for All: Transportation and Urban Growth.
                                                          (1975)
           SCHAEFFER, K.H. and SCLAR, E.
           Penguin Books Ltd. 1975. (182 pp.)

           An historical analysis of the development of
           transport in cities demonstrates that excessive
           growth of private motor transport, resulting in
           the growth and dispersion of urban areas, has led
           to an overall loss of access with accompanying
           social and economic problems. These include
           severely limited mobility for those without cars,
           a degree of community disintegration and the
           uneconomic functioning of urban areas. Some
           suggestions are put forward for transportation
           and land use concepts accompanied by fiscal
           policies which could lead to a better balance
           between privacy and community, a more equal dist-
           ribution of accessibility, and an economically
           more efficient urban environment.

3.3.2   Accessibility and Choice as Quantifiable Variables
           in Land Use Planning. (1972)
           IRELAND, J.V.
           Final Report to the Social Science Research Council.
                                                          1972 .

3.3.3   Accessibility in Basic Transportation Choice
           Behaviour. [*The Rôle of]   (1976)
           BURNS, L. and GOLOB, T.F.
           Transportation. Vol.5. No.2. June 1976. (pp. 175-
                                                          198)

           This paper was presented at the Seventh Annual
           Meeting of the Mid-Continent Section, Regional
           Science Association, Duluth, Minnesota, June 1975.
           It presents theory and models which result in the
           development of hypotheses linking accessibility
           measures with behavioural theories. A biblio-
           graphy is included and contains some fifty refer-
           ences relevant to studies of the relationship
           between accessibility and travel behaviour.

3.3.4   Accessibility of Various Social Groups to
                              Different Activities. (1977)

           MITCHELL, C.G.B. and TOWN, S.W.
           TRRL Supplementary Report SR 258. April 1977.
                                                          (17 pp.)

           This report was first presented as a paper at the
           5th British Regional Congress of the Permanent
           International Association of Road Congresses at
           Stirling in June 1976. It discusses the need for
           measures of accessibility that are sensitive to

variations in the travel patterns of different
sections of the population. The importance of
car ownership in determining personal mobility
is stressed. Using data from the 1972/3 National
Travel Survey it shows different distances that
people are prepared to travel by various modes;
socio-economic group membership is shown to have
a separate effect. The report looks at the
utility of travel time for providing a suitable
measure of accessibility and gives examples of
accessibility measures which use travel time.

3.3.5   Accessibility. [*Relationships between Land Use
                                    and] (1973)
          DAVIDSON, K.B.
          Greater London Council. R & D Report. Vol.378.
                                    1973.(38 pp.)

3.3.6   Accessibility Shapes Land Use. [*How] (1959)
          HANSEN, W.G.
          Journal of the American Institute of Planners.
                              Vol.25. 1959.(pp. 73-76)

3.3.7   Accessibility. [*The Measurement of Relative]
                                    (1975)
          BAXTER, R.S. and LENZI, G.
          Regional Studies. Vol.9. No.1. March 1975.(pp. 15-
                                    26)

          The paper presents a method of arriving at an
          accurate distance matrix at the urban scale
          using abstract network patterns incorporating
          geographical constraints.

3.3.8   Accessibility to Selected Neighbourhood Services.
          [*An Analysis of Individual Preferences for]
                                    (1970)
          PETERSON, G.L. and WORRALL, R.D.
          Highway Research Record No.305. Highway Research
          Board. Washington D.C. 1970. (pp. 99-111)

          In this paper a theory of individual preferences
          for accessibility to eight selected neighbourhood
          services is developed. This is based on a trade-
          off between the resident's desire for proximity
          to the service and its perceived potential irri-
          tant or nuisance value if it is located too close
          to the home.

3.3.9   Activity Patterns of Urban Residents. (1973)
          BRAIL, R.K. and CHAPIN, S.
          Environment and Behavior. Vol.5. No.2. June 1973.
                                    (pp. 163-190)

3.3.10   Buchanan's Law. [*A Summary of] (1974)
          LEWIS, H.
          Built Environment. Vol.3. No.7. July 1974. (p. 338).

3.3.11   Busways. [*Sweden's Small-scale] (1973)
          WHITE, P.R.
          Traffic Engineering and Control. Vol.15. No.6.
                                        October 1973. (p. 306)

          This article describes examples of individual
          busways constructed in new housing estates on the
          outskirts of several Swedish towns. Since these
          are built through the centre of the estates they
          can provide considerable economies for the bus
          operators through reductions in mileage and journey
          time as compared with conventional bus routes on
          perimeter roads. For residents they provide
          improved access to the bus stops and shorter
          journey times. The author recommends that similar
          busways be incorporated in all sizes of housing
          schemes in Britain.

3.3.12   Cost Benefit Analysis and Road Proposals for a
          Shopping Centre: A Case Study: Edgware. (1968)
          LICHFIELD, N. and CHAPMAN, H.
          Journal of Transport Economics and Policy. Vol.2.
                      No.3. September 1968. (pp. 280-320)

3.3.13   Cost Benefit Analysis in Town Planning: A Case
                              Study: Swanley. (1966)
          LICHFIELD, N.
          Urban Studies. Vol.3. No.3. November 1966. (pp. 215-
                                                        249)

3.3.14   Fair Play For All: a study of access to sport and
                          informal recreation. (1977)
          HILLMAN, M. and WHALLEY, A.
          P.E.P. Broadsheet No.571. 1977. (119 pp.)

          The Broadsheet reports on a study of the relation
          between mobility and travel, and participation in
          sport and informal recreation. The main aim of
          the study was to investigate how recreation bodies
          can give due attention to personal mobility and
          accessibility in policy and practice. The study
          showed that participation is affected by the
          transport available and by distance. Larger
          facilities give rise to longer journeys on average
          and are unlikely to serve the whole population in
          their estimated catchment areas. Their provision
          could be said to create areas of deficiency for
          people with restricted mobility. It was found that
          there was considerable potential for using bicycles
          to reach recreation facilities. Recommendations
          include the development of comprehensive policies
          and guidelines on establishing a fine network of
          local recreational facilities to complement existing

provision; the use of accessibility standards in policy-making to reflect the reality of personal mobility; and the compilation of inventories of local facilities with a recreation potential.

3.3.15   Land Use and Travel. (1975)
HILLMAN, M. and WHALLEY, A.
Built Environment. Vol.1. No.2. September 1975.
(pp. 105-111)

In this article the relationships between modal split, residential density and the distribution of facilities are discussed and the implications of these for planning and transport policy are examined. The authors outline the background to the need for a change in policy directed towards greater economy of travel. For planning this would mean achievement of higher housing densities, localisation of certain urban facilities, rehabilitation rather than extension of residential areas and more mixed land use patterns. For transport planning it would involve giving higher priority to non-motorised forms of transport and adopting measures to reduce dependence on the private car.

3.3.16   Land Use Planning. [*Walking and] (1975)
EVANS, E.W.
Unpublished M.Phil. Thesis. University College,
London.1975.

3.3.17   Land Use Structure.[*Transportation and] (1967)
JAMIESON, G.B., MACKAY, W.K. and LATCHFORD, J.C.R.
Urban Studies. Vol.4. No.3. November 1967. (pp. 201-217)

3.3.18   Location Trends of Specialist Services. (1971)
SCHILLER, R.K.
Regional Studies. Vol.5. No.1. April 1971. (pp. 1-10

Evidence is produced to show that specialist service in the Outer Metropolitan Area, around London, are less centrally located than would be expected by current theory. High income, car ownership and population dispersal are suggested as causes. It is argued that specialist services will tend to polarize in future between non-central locations serving car-based local consumers and metropolitan CBDs serving public transport-based commuters, tourists and distant visitors.

3.3.19   Mixed Blessing: The Motor in Britain. (1958)
BUCHANAN, C.D.
Leonard Hill (Books) Ltd. 1958. (232 pp.)

3.20   Modern Metropolis: [*The] Its Origins, Growth,
             Characteristics and Planning. (1967-1st. ed'n.)
         BLUMENFELD, H. (Selected essays edited by
                             Paul D. Spreiregen.)
         M.I.T. Press. Cambridge, Mass. 1967. (392 pp.)

3.21   Passenger Transport as an Urban Element. (1976)
         LEMBERG, K.
         In: 'Passenger Transport and the Environment'
                     (see ref. 4.5.7. below.)
         ed. Roy Cresswell. Paper read at Conference on
         Passenger Transport and the Environment held at
         the University of York. March 1976. (pp. 3-34)

         This paper presents an historical review of the
         effect of transport on urban form and of the
         interrelationships between land use and transport-
         ation. Problems arising from these interrelation-
         ships are discussed and conventional transport
         planning theories and practice aimed at providing
         solutions are critically examined. The rôle of
         recent technical and operational innovations is
         outlined. Copenhagen is used as a case study to
         illustrate the effects of changes in urban and
         regional planning on transport and on urban form
         since 1945. Briefer illustrations are drawn from
         the British new towns with a comparative examina-
         tion of the transport goals and achievements to
         date of Runcorn and Milton Keynes.

.22   Physical Planning. (1945)
         McCALLUM, I.R.M. (ed.)
         The Architectural Press. 1945.

.23   Population Density. [*Variations in Travel Between
         Individuals Living in Areas of Different] (1975)
         GOODWIN, P.B.
         Paper read at the PTRC Summer Annual Meeting.
         Urban Traffic Models Seminar (N). 1975.

.24   Residential Areas. [*Centrism and the Provision of
                             Services in] (1975)
         LOW, N.
         Urban Studies. Vol.12. No.2. June 1975. (pp. 177-
                                                    191)

.25   Residential Density. [*Automobile Ownership and]
                                            (1965)
         LANSING, J.B. and HENDRICKS, G.
         Survey Research Centre. University of Michigan. 1965.

.26   Residential Location and Urban Mobility. (1964)
         LANSING J.B. et al.
         Survey Research Centre, University of Michigan. 1964.

3.3.27   Residential Location Choice and Commuting by Men
           and Women Workers. [*A Model of] (1977)
           WHITE, M.J.
           Journal of Regional Science. Vol.17. No.1. April
                                1977. (pp. 41-52)

This paper presents an economic theory explaining
why women commute less than men. The investigation
is restricted to working women of households with
two wage earners and assumes that the household
acts with economic rationality with respect to
both jobs rather than just to the husband's. The
theory developed suggests that 2-worker households choose residential locations so as to minimise
the woman's journey to work rather than the man's.

3.3.28   Residential Location. [*The Economics of] (1973)
           EVANS, A.W.
           Macmillan. 1973. (293 pp.)

3.3.29   Road Capacity of City Centres. [*The] (1966)
           SMEED, R.J.
           Traffic Engineering and Control. Vol.8. No.7. July
                                     1966.

3.3.30   Road Space Required for Traffic in Towns. [*The]
                                        (1963)
           SMEED, R.J.
           Town Planning Review. Vol.33. No.4. January 1963.
                              (pp. 279-292)

3.3.31   1972/3 Road Traffic and Environment Survey. (1976)
           SOCIAL AND COMMUNITY PLANNING RESEARCH. May 1976.

3.3.32   Road Traffic. [*Town Planning and] (1942)
           TRIPP, H. ALKER.
           Edward Arnold & Co. London. 1942. (113 pp.)

In this book Alker Tripp set out the design
principles relating traffic control to town planning which became incorporated into the Ministry of
War Transport's manual: 'Design and Layout of
Roads in Urban Areas' (1946), later superseded by
'Roads in Urban Areas' (1966), and which were
largely followed and developed in 'Traffic in
Towns' (The 'Buchanan Report'- 1963). Road safety
is taken as the major objective and the recognition
of three classes of road-arterial, sub-arterial
and local-between which different types of traffic
would be distributed was seen as the key to achieving this. A series of 'precincts' within which
the local roads would carry no through-traffic,
would be created within a network of sub-arterial
roads. The general shape which a town's layout
and road pattern should form is also considered
and the ring and radial pattern generally recommended.

3.3.33   Roads and the Environment. (1972)
            BURT, M.E.
            TRRL Report LR 441.1972.

3.3.34   Traffic and the Environment.(1972)
            GREATER LONDON COUNCIL.
            Department of Highways and Transportation. Green Paper.
                                                            1972.

3.3.35   Traffic.[*Homes, Towns and] (1968 - 2nd edition)
            TETLOW, J. and GOSS, A.
            Faber. 1968. (272pp.)

            This book gives a background to British urban planning
            and examines its relationship with public transport.

3.3.36   Traffic in the Conurbations.(1971)
            VOORHEES, A.M. and Associates Ltd.
            British Road Federation. London. 1971 (48pp.)

3.3.37   Traffic Studies and Urban Congestion. (1968)
            SMEED, R. J.
            Journal of Transport Economics and Policy.Vol.2.No.1.
            January 1968. (pp.33-70)

3.3.38   Traffic.[*Towns Against] (1972)
            PLOWDEN, S.P.C.
            Andre Deutsch. London. 1972.(183pp.)

            The author's principal argument is that the problems
            associated with transport in towns will continue
            until a radical change of approach to them is made.
            The traditional town planning principle of accomm-
            odating all traffic demands is shown to be incompa-
            tible with the preservation of the town as a toler-
            able place to live in. Restrictions on the use of
            motor vehicles in towns, and the development of
            fast and efficient public transport systems are
            seen as essential in preserving the quality of the
            urban environment. The examples of Oxford, Central
            London and the London Motorway Box are used to
            illustrate the argument. The kind of measures which
            will need to be adopted if the problems are to be
            satisfactorily solved are presented, and a method
            of study is outlined as an alternative to the
            conventional transportation study, to help choose
            the measures to be adopted in a given situation.
            This would include examining all modes of travel
            including cycling and walking, and considering the
            quality as well as the capacity of the transport
            system. It should also take account of frustrated
            travel, of the pattern of road accidents, and of
            the environmental as well as the mobility aspects
            of transport.

3.3.39.   Traffic   [*Urban Survival and]: Economics of City
          Traffic   (1962)
          WILLIAMS, T.E.H. and MUNBY, D. (eds.)
          Paper read at a symposium held at King's College,
          University of Durham. 1961. Spon. 1962

3.3.40.   Transport and Regional Development: some preliminary
          results of the M.62 Project. (1974)
          GWILLIAM, K.M. and JUDGE, E.J.
          Paper presented to the Regional Studies Association.
          April 1974.

3.3.41.   Transportation Implications of Employment Trends in
          Central Cities and Suburbs. (1967)
          KANWIT, E.L. and ECKARTT, A.F.
          Highway Research Record No. 187. Highway Research
          Board. Washington D.C. 1967.

3.3.42.   Urban Development in the Analysis of Transportation
          Investment. [*Models of] : the case of North Central
          Texas (1977)
          TURNER, C.G. and ROARK, J.J.
          Paper read at the Annual Transportation Research
          Board Conference. January 1977. (27pp.)

3.3.43.   Urban Developments in Britain: Standards, Costs and
          Resources. 1964-2004. Vol.1. Population Trends and
          Housing.(1970)
          STONE, P.A.
          National Institute of Economic and Social Research.
          Cambridge University Press. 1970.

3.3.44.   Urban Form, Car Ownership and Public Policy: An
          Appraisal of"Traffic in Towns". (1964)
          BEESLEY, M.E. and KAIN, J.F.
          Urban Studies. Vol.1. No.3. November 1964. (pp.174-203)

3.3.45.   Urban Form in the Motor Age.(1969)
          SMIGIELSKI, K.
          Paper read at Town Planning Institute Conference.
          Newcastle. 1969.

3.3.46   Urban Land Market. [*A Theory of the] (1960)
          ALONSO, W.
          Papers and Proceedings of the Regional Science
          Association. Vol.6. (6th Annual Meeting). 1960

3.3.47.   Urban Mobility. [*Environmental Implications of Options
                                                      in] (1973)
          OECD. ENVIRONMENT DIRECTORATE.
          Organisation for Economic Co-operation and Development.
          Paris. September 1973.

3.48.   Urban Motorways and their Environment. (1968)
        KERENSKY, O.A.
        Rees Jeffreys Triennial Lecture. Town Planning Institute.
        London. 1968.

3.49.   Urban Settlements. [*The Structure, Size and Cost of]
                                                      (1973)
        STONE, P.A.
        National Institute of Economic and Social Research.
        Cambridge University Press. 1973. (302 pp.)

3.50.   Urban Structures. [*Bus Operation in Alternative] (1976)
        NEWBERRY, G.M.
        In:'Passenger Transport and the Environment'(see ref.
        4.5.7. below)
        ed. Roy Cresswell. Paper read at Conference on Passenger
        Transport and the Environment held at the   University of
        York. March 1976.(pp.35-56)

.3.51   Urbanisation. [*Developing Patterns of] (1970)
        COWAN,P. (ed.)
        Oliver and Boyd. 1970. (222pp.)
        First published results of the Centre for Environmental
        Studies Working Group. Most of these papers are also
        published in Urban Studies. Vol.6.No.3.November 1969.

OVERNMENT REPORTS AND PUBLICATIONS.

.3.52   Homes for Today and Tomorrow. (1961)
        MINISTRY OF HOUSING AND LOCAL GOVERNMENT ("Parker Morris
                                                  Report")
        H.M.S.O. 1961.

.3.53   Road Traffic. [*Research on] (1965)
        ROAD RESEARCH LABORATORY/DEPARTMENT OF SCIENTIFIC AND
                                    INDUSTRIAL RESEARCH.
        H.M.S.O. 1965.

.3.54   Roads in Urban Areas.(1966)
        (and Metric Supplement - 1974)
        DEPARTMENT OF THE ENVIRONMENT,SCOTTISH DEVELOPMENT
        DEPARTMENT and WELSH OFFICE.
        H.M.S.O. 1966. (96pp.)

        This manual summarises recommended standards of urban
        road design and layout which have been developed since
        the publication of the previous official authority on
        this subject, the Ministry of War Transport's 'Design
        and Layout of Roads in Built-up Areas', 1946. A short
        section on bus and coach services (pp.47-49) states the
        need for public transport to be planned to be as
        attractive an alternative as possible to the use of the
        private car in all towns, especially in central areas.
        The main physical factors affecting the siting and
        design of bus routes, stops, bays, shelters and terminals

are summarised and illustrated with diagrams and
photographs. A Metric Supplement (1974) gives
the metric dimensions to be used in place of those
in imperial units given in the main report.

3.3 Subsidiary References.

1.1 New Towns - Transport and Mobility.

1.1.1	Access and Mobility in New Towns. (1976)
1.1.2	Access, Travel and Transportation in New Communities. (1977)
1.1.3	Bus Transport in New Towns. (1959)
1.1.6	Demand Bus for a New Town. (1971)
1.1.7	Mobility in New Towns. (1970)
1.1.8	New Towns in Britain (their transport plans.) (1973)
1.1.10	Project for a Linear New Town. (1957)
1.1.12	Public Transport in its Exclusive Right of Way in Evry. (1973)
1.1.13	A Review of Public Transport in New Towns. (1974)
1.1.14	Public Transport in New Towns in Great Britain. (1971)
1.1.15	Public Transportation and the Needs of New Communities. (1972)
1.1.17-19	Transport and New Towns. Vol.1-3. (1976/7)
1.1.20	Transport Planning. (1968)
1.1.21	Transportation for a New Town. (1971)
1.1.22	Workshop on Transportation for New Towns and Communities.(1969)
1.1.24	Transportation Inputs in New Town Planning. (1969)
1.1.25	Transportation Planning for New Towns. (1969)
1.1.26	Urban Cluster Villages. (1976)
1.1.27	Urban Public Transport. (1971)
1.1.28	Urban Transportation: Problems and Progress. (1972)

1.2 New Towns - Non-Transport Aspects.

1.2.2	Aycliffe to Cumbernauld: a study of seven new towns in their regions. (1969)
1.2.5	British Townscapes. (1965)
1.2.13	Garden Cities of Tomorrow. (1965 edition.)
1.2.18	Progress in Master Plans. (1967)
1.2.21	Neighbourhood Shops in New Towns. (1976)
1.2.22	Neighbourhood Units in British New Towns. (1961)
1.2.24	New Communities U.S.A. (1976)
1.2.25	Recent Trends in New Town Densities. (1970)
1.2.26	New - Town Planning: principles and practice. (1976)
1.2.28	New Towns: A Comparative Atlas. (1972)
1.2.30	New Towns: analysis of activities and their densities. (1972)
1.2.31	New Towns: analysis of land uses.(1972)
1.2.32	The New Towns: The Answer to Megalopolis. (1969)
1.2.33	New Towns: the British Experience. (1972)
1.2.35	New Towns: the Evolution of Planning Criteria. (1972)
1.2.37	Perspectives on New Town Development. (1975)
1.2.38	Prairie Planning in the New Towns. (1953)
1.2.39	Recreational Planning in New Communities: A Review of British Experience. (1975)
1.2.40	Regions of Tomorrow: Towards the Open City. (1969)
1.2.49	United Nations Symposium on the Planning and Development of New Towns,held in Moscow, U.S.S.R. (Aug.-Sept. 1964)
1.2.55	Final Report of the New Towns Committee. (1946)

2.1 Runcorn.

2.1.1   Highway Hierarchy - or please don't bring your car into the
                                living room. (1975)
2.1.9   The Runcorn Plan for a Rapid Transit Bus Service. (1971)
2.1.11 Transportation Problems in Runcorn New Town. (1973)
2.1.12-16 [Runcorn New Town Master Plan and amendment documents.]

2.2 Skelmersdale.

2.2.2-5 [Skelmersdale New Town Planning Proposals.] (1964-5)

2.3 Telford.

2.3.3   Roads in Urban Areas: Brookside 4. (Undated)
2.3.6   Telford Transportation Study. (1976-7)
2.3.9-11 [Telford and Dawley Basic Plan Proposals.]

2.4 Other New Towns.

2.4.24 Irvine New Town: final report on planning proposals. (1967)
2.4.25 Irvine New Town Plan. (1971)
2.4.26 The Best of Both Worlds: transportation planning for Irvine
                                New Town. (1971)
2.4.27 Land Use and Transportation Integration in Irvine New Town.
                                                          (1975)
2.4.28 The Plan for Irvine. (1967)
2.4.29 The Plan for Milton Keynes. Vols. 1 & 2. (1970)
2.4.33 The Disadvantaged of Milton Keynes. (1973)
2.4.39 Changing Goals in Design: the Milton Keynes example. (1972)
2.4.43 Return to the Garden City - interim proposals for Milton Keynes.
                                                          (1969)
2.4.44 Expansion of Peterborough. Consultants' Proposal for
                                Designation.   (1966)
2.4.48 Redditch New Town. Report on Planning Proposals. (1965-7)
2.4.49 Redditch Town Centre Plan. (1969)
2.4.50-51 Stevenage Master Plan. Vols.1-4. (1965-6 and 1969)
2.4.57 Stevenage Public Transport: Cost Benefit Analysis.(1969)
2.4.62 Travel and Land Use in Stevenage. (1968)
2.4.65 Washington New Town Master Plan and Report. (1966)

3.1 Studies of Modal Choice Behaviour and Value of Travel Time.

3.1.33 Residential Location and the Journey to Work: an empirical
                                analysis. (1977)
3.1.36 Intra - Urban Journeys and Activity Linkages.   (1977)
3.1.45 Urban Structure and Modal Split in the Journey to Work. (1977)
3.1.71 The Structure of Movement and Household Travel Behaviour.(1969)
3.1.79 An Analysis of Urban Travel Demands. (1962)
3.1.88 Travel time Budgets and Mobility in Urban Areas. (1974)
3.1.92 Activity - Accessibility Models of Trip Generation. (1972)
3.1.101 A Study of House Prices as a Means of Establishing the Value of
        Journey Time, the Rate of Time Preference and the Valuation of
        Some Aspects of Environment in the London Metropolitan Region.
                                                          (1971)
3.1.116 Time Budgets and Models of Urban Activity Patterns. (1974)

3.2 Social Aspects of Mobility.

3.2.24   The Sunderland Hypermarket Survey. (1971)
3.2.25   Leisure in the North West. (1972)
3.2.26   The Living Suburb: Scheme for the redevelopment of Boston Manor.
                                                        (1958)
3.2.28   In the Market Place: the hypermarket debate. (1972)
3.2.29   Mobility and Accessibility in the Outer Metropolitan Area. (1974)
3.2.33   Rehousing of Old People: some planning implications. (1962)
3.2.37   Personal Mobility and Transport Policy. (1973)
3.2.41   Journeys to School: a survey of Secondary Schools in Berkshire
                                        and Surrey. (1977)
3.2.43   The Location of Primary Schools. (1968)
3.2.46   On Shoppers' Requirements for the Location of Shops in Towns.
                                                        (1974)
3.2.47   Shopping for Food. (Undated)
3.2.48   Shopping in Watford. (1971)
3.2.51   Social Costs of Hypermarket Developments. (1973)
3.2.57   Social Processes, Spatial Form and the Redistribution of Real
                                Income in an Urban System. (1971)
3.2.60   The Concept of Spatial Mobility and an Analytical Approach. (1975)
3.2.61   The Effects of Differing Levels of Spatial Mobility: a discussion.
                                                        (1976)
3.2.63   Transport Realities and Planning Policy. (1976)
3.2.65   Understanding Travel. (1978)
3.2.69   The Elderly at Home: a study of people aged sixty five and over
          living in the community in England in 1976. (1978)
3.2.73   Planning for Leisure. (1969)
3.2.77   Shopping Habits and Attitudes to Shop Hours in Great Britain. (1975)
3.2.78   The Future Pattern of Shopping. (1971)

3.4 General and Miscellaneous.

3.4.6   The Urban Transportation Problem. (1965)

4.1 Public Transport - Operational Aspects.

4.1.9   Vauxhall Bridge Bus Lane 12 Months after Study. (1969)
4.1.10   Assessment of the Effects of Introducing Reserved Bus Lanes.
                                                        (1969)
4.1.11   Bus Lanes in London. (1973)
4.1.13   Planning for the Bus. (1973)
4.1.14   Bus Priorities and Traffic Management (1974)
4.1.15   The Justification and Assessment of Bus Priorities. (1974)
4.1.16   Bus Priority. (1973)
4.1.17   Bus Priority in Greater London. (1972-3)
4.1.18   A Comparison of the Effectiveness of Separate Bus Priority
          Schemes and those Affecting Entire Networks. (1976)
4.1.27   Buses in Camden: A study of bus segregation in the central area
                                        of London. (1971)
4.1.89   Planning for Public Transport. (1976)
4.1.90   Planning for Public Transport: Variations on a Theme. (1977)

4.2 Public Transport - Marketing Approach.

4.2.4   Bus Promotion. (1975)
4.2.25   The Management of Urban Public Transport: a marketing perspective.
                                                        (1975)

4.4 Public Transport - Demonstration Projects and Innovatory Systems.

4.4.1   Bus System Experiments and Developments. (1976)
4.4.2   Cars for the Carless. (1974)
4.4.6   Major Urban Corridor Facilities: a New Concept. (1962)
4.4.35   Para-Transit: Neglected Options for Urban Mobility. (1976)
4.4.47   Zonal Taxi Systems: An Improvement in Local Mobility. (1976)

4.5 Public Transport - General and Miscellaneous.

4.5.7   Passenger Transport and the Environment: the integration of public passenger transport with the environment. (1976)
4.5.8   Public Attitudes to Transport in the Eastbourne, Bexhill and Hastings Area. (1975)

6.1 Non-Motorised Travel.

6.1.4   Planning for the Cyclist in Urban Areas.   (1968)
6.1.5   Feet and Pedals - few rights of way.   (1975)
6.1.6   The Peachtree City Path Experience.   (1974)
6.1.7   Pedestrian Planning and Design.   (1971)
6.1.8   Urban Space for Pedestrians.   (1975)
6.1.9   People First in Transport Planning: did they get it wrong at Radburn and will it be right at Cumbernauld? (1977)
6.1.11   Towards Effective Segregation.   (1975)

7.1 Transport Policy.

7.1.2   The Effect of the Bus Grant on Urban Transport.   (1974)
7.1.3   Changing Directions.   (1974)
7.1.5   Energy and Equity.   (1974)
7.1.6   Energy and the Environment.   (1974)
7.1.10   Getting Nowhere Fast. (1976)
7.1.12   The Economic and Social Impact of Investments in Public Transit. (1973)
7.1.16   New Deal for Motorway Victims.   (1972)
7.1.26   Effect of Traffic Engineering Methods on London. (1963)
7.1.27   An Evaluation of Two Proposals for Traffic Restraint in Central London.   (1967)
7.1.28   Study of Traffic Restraints in Singapore.   (1975)
7.1.37   The Comparative Study of Transport Systems: Swedish Urban Transport Policy and its Application in Britain.   (1974)
7.1.42   Urban Policies and the Motor Car. (1974)
7.1.44-61 [Specific Transport Plans.]
7.1.64   Cars for Cities. (1967)
7.1.65   The Future of Development Plans.   (1965)
7.1.68   New Roads in Towns: Report of the Urban Motorways Committee. (1972)
7.1.69   Planning and Transport: the Leeds Approach.   (1969)
7.1.72   Better Use of Town Roads: the report of a study of the means of restraint of traffic on urban roads.   (1967)
7.1.73   Traffic in Towns: a study of the long-term problems of traffic in urban areas. ["Crowther" and "Buchanan" Reports.] (1963)
7.1.78   Advisory Committee Report on Trunk Road Assessment. (1978)

3.4   General & Miscellaneous .

This subsection contains some general background literature
providing material relevant to several of the topics covered
in this bibliography.   THOMSON's Modern Transport Economics
(3.4.3) sets out the modern economist's approach to transport
problems, looking at transport as a whole rather than at
specific modes.   MEYER, KAIN and WOHL's The Urban Transportation Problem (3.4.6) examines problems arising from
peak work movements in and out of American city centres, and
includes a systematic investigation of patterns of transport
supply and demand and a consideration of the interrelationships between housing and urban transport.   The text by
PORTEOUS (3.4.1) and that edited by PROSHANSKY,ITTELSON
and RIVLIN (3.4.2) provide a basic introduction to studies
of the relationship between behaviour and the environment,
the former including a discussion of social aspects of new
town planning (mainly in the United States context).   Both
books provide numerous references for further investigation
in this field.

3.4.1   Environment and Behavior: planning and everyday
        life,(1977)
        PORTEOUS, J. DOUGLAS,
        Addison-Wesley Publishing Co. Inc., U.S.A. 1977.
        (446pp.)

        This book gives a comprehensive overview of the
        growing multi-disciplinary field of urban man-
        environment relations, divided into three sections:-
        behaviour, environment and planning. An initial
        account of human spatial behaviour is followed by an
        investigation of this behaviour in various
        environments, with a final discussion of the
        manipulation of both behaviour and environment via
        urban planning and design. The latter section
        includes a consideration of social aspects of new
        town planning. An appendix provides a guide to
        general sources, including conference proceedings,
        bibliographies, journals, organisations, information
        systems and compilations of research techniques.
        A bibliography containing over one thousand items is
        included.

3.4.2   Environmental Psychology: Man and his Physical Setting

        PROSHANSKY, H.M., ITTELSON, W.H., and RIVLIN, L.G.(eds
        Holt, Rinehart and Winston, Inc.. New York.1970.
        (690pp.)

        This book presents a collection of readings all
        dealing in one way or another with the relationship
        between behaviour and the environment,and which toget
        with introductory sections by the editors provide a
        comprehensive picture of environmental psychology.
        In attempting to define the boundaries of the growing
        field the editors reject a definition in terms of
        theory, arguing that there is as yet no adequate
        theory of the subject on which to base it, and sugges
        instead an operational definition for which the book's
        table of contents provides an outline. Between an
        opening section on theoretical approaches and a
        closing one on methodology there are a number of
        papers grouped into four sections which cover the
        main problem areas constituting environmental psychol
        viz:- 'Basic Psychological Processes and the Environm
        (including papers on perceptual learning and theory),
        'Individual Needs in the Organization of the Environme
        'Social Institutions and Environment Design', and
        'Environmental Planning'.Numerous references for
        further reading are given at the end of each subsecti

3.4.3   Transport Economics.[*Modern] (1974)
        THOMSON, J.M.
        Penguin Books Ltd.. 1974.(282pp.)

3.4.4. Transportation. [*The Citizen and] (1968)
CONSTANTINE, T.
In 'Urban Renewal. 1968' S. Millward (ed.):
proceedings of a symposium held at the Department
of Civil Engineering, University of Salford. 1968.

3.4.5. Urban Transportation Planning: Current Themes and
Future Prospects.(1977)
BONSALL,P., DALVI, M.Q., and HILLS, P.J. (eds.)
Abacus. 1977.

A collection of papers presented at the Urban Transport
Planning Conference held at the University of Leeds,
1976. Topics covered include Estimation of Demands
for Travel; Attitude Measurement and Evaluation.

3.4.6. Urban Transportation Problem. [*The] (1965)
MEYER, J.R., KAIN, J.F., and WOHL, M.
Harvard University Press, Cambridge, Mass. 1965.(427pp.)

This book presents a comprehensive examination of the
basic issues of the urban transportation problem,
focussing mainly on movement of passengers in and out
of cities during peak times. The first part is
concerned particularly with empirical testing of the
validity of various postulated hypotheses and solutions
to the problem, in order to provide a more rational
basis for decision-making. It analyses trends in the
urban context within which urban transport systems and
policies operate, examines characteristics of the
supply and demand for urban transport, and tests
hypotheses relating to the interaction between housing
and travel choices. Part II provides a series of cost
analyses. Part III develops the policy implications
of the findings presented in the first two Parts and
presents an evaluation of some less conventional means
of meeting urban travel need.

3.4   Subsidiary References.

1.1   New Towns- Transport and Mobility.

_1.1.4_   _The Characteristics of New Town Travel: A case study of Reston,_
Virginia. (1974)
_1.1.5_   _Commuting Flows and the Growth of London's New Towns, 1951-1971._
_(1977)_
_1.1.20_   _Transport Planning. (1968)_

2.1   Runcorn.

_2.1.2_   _People and Transportation - Runcorn New Town. (1974)_

2.2   Skelmersdale.

_2.2.1_   _Transportation in New Towns with Particular Reference to_
Skelmersdale. (1968)

2.4   Other New Towns.

2.4.6   *Traffic and Transport in Crawley. (1971)*
2.4.47   *Transport in Peterlee. (1961)*

7.1   Transport Policy.

7.1.73   *Traffic in Towns: a study of the long-term problems of traffic
           in urban areas. ("Crowther" and "Buchanan" Reports) (1963)*
7.1.74   *Transport Act. 1968 . (1970)*
7.1.76   *Transport Policy. (White Paper) (1977)*
7.1.77   *Transport Policy: A Consultation Document. (1976)*
7.1.79   *Urban Transport Planning. (1972)*

8.1   Survey Techniques: Behavioural and Attitudinal.

8.1.70   *The Application of Psychological Research and Theory to Urban
                                    Transportation Planning. (1975)*

8.2   Economic Evaluation.

8.2.1   *Notes on the State of the Art of Benefit-Cost Analysis as Related
                                    to Transportation Systems. (1966)*
8.2.4   *Cost-Benefit Scales for Urban Transportation. (1968)*
8.2.6   *A Rational Decision-Making Technique for Transportation Planning.
                                                                  (1967)*
8.2.9   *The Economics of Transport Appraisal. (1974)*

8.3   Research Techniques and Methodology – General and Miscellaneous.

8.3.24   *West Midlands Rural Travel Survey. (1972)*

9.1   Journals.

9.1.1-3:   [*Specialised bibliographical references to transport journals.*]
9.1.7-25: [*Transport Journals.*]

9.2   Bibliographies.

9.2.1-18: [*Transport Bibliographies.*]

9.3   Abstracting and Indexing Services.

9.3.1   *Architectural Periodicals Index. (Quarterly)*
9.3.2   *British Humanities Index. (Quarterly)*
9.3.3   *British Technology Index. (Monthly)*
9.3.5   *Current Literature in Traffic and Transportation. (Monthly)*
9.3.6   *Departments of the Environment and Transport Library Bulletin.
                                                          (Fortnightly)*
9.3.7   *Environmental Periodicals Bibliography. (Six times a year)*
9.3.9   *Geo Abstracts. (Six times a year)*
9.3.10   *HRIS Abstracts. (Quarterly)*
9.3.14   *Sage Urban Studies Abstracts. (Quarterly)*
9.3.18   *TRRL Information Storage and Retrieval System (On request, from
                                                                  1965)*

9.3.19	Transportation Research Abstracts. *(Six times a year)*
9.3.20	U.I.T.P. Biblio-Index: Verkehr. *(Quarterly)*
9.3.21	Urban Abstracts. *(Monthly)*
9.3.22	U.T.S.G. Famulus References. *(On request for members of U.T.S.G.)*

9.4 Research Registers.

9.4.1	Register of Research, 1977. Part II: Environmental Planning. *(1977)*
9.4.2	Register of Research, 1977: Part III: Roads and Transport. *(1977)*
9.4.3	Register of Surveys. *(1977)*
9.4.4	Research on Transport Economics. *(Twice a year)*
9.4.5	1977 World Survey of Current Research and Development on Roads and Road Transport. *(1977)*

9.5 Statistical Sources.

9.5.6-8	National Travel Survey. 1972/3.
9.5.14	Transport Statistics Great Britain. *(Annually.)*
9.5.15	Annual Abstract of Statistics. *(Annually.)*
9.5.16	Census of Population. *(1971)*
9.5.20	Monthly Digest of Statistics. *(Monthly)*
9.5.22	Regional Statistics. *(Annually)*
9.5.23	Social Trends. *(Annually)*

9.6 Other Sources.

9.6.2	National Index of Traffic and Transportation Surveys. *(1975)*
9.6.6	Transport and Communications: Statistical Sources. *(1975)*
9.6.10	Guide to Official Statistics. *(1976 and 1978)*
9.6.17	Sources of Economic and Business Statistics. *(1972)*

4. Public Transport.

4.1 Operational Aspects.

Section 4.1 concentrates on literature relevant to the operational aspects of public transport, drawn mainly from British experience. The emphasis is on bus transport: rail transport plays virtually no part in purely local travel in most new towns in the United Kingdom, although it does have a limited rôle in Telford. Many of the items on the marketing of public transport (4.2), some of those on ergonomic aspects (4.3), and virtually all the references describing demonstration projects and innovatory systems (4.4) are also relevant to the operation of public transport and have been cross-referenced at the end of this subsection. Other relevant material listed in the subsidiary references is drawn from sections 7.1 (Transport Policy), 3.1 (mainly relating to bus waiting times and journey times), 3.2 (particularly items concerned with fare concession schemes for the elderly and with school transport), 3.3 (the relation of bus operation to urban form), and the sections relating to transport in new towns (1.1 and 2.1-4)

Specific subject areas covered in this subsection include:-

- -Bus lanes and bus priority schemes.

- -One-man operation.

- -Fares policies and studies of fares elasticities.

- -Costing of bus operations.

- -Route planning strategy.

- -Organisational aspects of the bus industry and manpower problems.

- -Interchanges.

- -Demand for public transport, including studies of demand elasticities.

In addition several general studies have been included which cover various aspects of public transport operation and which form a useful introduction to the field. These include WHITE's Planning for Public Transport (4.1.89) which examines many aspects of public transport operation in Britain and relates them to both short-term and long-term Government policy. Specific topics covered include usage of public transport, organisation, bus design, pricing and costing, and urban network planning which is related to urban form. The book reviews and discusses much recent research in these areas and provides pointers for further reading. The texts by LANE, POWELL and PRESTWOOD SMITH (4.1.1), by HIBBS (4.1.4), and by LAMBDEN (4.1.5) also provide a useful background to studies of bus operation. GREY's Urban Fares Policy (4.1.58)

presents a detailed examination of fare structures taking
into account the social and other broader implications of
alternative fares policies.

The report of the Bradford Bus Study (4.1.2) describes the
results of a comprehensive investigation of bus operation
in Bradford which included detailed studies of bus routeing
costing, demand and promotion. Comparable major studies
by consultants of bus operation in new towns have been
carried out in Telford (2.3.1) and Glenrothes (2.4.11).

Journals which provide potential sources of up-to-date
material on bus operation are listed in subsection 9.1, and
relevant bibliographies in 9.2. The DEPARTMENTS OF THE
ENVIRONMENT AND TRANSPORT Headquarters Library's bibliography:
Buses in Urban Areas (9.2.3) brings together many references
to literature on bus operation published between 1970 and
1976, and the bibliography compiled by SMARE and BRUCE
(9.2.9) provides a review of literature on passenger transport
interchange up to 1974. The DEPARTMENTS OF THE ENVIRONMENT
AND TRANSPORT Headquarters Library's publication: U.K.
Transport Organisations (9.6.7) lists U.K. organisations and
Government departments concerned with transport.

4.1.1   Analytical Transport Planning.(1971)
LANE, R., POWELL, T.J. and PRESTWOOD SMITH, P.
Duckworth. London.1971. (283pp.)

4.1.2.   Bradford Bus Study : Final Report.(1976)
R. TRAVERS MORGAN & PARTNERS. January 1976.
                           (169 pp.)

The original reason for carrying out the
Bradford Bus Study was to establish how buses
should be rerouted on completion of the central
Transport Interchange. The study later
developed into a broader examination of the
existing bus system in Bradford and of its
future rôle. The report presents the findings
of the detailed studies of the present and
projected future rôle of buses in Bradford; bus
routeing, with particular consideration to the
rerouteing of buses on the opening of the
Transport Interchange ; bus costing and the
effects on costs of operational changes ; and
bus promotion, concerned with the means by which
bus travel can become more attractive and
competitive, and including an examination of the
factors affecting passenger demand. In the
course of the study major surveys were carried out
covering bus use, passenger origins and destinations,
bus running, and passenger attitudes. The methods
used in these are outlined in Appendix B and the
results of the Attitude Survey are summarised in
Appendix 7. Additional appendices give details
of other techniques used in the study and results
of these, covering bus network testing and
evaluation, aspects of rerouteing proposals, and
costing of bus operations.

4.1.3   Bradford Bus Study : Interim Report on Costing
of Bus Operations.(1974)
R.TRAVERS MORGAN & PARTNERS/ WEST YORKSHIRE
METROPOLITAN COUNTY.1974.

4.1.4   Bus and Coach Industry [*The] : its economics
and organisation.(1975)

HIBBS, J.
Dent. 1975.(224 pp.)

4.1.5   Bus and Coach Operation : Principles and
Practice for the Transport Student.(1969)
LAMBDEN, W.
lliffe. 4th Edition. 1969.

4.1.6   Bus and Rail Receipts 1970-72 [*An Analysis of Factors
        FAIRHURST, M.H.   Affecting]   (1973)
        London Transport Executive, Operational
        Research Report R.201   November 1973,

4.1.7   Bus Boarding and Alighting Times.(1973)
        CUNDILL, M.A. and WATTS,P.F.
        TRRL   Report LR 521. 1973.

4.1.8   Bus Improvements Survey, 1976. (1977)
        BRADLEY, J.and MAW, J.R.
        London Transport Executive. Marketing Memorandum
        M 52A. September 1977, (6 pp.)
        (See also ref.4.1.23 below)

        This Memorandum summarises the methods and
        findings of a survey which used priority
        evaluation research techniques for estimating
        the value to bus passengers of investment in
        waiting facilities at bus stations and stops.
        The main objective was to improve the method of
        allocating resources in this area by providing
        a basis for evaluation of projects in terms of
        London Transport's aim of maximising passenger
        mileage.   Respondents were presented with a
        set of alternative improvements from which
        they chose a 'package' within an overall financial
        limitation.   They then set a value on their
        chosen'package' by stating how much they would
        be prepared to pay on top of their regular fares to
        have these implemented.
        The main findings were that while improved bus
        services had the highest priority there was also
        a significant demand for better waiting facilities
        at stations and stops, especially for shelters
        and draught screens, toilets and information
        services.   There was also a demand for lower-
        cost facilities such as seating and clocks,
        but little interest in refreshment services.
        There was little demand for improvements to
        vehicles other than higher standards of
        cleanliness.   On average people were prepared
        to pay about 20% more in fares to have their
        chosen improvements implemented (an increase
        of 1½ to 2½ p. on an'average' journey).   The
        survey results were analysed to estimate the
        likely effects on passenger mileage of making
        the improvements postulated.   The key estimates
        are set out in the paper, and generally indicated
        that better waiting facilities would generate
        additional passenger miles.

4.1.9   Bus Lane 12 months after Study.[*Vauxhall Bridge]
                                              (1969)
        YATES, L.B
        G.L.C. Department of Highways and Transportation.
        Research Memorandum 178.   July 1969.

4.1.10   Bus Lanes. [*Assessment of the Effects of
         Introducing Reserved] (1969)
         FREBAULT, J.
         European Conference of Ministers of Transport. Paris. 1969.

4.1.11   Bus Lanes in London. (1973)
         RIDLEY, G., RUSHTON, P. and CRACKNELL, J.A.
         The Highway Engineer. Vol. XX No. 7. July 1973 (pp. 8 - 32)

4.1.12   Bus Operations [*Potential Methods of Improving] :
         some pointers from the Bradford Bus Study. (1975)
         SKINNER, R.J.
         Paper read at the PTRC Summer Annual Meeting.
         Seminar S. (Public Transport). July 1975.

4.1.13   Bus [* Planning for the] (1973)
         WEBSTER, A.T. and McGOWAN, J.
         TRRL Supplementary Report SR 6UC: "Moving People
         in Cities."
         Report of a conference held at the Transport and Road
         Research Laboratory, Crowthorne, Berkshire. April 1973.
                                            (pp. 95 - 101)

4.1.14   Bus Priorities and Traffic Management. (1974)
         LEVINSON, H.S.
         Paper read at the PTRC Summer Annual Meeting.
         Seminar S. (Public Transport). July 1974.

4.1.15   Bus Priorities. [*The Justification and Assessment of] (197
         RAPSON, G.H.
         Paper read at the PTRC Summer Annual Meeting.
         Seminar S. (Public Transport). July 1974.

4.1.16   Bus Priority. (1973)
         TRRL Report. LR. 570.
         Proceedings of a Symposium held at the Transport and
         Road Research Laboratory, Crowthorne, Berkshire, 1972. (197

4.1.17   Bus Priority in Greater London. (1972/3)
         Traffic Engineering and Control: a series of six papers
         in Vol. 14. November 1972 (pp. 324-6), December 1972
         (pp. 382-6), January 1973 (pp. 429-32), February 1973
         (pp. 482-5), March 1973 (pp. 522-5), April 1973 (pp. 592-4).

4.1.18   Bus Priority Schemes and those Affecting Entire Networks.
         [*A Comparison of the Effectiveness of Separate] (1976)
         WHITE, P.R. and HOLMES, R.W.
         Paper read at the PTRC Summer Annual Meeting. July 1976.

4.1.19   Bus Service. [*A Methodology for Planning] (1977)
         NICOLAIDIS, G. and KRISHNAN, K.S.
         Transportation. Vol. 6. No. 3. September 1977.
         (pp. 249-263)

.1.20   Bus Service Performance. [*A Study of Some Factors
Affecting]   (1977)
JACKSON, R.L., COE, G.A. and FINNAMORE, A.J.
TRRL Report LR 767. July 1977.

An examination of bus boarding and alighting
processes; methods of dealing with staff or
vehicle shortages; bus scheduling.

.1.21   Bus Services. [*Better]   (1973)
DALY, A.J. and ROGERS, K.G.
Local Government Operational Research Unit. (LGORU)
Report S.16. November 1973.   (14pp.)
Royal Institute of Public Administration.

.1.22   Bus Services. [*Measurement of Waiting Times in
Assessments of Operational Changes in]   (1977)
COE, G.A. and JACKSON, R.L.
TRRL Supplementary Report SR 298. 1977.

Discusses some of the difficulties likely to be
encountered in survey studies of urban bus services
when trying to measure changes in passenger waiting
times which are brought about by an operational change.

.1.23   Bus Station Improvements. [*Passenger Mileage
Estimates for] (1977)
BRADLEY, J. and MAW, J.R.
London Transport Executive. Marketing Technical
Note M T N.11. September 1977. (6pp.)

(see also ref. 4.1.8 above)

This Technical Note gives full details of the procedure
for calculating the effects on passenger mileage of
implementing the improvements postulated in the Bus
Improvements Survey, 1976. It also provides pointers
for further research to improve the methodology for
evaluating the effects of environmental improvements
for bus passengers.

.1.24   Bus. [*The Independent]   (1974)
TURNS, K.L.
David and Charles. 1974. (207 pp.)

.1.25   Bus Transportation Strategies. (1976)
TRANSPORTATION RESEARCH BOARD
Transportation Research Record No. 606. Transportation
Research Board. Washington D.C. 1976.

Papers concerned with the evaluation of levels of
bus service are included. A method is presented
for evaluating levels of comfort and convenience
together with other elements of service quality.

4.1.26   Bus Travel and the Next Ten Years. (1975)
          WEBSTER, F.V.
          Paper read at the Annual Conference of the
          Association of Public Passenger Transport
          (Incorporated). September 1975. (24 pp.)

          In the context of the decline in bus travel and
          increased level of subsidies in Britain since
          the 1950's the paper considers which operating
          policies are advantageous at present, likely
          trends in bus travel over the next ten years, and
          how these will be affected by overall planning
          decisions, transport policies and the state of
          the economy.   Comparisons are made with trends in
          bus patronage and subsidy levels in a number of
          other countries.   Some studies carried out by
          TRRL aimed at forecasting future demand for
          public transport and identifying promising
          operating policies are described.   Major
          conclusions are :-

          (i) The factors which have the greatest effect
          on public transport usage are car ownership
          levels, fares, level of service, reliability, and
          planning factors such as car-usage restraints
          and urban dispersal.
          (ii) Largescale service improvements paid for
          from higher fares are in general unlikely to be
          worthwhile in terms of increased numbers of
          passenger journeys.
          (iii) Reliability is one of the most important
          aspects of service, and improvements involving
          lower frequencies but greater reliability of
          service could be beneficial.
          (iv) There may be some scope for better utilisation
          of existing human and material resources in the
          bus industry but institutional problems may limit
          the extent of these.
          (v) Regarding future options, the adoption of a
          break-even policy involving higher fares and
          reduced services could cause considerable further
          losses in patronage by 1985.   Attempts to retain
          patronage levels by reducing fares and improving
          service would require substantial increases
          in subsidies.   The best choice would seem to lie
          somewhere between these two options.
          (see also ref. 4.5.18 below).

4.1.27   Buses in Camden (1971)
          LONDON BOROUGH OF CAMDEN.
          A study of bus segregation in the central area of
          London.
          Department of Planning and Communications. 1971. (48pp.)

4.1.28   Buses in Urban Areas. [*Ways of Helping]   (1968)
          ELLEN, E.R.
          Paper read at the 9th International Study Week in
          Traffic and Safety Engineering.   Munich.   September 1968.

4.1.29   Complimentary Bus Passes to Improve Ridership
on Bus Transit Systems.   [*The Use of]   (1976)
BROGAN, J.D., HEATHINGTON, K.W. and SATTERLEY, G.
Transportation Planning and Technology. Vol. 3.
No. 2. March 1976. (pp.103 -114)

4.1.30   Cost and Pricing in Road Passenger Transport.
[*A Study of Peak]   (1970)
TYSON, W.J.
Institute of Transport Journal.Vol.33.
November 1970.

4.1.31   Cost - Effectiveness in Urban Transportation.(1969)
DODSON, E.N.
Operations Research. May - June 1969.   Operations
Research Society of America.

4.1.32   Cost of Bus Transport in Urban Areas.   [*The Short
and Long-run]   (1975)
WABE J.S. and COLES, O.B.
Journal of Transport Economics and Policy.
Vol. IX. No. 2. May 1975. (pp. 127 - 140)

The authors find evidence of diseconomies of scale
in municipal bus operation.   They examine costs
between 1961 and 1971 and find that the cost of a
peak mile is increasing in proportion to total
cost.

4.1.33   Costing in the Bus Industry.   [*An Approach to
Operational]   (1973)
BEETHAM, A.
Paper read at the Second Seminar on Rural Transport.
Polytechnic of Central London. November 1973.

4.1.34   Costs in 1973.   [*Vehicle Operating]   (1974)
DAWSON, R.F.F. and VASS, P.
TRRL   Report   LR 661. 1974. (8pp.)

4.1.35   Demand.   [*Alternative Future Levels of Public
Transport] (1977)
WHITE, P.R.
Paper read at the Universities Transport Studies
Group (UTSG) Conference. January 1977. (17 pp.)

4.1.36   Demand, Cost and Efficiency in Urban Bus Operation.
[* Analysis of Recent Trends in]   (1976)
WHITE, P.R.
Paper read at the Eighth Annual Seminar on Public
Transport Operational Research. University of Leeds.
1976. (9 pp.)

The need for improved data on passenger demand at the
level of operators' whole networks is stressed and
the limitations of existing sources of statistics
are discussed.   An outline is given of the annual
survey of municipal and PTE operators conducted by
the   Bus and Coach   section of 'Motor Transport',

and of the statistical definitions used in the
survey. Trends for the 1970/1 and 1974/5
financial years are summarised, covering revenue
and passenger trips; working expenses, net deficits
and reserves; and vehicle utilisation, fleet
size and capital expenditure. The paper also
includes a discussion of some policy implications
and a brief summary of passenger trends in other
countries.

4.1.37 Demand, Cost and Efficiency in Urban Public
Transport. [*Further Analysis of Trends in](1977)
WHITE, P.R.
Paper read at the Ninth Annual Seminar on
Public Transport Operational Research. University
of Leeds. July 1977. (21pp.)

This paper updates the basic statistical data
presented in an earlier paper. (see ref. 4.1.36
above) to 1975/6, and gives further analysis
of some productivity measures. Trends in the
nationalised sectors of public transport in
Britain, and in urban systems elsewhere in Europe,
are discussed.

4.1.38 Demand Elasticities. [*Some Evidence of Transit]
(1973)
KEMP, M.A.
Transportation. Vol.2.6.1 April, 1973 (pp. 25.52)
Vol.2. No.1.
This paper draws together empirical evidence from
a variety of North American and European sources
about the magnitude of public transport price
elasticities and cross-elasticities. General
conclusions are that demand is inelastic with
respect to money price and that typically ridership is significantly more sensitive to changes
in the level of service (particularly door-to-door
journey time) than to changes in fares.
(This paper is a condensation of an Urban Institute
Working Paper of the same title, WP 708-52.
November 1971).

4.1.39 Demand for Bus and Rail Travel in London up to 1974.
[*Variations in the] (1975)
FAIRHURST, M.H. and MORRIS, P.J.
London Transport Executive. Economic Research
section. Report No. R.210.

This report contains a statistical analysis of
weekly bus and underground receipts up to the end
of 1973, and a number of analyses based on annual
data for 1953 - 73.
The main topics covered are:-
(i)   The response of travel to changes in fares.
(ii)   The effects of inflation and the level of
       real incomes.
(iii) Service level changes.
(iv)   Long-term trends.

4.1.40　Demand for Public Transport.　[*Elasticity of]　(1974)

DALY, A.J.and GALE, H.S.
TRRL　Report SR 68 UC. 1974. (36 pp.)

4.1.41　Demand for Transport in the SELNEC Area.
　　　　[*The Effects of Two Differential Pricing
Policies on]　　(1973)
TYSON, W.J.
Paper read at the　PTRC　Summer Annual Meeting.
1973.

4.1.42　Demand for Urban Bus Travel.　[*Estimating the]　(1975)

MULLEN, P.
Transportation. Vol.4. September 1975. (pp.231-252)

This paper investigates simple economic models of
bus demand, examines alternative variables that
can be used and discusses some alternative model
forms.　It demonstrates the results of a model
using data from twelve urban bus operators in
Britain and compares the results with those from
other types of study.　Average elasticities of
-0.31 with respect to fare changes and of +0.62
with respect to service quality changes are
derived.　It is estimated that fare rises accounted
for 13% of the 43% decline in passengers over the
preceding fifteen years and vehicle mileage
reductions for 14.3%.　Only an estimated 15.7%
was due to such factors as rising car ownership
which is often given as the cause of declining bus
patronage.　The results indicate that passengers
are　much more sensitive to changes in service than
they are to fare rises.　The author points to the
need for further research to establish more accurate
results for different types of passenger.

4.1.43　Demand for Urban Bus Travel.　[*The]　(1974)
MULLEN, K. and LEWIS,
Colin Buchanan and Partners　Research Paper. 1974.

4.1.44　Demand.　[*Public Transport] (1974)
COBBE, R.
Unpublished M. Sc. Thesis. Polytechnic of Central
London. 1974

4.1,45　Economic Change in the Road Passenger Transport
Industry. (1972)
RHYS, D.G.
Journal of Transport Economics and Policy. Vol.
VI. No. 3. September 1972.(pp.240 - 253)

The most significant developments in the road
passenger transport industry in recent years are
identified as the capital grants paid to operators
by the Ministry of Transport, the restructuring of
the bus operating sector, and changes in vehicle
design affecting the quality of buses.　These
three developments and the interactions between
them are discussed, and the economic consequences

examined. The author concludes that Government
grants towards the cost of new buses had not
(upto 1972) had any serious effect on design.
But there were deficiencies of design in the
standard rear-engined vehicles, and there was
danger of near-monopoly in production.

4.1.46   Economic Viability in Public Transport
         Undertakings. (1968)
         LATSCHA, W.
         Paper read at U.I.T.P conference. London. 1968.

4.1.47   Economies of Scale in Bus Transport: Some British
         Municipal Results. (1970)
         LEE, N. and STEDMAN, 1.
         Journal of Transport Economics and Policy.
         Vol. 4. No. 1. January 1970.

4.1.48   Effective Change in Large Organisations. (1966)
         GINZBERG, E. and REILLY, E.W.
         Columbia University Press. 1966.

4.1.49   Fare Deal - Your Choice. (1974)
         GREATER LONDON COUNCIL. 1974.

4.1.50   Fare-free Urban Transport Services [*Reduced
         Fare and]: Some case studies. (1974)
         KEMP, M.A.
         TRRL Supplementary Report SR 37 UC. 1974.
         (Paper read at the Symposium on Public Transport
         Fare Structure. TRRL. November 1973.)
         (see ref. 4.1.52 below)

4.1.51   Fare Levels.   [*Public Response to Change in]
                                                       (1974)
         SMITH, M.G. and McINTOSH, P.T.
         TRRL Supplementary Report SR 37 UC. 1974.
         (Paper read at the Symposium on Public Transport
         Fare Structure.   TRRL. November 1973.)
         (see ref. 4.1.52 below)

4.1.52   Fare Structure [* Symposium on Public Transport]:
         summary of the proceedings.   (1974)
         TRANSPORT AND ROAD RESEARCH LABORATORY.
         TRRL Supplementary Reports SR36 UC and SR 37 UC
         1974.
         (See refs. 4.1.50, and 4.1.51 above;
          4.1.55, 4.1.57 and 4.1.60 below)

4.1.53   Fares [* Low] and the Urban Transport Problem.
                                                       (1969)
         WILLIAMS, P.M.
         Urban Studies. Vol.6. No. 1. February 1969.
                         (pp. 83 - 92)

This article reports the results of a study
which attempted to determine the contribution
that adopting a policy of low standard fares
on public transport would make to solving the
urban transport problem. An interview survey
was carried out (1965) to investigate what
effect a reduction in fares to a comparatively
low standard level would have on the travelling
habits of car commuters working in Central
London. The results suggest that this policy
would persuade nearly half of the regular
car commuters to transfer to public transport,
resulting in a reduction of over one-third
in rush hour private car traffic. Even greater
numbers would transfer given improvements in
the speed and comfort of public transport,
although the clearer roads might also induce
some travellers who at present use public
transport to transfer to private cars. The
financial implications are considered, and it
was estimated that additional costs incurred
by the increase in peak-hour passengers would
be much greater than the additional revenue,
leading to substantial losses for public
transport operators. However there would be
considerable financial and social benefits from
the reduction in traffic congestion, and the
possible savings in congestion, accident and other
costs are examined in conjunction with some
suggestions on the sources of the necessary
subsidies.

4.1.54   Fares Elasticity Experiment. (1974)
         HEDGES, B. and PRESCOTT - CLARKE, P.
         Social and Community Planning Research Report
         No. 226. December 1974.

4.1.55   Fares Elasticity : Interpretation and Estimation.
                                                    (1974)
         SMITH, M.G., McINTOSH, P.T. and BLACK, I.
         TRRL Supplementary Report SR 37 UC. 1974.
         (Paper read at the Symposium on Public Transport
         Fare Structure. TRRL. November 1973.)
         (See ref. 4.1.52 above)

4.1.56   Fares on Transit Riding.   [*Effect of] (1968)
         CURTIN, J.F.
         Highway Research Record No. 213. Highway Research
         Board. Washington DC. 1968.

4.1.57   Fares Policy. [*The Rôle of Local Government in]
                                                    (1974)
         GREY, A.
         TRRL Supplementary Report SR 37 UC. 1974.
         (Paper read at the Symposium on Public Transport
         Fare Structure. TRRL. November 1973.)
         (see ref. 4.1.52 above)

4.1.58   Fares Policy.   [* Urban]   (1975)
          GREY, A .
          Saxon House/Lexington Books. 1975. (166pp.)

          The book presents a critique of conventional
          transport planning models and outlines an
          approach to urban fares policy which includes
          consideration of managerial and social
          implications and of the legal and organisational
          framework within which decisions are made.
          The aims and objectives for fares policy are set
          out under the general headings of social,
          environmental, financial and economic, and
          operational, and three categories of fares
          policy option are defined.   The impact on
          demand and receipts of general changes in fare
          level arising from fares policies is discussed, and
          current practice in fares policy in other (mainly
          Western European) countries is reviewed.   The
          book also includes an examination of the likely
          effects of fares changes on income redistribution
          and on improving travel opportunities for
          specific social groups.

4.1.59   Fares Revision on Work Journeys.   [*Analysis of
          the Effect of September 1969]   (1972)
          COLLINS, P.H. and LINDSAY, J.F.
          London Transport Executive. L.T. Report R.181.
          June 1972.

          The report describes an attempt to derive
          information on revenue yields and elasticities
          from sample survey data.   The difficulties
          involved in making this kind of analysis are
          revealed.

4.1.60   Fares Systems on Operational Efficiency   [* Effect
          of Alternative]:British experience. (1974)
          QUARMBY, D.A.
          TRRL   Supplementary Report SR 37 UC. 1974.
          Paper read at the Symposium on Public Transport
          Fare Structure. TRRL. November 1973.
          (See ref. 4.1.52 above)

4.1.61   Fares   [*Alternative Approaches to Public
          Transport] with their Revenue and Traffic
          Implications.   (1973)
          GUTNECHT, R.
          Paper read at U.I.T.P. Fortieth International
          Congress. 1973.

4.1.62   Free Public Transport. (1973)
          BAUM, H.J.
          Journal of Transport Economics and Policy.
          Vol. Vll. No. 1. January 1973. (pp. 3-19)

After a survey of transport studies in Germany
and elsewhere it is concluded that advocates
of free public transport have overestimated the
possible diversion from private cars, and
underestimated the cost, and that the benefit
would not go entirely to those in need.

4.1.63   Free Public Transport.   [*Some Data on the
         Effects of]   (1972)
         GOODWIN, P.B.
         Paper read at PTRC Urban Traffic Model Research
         Seminar. 1972.

4.1.64   Free Transit. (1970)
         DOMENCICH, T.A. and KRAFT, G.
         Heath Lexington Books. 1970. (115pp.)

4.1.65   Horizontal Dimension in a Bureaucracy. [*The]
                                                 (1961)
         LANDSBERGER, H.A.
         Administrative Science Quarterly. Vol. 6. 1961.
                        (pp. 298 - 333)

4.1.66   How Delhi made the Buses Run on Time. (1975)
         TINKER, J.
         New Scientist. Vol. 65. 9th. January 1975. (pp. 64-66)

4.1.67   Human Performance Requirements for an Innovative
         Transit Bus Operation (1976)

         BAUER, H.J.
         Human Factors. Vol. 18. No. 3. 1976.
                        (pp. 221 - 234)

Human performance requirements for an innovative
bus operation system utilising exclusive bus
lanes in a central area are described.
Requirements for both the bus company personnel
and bus passengers are discussed. Performance
levels achieved during a test and demonstration
of the system in Rochester, New York, are analysed.

4.1.68   Interchange.   [*Passenger Resistance to a Rural
         Bus-Bus] (1977)
         TEBB, R.G.P.
         TRRL Supplementary Report SR. 269. April 1977. (14pp.)

4.1.69   Interchanges on Merseyside. [*Public Transport]
                                          (1976)
         PEAT, MARWICK, MITCHELL & Co. with D.O.E. and
         MERSEYSIDE P.T.E.
         Summary Report. 1976.

4.1.70   Interchanges [* Passenger Transport]:   theory
          and practice on Merseyside.   (1973)
          MILLWARD, C., COLEMAN, A.H. and DUNFORD, J.E.
          Traffic Engineering and Control. Vol.14 No.12.
          April 1973. (pp.575 - 580)

4.1.71   Interchanges. [*The Design and Location of Urban
          Public Transport] (1973)
          WAGON, D.J., and COLLINS, P.H.
          Paper read at PTRC annual meeting, University of
          Sussex, 1973 and at the 19th Round Table of the
          European Conference of Ministers of Transport, Paris.

          Presents a review of literature on interchange
          design.

4.1.72   London Borough Buses : Hillingdon takes the
          initiative. (1977)
          BUSES. NO.270. September 1977. (pp.361-362)

          This article describes details of the planning and
          operation of a new bus service run by the London
          Borough of Hillingdon, using midibuses to link two
          hospitals, two stations and a village community.

4.1.73   London Borough of Haringey W.3 Bus Route Study. (1974)
          TREVELYAN, P. and WRIGHT, L.
          Paper read at PTRC Summer Annual Meeting, Seminar S
          (Public Transport). July 1974.

4.1.74   London Rail Study   (1975)
          GREATER LONDON COUNCIL. 1975.

4.1.75   Manpower Planning in the Public Sector of the
          Transport Industry. (1974)
          JENKINS, H.
          Paper read at the PTRC Summer Annual Meeting.
          July 1974. (pp. 47-66 of Proceedings)

4.1.76   Men who Manage. (1959)
          DALTON, M.
          John Wiley. 1959.

4.1.77   Midibus Operation in Cardiff : a Low Cost Approach
          to a Low Demand Problem. (1976)
          or: "The Great Little Buses of Cardiff".
          MONROE, R.E.
          Paper read at the PTRC Summer Annual Meeting.
          July 1976. (pp.109 -115 of Proceedings).

          Following rationalisation of bus services in Cardiff
          in 1973 a number of routes were withdrawn in an
          attempt to provide frequent, reliable and direct
          services to the central area along the main radial

corridors. Attempts were made to keep maximum home-to-bus stop walking distances to one-quarter of a mile. Midibus services were introduced on seven routes using three 25-seater vehicles to meet residual pockets of demand from people who found it difficult to walk these distances, those who wanted some intersurburban facilities, and those living in parts of Cardiff not served by conventional bus services. The paper describes details of the route pattern and operation of the midibus services and outlines service changes arising from a passenger questionnaire survey carried out after the first year of operation.

4.1.78   Multi-Journey Discount Ticket Systems. (1970)
HYDE, D.L.
Report to the Municipal Passenger Transport Association. 1970.

4.1.79   N.B.C. Regions Reorganised : National Travel Management Modified. (1977)
BUSES. No. 270. September 1977. (pp.360-361)

A short article outlining major changes about to come into effect in the regional structure of the National Bus Company and in its senior management. The number of regions has been extended frcm three to four with the creation of a new region: 'Wales and the Marches', and a map shows the revised regional boundaries.

4.1.80   Occupational Structure [*Changing]in the Road Passenger Transport Industry and its Implications for the Future. (1974)
BARNETT, D.C.
Paper read at the PTRC Summer Annual Meeting. July 1974. (pp.41 - 46 of Proceedings).

4.1.81   One-Man Bus Operation [*The Impact on Receipts of Conversion to] (1974)
FAIRHURST, M.H.
Journal of Transport Economics and Policy. Vol.VIII. No. 3. September, 1974. (pp. 223 - 236)

During 1972 a large study was performed within the London Transport Executive to assess whether one-man operated buses could or should be operated in Central London. This paper sets out the results of a receipts analysis of a set of suburban conversions, which was one of several contributions to the final evaluation. Receipts on many bus services converted

to OMO in 1972 had fallen by 10% to 20% by early
1972. However, the analysis presented in the
paper shows that when diversions to parallel
services on the same routes were excluded, receipts
losses due to OMO itself were on average only
3% to 4%. The paper discusses part of the work
done to identify and assess the relative importance of
the several factors which depressed receipts after
past conversions.

4.1.82   One-Man Buses. (1973)
         CONSUMERS' ASSOCIATION : 'Which?' Magazine.
         February 1973.

         An examination of the effects on passengers of
         conversion of two London bus routes to one-man
         operation in 1972, with some discussion of the
         wider implications for London's traffic.   Surveys
         were carried out on two routes immediately before
         and three weeks after conversion.   Records were
         made of the numbers of passengers boarding, bus
         stopping times, journey times between major
         stages and for the complete route, and the
         proportions of passengers using the automatic
         ticket machine after conversion.   The survey
         found a number of serious disadvantages in the
         design and operation of London's one-man buses:
         the service for the passenger was slower and less
         convenient, and there were adverse effects on
         traffic conditions generally.

4.1.83   One-Man Operation in Municipal Transport. (1970)
         FISHWICK, F.
         Institute of Transport Journal. Vol.33. March 1970.
                                (pp. 413-425)

4.1.84   One-Man Operation of Buses.   [*Cost Savings from]
                                                    (1972)
         BROWN, R.H. and NASH, C.A.
         Journal of Transport Economics and Policy. Vol. VI.
         No. 3. September 1972. (pp. 281-284)

         The findings from an investigation of the trading
         results of municipal bus undertakings from 1964
         to 1969 are summarised in this article.   These
         showed an average saving of 13.7% on buses
         converted to one-man operation.

4.1.85   Passenger Mileage : Theory and Practice. (1977)
         MAW, J.R., BRADLEY, J. and BERMINGHAM, T.P.
         London Transport Executive. Marketing Memorandum
         M.60. June 1977. (8pp.)

         The development of a decision-making criterion
         based on passenger - mile generation is London
         Transport's response to the need for public

transport operators to channel available resources
into those areas where they will best meet
passenger requirements. This paper summarises
the theoretical background to the estimates of
passenger mileage change used in the evaluation
of proposals affecting passengers' journey time
or their waiting environment. The first part of
the paper presents and discusses the concept of
generalised cost. The second part describes how
changes in generalised cost lead to changes in
the volume of travel. It sets out the calculation
procedures by which proportional changes in demand
are estimated by using the elasticity of demand,
and by which these are converted into estimated
passenger miles generated. The final part of the
paper relates the theories and calculations to the
actual changes in personal travel habits that
cause the observed fluctuations in travel demand,
and offers various explanations for the way in
which these changes in travel pattern occur.

4.1.86   Passenger Miles. [*An Analysis of Trends in Bus]
                                                    (1974)
         TYSON, W.J.
         Journal of Transport Economics and Policy.
         Vol. Vlll. No.1 January 1974. (pp. 40-47)

         This article describes a means of deriving
         passenger-mileage statistics for bus operation
         essentially from operators' fare scales, and
         shows the application of the method described
         in an empirical study of changes in average
         journey length.   Passenger-mileage is a much
         more meaningful measure of transport demand than
         passenger journeys, but few operators measure it,
         changes in passenger numbers being the basis of
         many policy decisions on, for instance, fares
         increases.   A comparison of trends in the two
         sets of statistics showed a significant difference
         between them: while the number of trips had
         declined, average trip length had increased.
         These results are contrasted with figures for
         London Transport and for Great Britain as a whole.

4.1.87   Passenger Miles. [*Measuring Bus] (1977)
         TYSON, W.J.
         Paper read at Rural Transport Seminar held at
         the Polytechnic of Central London.   November
         1977. (pp. 59-71 of Seminar proceedings).

4.1.88   Passenger Transport Operations. (1974)
         THE CHARTERED INSTITUTE OF PUBLIC FINANCE AND
         ACCOUNTANCY.
         Recommendations on a Standard Financial Statement
         and Route Costing System.   April 1974.

4.1.89   Public Transport. [*Planning for]   (1976)
         WHITE, P.R.
         Hutchinson & Co. Ltd., The Built Environment
         Series, London. 1976. (224 pp.)

         This is a basic textbook on public transport
         planning, giving a factual account of public
         transport systems in Britain and setting out
         practical guidelines for the more efficient
         utilisation of existing resources in the
         industry, mainly through specific improvements in
         service quality at minimum cost.   The organisation
         and control of transport industries in Britain
         are described within the context of the existing
         legal framework.   The basic principles of the
         design of bus and coach systems and of rail and
         rapid transit systems are set out, and costing
         and pricing structures are described.   Urban
         network planning is discussed in relation to urban
         form and its evolution, and there is a brief
         description of transport planning in British
         new towns.   Rural transport planning and
         intercity public transport are also examined.   The
         major elements in current British policy and
         likely trends over the next few years are considered.
         The book concludes with a discussion of long-term
         policy options, particularly in relation to
         subsidies and other financial considerations, and
         external factors likely to affect future policy
         are outlined.   Selected references are provided
         at the end of each chapter.

4.1.90   Public Transport [*Planning for]: Variations on
         a Theme . (1977)
         HAMILTON, T.D. and Young, T.D.
         Surveyor. Vol. 150, No. 4456. 3rd November 1977.
                                       (pp. 15-16)

         Four approaches to transport planning are
         examined: rural experiments, joint area studies,
         the 'Oxford approach', and 'viable network planning'.
         These are evaluated against the three basic components
         of transport planning : geography, scheduling
         and finance.

4.1.91   Recruitment and Retention of Bus Drivers in
         London. [*Problems of]   (1974)
         WEDDERBURN D., HOLDER, A., and REEVES, T.
         Paper read at the PTRC Summer Annual Meeting.
         July 1974.   (pp. 67-92 of Proceedings)

4.1.92   Recruitment and Wastage among Bus Drivers
          in London.1968-1973.   [*Factors Affecting]   (1974)
          COLLINS, P.H. and BATES, J.J.
          Paper read at the PTRC Summer Annual Meeting.
          July 1974.   (pp.93-105 of Proceedings.)

4.1.93   Route Costing and the Rural Bus Problem. (1974)
          MOYES, A. and WILLIS, E.
          Paper read at the Institute of British Geographers'
          Annual Conference.   Transport Group Symposium.
          University of East Anglia.1974.

4.1.94   Route Costing for Planning Purposes.   [*Bus]
          (1974)
          ARTHUR ANDERSEN & Co.
          TRRL   Supplementary Report SR 108 UC. 1974. (152pp.)

4.1.95   Routeing Strategy for Urban Passenger Transport
          Services. (1975)
          PARKER, G.B.
          Paper read at 6th. Annual Symposium on Operating
          Public Transport.
          Department of Civil Engineering.   University of
          Newcastle Upon Tyne. 1975.

4.1.96   Routes. [*Planning Urban Bus] : a study for Coventry
          City Council (1973)
          DALY, A.J., PHILLIPS, G.W., ROGERS, K.G., and
          SMITH,P.J.
          Local Government Operational Research Unit (LGORU).
          Report C.149. 1973. (47pp.)
          Royal Institute of Public Administration.

4.1.97   Urban Passenger Surface Transport.[*Measuring
          and Improving Productivity in] (1971)
          LEGRIS, R.
          Paper No.5, read at U.I.T.P. Conference. Rome. 1971.

4.1.98   Urban Passenger Transport.   [*Problems of](1967)
          SHARP, C.
          Leicester University Press. 1967. (118pp.)

4.1.99   Work Attitudes of Bus Drivers and Conductors.(1976)
          MULDREW, V.
          Cranfield Institute of Technology. Centre for
          Transport Studies.
          Memorandum No. 3. 1976. (63 pp.)

          This report presents the results of a study of work
          attitudes of a small group of platform staff from
          the principal depot of a large subsidiary of the
          National Bus Company.   The aim of the survey
          was to identify preferences within the particular
          grades of work   (one-man operator driver, crew
          driver, conductor) in order to assess the.impact
          that Dial-a-Ride operation may have upon the
          labour market in the industry.   Semi-structured
          interviews were conducted which examined attitudes

towards current job, management, unions, vehicles, one-man operations, and the travelling public, and which also provided data on individuals' job history and personal backgrounds. The study concluded through the examination of "profiles" for each grade, that Dial-a-Ride driving should offer significant benefits for crew drivers providing there is some attempt to assess the value placed on contact with people.
Appendix E identifies areas for further research in the bus industry, including further quantitative work on recruitment and retention of platform staff, data requirements for on-going manpower assessments, the scope for worker participation, and the relationship between various fare systems and boarding delays on OMO buses. Other appendices include a copy of the interview schedule, and detailed schedules of wage rates and wastage at the depot studied.

4.1.100 <u>Work Attitudes of Taxi Drivers.</u> (1976)
MULDREW, V.
Cranfield Institute of Technology. Centre for Transport Studies.
Memorandum No. 2. 1976. (40 pp.)

Work attitudes of a group of taxi drivers in a medium-sized provincial taxi firm are examined qualitatively in order to establish their work preferences and attitudes to Dial-a-Ride driving. The study concludes that the drivers employed on full-time taxi work do not perceive Dial-a Ride as currently operated within their firm as representing any improvement over their present work. Recommendations are made for further research into the structure, operation and wage structures of the provincial taxi industry, both licensed and unlicensed. Appendices include a copy of the semi-structured interview schedule used in the survey; notes on wage structures in the taxi industry; suggestions for further research; and selected analyses from the interview survey.

GOVERNMENT REPORTS AND PUBLICATIONS

4.1.101 <u>Concessionary Travel Schemes in England and Wales.</u>
[*Report of the Survey of] (1977)
DEPARTMENT OF TRANSPORT : Economics Transport and General Division. January 1977. (22 pp. plus Appendices)

This document reports the results of a survey of local authorities in England and Wales carried out by a Government working party in 1975 to ascertain details of the various concessionary travel schemes operated and to provide information on which forecasts of expenditure

on concessionary travel can be based. The
survey procedure is described and copies of the
local authority questionnaires used are appended.
The survey revealed wide variations in the type
and generosity of schemes in operation for the
elderly and for blind and other disabled persons.
The report concludes with a brief consideration
of the total cost of concessionary travel schemes
for the years 1975/6 and 1976/7.

4.1.102 One-Man Operation of Buses. [*Working Group on]
                                                        (1971)
         DEPARTMENT OF THE ENVIRONMENT. 1971.

4.1.103 Report of the Committee on Rural Bus Services.
                                                     (1961)
         (Chairman: Professor D.T. Jack)
         MINISTRY OF TRANSPORT.
         H.M.S.O. January 1961.

4.1 *Subsidiary References.*

1.1 New Towns - Transport and Mobility.

1.1.3   Bus Transport in New Towns. (1959)
1.1.6   Demand Bus for a New Town. (1971)
1.1.12   Public Transport in its Exclusive Right of Way in Evry. (1973)
1.1.25   Transportation Planning for New Towns. (1969)
1.1.27   Urban Public Transport. (1971)

2.1 Runcorn.

2.1.2-9 and 2.1.11 : [Runcorn Busway.]

2.3 Telford.

2.3.1   Bus Services for Telford: Report of the short term bus study.
*   (1976)*
2.3.2   Master Plan Policy: Public Transport Study. Bulletin 3. (1970)
2.3.5   The Telford Short Term Bus Study. (1976)
2.3.7   Telford Transportation Study:
*   1. An aid to the preliminary evaluation of long-term public*
*   transport options. (1976)*
*   2. New techniques in the modelling of trip generation and modal*
*   split. (1976)*

2.4 Other New Towns.

2.4.11   Glenrothes Area Public Transport Study: Final Report. (1977)
2.4.15   Harlow Bus Study. Final Report. (1976)
2.4.20   The Harlow Dial-a-Bus Service: some operational statistics. (1976)
2.4.21   The Harlow Dial-a-Ride Experiment. (1975)
2.4.22   How was the Harlow Dial-a-Ride Service Planned? (1974)
2.4.23   Some Preliminary Results of the Harlow Dial-a-Bus Experiment. (1975)

2.4.42   *Milton Keynes - So Far So Good.* *(1977)*
2.4.54   *Promoting Public Transport in a New Town: the Superbus Experiment*
           in Stevenage. (1973)
2.4.55   *Some results from the Second Stevenage Superbus Experiment. (1974)*
2.4.58   *Stevenage Superbus Experiment. (1973)*
2.4.59   *Stevenage Superbus Experiment: Summary Report. (1974)*
2.4.60   *Stevenage Superbus Public Transport Demonstration. (1974)*

3.1   Studies of Modal Choice Behaviour and Value of Travel Time.

3.1.8   *A Behavioural Explanation of the Association Between Bus and*
           Passenger Arrivals at a Bus Stop. (1974)
3.1.24   *Journey Times by Bus and Car in Central London in 1972. (1973)*
3.1.25   *Journey Times by Car and Bus in Central London. (1964)*
3.1.26   *Journey Times by Car and Bus in Central London: 1977 re-survey.*
           (1977)
3.1.29   *Public Transport Journey Times in London, 1970. (1971)*
3.1.37   *Car and Bus Journeys to and from Central London in Peak Hours.*
           (1969)
3.1.58   *Perception of Public Transport by the User. (1970)*
3.1.81   *Car and Bus Travel in Central Edinburgh. (1968)*
3.1.82   *A Theoretical Study of Bus and Car Travel in Central London.*
           (1972)
3.1.85   *An Exploratory Comparison of the Advantages of Cars and Buses for*
           Travel in Urban Areas. (1964)
3.1.90   *A Study of Travel Times by Private and Public Transport in Greater*
           London. (1967)
3.1.113 *Waiting Times for Buses in Central London. (1966)*
3.1.114 *Bus Passenger Waiting Times in Central Areas. (1970)*
3.1.115 *Bus Passenger Waiting Times in Greater Manchester. (1974)*

3.2   Social Aspects of Mobility.

3.2.1   *Age Concern on Transport. (1973)*
3.2.11   *Bus Passes and the Elderly: A Need for More Informed Policy*
           Making? (1976)
3.2.12   *An Examination of the Extent and Welfare Implications of Bus Use*
           by the Elderly in Harlow. (1977)
3.2.13   *Free Travel for the Elderly in London - 1974 Survey. (1975)*
3.2.16   *Travel Patterns of Elderly People Under a Concessionary Fares*
           Scheme. (1977)
3.2.17   *Some Implications of Fare Concessions for the Elderly. (1975)*
3.2.19   *Transport and the Elderly: problems and possible action. (1977)*
3.2.23   *Estimating the Use of Free Bus Passes in Reading - survey of the*
           number of trips by pass-holders. (1973)
3.2.40   *Cutting the Cost of School Buses. (1970)*
3.2.41   *Journeys to School: a survey of Secondary Schools in Berkshire*
           and Surrey. (1977)
3.2.42   *Report to D.E.S. Working Party on School Transport. (1972)*
3.2.67   *Crime and Vandalism in Public Transportation. (1974)*
3.2.74   *Rate Fund Expenditure and Rate Calls in 1975-6. (1974)*
3.2.75   *School Transport. (1973)*
3.2.76   *Revised Arrangements for School Travel: Consultation Document.*
           (1975)

9.2 Bibliographies.

9.2.3   *Buses in Urban Areas. 1970-1976.*   *(1976)*
9.2.5   *Control and Organisation of Transport.*   *(1975)*
9.2.9   *Passenger Transport Interchange Between Inland Surface Modes - a*
                   bibliography for 1968-1973.   *(1974)*

9.4 Research Registers.

9.4.14   *London Transport Executive: Planning Research Division: Lists of*
            Research Reports, Research Memoranda and Technical Notes.
9.4.16   *National Bus Company: Research Bulletin and Annual Report and*
                                          Accounts.

9.5 Statistical Sources.

9.5.2   *British Railways Board Annual Report and Accounts.*
9.5.3   *Business Monitor M1: Number of Road Vehicles, New Registrations.*
                                                     (Monthly)
9.5.4   *Motor Transport: Bus and Coach Supplement.*
9.5.10   *Proposed Increase in London Taxicab Fares.*   *(1968)*
9.5.11   *Road Accidents in Great Britain.*   *(Annually)*
9.5.13   *Traffic Commissioners' Annual Reports.*
9.5.14   *Transport Statistics Great Britain.*   *(Annually)*

9.6 Other Sources.

9.6.1   *The Little Red Book.*   *(Annually)*
9.6.7   *U.K. Transport Organisations.*   *(1976)*

4.2 Marketing Approach.

This subsection consists of literature relevant to the application of marketing strategies to public transport. Over the past fifteen years or so transport policy-makers and planners have become increasingly conscious of the need to promote public transport and restrain private car usage in towns. It has also become clear that large-scale capital-intensive transport innovations based on advanced technologies are unlikely to play a rôle in urban areas in the short and medium-term future. Attention has turned instead towards management rather than investment for solutions to most urban transport and mobility problems. The Transport Act 1968 (7.1.74) required the National Bus Company, which operates buses in most new towns, to operate commercially. It also inaugurated organisational and institutional changes which were partly intended to facilitate the adoption of modern management methods, including marketing. Since then there have been some signs of official recognition of the potential rôle of marketing strategies in enabling operators to halt or reduce the decline of urban public transport and to improve the quality of service offered to the public, and - in the wider context - in helping to alleviate problems of peak hour traffic congestion in urban areas. Evidence presented to the HOUSE OF COMMONS EXPENDITURE COMMITTEE on Urban Transport Planning in 1972 (7.1.79) indicated that public transport operators should pay far more attention to the public present-ation, promotion and marketing of their services. The 'negative class image' of the bus was also referred to. Two years later the INDEPENDENT COMMISSION FOR TRANSPORT's report Changing Directions (7.1.3) pointed to the need for bus operators to obtain a much better understanding of their markets. The Commission recommended that service improvements be introduced which would be tailored to the needs of the market, as identi-fied by the application of market research techniques, and that these should be promoted far more vigorously and effect-ively than had previously been the practice in the industry. The adoption of such an approach by the operators of local passenger transport services outside the conurbation PTE's has been relatively slow, but some National Bus Company sub-sidiaries have recently indicated a greater readiness to apply modern marketing techniques.

The amount of literature available relating to the application of marketing principles to public transport operation in this country is comparatively scanty and much of it refers to particular aspects of operation, notably information provision, or specific case studies. A good deal of the relevant material is contained in reports or papers which are included in other parts of the bibliography and brought together in the list of subsidiary references at the end of this subsection. The references contained in this subsection include the following:-

- General studies of the application of marketing strategies to public transport operation.
- Market identification and passenger demand studies undertaken as marketing exercises.

- Monitoring studies of the effectiveness of operational changes.

- Studies of consumer attitudes to public transport,
  including research into the image of public transport
  in relation to other transport modes, and into
  operators' 'corporate image'.

- Descriptive studies of measures undertaken to
  publicise existing services or service changes,including
  information provision, and assessments of the
  effectiveness of such measures.

ittle British literature is available of a general and
ieoretical nature concerning the application of marketing
:rategies to public transport. The major exception is The
inagement of Urban Public Transport:a marketing perspective,
/ HOVELL, JONES and MORAN, published in 1975 (4.2.25),which
^esents a carefully argued case for the adoption by operators
)articularly the conurbation PTE's) of comprehensive marketing
.rategies as the basis of their passenger transport management.
ie approach described would involve the thorough investigation
: market needs, the development and introduction of 'packages'
' improvements designed to satisfy the needs of selected
irket segments, the vigorous promotion of these improvements
> the relevant target segments, and regular monitoring of
ieir effectiveness. BROWN has written papers on the marketing
: public transport services with particular reference to
>ndon Transport (4.2.31 and 4.2.34), and a recent paper by
.SLEY *considers the development of a public transport marketing
rategy for British new towns, with special reference to
ncorn, Skelmersdale and Telford. Most other general and
eoretical studies relate to the North American context.
rticularly useful references are LOVELOCK's comprehensive
udy of the application of marketing strategies to transport-
ion systems (4.2.38), the article by VANIER and WOTRUBA which
esents a marketing procedural model which can be used by
ssenger transport operators, and the issue of Transportation
search Record devoted to Transit Marketing (4.2.36). Some
neral background literature on marketing has also been
cluded in this subsection, including KOTLER's Marketing
nagement: Analysis, Planning and Control (4.2.32), which is
basic text on the theory and techniques of marketing management.

VELL, JONES and MORAN (4.2.25) have underlined the importance
thorough research by public transport operators into their
rkets as a preliminary to developing service improvements.
ndon Transport Executive have made considerable use of market
search techniques in this context. The report Towards a
scription of L.T's Markets (4.2.29) outlines the present
ructure of London Transport's travel markets and discusses
ends likely to cause changes in travel patterns in the area.

Marketing Public Transit - towards a strategy for new towns.
LESLEY, L.J.S.   (1978)
Paper read at International Conference on Public Transport
Systems in Urban Areas. Gothenburg. June 1978.

Over the past few years the Eastern Counties Omnibus Co. has carried out a series of market research surveys of travel patterns and demand, which have been used as a basis for reorganising services. The findings of one of these surveys are presented in the Report on a Market Research Survey into Transport Demand: Waveney Valley Area (3.1.65). More recently the Midland Red Bus Company has initiated a Market Analysis Project involving detailed studies of passenger demand and attitudes to travel on an area basis, the assessment of existing provision in each area, reshaping the services to match supply to demand, publicising and promoting the services, and monitoring the revised services for cost effectiveness.* KIMBERLEY's report on the rail travel market of the Telford area (2.3.8) considers likely future travel demand patterns and ways in which British Rail could develop its full market potential in the area. Many of the references in subsection 4.4 of the bibliography and some of those in the new towns sections (1.1 to 2.4) contain accounts of market research exercises undertaken as preliminaries to various experimental projects. The paper by HENSHER, SMITH, HOOPER and STANLEY (4.2.48) describes the procedures and findings of an empirical market segmentation study carried out in the Sydney Metropolitan Area in order to identify a suitable site for the introduction of transport improvements likely to reduce the generalised cost of travel for transport disadvantaged groups. Survey techniques relevant to market research and market segmentation studies are covered in subsections 8.1 and 8.3, and discussed in the introduction to subsection 8.1. The book by KOTLER (4.2.32) also contains chapters on Market Segmentation (Ch.6) and Market Measuring and Forecasting (Ch.7). Subsection 8.3 includes papers describing techniques used in studies of London Transport's demand and supply markets (8.3. 5-6) and in the London Transport Executive Minibus Research Programme (8.3. 15-17). Other methodological papers and reports on the measurement of demand for public transport services are included in subsection 8.3. General studies of passenger transport demand are contained in subsection 4.1.

London Transport Executive has also used consumer research methods, in particular the trade-off 'priority evaluation' technique, as an aid to decision-making in planning investments in service improvements. The methods and findings of surveys in which these techniques were used are presented in the reports Passenger Evaluation of Underground Improvement (4.2.42) and Bus Improvements Survey 1976 (4.1.8), and in

---

*A description of the background to the project and an outline of the approach adopted are included in the article Midland Red's Market Analysis Project. Omnibus Magazine. May/June 1978 (pp.61-68). In May 1978 the National Bus Company reported to the Select Committee on Nationalised Industries that the Market Analysis Project is to be extended over the whole of its territory during the next three years

the article <u>Priority Research Techniques Applied to Public Transport Investment</u>, by <u>HATCH and FLACK</u> (4.2.43).

Monitoring the effectiveness of new or improved services in terms of revenue, ridership, passenger satisfaction and overall changes in travel patterns is an important aspect of marketing in the passenger transport industry. The Midland Red Bus Company is currently monitoring revised patterns of services for cost-effectiveness in separate areas within its territory-including the Telford area - as part of its Market Analysis Project. Most monitoring studies carried out in this country, however, have been reported by researchers rather than by operators. The book by <u>HOVELL, JONES and MORAN</u> includes summary descriptions of a series of experimental service improvements carried out in Merseyside and at Bolton in order to assess the effect on modal choice of specific variables within the 'marketing mix'. Collection and analysis of pre-and post-change data on passengers and revenue were central to the methodology used, and in most cases data are compared with similar sets of data collected from control routes where no service changes had been implemented. Most other monitoring studies have been concerned with assessing the effectiveness of a whole 'package' of improvements or a complete new service rather than with attempting to isolate individual elements and measure their effect. The Stevenage Superbus service and a number of experimental dial-a-ride services have been closely monitored and well-documented: reports on these are included in the subsidiary references at the end of this subsection, under the headings 2.4, and in subsection 4.4. A study of an experimental countryside rail service in the Yorkshire Dales including investigations of travel patterns and passenger attitudes is described in the Transport and Road Research Laboratory report by <u>GRIGG and SMITH</u> (4.2.41). In the United States the effects of projects initiated under the Urban Mass Transportation Administration demonstration programme have been studied in detail. One of the best-documented of these is the Skokie Swift commuter rail service in Chicago on which a series of monitoring studies was carried out over a two year period to determine passenger characteristics, travel patterns in the area, and the changes in these arising from the introduction of the new service (4.4.45). Many of the service improvements which have been monitored involve promotional fare reductions or experimental fare structures. General literature on fares and elasticities is included in subsection 4.1.

This subsection contains several references relating to consumer attitudes towards attributes of public transport, including studies carried out in the United States reported by <u>HILLE</u> (4.2.9), <u>BALKUS</u> (4.2.7) and <u>NATIONAL ANALYSTS INC.</u> (4.2.6). The paper prepared by <u>TEHAN and WACHS</u> for the U.S. Department of Transportation Urban Mass Transportation Administration (4.2.44) discusses a marketing approach for improving the quality and image of public transport through the satisfaction of a set of basic human needs as identified from a review of psychological literature. A number of more general modal choice studies also contain information on attitudes toward public transport which is relevant to assessments of consumer demand. These include papers and reports by PAINE, NASH, HILLE and BRUNNER (3.1.15-16), BRUNNING (3.1.17), GOLOB, CANTY and GUSTAFSON (3.1.18), HENSHER (3.1.19 and 3.1.57), GOLOB and DOBSON (3.1.59), DOBSON and NICOLAIDIS (3.1.60), GOLOB, DOBSON and SHETH (8.1.19), and WILSON's book, Journey to Work: Modal Split (3.1.32). The studies by Paine et al, Golob et al, and Wilson are reviewed in Chapter 2 of The Management of Urban Public Transport: a marketing perspective, by HOVELL, JONES and MORAN (4.2.25). The paper Perception of Public Transport by the User by STARK (3.1.58) examines bus users' images of the bus and attitudes to bus reliability, routes and interchange, and makes comparisons with attitudes to other modes. BEIER's article Marketing Programs for Mass Transit describes an empirical study carried out in the Minneapolis - St. Paul metropolitan area in an attempt to identify consumer attitudes towards mass transit as a basis for developing marketing programmes to attract ridership. Research carried out at Newcastle Upon Tyne University aimed at identifying the image of public transport in two housing estates in the Teesside conurbation through indirect attitudinal survey techniques is described in the report by LESLEY (4.2.13).

Research into their corporate image and the projection of a unique and favourable image to the public are aspects of promotion which have until recently been largely neglected by most passenger transport operators in this country. More attention is now being paid by the larger operators to the attainment of a recognisable image through such techniques as standardisation of signs and liveries, but very little literature is available on passenger transport operators' corporate image in the wider context. The chapter by WORCESTER in the Consumer Market Research Handbook (4.2.11) gives a general background to the concept of corporate image and the rôle which corporate image research can play in company policy. Research exercises in this field carried out by London Transport Executive between 1974 and 1977 are summarised in the report by DAY (4.2.10), which reveals a largely unfavourable image for London Transport in relation to a number of other public sector organisations and some private sector companies.

The contribution which a co-ordinated and favourable local image for operators could make towards strengthening local identity in new towns is touched upon in LESLEY's paper Marketing Public Transit - towards a strategy for new towns, and (in relation to Telford) in COLIN BUCHANAN and PARTNERS' Report of the Short Term Bus Study (2.3.1). Under the Midland Red Bus Company's Market Analysis Project bus services in each

area in which the marketing approach has been applied have
been given a local 'brand name'(for example 'Reddibus'in
Redditch and 'Tellus' in Telford) aimed at giving the bus
services a local identity to stimulate the interest of the
travelling public and the enthusiasm of local management
and employees.

The vigorous promotion of service improvements and of existing
services is a central aspect of a marketing approach to public
transport. HOVELL, JONES and MORAN (4.2.25) have categorised
the two main aims of advertising in the passenger transport
industry as making available service information and providing
persuasive communications in favour of public transport.
In practice most of the advertising effort in the industry,
particularly by bus operators, has been directed towards
providing service information, often in relation to service
changes. The literature available on the subject of passenger
transport publicity and advertising can be divided into studies
of passenger information needs and usage in relation to
provision; descriptions of advertising and promotional campaigns;
and attempts to assess the effectiveness of such campaigns.

The dissertation by TRENCHARD (4.2.16) describes a detailed
study of passenger information requirements and the role of
information provision in successful rail-bus interchange.
Several studies of passenger information requirements and
usage have been carried out by London Transport Executive:
the report by BOTTOM (4.2.17) describes the findings of a
survey of information required by bus passengers from conductors
in Central London; the report on the Underground Information
Survey by BRADLEY and MAW (4.2.21) describes a survey of
passenger use of and attitudes to information provision
on the London Underground which also attempted to identify
passenger priorities for improved information provision. The
accompanying Technical Note by MAW (4.2.22) outlines the way
in which estimates of passenger mileage likely to be generated
by the various kinds of improvement offered were derived from
the survey data.

A number of case studies of service improvements or innovations
include descriptive accounts of advertising and promotional
techniques used. The large scale publicity campaign which
accompanied the opening and running of the Chicago Transit
Authority's Skokie Swift commuter rail shuttle service was
a particularly important element in the success of the service:
20% of the first year's projected revenue was budgeted for
promotional purposes. The report Skokie Swift - the Commuters'
Friend by BUCK (4.4.45) gives a detailed account of the
promotional activities undertaken to publicise the service
and increase its attractiveness. In this country advertising
and public relations work undertaken in conjunction with the
Stevenage Superbus service is described in the Summary Report
of the Stevenage Superbus Experiment (2.4.59). Recent
publicity used to promote service reorganisation in the Midlands
is outlined in the article Midland Red's Market Analysis Project
Omnibus Magazine. May/June 1978).

Relatively little literature is available which attempts to assess the impact of advertising in the passenger transport industry, or to measure its effectiveness in terms of increase ridership or revenue. In most cases where advertising has been used its function has been to publicise a new or improve service and it has not been possible to isolate the effect of the advertising from that of the service change itself. Interesting exceptions are reported by Lesley and by Hovell, Jones and Moran. The University of Newcastle Upon Tyne repor by LESLEY (4.2.2) describes the methods and findings of a 'controlled experiment' to try and determine the effect on bus usage of advertising bus services where no change to fare or services was carried out. HOVELL, JONES and MORAN (4.2.25 have reported a monitoring study of an experimental promotion of an off-peak rail fare reduction on the Rock Ferry to Chest line which attempted to measure separately the effects on passenger demand of fare reduction and of promotion. Minimal promotion accompanied the fare reduction at one station and medium intensity promotion was carried out in the catchment area of a second station. A third station, with no fare reduction, was monitored as a control. The same authors have described studies of the effectiveness of advertising in stimulating passenger trips in Washington D.C. (4.2.15) and in Allegheny County (4.2.1) in the United States. The study reported by BRUCE and ENNOR (4.2.20) included an attempt to assess the success (in terms of public awareness) of a campaign aimed at publicising the takeover in 1973 of Sunderland Corporation bus services by Tyneside PTE, and the provision of a new timetable.

4.2.1 Advertising and Promotion Demonstration Program. (1970)
PORT AUTHORITY OF ALLEGHENY COUNTY and TRANSPORT
RESEARCH INSTITUTE OF CARNEGIE-MELLON UNIVERSITY.
PAMTD - 7 PITTSBURGH. 1970.

The report describes a demonstration project in which
the effectiveness of advertising in stimulating off-
peak riding was studied. Following household distribution of maps and literature there was a 3½% increase
in revenue, and the costs of the campaign were recovered
within six months. Radio and television promotion
were later used, but had little effect on ridership.

4.2.2 Advertising Bus Services in Two Housing Estates in
the Teesside Conurbation. [*The Effect of] (1974)
LESLEY, L.J.S.

Action Report No.5 (Report to Cleveland County Department of Engineering). University of Newcastle Upon Tyne.
Transport Operations Research Group. August 1974.
(7 pp. plus appendices).

Previous advertising of local bus services has been
associated with alterations in the services, so it has
not been possible to isolate the effect on ridership
of the advertising itself. This report describes a
'controlled experiment' to try and determine the effect
of advertising on local bus usage in two housing estates
in the Teesside Conurbation, in a context of no change
to bus services or to fares during the survey period.
Promotional leaflets were delivered to houses on the
estates and analyses were made of bus ridership levels
and bus revenue data. These showed no significant
change during the survey period, indicating that the
advertising had had no effect on bus usage. It is
concluded that future studies of this kind should first
aim at identifying areas of steady bus demand which
would be the best sites for experimental work since any
change could be readily detected. Where there was a
high variability of demand, as in the estates surveyed,
it would be necessary to collect ridership data over a
longer period.

4.2.3 Attractiveness of Public Transport. [*Increasing the]
BENNETT, R.F.   (1971)
Paper read at U.I.T.P. Conference. Rome. 1971.

4.2.4 Bus Promotion. (1975)
PARKER, G.B.
Paper read at a Conference on Transport for Society.
The Institute of Civil Engineers. 1975.

The paper reviews the background to the present position
of bus services in Britain, examines recent efforts to
promote bus transport and indicates the most urgent
and promising areas of bus promotion in the future.
Promotion, through the advancement of the science and
practice of bus operation, is advocated and a number
of fundamental questions concerning bus operation are

examined. These include the rôle of buses, the financing of bus operation, the estimation and stimulation of demand, the costing of bus operations, the style of operation, the rôle of traffic management and restraint, and the relationship between bus promotion and town planning. The commercial and social rôles of bus transport are also discussed. A flexible and innovative approach to marketing and operating is proposed, with stress on the need for greater integration of bus and town planning procedures.

4.2.5 Communications with Passengers. (1976)
CLAYTON, D.G.E
Chartered Institute of Transport Journal. Vol.37.No.3. March 1976 (pp.81-85).

A review of some of the gaps in the information required by passengers for comfortable and satisfactory journey-making.

4.2.6 Commuter Attitudes Towards Rapid Transit Systems.
[*A Survey of] Vol.2. (1963)
NATIONAL ANALYSTS INC.
For the National Capital Transportation Agency (now the Washington Metropolitan Area Transit Authority).
March 1963.

4.2.7 Consumer Motivation.[*Transportation Issues in] (1973)
BALKUS, K.
Highway Research Record No.439. Highway Research Board. Washington D.C. 1973. (pp.1-9)

This paper concerns an investigation of consumer motivation regarding transportation issues. Instead of isolating transportation from the cultural context the study explores the patterns of consumer motivation regarding all goods and services and then observes how the transportation issues appear among them, thus providing a more comprehensive view of the issue. The study employed the Delphi technique for obtaining information from a group of experts.

4.2.8 Consumer Response to Public Transport Improvements and Car Restraint: some practical findings. (1977)
HEGGIE, I.G.
Policy and Politics. Vol.5. No.4. June 1977.(pp.47-69)

The paper reviews studies of and measures to encourage public transport use and to restrain cars in the U.K. These are shown to have been generally unsuccessful, largely as a result of over-estimating the effects of the growth of car ownership and under-estimating the effects of rapidly rising public transport fares.

4.2.9 Consumer Viewpoint.[*Studying Transportation from the]: some recommendations. (1967)
HILLE, S.J.
Maryland University. PB 176484. September 1967.

4.2.10 Corporate Image Research. (1977)
DAY, D.J.
London Transport Executive. Market Development Office. Marketing Memorandum M.57. April 1977.(5pp.)

The report summarises the results of several market
research exercises carried out between 1974 and 1977
to identify the public's image of London Transport.
Group discussions and interview surveys were conducted
in 1974 to compare London Transport's image with those
of other public sector bodies and of private sector
companies.
A consistent and largely unfavourable picture emerged.
London Transport was generally seen as less efficient
and less advanced in the use of modern technology and
equipment than private sector companies and most other
public sector organisations. Its reputation for staff
friendliness and helpfulness was particularly poor.
Comparison of the results of surveys carried out in
1976/7 with the earlier surveys revealed shifts in
public attitudes to staff payment and to quality of
service. London Transport staff were seen as being
poorly paid in 1974, but reasonably well paid in 1976;
and an increasing proportion of people thought that the
quality of service was deteriorating. The main reasons
for deficiencies in the bus services in 1976 were seen
to be insufficient management control, staff shortages
and traffic congestion.

2.11   Corporate Image Research. (1972)
       WORCESTER, R.M.
       In: 'The Consumer Market Research Handbook' (ed.
       R.M. Worcester) McGraw-Hill Book Company (U.K.) Ltd.,
       1972. (pp. 505-518)
       (see ref. 8.1.27 below)

The concept of corporate image is defined as:..."the
net result of interaction of all experiences, impressions,
beliefs, feelings, and knowledge people have about a
company". The role and purpose of corporate image
research are discussed in the context of four major
categories of image influence,viz:- the image of the
product class as a whole; the image of the brand within
the product class; the image of users of the brand; and
the corporate image of the company behind the brand. The
major ingredients of a good corporate image emerging from
public opinion surveys are a company's reputation as
a good employer and being fair to its employees, and
the high standard, quality and reliability of its products.

The influence of image on behaviour is examined and
illustrated, and some indication is given of possible
practical applications of corporate image research
findings to company policy. The principal methods
of research in this field are discussed and the
importance of examining a company's public image
in relation to that of other companies rather than in
isolation is stressed.   Employee attitude surveys
are an important aspect of corporate image research
and methods of conducting these are examined and
compared. It is concluded that although relatively
little attention has so far been paid to corporate
image in this country, research in this field is becoming
increasingly important in helping management to
understand and to evaluate its significance and
effects.

4.2.12   Image. [*Improving the] (1974)
          LESLEY, L.J.S.
          Motor Transport. Bus and Coach Supplement.
          March 1st 1974.

          The scope for advertising local bus services is
          examined. A Newcastle Upon Tyne University survey
          in Sunderland indicated that over one-third of car
          users interviewed did not know about public
          transport adequacy and would presumably be responsive
          to more information about public transport services.
          Most public transport advertising is directed towards
          people who already use the services. Of that
          directed towards non-users, most is concerned with
          long-distance rail or coach services. There is
          virtually no advertising of local services directed
          towards non-users yet most journeys are short-distance
          and start or end at home. There should therefore be
          considerable scope for advertising local bus services
          by house-to-house distribution of promotional
          material. If operators used ½% of turnover to
          promote local services, public transport's image
          would be improved and the increased patronage should
          pay for the cost.

4.2.13   Image of Public Transport in Two Housing Estates in
          the Teesside Conurbation. [*The] (1974)
          LESLEY, L.J.S.
          Action Report No.4. (Report to Cleveland. County
          Department of Engineering). University of Newcastle
          Upon Tyne. Transport Operations Research Group.
          August 1974 (7pp. plus appendices).

          This report describes an attempt to measure attitudes
          to users of various transport modes among residents
          of two housing estates in the Teesside conurbation by
          using an attitude test known as the 'Compound Scale
          of Facial Attributes'. A series of schematic
          faces was used, calibrated from the results of
          field experiments by the Department of Psychology at
          Newcastle Upon Tyne University for five different
          attributes: happiness, age, good looks, intelligence
          and likeability. The faces were used in interviews
          with residents and the results analysed to identify
          respondents' images of users of various forms of
          transport. Women were shown to make more distinctions
          than men between users of different transport modes.
          In general, public transport users were less
          favourably viewed than were private transport users.

          The test was found to be simple to administer, the
          response rate was relatively high and the results
          showed an overall consistent pattern. However,
          whether it could usefully be applied on a wider scale
          is not clear since the calibration of the faces may
          need to be altered from area to area.

4.2.14   Importance of Service Features to Passengers and
          the Effects on Traffic. [*The] (1966)
          RESEARCH PROJECTS LTD.
          London Transport Board. October 1966.

4.2.15   Information Aids. [*Transit] (1969)
          WASHINGTON METROPOLITAN AREA TRANSIT COMMISSION
          and SIDNEY HOLLANDER ASSOC.
          INT-MTD-10. 1969.

          The report describes a demonstration project
          aimed at testing the hypothesis that informational
          aids would increase passenger trips, improve
          attitudes towards public transport and improve
          route knowledge in Washington D.C.

4.2.16   Information and its use in rail-bus interchange.
          [*Passenger] (1975)
          TRENCHARD, M.R.
          Unpublished M.Sc.Dissertation. University of
          Newcastle Upon Tyne. 1975. (150pp.)

          This study looks at passenger information requirements
          and assesses the importance of their relationship with
          the journey process.   General introductory sections
          define the parameters of passenger information, examine
          why it is necessary and establish criteria for when and
          where it should be provided.   The journey process
          including interchange and the types of passenger involved
          with this journey process are defined.   A detailed study
          of the provision of passenger information within the
          rail-bus interchange process is described, an assessment
          being made of a selection of stations where rail-bus
          interchange occurs, to try and establish the rôle that
          passenger information plays in successful interchange.
          The rôle of the operator in information-provision is also
          examined.   Recommendations are made for future inform-
          ation provision to benefit the user, and for further
          research into passenger information and its effects on
          the utility of interchange.

4.2.17   Information. [*Conductors and Passenger] (1975)
          BOTTOM, C.G.
           London Transport Executive. Operational Research
          Memorandum M.309. November 1975. (7pp.)

          Bus conductors in Central London answer passengers'
          questions and have to some extent a public relations
          function for London Transport. This memorandum
          describes a survey of six crew-operated routes
          covering Inner London to assess the extent of
          passenger demand for information by determining
          the times and places questions were asked, the
          nature of the questions and answers, and the amount
          of delay incurred. The objective of the
          investigation was to try and estimate the effects
          on operability of one-man buses in Central London

of the conductors' information-providing function.
The survey showed that overall about half the
questions were asked from the kerb, one-quarter
from the platform and one-quarter by passengers
already riding on the bus. Most questions required
confirmation of existing knowledge rather than new
information and needed only very brief answers.
Two-thirds of the questions asked before or during
boarding were not considered to obstruct boarding.
The memorandum concludes that questions were likely
to delay one-man operated buses only occasionally in
Central London, and that particularly sensitive
routes could not be identified. Even if the effect
of OMO conversion were to double the obstructions
to boarding this would be most unlikely to increase
journey times by more than 1%. Improved publicity
at stops and inside buses and the use of a public
address system inside the buses could help to satisfy
passenger demand for information and reduce the number
of questions asked.

4.2.18 Information Control as a Power Resource.(1972)
PETTIGREW, A.M.
Sociology. Vol.6. 1972.(pp.187-204)

4.2.19 Information Problems [*Urban Railway Passenger]: A
Case Study. (1976)
OSBORN, S.E.
Chartered Institute of Transport Journal. Vol.37.
No.6.Sept. 1976.(pp.175-177)

The results of a survey conducted by an Underground
railway guard on the Bakerloo Line between April
and October, 1975.

4.2.20 Information [*Public Awareness of Transport Agencies
and]: a small-scale study in Sunderland.(1976)
BRUCE, S. and ENNOR, P.D.
Working Paper No. 17. University of Newcastle Upon
Tyne. Transport Operations Research Group. March
1976.(32pp).

The paper describes a study made in Sunderland between
March and August 1973 to gauge public awareness of
local public transport operators and of a new timetable, in a changing situation. One interview survey
was carried out before, and three after, the
takeover of Sunderland Corporation green buses by
the Tyneside P.T.E. There was an accompanying
publicity campaign within Sunderland and on the
buses and a widely advertised pocket timetable was
distributed through local shops. The surveys
indicated limited success in impressing the new
operator's image on public consciousness. Before
the takeover three-quarters of respondents correctly
answered that the green buses were owned by

Sunderland Corporation. Twenty weeks after it over one-half still thought that the green buses were Corporation-owned, only 28% correctly knew the name of the new operator, and less than one-quarter could identify correctly the PTE's symbol. Awareness of the new operator was consistently higher among respondents who had had maximum exposure to the publicity (those living within Sunderland and those travelling regularly on the green buses). The publicity for the new timetable also appeared to have had some effect. The proportion who said that they would use a timetable to find out details of unfamiliar bus routes and times, although not high, showed a definite increase after the publicity campaign and again was higher among those most exposed to the advertising.

21   Information Survey. [*Underground] (1975)
      BRADLEY, J. and MAW, J.R.
      London Transport Executive. Marketing Office.
      Marketing Memorandum M.35. October 1975. (5pp.)

This report describes a survey carried out to determine passengers' use of and attitudes to the provision of information on the Underground.

Respondents were asked about their timetable knowledge and usage, then about their opinions on fixed information about routes and station layouts, and on information as to the state of the service. Respondents were also invited to 'spend' ten points between five investment options relating to Underground travel, including information provision. The results showed that passengers were reasonably satisfied with existing information on routes and station layouts but would like more widespread provision of timetable boards, especially at stations with infrequent services. They would also like a much greater use of public address systems both on trains and at stations, particularly for providing information about unexpected delays.

2.22 Information. [*The Benefits of Improving Railway]
      (1976)
      MAW J.R.
      London Transport Executive. Marketing Office. Marketing
      Technical Note MTN 8. August 1976. (6pp.).

This technical note describes the method by which estimates of passenger mileage generation were derived from London Transport's survey of the usefulness of the various types of information available on the Underground. An appendix sets out for individual stations the traffic generation estimates for the main kinds of improvement offered.

4.2.23 Information to Bus Passengers. [*The Use of Computers for Providing] (1975)
WREN, M.B.
London Transport Executive. Operational Research Memorandum M304. January 1975. (8pp.)

This memorandum describes an initial investigation into the possibility of providing improved information to bus passengers on a large scale using computerised techniques. It concludes that computers would seem to have considerable potential in the provision of bus information, particularly in the production of bus maps and bus stop displays. Further investigation into the costs and benefits involved is recommended.

4.2.24 Management of Innovation. [*The] (1961)
BURNS, T. and STALKER, G.M.
Tavistock Publications. 1961.

4.2.25 Management of Urban Public Transport [*The] : a marketing perspective. (1975)
HOVELL, P.J., JONES, W.H. and MORAN, A.J.
Saxon House/Lexington Books (D.C.Heath Ltd.) (263pp.)

The authors present the 'marketing mix' as the keystone of their management philosophy for public transport. This involves a combination of detailed market research to ascertain consumers' travel needs, the development of a 'package' of satisfactions to meet selected consumers' needs, and vigorous promotion of any changes introduced. In Part I public transport is set in the environmental framework. Trends towards the dispersal of urban form and functions are examined, their implications discussed, and a case presented for political intervention to curb these trends. The problems of public transport in major urban areas since 1950 are studied in the context of the dispersal trends. Factors affecting the demand for travel and modal choice are examined and the future of public transport in relation to relevant technological changes and political attitudes is briefly reviewed. In Part II the strategic and marketing activities of the British PTEs are described and evaluated, with comparisons from 28 Metropolitan are from North America and Europe. The nature of marketing and its rôle in public transport are outlined Recommendations are made for the integration of marketing with the corporate, transport and operational planning functions and for the most effective organisational structure options for accommodating these functions. Part III identifies ways in which public transport operators can develop more competitive and professional services. An analysis is made of relevant secondary data, drawing from market research surveys and demand modelling

exercises concerned with establishing passenger
priority evaluations, and from the published findings
of (mainly U.S.) demonstration projects. Primary data
is then presented from a number of experimental
projects carried out in the Merseyside and Manchester
areas which involved the main elements of the
'marketing mix' and represent the practical application
of the market research-based methodology described by
the authors. The market implications of the
secondary and primary research findings are discussed
and set in the context of a total strategy which
also embraces the political and organisational aspects.
The book includes an extensive bibliography of
publications relevant to the marketing of public
transport.

4.2.26   Managing a Transport Business. (1963)
         BARRY, W.S.
         George Allen & Unwin Ltd. London. 1963. (210pp.)

         See Ch. XVI (pp. 162-176): Marketing Management.

         Differences between transport marketing and classical
         marketing are outlined, and mechanical and economic
         aspects of public transport marketing are discussed
         in this chapter.

4.2.27   Market Analysis for the National Bus Company. (1973)
         KNIGHT, D., SLEVIN, R. and BULL, H.C.
         Cranfield Institute of Technology. Centre for
         Transport Studies. 1973.

4.2.28   Market Information. [*Better Management of] (1966)
         UHL, K.P.
         Business Horizons. Vol.9. Spring 1966. (pp.75-81)

4.2.29   Markets. [*Towards a Description of L.T's.] (Undated)
         LONDON TRANSPORT EXECUTIVE. Marketing Office. (8pp.)

         This paper outlines the present structure of London
         Transport's travel markets and describes the way in
         which passengers react to changes in the cost of travel
         by transferring between modes or markets.   It also
         summarises underlying social and economic trends in
         London which are gradually changing travel patterns
         and habits, with particular reference to population
         trends and associated changes in the level of economic
         activity, and to changes in the extent of car
         ownership and use.

         In discussing London Transport's travel market the
         paper identifies three separate markets: the Central
         Area Market (trips wholly contained within the Central
         Area - 12% of total trips); the Suburban Market
         (trips within and between non-Central Area sectors

- 80% of total trips) and the Radial Market (trips from non-Central Area zones to the Central Area - 18% of total trips). Detailed analyses, including modal splits, are presented for each market.

4.2.30   Marketing Concept to Urban Passenger Transport. [*Applying the] (1969)
HOVELL, P.J.
British Journal of Marketing. No.3. Summer 1969. (pp. 152-163)

4.2.31   Marketing in London Transport. (1973)
BROWN, A.C.N.
Paper read at PTRC Meeting at the University of Sussex. January 1973.

4.2.32   Marketing Management: Analysis, Planning and Control. (1st ed. 1967, 2nd ed. 1973)
KOTLER, P.
Prentice-Hall Inc.New Jersey.1967 and 1973.(2nd ed.885pp.

This book is a basic text on marketing management, incorporating the quantitative and behavioural tools, concepts and models designed to improve marketing decision-making.   Section II, entitled 'Analyzing Marketing Opportunities' (pp.51 - 228), includes chapters on Market Segmentation (Chapter 6, pp.165 -191) and Market Measurement and Forecasting (Chapter 7, pp. 192 - 228).

4.2.33   Marketing Management. [*Motivational Research and] (1957)
NEWMAN, J.W.
Harvard University Press. 1957.

4.2.34   Marketing of Public Transport Services. [*The Development and] (1973)
BROWN, A.C.N.
Paper read at the Symposium on Promoting Public Transport. University of Newcastle Upon Tyne. April 1973.

4.2.35   Marketing Programs for Mass Transit. (1972)
BEIER, F.J.
Traffic Quarterly. Vol.26. No.4. October 1972. (pp. 533-545)

4.2.36   Marketing. [*Transit] (1976)
TRANSPORTATION RESEARCH BOARD
Transportation Research Record No.590.   Transportation Research Board. Washington D.C. 1976.

4.2.37   Marketing Urban Mass Transit. (1965)
SCHNEIDER, L.M.
Harvard University Press. 1965.

4.2.38   Marketing Urban Transit. [*Consumer Oriented Approaches
         to] (1973)
         LOVELOCK, C.H.
         Graduate School of Business.   Stanford University,
         California.   P.B. 220   781.   March 1973. (425pp.)

         This paper discusses the application of marketing
         strategies to transportation systems and presents
         evidence to suggest that relatively inexpensive
         marketing and communications strategies might be
         effective in stimulating use of public transport.

4.2.39   Mass Transit: devising a research-based marketing
         plan. (1977)
         VANIER, D.J. and WOTRUBA, T.R.
         Transportation Research.   Vol.11.   No.4. August 1977.
         (pp. 245-253)

         This study presents a marketing procedural model that
         can be operationally used by marketing managers.   The
         model enables the user to assess his company's perform-
         ance on the various attributes of the marketing mix.
         It is applied here specifically to mass transit and
         is tested empirically.   Within this context it permits
         transit marketing to aim at increasing usage by existing
         passengers and at attracting new users.   The article
         describes research conducted under the auspices of the
         United States Urban Mass Transportation Administration
         and a bus operator in a large metropolitan area in the
         south western U.S.A. using matched samples of bus riders
         and non-riders.

4.2.40   Mix of Demands. [*The] (1972)
         KULASH, D.J.
         Urban Institute Working Paper.   708-67.
         Washington D.C.   March 1972.

4.2.41   Opinion Survey of the Yorkshire Dales Rail Services
         in 1975. [*An] (1977)
         GRIGG, A.O. and SMITH, P.G.
         TRRL Report   LR 769. November 1977. (20pp.)

         In 1975 the Transport and Road Research Laboratory
         monitored the use of an experimental countryside rail
         service - Dales Rail - undertaken by the Yorkshire
         Dales National Park Committee.   This involved the
         re-opening of five disused stations between Settle
         and Appleby for charter train services with connecting
         buses on certain weekends between May and September.
         The report presents and discusses the findings of four
         questionnaire surveys carried out among car drivers,
         walkers and rail passengers to assess people's
         attitudes to the service.   The survey indicated that
         Dales Rail was going some way towards meeting a
         transport demand both from those who had no alternative
         form of transport and from those who preferred to

leave their cars at home.   The attitudes of people
using the service to travel out of the Dales suggested
a social need for a service of this type.

4.2.42   Passenger Evaluation of Underground Improvements. (1976
         MAW, J.R. and BRADLEY, J.
         London Transport Executive.   Market Development Office.
         Greater London Intelligence Journal No.37. December 197(
         (pp.28-31)
         (see also ref. 4.2.43 and 4.2.47 below)

         This paper summarises the methods and results of three
         surveys undertaken by Opinion Research Centre for
         London Transport in 1973, 1974 and 1975.   The surveys
         were carried out to estimate the relative value for
         money of various postulated improvements to Underground
         travel, using the 'priority evaluation' technique in
         which respondents were asked to choose between competin(
         projects within an overall financial constraint.   The
         surveys revealed considerable support for updating the
         Underground and improving the services and facilities
         generally, and there were indications that improved
         standards would generate additional journeys.   However
         demand for individual improvements varied considerably
         between stations depending on local conditions and
         passengers' perception of the quality of service offere(
         there.   A selective approach would therefore be
         required in planning and implementing improvements.
         The paper concludes by indicating ways in which the
         results of this research are being applied by London
         Transport in planning improvements to the Underground
         system.

4.2.43   Priority Research Techniques Applied to Public
         Transport Investment.   (1974)
         HATCH, D. and FLACK, M.
         Journal of the Market Research Society. Vol.16.
         No.1   January 1974.   (pp.1 - 11)
         (see also ref. 4.2.42 above)

         This article describes an attempt to develop and apply
         consumer preference and priority techniques so that the
         allocation of resources to alternative public transport
         improvements could take account of the priorities of
         passengers.   The example of research on the London
         Underground railway system is used.

4.2.44   Psychological Needs in Mass Transit. [*The Rôle of] (197
         TEHAN, C. and WACHS, M.
         University of California, Los Angeles, School of
         Architecture and Urban Planning.   Prepared for the U.S.
         Department of Transportation,   Urban Mass Transportatior
         Administration.   December 1972.

This paper decribes a review of recent psychological
literature which was used to identify a set of basic
human needs which could be applied to improve the image
and quality of mass transit. The marketing of a
psychological approach so as to maximize the attractiveness of public transport is discussed.

4.2.45   Reinforcement Procedure on Bus Ridership. [*Effects
         of a Token] (1974)
         EVERETT, P.B., HAYWARD, S.C. and MEYERS, A.W.
         Journal of Applied Behavior Analysis. Vol.7. No. 1
         1974. (pp. 1 - 9)

4.2.46   Reinforcement Procedure to Increase Bus Ridership.
         [*The Use of the] (1973)
         EVERETT, P.B.
         Paper read at the 81st Annual Convention of the
         American Psychological Association, 1973. (Vol.8,
         pp. 897-898 of Proceedings).

4.2.47   Traffic Generation Estimates for the Station
         Improvement Programme. (1977)
         BRADLEY, J., MAW, J.R. and MUIR, R.M.
         London Transport Executive, Marketing Office.
         Marketing Technical Note MTN 10. July 1977. (8pp.)
         (see also ref. 4.2.42 above).

This technical note outlines the method used to
calculate estimates of increased traffic generation
from passengers' evaluation of Underground improvements,
as indicated in three surveys carried out between
1973 and 1975.

4.2.48   Transport Improvement Proposals. [*An Approach to
         Developing] (1976)
         HENSHER, D.A., SMITH, R.A., HOOPER, P.G. and
         STANLEY, J.K.
         Commonwealth Bureau of Roads. Occasional Paper
         No.2. 1976. (128pp.)

The paper presents a systematic planning approach
for identifying deficiencies in urban public
transport and developing remedial improvements.
Sydney is used as a case study and the paper describes
the procedures and findings of an empirical market
segmentation study undertaken to identify the ranking
of all urban locations in the Sydney Metropolitan
Area with respect to transport service, and the
selection of transport/location disadvantaged groups
of travellers. A particular travel corridor was
identified which had a sufficient number of work
journeys to justify an investigation of transport
improvements likely to meet the criterion of reducing
the generalised cost of travel for the transport
disadvantaged groups. Cost benefit and financial
analyses of the proposed improvements are set out
to assess their impact on consumers and operators.

4.2 Subsidiary References.

1.1 New Towns - Transport and Mobility.

1.1.6   Demand Bus for a New Town. (1971)
1.1.15   Public Transportation and the Needs of New Communities. (1972)
1.1.21   Transportation for a New Town. (1971)
1.1.23   Transportation Innovations in New Communities Abroad. (1973)
1.1.26   Urban Cluster Villages. (1976)

2.3 Telford.

2.3.1   Bus Services for Telford: Report of the short term bus study.
          (1976)
2.3.8   Telford - Whose Opportunity? An Appraisal of Changes in the Rail
          Travel Market of the Telford Area. (1978)

2.4 Other New Towns

2.4.11   Glenrothes Area Public Transport Study: Final Report. (1977)
2.4.15   Harlow Bus Study. Final Report. (1976)
2.4.54   Promoting Public Transport in a New Town: the Superbus Experiment
          in Stevenage. (1973)
2.4.58   Stevenage Superbus Experiment. (1973)
2.4.59   Stevenage Superbus Experiment: Summary Report. (1974)

3.1 Studies of Modal Choice Behaviour and Value of Travel Time.

3.1.15   Consumer Attitudes toward Auto versus Public Transport Alternative
          (1969)
3.1.16   Consumer Conceived Attributes of Transportation: An Attitude Stud
          (1967)
3.1.17   Measuring and Interpreting Consumer Preferences. (1970)
3.1.18   An Analysis of Consumer Preferences for a Public Transportation
          System. (1972)
3.1.19   Consumer Preferences in Urban Trip-Making. (1974)
3.1.20   Consumer Response to Public Transport Improvements and Car Restrai
          some practical findings. (1977)
3.1.41   Modal Choice and the Value of Travel Time. (1976)
3.1.53   Report of a Study into the Motivation and Attitudes of Passengers
          and Potential Passengers of London Transport Buses. (1968)
3.1.58   Perception of Public Transport by the User. (1970)
3.1.61   A Pilot Study of Relationships between Socio-Economic Factors, User
          Attitudes and Preferences, and Urban Transportation System Attribut
          (1969
3.1.65   Report on a Market Research Survey into Transport Demand: Waveney
          Valley Area. (1976)

3.2 Social Aspects of Mobility.

3.2.49   Some Social Aspects of Public Passenger Transport. (1977)

4.1 Public Transport - Operational Aspects.

4.1.2   Bradford Bus Study: Final Report. (1976)
4.1.8   Bus Improvement Survey, 1976. (London Transport, 1977)

8.3.8	Passenger Transport Demand in Urban Areas: Methodology for analysing and forecasting. (1976)
8.3.9	Demand Responsive Diversions on a Rural Bus Service. (1975)
8.3.27	Spatial Orientation in a Subway System. (1976)
8.3.29	Successive Overlays - a Small City Transit Surveying Process. (1974)

9.1 Journals.

9.1.44	European Journal of Marketing. (Quarterly)
9.1.46	Journal of Advertising Research (Six times a year)
9.1.47	Journal of Applied Psychology. (Six times a year)
9.1.48	Journal of Marketing. (Quarterly)
9.1.49	Journal of Marketing Research. (Quarterly)
9.1.54	Psychological Review. (Six times a year)
9.1.55	Public Opinion Quarterly (Quarterly)

9.2 Bibliographies.

9.2.1	Annotated bibliography of the application of behavior and attitude research to transportation system planning and design. (1976)
9.2.35	Bibliography on Methods of Social and Business Research. (1973)
9.2.38	Indexes to Survey Methodology Literature. (1974)

9.3 Abstracting and Indexing Services.

9.3.11	Market Research Abstracts. (Twice a year)
9.3.13	Psychological Abstracts. (Monthly)
9.3.17	Sociological Abstracts. (Five times a year)

9.4 Research Registers.

9.4.16	National Bus Company: Research Bulletin and Annual Report and Accounts.

9.5 Statistical Sources.

9.5.2	British Railways Board Annual Report and Accounts.

4.3 Ergonomic Aspects.

The desirability of increasing the attractiveness of public
transport to non-users and of improving the service offered
to existing users is generally accepted. One of the ways in
which this can be done is by improving the comfort and other
design aspects of public transport vehicles and infrastructure
through the application of ergonomic design techniques. This
subsection brings together a number of references relevant
to the 'human factors' approach to public transport design,
including the following:-

- Several basic texts on human factors in engineering
  design generally.

- Studies which have attempted objective measurements
  of particular physical factors which have a significant
  bearing on degrees of comfort or discomfort experienced
  during travelling. Noise, temperature and vibration
  levels have received the most attention, and some
  general literature has been included in addition to
  studies examining these aspects in the passenger
  environment context.

- Investigations of human physiological and psychological
  reactions to noise, temperature and vibration levels.
  Some studies which concentrate on describing methodologies used to measure these reactions have been
  included in section 8 of the bibliography and are listed
  in the subsidiary references at the end of this subsection.

- Detailed studies of passengers' physical requirements
  in the design of various static features in vehicles
  and terminals, such as step height, seats, personal
  and luggage space provision, and the location of
  handrests.

- Some studies of the psychological and social aspects
  of public transport usage, including the effects of
  crowding and of seating arrangements.

Several comprehensive texts on the subject of human factors
engineering are available, based largely on United States
experience. McCORMICK's Human Factors in Engineering and
Design (4.3.26) contains a section on public transport systems
which outlines the rôle of ergonomics in public transport
design and includes a discussion of relevant U.S. research on
consumer preferences in vehicle and infrastructure design. A
number of useful references are given. CANTILLI's book,
Programming Environmental Improvements in Public Transportation
(4.3.14) outlines the development of a methodology designed to
measure public reactions and preferences regarding various
aspects of the passenger environment, and describes its application in the New York City transit system.

BELL (4.3.40) has reported a study carried out at Newcastle
Upon Tyne University which made objective measurements of
noise, temperature and lighting levels in urban buses to try and
discover whether these levels varied significantly according
to type of bus, position in the bus or location on the route.
Much work has been carried out aimed at investigating human
reactions to factors such as noise, temperature and vibration,
and at identifying their long and short-term side effects. The
physiological and stress effects of noise, for instance, have
received considerable attention and are discussed in the
articles by MØLLER (4.3.39)', BRYAN (4.3.37) and others. The
literature included in this subsection includes both general
studies of the effects of these factors, and reports of research
specific to vehicular environments. These studies have obvious
relevance both in attempting to establish parameters of
tolerable comfort levels and in identifying physiological side
effects. However, much of the United States research effort in
this field has been related to the aerospace and military
research programmes and has been conducted in laboratory situations. Other approaches to measuring comfort have concentrated
on identifying sub-attributes of comfort and have applied
psychometric techniques to measuring passenger preferences and
attitudes to these sub-attributes. NICOLAIDIS' paper,
Quantification of the Comfort Variable (8.1.77) describes a
study in which a quantitative index of comfort was defined which
indicates the level of comfort of a particular travel mode to
a particular individual. While this type of approach can
contribute towards an improved understanding of the travel mode
decision process it can have little relevance to improving
the design of the passenger environment unless related to
physical measurements of the attributes identified. The
articles by OBORNE (4.3.61-62) and OBORNE and CLARK (8.1.84-85)
point out the importance of measuring subjective passenger
reactions in actual fare-paying situations (on the assumption
that this situation is itself a factor which influences passengers'
reactions), and of relating these to simultaneous physical
measurements of the parameters involved. The series of articles,
arising from research carried out at Swansea University,
discusses methodological approaches for measuring the interaction between passengers and the less tangible aspects of
the passenger environment, concentrating particularly on the
effects of motion.

Relatively little research has been published particularly
in this country, which relates human factors to bus design.
Interesting exceptions are the paper by BROOKS (4.3.57) and
the report by BROOKS, RUFFELL-SMITH and WARD (4.3.11),
describing a study carried out by British Leyland under contract
to the Transport and Road Research Laboratory which attempted
to relate human requirements to static elements of bus design.
BROOKS has pointed out in Vehicle Design for People (4.3.57)
that most American research in this field has been based on

laboratory experiments among young healthy pilots or military personnel and that vehicle design should be more closely related to the physical capabilities and requirements of the general public, including the elderly and partially disabled. The British Leyland study involved a series of trials using elderly and ambulant disabled subjects in a static mock-up of a bus as an aid to the design of such features as step height, seat spacing and handrails.

Several of the references in this subsection have been derived from the British journals Ergonomics and Applied Ergonomics. The American periodicals Human Factors and High Speed Ground Transportation also contain literature relevant to the ergonomic aspects of passenger transport. Abstracts of current ergonomics publications are published quarterly in Ergonomics Abstracts (9.3.8) by Birmingham University's ERGONOMICS INFORMATION ANALYSIS CENTRE, and a selection of these abstracts is presented in the journal Ergonomics three times a year. The INSTITUTE FOR CONSUMER ERGONOMICS at Loughborough University of Technology publishes a list of reports and papers produced by or under the supervision of staff of the Institute (9.4.13), and a number of these are relevant to public transport studies.

.3.1   Ageing. [*Biology of] (1957)
        HOBSON, W.
        Institute of Biology. 1957.

.3.2   Anxiety.[*National Differences in] (1971)
        LYNN, R.
        Economic and Social Research Institute. Paper No. 59.
                                                        1971.

.3.3   Behavior and Transit Vehicle Design. (1972)
        LEPPER, R.
        Paper read at Man-Transportation Interface, Specialty
        Conference.   American Society of Civil Engineers. 1972.
                (pp. 37-48 of Conference Proceedings).

        Rider satisfaction within public transport vehicles
        has both physiological and psychological aspects.
        If public transport is to offer serious competition
        to the private car it must offer some degree of
        insulation from the stress arising from person-to-
        person contact with strangers.   One method of achiev-
        ing this would be to provide single seats set at
        angular axes.

.3.4   Behaviour, Body Mechanics and Discomfort.(1969)
        BRANTON, P.
        Ergonomics. Vol. 12. No. 2. March 1969. (pp. 316-327)

        The paper reviews previous behavioural research on
        sitting and seats, points to gaps in the research
        and suggests ways of filling these.

.3.5   Behavior - contingent Design and Transportation
                                        Networks.(1969)
        STUDER, R.G.
        High Speed Ground Transportation Journal. Vol. 3.
                        No. 2. May 1969. (pp. 220-229)

.3.6   Behavioral Perspective for Transportation Planning.
                                        (1972)
        HAYWARD, D.G.
        Paper read at Man-Transportation Interface, Specialty
        Conference.   American Society of Civil Engineers. 1972.
                (pp. 27-36 of Conference Proceedings).

3.7   Behavior Studies for Automatic Transit Systems.
                        [*Passenger] (1976)
        ASHFORD, N.J., FEENEY, R.J., KIRK, N.S., RICHARDSON, J.
                        and STROUD, P.G.
        Transportation Research Record. No. 559: 'Transit
        Planning'.   Transportation Research Board. Washington
                        DC. 1976.

4.3.8   Comfort Limitations of High-Speed Ground Transportation
                [*Literature Survey of Passenger] (1965)
         CARSTENS, J.P. et al.
         Dept. of Commerce, FCST 1: PB. 168. July 1965.
         (Report by United Aircraft Corporation for the Office
              of High-Speed Ground Transportation).

4.3.9   Comfort. [*The Assessment of Chair] (1969)
         SHACKEL, B., CHIDSEY, K.D. and SHIPLEY, P.
         Ergonomics. Vol. 12. No. 2. March 1969. (pp. 269-306)

         This paper describes a series of studies made on
         behalf of and in conjunction with the Consumers'
         Association to explore the general area of seating
         comfort from the user's viewpoint. The results of
         field studies are summarised, various methodologies
         discussed, and areas for further research are indicated.

4.3.10   Comfort. [*The Specification of the Environment Inside
         Passenger Carrying Vehicles from the Point of View of
                                          Passenger] (1970)
         CLARKE, M.J.
         Paper read at Universities Transport Studies Group
              (UTSG) Conference. Cranfield. January 1970.

4.3.11   Elderly and Ambulant Disabled Persons. [*An Investigation
         of Factors Affecting the Use of Buses by Both] (1974)
         BROOKS, B.M., RUFFELL-SMITH, H.P. and WARD, J.S.
         TRRL/British Leyland U.K. Ltd. Contract Report.
         No. CON/3140/32. 1974. (115 pp.)

         This report describes a series of tests made to
         identify aspects of bus design which involve difficulty
         for elderly and disabled persons, and to establish ways
         of reducing the difficulties. The relevant anthropo-
         metric dimensions, neurological and orthopaedic disabil-
         ities and mobility limitations of approximately 100
         elderly and 100 ambulant disabled persons were recorded.
         Current bus usage was noted and nearly 70% of the
         elderly subjects were found to use buses more than
         once a week, but nearly half of the ambulant disabled
         persons seldom or never travelled on buses. The
         subjects' ability to negotiate steps of various
         heights and to pull, twist and reach with their arms
         were recorded and filmed in a mock-up of a static bus.
         Preferences for step heights; seat height, position and
         spacing; and handrail positions and dimensions were
         established. The height of entry and exit steps was
         shown to cause the greatest problems, 86% of the bus
         users having difficulties. The report suggests that
         this problem be overcome by a series of 7 inch high
         steps, the bottom one being retractable. Difficulties
         in getting in and out of seats affected half of the
         bus-using subjects.

Statistical appendices present tabulated results of
the tests, together with details of current bus usage,
types of problem usually encountered on buses, and
data on the subjects' age, sex, anthropometry and
types of disability suffered. Illustrations include
diagrams of seat spacing, pitch and handrail positions
and photographs of the trials.
(see also ref. 4.3.57 below).

4.3.12   Environment. [*Ergonomic Research Contributions to
                     the Design of the Passenger] (1972)
           BRANTON, P.
           Paper read at a Conference on Passenger Environment
           sponsored by the Institution of Mechanical Engineers.
                            London. March 1972.

4.3.13   Environmental Factors in Passenger Terminal Design.
                                                       (1970)
           FRUIN, J.J.
           Paper read at the American Society of Civil Engineers
           Annual and National Environmental Engineering Meeting,
           New York. October 1970. Meeting preprint 1280.

4.3.14   Environmental Improvements in Public Transportation.
                                     [*Programming] (1974)
           CANTILLI, E.J.
           Lexington/Heath Books. Lexington, Mass. 1974. (151 pp.)

           This book discusses the development of a resource-
           allocation index as a guide to apportioning funds for
           the improvement of mass transportation facilities.
           The index is based on user opinion and also takes
           into account the need to quantify the 'intangibles'
           of everyday amenities, the need to relate improvement
           to meaningful degrees of change, and considerations
           of cost-effectiveness. Part I of the book discusses
           existing techniques for assessing 'community values'
           and cost-effectiveness, and for measuring selected
           human environmental factors. In Part II the allocation
           technique is developed and its application in test
           surveys on the New York City transit system described.
           Part III discusses the application of the methodology
           and the evaluation of the results. The author concludes
           that the methodology presented is a feasible means of
           combining the tangible and the intangible factors
           in numerical indices which incorporate the public's
           expressed wishes and desires regarding transportation
           systems. An appendix provides notes on the analytical
           method and presents a computer programme for the
           allocation of costs in environmental amenities. A
           substantial list of references is also included.

4.3.15   Ergonomics and the Quality of Living,(1972)
           FERGUSON, D.
           Applied Ergonomics. Vol. 3. No.2. June 1972.(pp. 70-74)

4.3.16   Ergonomics: Man in his Working Environment.(1965)
MURRELL, K.F.H.
Chapman and Hall London. 1965. (496 pp.)

4.3.17   Heat and Noise [*Effects of Combined] on Human
Performance. Psychology and Subjective Estimates of
                   Comfort and Performance. (1965)
DEAN, R.D. and McGOTHLEN, C.L.
Paper read at the Annual Technical Meeting of the
Institute of Environmental Sciences. Chicago. April
                                         1965.

4.3.18   Heat Stress [*Effects of] on the Performance of Two
Tasks Running Concurrently.(1970)
PROVINS, K.A. and BELL, C.R.
Journal of Applied Psychology.Vol. 85. No.1. 1970.

4.3.19   Human Body in Equipment Design.[*The] (1966)
DAMON, A., STOUDT, W., and McFARLAND, R.A.
Harvard University Press. 1966.

4.3.20   Human Commotion [*The] - Human Factors in Transport-
                                  ation.(1972)
MILLAR, A. E. (ed.)
NASA-ASEE Report, Contract NGT 47-003-028.
Langley Research Centre and Old Dominion Research
                            Foundation.1972.

4.3.21   Human Engineering.(1967)
DE FONSEKA, C.P.
Department of Transportation and Environmental
Planning Research Journal. April 1967. University of
                                 Birmingham.

4.3.22   Human Engineering Guide for Equipment Designers.
                        (2nd. ed'n) 1964.
WOODSON, W.E. and CONOVER, D.W.
University of California Press, Berkeley. 1964.

4.3.23   Human Engineering Guide to Equipment Design.(1963)
MORGAN, C.T., COOK, J.S., CHAPANIS, A. and LUND, M.W.
McGraw - Hill. 1963.

4.3.24   Human Factors and Ergonomic Considerations in the Design
                    of Automatic Transit Systems.(1975)
ASHFORD, N.J. and KIRK, N.S.
Paper read at NATO Conference on Transportation and
Urban Life. Munich. September 1975.

4.3.25   Human Factors Engineering. [*Public Transportation and]
                                (1970)
BAUER, H.J.
Research Publication GMR-9982. Research Laboratories.
General Motors Corporation. Warren, Michigan. April 1970.

4.3.26   Human Factors in Engineering and Design. (4th edition-
                                                        1974)
         McCORMICK, E.J.
         McGraw - Hill. 1974.
         Chapter 17: The Living Environment: Services and
         Related Facilities.Subsection on Public Transportation
                                          Systems.(pp. 431-441)

The two main aims of human factors engineers in
relation to public transport are defined as making
more people want to use the service and gaining support
at the community level through a new and more positive
image. Transportation systems should be designed
with the main requirements of potential users in mind,
but the requirements of operating and maintenance
personnel should also be considered. Design features
relevant to users can be divided into those concerned
with physical aspects of convenience and mobility,
and those concerned with their more aesthetic,
psychological and subjective values and preferences.

Designers of urban transportation systems have tended
to neglect the consumer mobility aspect from two
particular angles - the provision of certain functional
requirements (such as loading and unloading of passengers;
methods of obtaining tickets), and special provision for
certain groups of users - the very young, the very old
and the handicapped. These requirements are outlined,
with reference to relevant research. The findings
and methodologies of several U.S. consumer preference
studies regarding transportation are also summarised,
and possible alternative future urban transportation
systems are briefly discussed in relation to the requirements of potential users. A number of references are
listed, mainly relating to U.S. research into ergonomic
aspects of public transport and into user preferences.

.3.27   Human Factors in Urban TransportationSystems. (1975)
         HOAG, L.   and ADAMS, S.K.
         Human Factors. Vol. 17. No.2. 1975. (pp. 119-131)

.3.28   Humanscale 1/2/3 . (1974)
         DIFFRIENT, N., TILLEY, A.R. and BARDAGJY, J.C.
         Henry Dreyfus Associates. The M.I.T. Press. 1974.

3.29   Let's Design a British Coach to Beat the Continentals.
                                                        (1976)
         LLOYD, D.
         Commercial Motor. Vol. 144. December 10th. 1976.(pp. 32-
3.30   Man and Motor Cars: An Ergonomic Study.(1966)   36)
         BLACK, S.
         Secker and Warburg. 1966.

3.31   Motion Discomfort and Transportation Guideway Form.(1974)
         DAIS, J.L. and BALACHANDRA, M.
         Transportation Research. Vol.8. No. 6. December 1974.
                                          (pp. 523-532)

4.3.32   Noise. (1967)
         HARRIS, C.M.
         Environmental Science and Technology. April 1967.

4.3.33   Noise. [*A Review of Road Traffic] (1970)
         WORKING GROUP ON RESEARCH INTO ROAD TRAFFIC NOISE.
         TRRL   Report LR 357. 1970.

4.3.34   Noise [*Community] and Hearing Loss. (1966)
         DOUGHERTY, J.D.
         New England Journal of Medicine. October 6th. 1966.

4.3.35   Noise and Vibration Levels in Rapid Transit Vehicle
                             Systems. [*Comparison of] (19
         DAVIS, E.W.
         Operations Research Inc. for National Capital Transpo
         ation Agency. April 1964.

4.3.36   Noise in Mass - Transit Systems. (1967)
         SALMON, V.
         Stanford Research Institute Journal, No. 16. September
                                                          1967.

4.3.37   Noise Laws Don't Protect the Sensitive. (1973)
         BRYAN, M.
         New Scientist. 27th September 1973.

4.3.38   Noise Levels. [*Human Performance as a Function of
                             Changes in Acoustic] (1965)
         SHOENBURGER, R.W. and HARRIS, C.S.
         Journal of Engineering Psychology. Vol. 4. No.4. 1965.

4.3.39   Noise Standards? [*How Good are Work] (1977)
         MØLLER, A.
         New Scientist. 27th. January. 1977. (pp. 192-194)

         A critical examination of current standards of
         tolerable noise levels with reference to working
         environments, which could have relevance for staff
         working on public transport vehicles and for regular
         passengers. Conventional methods of measuring noise
         energy in dBA may not give measures that are relevant
         to the inner ear, and in particular transient high
         noise levels damage the ear more than is reflected
         in their weighting in sound level meters. It is
         argued that the noise standards adopted by most
         western countries are too low. Many people exposed
         to noise of much lower intensity than the present
         upper limit of tolerable noise level (85 or 90 dBA
         for eight hours exposure) may experience various
         noise - related discomforts and slight impairments
         of hearing which can cause a significant reduction
         in the quality of life. The author suggests that
         the upper limit of tolerable noise levels be reduced
         to about 75dBA. Current noise standards also ignore
         the non - hearing physiological effects of noise
         exposure. The stress effects of noise can lead to

short-term increases in heart rate and blood
pressure and in the secretion of a number of
important hormones. Little is known of the effects
on human health of long-term exposure to loud or
intermittent noise but there are indications of
higher-than-average incidences of cardiovascular
disease and diabetes among workers exposed to loud
noise, and the author points to the need for further
research in this field.

4.3.40   Noise, Temperature and Lighting Levels on Urban Buses.
                                    [*A Study of] (1976)
          BELL, M.C.
          University of Newcastle Upon Tyne. Transport
          Operations Research Group. Working Paper No. 16.
                                February 1976.(17 pp.)

          The paper describes the methods and findings of studies
          made in urban buses on Tyneside to measure levels of
          temperature, light intensity and noise climate. The
          aim of the studies was to discover whether there were
          any significant variations in these parameters between
          different positions within the buses, between different
          buses and between different locations on the route.
          There were found to be no statistically significant
          differences in measured light intensity between buses,
          within buses, or between different positions on the
          route. Temperatures inside the buses were found to
          correlate with those outside, as expected. The
          measurements of the noise climate inside two single-
          deck and two double-deck buses indicated that the
          character of the noise varied between different buses.

4.3.41   Noise. [*The Anatomy of] (1967)
          BERANEK, L.L. and MILLER, L.N.
          Machine Design. September 14th. 1967.

          (see also refs. 4.3.17 above and 4.3.68 below.)

4.3.42   Physiological Psychology.(1965)
          MORGAN, C.T.
          McGraw-Hill. 1965

4.3.43   Psychological Design Factors in Urban Public
                                Transportation Vehicles.(1974)
          ADAMS, S.K. and HOAG, L.
          Paper read at the 18th. Annual Meeting of the Human
          Factors Society and published in: "Benefits for
          Mankind", edited by E.L. Saenger and M. Kirkpatrick.
                                1974. (pp. 5-8).

          The paper discusses important psychological variables,
          such as personal space, aesthetics, situation control
          and privacy, and makes recommendations for improving
          the design of urban public transport vehicles from
          these aspects.

4.3.44   Psychological Dynamics. [*Passenger] (1968)
SOLOMON, K.M., SOLOMON, R.J. and SILIEN, J.S.
H.804. U.S. Dept. of Transportation.Urban Mass
            Transportation Administration. June 1968.

4.3.45   Psychological Factors Affecting Urban Travel:
responses to crowding in transit vehicles. (1972)
YANCEY, L.L.
Florida State University Transportation Center,
June 1972. Sponsored by U.S. Dept. of Transportation.
Urban Mass Transportation Administration. (PB 215 625)

The report describes the development and testing of
a survey technique for examining psychological responses
to crowding in public transport vehicles.

4.3.46   Rides, Trips and Moves on a Bus. (1970)
TOMLINSON, G.
Sacramento Transit Authority. Interim Technical
    Report No. 6. December 1970. PB 197 817 (99 pp.)

An examination of the social setting of the bus which
looks at what people do on buses and how they choose
seats. The investigations were carried out on a
demonstration crosstown bus service in Sacramento,
California. The report provides some suggestions
that the sociology of a bus has a relationship with
the nationwide (U.S.) decline in mass transit patronage.

4.3.47   Sick Transit.(1970)
EVANS, R.
Humble Way. Vol. 9. 1970.

4.3.48   Sociology of Public Transit. [*Toward a] (1967)
MORRIS, D. and LEVINE, S.
Social Problems. Vol. 15. No. 1. 1967 (pp. 84-91)

An examination of the stressful sociological characteristics of short trips on public transport.

4.3.49   Stress at the Wheel.(1969)
HOFFMANN, H.
Paper read at a Symposium on the Human Factors of
Road Accidents. World Health Organisation. Geneva.
                               February 1969.
4.3.50   Temperature Fluctuations. [*Adaptation of the Body to]
                                      (1966)
SHAKHBAZYAN, G. Kh. and SCHLEYFMAN, F.M.
'Vestnik' of the USSR Academy of Medical Sciences.
               Vol. XXI. No. 8. 1966.

4.3.51   Thermal Tolerance Limits for Unimpaired Mental
                    Performance. [*Upper] (1965)
WING, R.F.
Aerospace Medicine. October 1965.

3.52   Thermoregulatory Function in Men and Women. [*Compari-
                                     son of] (1969)
        FOX, R.H. et al.
        Journal of Applied Physiology. Vol. 26. No. 4. April
                                              1969.
        (see also refs. 4.3.17, 4.3.18 and 4.3.40 above.)

3.53   Train Seats [*An Evaluation of] by Observation of
        Sitting Behaviour. (1967)
        BRANTON, P. and GRAYSON, G.
        Ergonomics. Vol. 10. No. 1. January 1967. (pp. 35-51)

        The paper describes a study which used an 'ecological'
        approach to the evaluation of train seats. The sitting
        behaviour of travellers on a British Rail experimental
        train was recorded by two techniques: by using observa-
        tions of changes in sitting postures and by time-lapse
        films of a selected sample of subjects. High correla-
        tions between the two techniques were found. Two
        types of seat were studied. Frequency of occurrence,
        duration, and sequences of postures were recorded
        to arrive at quantitative comparisons, and the two
        seat-types were found to give rise to significant
        differences in passenger sitting behaviour.

3.54   Transit Car Features. [*A Discussion of] (1964)
        SHEENAN, J.K.
        Operations Research Inc. for National Capital
                                 Transportation Agency. June 1964.

3.55   Transportation and the Person. (1969)
        CRAIK, K.H.
        High Speed Ground Transportation Journal. Vol.3.No. 1.
                                 January 1969. (pp. 86-91)

        A consideration of the contributions environmental
        psychology can make to understanding the interplay
        between transportation systems and behavioural systems.

3.56   Travel Barriers.(1970)
        U.S. DEPARTMENT OF TRANSPORTATION.
        National Information Service. PB. 187-237. 1970.

3.57   Vehicle Design for People,(1976)
        BROOKS, B.M.
        In: Passenger Transport and the Environment. ed.
                                     R. Cresswell.
             Paper read at Conference on Passenger Transport
             and the Environment held at the University of
             York.   March 1976. (pp. 246-264)

        This chapter describes studies relating to the
        interaction between passengers, driver and vehicle
        design configuration on public transport vehicles.
        The dimensional, comfort and safety requirements of
        both driver and passengers are outlined and the
        implications of these for vehicle design are

discussed. Trials carried out by British Leyland
under contract to the Transport and Road Research
Laboratory are described to illustrate how passenger
requirements can be determined. A brief description
is given of the Leyland B15 prototype bus to demonstrat
how the results of such studies can be used to influenc
bus design.
(see refs. 4.3.11 above and 4.5.7 below.)

4.3.58   Vehicle Design [*Transit] and Rider Satisfaction. (1970
         MOORHEAD, R. and LEPPER, R.
         Urban and Social Change Review. Vol. 4. No. 1. Fall 197
                                              (pp. 6-10)

An attempt is made to identify the principles underlying passenger irritations in urban public transport
vehicles, and to propose a solution which would give
greater independence and satisfaction within existing
vehicles. This could be achieved by the adoption of
a diagonal-axis seating arrangement.

4.3.59   Vehicle Riding Properties. [*The Determination of]
                                                   (1962)
         BATCHELOR, G.H.
         Railway Gazette. July 27th. 1962. (pp. 97-100).

4.3.60   Vehicle Seating Accommodation. [*Devices for Use in
                    Defining and Measuring] (1974)
         SAEJ 826b.
         1975 SAE Handbook, 1974.

4.3.61   Vibration and Passenger Comfort. (1977)
         OBORNE, D.J.
         Applied Ergonomics. Vol. 8. No. 2. June 1977 (pp.97-
                                                       101)

The maintenance of passenger comfort has become an
important consideration for vehicle designers in
recent years, and this paper examines the relationship
between vehicular vibration and passenger comfort. The
results of a number of laboratory experiments dating
from the early 1930's are reviewed and the limitations
of indices and standards developed under laboratory
conditions are identified. The paper describes the
results and relative merits of field investigations
carried out by Swansea University between 1969 and
1973, using questionnaires distributed to actual fare-
paying passengers on various types of public transport
vehicles. Attempts were made to relate the questionnaire results to vibration measurements carried out
during the journeys. It was found that at lower
intensity levels high-frequency vibration (due to the
engine) is more important to passenger comfort, but
that as intensity levels increase lower-frequency
motion is more important. The paper concludes that
although the measurement errors and problems incurred
during such field investigations are much greater than i
laboratory studies, the results may be of more
relevance and value to design engineers.

4.3.62   Vibration and Passenger Comfort. [*A Critical
           Assessment of Studies Relating Whole-Body] (1976)
           OBORNE, D.J.
           Ergonomics. Vol. 19. No.6. November 1976. (pp. 751-
                                                          774).

           This paper critically reviews the major work which
           has been carried out over the past forty years to
           investigate the relationship between whole-body
           vibration and comfort. Much of the work is shown
           to be inadequate from most practical standpoints. The
           paper indicates that attempts which have been made to
           draw the field together to produce curves of equal
           comfort (including an International Standard) have not
           significantly increased knowledge of how people react
           to whole-body vibration. To remedy this situation
           more controlled experimental work, with the emphasis
           on human and passenger response to vibration, is
           recommended. The paper includes a substantial
           bibliography of works on vibration and comfort.

4.3.63   Vibration. [*Guide for the Evaluation of Human
                Exposure to Whole-Body] (1974)
           INTERNATIONAL ORGANISATION FOR STANDARDIZATION.
           ISO. 2631. 1974.

4.3.64   Vibration. [*Guide to the Evaluation of Human Exposure
                          to Whole-Body] (1974)
           BRITISH STANDARDS INSTITUTE.
           Draft for Development. DD. 32. March 1974. (20 pp.)

           This Draft for Development defines and gives numerical
           values for limits of exposure for mechanical vibrations
           transmitted to the body in the frequency range 1 Hz to
           80 Hz. Recommended limits are given for use according
           to the three generally recognised criteria of preserv-
           ing comfort, working efficiency, and safety or health.
           According to these criteria the recommended limits
           are specified in terms of vibration frequency, accelera-
           tion magnitude, exposure time and the direction of
           vibration relative to the torso. Because of the wide
           variety of possible conditions and effects of human
           exposure to vibrations and the shortage of firm data
           these recommendations constitute provisional guidance
           only and not a British Standard.

4.3.65   Vibration on Man. [*A Study of the Influence of] (1958)
           DIECKMANN, D.
           Ergonomics. Vol.1. No.4. August 1958. (pp. 347-355).

           The article describes an examination by physical and
           physiological methods of the effects on the human being
           of vertical and horizontal vibrations up to 100 cycles

per second. Resonance phenomena are described and a strain scale is given for vertical and horizontal vibration excitation. Vibration measurements in a railway carriage provide an example for typical resonance phenomena experienced by passengers sitting on seats.

4.3.66   Vibration. [*Passengers' Reaction to] (1972)
BARTWELL, F.T. and CLARKE, M.J.
Paper C23/72 read at a Conference on Passenger Environment sponsored by the Institution of Mechanical Engineers. London. March 1972.

Includes a section on questionnaire studies of passenger reaction, and bibliography.

4.3.67   Vibration Perceptibility and Annoyance. [*A Scale for the Degrees of] (1968)
SOLIMAN, J.I.
Ergonomics. Vol. 11. No. 2. March 1968. (pp. 101-122)

The paper reviews the work of previous investigators in the field of human susceptibility to vibrations. Criteria for permissible vibrations with regard to their effect on human beings (thresholds of perception and annoyance) are suggested and it is recommended that these could serve as a basis for a British Standard specification.
(see also ref. 4.3.35 above).

GOVERNMENT REPORTS AND PUBLICATIONS.

4.3.68   Noise Units. [*A Guide to] (1973)
NOISE ADVISORY COUNCIL.
H.M.S.O. 1973. (7 pp.)

4.3 Subsidiary References.

3.1 Studies of Modal Choice Behaviour and Value of Travel Time.

3.1.53   *Report of a Study into the Motivation and Attitudes of Passengers and Potential Passengers of London Transport Buses. (1968)*
3.1.108 *Human Effort and the Value of Travel Time. (1976)*

3.2 Social Aspects of Mobility.

3.2.1   *Age Concern on Transport. (1973 edition.)*
3.2.8   *Planning for Disabled People in the Urban Environment. (1969)*
3.2.19   *Transport and the Elderly: problems and possible action. (1977)*
3.2.69   *The Elderly at Home: a study of people aged sixty five and over living in the community in England in 1976. (1978)*
3.2.70   *Handicapped and Impaired in Great Britain. (1971)*

3.4 Transport and Mobility - General and Miscellaneous.

3.4.1   *Environment and Behavior: planning and everyday life.* (1977)
3.4.2   *Environmental Psychology: Man and his Physical Setting.* (1970)

4.1 Public Transport - Operational Aspects.

4.1.25   *Bus Transportation Strategies.* (1976)
4.1.67   *Human Performance Requirements for an Innovative Transit Bus Operation.* (1976)
4.1.71   *The Design and Location of Urban Public Transport Interchanges.* (1973)
4.1.82   *One-Man Buses.* (1973)

4.2 Public Transport - Marketing Approach.

4.2.44   *The Rôle of Psychological Needs in Mass Transit.* (1972)

4.4 Public Transport - Demonstration Projects and Innovatory Systems.

4.4.34   *General Concepts Concerning New Transport System Characteristics.* (1974)

4.5 Public Transport - General and Miscellaneous.

4.5.7   *Passenger Transport and the Environment: the integration of public passenger transport with the environment.* (1976)

5.1 Private Motor Transport.

5.1.15   *Medical Aspects of Fitness to Drive Vehicles.* (1968)

8.1 Survey Techniques - Behavioural and Attitudinal.

8.1.35   *Human Factors/Ergonomics: Research Methods.* (1971)
8.1.70   *The Application of Psychological Research and Theory to Urban Transportation Planning.* (1975)
8.1.77   *Quantification of the Comfort Variable.* (1975)
8.1.84   *The Development of Questionnaire Surveys for the Investigation of Passenger Comfort.* (1973)
8.1.85   *Questionnaire Surveys of Passenger Comfort.* (1975)
8.1.92   *Examples of the Use of Rating Scales in Ergonomics Research.* (1976)
8.1.93   *Multidimensional Scaling of an Aircraft Handling Rating Scale.* (1969)
8.1.96   *An Application of Mulitidimensional Scaling Techniques to the Quantification of the Comfort Variable for Use in Binary Disaggregate Mode Choice Models.* (1974)

8.3 Research Techniques and Methodology - General and Miscellaneous.

8.3.18   *A Model of Vehicle Comfort and a Method for its Assessment.* (1973)

9.1 Journals.

9.1.41   *Applied Ergonomics.*   *(Quarterly)*
9.1.43   *Ergonomics.*   *(Six times a year.)*
9.1.45   *Human Factors.*   *(Six times a year.)*

9.2 Bibliographies.

9.2.1   *Annotated bibliography of the application of behavior and attitude research to transportation system planning and design.*
                                               (1976)
9.2.3   *Buses in Urban Areas. 1970-1976. (1976)*
9.2.4   *Bibliography: Control and Communication. (1976)*
9.2.7   *Environmental effects of urban road traffic - an annotated bibliography. (1972)*

9.3 Abstracting and Indexing Services.

9.3.8   *Ergonomics Abstracts.*   *(Quarterly)*
9.3.13   *Psychological Abstracts.*   *(Monthly)*

9.4 Research Registers.

9.4.13   *Institute for Consumer Ergonomics: list of reports and publications.*

4.4   Demonstration Projects and Innovatory Systems .

Growing congestion in urban areas together with the need both
to arrest the decline in public transport usage and to improve
the nature of the service offered to people without a car
available have prompted a number of new approaches to public
transport provision since the mid-1960's. This subsection
brings together reports of a number of case studies of experimental and innovatory services, and some more general assessments. The case study reports include descriptions of feasibility studies and other preliminary research, and some results
in terms of operating experience and of passenger usage and
reactions. The services and systems covered can be classified
as follows:

- Experimental bus services using conventional stage-
  carriage buses, midibuses or minibuses en a fixed
  line-haul basis, including stage bus diversions, bus-
  rail feeder services, and express bus services.

- More unconventional 'demand-responsive' services which
  attempt to match the convenience of the private car or
  to provide public road transport in areas where it
  would be impractical to operate normal stage carriage
  bus services. This group includes various types of
  dial-a-ride service, postbuses, hail-stop minibuses
  and shared taxis or jitneys operating on fixed routes.

- Larger-scale innovatory systems involving much heavier
  investment in new or modified transport infrastructure.
  These systems include busways, monorails and minitram
  systems.

Demonstration projects involving improvements to existing operation through bus priority schemes and fares experiments are
included in subsection 4.1 (Operational Aspects of Public
Transport).

All three types of experimental service identified above have
been tried out in British new towns, and have been closely
monitored and widely reported. A number of relevant studies
have been listed in sections 1.1 and 2.1-4 and cross-referenced
at the end of this subsection. These include in particular
the studies of the Runcorn Busway, the Stevenage Superbus
service and those of the Harlow and Milton Keynes dial-a-ride
services.

Examples of 'conventional' experimental bus services in Britain
are described in the reports of the Stevenage Superbus service
2.4.54-55 and 2.4.57-60), the Peak Park Pathfinder Services
(4.4.36), the Surrey Ramblers' Bus (4.4.42), the Cardiff Midibus (4.1.77) and of experimental bus services in Devon (4.4.40).
The Management of Urban Public Transport: a marketing perspective by HOVELL, JONES and MORAN (4.2.25) includes detailed

studies of a range of experimental bus service schemes
including the Hale Barns Executive Express commuter coach
service and the Formby bus-rail feeder service. This project
was examined in detail under the programme drawn up by the
Government Working Group on Bus Demonstration Projects (4.4.54)
and is further described in the reports by HOVELL and JONES
(4.4.22), and JONES (4.4.23), and in the DEPARTMENT OF THE
ENVIRONMENT's official report (4.4.53).

The Department of the Environment has carried out a major
research programme on dial-a-ride to ascertain whether it has
a potentially useful rôle in Britain. Experimental schemes
in Harlow, Solihull, Maidstone and elsewhere have been monitored in detail by TRRL and Cranfield Institute of Technology
Centre for Transport Studies. Much of the material arising
from this British research and experience from the early 1970's
is gathered together in the Proceedings of the Symposium on
Dial-a-Bus Services - 1974 (4.4.14), in MITCHELL and SLEVIN's
paper: Dial-a-Ride in Britain: Experience to mid - 1974 and
Research Programme (4.4.16) and in the TRRL report of the
1977 Symposium on Unconventional Bus Services (4.4.52).

The article by GUY on local shopping facilities in new towns
(1.2.21) points out that in several new towns residents are
in effect creating their own public transport by forming groups
and shopping by taxi, which could be a more appropriate method
of providing public transport than conventional bus services
in low-density areas difficult to serve adequately and at
reasonable fare-levels by buses. Most research on taxi usage
and operation in this country which has been published to date
has focussed on the London taxicab trade. Very little detailed
information on the provision and usage of taxis and hire cars
in British new towns is available, but some of the major studies
of taxi operation and use in the London area have a wider
relevance and provide useful background information. The
NATIONAL BOARD FOR PRICES AND INCOMES' report Proposed Increases
in London Taxicab Fares, published in 1968 (9.5.10) presents
statistical information relating to taxi operation and usage
in London, including details of journey characteristics, length
of jobs and availability of cabs by time of day. The 1970
Report of the Departmental Committee on the London Taxicab Trade
(4.5.21) [the 'Maxwell Stamp' Report] summarised the findings
of a three-year investigation and included recommendations for
further research into the feasibility of new systems such as
commuter minibus services and more versatile taxi systems
along the lines of those developed in some European cities.
The report by DOGANIS and LOWE, Alternative Taxicab Systems:
A London Case Study (4.4.48) describes a study carried out at the
Polytechnic of Central London as part of the wider search for a
transport mode which can effectively bridge the gap between the
private car and the more tradtional forms of public transport.
The study aimed to establish a thorough understanding of the
operation of the London taxicab trade and to consider the
feasibility of alternative taxicab systems within existing

technology. The report includes a description of new 'personalised transit' systems (Volume 1, Chapter 5) and an examination of alternative patterns of taxicab operations, including zonal taxi systems in residential areas and various kinds of taxi sharing schemes. Suggestions for a number of regulatory changes are also made. The authors point out in the introduction that while the study was specifically concerned with the London area several of the findings and conclusions would appear to be relevant to other large urban or suburban areas. The article by LOWE, Zonal Taxi Systems:An Improvement in Local Mobility (4.4.47), examines the feasibility of a zonal taxi system connecting residential areas with local centres, which could have relevance to some new towns. Taxis would operate along predetermined regular routes and schedules on a hail-stop basis with relatively low flat-rate fares. Some qualitative information on usage of and attitudes to taxis, based on depth interviews carried out by Social and Community Planning Research with a small sample of residents of Old Harlow, is contained in the report Attitudes to Transport Provision in Old Harlow by MORTON-WILLIAMS and BUTLER (2.4.14). This study indicated that the residents interviewed could be classified into 'taxi-users', people who readily considered taxis as a possible means of transport, and 'non-users' who never or rarely did so. This distinction was related partly to income, but was mainly an attitude of mind. Taxis were used mainly by non-car owners or non-drivers in car owning households, as an alternative to buses, to take the physical strain out of travelling or to make good deficiencies in the bus service.

The study reported by MULDREW in Work Attitudes of Taxi Drivers (4.1.100) examined the attitudes to Dial-a-Ride driving of a small group of taxi drivers in a provincial taxi firm which also operated a Dial-a-Ride service. The findings indicated that full-time taxi drivers did not consider Dial-a-Ride driving as representing any improvement over their present work. A survey of bus crews by the same author reported in Work Attitudes of Bus Drivers and Conductors (4.1.99) concluded that Dial-a-Ride driving could offer significant benefits for crew drivers.

Although the emphasis in this part of the bibliography is on British experience, in order to widen the frame of reference some material relating to experimental and innovatory services in the United States has been incorporated. This includes several TRANSPORTATION RESEARCH BOARD/HIGHWAY RESEARCH BOARD reports on demand-responsive transportation (4.4.8-10) and the major study of para-transit operation in the U.S.A. by KIRBY, BUTT et al. (4.4.35). Some case-studies of successful demonstration projects have also been incorporated, including an article on the Decatur and Peoria Premium Special Services (4.4.7) on which the Stevenage Superbus service was partially modelled, and the CHIGAGO TRANSIT AUTHORITY's report of the

Skokie Swift demonstration rail commuter shuttle service.
The Economic and Social Impact of Investments in Public Transit
by SHELDON and BRANDWEIN (7.1.12) describes a number of
demonstration projects in the United States and includes a
substantial bibliography containing many references to projects
carried out under the U.S. federally aided Urban Mass
Transportation Administration demonstration programme of the
1960's. The book by HOVELL, JONES and MORAN (4.2.25) also
provides many references and includes studies of a range of
international demonstration projects.

Many other items listed in this subsection provide pointers
for further reading. Additional references are incorporated
in the bibliography Buses in Urban Areas 1970-1976 (9.2.3)
which contains subsections on 'Busways' (relating principally
to the Runcorn Busway), 'Rapid Transport', 'Demand-Actuated
Travel and Minibuses', and 'Design and New Technology'.

4.4.1. Bus System Experiments and Developments.(1976)
JACKSON, M.W.
Paper read at a Conference on Passenger Transport and
the Environment held at the University of York, March
1976 and published as Chapter 6 in: 'Passenger Transport
and the Environment', ed. R. Cresswell (pp. 115-137)
(see ref. 4.5.7. below)

4.4.2. Cars for the Carless.(1974)
BENDIXSON, T.
Built Environment. Vol. 3. No.11. November 1974.
(pp.582-583)

This article gives a brief review of dial-a-ride
developments in the United States and Britain. The
factors which contribute to successful operation are
discussed, the most significant being identified as
high levels of telephone installations, high residential density and low fares.

4.4.3. Chauffeur Coach Service. [*Studies of the Harrogate]
(1977)
TUNBRIDGE, R.J.
TRRL Supplementary Report   SR 253.April 1977.(20pp.)

The report describes a series of studies of the
Harrogate minibus service carried out by TRRL in 1973
and 1974.   The studies comprised:-

(i)   Timing measurements of radio usage.
(ii)   Operational observations of boarding and alight-
        ing locations and times, and details of articles
        of luggage carried.
(iii)   An on-vehicle questionnaire survey to ascertain
        the types of people using the service.

The on-vehicle survey showed that 83% of passengers
used the service for shopping; approximately 84% of
users were female and almost half the users were aged
65 years or over.   Nearly 60% were non-car owners
and at the time of travel 90% of users did not have
a car available to them.   Approximately half of those
interviewed previously travelled by stage-carriage
bus.   The proportion having a telephone was high
(72%), although in practice the number of telephone
requests for diversion from the fixed route have
amounted to less than 10% of the total patronage.

4.4.4. Chauffeur Coach - An Experiment by the West Yorkshire
Road Car Company in Personalised Transport at
Harrogate.(1974)
DAYKIN, P.
Paper read at the PTRC Summer Annual Meeting. July
1974 (pp. 161-177 of Conference proceedings)

The conception, planning, development and operating
experience of the Harrogate Chauffeur Coach service

are reviewed in this paper. The main objective of the experiment, which commenced in October 1972, was to discover whether there was a market for a quality public transport service at a higher-than-usual price. It was hoped to regain to public transport a proportion of the off-peak car-borne shopping trips from residential areas to the town centre, using a high quality service which combined convenience and personal service with greater passenger comfort than normally offered by buses. The experimental system was designed as a hail-stop service operating on a series of basic fixed routes, but with provision for telephoned request pick-ups in certain areas. Details are given of costs, revenues and numbers of passengers carried, and an analysis of the service by areas covered identifies those of weak demand, which were likely to be abandoned and those which seemed to offer a greater potential for future development.

4.4.5. Chesapeake Mass Transportation Demonstration Project.
                                                      (1969)
        WILBUR SMITH and ASSOCIATES.
        Department of Housing and Urban Development.VA-MTD-1

4.4.6. Corridor Facilities [*Major Urban]: a New Concept.
                                                      (1962)
        QUINBY, H.D.
        Traffic Quarterly. Vol.16. No.2.   April 1962.
                                                (pp.242-259)

4.4.7. Decatur and Peoria Premium Special Services.[*The]
                                                      (1967)
        PASSENGER TRANSPORT.   May 1967. (pp.183-187)

4.4.8. Demand-Actuated Transportation Systems.(1971)
        HIGHWAY RESEARCH BOARD.
        Special Report No. 124. Washington D.C. 1971.

4.4.9. Demand-Responsive Transportation Systems and Other
        Paratransit Services.(1976)
        TRANSPORTATION RESEARCH BOARD
        Transportation Research Record No. 608. Washington
                                    D.C. 1976 (134 pp.)

4.4.10.Demand-Responsive Transportation Systems.[*Operational
        Experience with] (1972)
        ROOS, D.
        Highway Research Record No. 397. Highway Research
        Board.
        Washington D.C. 1972.
        (Paper read at the 51st meeting on New Transportation
        Systems and Technology. 1972).

4.4.11.Dial-a-Bus: London Transport's Experience.(1975)
        SYMONDS, A.A.S., and DAY, D.J.
        Paper read at the PTRC Summer Annual Meeting,
        Seminar S-Public Transport. July 1975.

4.4.12. Dial-a-Bus Ridership in Small Urban Areas. [*Forecasting]
HARTGEN, D.T. and KECK, C.A. (1974)
Preliminary Research Report 60. New York State
Department of Transportation. Albany. New York.1974.

4.4.13. Dial-a-Bus Services.[*The Preliminary Design of Many-
to-Few] (1977)
TUNBRIDGE, R.J. and MITCHELL, C.G.B.
TRRL Report   LR 789.   September 1977. (9pp.)

Estimates are provided of the distances to be
travelled to connect different numbers of collection
or set-down points in service areas of different
sizes and shapes. This information allows the round-
trip time, the required vehicle capacity and the
productivity of the dial-a-bus service to be estimated
for an assumed level of demand. Mean tour distances
and standard deviations are set out for three different
operating strategies for service areas of a number
of sizes and shapes.

4.4.14. Dial-a-Bus Services.[*The Proceedings of the Symposium
on](1974)
SLEVIN, R. (ed.)
Cranfield Institute of Technology. Centre for
Transport Studies.   September 1974.   (150pp.)
(Contains a bibliography)
The Symposium was sponsored by the Transport and Road
Research Laboratory and the Ford Motor Company.

4.4.15. Dial-a-Bus Work? [*How Does] (1975)
ALDOUS, A.
The Architects' Journal. Vol. 161. No. 9.
26th February 1975   (pp.460-461)

An examination of two dial-a-bus systems after some
months in use, at Old Harlow and at Hampstead Garden
Suburb.

4.4.16. Dial-a-Ride in Britain: Experience to mid-1974 and
Research Programme.(1974)
MITCHELL, C.G.B.   and   SLEVIN, R.
Paper read at the PTRC Summer Annual Meeting.
July 1974.   (pp. 203-245 of Conference Proceedings)

The results of small-scale operations of dial-a-ride
systems in Maidstone, Harrogate, Abingdon, Carterton
and Eastbourne are reviewed. Despite institutional
restrictions on the services two of the operations
were close to financial viability when all revenue
is included in the balance. The plans for an
experimental dial-a-ride system in Harlow are
described, and the programme of research and evaluations
of dial-a-ride to be undertaken by the Cranfield
Centre for Transport Studies is summarised.

4.4.17. Dial-a-Ride in Carterton: a review of residents'
        travel patterns. (1975)
        OCHOJNA, A.D.
        Cranfield Institute of Technology. Centre for
        Transport Studies. Report No. 8. June 1975. (58pp.)

4.4.18. Dial-a-Ride in Maidstone. (1973).
        SLEVIN, R. and OCHOJNA, A.D.
        Cranfield Institute of Technology. Centre for
        Transport Studies. Report No. 6. August 1973 (63pp.)

        Report of research undertaken for the Transport and
        Road Research Laboratory, Public Transport Section.

4.4.19. Dial-a-Ride: Pick-me-up or flash-in-the-pan? (1975)
        RICHARDS, B.
        Architectural Design. Vol XLV. December 1975.
                                        (pp.777-778)

4.4.20. Dial-a-Ride. [*Telephone Facilities for] (1974)
        SOUTHALL, J.A.
        Telecommunications Consultancy Service Report No. 3.
        for Cranfield Institute of Technology Centre for
        Transport Studies. November 1974. (71pp.)

        This report presents a guide to the setting up of
        telephone equipment for dial-a-ride operations, the
        space it requires, facilities it offers, level of
        complexity of its operation and possible technical
        or operational problems. It also gives suggestions
        for the most appropriate choice of telephone equip-
        ment for various dial-a-ride operations and the
        effects of this on the control room and on dial-a-ride
        operation generally, and outlines methods of
        ordering and payment or rental for these. Tabulated
        appendices give statistics on mean delay of answered
        calls and probability of loss, and distribution of
        delays of answered calls.

4.4.21. Formby Bus-Rail Demonstration Project [*The] : A Pre-
        Service Feasibility Study.   (1970)
        HOVELL, P.J. and JONES, W.H.
        University of Liverpool. August 1970.

4.4.22. Formby Bus-Rail Demonstration Project [*The] : A Study
        of its Effect on Modal Split for the Journey to Work.
                                                        (1971)
        HOVELL, P.J. and JONES, W.H.
        University of Liverpool. July 1971.

4.4.23. Formby Bus-Rail Demonstration Project [*The] : A
        Survey Analysis of the Changed Demand Pattern. (1972)
        JONES, W.H.
        University of Liverpool. July 1972.

        (see also ref. 4.4.53. below)

4.4.24. Future Urban Transport Technology. (1976)
BAKER, R.C.
Paper read at a Conference on Passenger Transport
and the Environment held at the University of York,
March 1976 and published as Chapter 9 in 'Passenger
Transport and the Environment', ed. R. Cresswell
(pp. 191-206).

(see ref. 4.5.7. below)

4.4.25. Intermediate Solutions. (1975)
ROBERTS, J . and McGLYNN, R.
Built Environment. Vol. 1. No. 2. September 1975.
(pp. 112-116)

An outline of international experimental and
operational examples of alternatives to the private
car.

4.4.26. Metro Flyer [*The] : A Suburban Express Bus Service
to Downtown Area, Baltimore County - Baltimore City. (1967)

MARYLAND METROPOLITAN TRANSIT AUTHORITY.
PB 177030. 1967.

4.4.27. Metro Guideway [*The] : An Integrated Automobile,
Transit and Freight Transportation System. (1972)
CANTY, E.T.
General Motors Research Publication GMR-1136. Warren,
Michigan, 1972. (Also published in Highway Research
Record No. 397, Highway Research Board, Washington
D.C. 1972).

4.4.28. Minibus in Washington D.C. [*The] - Final Report. (1965)

WASHINGTON METROPOLITAN AREA RAPID TRANSIT COMMISSION.
DC-MTD-2 May 1965.

4.4.29. Minibus Service.[*Attitudes towards the London
Transport] (1973)
HEDGES, B. and SMITH, D.
Social and Community Planning Research.   February 1973.

4.4.30. Minitrams and New Addington. (1975)
PRESCOTT-CLARKE, P.
Social and Community Planning Research.   Report No.354.
February 1975.   (84pp. plus Appendices).

This report describes the methods and findings of
investigations conducted in 1974 into what improvements
New Addington residents would like to see in their
local public and private transport systems and into
their likely attitudes to a suggested new mode of
public transport between New Addington and Croydon,
consisting of a light rapid transport system on a
fixed track.   The research techniques reported on
were a series of informal group discussions and a
structured attitude interview survey among randomly
selected adults.

4.4.31. Monorail.[*The Case for the] (1965)
BUCKS. DEPARTMENTS OF ARCHITECTURE AND PLANNING.
Bucks.County Council. Aylesbury. April 1965.

4.4.32. New Systems of Urban Transportation.[*Case Studies
of Seven] (1969)
CANTY, E.T. and SOBEY, A.J.
General Motors Research Publication GMR-845. Warren,
Michigan. January 1969.

4.4.33. New Technology in Urban Transport.(1972)
MITCHELL, C.G.B.
Proceedings of the Institution of Civil Engineers.
Vol. 52. August 1972. (pp. 127-147)

4.4.34. New Transport System Characteristics.[*General
Concepts Concerning] (1974)
VALERO, J.
Report No. 7 of Conference on Urban Transport
Services, Theme No. 2: Present and Future Transport
Systems. Madrid, Spain. October 1974. (33pp.)

(Gestion del Servicio de Transporte Urbano de
Viajeros. Tema 2: Sistemas de Transporte Presentes
y Futuros. Ponencia 7: Ideas Generales Acerca de
las Caracteristicas de los Nuevos Sistemas de Transporte.)

I Mesa Redonda 'Gestion del Servicio de Transporte
Urban de Viajeros'. Instituto de Estudios de
Administration Local-Centro de Documentation, Joaquin
Garcia Morato 7, Madrid, Spain.

This paper reviews the difficulties arising in
urban transport systems and the remedial methods of
solving them. Present and future transport systems
are examined from the financial aspect and from those
of time and comfort (the possibility of finding a
seat, not too close contact with other travellers,
personal safety, the environment inside the vehicle,
and the vehicle's aesthetic aspect). An integrated
transport system is recommended.

4.4.35 Para - Transit: Neglected Options for Urban Mobility.(1976)
KIRBY, R.F., BUTT, K.U., KEMP, M.A., McGILLIVRAY, R.G.
and WOHL, M.
The Urban Institute. Washington DC.1976. (334pp.)

This report describes the findings of a study financed
by the U.S. Department of Transport to investigate
existing para-transit operations in the U.S.A. (car-
sharing, jitneys and dial-a-ride services). It also
assessed the potential of such operations for improving
mobility for both car and non-car owners in the dispersed U.S. suburban land use pattern. Four main
areas are identified in which para-transit could
contribute to improved mobility : suburb to city
centre work journeys; suburban non-car owners'
leisure trips; public transport feeder services;
and travel within the CBD. Numerous detailed case
studies are presented and a bibliography containing
over 200 references to U.S. para-transit operations
is included.

4.4.36.   Peak Park Pathfinder Services. (1974)
          SMITH, M.
          Paper read at Rural Transport Seminar held at the
          Polytechnic of Central London. November 1974.
          (pp. 26-29 of Seminar proceedings).

          Experimental bus and minibus services in Derbyshire
          are described in this paper.

4.4.37   Personalized Bus Service for Heathrow Airport Staff.
          [*Experience with a] (1974)
          HERATY, M.J. and DAY, D.J.
          Paper read at the PTRC Summer Annual Meeting.
          July 1974.

4.4.38   Postbus [*The] - a new element in Britain's rural
          transport pattern. (1977)
          TURNOCK, D.
          Geography. Vol.62.Part 2.No.275. April 1977.
          (pp.112-118)

4.4.39   Postbus Network. [*The Scottish] (1975)
          TRODDEN, C.W. (Scottish Postal Board)
          Paper read at the PTRC Summer Annual Meeting.
          Seminar S - Public Transport.July 1975.

4.4.40   Public Transport in Devon.[*Further Progress with](1975)
          AWDAS, D.
          Paper read at Rural Transport Seminar held at the
          Polytechnic of Central London. November 1975.(pp.66-
          73 of Seminar proceedings)
          This paper includes sections on experimental bus
          services, and on publicity and marketing.

4.4.41   Public Transport.[*Promotion of Urban] (1973)
          EUROPEAN CONFERENCE OF MINISTERS OF TRANSPORT.
          December 1973(86pp.)

          The results of a study of promotional measures
          concerning urban public transport in European towns
          are summarised.   The aims of the study were to
          record the various measures taken to attract more
          custom to public transport and to assess the main
          results.   Particular stress is laid on promotional
          experiments.   Questionnaires were sent out and
          returned from 23 towns in ten different European
          countries. The information from these forms the
          basis of a general description, followed by a
          more detailed investigation and assessment of the
          various types of promotional improvement being
          implemented.   These are classified into three
          types (measures relating to roads and their
          utilisation;   improvements in conventional transport
          operation through measures taken in the under-
          taking; and operational improvements made by
          introducing 'new services') and discussed under
          these three headings.   Two annexes present summaries

of specific public transport promotional schemes in 15 individual European towns (including Derby, Manchester, Teesside and Stevenage in Britain), and a report on measures for promoting the utilisation of urban public transport in Japan.

4.4.42.   Ramblers' Bus [*The] :   Service 417 to the Surrey Hills.(1977)
GARRARD, B.J.
Buses. No.270.September 1977.(pp.363-364)

An account of a small experimental bus project carried out in Surrey in summer 1977, illustrating co-operation between Surrey County Council, who initiated the scheme, and the bus operators (London Country Bus Services). The bus service operated on a circular route from Dorking on Sundays and public holidays, catering for people without a car available who wished to visit the countryside. The timetable was designed to link with train and Green Line services from London. The aim of the service was principally to take walkers to a convenient starting point from which to walk back to Dorking, but it was also used by many people (especially local elderly people) for a country leisure ride.

4.4.43.   Rapid Transit System. [*Road Transport in a](1968)
BENNETT, R.F.
Institute of Transport Journal. Vol.31. March 1968. (pp.333-344)

4.4.44   Rural Transport Innovation.[*An Independent View of](1977
PEDDLE, J.
Paper road at Rural Transport Seminar held at the Polytechnic of Central London. November 1977. (pp.26-58 of Seminar Proceedings).

4.4.45   Skokie Swift - the Commuters' Friend.(1968)
BUCK, T.
Mass Transportation Demonstration Project - Final Report. Chicago Transit Authority. Chicago.1968. (65 pp.)

The report describes the development, progress and achievements of the Skokie Swift high-speed 2-station commuter shuttle service, linking the medium-density suburb of Skokie, Illinois, to Chicago's main-line rapid transit line at the City boundary. Park and ride facilities were provided at the outer terminal and feeder bus services were co-ordinated with the service. The scheme began in 1964 as a locally-sponsored two-year mass demonstration project with federal aid, authorised by the 1961 National Housing Act. Ridership was substantially higher than expected, amounting to approximately 7,000 per weekday after two years and surveys showed that approximately 20% of passengers had

switched from cars.   Over the 2-year period
operating costs were covered by fares collected.
Because of its success, at the end of the 2-year
experimental period the service was continued
by the Chicago Transit Authority as part of its
permanent mass transportation system.   The report
describes the extensive promotional campaign
carried out before and after the service began,
which was a significant element in its immediate
success.   It also summarises the findings of
surveys carried out before the service began and
at various stages afterwards, to determine passenger
characteristics, travel patterns in the area and
the changes in these resulting from the new
element in modal choice availability.   An appendix
contains details of the survey methods and results.

4.4.46.   Taxi Systems [*Self-drive]:   a preliminary feasibility
           study.(1974)
           BEAUMONT LEWIS, C.
           TRRL Supplementary Report SR 38UC.1974. (52pp.)

4.4.47.   Taxi Systems [*Zonal]:   An Improvement in Local
           Mobility. (1976)
           LOWE, S.R.
           Traffic Engineering and Control.Vol.17.No.12.
           December 1976.(pp.520-521)

           Because bus routes in London tend to use main
           roads on the edges of residential areas, residents
           are often not well served by public transport for
           local trips within their neighbourhood, and most
           trips to local shopping centres have to be made
           on foot or by private car when available.   Normal
           taxi services and conventional dial-a-ride schemes
           may offer an alternative to some, but usage is
           limited by the cost of taxi fares, the difficulty
           of obtaining a taxi on the street within residential
           areas, and the necessity to have easy access to a
           telephone.   A 'zonal' taxi service within each
           residential area could considerably improve local
           mobility, particularly for people without a car,
           those unable to walk far and unable to afford
           normal taxi fares, and people without telephones.
           It could also benefit public transport services
           by providing improved access to these.   This
           article examines the feasibility of such a system,
           based on predetermined regular routes and schedules
           connecting the residential neighbourhoods with the
           local centre and covering most roads in the area,
           operating on a hail-stop basis.   Journeys would
           average about one mile in length and flat fares
           would be charged, the level of these depending on
           household density within each area of operation.
           A model is developed which indicates that a flat
           fare of approximately 5p. in high density areas and
           21p. in low density areas (at mid - 1975 prices)

would permit viable operation, unlike conventional
dial-a-ride schemes, which have usually incurred
heavy financial losses. Such fares should be low
enough to attract sufficient passengers yet
sufficiently attractive to cab-drivers to encourage
their participation. The improved quality of
local transport facilities should also generate
additional trips per household per day.

4.4.48.   Taxicab Systems [*Alternative]:   A London Case
          Study. (1976)
          DOGANIS, R.S. and LOWE, S.R.
          Polytechnic of Central London. April 1976.
          Vol.I (240 pp.)
          Vol.II Appendices (128 pp.)

          The report describes the findings and conclusions
          of a three-year study of the London taxicab trade.
          Volume I includes an examination of the legislative
          and institutional factors affecting the trade and
          of differences between the taxi and hire car trades,
          and an evaluation of its cost and revenue structure.
          The pattern of demand for taxi and hire car trips
          in London is outlined, using data from pre-existing
          sources, including the Greater London Transportation
          Study.   The study also involved an analysis of a
          number of foreign taxicab systems and an assessment
          of their relevance to London, and an examination of
          'personalised transit' systems, including dial-a-
          ride systems.   Possibilities for alternative
          patterns of taxicab operations are discussed and
          the legislative constraints to changes in the
          pattern of the London taxicab trade are outlined.

          Volume II presents details of several of the
           surveys undertaken for the research programme.
          These comprise a comparative description of taxi
          operations in six European cities (Amsterdam,
          Brussels, Copenhagen, London, Madrid and Paris);
          variations in the geographical distribution of the
          private car hire trade in Greater London; an
          analysis of taxi hirings at Central London rail
          terminals; a mathematical model of a two-class
          taxicab system; and a description of the legal
          framework for taxicab and bus operations in
          London.

4.4.49   Tomorrow's Transportation: new systems for the
          urban future. (1968)
          U.S. DEPARTMENT OF HOUSING AND URBAN DEVELOPMENT.
          Washington D.C.1968.

4.4.50   Town-Flyer : Atlanta's City Centre Shuttle Bus.(1972)
          CITY OF ATLANTA DEPARTMENT OF PLANNING and ERIC HILL &
          ASSOCIATES.
          SA-MTD-1,2. 1972.

4.4.51.   Transit Demonstrations Really Shown? [*What Have](1971)
          SMITH, C.O.
          Transportation Engineering Journal of A.S.C.E.
          (Proceedings of the American Society of Civil
          Engineers) Vol.97.No.T.E.2.1971.(pp.325-331)

          The paper presents the results of an analysis
          of 25 U.S. Federal mass transportation demonstration
          projects, covering both rail and bus experiments
          in a variety of areas. The principal common
          findings are outlined under broad headings
          including feeder buses, minibuses, express
          service, transfers, parking, fares and deficits,
          level of service, and ridership.

4.4.52   Unconventional Bus Services [*Symposium on]:
          summaries of papers and discussions. (1977)
          TRANSPORT AND ROAD RESEARCH LABORATORY.
          TRRL Supplementary Report SR 336. October 1977.(43pp.)
          The Proceedings of a Symposium held at the Transport
          and Road Research Laboratory, Crowthorne, Berkshire.
          October 6th. and 7th. 1976.

          The following papers and discussions following them
          are summarised in this report:

          Paper 1:   BALCOMBE, R.J.   The rôle of unconventional
                                        bus services in public
                                        transport.

          Paper 2:   MITCHELL, C.G.B.   Social Aspects of public
                                        transport.(see ref.3.2.49
                                                    above).

          Paper 3:   OXLEY, P.R.   Dial-a-Ride in the U.K:
                                        a general study.

          Paper 4:   GUENTHER, K.W.   Dial-a-Ride in the U.S.A:
                                        a case study.

          Paper 5:   LLOYD, F.J.   Dial-a-Ride in the U.K:
                                        a case study.

          Paper 6:   MARTIN, P.H.   Comparative assessment of
                                        unconventional bus systems.

          Paper 7:   ENNOR, P.D.   Public transport in rural
                                        areas: a review.

          Paper 8:   CARPENTER, T.C.   Postbuses in Scotland.

          Paper 9:   WILKES, P.F.   The Norfolk Community Bus I.

          Paper 10: MADGETT, J.   The Norfolk Community Bus II.

          Paper 11: MADGETT, J.   Rural Midibus experiments.

          Paper 12: HAWKER,Mrs.M.E.   Social Transport.

          Paper 13: DICKINSON, D.W.   Stage bus diversion schemes.

          Paper 14: DAVISON, P.   National Park buses.

          Paper 15: MILEFANTI,D.C.   The rural transport
                                        experiments.

          The Summary of the Proceedings by the Symposium
          Chairman, M. Grimmer, is also included.

4.4.53   Bus Demonstration Project: Summary Report No.6.
          Formby Bus Feeder Service to the Local Railway
          Station (1974).
          DEPARTMENT OF THE ENVIRONMENT.
          H.M.S.O. 1974.(20 pp.)
          (See also refs. 4.4.21 - 23 above).

4.4.54   Bus Demonstration Projects. [*Working Group on](1970)
          DEPARTMENT OF THE ENVIRONMENT. Report to the Minister
          H.M.S.O. 1970.

4.4.55   Minibus Act.(1977)
          DEPARTMENT OF TRANSPORT.
          H.M.S.O. 1977.

4.4.56   Passenger Vehicles (Experimental Areas) Act. (1977)
          DEPARTMENT OF TRANSPORT.
          H.M.S.O. 1977.

4.4   Subsidiary References.

1.1   New Towns - Transport and Mobility.

1.1.6   Demand Bus for a New Town. (1971)
1.1.12   Public Transport in its Exclusive Right of Way in Evry. (1973)
1.1.13   A Review of Public Transport in New Towns. (1974)
1.1.14   Public Transport in New Towns in Great Britain. (1971)
1.1.15   Public Transportation and the Needs of New Communities. (1972)
1.1.18   Transport and New Towns. Volume Two. (1976)
1.1.19   Transport and New Towns. Volume Three. (1977)
1.1.21   Transportation for a New Town. (1971)
1.1.22   Workshop on Transportation for New Towns and Communities. (1969)
1.1.23   Transportation Innovations in New Communities Abroad. (1973)
1.1.25   Transportation Planning for New Towns. (1969)
1.1.28   Urban Transportation: Problems and Progress. (1972)

2.1   Runcorn.

2.1.2-9 and 2.1.11 : [Runcorn Busway.]

2.4   Other New Towns.

2.4.14 and 2.4.16-23 : [Harlow Dial-a-Bus service.]
2.4.31   Dial-a-Bus News Letter No.1 (1975) [Milton Keynes.]
2.4.32   Concern No.3 (1975) [Milton Keynes transport planning seminar
                                                           edition.]
2.4.42   Milton Keynes - So Far So Good. (1977)
2.4.54-55 and 2.4.57-60 : [Stevenage Superbus Experiment.]

3.1 Studies of Modal Choice Behaviour and Value of Travel Time.

3.1.38   *Minibus Service W9 : Bus/Minibus Modal Choice Analysis and Cost-Benefit Assessment. (1975)*

3.1.41   *Modal Choice and the Value of Travel Time. (1976)*

3.1.42   *An Investigation of Modal Choice for Dual-Mode Transit, People Mover and Personal Rapid Transit Systems. (1974)*

3.1.100   *Value of Commuters' Travel Time - A Study in Urban Transportation. (1968)*

3.2 Social Aspects of Mobility.

3.2.49   *Some Social Aspects of Public Passenger Transport. (1977)*

3.3 Interaction between Land Use and Travel.

3.3.11   *Sweden's Small-scale Busways. (1973)*

3.3.21   *Passenger Transport as an Urban Element. (1976)*

3.3.50   *Bus Operation in Alternative Urban Structures. (1976)*

3.4 Transport and Mobility - General and Miscellaneous.

3.4.6   *The Urban Transportation Problem. (1965)*

4.1 Public Transport - Operational Aspects.

4.1.67   *Human Performance Requirements for an Innovative Transit Bus Operation. (1976)*

4.1.72   *London Borough Buses: Hillingdon takes the initiative. (1977)*

4.1.77   *Midibus Operation in Cardiff: a Low Cost Approach to a Low Demand Problem. (1976)*

4.1.89   *Planning for Public Transport. (1976)*

4.1.99   *Work Attitudes of Bus Drivers and Conductors. (1976)*

4.1.100   *Work Attitudes of Taxi Drivers. (1976)*

4.2 Public Transport - Marketing Approach.

4.2.6   *A Survey of Commuter Attitudes towards Rapid Transit Systems, Vol.2. (1963)*

4.2.24   *The Management of Innovation. (1961)*

4.2.25   *The Management of Urban Public Transport: a marketing perspective. (1975)*

4.2.41   *An Opinion Survey of the Yorkshire Dales Rail Services in 1975. (1977)*

4.3 Public Transport - Ergonomic Aspects.

4.3.7   *Passenger Behavior Studies for Automatic Transit Systems. (1976)*

4.3.8   *Literature Survey of Passenger Comfort Limitations of High-Speed Ground Transportation. (1965)*

4.3.24   *Human Factors and Ergonomic Considerations in the Design of Automatic Transit Systems. (1975)*

4.3.26   *Human Factors in Engineering and Design. (1974)*

4.3.31   *Motion Discomfort and Transportation Guideway Form. (1974)*

4.3.35   *Comparison of Noise and Vibration Levels in Rapid Transit Vehicle Systems. (1964)*

4.3.36	Rides, Trips and Moves on a Bus. (1970)
4.3.53	An Evaluation of Train Seats by Observation of Sitting Behaviour. (1967)
4.3.57	Vehicle Design for People. (1976)

4.5   Public Transport - General amd Miscellaneous.

4.5.7	Passenger Transport and the Environment: the integration of public passenger transport with the environment. (1976)
4.5.9	Public Transport in Bedfordshire: Facts, Views, Issues, Options. (1974)
4.5.13	Public Transport for Rural Communities. (1977)
4.5.21	Report of the Departmental Committee on the London Taxicab Trade. (1970)

7.1   Transport Policy.

7.1.12	The Economic and Social Impact of Investments in Public Transit. (1973)
7.1.37	The Comparative Study of Transport Systems: Swedish Urban Transport Policy and its Application in Britain. (1974)
7.1.73	Traffic in Towns: a study of the long-term problems of traffic in urban areas. ("Crowther" and "Buchanan" Reports.) (1973)

8.1   Survey Techniques: Behavioural and Attitudinal.

| 8.1.94 | Multidimensional Scaling of Consumer Preferences for a Public Transportation System. (1974) |
| 8.1.114 | User Preferences for a Demand-Responsive Transportation System: A case - study report. (1971) |

8.3   Research Techniques and Methodology: General and Miscellaneous.

8.3.15	Home Interview Phase of the Minibus Research Programme. (1973)
8.3.16	On-Bus Phase of the Minibus Research Programme. (1973)
8.3.17	L.T. Minibus Study. (1974)

9.2   Bibliographies.

9.2.3	Buses in Urban Areas. 1970 - 1976. (1976)
9.2.4	Bibliography: Control and Communication. (1976)
9.2.9	Passenger Transport Interchange Between Inland Surface Modes - a bibliography for 1968-1973. (1974)
9.2.11	Rapid Transit: a select reading list. (1970)

4.5 General and Miscellaneous.

A number of references relating to aspects of public transport
which fall outside the specific scope of subsections 4.1 to
4.5 are brought together in this subsection, together with
some more general material on public transport which provides
useful background to a study of public transport in new towns.
The following are among the specific subject areas covered:-

- Studies of community attitudes to public transport.

- Usage of public transport in urban areas.

- Public transport in rural areas.

The A.M.V. report Public Transport in Bedfordshire: Facts,
Views, Issues, Options (4.5.9) describes a largescale study
which included detailed investigation of both public transport provision and needs and of the viewpoints of all sectors
of the community involved with public transport. Other
studies involving qualitative investigations into community
needs for and attitudes to public transport are described in
A.M.V's Sheffield and Rotherham Land Use/Transportation Study
Community Involvement Programme report (4.5.3) and in
Summary of the Issues Raised by the Public through the
Community Involvement Programme (4.5.4).

The collected conference papers published as Passenger
Transport and the Environment (4.5.7) provide useful material
on a range of topics relating to the environmental aspects
of public transport. It includes papers which consider the
relationship between public transport and urban form, the
rôle of bus system experiments and innovatory systems,possible
improvements in technology and in the legislative and
administrative framework, and the design aspects of public
transport vehicles and infrastructure. Several of the papers
are included in relevant sections elsewhere in the bibliography.

4.5.1   Attitudes and Beliefs Underlying the Use of Local
         Bus Services: [*An Examination of] (1975)
         THOMAS, K. and BULL, H.C.
         Cranfield Institute of Technology. Centre for
         Transport Studies. September 1975.(50pp.)

4.5.2   Bus Travel in Town Centres.(1969)
         LYONS, D.J.
         Traffic Engineering and Control. Vol.11. No.1.May
                                          1969. (pp.20-23)

4.5.3   Community Involvement Programme. Household Reviews.
         Report on Phases 1 and 2. (Sheffield and Rotherham
         Land Use/Transportation Study.) (1977)
         A.M.V. Ltd. (ALAN M. VOORHEES). 1977. (29pp.)

         The methods and findings of studies conducted as
         part of the Community Involvement Programme within the
         Sheffield and Rotherham Land Use/Transportation Study
         are described in this report. Data for the study
         was derived from discussions with representatives of
         local organised groups, a largescale household interview
         survey providing details of trip-making patterns and
         some basic attitudinal data, and extended interviews
         with a small sample of households. The report is
         concerned largely with the interpretation of the data
         accumulated by the first two phases of the detailed
         interview programme.

4.5.4   Community Involvement Programme. [*Summary of the
         Issues Raised by the Public through the] (1976)
         WYTCONSULT (Freeman, Fox & Associates; Martin and
         Voorhees Associates and Seconded County Staff)
         Document 108. West Yorkshire Transportation Studies.
                                          August 1976.(42pp.)

         The objectives of the West Yorkshire Community
         Involvement Programme are set out and the techniques
         used in achieving these objectives are outlined. The
         major part of the report is concerned with describing
         the principal findings of the studies and discussing
         the issues raised by them and the implications arising
         from the general conclusions. The report concludes by
         summarising the input which the Community Involvement
         Programme has had to various other studies within the
         West Yorkshire Transportation Study.

4.5.5   Comprehensive Approach to Transport. [*The] (1977)
         BODGER, J.M.
         Chartered Institute of Transport Journal. Vol.38.No.1.
                                          November 1977. (pp.11-15)

         A review of the rôle of bus transport in urban
         transport planning.

4.5.6   Modern Transit.(1974)
         GAPP, P.
         Metropolitan. March/April 1974.

264

4.5.7 Passenger Transport and the Environment: the integration of public passenger transport with the environment.(1976)
CRESSWELL, R. (ed.)
Leonard Hill. 1976
Proceedings of a Conference held at the University of York in March 1976 and organised by the Construction Industry Conference Centre Ltd., in association with other bodies. (299 pp.)

Conference papers and discussions relating to the integration of public transport with the urban environment are presented in this book. Aspects covered move from the overall structure and design of towns and cities down to the detailed design of buses, trains, stations and bus stops. Part One, Public Transport in the Urban Structure, is concerned with the public transport system in both established and newly-developed urban areas. The need for public transport to be a key factor at the design stage of new major urban areas is considered to be of paramount importance, with a planned relationship between the location of people and the picking-up points of the public transport system Part Two, Passenger Transport in the Local Environment, considers the part which public transport could play in providing for adequate accessibility in towns and cities without the alternative need for major environmental changes to cater for cars. Urban conservation schemes and the pedestrianisation of parts of town and city centres are ways in which this could be achieved and the relationship of public transport with such schemes is discussed. This section also includes a review of bus system experiments and developments. Part Three, New Developments in Passenger Transport, considers changes in the legislative, financial and technological aspects of public transport which could secure its improvement and increased attraction to the public. In Part Four, Design for Public Transport, the importance of good design is discussed in relation both to vehicles and to transport infrastructure. (see also refs. 3.3.21, 3.3.50, 4.3.57, 4.4.1, and 4.4.24 above)

4.5.8 Public Attitudes to Transport in the Eastbourne, Bexhill and Hastings Area.(1975)
SMITH, D.
Social and Community Planning Research. Report No. P.341. December 1975.

The report describes the findings of an interview survey carried out to obtain information about public attitudes to transport problems. The survey formed part of a programme of research undertaken by East Sussex County Council to help plan the County's short and long-term transport strategy. The first section assesses whether existing transport facilities meet residents' requirements in terms of environmental standards. In Section II residents' views on existing public transport provision and on the kind of improvement they want are presented. The problem of traffic congestion is then examined and residents' views on ways of solving it discussed. General conclusions are drawn and four pointers for those concerned with regional planning are shown to have emerged from the survey. These are that the public would be likely to find the following developments acceptable:-

(i) Movement towards pedestrianised areas and greater protection for pedestrians crossing busy roads.

(ii) Increased priority to buses for rush hour travel, combining some positive encouragement to motorists to switch to buses with restrictive policies.

(iii) Improved parking facilities in special parking areas adjacent to or conveniently linked to pedestrianised areas by bus services.

(iv) Greater control over heavy lorry movement to reduce pedestrian dangers and to remove the larger, noisier vehicles from residential areas.

Methodological details and a copy of the questionnaire are contained in the Appendicies.

4.5.9   Public Transport in Bedfordshire: Facts, Views, Issues, Options. (1974)
A.M.V. (ALAN M. VOORHEES and ASSOCIATES).
July 1974 . (154pp.)
(See also ref. 8.3.23 below.)

The report presents the results of a comprehensive study of public transport carried out in Bedfordshire between 1972 and 1974 in order to provide the County Council with sufficient information to enable public transport policies to be developed. The main issues relating to public transport in the county are identified and a framework suggested to help formulate relevant policies. Emphasis was placed on obtaining a detailed understanding of the relationship between public transport and the needs and lifestyles of the communities in the county. The work programme covered four main aspects:-

(i) Study of public transport operation - providing a detailed account of the provision and use of public transport in Bedfordshire as at 1972 (and of the major subsequent trends).

(ii) Study of communities in relation to public transport - in order to show how public transport relates to and affects the population in different areas.

(iii) Study of viewpoints - including an evaluation of the needs, views and problems of public transport patrons, operators and their staff, public officials, politicians and other segments of the community.

(iv) Study of transport policies and innovations – involving research into experience with transport policies and innovations being tried in other parts of the country.

4.5.10　Public Transport in Towns and Cities of Britain and Ireland. [*Use of] (1974)
WHITE, P.R.
Journal of Transport Economics and Policy. Vol. VIII No. 1. January 1974. (pp. 26–39)

4.5.11　Public Transport. [*Research and] (1974)
WEBSTER, F.V.
TRRL Supplementary Report SR 76 UC. 1974.

4.5.12　Public Transport. [*Survey of] (1972)
NATIONAL COUNCIL OF WOMEN. 1972.

4.5.13　Rural Communities. [*Public Transport for] (1977)
BETTS, T.J. and HOLMES, K.
Paper read at a Rural Transport Seminar held at the Polytechnic of Central London. November 1977. (pp. 11–25 of the Seminar Proceedings).

4.5.14　Rural Transport Problem among Norwich Commuter Villages. [*Some Aspects of the] (1975)
HOARE, A.G.
Journal of Transport Economics and Policy. Vol. IX No. 2. 1975. (pp. 141–153)

(Paper read at the Institute of British Geographers' Transport Group Symposium. University of East Anglia. January 1974).

This paper describes a survey carried out in East Anglia which related attitudes towards public transport to characteristics of respondents and villages in which they lived. Poor public transport was found to be more likely to be perceived as a major drawback by village residents who had previously lived in Norwich than by long-term residents.

4.5.15　Rural Transport: What Future Now? (1971)
GRIFFITHS, E.
Paper read at Rural District Councils Association Transport Conference. 19th. October 1971.

4.5.16　Urban Areas. [*Public Transport's Rôle in] (1968)
BENNETT, R.F. and McCORQUODALE, D.
Traffic Engineering and Control. Vol 9. No. 12. April 1968. (pp. 596–601)

4.5.17　Urban Areas. [*Use of Public Transport in] (1962)
SCHNORE, L.E.
Traffic Quarterly. Vol. 16. No. 4. October 1962. (pp. 488–499)

4.5.18   Urban Passenger Transport: Some trends and prospects.
                                                           (1977)
         WEBSTER, F.V.
         TRRL Report No. LR 771. 1977.(37pp.)

         This report was first presented as a paper to the 10th
         Symposium on 'The Future of Conurbation Transport',
         University of Manchester, Department of Extra-Mural
         Studies in October 1976.   The trends in patronage by
         the main modes of public transport over the past twenty
         years are described, and quantitative explanations
         given, where possible, of the changes which have taken
         place in terms of the main service variables, fare
         levels, and the socio-economic variables which are
         mainly responsible for the background trends.   The
         social consequences of these trends are discussed.
         The results of various travel surveys are described in
         relation to the travel 'needs' and 'desires' of
         individuals.   Current work on the evaluation of the
         main factors affecting public transport patronage is
         described and the latest information on elasticities
         with respect to fares, service levels etc., is
         summarised.   A TRRL model is used to see how bus
         patronage is likely to be affected over the next ten
         years if a break-even policy is applied, and, alterna-
         tively how the subsidy level will grow if attempts are
         made to hold on to the present levels of bus patronage.
         (see also ref. 4.1.26 above).

4.5.19   Urban Public Transportation. [*Mobility Evaluation
                                             for] (1976)
         POPPER, R.J. and HOEL, L.A.
         Transportation Planning and Technology. Vol.3.1976.
                                               (pp.131-141)

4.5.20   Urban Transportation. (1969)
         VOORHEES, A.M. and KEITH, R.A.
         Consulting Engineer. Vol.32. No.3. March 1969.
                                               (pp.130-136)

GOVERNMENT REPORTS AND PUBLICATIONS.

4.5.21   London Taxicab   Trade. [*Report of the Departmental
                                     Committee on the] (1970)
         Chairman: Rt.Hon. A. Maxwell Stamp.
         H.M.S.O. Cmnd. 4483. 1970

4.5.22   Public Transport and Traffic.(1967)
         MINISTRY OF TRANSPORT.
         H.M.S.O. Cmnd. 3481. 1967.

4.5.23   Rural Transport in Devon.[*Study of] (1971)
         DEPARTMENT OF THE ENVIRONMENT.1971.

4.5 Subsidiary References.

1.1 New Towns - Transport and Mobility.

1.1.9   The New Towns in the London Transport Area and their Passenger Transport. (1959)
1.1.11   Public Transport in a New City. (1967)
1.1.13   A Review of Public Transport in New Towns. (1974)
1.1.14   Public Transport in New Towns in Great Britain. (1971)
1.1.16   Transport and Mobility in Durham New Towns. (1974-5)
1.1.26   Urban Cluster Villages. (1976)

1.2 New Towns - Non-Transport Aspects.

1.2.55   Final Report of the New Towns Committee. (1946)

2.3 Telford.

2.3.4   Telford Bus Use Attitude Survey: An investigation of citizen attitudes towards public transportation in Telford. (1976)
2.3.14   A Facility Survey of Telford Development Corporation Industrial Estates (1974)

2.4 Other New Towns.

2.4.37   Public Transport in the City. (1975) [Milton Keynes]
2.4.38   Public Transport in Milton Keynes: Report of the Working Party. (1974)

3.1 Studies of Modal Choice Behaviour and Value of Travel Time.

3.1.14   A Theoretical Estimate of the effect of London Car Commuters Transferring to Bus Travel. (1968)
3.1.32   Journey to Work: Modal Split. (1967)
3.1.60   Preferences for Transit Service by Homogeneous Groups of Individuals. (1974)
3.1.68   Need as a Criterion for Transportation Planning. (1973)
3.1.97   Urban Mobility. (1970)
3.1.98   Psychological Determinants of User Behaviour. (1977)
3.1.99   The Effects on Transport Benefit Evaluation of User Misperception of Costs. (1974)

3.2 Social Aspects of Mobility.

3.2.3   Automobile and Public Transportation for Retired People. (1971)
3.2.14   Lifestyles and the Transportation Needs of the Elderly in Los Angeles. (1976)
3.2.20   Employment, Mobility and Public Transportation. (1971)
3.2.71   Travelling Expenses and Transport for Hospital Patients and Visitors . (1973)

3.3 Interaction between Land Use and Travel.

3.3.35   Homes, Towns and Traffic. (1968)

3.4 *Transport and Mobility - General and Miscellaneous.*

3.4.6   *The Urban Transportation Problem.* (1965)

5.1 *Private Motor Transport.*

5.1.16   *The Possible Effects of Petrol Rationing on Travel in London.*
                                                                    (1975)

7.1 *Transport Policy.*

7.1.15   *Public Transport and Local Government Reorganisation.* (1975)
7.1.20   *Priority for Passengers.* (1976)
7.1.44   *Plan for Public Transportation.* (1974)
7.1.51   *Public Transport Plan for the Future.* (1973)
7.1.52   *Mass Transportation in Massachussetts.* (1964)
7.1.56   *Mass Transportation in a Small City.* (1968)
7.1.59   *People and Transport - the future of Public Transport in*
                                              Sunderland. (1964)
7.1.61   *Public Transport for West Yorkshire.* (1975)
7.1.62   *The Rôle of British Rail in Public Transport.* (1977)
7.1.76   *Transport Policy.* [*White Paper*]. (1977)
7.1.77   *Transport Policy: A Consultation Document.* (1976)
7.1.79   *Urban Transport Planning.* (1972)

8.2 *Economic Evaluation.*

8.2.7   *A Procedure for Determining Economic Base Levels for Public*
           Transport Services for Transportation Study Design Years. (1973)
8.2.8   *Economics and Methodology in Urban Transport Planning.* (1969)
8.2.17   *Estimating the Social Benefit of Constructing an Underground*
                                              Railway in London. (1963)

9.1 *Journals.*

9.1.7 - 25 [*Transport Journals*]

9.2 *Bibliographies.*

9.2.12   *Road Passenger Transport.* (1976)
9.2.13   *Transport Policies and Planning.* (1977)
9.2.15   *Transport: Sources of information together with a short*
                                              bibliography. (1973)
9.2.17   *Transportation Systems Bibliography.* (1974)

9.3 *Abstracting and Indexing Services.*

9.3.6   *Departments of the Environment and Transport Library Bulletin.*
                                              (*Fortnightly*)
9.3.18   *TRRL Information Storage and Retrieval System.* (*On request*)
9.3.19   *Transportation Research Abstracts.* (*Six times a year*)

9.4 *Research Registers.*

9.4.1   *Register of Research, 1977. Part II: Environmental Planning.*
                                              (*1977*)

9.4.2	*Register of Research, 1977. Part III Roads and Transport.*
	(1977)
9.4.4	*Research on Transport Economics. (Twice a year)*
9.4.5	*1977 World Survey of Current Research and Development on Roads and Road Transport. (1977)*

9.5 Statistical Sources.

9.5.1	*Basic Road Statistics. (Annually)*
9.5.6-8	*National Travel Survey 1972/73*
9.5.14	*Transport Statistics Great Britain. (Annually)*
9.5.15	*Annual Abstract of Statistics. (Annually)*
9.5.20	*Monthly Digest of Statistics. (Monthly)*
9.5.22	*Regional Statistics. (Annually)*

9.6 Other Sources of Information.

9.6.6	*Transport and Communications. (1975)*
9.6.10	*Guide to Official Statistics. (1976 and 1978)*

5. Private Motor Transport.

Car ownership and availability are crucial factors in modal choice decisions which both affect and are affected by the level of public transport provision in a given area. This section draws together a number of references on these aspects and on some factors affecting car usage, including motoring costs. Some literature which is relevant to car ownership and usage and to the effects of road traffic is included in other parts of the bibliography and cross-referenced at the end of this section. This includes material relating to the environmental and planning aspects of roads and road traffic (subsection 3.3); policy-oriented studies and official policy documents relating to roads and traffic (section 7.1); studies reporting measurements of journey times by car and other modes (subsection 3.1); and statistical sources (subsection 9.5). Forecasts of car ownership and future traffic volumes in new towns as a basis for road network proposals are contained in individual new town master plan documents. Figures of current car ownership in new towns and in some cases other aspects of private motor transport, such as garaging facilities, licence holding and petrol purchases, are given in the reports of household surveys carried out in specific new towns. These also usually include details of modal splits for various journey purposes (subsections 2.1-2.4).

From the early 1950's the Road Research Laboratory (now the Transport and Road Research Laboratory) have been making forecasts of future traffic volumes, based partly on annual 50-point traffic censuses, which have been used as a basis for the national road-building programme. Recent forecasts are set out in two TRRL reports by TANNER (5.1.4 and 5.1.20). In the last few years these forecasts have been the subject of a considerable amount of criticism. THE INDEPENDENT COMMISSION ON TRANSPORT'S report Changing Directions (7.1.3) includes a critical examination of the TRRL methods of predicting future car ownership and travel, and recommends much greater sophistication in future forecasting procedures taking into account studies of the causal and behavioural determinants of car ownership. The Commission recommend extensive research into the determinants of car ownership and use, with special regard to 'unwanted ownership'. Specific research proposals include large-scale surveys to monitor the growth of car ownership in relation to external factors which can be influenced by policy measures such as levels of service offered by alternative means of transport; and experiments in specific places to identify the effects of different combinations of restraint on the use of cars, and of improvements in walking, cycling and public transport facilities on car ownership and consumer satisfaction. The Government's Consultation Document on Transport Policy (7.1.77) outlines the assumptions and methods used in the calculation of the official national car ownership and traffic forecasts (Volume 2, Paper 7). It also sets out some of the commonly levelled criticisms both of specific aspects of the techniques used, and of the way in which the forecasts have been used as a basis for road-planning. The Consultation Document stated the Government's intention to seek

.n independent assessment of its road scheme appraisal techniques,
ncluding traffic forecasts. The conclusions of the Committee
et up to do this which was chaired by Sir George Leitch are
et out in the Advisory Committee Report on Trunk Road Assessment,
ublished in January 1978 (7.1.78). The report recommends the
eplacement of the extrapolatory forecasting method hitherto
sed by a 'causal model' which could be made more sensitive to
ocial and economic factors affecting car ownership, including
ncome, family structure, and the availability of public
ransport.

he two articles by MULLEN and WHITE in Traffic Engineering
nd Control (5.1.2) review critically both the national approach
o car ownership forecasting and other approaches which have
llowed for differences in income and residential density but
ave given less attention to possible trends in time. It is
uggested that future growth in car ownership - particularly
f second cars - will be increasingly sensitive to transport
olicies, especially those relating to future levels of public
ransport provision and to traffic restraint measures. The
uthors describe the person-based model of car ownership used
n the Telford Transportation Study which related car ownership
o person-type within the household, to individual rather than
ousehold incomes, and to alternative levels of public transport
uality. The need for considerable further research into the
roblems and methods of forecasting car ownership and usage is
tressed, and the authors point to the ownership and use of
ousehold cars in relation to household structure, and the effects
f public transport on car ownership as two particular subjects
equiring more investigation. Further details of the forecasting
echniques and assumptions used in the Telford Transportation
tudy model are given in the two-part article by PIKE,FULLER
nd WHITE and by MULLEN, BURSEY and WHITE (2.3.7).

espite the clear need for much more detailed research into the
otivation of car ownership and usage, relatively little British
ork has been published in these fields although investigations
re currently under way at the Transport and Road Research
aboratory and elsewhere. The results of a theoretical study
f car ownership decisions which was conducted in the United
tates are presented in the paper by BURNS, GOLOB and NICOLAIDIS
5.1.11). The article by BECKMANN and BURNS (5.1.10) discusses
he need for a better understanding of household car allocation
ecisions in relation to overall household travel behaviour,
nd attempts to develop a theory of urban households' decision-
aking in allocating the use of their cars between various travel
urposes. ARCHER, BULL and LUCAROTTI (5.1.1) describe an
mpirical quantitative study into car availability and usage
arried out in Cambridge in 1973 and discuss methodological
spects of the survey techniques used. A major conclusion from
his study was that much more research should be carried out into
actors affecting car purchase, including the less easily
uantifiable psychological factors.

5.   PRIVATE MOTOR TRANSPORT

5.1.1   Car Availability. [*Initial Study of] (1974)
ARCHER, P.R., BULL, H.C. and LUCAROTTI, P.S.K.
Cranfield Institute of Technology. Centre for
Transport Studies. Memorandum No.138. April 1974.
(71 pp.)

A household interview survey on car availability
and use carried out in Cambridge in 1973 is
described in this report. A critical account is
given of the questionnaire design, fieldwork
programme and methods of data analysis. Copies
of the questionnaire and interviewer briefing
notes are appended. The two main conclusions are
that car availability is not synonymous with household car ownership (and that consequently statistic
of car ownership and licence possession are inaccur
ate indicators of car availability) and that the
rate of use of available cars is very high, indepen
dent of sex and trip purpose: it was found that if
a car was available it was used for at least 78%
of non-walk trips. This implies that car availability is of paramount importance in modal choice
decisions. Three main areas for further research
are identified: more accurate measurements of car
availability to passengers; investigations of the
differences between daytime and evening availabil-
ities; and research into the factors which influenc
the decision to purchase a car.

5.1.2   Car Ownership [*Forecasting]: a new approach.
(1977)
MULLEN, P. and WHITE, M.

Part 1:   Traffic Engineering and Control. Vol.18
No.7/8. July/August 1977.(pp. 354-356)
Part 2:   Traffic Engineering and Control. Vol.18
No.9. September 1977.(pp. 422-426)

5.1.3   Car Ownership in the London Metropolitan Region.
(1973)
WILLMOTT, P.
Quarterly Bulletin of the Intelligence Unit.No.23.
Greater London Council. June 1973. (pp. 5-19)

5.1.4   Car Ownership Trends and Forecasts.(1977)
TANNER, J.C.
TRRL. Report LR 799. October 1977.

5.1.5   Car Rental Market [*The]: What of the Future?
(1977)
COUSINS, S.
Paper read at the British Vehicle Rental and
Leasing Associations's Rental Seminar. April 1977.

5.1.6   Cars? [*How Many More] (1973)
         HEDGES, B. and SMITH, D.
         Social and Community Planning Research. 1973.

5.1.7   Cost of Motoring to the Consumer. [*The] (1977)
         POTTER, S.
         Sustran Research Report No.1. June 1977. (21 pp.)
         The Open University. New Towns Study Unit.

         An examination of the Autombile Association and
         Family Expenditure Survey estimates. The study
         is part of a research project funded by the
         Nuffield Foundation, the main objective of which
         is the secondary analysis of existing statistics
         for transport policy decisions.

         (This paper has been revised by the author and
         renamed: Estimates of Private Motoring Costs and
         Mileage Allowance Calculations for Research and
         Industry. New Towns Study Unit. 1978).

5.1.8   Costs. [*Index of Motoring] (Annually)
         AUTOMOBILE ASSOCIATION.
         Drive Magazine. (October each year since 1975.)

         The Index gives figures for car running costs
         compiled from a household survey of some 1,000
         motorists per month. Information is presented on
         costs of petrol, oil,servicing/repairs, insurance
         and 'other' costs, and variations according to
         model of car and engine size are given.

5.1.9   Costs. [*Schedule of Estimated Vehicle Running]
                                             (Annually)
         AUTOMOBILE ASSOCIATION TECHNICAL SERVICES.
         A.A. Publications Division. Basingstoke.

         Annually published estimates for the standing and
         running costs of private cars, taking all costs
         into account (including depreciation.)

5.1.10   Household Automobile Allocation Decisions. [*A
                                       Theory of] (1976)
         BECKMANN, M.J. and BURNS, L.D.
         Transportation Science. Vol.10. No.1. February
                                   1976.(pp. 72-84)

         A theory of the decision-making behaviour of
         urban households in allocating the use of their
         cars among essential travel purposes is developed.
         This theory begins to assess interdependence of
         household members with respect to their trip-
         making behaviour. Mathematical programmes are
         developed based on the assumption that households
         attempt to minimise travel costs (in terms of
         both time and money) required to achieve essential
         purposes subject to constraints on car availabil-
         ity.

5.1.11 Household Automobile Ownership Decisions.
       [*Theory of Urban] (1976)
      BURNS, L.D., GOLOB, T.F. and NICOLAIDIS, G.
      Transportation Research Record No.569. Transporta-
      tion Research Board. Washington D.C. 1976.

5.1.12 Household Car Ownership. [*The Distribution of]
                  (1977)
      DOWNES, J.D.
      TRRL Supplementary Report SR 250. February 1977.
                  (18 pp.)

      Data from the 1971 National Population Census are
      used to develop a mathematical relationship between
      the average number of cars per household for an
      area and the proportions of households with diff-
      erent numbers of cars within the area. The rela-
      tionship may be interpreted to mean that a house-
      hold is twice as likely to acquire a first car
      than to acquire a second car. Similar data from
      the 1962 and 1971 Reading Area Travel Surveys give
      a modified relationship which suggests some under-
      recording in the surveys of those cars supplied
      by employers which householders can use.

5.1.13 Households. [*The Future Proportions of Non-Car
      Owning and Multi-Car Owning Households.] (1970)
      PAILING, K.B. and SOLESBURY, W.
      Traffic Engineering and Control. Vol.11. No.9.
             September 1970.(pp. 244-247)

5.1.14 Households With and Without Cars in 1970.
          [*Characteristics of] (1974)
      TULPULE, A.H.
      TRRL Supplementary Report SR 64 UC . 1974.

5.1.15 Medical Aspects of Fitness to Drive Vehicles.
                  (1968)
      NORMAN, L.G. (ed.)
      The Medical Commission on Accident Prevention,
      Royal College of Surgeons. 1968.

5.1.16 Petrol Rationing on Travel in London. [*The
          Possible Effects of] (1975)
      COLLINS, P.H. and FLOWER, S.P.
      Economic Research Report R.214 Economic Research
      Section. Economic and Operational Research Office.
      London Transport Executive. May 1975.(15 pp. plus
                  appendices)

      The report describes the results of a survey of
      1,000 car owning households in the Greater London
      area carried out in December 1973 for London
      Transport to try and discover car users' likely
      response to petrol rationing at a time when the
      threat of petrol rationing was imminent. The
      results showed that the present pattern of car

usage is strongly oriented towards those trips where the public transport alternative is markedly less satisfactory. Of the trips made by car at the time of the survey 60% would continue to use the car; 24% would be suppressed; 9% would be diverted to bus services and 5% diverted to rail. The study suggests that a 50% petrol price increase would result in increases of approximately 2% on bus receipts and 1% on rail receipts, other things being equal. Appendices include details of the sampling and research methods used, a copy of the questionnaire, some tables of information on the sample, a note of problems and reservations concerning the sample, and a summary of research findings on the effect of petrol price changes.

5.1.17   <u>Road Accident Pattern in G.B.</u> [*Some Recent Trends in] (1968)
MUNDEN, J.M.
RRL Report LR 168. 1968.

5.1.18   <u>Road Accidents in Great Britain</u>. [*Cost of] (1967)
DAWSON, R.F.F.
TRRL Report LR 79. 1967.

5.1.19   <u>Road Accidents in Great Britain</u>. [*Current Cost of] (1971)
DAWSON, R.F.F.
TRRL Report LR 396. 1971.

5.1.20   <u>Vehicles and Traffic in G.B.</u> [*Forecasts of]: 1974 Revision (1974)
TANNER, J. C.
TRRL Report LR 650. 1974.

(1972 Revision by A.H. Tulpule - TRRL Report LR 543. 1973)

5.1 Subsidiary References.

1.1 New Towns - Transport and Mobility.

1.1.1   Access and Mobility in New Towns. (1976)
1.1.7   Mobility in New Towns. (1970)
1.1.18   Transport and New Towns. Volume Two. (1976)
1.1.19   Transport and New Towns. Volume Three.(1977)

1.2 New Towns - Non-Transport Aspects.

1.2.23   Transportation Innovations in New Communities Abroad. (1973)

2.1 Runcorn.

2.1.1   Highway Hierarchy - or please don't bring your car into the living room. (1975)
2.1.6   Runcorn Busway Study. (1976)
2.1.14   Runcorn New Town Master Plan. (1967)

2.2 Skelmersdale.

2.2.2   Skelmersdale New Town Planning Proposals. (1964)
2.2.8   Skelmersdale New Town Population and Social Surveys. (Annually)

2.3 Telford.

2.3.3   Roads in Urban Areas: Brookside 4. (Undated)
2.3.6   Telford Transportation Study. (1976/7)
2.3.7   Telford Transportation Study:
         2. New techniques in the modelling of trip generation and
                                 modal split. (1976)
2.3.11 Telford Basic Plan Proposals. (1973)
2.3.21 Telford Social Survey. (1973)

2.4 Other New Towns.

2.4.6   Traffic and Transport in Crawley. (1971)
2.4.13 Harlow 1976 Household Survey. (1977)
2.4.32 Concern No.3. [Milton Keynes transport planning seminar edition.]
                                                                  (1975)

3.1 Studies of Modal Choice Behaviour and Value of Travel Time.

3.1.14 A Theoretical Estimate of the Effect of London Car Commuters
                         Transferring to Bus Travel. (1968)
3.1.15 Consumer Attitudes Toward Auto versus Public Transport Alterna-
                                                         tives. (1969)
3.1.20 Consumer Response to Public Transport Improvements and Car
         Restraint: some practical findings. (1977)
3.1.24 Journey Times by Bus and Car in Central London in 1972.   (1973)
3.1.25 Journey Times by Car and Bus in Central London. (1964)
3.1.26 Journey Times by Car and Bus in Central London: 1977 re-survey.
                                                                  (1977)
3.1.27 Journey Times by Car in Central London. (1969)
3.1.28 Car Journey Times in London, 1970. (1971)
3.1.37 Car and Bus Journeys to and from Central London in Peak Hours.
                                                                  (1969)
3.1.62 The Influence of Car Ownership on Shopping Habits. (1964)
3.1.67 Mid Glamorgan Transport Use and Attitude Survey.   (1976)
3.1.81 Car and Bus Travel in Central Edinburgh. (1968)
3.1.82 A Theoretical Study of Bus and Car Travel in Central London. (1972)
3.1.85 An Exploratory Comparison of the Advantages of Cars and Buses for
                                 Travel in Urban Areas. (1964)
3.1.90 A Study of Travel Times by Private and Public Transport in Greater
                                                   London. (1967)
3.1.103 The Value of Time for Commuting Motorists as a Function of their
         Income Level and Amount of Time Saved. (1970)

3.2 Social Aspects of Mobility.

3.2.3   Automobile and Public Transportation for Retired People. (1971)
3.2.4   On the Driving of Automobiles by Older People. (1964)
3.2.37 Personal Mobility and Transport Policy. (1973)
3.2.63 Transport Realities and Planning Policy. (1976)

9.4 Research Registers.

9.4.2	Register of Research, 1977: Part III: Roads and Transport. (1977)
9.4.5	1977 World Survey of Current Research and Development on Roads and Road Transport. (1977)

9.5 Statistical Sources.

9.5.1	Basic Road Statistics. (Annually)
9.5.3	Business Monitor M1: Number of Road Vehicles, New Registrations. (Monthly)
9.5.9	Policy for Roads: England. 1978. (Annually)
9.5.11	Road Accidents in Great Britain. (Annually)
9.5.12	Roads in England: Report by the Secretary of State for the Environment for the Year. (Annually, up to 1975-76)
9.5.14	Transport Statistics Great Britain. (Annually, from 1976.)
9.5.15	Annual Abstract of Statistics. (Annually)
9.5.16	Census of Population. (Every ten years.)
9.5.17	Family Expenditure Survey. (Annually.)
9.5.20	Monthly Digest of Statistics. (Monthly.)
9.5.22	Regional Statistics. (Annually)

9.6 Other Sources of Information.

9.6.2	National Index of Traffic and Transportation Surveys. (1975)
9.6.4	Road Safety. (1973)
9.6.5	Road Traffic Engineering and Control. (1973)
9.6.10	Guide to Official Statistics. (1976 and 1978)

6. Non-Motorised Travel.

This section together with the appended subsidiary references comprises a selection of recent literature relating to pedestrian and cycling movement. Some of the items listed cover more than one aspect of non-mechanised movement, but in general three main types of material can be identified:-

- Policy-oriented studies pointing to the importance of walking and cycling as alternatives to motorised transport.

- Studies of the design aspects of planning for pedestrians and cyclists, including segregated layouts and safety considerations.

- Studies of pedestrian and cycling movement and activity.

Conventional transport planning based on land use/transportation studies has paid little attention to the rôle of non-motorised movement. ILLICH's book Energy and Equity (7.1.5) sets out on broad philosophical grounds radical arguments against high-speed mechanised mobility and in favour of access by non-mechanised transport (foot and cycle) to small-scale local facilities. More realistically, HILLMAN, WHALLEY and HENDERSON have pointed out that although walking is the most commonly and universally used mode of transport, Government policies have concentrated on motorised movement, often at the expense of the pedestrian. Their books: Personal Mobility and Transport Policy (3.2.37) and Transport Realities and Planning Policy (3.2.63) call for a reversal of priorities in Government transport policies so as to give first place to pedestrian movement, combined with land use policies directed at reducing the need for motorised movement. Similar proposals are set out in THE INDEPENDENT COMMISSION ON TRANSPORT's report Changing Directions (7.1.3) which recommends that travel studies should always include movements by pedestrians and cycles, and that measures should be taken to increase accessibility through locational and land use planning directed towards keeping journeys short. Where possible facilities should be sited within easy reach of users by foot and cycle (and public transport) and local authorities should aim to create a safe and convenient walking environment throughout urban areas - not just in pedestrian precincts - and in the longterm to provide comprehensive cycle networks. More and safer pedestrian activity is also an important concomitant of the 'low movement' policy advocated in HAMER's; Getting Nowhere Fast (7.1.10), arising from an examination of the ecological and environmental implications of the increased mobility policy implicit in the Government's 1976 Consultation Document on Transport Policy (7.1.77). The effect at policy level of these and other studies reflected in the 1977 Transport Policy White Paper (7.1.76) which indicates Government recognition of the need to reduce absolute dependence on transport and the length and number of journeys made, and to plan more consciously for pedestrians.

edestrian - and to a lesser extent cycle - movement have been
iven considerable attention in a number of new town master
lans, usually in a context of segregated layouts. POTTER
(.1.18 - 19) has examined the importance given to pedestrian
nd cycle movement in new town master plans and has demonstrated
ne conflicts between the optimal requirements of the pedestrian
nd cyclist and those of motorised transport, and the problems
nvolved in reconciling these conflicts. POTTER's article
n Town and Country Planning, February 1977 (6.1.9) looks at
edestrian problems within a segregated Radburn layout, with
articular reference to Cumbernauld, and indicates that the
evel of pedestrian mobility and safety provided by conventional
egregated layouts is less than ideal. The article suggests
hat the 1975 Cumbernauld Extension Plan's 'inverted Radburn'
ayout which adapts vehicle needs to those of the pedestrian
ould improve both pedestrian mobility and safety. Similar
pproaches have been adopted in the Brookside 4 estate at
lford (2.3.3) and in the Brow estate at Runcorn. A major
rinciple underlying the design of Skelmersdale, as outlined
n WILSON and WOMERSLEY's Basic Plan (2.2.2), was that a large
roportion of the new town's population should live within
asy access by foot both of the town centre and surrounding
reas of open space. The provision of a footpath system to
acilitate easy and safe pedestrian movement was an important
spect of this policy. The reports of the DEVELOPMENT
ORPORATION's annual Skelmersdale New Town Population and
ocial Surveys (2.2.8) contain the results of a regular
onitoring of residents' usage and opinions of the footpath
stem.

ie paper by TREVELYAN (6.1.12) brings together a range of
uantitative data on walking distances in and to urban central
eas, indicating that most people do not walk further than
5 km. The author points out the significance of the walk
de to central area planning decisions and suggests that
lking should be adopted as a starting point in transport
licy formulation. In 1974 the Department of the Environment
mmissioned a study entitled 'Improving the Pedestrian's
vironment', which sought a comprehensive understanding of
destrian activity, problems and needs. The literature review
d annotated bibliography resulting from this study - The
destrian: Planning and Research, by ELKINGTON, McGLYNN and
BERTS (9.2.10) - is a useful compilation and assessment of
ailable literature relating to pedestrian movement and of U.K.
gislation relating to the pedestrian . The books by FRUIN
.1.7) and by PUSHKAREV and ZUPAN (6.1.8), which consider
 detail the design aspects of urban pedestrians' requirements,
so contain many bibliographical references.

ferences to literature on cycle transport are provided
 the POLYTECHNIC OF CENTRAL LONDON's Bibliography of Bicycle
ansportation (9.2.2). PERRATON's article: Planning for the
clist in Urban Areas (6.1.4) examines the role and design
 cycleways in some British new towns, including Stevenage
ere the provision of a cycleway network has affected the
dal split pattern for internal journeys to work. Proposals
r cycleway provision in Peterborough are set out in the
VELOPMENT CORPORATION's report: Cycleways for Greater
terborough (2.4.45).

6. NON-MOTORISED TRAVEL

6.1.1   Before the Traffic Grinds to a Halt. (1974)
         BRITISH CYCLING BUREAU. 1974.

6.1.2   Bicycle. [*The Return of the] (1975)
         BENDIXSON, T.
         New Society. 12th June 1975. (pp. 651-652)

6.1.3   Bicycle in a Modern Society. [*The Future of the]
                                                     (1968)
         CLAXTON, E.C.
         Journal of the Royal Society of Arts. January 1968.

6.1.4   Cyclist in Urban Areas. [*Planning for the] (1968)
         PERRATON, J.K.
         Town Planning Review. Vol. 39. No. 2. July 1968.
         (pp. 149 - 162)
         The paper considers whether more cycleways should
         be provided in urban areas and examines some
         aspects of their planning.   It includes reference to
         the rôle, functioning and design of cycleways in
         British new towns.

6.1.5   Feet and Pedals - few rights of way. (1975)
         MAY, P. and McKEE, W.
         Built Environment. Vol. 1. No. 2. September 1975.
                                    (pp. 117-118)

         A comment on aspects of distress, danger and
         nuisance suffered by the non-motorised public.

6.1.6   Peachtree City Path Experience. [*The] (1974)
         KOONS, E.R.
         Paper read at the First International Pedestrian
          Bicycle Seminar. May 1974. London. (pp. 139-143
         of the Seminar Proceedings)

         The paper describes Peachtree City's facilities
         for pedestrians and cyclists which have become
         a parameter for town planning.   The initial
         concentration   on the need for school children
         to reach primary school and return safely without
         crossing a road has developed into an encouragement
         by the city of the use of electric vehicles and
         golf carts as an alternative to the private motor
         car.   A regulation has been passed permitting
         legal operation of these types of vehicle in
         the city's streets.

6.1.7 Pedestrian Planning and Design. (1971)
FRUIN, J.J.
Naudep Press. New York. 1971. (206 pp.)

The book attempts to establish the importance of
walking in urban design and to identify the problems
of pedestrians in modern cities. The human
physiological and psychological factors that affect
the planning and design of pedestrian spaces are
examined and the traffic and space characteristics
of pedestrians are analysed. The objectives of
pedestrian planning programmes, study procedures
and methods of plan implementation are illustrated
and some projects for the improvement of the
pedestrian environment are reviewed.

6.1.8 Pedestrians. [*Urban Space for] (1975)
PUSHKAREV, B.S. and ZUPAN, J.M.
A report of the Regional Plan Association.
The M.I.T. Press,
Cambridge, Mass. and London. 1975. (162 pp.)

This comprehensive examination of pedestrians'
requirements includes an analysis of pedestrian
travel demand by trip generation, length and
purpose; an assessment of pedestrian space
requirements arising from the estimated demand;
and a consideration of the design implications
of these space requirements. A number of
bibliographical references is included.

6.1.9 People First in Transport Planning: did they
get it wrong at Radburn and will it be right
at Cumbernauld? (1977)
POTTER, S.
Town and Country Planning. Vol. 45. No.2.
February 1977. (pp. 76-81)

6.1.10 Road Safety. [*Two Experiments on Methods of
Training Children in] (1971)
COLBORNE, H.V.
TRRL Report LR 404. 1971 (11 pp.)

6.1.11 Segregation. [*Towards Effective] (1975)
CLAXTON, E.C.
International Federation of Pedestrian
Associations.
Paper read at the Second International Seminar
on the Planning, Design and Implementation of
Bicycle and Pedestrian Facilities. 1975.
(pp. 141-158 of the Seminar Proceedings).

Segregating different types of road users is
seen as the most positive way of eliminating
collisions between motor vehicles and

pedestrians or cyclists. Much of the segregation to date has been partial and unattractive. A total reappraisal of the units making up the traffic pattern is required, in order to achieve equality of opportunity to travel safely and conveniently by all modes. The paper discusses the urban pattern, crossing the road, grade separation, public transport, and costs.

6.1.12   Walk Trip. [*The Characteristics of the] (1973)
            TREVELYAN, P.
            Paper read at the PTRC Summer Annual Meeting.
            Seminar F: Urban Traffic Models. June 1973 (22 pp.)
            (See also comments on this paper by C.G.B. Mitchell).

6.1.13   Walking and Riding. (1973)
            BENDIXSON, T.
            Paper read at Session 9 of the Symposium:
            'Transport and Environment: Policies, Plans and
            Practice', held at the University of Southampton.
            April 1973. Proceedings published by the
            Southampton University Press. 1973.

6.1 Subsidiary References.

1.1 New Towns - Transport and Mobility.

1.1.1   *Access and Mobility in New Towns. (1976)*
1.1.7   *Mobility in New Towns. (1970)*
1.1.17   *Transport and New Towns. Volume One. (1976)*
1.1.18   *Transport and New Towns. Volume Two. (1976)*
1.1.19   *Transport and New Towns. Volume Three. (1977)*

2.1 Runcorn.

2.1.6   *Runcorn Busway Study. (1976)*
2.1.14   *Runcorn New Town Master Plan. (1967)*

2.2 Skelmersdale.

2.2.2   *Skelmersdale New Town Planning Proposals. (1964)*
2.2.8   *Skelmersdale New Town Population and Social Surveys. (Annually)*

2.3 Telford.

2.3.3.   *Roads in Urban Areas: Brookside 4. (Undated)*
2.3.6   *Telford Transportation Study. (1976/7)*

2.4 Other New Towns.

2.4.32   *Concern No.3. [Milton Keynes transport planning seminar edition.]*
                                                          (1975)
2.4.45   *Cycleways for Greater Peterborough. (1973)*

3.1 Studies of Modal Choice Behaviour and Value of Travel Time.

3.1.39   *Modal Choice and the Pedestrian. (1969)*

7. Transport Policy.

This subsection includes a number of studies relevant to transport policy in Great Britain at both national and local levels. It also lists a selection of specific transport plans (7.1.44 - 61) and the more important Government reports and legislation concerned with roads and transport published during the past fifteen years. References are included on the following specific aspects of transport policy:-

- Traffic restraint measures.

- Transport Policies and Programmes.

- The financing of public transport.

- Transportation studies.

- The administrative background to transport planning and policy.

Economic evaluation of transport projects as a tool of transport policy is covered in subsection 8.2. Many of the references in other parts of the bibliography have policy implications and the most relevant of these are included in the list of subsidiary references at the end of this section.

STARKIE's Transportation Planning, Policy and Analysis (7.1.38) reviews various aspects of British transport policy and provides a useful introduction to the evolution of policy from the mid-1950's and to the administrative framework of transport planning and policy. The book traces substantial changes in transport policy over this period and points to recent fundamental changes in the perception of transport problems. WHITE's book, Planning for Public Transport (4.1.89) contains a concise review of short and long-term policy issues affecting public transport.

Several important general studies published since 1973 have both examined and attempted to influence transport policy, and have contributed towards changing the perception of the urban transport problem from one of traffic congestion to be solved by increased road-building and other 'engineering' measures, to a broader consideration of the transport needs of all sectors of the community including those without the use of a car, an awareness that the function of transport is to give access to facilities and people rather than mobility per se, and concern with measures to protect society from the adverse environmental consequences of traffic. The most comprehensive of these is the report of the INDEPENDENT COMMISSION ON TRANSPORT, Changing Directions (7.1.3) published in 1974, which includes a fundamental reappraisal of the rôle of transport, of transport policy and of decision-making processes. It points to the need for radical changes in the process of decision-making based on a thorough understanding of the function of transport, and makes many general and specific policy recommendations. The Friends of the Earth report, Getting Nowhere Fast, by HAMER (7.1.10) is a more specific examination of the consequences of the policy of increasing mobility as implied in the Government's 1976 Consultation Document on Transport Policy. The report concludes that the Consultation Document's proposals could lead to a transport system which was neither efficient nor desirable and suggests instead a low movement policy, to be attained by manipulating the land use pattern and adopting fiscal, traffic restraint and other measures designed to reduce the attractiveness of private car ownership and usage. The work of HILLMAN et al pinpoints the problems of access and mobility of people rather than vehicles and looks at the mobility needs and opportunities of different sectors of the community, focussing particularly on those without the optional use of a car and on individuals rather than households. Recommendations are set out in Personal Mobility and Transport Policy (3.2.37) and in Transport Realities and Planning Policy (3.2.63) for a more equitable national transport policy directed towards providing an adequate level of access to all groups, giving first priority to pedestrian movements, followed by cycles and public transport. Proposals are also made for urban land use policies aimed at reducing the need for movement.

Two more general books published in the early 1970's which fundamentally question the economic basis of modern society and suggest radical alternatives have had some influence on subsequent thinking on transport problems. ILLICH's Energy and Equity (7.1.5) argues that the high-speed mobility of a minority leads to reduced mobility and freedom for the majority, overconsumption of energy resources, the destruction of the physical environment and the disintegration of society. The author recommends policies aimed at reducing energy consumption and improving equity in transport through limiting motorised traffic (particularly at high speeds) and replacing large specialised economic structures by smaller-scale institutions at local level which would reduce the need for high-speed motorised mobility. SCHUMACHER's Small is Beautiful (7.1.21) presents evidence to indicate that small-scale integrated industrial units using local labour and resources can often be more efficient than giant organisations. Although not specifically concerned with transport, Schumacher's carefully argued case against the large-scale profit-based economic structures of the Western world in favour of smaller organisations at local level, and of a technology emphasising people rather than products and profits, clearly has implications for transport and mobility.

The HOUSE OF COMMONS Expenditure Committee's report on Urban Transport Planning (7.1.79) published in 1972 contains much background material to official policy and thinking on transport in the early 1970's with particular reference to the balance between public transport and private car use in the large conurbations. The Report includes recommendations for

and planning. The emphasis is on material published since the reorganisation of local government and introduction of the Transport Policies and Programmes system in England and Wales in 1974, as a result of the Local Government Act 1972, and a number of references on Transport Policies and Programmes are included. Under this system the county authorities are responsible for submitting to the Department of Transport an annual Transport Policies and Programme (TPP) document, setting out their overall transport planning objectives for the county area (including any new towns which lie within the county) together with progress made in achieving these objectives, current proposals, and a financial statement of desired expediture. This is used by the Department as a basis for determining the total level of approved expenditure for each county and the threshold figure to be paid to the county via the Rate Support Grant (R SG).   The separate Transport Supplementary Grant (TSG) makes up a fixed proportion of the difference between the threshold figure and the total approved expenditure. Some early reactions to the proposed TPP and TSG systems are set out in the papers to the PTRC by COOPER (7.1.31) and COLLIER (7.1.32) in 1973. A more recent article by COLE and TYSON in the Chartered Institute of Transport Journal (7.1.7) describes the development of a methodology for evaluating the consequences of various policies on public transport performance for the Transport Policies and Programme.

7.1.1. Ad Hoc Governments: Special Purpose Transportation
Authorities in Britain and the U.S. (1974)
SMITH, R.K.
Sage Publications. London. 1974.

7.1.2 Bus Grant on Urban Transport. [*The Effect of
the] (1974)
KERRIDGE, M.S.P.
Journal of Transport Economics and Policy.
Vol. Vlll. No.3. September 1974. (pp.237-243)

The effects of the Department of the Environment's
50% bus grant towards the cost of approved vehicles
are discussed from both the operators' and the
consumers' viewpoints, and some external effects
are considered.   It is concluded that the grant
scheme discriminates in favour of rear-engined
rather than front-engined double-deck buses.
This gives an artificial impetus to one-man
operation which has serious disadvantages in
congested areas.   The author suggests that the
bus grant scheme should instead apply to all buses
on condition that they reach a minimum level of
passenger comfort.   However, more effective aid
could be provided in other ways, such as the
implementation of road and traffic measures which
would enable the operation of faster and more
direct bus services in urban areas.

7.1.3 Changing Directions. (1974)
THE INDEPENDENT COMMISSION ON TRANSPORT.
Coronet Books. London. 1974.   (365 pp.)

The report of the Independent Commission on
Transport presents a critical review of the
overall transport situation in Britain in the early
1970's, considering in particular the social priorities,
value judgements and ethical questions raised by
transport.   The report argues that solutions
to the problems depend largely on a fundamental
understanding of the way in which transport shapes the
community and that the problems, which are mainly
organisational and political, can be solved within
present technology given the right will and
attitudes.   The costs of transport are considered
in detail.   The concept of mobility is examined
and it is argued that the real goal of transport
is not ease of movement but access to people and
facilities.   The process of decision-making in
transport is discussed and radical changes called
for.   A number of both general and detailed
policy recommendations are made, and these are set
out separately for urban, rural and inter-urban
transport.   Appendices give details of specific
aspects of transport and mobility, such as the urban

mobility problems of the elderly, and the impact
on rural life of declining public transport
services.

7.1.4   Economic Growth. [*The Costs of] (1967)
MISHAN, E.J.
Penguin Books. 1967.

7.1.5   Energy and Equity. (1974)
ILLICH, I.D.
Calder and Boyars Ltd., London. 1974. (96 pp.)

The author argues that after passing certain thresholds in energy consumption, transport dictates the
pattern of the social environment and in providing
increased mobility for a minority leads to reduced
mobility and loss of freedom for the majority.
Overconsumption of energy, as indicated in high-
speed mobility, is seen as destroying the physical
environment and causing the disintegration of
society and loss of equity. Speed is seen as both
a source and a tool of manipulative political power
in both rich and poor countries. The case is put
forward for radical political decisions to reduce
energy consumption in transport through limiting
traffic, and for the replacement of large specialised economic structures by small-scale institutions
at the community level.

7.1.6   Energy and the Environment. (1974)
ROYAL SOCIETY OF ARTS - COMMISSION FOR ENVIRONMENTAL
CONSERVATION. 1974.

7.1.7   Financial Performance for the Transport Policies
and Programme. [*Forecasts of Public Transport]
                                        (1977)
COLE, W.S. and TYSON, W.J.
Chartered Institute of Transport Journal. Vol. 37.
No.9. March 1977. (pp. 266-269)

An outline of the methodology developed by Cheshire
County Council to evaluate the consequences of
various policies on public transport services.
(See also refs. 7.1.31 & 7.1.32 below)

7.1.8   Financing of Capital and Revenue Costs of Public
           Transport Undertakings. [*The] (1973)
ELLEN, E.R. and PHILLIPS, I.
U.I.T.P. 40th International Congress. 1973

7.1.9   Financing of Public Transport.[*The] (1972)
TYSON, W.J.
Local Government Finance. Vol.6. August 1972. (pp.273-
                                          276)

7.1.10   Getting Nowhere Fast. (1976)
          HAMER, M.
          Friends of the Earth Ltd. London.1976. (90 pp.)

          This report examines the consequences of the Consultati
          Document's policy of increasing movement under five hea
          ings:- Land Use Planning; Energy; Alternative Passenger
          Transport Modes; Noise and Pollution; and Safety. The
          distinction between movement, the means by which access
          to facilities is achieved, and access, which is the
          purpose of transport, is stressed. In failing to defin
          the purpose of transport the Government's Consultation
          Document confuses movement and access. It is concluded
          that the policies advocated in the Consultation Documen
          could produce a transportation system which was neither
          efficient nor desirable. An alternative approach to
          transport planning is proposed. This would seek to min
          mise the need to move through manipulating the land use
          pattern towards a more nucleated settlement pattern wit
          smaller, more dispersed employment units and other faci
          ties. Fiscal, traffic restraint and other Government
          measures designed to make car ownership and usage more
          difficult and less attractive should be adopted. The
          consequences of a low movement policy on land and energ
          requirements, public transport usage, car ownership, noi
          pollution and safety are examined. It is concluded tha
          this approach would be a viable option and that a more
          thorough examination of this and other policy options
          should be made.

7.1.11   Investment in Urban Transport. [*Distributional
          Aspects of] (1973)
          DALVI. M.Q.
          Working Paper 26. Institute for Transport Studies.
          University of Leeds. 1973

          The income distributional effects of investment
          in urban transport are investigated on the basis
          of evidence drawn from the British transportation
          studies. It is shown that the overall impact of
          proposed investments is regressive, owing to the
          implicit bias of transport planning modelling in
          favour of the private car and the high correlation
          existing between income and car ownership and usage.
          It recommends that future transportation studies
          pay greater attention to the distributional effects
          of transport investments.

7.1.12   Investments in Public Transit. [*The Economic and
          Social Impact of] (1973)
          SHELDON, N.W. and BRANDWEIN,R.
          Lexington Books. D.C. Heath & Co. 1973.(170 pp.)

          Broad urban goals are identified and related to a
          set of urban transportation objectives to help achieve
          these goals. In Part I the rôle of public transport
          in meeting these objectives is examined in terms of
          economic efficiency, equity, and social benefits.
          The examination is made in terms of three categories
          according to the type of group affected : users,
          operators and the community. Part II presents
          the results from a study of specific transit systems

including the San Francisco Bay Area Rapid
Transit (BART) System, the Cleveland Transit
System, bus dial-a-ride systems and the Skokie
Swift commuter rail service. The programmes
are divided into three major categories;
rapid rail, bus transit and commuter rail
services, and each is examined in terms of the
extent to which it meets the urban goals
identified. The discussion of each system first
establishes the need for an alternative to
private car transport within the particular area,
and then focuses on the social and economic
benefits to users, operators and the community.
In Part 111 the findings from the case studies
are summarised and examined in relation to a
set of major questions posed in the book,
focusing on the basic problem of whether urban
transportation policy should be directed towards
making provision mainly for private car transport
or whether increased provision should be made for
developing, expanding and/or improving one or
more of the public transit modes. Conclusions
from the studies are presented in the form of a
series of policy guidelines. A bibliography is
included containing some two hundred items, mainly
relating to specific public transport developments and
projects in the United States during the late
1960's and early 1970's.

7.1.13   Land Compensation Act 1973. [*A Guide to the]
                                              (1974)
         MOORE, V.
         Estates Gazette. London. 1974. (64pp.)

7.1.14   Local Government Finance. [*A New Look at] (1974)
         ASSOCIATION OF DISTRICT COUNCILS. 1974. (two parts)

7.1.15   Local Government Reorganisation. [*Public
         Transport and]   (1975)
         SMITH, L.H.
         Chartered Institute of Transport Journal.
         Vol. 36. No. 8. January 1975. (pp.185-190)

7.1.16   Motorway Victims. [*New Deal for]   (1972)
         MURPHY, C.
         Official Architecture and Planning. Vol. 35.
         No. 2. February 1972. (pp.81-84)

7.1.17   Municipal Transport. [*The Rise and Decline of]
                                              (1962)
         SLEEMAN, J.
         Scottish Journal of Political Economy. Vol. 9.February
         1962.   (pp. 46-64)
         also in : Journal of the Municipal Passenger
         Transport Association,and reprinted separately
         by the Omnibus Society.

7.1.18   New Authorities. [*Setting up the] (1972)
           LONG, J. and NORTON, A.
           Charles Knight. London. 1972 (164pp.)

7.1.19   New Local Authorities: Management and Structure.
           [*The] (1972)
           BAINS, M.A. (Chairman)
           Report of the Working Group of Local Authority
           Associations. 1972.

7.1.20   Priority for Passengers. (1976)
           NATIONAL CONSUMER COUNCIL. London. August 1976. (16pp.)
           Comments by the National Consumer Council presenting a
           consumer view of the Government's Consultation Document
           on Transport Policy (ref. 7.1.77 below), incorporating
           evidence submitted by some 55 organisations and
           informed individuals.

7.1.21   Small is Beautiful: A Study of Economics as if
           People Mattered. (1973)
           SCHUMACHER, E.F.
           Blond and Briggs Ltd. London. 1973. (255pp.)

           The author critically examines the economic structure of
           the Western world, producing evidence to indicate that
           the current pursuit of money profits which has involved
           the development of giant organisations and increased
           specialisation, has in fact resulted in economic ineffic-
           iency, environmental pollution and inhumane working
           conditions. The case is presented for a system of
           'Intermediate Technology' based on smaller working units,
           communal ownership and regional workplaces using local
           labour and resources, the emphasis being on the person
           rather than the product.

7.1.22   Subsidies and Benefit - Cost Considerations.
           [*Rail Passenger] (1971)
           SHIPMAN, W.D.
           Journal of Transport Economics and Policy.
           Vol. V. No.1. January 1971. (pp.4 - 37)

7.1.23   Subsidies for Public Transit. [*Optimal] (1975)
           JACKSON, R.
           Journal of Transport Economics and Policy.
           Vol. IX. No.1. January 1975. (pp. 3-15)

           In this paper a model is developed to estimate the
           optimal fare subsidy for public transit. The model is
           extended to estimate optimal subsidies for increasing
           the speed of public transit rather than lowering fares.
           It is concluded that no significant improvement is
           apparent unless marginal social cost per car passenger
           mile is at least 80% above private cost in the highway
           sector.

7.1.24   Supplementary Licensing. [*A Study in] (1974)
           GREATER LONDON COUNCIL
           G.L.C. London. 1974.

7.1.25   Survey Research in Policy Analysis. [*The Use of]
                                                   (1975)
         SHOSTAK, L.A. and FULLER, S.F.

         Paper read at the Centre for Environmental
         Studies' New Towns Seminar. London. October 1975.

7.1.26   Traffic Engineering Methods on London. [*Effect
                                          of] (1963)
         CHURCHILL, J.D.C.
         Traffic Engineering and Control. Vol.4. No.9.
                  January 1963. (pp. 505-509)

7.1.27   Traffic Restraint in Central London. [*An
                Evaluation of Two Proposals for   (1967)
         THOMSON , J.M.
         Journal of the Royal Statistical Society, Series
         A. Vol.130. Part 3. 1967. (pp. 327-377)

7.1.28   Traffic Restraints in Singapore. [*Study of]
                                          (1975)
         GEOK, LIM LEONG, WATSON, P.L. and HOLLAND, E.P.
         INTERNATIONAL BANK FOR RECONSTRUCTION and
                                 DEVELOPMENT.
         Technical Memorandum No.5. Paper read at the
         Conference on "Better Towns with Less Traffic".
                  O.E.C.D.,Paris, April 1975. (30 pp.)

         Two major transportation studies carried out in
         Singapore between 1967 and 1974 concluded that
         restraints on both car ownership and car usage
         would be necessary in the city before 1992. These
         measures would form part of a wider transportation
         strategy for Singapore which would also involve
         the expansion and upgrading of bus services,
         public campaigns to promote staggered working hours
         and car pools, a modest programme of road develop-
         ment, and the adoption of land use strategies
         aimed at minimising the need to travel. A 25% to
         30% reduction in peak hour traffic was estimated
         to be required to restore reasonably good traffic
         conditions for the present. The paper describes
         a proposed supplementary licence scheme for private
         car access into a 'Restricted Zone' within the
         central area, which would be combined with increased
         parking charges in the centre. It also outlines
         a proposed complementary Park and Ride Scheme.

         A supplementary report describes a proposed monitor-
         ing study of the likely impacts of the Area Licence
         and Park and Ride schemes on travel behaviour,
         traffic conditions, business activity and the
         environment.

7.1.29   Transport for Passengers. (1971)
      HIBBS, J.
      Institute of Economic Affairs. Hobart Paper 23.
      Second edition 1971. (First edition 1963) (95 pp.)

      The paper outlines the organisation, historical
      development and economic structure of the bus
      and coach passenger industry. The licensing
      system is critically examined and is shown to
      have been a factor in preventing the industry
      from responding to consumers' requirements. The
      author argues for a return to a fully competitive
      market and for other legal and institutional
      reforms which would enable the industry to
      develop in response to changing consumer needs
      and preferences. The question of subsidy provis-
      ion is discussed and the shortcomings of cross-
      subsidisation in particular are identified. A
      radically altered approach to costing, including
      the removal of cross-subsidisation, is seen as
      essential for the solution of the bus industry's
      problems in both urban and rural areas.

7.1.30   Transport Organisation in a Great City: the case
                of London. (1974)
      COLLINS, M.F. and PHAROAH, T.M.
      Allen and Unwin. London. 1974. (660 pp.)

7.1.31   Transport Policies and Programmes - a Local
               Authority View. (1973)

      COOPER, J.B.
      Paper read at a seminar organised by PTRC at the
      University of Sussex. June 1973.

7.1.32   Transport Policies and Programmes Associated
           with Transport Grant. (1973)
      COLLIER, J.C.
      Paper read at a seminar organised by PTRC at the
      University of Sussex. June 1973.
      (See also ref. 7.1.7 above)

7.1.33   Transport Policy. [*Sociological Implications
                of] (1975)
      SIMMIE, J.
      The Planner. Vol.61. No.9. 1975 (pp.336-338)

7.1.34   Transport Policy, the Report of a Study Group.
                   (1975)
      HUCKFIELD, L. (Chairman)
      Socialist Commentary. London. April 1975.

7.1.35   Transport Problem. [*The] (1975 Edition)
      FOSTER, C.D.
      Croom Helm. London. 1975. (1st. edition in 1963)
                  (356 pp.)

7.1.36   Transport Reform Movement. (1974)
          KIMBER, R., RICHARDSON, J.J., BROOKES, S.K.
          Political Quarterly. Vol.45. No.2. 1974. (pp 190-
                                                      205)

7.1.37   Transport Systems [*The Comparative Study of] :
          Swedish Urban Transport Policy and its Application
                                    in Britain. (1974)
          WHITE, P.R.
          International Journal of Transport Economics.
          Vol.1. No.1. April 1974. Rome. (pp. 78-90)

          This article presents a methodology for the
          comparative study of transport systems, postula-
          ting three stages: (1) adopting some measure of
          system performance with relation to planning
          objectives; (2) identifying the planning and
          operating techniques associated with this
          performance; (3) insofar as system performance is
          better than in other areas in which the same
          objectives apply (i.e. Britain) to evaluate the
          differences in the planning context which may
          affect their application. This methodology is
          used to examine the performance of public trans-
          port systems in Stockholm and Gothenburg, and
          several factors considered as leading to the
          success of Sweden's public transport and applic-
          able to other countries are identified, viz:-
          investment in rapid transit; good off-peak
          services; simple fare structures to encourage
          bus/rapid transit interchange; related land use
          planning; and marketing of the services operated.
          The application of these factors to public trans-
          port in Britain is discussed, and the conclusion
          reached that specific techniques play a vital
          but secondary rôle to the attitudes of planners
          and managers towards public transport, which may
          be the long-term key to its success.

7.1.38   Transportation Planning, Policy and Analysis.
                                                (1976)
          STARKIE, D.N.M.
          Pergamon Press Ltd., Urban and Regional Planning
                        Series. Vol.13.1976. (147 pp.)

          The book's theme concerns the interrelationship
          between transport policy and transport planning
          analysis. The author argues that if analytical
          methods are to play a part in shaping decisions
          they must be related to policy matters and must
          evolve concurrently with policy issues. Various
          aspects of transport policy are reviewed and trends
          and developments that have taken place over the
          past twenty years are identified, the emphasis
          being on policies relating to transport administ-
          ration, to urban transport and to the evaluation
          of different transport proposals. Significant

changes are shown to have taken place in
Government policy over this period. The development of the use of systems planning techniques in
transport planning is outlined and the relationship between the new methodology and evolving
policies discussed. Appendix B gives a description of a typical transportation planning package (COMPACT).

7.1.39   Transportation Studies: a critical assessment.
                                              (1968)
          SPENCE,R.
          Paper read at the Transportation Engineering
          Conference. Institution of Civil Engineers.
          London. 1968.

7.1.40   Transportation Studies: a review of results to
                    date from typical areas. (1968)
          MARTIN, B.V.
          Paper read at the Transportation Engineering
          Conference. Institution of Civil Engineers.
          London. 1968.

7.1.41   Transportation Studies: a review of results to
          date from typical areas - West Midlands Conurbation.
                                              (1968)
          BORG, N.
          Paper read at the Transportation Engineering
          Conference. Institution of Civil Engineers.
          London. 1968.

7.1.42   Urban Policies and the Motor Car.   (1974)
          DONNISON, D.V.
          In: Social and Political Consequences of the Motor
          Car. ed. P.M. Townroe. Newton Abbot. David and
          Charles. 1974.   Chapter 5.   (pp. 62-75)

7.1.43   Urban Transport Policy. [*Appraising]:the new
                                        regime.(1974)
          GWILLIAM, K.M.
          Paper read at the PTRC Summer Annual Meeting. 1974.

SPECIFIC TRANSPORT PLANS

7.1.44   Plan for Public Transportation. (1974)
          ANN ARBOR TRANSPORTATION AUTHORITY. 1974.

7.1.45   Belfast.[*Travel in] (1968)
          R. TRAVERS MORGAN & PARTNERS.1968

7.1.46   Cambridge Transportation Plan: Final Report.(1972)
          R. TRAVERS MORGAN & PARTNERS. 1972.

7.1.47   East Central Scotland. [*Land Use Transportation
                                  Study for] (1968)
          FREEMAN, FOX, WILBUR SMITH & ASSOCIATES.
          Scottish Development Department. 1968.

7.1.48   Leicester Traffic Plan. (1964)
SMIGIELSKI, K.
Leicester Corporation. 1964.

7.1.49   Greater London Development Plan. [*The] (1969)
GREATER LONDON COUNCIL.
G.L.C. London.1969.

7.1.50   London's Roads - a Programme for Action. (1967)
GREATER LONDON COUNCIL.
G.L.C. London. 1967.

7.1.51   Public Transport Plan for the Future. (1973)
GREATER MANCHESTER P.T.E. January 1973.

7.1.52   Massachussetts. [*Mass Transportation in] (1964)
MALONEY, J.F. and Associates.
Transportation Commonwealth of Massuchussetts. PB
174422. July 1964.

7.1.53   Merseyside. [*A Transport Plan for] (1972)
MERSEYSIDE P.T.E. March 1972.

7.1.54   Merseyside Area Land - Use Transportation Study.
Technical Report No.24. (1969)
TRAFFIC RESEARCH CORPORATION. 1969.

7.1.55   Mosborough Master Plan: Interim Report. (1968)
CULPIN, CLIFFORD and PARTNERS.
Sheffield City Council. 1968.

7.1.56   Mass Transportation in a Small City. (1968)
BLACKMAN, JOHN ASSOCIATES.
Newcastle Transit Authority. Newcastle,
Pennsylvania. 1968.

7.1.57   Nottingham's New Transportation Policy. (1973)
TRENCH,S. and SLACK, J.A.
Traffic Engineering and Control. Vol.15. No.4/5.
August/September 1973. (pp. 200-204)

7.1.58   South East. [*Strategic Plan for the] Interim
Report.(1976)
STANDING CONFERENCE OF LONDON AND SOUTH EAST
REGIONAL PLANNING. 1976.

7.1.59   People and Transport - the future of Public
Transport in Sunderland. (1964)
MORTON, N.
Sunderland Corporation. Transport Department. 1964.

7.1.60   West Midlands. [*A Passenger Transport Development
Plan for the] (1972)
WEST MIDLANDS P.T.E. November 1972.

7.1.61   West Yorkshire: [*Public Transport for] (1975)
          Joint Statement by WEST YORKSHIRE METROPOLITAN
          COUNTY COUNCIL and WEST YORKSHIRE PASSENGER
          TRANSPORT EXECUTIVE. April 1975.

GOVERNMENT REPORTS and PUBLICATIONS.

7.1.62   British Rail in Public Transport.[*The Rôle of]
                                                   (1977)
          First Report from the Select Committee on
          Nationalised Industries. Session 1976-77.

          Volume 1:   Report and Proceedings of the Committee.
                       (136 pp.)
          Volume II: Minutes of Evidence. (431 pp.)
          Volume III: Appendices. (245 pp.)

          HOUSE OF COMMONS.
          H.M.S.O. April 1977.

7.1.63   British Railways. [*The Reshaping of] (1963)
          ('The Beeching Report')
          BRITISH RAILWAYS BOARD.

          Volume I: Report.
          Volume II: Maps.

          H.M.S.O. 1963.

7.1.64   Cars for Cities. (1967)
          MINISTRY OF TRANSPORT.
          H.M.S.O. 1967.

7.1.65   Development Plans. [*The Future of] (1965)
          MINISTRY OF HOUSING AND LOCAL GOVERNMENT, MINISTRY
          OF TRANSPORT and SCOTTISH DEVELOPMENT DEPARTMENT.
          Planning Advisory Group. (Chairman: J.V. Pugh).
          H.M.S.O. 1965. (73 pp.)

7.1.66   Nationalised Industries: A Review of Economic and
                                   Financial Objectives. (1967)
          TREASURY. Cmnd. 3437
          H.M.S.O. 1967.

7.1.67   Nationalised Industries. [*A Study of U.K.]: their
          rôle in the economy and control in the future.
                                                   (1976)
          NATIONAL ECONOMIC DEVELOPMENT OFFICE.
          H.M.S.O. November 1976.

7.1.68   New Roads in Towns: Report of the Urban Motorways
                                   Committee. (1972)
          DEPARTMENT OF THE ENVIRONMENT.
          H.M.S.O. 1972.

7.1.69   Planning and Transport: the Leeds Approach. (1969)
          LEEDS CITY COUNCIL, MINISTRY OF TRANSPORT, MINISTRY
          OF HOUSING AND LOCAL GOVERNMENT.
          H.M.S.O. 1969

7.1.70   Public Expenditure on Transport. [*Report on]
                                                      (1974)
          First Report from the Expenditure Committee.
          (Environment Sub-committee). Session 1974.
          HOUSE OF COMMONS.
          H.M.S.O. July 1974.

7.1.71   Public Expenditure to 1979/80. (1976)
          TREASURY. Cmnd. 6393.
          H.M.S.O. 1976.
          (Also available for earlier years)

7.1.72   Town Roads [*Better Use of]: the report of a
          study of the means of restraint of traffic on urban
                                              roads. (1967)
          MINISTRY OF TRANSPORT.
          H.M.S.O. 1967.

          This report presents the results of a Government
          study of the scope for relieving congestion on
          urban roads by restraints on the use of vehicles.
          The basic objective of traffic restraint is
          defined as getting the best use out of scarce
          road space by inhibiting those uses which cost more
          to others than they benefit the users. The main
          conclusions are that intensified parking controls
          offer the most promising short-term method of
          restraint, and that direct road pricing seems
          potentially the most efficient long-term approach.
          Further research into the feasibility of road
          pricing is recommended.

7.1.73   Traffic in Towns: a study of the long-term problems
          of traffic in urban areas. Reports of the Steering
          Group ('Crowther Report') and Working Group
                                    ('Buchanan Report'.)(1963)
          MINISTRY OF TRANSPORT.
          H.M.S.O. 1963. (236 pp.)

7.1.74   Transport Act. 1968 (1970)
          MINISTRY OF TRANSPORT. H.M.S.O. 1970.

7.1.75   Transport Planning: The Men for the Job: a report
          to the Ministry of Transport by Lady Sharp. (1970)
          MINISTRY OF TRANSPORT.
          H.M.S.O. January 1970. (143 pp.)

7.1.76   Transport Policy. (White Paper) (1977)
          DEPARTMENT OF TRANSPORT, SCOTTISH DEVELOPMENT
          DEPARTMENT, WELSH OFFICE. Cmnd. 6836.
          H.M.S.O. 1977. (76 pp.)

7.1.77   Transport Policy: A Consultation Document. (1976)
                DEPARTMENT OF THE ENVIRONMENT. 2 Vols.
                H.M.S.O. 1976. (98 pp. and 130 pp.)

7.1.78   Trunk Road Assessment. [*Advisory Committee Report
                                       on] (1978)
                (Chairman: Sir George Leitch)
                DEPARTMENT OF TRANSPORT.
                H.M.S.O. January 1978.

7.1.79   Urban Transport Planning. (1972)
                Second Report from the Expenditure Committee
                (Environment and Home Office Sub-Committee).
                                      Session 1972-73.
                Volume I: Report and Appendix (59 pp.)
                Volume II: Minutes of Evidence (510 pp.)
                Volume III: Appendices and Index (118 pp.)

                HOUSE OF COMMONS.
                H.M.S.O. December 1972.

7.1 Subsidiary References.

1.1 New Towns - Transport and Mobility.

1.1.1   Access and Mobility in New Towns. (1976)
1.1.8   New Towns in Britain (their transport plans). (1973)
1.1.14   Public Transport in New Towns in Great Britain. (1971)
1.1.18   Transport and New Towns. Volume Two. (1976)
1.1.19   Transport and New Towns. Volume Three.(1977)
1.1.20   Transport Planning. (1968)
1.1.24   Transportation Inputs in New Town Planning. (1969)
1.1.26   Urban Cluster Villages. (1976)
1.1.29   Financing of New Town Transport Requirements.(1976)

1.2 New Towns - Non-Transport Aspects.

1.2.26   New - Town Planning: principles and practice. (1976)
1.2.50   Commission for the New Towns: Annual Reports.
1.2.51   Annual Reports of the Development Corporations.
1.2.55   Final Report of the New Towns Committee. (1946)

2.1 Runcorn.

2.1.6   Runcorn Busway Study. (1976)
2.1.9   The Runcorn Plan for a Rapid Transit Bus Service. (1971)
2.1.12-16 [Runcorn New Town Master Plan and amendment documents.]

2.2 Skelmersdale.

2.2.2   Skelmersdale New Town Planning Proposals. (1964)

2.3 Telford.

2.3.1   Bus Services for Telford: Report of the short term bus study.
*   (1976)*

| 3.1.67 | Mid Glamorgan Transport Use and Attitude Survey. (1976) |
| 3.1.111 | The Value of Travel Time Savings - U.K. Studies, Transportation and Environment: Policies, Plans, Practice. (1973) |

3.2   Social Aspects of Mobility.

3.2.1	Age Concern on Transport. (1973 edition.)
3.2.11	Bus Passes and the Elderly: A Need for More Informed Policy Making? (1976)
3.2.12	An Examination of the Extent and Welfare Implications of Bus Use by the Elderly in Harlow. (1977)
3.2.13	Free Travel for the Elderly in London - 1974 Survey. (1975)
3.2.14	Lifestyles and the Transportation Needs of the Elderly in Los Angeles. (1976)
3.2.16	Travel Patterns of Elderly People Under a Concessionary Fares Scheme . (1977)
3.2.17	Some Implications of Fare Concessions for the Elderly. (1975)
3.2.18	The Organisation of Voluntary Service: a study of domiciliary visiting of the elderly. (1972)
3.2.19	Transport and the Elderly: problems and possible action. (1977)
3.2.23	Estimating the Use of Free Bus Passes in Reading - survey of the number of trips by pass-holders. (1973)
3.2.26	The Living Suburb: scheme for the redevelopment of Boston Manor. (1958)
3.2.33	Rehousing of Old People: some planning implications. (1962)
3.2.37	Personal Mobility and Transport Policy. (1973)
3.2.38	Cutting the Cost of School Buses. (1970)
3.2.42	Report to D.E.S. Working Party on School Transport. (1972)
3.2.43	The Location of Primary Schools. (1968)
3.2.51	Social Costs of Hypermarket Developments. (1973)
3.2.55	Social Goals for Transport Policy. (1975)
3.2.57	Social Processes, Spatial Form and the Redistribution of Real Income in an Urban System. (1971)
3.2.59	Sociological Implications of Transport Planning. (1972)
3.2.61	The Effects of Differing Levels of Spatial Mobility: a discussion (1976)
3.2.63	Transport Realities and Planning Policy. (1976)
3.2.64	Travel Needs of Individuals. (1974)
3.2.65	Understanding Travel. (1978)
3.2.71	Travelling Expenses and Transport for Hospital Patients and Visitors. (1973)
3.2.72	Hospital Plan for England and Wales. (1962/3/4)
3.2.73	Planning for Leisure. (1969)
3.2.74	Rate Fund Expenditure and Rate Calls in 1975-6. (1974)
3.2.75	School Transport. (1973)
3.2.76	Revised Arrangements for School Travel: Consultation Document. (1975)
3.2.77	Shopping Habits and Attitudes to Shop Hours in Great Britain.(1975)
3.2.78	The Future Pattern of Shopping. (1971)
3.2.80	Changing Patterns of Working Hours. (1975)

3.3   Interaction between Land Use and Travel.

| 3.3.1 | Access for All: Transportation and Urban Growth. (1975) |
| 3.3.2 | Accessibility and Choice as Quantifiable Variables in Land Use Planning. (1972) |

3.3.10	*A Summary of Buchanan's Law. (1974)*
3.3.11	*Sweden's Small-scale Busways. (1973)*
3.3.14	*Fair Play For All: a study of access to sport and informal recreation. (1977)*
3.3.15	*Land Use and Travel. (1975)*
3.3.16	*Walking and Land Use Planning. (1975)*
3.3.19	*Mixed Blessing: The Motor in Britain. (1958)*
3.3.21	*Passenger Transport as an Urban Element.(1976)*
3.3.29	*The Road Capacity of City Centres. (1966)*
3.3.32	*Town Planning and Road Traffic. (1942)*
3.3.35	*Homes, Towns and Traffic. (1968 edition)*
3.3.36	*Traffic in the Conurbations. (1971)*
3.3.37	*Traffic Studies and Urban Congestion. (1968)*
3.3.38	*Towns Against Traffic. (1972)*
3.3.39	*Urban Survival and Traffic: Economics of City Traffic. (1962)*
3.3.40	*Transport and Regional Development: some preliminary results of the M62 Project. (1974)*
3.3.42	*Models of Urban Development in the Analysis of Transportation Investment: the case of North Central Texas. (1977)*
3.3.44	*Urban Form, Car Ownership and Public Policy: An Appraisal of "Traffic in Towns." (1964)*
3.3.47	*Environmental Implications of Options in Urban Mobility. (1973)*
3.3.48	*Urban Motorways and their Environment. (1968)*
3.3.54	*Roads in Urban Areas. (1966)*

3.4 Transport and Mobility - General and Miscellaneous.

3.4.4	*The Citizen and Transportation. (1968)*
3.4.5	*Urban Transportation Planning: Current Themes and Future Prospects. (1977)*
3.4.6	*The Urban Transportation Problem. (1965)*

4.1 Public Transport - Operational Aspects.

4.1.2	*Bradford Bus Study: Final Report. (1976)*
4.1.4	*The Bus and Coach Industry: its economics and organisation. (1975)*
4.1.9	*Vauxhall Bridge Bus Lane 12 months after Study. (1969)*
4.1.10	*Assessment of the Effects of Introducing Reserved Bus Lanes. (1969)*
4.1.11	*Bus Lanes in London. (1973)*
4.1.13	*Planning for the Bus. (1973)*
4.1.14	*Bus Priorities and Traffic Management. (1974)*
4.1.15	*The Justification and Assessment of Bus Priorities. (1974)*
4.1.16	*Bus Priority. (1973)*
4.1.17	*Bus Priority in Greater London. (1972/3)*
4.1.18	*A Comparison of the Effectiveness of Separate Bus Priority Schemes and those Affecting Entire Networks. (1976)*
4.1.24	*The Independent Bus. (1974)*
4.1.26	*Bus Travel and the Next Ten Years. (1975)*
4.1.27	*Buses in Camden. (1971)*
4.1.35	*Alternative Future Levels of Public Transport Demand. (1977)*
4.1.41	*The Effects of Two Differential Pricing Policies on Demand for Transport in the SELNEC Area. (1973)*
4.1.45	*Economic Change in the Road Passenger Transport Industry. (1972)*
4.1.49	*Fare Deal - Your Choice. (1974)*
4.1.50	*Reduced Fare and Fare - Free Urban Transport Services. (1974)*
4.1.51	*Public Response to Change in Fare Levels. (1974)*

4.1.52	Symposium on Public Transport Fare Structure: summary of the proceedings. (1974)
4.1.53	Low Fares and the Urban Transport Problem. (1969)
4.1.57	The Rôle of Local Government in Fares Policy. (1974)
4.1.58	Urban Fares Policy. (1975)
4.1.59	Analysis of the Effect of September 1969 Fares Revision on Work Journeys. (1972)
4.1.60	Effect of Alternative Fares Systems on Operational Efficiency: British Experience. (1974)
4.1.61	Alternative Approaches to Public Transport Fares with their Revenue and Traffic Implications. (1973)
4.1.62	Free Public Transport. (1973)
4.1.63	Some Data on the Effects of Free Public Transport. (1972)
4.1.64	Free Transit. (1970)
4.1.89	Planning for Public Transport. (1976)
4.1.90	Planning for Public Transport: Variations on a Theme. (1977)
4.1.93	Route Costing and the Rural Bus Problem. (1974)
4.1.94	Bus Route Costing for Planning Purposes. (1974)
4.1.95	Routeing Strategy for Urban Passenger Transport Services. (1975)
4.1.96	Planning Urban Bus Routes: a study for Coventry City Council. (1973)
4.1.98	Problems of Urban Passenger Transport. (1967)
4.1.101	Report of the Survey of Concessionary Travel Schemes in England and Wales. (1977)
4.1.102	Working Group on One-Man Operation of Buses. (1971)
4.1.103	Report of the Committee on Rural Bus Services. (1961)

4.2 Public Transport - Marketing Approach.

4.2.8	Consumer Response to Public Transport Improvements and Car Restraint: some practical findings. (1977)
4.2.25	The Management of Urban Public Transport: a marketing perspective. (1975)

4.3 Public Transport - Ergonomic Aspects.

4.3.39	How Good are Work Noise Standards? (1977)

4.4 Public Transport - Demonstration Projects and Innovatory Systems.

4.4.25	Intermediate Solutions. (1975)
4.4.43	Road Transport in Rapid Transit Systems. (1968)
4.4.48	Alternative Taxicab Systems: A London Case Study. (1976)
4.4.49	Tomorrow's Transportation: new systems for the urban future. (1968)
4.4.54	Working Group on Bus Demonstration Projects. (1970)
4.4.55	Minibus Act. (1977)
4.4.56	Passenger Vehicles (Experimental Areas) Act. (1977)

4.5 Public Transport - General and Miscellaneous.

4.5.3	Community Involvement Programme. Household Reviews. Report on Phases 1 and 2. (Sheffield and Rotherham Land Use/Transportation Study.) (1977)

8.2.16	Metropolitan Plan Making – an Analysis of Experience with The Preparation and Evaluation of Alternative Land Use and Transportation Plans. (1970)
8.2.17	Estimating the Social Benefit of Constructing an Underground Railway in London. (1963)
8.2.18	Social Cost-Benefit Study of the Manchester – Glossop and Manchester – Marple/New Mills Suburban Railway Services. (1972)
8.2.20	An Overview of Transport Technology Assessment. (1975)
8.2.21	Getting the Best Roads for our Money: the COBA Method of Appraisal. (1972)

8.3 Research Techniques and Methodology – General and Miscellaneous.

8.3.5	Modelling London Transport's Demand and Supply Markets. (1975)
8.3.14	Information Availability and Travel Characteristics in Developing Cities. (1977)
8.3.21	Program Background. (1972)

9.2. Bibliographies.

9.2.3	Buses in Urban Areas. 1970-1976. (1976)
9.2.8	Land Use/Transportation Studies: A Select Bibliography. (1977)
9.2.10	The Pedestrian: Planning and Research. (1976)
9.2.13	Transport Policies and Planning. (1977)
9.2.14	Transport Policy Consultation Document 1976. (1977)
9.2.37	Structure Plans: A. Structure Plan documents. (1976) B. The literature and debate on structure plans and structure planning. (1976)

9.3 Abstracting and Indexing Services.

9.3.6	Departments of the Environment and Transport Library Bulletin. (Fortnightly)
9.3.9	Geo Abstracts. (Six times a Year)
9.3.14	Sage Urban Studies Abstracts. (Quarterly)
9.3.21	Urban Abstracts. (Monthly)

9.4 Research Registers.

9.4.1	Register of Research, 1977, Part II: Environmental Planning. (1977)
9.4.2	Register of Research, 1977, Part III: Roads and Transport. (1977)

9.5 Statistical Sources.

9.5.1	Basic Road Statistics. (Annually)
9.5.2	British Railways Board Annual Report and Accounts.
9.5.5	National Bus Company Annual Report and Accounts.
9.5.9	Policy for Roads: England. 1978. (Annually)
9.5.10	Proposed Increase in London Taxicab Fares. (1968)
9.5.12	Roads in England: Report by the Secretary of State for the Environment for the Year. (Annually up to 1975/76.)
9.5.13	Traffic Commissioners' Annual Reports.

9.6 Other Sources of Information.

9.6.4	Road Safety. (1973)
9.6.5	Road Traffic Engineering and Control. (1973)
9.6.7	U.K. Transport Organisations. (1976)
9.6.8	DOE Annual List of Publications . (Annually)
9.6.11	Hansard. (Daily, Weekly and Sessional)
9.6.16	Sourcebook of Planning Information. (1971)
9.6.20	Town and Country Planning. (1974)

8. Research Techniques

and Methodology.

8.1   Survey Techniques : Behavioural & Attitudinal .

Section 8 of this bibliography contains references to a
wide range of literature on research techniques and methodologies which could be useful in studying transport and
mobility in new towns. Subsection 8.1 covers techniques of
survey design, data gathering, and data processing and
analysis in behavioural and attitudinal research, and some
theoretical material on attitude studies. Subsection 8.2
brings together some references on economic evaluation
methodology, and subsection 8.3 contains miscellaneous items
concerned with techniques relevant to transportation research.
Reports of surveys of various kinds, usually containing some
methodological background details, are included in several
parts of the bibliography. These are cross-referenced at
the end of this subsection together with some studies
relating to the application of behavioural and attitudinal
modelling and consumer preference techniques in transport
research and planning, from subsections 3.1 and 4.2.
Journals and abstracting and indexing services which regularly
contain material on behavioural and attitudinal research
methodology are listed under the headings 9.1 and 9.3 at the
end of this subsection.

A number of useful basic textbooks have been written giving
comprehensive coverage of both the theoretical and practical
aspects of social research techniques in general and survey
methodology in particular. The books by MOSER and KALTON
(8.1.100), GOODE and HATT (8.1.103), FESTINGER and KATZ
(8.1.23), and SELLTIZ, JAHODA, DEUTSCH and COOK (8.1.101)
cover most aspects of qualitative and quantitative social
research methodology from the design to the report stages.
The recent publication Survey Research Practice (8.1.109)
by HOINVILLE, JOWELL and Associates presents much valuable
practical information and advice on survey design, data
collection and data preparation derived largely from survey
experience with Social and Community Planning Research. The
Consumer Market Research Handbook (8.1.27) edited by WORCESTER
also includes useful practical material on the techniques
and applications of consumer market research, drawn from
the experience of practising market researchers. The book
by BURTON and CHERRY (8.1.104) deals specifically with survey
and analysis techniques suitable for use by planners, and
Behavioral Research Methods in Environmental Design (8.1.22)
edited by MICHELSON contains contributions on several methodological approaches which can usefully be applied in environmental research. The U.S. DEPARTMENT OF TRANSPORTATION's
Effective Citizen Participation in Transportation Planning
(8.1.25)discusses various techniques which can be used to aid
public participation in transport planning, including
focussed group discussions and questionnaire surveys of
citizens' attitudes and opinions. The book edited by GLOCK
(8.1.105) examines the applications of survey research
techniques in a number of fields, and that by RAJ (8.1.110)
includes a discussion of survey methodology in transport
research.

Specific aspects of survey design, execution and analysis
covered in this subsection include:-

- Survey design in general.
- Sampling techniques.
- Questionnaire design.
- Fieldwork organisation.
- Interviewing in structured questionnaire surveys.
- Postal surveys.
- Coding, editing and processing of quantitative
  survey data.
- Classification of survey respondents.
- Statistical techniques in data analysis, including
  multivariate analysis.
- Qualitative research techniques, including tape-
  recorded depth interviews and group discussions.
- Processing and analysis of qualitative research data.
- Attitude measurement techniques, including both
  scaling and non-scaling methods.
- Market Segmentation.

The books by OPPENHEIM (8.1.80 - Chapter 1) and MOSER and
KALTON (8.1.100 - Chapter 2) both contain chapters discussing
problems involved in the overall design and planning of
surveys.   The authors emphasise the importance of careful
preliminary work to ensure that the survey techniques
employed will supply the information required by the researchers
as accurately as possible within the limits of what is
practically feasible in terms of cost, time and labour.   A
general introduction to research design is also provided in
the preliminary chapters of Research Methods in Social Relations
(8.1.101) by SELLTIZ et al.

In the great majority of surveys coverage of the whole target
population is not necessary or practicable.   The selection
of a proportion which will be representative of the whole
necessitates the use of sampling, and this is a major aspect
of survey methodology which is widely covered in the literature.
Chapters 3 to 8 of MOSER and KALTON's Survey Methods in
Social Investigation (8.1.100) give a good basic background
to sampling theory and techniques.   A detailed description
is given of a random sample design used in a national market
research survey to illustrate the process of drawing up a
sample, and the problems arising from non-response are fully
discussed.   HOINVILLE and JOWELL's book Survey Research
Practice (8.1.109 - Chapter 4) outlines the main theoretical
concepts underlying sample design and then concentrates on
the practical issues involved in the use of probability
sampling methods.   Both these books provide a number of

suggestions for further reading on the subject. Other general
introductions to sampling theory and methods are included in
the books by GOODE and HATT (8.1.103 - Chapter 14), by
SELLTIZ et al (8.1.101 - Appendix B), and in Research Methods
in the Behavioral Sciences,edited by FESTINGER and KATZ (8.1.23).
BURTON and CHERRY (8.1.104) discuss the use of sampling
methods in planning surveys, and the Handbook for Interviewers
by ATKINSON, published by the Office of Population Censuses
and Surveys (8.1.116) describes aspects of sampling procedures
relevant to interviewers in the field. The literature on
sampling techniques concentrates largely on probability
(random) methods. Non-probability methods, of which the most
common is quota sampling, are widely used in commercial market
research and public opinion polls for practical reasons of
time and cost, and are often satisfactory for the purpose
required. These techniques do, however, contain statistical
weaknesses which can give rise to potentially serious bias and
are not suitable for use in surveys in which it is important
that the results are based on statistically sound methods.
MOSER and KALTON's book (8.1.100) includes a discussion of
non-random techniques, setting out clearly the advantages for
and against quota sampling and outlining the results of a
research programme comparing quota and random sampling methods
which was carried out by the London School of Economics in
the early 1950's. Briefer outlines of the relative advantages
and disadvantages of quota sampling are given by HOINVILLE
and JOWELL (8.1.109), GOODE and HATT (8.1.103), and SELLTIZ
et al (8.1.101). Practical aspects of the application of quota
sampling are discussed in the article by WEINBERGER (8.1.89)
and in Chapter 3 (by COLLINS) in the Consumer Market Research
Handbook (8.1.27). In the planning and transport research
fields descriptions of sampling techniques applied in specific
studies are often given in methodological reports of general
household or travel surveys, in varying degrees of detail.
Examples included in this bibliography are provided by the
reports of the Runcorn Travel Survey (2.1.10) and of the West
Midlands Rural Travel Survey (8.3.24) published by Social and
Community Planning Research, and the Technical Report of the
Harlow 1976 Household Survey (2.4.13 - Volume 6). The Building
Research Establishment's Current Paper Monitoring in Practice:
a household survey, its use and potential for local authorities
and new towns (8.1.63) describes the sampling technique and
other methodological aspects of a household survey conducted
in Washington New Town in 1974.

Questionnaire design is another major topic central to most
general texts on survey methodology, and has been the subject
of several specialised books and numerous articles in relevant
journals. Basic texts which are specifically concerned with
questionnaire design include OPPENHEIM's Questionnaire Design
and Attitude Measurement (8.1.80), PAYNE's The Art of Asking
Questions (8.1.88) and The Dynamics of Interviewing by KAHN
and CANNELL (8.1.43). The general texts on social research

already referred to include fairly detailed discussions
of the layout of structured questionnaires and of question
wording. Research Methods in Social Relations by SELLTIZ et al
(8.1.101) includes a general discussion of question content
(Chapter 7) and also provides as an Appendix a guide for
questionnaire construction which gives a number of practical
examples to illustrate some of the problems and pitfalls
involved in formulating questions and incorporating them into
a questionnaire format. Other useful sources of practical
advice on questionnaire layout and question content, wording
and order include the chapter by MORTON-WILLIAMS in the
Consumer Market Research Handbook (8.1.27), Chapter 13 of
MOSER and KALTON's Survey Methods in Social Investigation
(8.1.100) and SOCIAL AND COMMUNITY PLANNING RESEARCH's
Questionnaire Design Manual (8.1.81) and Survey Research
Practice (8.1.109). All these sources contain examples of
questionnaire layouts. The articles by BELKIN and LIBERMAN
(8.1.79) and LAURENT (8.1.78) discuss the effects on respondents
of question wording and length, and the paper by BELSON
(8.1.87) describes the results of research on respondents'
understanding of survey questions. The development of questionnaires to obtain subjective information from passengers on
noise and vibration experienced while travelling on various
types of vehicle is described in two articles by OBORNE
and CLARKE (8.1.84-85).

Personal interviewing is the most common method of collecting
survey information from respondents. The classic texts by
KAHN and CANNELL (8.1.43) and HYMAN et al (8.1.41) give a good
background to the subject of survey interviewing, and the
Office of Population Censuses and Surveys' Handbook for
Interviewers by ATKINSON (8.1.116) provides a detailed guide
to interviewing procedures. Chapter 12 in MOSER and KALTON's
Survey Methods in Social Investigation (8.1.100) gives a clear
outline of the interviewer's task and of the selection and
training of interviewers. The effect of interviewers on
response errors is examined in detail in Chapter 15 of this
book. Other helpful guides to interviewing are included in
the texts by GOODE and HATT (8.1.103 - Chapter 13), by SELLTIZ
et al, which contains an appendix on the art of interviewing
(8.1.101) and by HOINVILLE and JOWELL (8.1.109 - Chapter 5),
and in the chapter by DRAKEFORD in the Consumer Market Research
Handbook (8.1.27 - Chapter 5). The latter chapter, together
with Chapter 6 of HOINVILLE and JOWELL's book (8.1.109),
Chapter 12 of MOSER and KALTON's text (8.1.100) and the Office
of Population Censuses and Surveys' Handbook for Interviewers
(8.1.116) also contain much useful information on practical
aspects of fieldwork organisation.

As an alternative to personal interviewing postal questionnaires
can, where suitable for the nature of the survey, offer
substantial advantages of cost and convenience and may also be
preferable on other grounds - for instance, where the presence

of an interviewer may have an inhibiting effect on the
respondent or where questions require time for reflection
or for checking records. Satisfactory and sometimes high
response rates can be obtained in postal surveys: a number
of Government social surveys carried out by post have achieved
response rates of around 90%. In the 1976 Runcorn Household
Census (2.1.20) a postal questionnaire sent by the Runcorn
Development Corporation to all households in the new town,
followed by a postal reminder to households who had not replied
after ten days, produced a 70% response rate. (Personal
calls on remaining non-respondents resulted in a final
response rate of 78%). HILLMAN, WHALLEY and HENDERSON have
described in Transport Realities and Planning Policy (3.2.63)
a postal survey in which questionnaires on mobility and
accessibility were sent to a sample of 24,000 electors in the
Outer Metropolitan Area. The initial mail-out and two
reminders produced an overall response rate of over 76%. In
practice, however, responses to postal surveys have varied
widely, largely owing to the difficulty of motivating respondents sufficiently to fill in and return the forms when no
personal contact is involved. Much of the literature available
on postal surveys is therefore concerned with the problem of
maximising response rates through the design of the questionnaire and accompanying letter and the use of incentives and
other techniques. The articles by FRANCEL (8.1.47), KEANE
(8.1.49) and FORD (8.1.51), for instance, all focus on methods
for improving the response to mailed questionnaire surveys.
The book Professional Mail Surveys by ERDOS (8.1.50) gives a
comprehensive treatment of the subject. The chapter by ALLT
in the Consumer Market Research Handbook (8.1.27 - Chapter 9)
usefully outlines the advantages and disadvantages of mail
surveys and discusses when they may or should be used. Various
aspects of questionnaire design, sampling techniques and
methods of response maximisation in mail surveys are examined.
Chapter 7 of Survey Research Practice (8.1.109) and Chapter 11
of MOSER and KALTON's book (8.1.100) also provide practical
guidance on postal survey procedures. These authors all
give suggestions for further reading on the subject. A
substantial bibliography and a review of the literature
available up to 1961 are included in the article Research on
Mail Surveys by SCOTT (8.1.52) which is widely cited as being
an important source of information on postal questionnaire
surveys.

The majority of the literature on survey methodology focuses
on the survey design and data collection processes and on
techniques of statistical analysis. Less attention has been
paid in the literature to the data processing stages in
quantitative surveys - editing, coding, card-punching and
preliminary analysis by hand, machine or computer. Yet
meticulous editing to eliminate errors as far as possible
from the new survey material, and accurate coding following
a coding frame carefully compiled to classify answers into

categories which will fit the needs of the particular survey have an extremely important bearing on the reliability and usefulness of the survey results. Good introductions to these procedures are given in Chapter 16 of MOSER and KALTON's book (8.1.100) and the chapter on Data Preparation in Survey Research Practice (8.1.109 - Chapter 8). MOSER and KALTON discuss in some detail the problem of variability of coding between different coders and describe an experiment which revealed considerable discrepancies between different coders and with the same coder at different times in dealing with multi-coding of open-ended questions. These chapters both identify sources for further reading on specific aspects such as the reliability of coding. The chapter by ROUGHTON in the Consumer Market Research Handbook (8.1.27 - Chapter 11) gives a clear outline of the procedures involved in editing and coding and in hand, mechanical and computer analysis. It also contains a brief guide to the better-known computer packages available in Britain at the time of publication (1972). The book by OPPENHEIM (8.1.80 - Chapter 9) also describes the main processes involved in data preparation and analysis and includes a useful discussion of the problems involved in compiling and designing satisfactory coding frames.

Most surveys use one or more classification schemes so as to disaggregate subgroups within the total sample as a basis for identifying possible variations in patterns of behaviour or attitudes between different subgroups. The Handbook for Interviewers by ATKINSON, published by the Office of Population Censuses and Surveys (8.1.116) contains a chapter on 'Classification Standard Definitions' which sets out detailed definitions of twelve commonly collected items of classification information. The article Classifying Market Survey Respondents by JOYCE and CHANNON (8.1.57), the Classification Manual for Household Interview Surveys in Great Britain (8.1.36) by HOINVILLE and JOWELL, and the chapter on 'Classifying Respondents' in the book by the same authors (8.1.109) also provide detailed treatments of definitions and classification questions. The latter source examines a selection of the most widely used variables and illustrates the ways in which they can be categorised. The book Sources of Social Statistics by EDWARDS (9.6.18) includes a discussion of some of the main classification systems used in official economic and social statistical series.

Useful general introductions to the statistical analysis of quantitative survey data are contained in the books by OPPENHEIM (8.1.80 - Chapter 9 and Appendix III), MOSER and KALTON (8.1.100 - Chapter 17), GOODE and HATT (8.1.103 - Chapter 20), and SELLTIZ et al (8.1.101 - Chapter 11). Chapter 12 of the Consumer Market Research Handbook, by HARRIS, is concerned with elementary statistics obtained from survey tabulations and the testing of statistical hypotheses by significance tests to show whether observed differences in the data are due to sampling errors. Much more detailed treatments are provided by the basic textbooks on statistical techniques in research surveys, such as those by FISHER (8.1.107) and FERBER (8.1.108). Some of the methodological survey reports which have been incorporated in this bibliography set out details of the statistical analysis techniques used or referred to, and discuss their application. For example, the report by REES, DIX and CLYDE (8.1.10) describing an attitude survey carried out in Liverpool by the University of Leeds includes an appendix on statistical methods which discusses stepwise multi-linear regression analysis, factor analysis and the Hotelling T - squared test. In recent years multivariate statistical techniques, which enable the relationship between many variables to be examined simultaneously, have been increasingly used in survey analysis. This is largely due to the development of computer analysis in this area and to advancements in computer technology. In Chapter 13 of the Consumer Market Research Handbook (8.1.27), HOLMES gives a straightforward account of the use of multivariate statistical techniques in the analysis of market research data. The kind of practical problems to which such methods can usefully be applied are described and the main techniques which come under the general heading of multivariate analysis are outlined. The books Multivariate Statistical Methods by MORRISON (8.1.68) and Multiple Factor Analysis by THURSTONE (8.1.67) give more advanced and detailed descriptions of these techniques.

The preceding paragraphs have referred principally to the use of structured survey techniques in quantitative studies. The qualitative research techniques of social investigation are also applicable to studies of travel behaviour and motivations. The introduction to subsection 3.1 has referred to the comparatively recent development of the use of in-depth research techniques in the transport field, citing in particular work carried out at Oxford University and reported by HEGGIE (8.3.26) and DIX (8.1.42). Travel studies conducted by the social research institute, Social and Community Planning Research, have made considerable use of the two main techniques of qualitative research - the depth interview and the group discussion - both as a preliminary stage in largescale studies to provide a basis for developing structured questionnaires, and as a research tool in their own right to increase researchers' depth of understanding of the factors and motivations which influence travel behaviour. Research Methods in Social Relations by SELLTIZ et al (8.1.101) and Research Methods in the Behavioral Sciences edited by FESTINGER and KATZ (8.1.23) provide a general background to the use of qualitative techniques in social research. The technical manual Depth Interviews and Group Discussions published by SOCIAL AND COMMUNITY PLANNING RESEARCH (8.1.45), the chapter on unstructured design work in Survey Research Practice (8.1.109 - Chapter 2), and the chapter by SAMPSON in the Consumer Market Research Handbook (8.1.27 - Chapter 1) give practical guidance on procedures in group discussions, unstructured and semi-structured (focussed) interviewing, and provide references for further reading. The rôle of tape recorded interviews in social research is discussed in the article by BUCHER, FRITZ and QUARANTELLI (8.1.111) and the effect of tape recording on response in survey interviews is examined in the article by BELSON (8.1.11 3). Unstructured and focussed interviews are also the

subject of articles by BERENT (8.1.37), GOLDMAN (8.1.39),
the book by MERTON, FISKE and KENDALL (8.1.38) and the chapter
by WELLS in the Handbook of Marketing Research, edited by
Ferber (8.1.40). The book by BANAKA (8.1.44) deals in detail
with training for depth interviewing. The use and potential
of focussed group discussions and tape recorded interviewing
in promoting public participation in transportation planning
is outlined in Effective Citizen Participation in Transportation
Planning (8.1.25), and the paper by DIX (8.1.42) describes the
use of tape recorded unstructured household interviews in a
smallscale survey of household travel activities in Oxfordshire.

SAMPSON (8.1.27) has pointed out that the growing emphasis on
qualitative research in recent years has not been accompanied
by a parallel increase in attention to methodology. This applies
in particular to the analysis and interpretation of unstructured
survey data, which remains largely a matter of individual skill
in objectively extracting and presenting material relevant to
the purpose of the survey. The chapter on 'Some Problems in
Qualitative and Case Analysis' in GOODE and HATT's Methods in
Social Research (8.1.103) contains a useful discussion of
qualitative coding, the application of qualitative coding in
content analysis of unstructured research data, and the analysis
of case studies. A brief outline of the analysis of tape
recorded interviews and group discussions is given in Survey
Research Practice (8.1.109 - pp. 24-25). The chapter by HOLSTI,
LOOMBA and NORTH in the Handbook of Social Psychology (8.1.28)
focuses on content analysis, although the authors are concerned
more with the use of the technique for analysing written items
such as newspapers than with its use in abstracting relevant
and significant data from unstructured interviews and discussions.

The application of attitudinal research techniques in modal
choice studies has been referred to in the introduction to
subsection 3.1 Over the past decade a number of studies have
been carried out, particularly in the United States, which have
attempted to quantify the attitudinal factors in mode choice
decisions, and attitudinal modelling has been developed to
supplement the behavioural models used in travel demand forecasting. Attitudinal techniques have also been used in assessments of likely reactions to alternative transport policies and
changes in service provision, and in the ergonomics field as
a basis for improving vehicle and infrastructure design.

The development of measuring techniques to enable comparisons
to be made between the attitudes of different groups of people
has generated an enormous volume of literature over the past
fifty years. Original sources for early work involving the
development of unidimensional scaling methods include the book
by THURSTONE and CHAVE (8.1.13) and the articles by THURSTONE
(8.1.17) and LIKERT (8.1.16). The cumulative scaling technique
using the scalogram is introduced by GUTTMAN in the article
A Basis for Scaling Qualitative Data (8.1.95) and in the chapter
in Measuring and Prediction, edited by STOUFFER (8.1.97).
The articles by Thurstone, Likert and Guttman, together with a

number of other important early papers and some more recent
work, are brought together in Readings in Attitude Theory
and Measurement, edited by FISHBEIN (8.1.14), which gives a
basic introduction to the theory underlying attitude measurement and to the techniques which have been developed. The
books by OPPENHEIM (8.1.80 - Chapters 5-8), SELLTIZ et al
(8.1.101 - Chapter 10) and GOODE and HATT (8.1.103-Chapters
15-17) provide a good background to the theory and application
of attitude scaling techniques. The chapter on Scaling Methods
in MOSER and KALTON's Survey Methods in Social Investigation
(8.1.100 - Chapter 14) gives a clear exposition of the principal
scaling methods used in survey research. A concise outline of
the Thurstone method of equal-appearing intervals, the Likert
method of summated ratings, and Guttman cumulative scales is
included as an appendix to SOCIAL AND COMMUNITY PLANNING
RESEARCH's Questionnaire Design Manual (8.1.81). More advanced
textbook references include Techniques of Attitude Scale
Construction by EDWARDS (8.1.9), and GUILFORD's Psychometric
Methods (8.1.72). Other references which discuss various
problems arising from the principal scaling techniques include
the article by EDWARDS and KENNEY comparing the Thurstone and
Likert techniques (8.1.8) and that by HOVLAND and SHERIF which
considers the effect of the panel judge's own opinions on the
ordering of items in the Thurstone scaling procedure (8.1.5).
Both are reprinted in Readings in Attitude Theory and Measurement
edited by FISHBEIN (8.1.14). The paper by DRAKEFORD (8.1.7)
examines piloting techniques used prior to attitude quantificatio
and the report by BELSON (8.1.91) describes the results of
investigations into the effect on the distribution of answers of
reversing the order of presentation in verbal rating scales.
These indicated advantages in placing negative response categories at the top of the scale. The semantic differential
technique developed by Osgood and his colleagues as part of
their research on the meaning of concepts is described by OSGOOD,
SUCI and TANNENBAUM in The Measurement of Meaning (8.1.61) and
in the chapter by OSGOOD in Readings in Attitude Theory and
Measurement (8.1.14). The technique, utilising a self-completion
scale whose ends are described by adjectives which are polar
opposites, to which factor analysis is then applied, has subsequently been widely used in attitude research and is discussed
in the basic texts on survey methodology already referred to.
The chapter on The Semantic Differential and Other Paper-and-
Pencil Tests in Behavioral Research Methods in Environmental
Design, edited by MICHELSON (8.1.22 - Chapter 2) pinpoints
a number of problems associated with the use of the semantic
differential in environmental studies. MACOURT has reported
an investigation of the consistency of responses to semantic
differential scales in questionnaire surveys of residents'
attitudes to the new town of Newton Aycliffe (8.1.98). This
study indicated that a large proportion of respondents were
unable to use the scaling method satisfactorily and that of those
who did, many were unable to produce consistent responses when
filling in identical scales in an interviewer-conducted and a
postal questionnaire. HALL (8.1.117) has discussed the problem

Most attitudinal research in the transport field has utilised verbal, numerical or diagrammatic scaling techniques or direct questioning through open-ended questions. Very little use has been made of projective or other indirect techniques, such as sentence - completion or cartoon caption-filling, for eliciting attitudinal information. However, LESLEY has reported the application of a test using schematic faces in a study which attempted to identify the image of public transport and other forms of transport in two housing estates in Teesside (4.2.13). The Compound Scale of Facial Attributes used in this study is a version of the Facial Attribute Differential Test described in the article by FISHER and COX (8.1.30) and in the thesis by COX (8.1.31), and is a more complex and less direct technique than the simple schematic faces scales sometimes used in consumer research. General introductions to projective and other indirect techniques are provided by relevant chapters in the books by OPPENHEIM (8.1.80 - Chapter 7), SELLTIZ et al (8.1.101 - Chapter 8), and HENRY (8.1.64 - Chapter 4).

In the recent past some transport researchers have shown interest in the application of consumer research theory and techniques to travel demand research, and there have also been signs of an increasingly consumer-based approach in operational transport planning. Market segmentation is a central concept in modern marketing and consumer research and has generated a large volume of literature. A useful general introduction which also gives many further references is provided by LUNN's chapter, Market Segmentation - An Overview, in the book The Effective Use of Market Research, edited by AUCAMP (8.1.54 - Chapter 5). The distinction is made between the marketing interpretation of market segmentation as a strategy whereby products are directed towards specific target groups rather than at the whole population, and the researcher's perspective of market segmentation as a methodological approach geared to a comprehensive description of the market as a background to marketing action. An outline is given of the criteria used for defining target groups, ways of measuring these criteria, and ways of grouping consumers in terms of these criteria. The chapter, Different Uses of Market Segmentation by CLUNIES-ROSS in the same book, LUNN's chapter in the Consumer Market Research Handbook (8.1.27 - Chapter 14) and the chapter on Market Segmentation in KOTLER's Marketing Management: Analysis, Planning and Control (4.2.32) also provide general background reading on the subject. As a methodological approach which utilises many of the specific techniques referred to in this introduction, market segmentation has considerable relevance to transport research and planning, for instance in improving behavioural travel demand models, in identifying groups likely to be affected by changes in transport provision, and in developing and promoting service improvements directed towards specific target groups. In the latter context the market segmentation approach is central to the marketing philosophy presented by HOVELL, JONES and MORAN in The Management of Urban Public Transport: a marketing perspective (4.2.25).

of the optimum length of semantic differential scales as used in subjective measures of the 'quality of life' and concluded that a 9-point scale is preferable to 7-point and 10-point scales.

In the late 1960's and early 1970's Golob and others,principally in the United States, developed the application of unidimensional scaling techniques in studies which sought to quantify preferences and perceptions relevant to the use of transportation systems. A 7-point Likert scale was used in the Baltimore and Philadelphia studies reported by PAINE et al (3.1.15 and 3.1.16), and the paper Analysis of Consumer Preferences for a Public Transportation System by GOLOB, CANTY and GUSTAFSON (3.1.18) describes the use of the Thurstone paired comparison technique for measuring preferences for attributes of a new transportation concept, the demand-responsive jitney. A review of the use of psychometric scaling techniques in transportation research up to 1973 is included in Assessment of Preferences and Perceptions towards Attributes of Transportation Alternatives by GOLOB and DOBSON (3.1.59). The paper Attitude-Behavior Models for Public Systems Planning and Design, by GOLOB and RECKER (8.1.2) contains a general discussion of the concept of an attitude and of techniques of measuring it, in the context of potential application in public facilities planning and design. An empirical example is described in which 6-point scales were used for respondents' rating of twenty-five attributes of bus and car modes for work journeys. In this country, the market analysis study carried out by Cranfield Institute of Technology Centre for Transport Studies for the National Bus Company, reported by KNIGHT, SLEVIN and BULL (4.2.27), used the paired comparison technique, and THOMAS and BULL (4.5.1) have described the use of rating scales in another survey carried out by the Centre for Transport Studies at Cranfield, which attempted to relate beliefs and attitudes to travel behaviour for off-peak shopping trips. The report by REES, DIX and CLYDE (8.1.10) includes a detailed description of the theoretical background and methodological aspects of a study which used a variant of the semantic differential scaling technique in a survey of pedestrians' attitudes to two Liverpool shopping streets before and after pedestrianisation. Ten-centimetre 21-point self-completion scales were used, with a standard (good-bad) bipolar description The articles by OBORNE (8.1.92) and OBORNE and CLARKE (8.1.84-85) discuss the use of unidimensional rating scales in ergonomics research to obtain quantifiable subjective information from passengers on the intensity of noise and vibration experienced in transit. Since the mid-1970's more complex multidimensional scaling techniques have been used by some investigators in studies of travel perception and preference. For instance NICOLAIDIS,in Quantification of the Comfort Variable (8.1.77) has described the use of multidimensional scaling in a study which attempted to define and measure sub-attributes of 'comfort' as perceived by individual travellers.

In the past few years Hensher and others have developed the application of market segmentation in the field of travel demand research. The article in Transportation by HENSHER (8.1.55) discusses the use of the methodology in travel behaviour studies, and the chapters by HENSHER and by LOUVIERE, OSTRESH, MENLEY and MEYER in Behavioral Travel-Demand Models (3.1.10 - Chapter's 14 and 15) examine the use of market segmentation strategies in behavioural travel demand modelling and point to the need for research into other potential applications of the approach in transportation research. The Commonwealth Bureau of Roads' Occasional Paper by HENSHER, SMITH, HOOPER and STANLEY (4.2.48) describes an approach for identifying and analysing suitable improvements for particular consumer segments which could be used in the field of urban transport improvements. An empirical study undertaken in the Sydney Metropolitan area is described, in which transport disadvantaged areas were identified using market segmentation, and the techniques used are set out in some detail.

Bibliographies devoted to literature on survey methodology include BELSON and THOMPSON's Bibliography on Methods of Social and Business Research - 1973 (9.2.35), and the U.S. BUREAU OF THE CENSUS'S Index to Survey Methodology Literature - 1974 (9.2.38). Useful annotated guides to further reading on specific aspects of survey methodology are provided at the end of each chapter in the books by OPPENHEIM (8.1.80), MOSER and KALTON (8.1.100), and HOINVILLE and JOWELL (8.1.109). The latter two books also contain fairly substantial bibliographies. Lists of further reading on individual topics are also given in the Consumer Market Research Handbook (8.1.27) and in Methods in Social Research by GOODE and HATT (8.1.103). Most of the other general textbooks referred to in this introduction, and many of the journal articles, incorporate suggestions for further reading. On the specific subject of postal surveys the article by SCOTT (8.1.52) provides an extensive bibliography of material published up to 1961, and more recent material is listed in the book by ERDOS (8.1.50) and in the relevant chapters of more general textbooks. British and American journals which regularly contain contributions on aspects of survey methodology are listed under the heading 9.1 at the end of this subsection, and relevant abstracting and indexing services are listed under the heading 9.3. Readings in Attitude Theory and Measurement, edited by FISHBEIN (8.1.14), and OPPENHEIM's Questionnaire Design and Attitude Measurement both contain references to further reading on attitudinal theory and techniques. The Annotated Bibliography of the Application of Behavior and Attitude Research to Transportation System Planning and Design by SHEPARD (9.2.1) includes a section on psychometric techniques which forms the major part of the bibliography. A number of references are provided (mainly to material of United States origin) on scaling and non-scaling techniques and on attitude

surveys. Many of the reports and papers concerned with the
application of attitudinal measurement and modelling techniques
to transport research and planning in the U.S.A. are well-
referenced. These include GOLOB and RECKER's Attitude-
Behavior Models for Public Systems Planning and Design (8.1.2),
An Analysis of Consumer Preferences for a Public Transportation
System by GOLOB, CANTY and GUSTAFSON (3.1.18), and Assessment
of Preferences and Perceptions towards Attributes of Transportation Alternatives by GOLOB and DOBSON (3.1.59).

8.1.1　Attitude and Opinion Research. [*The Intensity
Component in] (1950)
SUCHMAN, E. A.
In: Measurement and Prediction. S.A. Stouffer (ed.)
Princeton University Press. Princeton, New Jersey. 1950.

8.1.2　Attitude - Behavior　Models for Public Systems
Planning and Design. (1975)
GOLOB, T.F. and RECKER, W.W.
Paper read at the Specialty Conference on Human
Factors in Civil Engineering Planning, Design and
Education. Buffalo. New York.
June　1975. A.S.C.E. and N.S.F.　co-sponsors.
General Motors Research Laboratories Publication
GMR-1906. (37 pp.)

This theoretical paper explores potential applications
of behavioural choice models in the planning and
design of public systems, focussing on choice models
involving attitudinal variables. Areas of application
include environmental design, structures and general
cost benefit analysis of systems. The paper includes
a discussion of the concept of an attitude and an
evaluation of attitude measurement techniques using
various scaling preference methods. Model· e
investigated for explaining overall preference or
choice of alternatives in terms of perceptions of the
characteristics of the alternatives. An approach
is proposed in which all relevant aspects of a design,
both objective and subjective, are treated as integral
to the design process. To demonstrate the applicability
of the approach an empirical example is presented in
which policies concerning improvements in a public
transport bus system can initially be formulated using
information obtained from an attitudinal model of
urban residents' choice of travel mode for their work
and shopping trips. A reference section contains over
seventy items relevant to the theoretical　aspects of
attitude measurement.

8.1.3　Attitude Measurement. (1954)
GREEN, B.F
In: Handbook of Social Psychology. G. Lindzey.(ed.)
Addison-Wesley Publishing Co. Cambridge, Mass. 1954.

8.1.4　Attitude Measurement in the Forecasting of Off-Peak
Behaviour.[*The Use of] (1977)
THOMAS, K.
In: Urban Transportation Planning: Current Themes and
Future Prospects.
P. Bonsall, M.Q. Dalvi and P.J. Hills.(eds.)
(see ref. 3. 4. 5 above)

333

8.1.5   Attitude Measurement: [*Judgmental Phenomena and Scales of]
         item displacement in Thurstone Scales. (1952)
         HOVLAND, C.I. and SHERIF, M.
         The Journal of Abnormal and Social Psychology. Vol.XLVII
         1952. (pp.822-832)
         (Reprinted in: Readings in Attitude Theory and
         Measurement. 1967. pp.236-248 M. Fishbein (ed.) - see ref.
         8.1.14 below)
         This study reveals the influence of the panel judge's
         own opinions on his arrangement of items in the
         Thurstone scaling procedure.

8.1.6   Attitude. [*Measures of Social Psychological] (1969)
         ROBINSON, J.P. and SHAUER, P.K.
         Ann Arbor: Survey Research Center. Institute for
         Social Research. University of Michigan. 1969.

8.1.7   Attitude Quantification. [*A Critical Appraisal of
         Pilot Techniques used Prior to] (1970)
         DRAKEFORD, J.
         Paper read at ESOMAR Seminar on Attitude and Motivation
         Research. Elsinore. 1970.

8.1.8   Attitude Scale Construction. [*A Comparison of the
         Thurstone and Likert Techniques of] (1946)
         EDWARDS, A.L. and KENNEY,K.C.
         Journal of Applied Psychology. Vol. XXX. 1946.
                                           (pp. 72-83)
         (Reprinted in:Readings in Attitude Theory and
         Measurement. 1967. pp. 249-256.
         M. Fishbein (ed.) - see ref. 8.1.14 below).

         This article presents a comparison and evaluation of
         the two most frequently used methods of measuring
         social attitudes - the 'method of equal appearing
         intervals' developed by Thurstone and Chave (see ref.
         8.1.13 below) and that of 'summated ratings'
         developed by Likert (see ref. 8.1.16 below). A
         discussion of the theoretical aspects of each method is
         followed by a description of an empirical study in
         which both scaling techniques were used independently
         with the same group of subjects. The study findings
         indicated that scores obtained from the two differently
         constructed scales were comparable; that scales
         constructed by the Likert method yield higher
         reliability coefficients with fewer items than scales
         constructed by the Thurstone method; that the Likert
         technique is less time-consuming and less laborious
         than that of Thurstone; and that there was nothing
         of a practical nature to confirm that a judging group,
         as used in the Thurstone technique, is a prerequisite
         for the construction of an adequate attitude scale.

8.1.9   Attitude Scale Construction. [*Techniques of](1957)
         EDWARDS, A.L.
         Appleton-Century-Crofts. New York. 1957.

8.1.10   Attitude Survey in two Liverpool Shopping Streets before
          the Implementation of Traffic Schemes. [*A Structured |
                                                              (1975)
          REES, F.J., DIX, M. and CLYDE, C.
          University of Leeds. Institute for Transport Studies.
          Working Paper 64. August 1975. (49 pp plus appendices).

          The plan to pedestrianize a major shopping street in
          Liverpool gave the opportunity for attitude surveys of
          pedestrians to be carried out before and after the change,
          in order to ascertain how the change had been perceived
          by the public. An attitude scaling technique was applied
          to eight basic attributes of Church Street which had
          been identified in a previous tape recorded survey. This
          paper describes how the 'before' survey was carried out
          and describes its results. It also presents a review
          of attitude measurement techniques and discusses the
          theoretical aspects of the survey method used. The
          development of the final questionnaire through several
          pilot stages is outlined in an appendix. Other appendices
          include copies of the final and various draft pilot
          questionnaires; the Interviewers' Instructions; details
          of a Control Survey; and details of the statistical
          methods used in the analysis.

8.1.11   Attitude Surveys in Transportation Planning and Impact
          Studies [*Application of]: A case study of Southwest
                                          Washington D.C. (1975)
          STEIN, M.M.
          Traffic Quarterly. Vol. 29. No. 1. January 1975. (pp. 51-
                                                                  64).

8.1.12   Attitude Techniques in Action. (1970)
          SHAFFER, M.T.
          Highway Research Record No. 305. Highway Research Board.
                                          Washington D.C. 1970

8.1.13   Attitude. [*The Measurement of] (1929)
          THURSTONE, L.L. and CHAVE, E.J.
          University of Chicago Press. Chicago. 1929. (109 pp.)

          This book is the sourcebook for the Thurstone scaling
          technique.

8.1.14   Attitude Theory and Measurement. [*Readings in]
                                                        (1967)
          FISHBEIN, M. (ed.)
          John Wiley & Sons, Inc., New York. 1967. (499 pp.)
          (see also refs. 8.1.5. and 8.1.8 above, and 8.1.15
          to 8.1.18, and 8.1.95 below).

          This book brings together some fifty important
          historical and contemporary articles on attitude
          theory and measurement, arranged under the headings:
          Historical Foundations; Attitude Measurement; and
          Attitude Theory. Approximately half of the book is
          concerned with attitude measurement, the articles
          relating primarily to the theory underlying attitude
          measurement rather than with the measurement process

335

per se. This section is divided into the following four subsections:-

A. Standardized Measurement Techniques: including reprints of or excerpts from original writings on scaling techniques by L.L. Thurstone (ref.8.1.17), R. Likert (ref. 8.1.16), and L. Guttman (ref.8.1.95), and a more recent contribution on semantic differentials by C.E. Osgood.

B. Multidimensional Measurement Techniques.

C. Alternative Measurement Techniques. (see ref. 8.1.18)

D. Problems and Perspectives in Attitude Measurement: including several articles which critically examine, compare and discuss some of the basic measurement techniques presented in the preceding subsections. (see refs. 8.1.5 and 8.1.8 above.)

8.1.15   Attitudes. (1967)
ALLPORT, G.W.
In: Readings in Attitude Theory and Measurement. 1967. (pp. 3-13) M. Fishbein (ed.) - see ref. 8.1.14 above.

Excerpted from an article in: Handbook of Social Psychology. C. Murchison (ed.). Clark University Press, Worcester, Mass. 1935.

The author reviews the history of the concept of attitude, discusses alternative definitions, and summarises three methods of measuring attitudes.

8.1.16   Attitudes. [*A Technique for the Measurement of] (1932)
LIKERT, R.
Archives of Psychology. Vol. 22. No. 140. 1932.
            Columbia University Press, New York.

An excerpt from the Appendix, entitled: "The Method of Constructing an Attitude Scale" is reprinted in: Readings in Attitude Theory and Measurement. 1967. pp. 90-95. M. Fishbein (ed.) - see ref. 8.1.14 above.

8.1.17   Attitudes can be Measured. (1928)
THURSTONE, L.L.
American Journal of Sociology. Vol. 33. 1928. (pp. 529-554) (Reprinted in: Readings in Attitude Theory and Measurement. 1967. pp. 77-89. M. Fishbein (ed.) - see ref. 8.1.14 above).

In this early paper by Thurstone the problem of measuring attitudes and opinions is discussed and a scaling technique solution which could be applied under certain circumstances is outlined.

8.1.18   Attitudes. [*The Indirect Assessment of Social]
                                                    (1950)
          CAMPBELL, D.T.
          Psychological Bulletin. Vol. XLVII. 1950.
              (pp. 15-38)
          (Reprinted in:Readings in Attitude Theory and
          Measurement. 1967. pp. 163-179. M. Fishbein (ed.) -
          see ref. 8.1.14 above).

          This paper discusses the problem of the indirect
          measurement of social attitudes and of prejudice,
          and reviews a number of attempts at obtaining such
          measurements. (prior to 1950).

8.1.19   Attribute Importance   in Public and Private Transport-
                                ation. [*Perceived](1973)
          GOLOB, T.F.,DOBSON, R. and SHETH, J.N.
          Faculty Working Paper No. 129. College of Commerce
          and Business Administration. University of Illinois at
          Urbana-Champaign. August 1973.
          Also in: Advancing, Applying and Teaching the Decision
          Sciences. M.W.Hopfe. (ed.) (Proceedings of the Fifth
          Annual Meeting of the American Institute for Decision
          Sciences. 1973. pp. 7-10).

          The paper describes the methods and findings of a
          survey in which 500 mail panel respondents rated
          attributes of a private and a public system of urban
          transport on a seven-point importance scale. Factor
          analysis was then applied to the data.

8.1.20   Attribute Meaning in Empirical Concept Testing.
                        [*Testing the Consistency of] (1975)
          GENSCH, D.H. and GOLOB, T.F.
          Journal of Marketing Research. Vol. 12. No. 3. August
                                1975. (pp. 348-354).

8.1.21   Attributes. [*Resource Paper on Product] (1973)
          SHERRET, A. and WALLACE, J.P. III.
          Highway Research Board Special Report No. 143.
          Washington D.C. 1973 (pp. 146-174)

8.1.22   Behavioral Research Methods in Environmental Design.
                                                    (1975)
          MICHELSON, W. (ed.)
          Community Development Series.
          Dowden, Hutchinson & Ross, Inc., Strondsburg,
          Pennsylvania. (Distributed by Halsted Press - a
          division of John Wiley & Sons, Inc.) (316 pp.)

          This collection of papers attempts to provide a
          theoretical basis for the application of social
          science techniques to environmental studies. Each
          section presents a clear discussion of a particular
          methodological approach, describes its relevance to
          research in environmental design, gives advice about
          its use in this field, and describes its application

with reference to a particular environment-oriented research project. Substantial reference lists are appended to each section. Topics covered include:-
Ch.2: The Semantic Differential and Other Paper-and Pencil Tests, by R.B. Bechtel (pp. 41-78)
Ch.3: Trade-Off Games, by I.M. Robinson, W.C. Baer, T.K. Banerjee and P.G. Flachsbart (pp. 79-118)
Ch.4. Survey Research, by R.W. Marans. (pp. 119-179)
Ch.5. The Time Budget, by W. Michelson and P. Reed. (pp. 180-234)

8.1.23   Behavioral Sciences. [*Research Methods in the]
                                        (1953)
          FESTINGER, L.F. and KATZ, D.K. (eds.)
          Holt, Rinehart and Winston. New York. 1953,
          and Dryden Press. New York. 1953.(2nd edition 1966-
                                                   660 pp.)
          (see also ref. 8.1.74 below).

8.1.24   Category Analysis to Smallscale Household Travel
          Surveys. [*A Pragmatic Application of] (1976)
          OCHOJNA, A.D. and MACBRIAR, I.D.
          Traffic Engineering and Control. Vol. 17. No. 7.
                    July 1976. (pp. 293-295)

8.1.25   Citizen Participation in Transportation Planning.
                              [*Effective] (1976)
          Vol. I: Community Involvement Processes. (129 pp.)
          Vol. II: A Catalog of Techniques. (298 pp.)
          U.S. DEPARTMENT OF TRANSPORTATION (Federal Highway
                    Administration). Washington D.C. 1976.

          Volume I of this report presents a general discussion
          of the rôle of citizen participation in the transport-
          ation planning process, followed by eight case studies
          which illustrate the application of various techniques
          used either singly or in combination.

          Volume II identifies and describes 37 techniques for
          citizen participation in transportation planning,
          grouping these into 34 'Direct Participatory Techniques',
          such as Game Simulation, Fishbowl Planning and Workshops;
          and 3 'Indirect Participatory Techniques', consisting
          of Delphi , Focused Group Discussions and Surveys of
          Citizens' Attitudes and Opinions. The techniques are
          presented alphabetically in a standard format consisting
          of: description; potential for resolving issues;
          positive and negative features; costs involved; program
          utilization, and bibliography.

8.1.26   Consumer Demand - a new approach. (1971)
          LANCASTER, K.
          Columbia University Press. 1971.

Consumer Market Research Handbook. (1972)
WORCESTER, R.M. (ed.)
McGraw-Hill Book Company (U.K.) Limited. 1972 (686 pp.)

The volume contains a collection of writings by
practising consumer market researchers which give a
comprehensive summary of consumer research techniques
and applications. Part One covers techniques of data
collection and analysis, and Part Two is concerned with
the uses of consumer market research. Topics covered
in the data collection section include: Qualitative
Research and Motivation Research (by P. Sampson);
Sampling (by M. Collins); Questionnaire Design (by
J. Morton-Williams); Interviewing and Field Control
(by J.F. Drakeford); and Mail Surveys (by B. Allt).
The section on data analysis includes chapters on
Coding, Editing and Processing (by G.R. Roughton);
Statistics and Significance Testing (by P.T. Harris);
and Multivariate Analysis of Market Research Data (by
C. Holmes). Market Segmentation and Corporate Image
Research are among the aspects covered in Part Two.
Each section is preceded by an introductory passage,
and the individual chapters are followed by lists of
relevant references. The book focuses on British work,
but references to work being done in North America,
Europe and elsewhere are also included.

8.1.28 Content Analysis.(1967)
        HOLSTI, O.R., LOOMBA, J.K. and NORTH, R.C.
        In: The Handbook of Social Psychology. G. Lindzey
        and E. Aronson (eds.) Addison-Wesley Publishing Co.
        Cambridge, Mass. 1967.

8.1.29 Critical Evaluation of the Relative Efficiency of
        Three Techniques in Item Analysis. [*A] (1952)
        KUANG, H.P.
        Educational and Psychological Measurement. Vol. XII.
                1952. (pp. 248-266)

8.1.30 Development and Initial Application of the Facial
                        Attribute Differential Test. (1971)
        FISHER, G.H. and COX, R.
        Bulletin of the British Psychological Society. Vol.24.
                        No. 84. 1971. (pp. 259-260).

8.1.31 Developmental Study in Person Perception. [*A .] (1971)
        COX, R.
        M. Sc. Thesis. University of Newcastle upon Tyne. 1971.

8.1.32 Econometric Methods. (1972)
        JOHNSON, J.
        McGraw-Hill Book Company. New York. 1972.

8.1.33 Errors in Surveys. [*On] (1944)
        DEMING, W.E.
        American Sociological Review. Vol. 9. August 1944.
                                (pp. 359-369)

8.1.34   Exploratory Research Techniques. [*An Examination of]
                                                        (1969)
          SAMPSON, P.
          Paper read at ESOMAR Congress. 1969.

8.1.35   Human Factors/Ergonomics: Research Methods. (1971)
          MITCHELSON, D.L., and DAMODARAN, L.
          Conference Report by NATO Advanced Study Institute.
          Bellagio, Italy. Applied Ergonomics. Vol. 2. No. 3.
                              September 1971.(pp. 252-254)

8.1.36   Interview Surveys in Great Britain. [*Classification
                              Manual for Household] (1969)
          HOINVILLE, G. and JOWELL, R.
          Social and Community Planning Research. 1969. (78 pp.)
          (see also ref. 8.1.109 below).

8.1.37   Interview. [*The Depth] (1966)
          BERENT, P.H.
          Journal of Advertising Research. Vol. 6. No. 2. April
                                                            1966.

8.1.38   Interview. [*The Focused] (1956)
          MERTON, R.K., FISKE, M. and KENDALL, P.
          The Free Press. Glencoe, Illinois. 1956.

8.1.39   Interview. [*The Group Depth] (1962)
          GOLDMAN, A.E.
          Journal of Marketing. Vol. 26. 1962.(pp. 61-68)

8.1.40   Interviewing. [*Group] (1974)
          WELLS, W.D.
          In: The Handbook of Marketing Research. R. Ferber (ed.)
          McGraw-Hill Book Company Ltd. New York. 1974.

8.1.41   Interviewing in Social Research. (1954)
          HYMAN, H.H. et al.
          University of Chicago Press, Chicago. 1954.

8.1.42   Interviewing Techniques to the Study of Travel
          Behaviour [*Application of In-Depth] : some prelimin-
          ary results. (1975)
          DIX, M.C.
          Oxford University Transport Studies Unit. Working
          Paper No. 9. October 1975. (22pp. plus Appendix)

          The paper describes the development of a methodology
          to aid in the understanding of the travel decision
          process. It presents some tentative findings from a
          small pre-pilot survey of household activities carried
          out in a commuter village near Oxford, using the
          diary technique in conjunction with tape-recorded
          unstructured household interviews.

8.1.43   Interviewing [*The Dynamics of]: theory, technique
                                              and cases. (1957)
         KAHN,R.L. and CANNELL, C.F.
         John Wiley & Sons, Inc. New York. 1957.

         A basic text book on surveys, interviewing and
         questionnaire design, including a full treatment of
         sources of interviewer bias.

8.1.44   Interviewing. [*Training in Depth]   (1971)
         BANAKA, W.H.
         Harper & Row. 1971

8.1.45   Interviews [*Depth] and Group Discussions. (1972)
         SOCIAL AND COMMUNITY PLANNING RESEARCH.
         Technical Manual No.4.
         Research Publications Ltd. 1972. (73 pp.)
         (see also ref. 8.1.109 below).

8.1.46   Magical Number Seven, Plus or Minus Two [*The]:
         Some limits on our capacity for processing information.
                                                       (1956)
         MILLER, G.A.
         Psychological Review. Vol. 62.   1956. (pp. 81-97).

8.1.47   Mail-Administered Questionnaires: A Success Story.(1966)
         FRANCEL, E.G.
         Journal of Marketing Research. Vol. 3. No. 3. February
                                                           1966.

8.1.48   Mail Panel Survey. [*Personal Interview Versus] (1964)
         NUCKOLS, R.C.
         Journal of Marketing Research. Vol. 1. No. 1. February
                                                           1964.

8.1.49   Mail Surveys. [*Low Cost, High Return] (1963)
         KEANE, J.G.
         Journal of Marketing. Vol. 27. No. 3. 1963.

8.1.50   Mail Surveys. [*Professional] (1970)
         ERDOS, P.L.
         McGraw-Hill Book Co., New York. 1970. (304 pp.)

8.1.51   Mail Surveys. [*Questionnaire Appearance and Response
                                         Rates in] (1968)
         FORD, N.M.
         Journal of Advertising Research. Vol. 8. No. 3.
                                              June 1968.

8.1.52   Mail Surveys. [*Research on] (1961)
         SCOTT, C.
         Journal of the Royal Statistical Society. Series A.
                 Vol. XXIV. 1961. (pp. 143-195)

         Includes a full review of the literature on mail
         questionnaire surveys up to 1961 and an extensive
                                              bibliography.

8.1.53   Market Projections. [*Quantifying the Passenger
                    Selection Process for Accurate] (1972)
          CLAPP, R.G., HOLLIGAN, P.E., JAIN, S.C. and LIPPKE, B. R.
          Transportation Research. Vol. 6. No. 3. September 1972.
                                              (pp. 275-285)

8.1.54   Market Research. [*The Effective Use of] (1971)
          AUCAMP, J. (ed).
          Staples Press. London. 1971. (320 pp.)

          This book, written by practising market researchers,
          summarises the different types of market research and
          indicates their practical applications. Part One
          outlines the information needs of management and
          discusses the concept of market research as an infor-
          mation system closely integrated with the operations
          of a company's marketing division. Part Two consists
          of studies of the main market research techniques,
          and includes chapters on qualitative research, behaviour
          and attitude research, and market segmentation. Part
          Three includes a number of case histories showing how
          research results were used to guide marketing action
          and to measure its effects.

8.1.55   Market Segmentation as a Mechanism in Allowing for
          Variability of Traveller Behaviour. (1976)
          HENSHER, D.A.
          Transportation. Vol. 5.   September 1976. (pp. 257-284)

8.1.56   Market Segmentation: Group versus Individual Behaviour.
                                              (1968)
          BASS, F.M. et.al.
          Journal of Marketing Research. Vol. 5.   August 1968.

8.1.57   Market Survey Respondents. [*Classifying] (1966)
          JOYCE, T. and CHANNON, C.
          Applied Statistics. Vol. XV. No. 3.   1966.

8.1.58   Mathematics, Measurement and Psychophysics. (1951)
          STEVENS, S.S.
          In: Handbook of Experimental Psychology. S.S. Stevens
                                              (ed.)
          John Wiley & Sons, Inc. New York. 1951.

          This chapter provides an introduction to various
          techniques of psychological measurement.

8.1.59   Measurement and Analysis of the Quality of Life. (1972)
          DALKEY, N.C., LEWIS, R. and SNYDER, D.
          In: Studies in the Quality of Life, Delphi and Decision-
          making. N.C. Dalkey, D.O.Rourke, R. Lewis and D. Snyder.
          Lexington Books. D.C. Heath & Co. 1972.

8.1.60   Measurement of Community Values. [*Basic Approaches to
                                              the] (1970)
          WACHS, M.
          Highway Research Record No. 305. Highway Research Board.
          Washington D.C. 1970.

8.1.61   Measurement of Meaning [*The] (1957)
         OSGOOD, C.E., SUCI, G.J. and TANNENBAUM, P.H.
         University of Illinois Press. Urbana. Illinois. 1957.
                                                    (342 pp.)

8.1.62   Measurement of Values. [*The] (1959)
         THURSTONE, L.L.
         University of Chicago Press. Chicago. 1959.

8.1.63   Monitoring in Practice. A household survey: its use
         and potential for local authorities and new towns.
                                                    (1976)
         ADDERSON, I.M., POUNTNEY, M.T. and HOLE, W.V.
         Building Research Establishment. Current Paper CP 31/76.
                                               1976. (15 pp.)

         The paper describes a household survey carried out
         by Washington Development Corporation and the
         Building Research Station to monitor selected aspects
         of the development of Washington New Town. Survey
         content, method of analysis, type of output and
         further potential of the data are covered, in addition
         to administrative procedures and costs.

8.1.64   Motivation Research. (1958)
         HENRY, H.
         Crosby Lockwood & Son. London. 1958.

8.1.65   Motivation to Work. [*The] (1959)
         HERZBERG, F. et al.
         John Wiley & Sons, Inc. New York. 1959.

8.1.66   Motivational Research. [*The Origins of] (1969)
         COLLINS, L. and MONTGOMERY, C.
         British Journal of Marketing.   Summer 1969.

8.1.67   Multiple Factor Analysis.(1947)
         THURSTONE, L.L.
         University of Chicago Press. Chicago. 1947.

8.1.68   Multivariate Statistical Methods. (1967).
         MORRISON, D. F.
         McGraw-Hill Book Co. 1967.

8.1.69   Psychological Measurement Techniques to Travel
         Demand Estimation. [*On the Application of] (1977)
         STOPHER, P.R.
         Environment and Behavior. Vol. 9. No. 1. March 1977.
                                               (pp. 67-80).

8.1.70   Psychological Research and Theory to Urban
         Transportation Planning. [*The Application of]
                                                    (1975)
         DOBSON,R.
         Paper read at the Specialty Conference on Human
         Factors in Civil Engineering Planning and Design,
         State University of New York. Buffalo, New York.
                                                    1975.

8.1.71   Psychological Testing. [*Essentials of] (1960)
          CRONBACH, L.J.
          Harper. New York. 1960.

8.1.72   Psychometric Methods. (1954)
          GUILFORD, J.P.
          McGraw-Hill Book Co. New York. 1954.

8.1.73   Qualitative Data. [*Analyzing] (1961)
          MAXWELL, A.E.
          Methuen. London. 1961.

8.1.74   Qualitative Material Research Methods. [*Analysis of]
                                                          (1966)
          CARTWRIGHT, D.P.
          In: Research Methods in the Behavioral Sciences.
          L.F. Festinger and D.K. Katz. (eds.) 1966.
          (see ref. 8.1.23 above.)

8.1.75   Qualitative Measurement of Public Opinion: The
          Quintamensional Plan of Question Design. (1947)
          GALLUP, G.H.
          American Institute of Public Opinion. Princeton,
                                         New Jersey. 1947.

8.1.76   Qualitative Research. [*A New Look at] (1967)
          SAMPSON, P.
          Paper read at Market Research Society Seminar on
          Psychological Methods in Market Research. 1967.

8.1.77   Quantification of the Comfort Variable. (1975)
          NICOLAIDIS, G.
          Transportation Research. Vol. 9. No. 1. February 1975.
                                         (pp. 55-66).

          A study which used modern psychometric techniques to
          develop a set of quantitative measures of comfort as
          perceived by individual travellers is described in
          this paper. Multidimensional scaling techniques and
          more specifically the Individual Differences Scaling
          model (statistical details of which are presented in
          an appendix) were used to define principal factors
          describing comfort. Comfort indices were then derived
          and preliminary analysis supported the argument that
          comfort, as measured in the study, does influence
          travellers' mode selection. It is concluded that this
          application of multidimensional scaling techniques to
          the study of qualitative aspects of transport is
          promising, and that more research is needed to quantif
          other qualitative variables, such as convenience,
          reliability, safety and accessibility, in order to
          obtain a better and more complete understanding of the
          travel mode decision process.

344

8.1.78   Question Length on Reporting Behavior in the Survey
          Interview. [*Effects of] (1972)
          LAURENT, A.
          Journal of the American Statistical Association. Vol.67.
                              No. 338. 1972. (pp. 298-305)

8.1.79   Question Wording on Response Distribution. [*Effect of]
                                                      (1967)
          BELKIN, M. and LIBERMAN, S.
          Journal of Marketing Research. Vol. 4. 1967. (pp. 312-
                                                              313)

8.1.80   Questionnaire Design and Attitude Measurement. (1966).
          OPPENHEIM, A.N.
          Heinemann. London. 1966. (298 pp.)

          A clear textbook outlining procedures for the design
          of surveys and questionnaires and techniques for the
          measurement of attitudes. Problems of survey and
          questionnaire design are discussed, attitude-scaling
          and projective techniques are examined, and a chapter
          on quantification of questionnaire data is included.
          Each chapter is followed by an annotated list of
          relevant references. Appendices include Scales of
          Occupational Prestige, a short test of statistical
          knowledge, and monographs for testing the statistical
          significance of differences between percentages.

8.1.81   Questionnaire Design Manual. (1972)
          SOCIAL AND COMMUNITY PLANNING RESEARCH.
          Technical Manual No. 5. 1972. (88 pp.)

          This manual describes and discusses the stages
          involved in questionnaire design, basic principles
          of information gathering, types of question to avoid,
          and the layout of questionnaires. Appendices present
          an outline of the Thurstone, Likert and Guttmann
          scaling techniques and examples of the layout of
          interviewer-administered and self-completion
          questionnaires.
          (see also ref. 8.1.109 below.)

8.1.82   Questionnaire Items. [*A Guide for Developing] (1970)
          JACOBS, O.
          National Technical Information Service. Springfield,
                                          Virginia. 1970.

8.1.83   Questionnaire Responses. [*Traits Affecting] (1970)
          OGNIBENE, P.
          Journal of Advertising Research. Vol. 10. No. 3.
                              June 1970. (pp. 18-20)

8.1.84   Questionnaire Surveys for the Investigation of
          Passenger Comfort. [*The Development of] (1973)
          OBORNE, D.J. and CLARKE, M.J.
          Ergonomics. Vol. 16. No. 6. November 1973. (pp. 855-
                                                           869)

          This article reports the progress (to 1973) of a
          research programme carried out by Swansea University
          with the aims of obtaining subjective information on
          passenger comfort as affected by vibration and noise
          while in motion, and of developing suitable question-
          naires as a tool for obtaining such information. A
          series of self-completion questionnaire surveys was
          conducted among actual passengers in a fare-paying
          situation, on hovercraft, helicopters and trains. The
          questions asked consisted mainly of those in which
          passengers were asked to describe the intensities of
          noise and vibration experienced, and those in which
          they were asked to rate the extent to which these
          features were present, using unidimensional scales.
          Various methodological improvements and refinements
          were incorporated as the research progressed and the
          authors concluded that the results demonstrated the
          usefulness of the questionnaire technique in obtaining
          from the passengers themselves reliable and measurable
          subjective information on comfort experienced. They
          also provided indications for further research and
          were found to have the additional advantage of promot-
          ing favourable public relations between the transport
          operators and customers.

8.1.85   Questionnaire Surveys of Passenger Comfort.(1975)
          OBORNE, D.J. and CLARKE, M.J.
          Applied Ergonomics. Vol. 6 No. 2. June 1975. (pp. 97-
                                                           103)

          The paper uses data obtained from questionnaire
          surveys of passenger comfort on moving public
          transport vehicles as a basis for discussing the
          quantitative assessment of subjective information
          on passenger reaction to noise and vibration
          experienced. Methods of obtaining and analysing
          the information are discussed, and a comparison is
          made between the application of the graphic and the
          numerical rating scales. The authors identify
          several drawbacks in the use of the graphic rating
          scale and conclude that the numerical scale has
          overall advantages in application and interpretation.

8.1.86   Questionnaires. [*Documentation for the Metro
          Guideway Home-Interview and Leave-Behind] (1973)
          DOBSON, R.
          General Motors Research Publication. GMR-1511.
                                          Warren, Michigan. 1973.

8.1.87   Questions. [*Respondent Understanding of Survey]
                                                        (1968)
          BELSON, W.A.
          Polls, Survey Research Centre Reprint Series 40,
                          Vol. 3. No. 4. (pp. 1-13)
          The London School of Economics. 1968.

8.1.88   Questions. [*The Art of Asking] (1951)
          PAYNE, S.L.
          Princeton University Press. Princeton, New Jersey.
                          1951. (263 pp.)

8.1.89   Quota Sample Right. [*Getting the] (1973)
          WEINBERGER, M.
          Journal of Advertising Research. Vol. 13. No. 5.
                          October 1973. (pp. 69-72)

8.1.90   Rank Correlation Methods. (1948)
          KENDALL, M.G.
          Griffin. London. 1948, and Hafner, New York. 1955

8.1.91   Rating Scales. [*A Study of the Effects of Reversing
          the Order of Presentation of Verbal] (1965)
          BELSON, W.A.
          Survey Research Centre Report. The London School of
                                        Economics. 1965.

8.1.92   Rating Scales in Ergonomics Research. [*Examples of
                          the Use of] (1976)
          OBORNE, D.J.
          Applied Ergonomics. Vol. 7. No.4. December 1976 (pp.201-
                                                        204)
8.1.93   Scaling of an Aircraft Handling Rating Scale.
                          [*Multidimensional] (1969)
          MURRELL, J.F.
          Ergonomics. Vol. 12. No. 6. November 1969. (pp. 925-
                                                        933)

8.1.94   Scaling of Consumer Preferences for a Public
             Transportation System. [*Multidimensional] (1974)
          DOBSON, R., GOLOB, T.F. and GUSTAFSON, R.L.
          Socio-Economic Planning Sciences. Vol. 8. No. 1.
                          February 1974. (pp. 23-36).

          Two multidimensional scaling models are applied to
          data on preference choices for system attributes
          in order to measure consumer attitudes towards a
          proposed new public transportation system.

8.1.95   Scaling Qualitative Data. [*A Basis for] (1944)
          GUTTMAN, L.
          American Sociological Review. Vol. 9. 1944. (pp. 139-
                                                        150)
          (Reprinted in: Readings in Attitude Theory and Measure-
          ment. 1967. pp. 96-107. M. Fishbein (ed.) - see ref.
                                        8.1.14 above.)

          In this paper Guttman discusses what is meant by a

scale, and suggests an approach to the problem of
quantifying qualitative data which involves
presenting the results of the analysis in the form
of a 'scalogram' which shows at a glance the configur-
ation of the qualitative data.

8.1.96   Scaling Techniques to the Quantification of the Comfor*
          Variable for Use in Binary Disaggregate Mode Choice
          Models. [*An Application of Multidimensional] (1974).
          NICOLAIDIS, G.
          Unpublished PhD. Dissertation. Cornell University.
          Ithaca, New York. 1974.

8.1.97   Scalogram Analysis. [*The Basis for] (1950)
          GUTTMAN, L.
          In: Measurement and Prediction. S.A. Stouffer (ed.)
          Princeton University Press. Princeton, New Jersey.
                                                              1950.

          This is the principal source for the Guttman scaling
          technique and its theoretical background.

8.1.98   Semantic Differential Scales. [*An Investigation of
          the Consistency of Responses to]. (1976).
          MACOURT, M.P.A.
          Durham University North East Area Study. Working
                              Paper No.24. 1976. (35 pp.)

8.1.99   Semantic Profiles for 360 Words. [*An Atlas of] (1958
          JENKINS, J.J., RUSSELL, W.A. and SUCI, G.J.
          American Journal of Psychology. Vol. LXXI. 1958.
                                              (pp. 688-699).

8.1.100   Social Investigation. [*Survey Methods in](1958.
                                              Revised 1971).
          MOSER, C.A. and KALTON, G.
          Heinemann, London. 1971. (549 pp. in paperback edition
          also: Basic Books Inc., New York. 1972.

          This basic textbook gives a comprehensive account of
          the methods used in social surveys, covering all the
          stages of a survey, from the original planning to the
          drafting of the final report. A substantial part of
          the book is devoted to the treatment of sampling
          techniques. Other aspects covered include mail
          questionnaires; interviewing; questionnaire design;
          scaling methods; response errors; processing of the
          data; and the analysis, interpretation and present-
          ation of the data. Notes on reading are given at the
          end of each chapter, and a bibliography is also
          included.

8.1.101   Social Relations. [*Research Methods in] (1951.
                                  Revised 1959 and 1965).
          SELLTIZ, C., JAHODA, M., DEUTSCII, M. and COOK, S.W.
          Methuen & Co., Ltd. London. 1965. (622 pp.)

          The book covers every stage of the research process,

with the emphasis on the practical applications of
the research. The first chapters are concerned with
general aspects of the research process and design,
and selection of and formulation of a research problem.
Subsequent chapters deal with general problems of
measurement, questionnaires and interviews, the use
of secondary data as source material and the application of scaling techniques. The analysis and interpretation of the data, preparation and presentation
of the research report, and the application of the
research are also covered. Appendices provide
technical details on sampling, questionnaire construction and interviewing procedure, and on estimating
the time and personnel needed for a study. A
bibliography is included.

8.1.102　Social Research and New Communities. (1968)
　　　　　WILLMOTT, P.
　　　　　Journal of the American Institute of Planners. Vol.34.
　　　　　　　No.6. November 1968. (pp. 387-397).

8.1.103　Social Research. [*Methods in] (1952)
　　　　　GOODE, W.J. and HATT, P.K.
　　　　　McGraw-Hill Series in Sociology.
　　　　　McGraw-Hill Book Co. New York. 1952. (386 pp.)

　　　　　In this textbook on social research methods the
　　　　　authors attempt to show how the principles of
　　　　　scientific method apply to the field of sociology.
　　　　　The first chapters deal with general and basic
　　　　　problems of the relation between the foundations of
　　　　　science and social data. The remaining two-thirds
　　　　　of the book cover a variety of empirical tools
　　　　　commonly used in sociological research, drawing
　　　　　examples from specific research experience . Topics
　　　　　covered include use of the library; questionnaire
　　　　　construction; mailed surveys; interviewing;
　　　　　probability and sampling; scaling techniques;
　　　　　research in population; analysis of quantitative
　　　　　and qualitative data (including content analysis);
　　　　　and report preparation.

8.1.104　Social Research Techniques for Planners. (1970)
　　　　　BURTON, T.L. and CHERRY, G.E.
　　　　　George Allen and Unwin. London. 1970 (137 pp.)

　　　　　This book is an introduction to social surveys for
　　　　　planning purposes and presents a review of question-
　　　　　naire design, sampling techniques and data analysis.

8.1.105　Social Sciences. [*Survey Research in the] (1967)
　　　　　GLOCK, C.V. (ed.)
　　　　　Russell Sage Foundation. New York. 1967.

8.1.106　SPSS Statistical Package for the Social Sciences.
　　　　　　　　　　　　　　　　　　　　　　　　　(1970)
　　　　　NIE, N.H., BENT, D. and HULL, C.
　　　　　McGraw-Hill Book Co. New York. 1970.

8.1.107   Statistical Methods for Research Workers. (1950)
          FISHER, R.A.
          Hafner. New York. 1950.
          (14th edition published by Oliver and Boyd. Edinburgh.
                                                  1970. 362 pp.)

          This textbook describes and explains techniques for
          applying statistical tests to quantitative data
          accumulated from research surveys, and includes
          many illustrative examples. The subjects covered
          include: Diagrams; Distributions;Tests of Goodness
          of Fit, Independence and Homogeneity; the Correlation
          Coefficient; Tests of Significance of Means,
          Differences of Means and Regression Coefficients; and
          the Principles of Statistical Estimation.

8.1.108   Statistical Techniques in Market Research. (1949)
          FERBER, R.
          McGraw-Hill Book Co. New York. 1949 (556 pp.)

8.1.109   Survey Research Practice. (1978).
          HOINVILLE, G., JOWELL, R. and ASSOCIATES.
          Social and Community Planning Research.
          Heinemann. London. March 1978. (228 pp.)

          This book is a practical manual covering the
          organisational aspects of conducting sample surveys.
          The main emphasis is on the survey design and data
          collection stages, but chapters are also included on
          data preparation and classifications. Subjects
          covered include the conduct of qualitative survey
          research (group discussions and depth interviews),
          questionnaire construction, sampling, interviewing,
          organising fieldwork, and postal survey procedures.
          The book includes a bibliography, and notes on
          further reading are provided at the end of each
          chapter.
          (see also refs. 8.1.36, 8.1.45 and 8.1.81 above.)

8.1.110   Surveys. [*The Design of Sample] (1972)
          RAJ, D.
          McGraw-Hill Book Co. New York. 1972.

          Includes a section on methodology for transport
          surveys.

8.1.111   Tape Recorded Interviews in Social Research. (1956)
          BUCHER, R., FRITZ, C.E. and QUARANTELLI, E.L.
          American Sociological Review. Vol. 21. 1956. (pp.359-
                                                             364)

8.1.112   Tape Recorders to Find Impressions of Church Street,
                     Liverpool. [*A Survey Using] (1973)
          REES, F.J.
          University of Leeds. Institute of Transport Studies.
             Working Paper 54. 1973. (37 pp. plus appendices).

          This document reports on the first of a series of

surveys carried out before and after pedestrianisation
of Church Street and Lord Street, Liverpool, to find
out reactions to the environmental changes brought
about. The aim of this survey, carried out in April,
1973, was to obtain tape recordings of a broad range
of impressions and perceptions of Church Street
before pedestrianisation from people using it, and
to condense these impressions into a small number of
factors. 1,823 tape recorded interviews were conducted,
of which two-thirds were with women. These provided
3,891 separate impressions which were grouped into
37 main factors (27 unfavourable and 10 favourable).
This gave sufficient information from which to
select descriptive factors for use in further surveys.
The report describes the implementation of the pilot
and main surveys, analysis of the survey data, and
potential uses of the data obtained. Appendices
include copies of the interviewers' notes, excerpts
from transcripts of the tape recordings covering
approximately 5 minutes, and details of the equipment
used.

8.1.113 Tape Recording: its Effect on Accuracy of Response
in Survey Interviews. (1967)
BELSON, W.A.
Journal of Marketing Research. Vol. 4. 1967. (pp. 253-
260)

8.1.114 User Preferences for a Demand -Responsive Transport-
ation System: A case-study report. (1971)
GUSTAFSON, R.L., CURD, H.V. and GOLOB, T.F.
Highway Research Record No. 367. Highway Research
Board. Washington D.C. 1971. (pp. 31-45).
Also: General Motors Corporation Research Publication
        Warren, Michigan.   January 1971.

This paper discusses the measurement of user preferences for a demand-responsive transportation system
and describes a study which consisted of three phases:
survey design, adaptation of psychological scaling
techniques, and the fieldwork and analysis of an
attitudinal survey.

GOVERNMENT REPORTS AND PUBLICATIONS.

8.1.115 Classification of Occupations. [*The] (1970)
OFFICE OF POPULATION CENSUSES AND SURVEYS.
H.M.S.O. 1970.

8.1.116 Interviewers. [*A Handbook for] (1971)
ATKINSON, J.
Office of Population Censuses and Surveys. Social
Survey Division. 1971. (169 pp.)

This manual, originally produced for Government
Social Survey interviewing staff, describes the
practise and procedures of structured interviewing.
Topics covered include sampling technique; the

public relations rôle of the interviewer (including
instructions on the approach to employ with the
public and on the conduct of the interview);
instruction in structured interviewing (including
classification standard definitions); the sequence
of an interview; and the organisation of fieldwork.
The Handbook also includes a glossary of the terms
used most often in social survey research.

8.1.117   Quality of Life in Britain: 1971 to 1975.
[*Subjective Measures of] Some Developments and
Trends. (1976)
HALL, J.
In: Social Trends. No. 7. Central Statistical Office.
H.M.S.O. 1976. (pp. 47-60)

This paper reviews recent work in measuring 'quality
of life' as experienced by individuals rather than
as gauged by financial or socio-economic indices.
It describes and assesses various subjective
indicators which have been used to measure changes
in, and changing perceptions of, 'quality of life'
over a span of years.

8.1 Subsidiary References.

1.1 New Towns - Transport and Mobility.

1.1.16   Transport and Mobility in Durham New Towns. (1974-5)

1.2 New Towns - Non-Transport Aspects.

1.2.1   Survey of Attitudes to New Towns in County Durham. (1975)

2.1 Runcorn.

2.1.10   Runcorn Travel Survey. (1973)
2.1.17   Home Interview Social Survey. (1966)
2.1.18   The Leisure Activities of Young Children: A Preliminary Report.
(1971)
2.1.20   1976 Runcorn Household Census. (1976)
2.1.21   1969 Social Survey: the First 500 Families. (1969)
2.1.22   Statistical Profile of Runcorn New Town. (1964)
2.1.24   Creating a Community: A Study of Runcorn New Town. (1973)
2.1.25   Runcorn: A Second Look. (1975)

2.2 Skelmersdale.

2.2.8   Skelmersdale New Town Population and Social Surveys. (Annually)

2.3 Telford.

*2.3.4   Telford Bus Use Attitude Survey: An investigation of citizen
attitudes towards public transportation in Telford. (1976)*
*2.3.13   Executive Housing Survey: a study of attitudes in the medium
to upper private housing market. (1976)*

3.1.42   *An Investigation of Modal Choice for Dual-Mode Transit, People Mover and Personal Rapid Transit systems. (1974)*

3.1.53   *Report of a Study into the Motivation and Attitudes of Passengers and Potential Passengers of London Transport Buses. (1968)*

3.1.59   *Assessment of Preferences and Perceptions toward Attributes of Transportation Alternatives. (1974)*

3.1.60   *Preferences for Transit Service by Homogeneous Groups of Individuals. (1974)*

3.1.62   *The Influence of Car Ownership on Shopping Habits. (1964)*

3.1.65   *Report on a Market Research Survey into Transport Demand: Waveney Valley Area. (1976)*

3.1.67   *Mid-Glamorgan Transport Use and Attitude Survey. (1976)*

3.1.80   *Road Talk: Travel in Britain. (1978)*

3.1.91   *Research into the Urban Traveller's Behaviour. (1971)*

3.2 *Social Aspects of Mobility.*

3.2.1   *Age Concern on Transport. (1973 edition.)*

3.2.9   *A Study of Travel Behaviour of the Elderly. (1976)*

3.2.10   *Attitudes of the Retired and the Elderly. (1974)*

3.2.12   *An Examination of the Extent and Welfare Implications of Bus Use by the Elderly in Harlow. (1977)*

3.2.13   *Free Travel for the Elderly in London - 1974 Survey. (1975)*

3.2.14   *Lifestyles and the Transportation Needs of the Elderly in Los Angeles. (1976)*

3.2.16   *Travel Patterns of Elderly People Under a Concessionary Fares Scheme. (1977)*

3.2.23   *Estimating the Use of Free Bus Passes in Reading - survey of the number of trips by pass-holders. (1973)*

3.2.24   *The Sunderland Hypermarket Survey. (1971)*

3.2.25   *Leisure in the North West. (1972)*

3.2.29   *Mobility and Accessibility in the Outer Metropolitan Area.(1974)*

3.2.35   *The Olney Residents' Survey. (1974 and 1975)*

3.2.37   *Personal Mobility and Transport Policy. (1973)*

3.2.41   *Journeys to School: a survey of Secondary Schools in Berkshire and Surrey. (1977)*

3.2.46   *On Shoppers' Requirements for the Location of Shops in Towns. (1974)*

3.2.48   *Shopping in Watford. (1971)*

3.2.63   *Transport Realities and Planning Policy. (1976)*

3.2.69   *The Elderly at Home: a study of people aged sixty five and over living in the community in England in 1976. (1978)*

3.2.73   *Planning for Leisure. (1969)*

3.2.77   *Shopping Habits and Attitudes to Shop Hours in Great Britain. (1975)*

3.2.79   *A Survey of Women's Employment. (1968)*

3.3 *Interaction between Land Use and Travel*

3.3.14   *Fair Play For All: a study of access to sport and informal recreation. (1977)*

3.4 *Transport and Mobility - General and Miscellaneous.*

3.4.5   *Urban Transportation Planning: Current Themes and Future Prospects. (1977)*

4.1 Public Transport – Operational Aspects.

4.1.2   *Bradford Bus Study: Final Report. (1976)*
4.1.101 *Report on the Survey of Concessionary Travel Schemes in England and Wales.*

4.2 Public Transport – Marketing Approach.

4.2.1   *Advertising and Promotion Demonstration Program. (1970)*
4.2.2   *The Effect of Advertising Bus Services in Two Housing Estates in the Teesside Conurbation. (1974)*
4.2.6   *A Survey of Commuter Attitudes Towards Rapid Transit Systems. (1963)*
4.2.7   *Transportation Issues in Consumer Motivation. (1973)*
4.2.9   *Studying Transportation from the Consumer Viewpoint: some recommendations. (1967)*
4.2.10   *Corporate Image Research. [London Transport] (1977)*
4.2.11   *Corporate Image Research. (1972)*
4.2.13   *The Image of Public Transport in Two Housing Estates in the Teesside Conurbation. (1974)*
4.2.20   *Public Awareness of Transport Agencies and Information: a small-scale study in Sunderland. (1976)*
4.2.41   *An Opinion Survey of the Yorkshire Dales Rail Service in 1975. (1977)*

4.3 Public Transport – Ergonomic Aspects.

4.3.26   *Human Factors in Engineering and Design. (1974 edition)*

4.4 Public Transport – Demonstration Projects and Innovatory Systems.

4.4.29   *Attitudes towards the London Transport Minibus Service. (1973)*
4.4.30   *Minitrams and New Addington. (1975)*

4.5 Public Transport – General and Miscellaneous.

4.5.1   *An Examination of Attitudes and Beliefs Underlying the Use of Local Bus Services. (1975)*
4.5.8   *Public Attitudes to Transport in the Eastbourne, Bexhill and Hastings Area. (1975)*
4.5.14   *Some Aspects of the Rural Transport Problem among Norwich Commuter Villages. (1975)*

5.1 Private Motor Transport.

5.1.1   *Initial Study of Car Availability. (1974)*
5.1.16   *The Possible Effects of Petrol Rationing on Travel in London. (1975)*

9.1 Journals.

9.1.44   *European Journal of Marketing. (Quarterly)*
9.1.46   *Journal of Advertising Research. (Six times a year)*
9.1.47   *Journal of Applied Psychology. (Six times a year)*
9.1.48   *Journal of Marketing. (Quarterly)*
9.1.49   *Journal of Marketing Research. (Quarterly)*
9.1.50   *Journal of the Royal Statistical Society.*

9.1.54   Psychological Review. (Six time a year)
9.1.55   Public Opinion Quarterly. (Quarterly)

9.2 Biliographies.

9.2.1   Annotated bibliography of the application of behavior and
         attitude research to transportation system planning and
         design. (1976)
9.2.36   Bibiliography on Methods of Social and Business Research. (1973)
9.2.38   Indexes to Survey Methodology Literature. (1974)

9.3 Abstracting and Indexing Services.

9.3.11   Market Research Abstracts. (Twice a year)
9.3.13   Psychological Abstracts. (Monthly)
9.3.15   Social Sciences Citation Index. (Annually)
9.3.16   Social Sciences Index. (Quarterly)
9.3.17   Sociological Abstracts. (Five times a year)

9.5 Statistical Sources.

9.5.6-8 National Travel Survey 1972/73.

9.6 Other Soures of Information.

9.6.18   Sources of Social Statistics.

8.2   Economic   Evaluation .

This subsection together with the appended subsidiary references brings together selected material concerned with the
evaluation of alternative transport projects. Some general
items relating to planning evaluation have been included in
an attempt to set transport decision-making within a wider
frame of reference. Since economic evaluation of alternative
transport investments as an aid to decision-making is basically
an instrument of policy, much of the literature which focuses
on transport policy issues includes a consideration of evaluation methodology. Thus, a number of important and topical
references to the subject matter covered by this subsection
are listed in the section of the bibliography dealing with
transport policy (7.1) and are cross-referenced at the end
of this subsection. The subsidiary references also include
some cost benefit analysis case studies, and several of the
most relevant items concerned with modal choice and the value
of travel time (subsection 3.1). These whole subject areas,
however, are important components of cost benefit analysis in
transport studies, and many of the items listed in subsection 3.1
provide useful supportive material to the subject matter
covered in this subsection.

STARKIE'S book, Transportation Planning, Policy and Analysis
(7.1.38) traces the increasing replacement of technical
engineering criteria by economic evaluation criteria during
the 1960's as a basis for deciding between alternative transport
investments. This was related to the concern with formulating
and evaluating alternative strategies which was the keystone
of the systems-based approach to transport planning generally
adopted in this country at that time. The development of
systematic evaluation techniques based on economic criteria
also reflected both the prevailing perception of the urban
transport problem as primarily one of traffic congestion which
could be solved by providing additional roads, and the existence
of more clearly defined Government guidelines on transport
investment and phasing than had previously been provided.
THOMSON'S Modern Transport Economics (3.4.3) sets out the
economist's approach to transport planning and includes a
general discussion of economic evaluation and a detailed
examination of the evaluation of improvements to transport
infrastructure, supported by case studies.

The methods of investment appraisal used by the Departments of
the Environment/Transport in public sector transport are
outlined in the report Getting the Best Roads for our Money:
the COBA Method of Appraisal (8.2.21), and in Paper 5 of the
DEPARTMENT OF THE ENVIRONMENT'S 1976 Consultation Document on
Transport Policy (7.1.77). The Consultation Document also
describes some of the practical problems arising from the
application of these methods. During the 1970's there has been
increasing recognition of the shortcomings in the evaluation
techniques currently used. Together with general changes in

357

the economic climate, in the perception of transport problems
and of the perceived means required to solve them, this has
led to a re-examination of the validity of the conventional
economic assessment approaches in transport planning (in
particular, cost benefit analysis) and of their relevance to
the actual decision-making process. Much of this questioning
was prompted by the Government's rejection of the majority findings
of the independent Committee on the Third London Airport,
published in 1971 (the 'Roskilll Commission'), which were based
on highly sophisticated economic evaluation techniques. This
has been widely cited as a classic example of the failure of
such techniques to provide a sound basis for policy formulation.

The INDEPENDENT COMMISSION ON TRANSPORT'S report, Changing
Directions (7.1.3), examines the rôle of cost benefit analysis
as an instrument of transport decision-making, discussing both
general problems including those arising from the complexity
of economic interrelationships, and a number of specific
methodological difficulties. The report recommends that more
work be done to refine the measurement of intangibles and that
the cost benefit analysis technique be used more consistently
and with a wider frame of reference. It concludes that although
the technique is an important component of the decision-making
process it is not adequate as a basis for decision-making on its
own, and is unlikely ever to be able to dispense with the need
for broad value judgments on aesthetic and environmental effects
and on moral and political issues. This point is borne out by
the cost benefit analysis described by POTTER in Volume 3 of
Transport and New Towns (1.1.19). In this study of alternative
transport plans for a theoretical new town cost benefit analysis
revealed clear overall benefits in public transport and pedestrian/
public transport oriented designs as compared with a car oriented
design. But the technique was unable to indicate a clear
advantage between the two non-car oriented designs and the author
concluded that a subjective value judgment would be needed to
decide the balance of advantages between these two designs.

The Government's Consultation Document on Transport Policy
(7.1.77), recognising the growing volume of criticism of official
economic evaluation procedures for road schemes and particularly
of cost benefit analysis techniques, recommended an independent
assessment of these procedures. This led to the setting up of
the Advisory Committee on Trunk Road Assessment, under the Chairmanship of Sir George Leitch. The Report of the Advisory
Committee on Trunk Road Assessment (7.1.78) recommended a broad-
ening of the assessment process, in which a 'framework' document
would set out alongside the cost benefit calculations of tangible
factors, the intangible costs and benefits less easily expressed
in monetary terms. The difficulty involved in applying monetary
measures to intangibles is generally considered to be one of the
major problems raised by conventional cost benefit analysis
techniques. Awareness of this and of other limitations has led
to various attempts to develop satisfactory alternative approaches
to transport assessment. SHELDON and BRANDWEIN in The Economic
and Social Impact of Investments in Public Transit (7.1.12)
report the use of a goals achievement methodology as an expanded

form of cost benefit analysis which provided a basis for
evaluating the tangible and intangible impacts of a large
number of transport projects in the U.S.A.

LICHFIELD'S Stevenage Public Transport: Cost Benefit Analysis
(2.4.57), published in 1969 is a more broad-based approach
to a particular urban transport situation which sought to
discover whether a community as a whole would benefit if some
people were persuaded to use public transport in preference
to cars as an alternative to costly extensions of the road
system. The study considered the alternative courses of action
from the point of view of various sectors of the community
who would be affected, and the methodology used included both
the planning balance sheet and a financial operating analysis.
The planning balance sheet involved the analysis of measurable
costs and benefits in monetary terms (social cost benefit
analysis) and the non-monetary assessment of intangible costs
and benefits on a subjectively based points system. The two-
volume report of the study contains a substantial amount of
methodological detail and the article in Journal of Transport
Economics and Policy by LICHFIELD and CHAPMAN (2.4.64) uses
the analysis to illustrate a general discussion of the urban
transport problem and a more detailed examination of the rôle
of the planning balance sheet technique in transport investment
decisions, LICHFIELD'S Edgware (3.3.12) and Swanley (3.3.13)
studies provide further examples of the application of the
planning balance sheet approach.

 ASHFORD and CLARK'S paper (8.2.20) critically reviews both
conventional cost benefit analysis and other methods currently
used in transport technology assessment, including the planning
balance sheet and goals achievement matrices. The authors
show how inadequacies in analytic techniques as currently used,
together with a more fundamental gap between the assumptions
on which studies are based and the major 'real world' issues
as perceived by the decision-makers, have resulted in the
recommendations of some costly and expert studies being rejected
at the point of decision taking. A number of suggestions are
put forward for improving the quality and relevance of assessment techniques in transport planning.

8.2.1.   Benefit-Cost Analysis as Related to Transportation
         Systems. [*Notes on the State of the Art of] (1966)
         CRUMLISH, J.D.
         U.S. Department of Commerce. Bureau of Standards.
         N.B.S. Technical Note 294. 1966.

8.2.2.   Cost-Benefit Analysis: a survey. (1965)
         PREST, A.R. and TURVEY, R.
         Economic Journal. Vol. 75. December 1965.(pp.683-731)

8.2.3.   Cost-Benefit Analysis in City Planning.(1960)
         LICHFIELD,N.
         Journal of the American Institute of Planners. Vol.26.
         No.5.November 1960. (pp.273-279)

8.2.4.   Cost-Benefit Scales for Urban Transportation.(1968)
         DODSON,E.N.
         Systems Analysis of Urban Transportation. Vol.3.
         General Research Corporation. Santa Barbara. January
         1968.
         (see also refs: 3.2.12-13 above and 8.2.17-19 below.)

8.2.5.   Decision-making in Economics and Behavioral Science.
         [*Theories of] (1959)
         SIMON,H.A.
         American Economic Review. Vol. 49 June 1959. (pp.253-
                                                             283)
8.2.6.   Decision-making Technique for Transportation Planning.
         [*A Rational] (1967)
         JESSIMAN,W. et al.
         Highway Research Record No.180. Highway Research Board.
         Washington D.C. 1967.

8.2.7.   Economic Base Levels for Public Transport Services
         for Transportation Study Design Years. [*A Procedure
         for Determining] (1973)
         HILL, G.J.
         Paper read at the PTRC Summer Annual Meeting.June 1973.

8.2.8.   Economics and Methodology in Urban Transport Planning
                                                           (1969)
         KIRWAN,R.M.
         In: Orr,S. and Cullingworth,J.B. (eds): Regional
         and Urban Studies.
         Allen and Unwin. London. 1969.

8.2.9.   Economics of Transport Appraisal. [*The](1974)
         HARRISON,A.J.
         Croom Helm. London. 1974. (293pp.)

8.2.10   Evaluating Alternative Plans. [* A Goals Achievement
         Matrix for] (1968)
         HILL,M.
         Journal of the American Institute of Planners. Vol.34.
         No.1.January 1968 (pp.19-29).

8.2.11   Evaluating Urban Transportation Planning in Terms
          of User Benefit. [*A Method for] (1975)
          KOBOYASHI, K., AOKI,Y. and TANI,A.
          Transportation Research. Vol.9.No.1. February 1975.
          (pp.67-79)

          This paper presents a methodology for evaluating the
          impacts of urban transport systems on society from
          the user's viewpoint. The evaluation is developed
          in terms of time, cost, convenience and comfort.

8.2.12.   Evaluation in the Planning Process. (1975)
          LICHFIELD, N.,KETTLE, P. and WHITBREAD, M.
          Urban and Regional Planning Series. Vol. 10.
          Pergamon Press, Oxford. 1975 (344pp.)

8.2.13.   Evaluation in the Planning Process- the Case of
          Accessibility.(1972)
          WHITBREAD, M.
          Working Paper No. 10.Planning Methodology Research
          Unit. School of Environmental Studies. University
          College, London. 1972. (38pp.)

8.2.14.   Evaluation Methodology of Urban and Regional Plans:
          A Review.(1970)
          LICHFIELD, N.
          Regional Studies. Vol.4. No.2. August 1970.(pp.151-165)
          This special issue of Regional Studies is devoted
          to evaluation methods in urban and regional planning.

8.2.15.   Evaluation: [*Plan] A review of research relevant
          to the choice of objectives and criteria for plan
          evaluation. (1973)
          PERRATON, J.K.
          Working Paper No.67. Centre for Land Use and Built
          Form Studies, Cambridge. 1973.

8.2.16.   Metropolitan Plan Making-an Analysis of Experience
          with the Preparation andEvaluation of Alternative
          Land Use and Transportation Plans. (1970)
          BOYCE, C.E., DAY.N.D. and McDONALD,C.
          Regional Science Research Institute, Philadelphia.
          1970.

8.2.17.   Social Benefit of Constructing an Underground
          Railway in London. [*Estimating the] (1963)
          FOSTER, C.D. and BEESLEY, M.E.
          Journal of the Royal Statistical Society. Series A.
          (General). Vol.126, Part 1. 1963 (pp.46-78)

8.2.18   Social Cost-Benefit Study of the Manchester-Glossop
          and Manchester-Marple/New Mills Suburban Railway
          Services. (1972)
          FOSTER,C.D.
          British Railways Board, Midland Region. London.1972.

8.2.19. Social Costs and Benefits in Urban Transportation.
         [*Identification of] (1968)
         SORENSON,J.L.
         Systems Analysis of Urban Transportation. Vol.3:
         Network Flow Analyses. General Research Corporation.
         Santa Barbara. January 1968.
         (see also refs. 3.2.12-13 and 8.2.1-4 above.)

8.2.20. Transport Technology Assessment. [*An Overview of]
                                                      (1975)
         ASHFORD,N.J. and CLARK,J.M.
         Transportation Planning and Technology. Vol.3.
         December 1975.(pp.31-43).

         This paper presents a critical review of the methods
         currently used in transport technology assessment,
         focussing particularly on travel demand forecasting.
         The authors investigate the reasons for the gulf
         which often exists between the assumptions inherent
         in many complex analytical assessment studies and
         the major issues as perceived by the decision makers.
         It is suggested that although serious deficiencies
         exist throughout the assessment process, the root
         of the problem lies in the procedures adopted for
         evaluation. Accordingly a number of existing
         evaluation techniques are examined, including cost
         benefit analysis, the planning balance sheet and
         goals achievement matrices. On the basis of the
         shortcomings which are exposed, six areas of import-
         ant assessment criteria are isolated. Finally a
         more realistic and applicable framework for assess-
         ment is proposed which it is believed can take more
         explicit account of all relevant assessment criteria.

GOVERNMENT REPORTS AND PUBLICATIONS.

8.2.21. Getting the Best Roads for our Money: the COBA
         Method of Appraisal. (1972)
         DEPARTMENT OF THE ENVIRONMENT.
         H.M.S.O. 1972.

8.2 Subsidiary References.

1.1 New Towns - Transport and Mobility.

1.1.19   Transport and New Towns. Volume Three. (1977)

2.1 Runcorn.

2.1.6   Runcorn Busway Study. (1976)

362

2.3 Telford.

2.3.7   Telford Transportation Study:
1. An aid to the preliminary evaluation of long-term public transport options. (1976)
2. New techniques in the modelling of trip generation and modal split. (1976)

2.4 Other New Towns.

2.4.57   Stevenage Public Transport: Cost Benefit Analysis. (1969)
2.4.64   The Urban Transport Problem and Modal Choice. (1971)

3.1 Studies of Modal Choice Behaviour and Value of Travel Time.

3.1.38   Minibus Service W9: Bus/Minibus Modal Choice Analysis and Cost-Benefit Assessment. (1975)
3.1.41   Modal Choice and Value of Travel Time. (1976)
3.1.52   Choice of Mode of Transport: a) Psychological Motivation.
                    b) The Economic Approach. (1969)
3.1.59   Assessment of Preferences and Perceptions toward Attributes of Transportation Alternatives. (1974)
3.1.99   The Effects on Transport Benefit Evaluation of User Misperception of Costs. (1974)

3.3 Interaction between Land Use and Travel.

3.3.12   Cost Benefit Analysis and Road Proposals for a Shopping Centre: A Case Study: Edgware. (1968)
3.3.13   Cost Benefit Analysis in Town Planning: A Case Study: Swanley (1966)
3.3.28   The Economics of Residential Location. (1973)
3.3.38   Towns Against Traffic. (1972)
3.3.39   Urban Survival and Traffic: Economics of City Traffic. (1962)
3.3.42   Models of Urban Development in the Analysis of Transportation Investment: the case of North Central Texas. (1977)
3.3.46   A Theory of the Urban Land Market. (1960)
3.3.49   The Structure, Size and Cost of Urban Settlements. (1973)

3.4 Transport and Mobility – General and Miscellaneous.

3.4.3   Modern Transport Economics. (1974)
3.4.6   The Urban Transportation Problem. (1965)

4.1 Public Transport – Operational Aspects.

4.1.1   Analytical Transport Planning. (1971)
4.1.2   Bradford Bus Study: Final Report. (1976)
4.1.3   Bradford Bus Study: Interim Report on Costing of Bus Operations. (1974)
4.1.4   The Bus and Coach Industry: its economic and organisation.
4.1.8   Bus Improvements Survey, 1976. (1977)
4.1.23   Passenger Mileage Estimates for Bus Station Improvements. (1977)

4.2 Public Transport – Marketing Approach.

4.2.48   An Approach to Developing Transport Improvement Proposals. (1976)

This subsection brings together methodological literature relevant to transport research which falls outside the specific scope of subsections 8.1 (behavioural and attitudinal survey techniques) and 8.2 (economic evaluation methodology). The material includes several papers and reports on techniques of travel demand measurement, literature describing methodologies used in particular travel studies, and a number of miscellaneous technical papers and reports. The subsidiary references list items from other sections of the bibliography which contain relevant methodological information.

8.3.1. Cognitive-conative consistency. [*Triadic Consistency: a statment of effective] (1967)
INSKO,C.A. and SCHOPLER,J.
Psychological Review. Vol.74. 1967. (pp. 361-376)

8.3.2. Cognitive Dissonance.[*A Theory of] (1957)
FESTINGER,L.
Stanford University Press. 1957; and Tavistock, London.
1957. (291 pp.)

8.3.3. Cognitive Transformation of Information from Urban Geographic Fields to Mental Maps. (1976)
BECK,R.J. and WOOD,D.
Environment and Behavior. Vol.8.No.2. June 1976 (pp.199-238)

8.3.4. Defining Minimum Socially Acceptable Levels of Mobility in Rural Areas. (1975)
STANLEY,R.A.
Paper read at the Institute of British Geographers' Transport Geography Study Group Conference. University of Birmingham. September 1975.

8.3.5. Demand and Supply Markets. [*Modelling London Transport's]
(1975)
FAIRHURST, M.H.
London Transport Executive. Economic Research Section. Technical Note TN90. June 1975. (25pp.)
(see also TN92 - ref.8.3.6 below)

A programme of work to establish a model of the demand and supply markets in which London Transport operates is described. The model attempts to:-

   (i)   provide a broad framework within which a wide variety of factors affecting London Transport's demand and supply markets can interact on a consistent set of assumptions;
   (ii) stratify these markets in greater detail than was previously possible;
   (iii) explicitly make allowance for alternative GLC policies towards the private car;
   (iv) relate all of the above to the likely trends in London's structure and economy.

The note describes in some detail the way in which various parts of the model will work and closes with a statement of current progress in setting up the model and likely progress in the immediate future.

8.3.6.   Demand and User Cost. [*Choice,] (1975)
          FAIRHURST,M.H.
          London Transport-Executive. Economic Research
          Section. Technical Note TN92.August 1975. (15pp.)

          This Technical Note provides further details of the
          proposed model of London Transport's demand and
          supply markets outlined in Technical Note 90. (see
          ref. 8.3.5. above). It sets out the form of the
          relationships that are to be used in the model to
          estimate changes in trip making (primarily as a
          result of user cost changes), together with the more
          standard transportation models from which they are
          derived. Some general problems associated with
          such models are discussed and the approach to be
          taken in the model is set out. The topics covered
          are:-

                (i) the unit in which changes in user costs are
                    to be measured;
               (ii) the effects of variations in the availability
                    of modes.

8.3.7.   Demand. [*Applications of Information-Processing
          Theory to the Analysis of Urban Travel (1977)
          LOUVIERE,J.J. and NORMAN,K.L.
          Environment and Behavior Vol.9 No.1. March 1977
                                         (pp.91-106)

8.3.8.   Demand in Urban Areas: [*Passenger Transport]:
          Methodology for analysing and forecasting. (1976)
          BONNAFOUS,A. and GERARDIN,B.
          European Conference of Ministers of Transport (ECMT).
          Report of the 32nd. Round Table on Transport Economics
          held in Paris, December 1975. Economic Research
          Centre, Paris. 1976. (82pp.)

          This paper is concerned with urban transport demand
          modelling. It identifies three major requirements
          for an operational model:- relevance, measurability
          and consistency, which prove to be more or less
          contradictory when analysed. Various problems
          involved in meeting these three requirements are
          discussed, relevant recent work reviewed, and
          potential new approaches suggested. An Annex
          presents an outline of a number of typical demand
          models referred to in the paper, with bibliographical
          details. The report concludes with a summary of the
          subsequent discussion on the paper.

8.3.9.　**Demand Responsive Diversions on a Rural Bus Service.**
　　　　　　　　　　　　　　　　　　　　(1975)
　　　　GALLOP,K.R.
　　　　Paper read at a Rural Transport Seminar held at the
　　　　Polytechnic of Central London. November 1975, (pp.35-42
　　　　of Seminar Proceedings.)

　　　　The paper describes surveys carried out as part of
　　　　a feasibility study for the planning of possible
　　　　bus service improvements in the Dorchester-Wareham
　　　　corridor in South Dorset. The investigations
　　　　described include an examination of present (mid-
　　　　1970's) provision of services compared with that in
　　　　the mid-1960's, and an On-Bus Survey and Household
　　　　Interview Survey which established the present pattern
　　　　of journey-making behaviour in the area and gave
　　　　indications of deficiencies in bus service provision
　　　　and of opportunities for improvements. Arising from
　　　　the findings of the studies a proposal for a demand
　　　　responsive diversion to an existing inter-urban bus
　　　　route is outlined. The proposal is considered to
　　　　be practical and capable of implementation, and to
　　　　have relevance to poorly-served areas in other parts
　　　　of the country.

8.3.10　**Determination of Functional Sub-Regions Within an
　　　　Urban Area for Transportation Planning.** (1974)
　　　　GOLOB,T.F., HEPPER,S.J. and PERSHING,J.J.
　　　　Transportation Research Record No. 526.Transportation
　　　　Research Board. Washington D.C. 1974. (pp.16-26)
　　　　(This paper was read at the 53rd. Annual Meeting
　　　　of the Highway Research Board at Washington D.C.,
　　　　　　　　　　　　　　　　January 1974)

　　　　The paper presents a technique for using area-wide
　　　　travel, land use and population data to divide an urban
　　　　area into a set of functional sub-regions. Results
　　　　from an application of the technique in the Detroit
　　　　area are included as a case study.

8.3.11.　**Distance Estimation in Cities.**(1975)
　　　　CANTER,D. and TAGG,S.K.
　　　　Environment and Behavior. Vol.7. No.1. March 1975.
　　　　　　　　　　　　　　　　　　(pp.59-80)

8.3.12.　**Gaming Approach to the Study of Travel Behaviour in
　　　　　　　　　　　　　　　　Oxford.** [*A] (1976)
　　　　JONES,P.M.
　　　　Oxford University, Transport Studies Unit. Working
　　　　　　　　　　　　　　Paper No.18. 1976.
　　　　A subsequent version of this Working Paper is available
　　　　under the title: Assessing Policy Impacts Using the
　　　　Household Activity - Travel Simulator (1977).

8.3.13.   Gravity Distribution Model. [*A] (1971/2).
           GOOD, G.E.
                 Part 1:   Traffic Engineering and Control. Vol.12,
                           No.12.December 1971.
                 Part 2:   Traffic Engineering and Control. Vol.13,
                           No.1. January 1972(pp.391

8.3.14.   Information Availability and Travel Characteristics
           in Developing Cities.(1977)
           NATHANIEL LICHFIELD AND PARTNERS
           International Bank for Reconstruction and Development
           Urban and Regional Economics Division. Development
           Economics Department.
           Phase I City Study. Urban Transport Sector Working
           Paper. (Draft). June 1977. (58pp.)

           This paper presents an analysis of developing countri
           city transport study information, based on fourteen c
           studies from Central and South America , Africa and
           Asia. Section 2 describes the availability of major
           data sets across the sample of cities and comments on
           more significant attributes. Section 3 summarizes
           the inter-city relationships developed for specific
           travel characteristics in terms of graphical plots,
           regression equations and statistics. Particular
           emphasis is placed on the analysis of modal substitut
           at different income levels.

8.3.15.   Minibus Research Programme. [*Home Interview Phase of
                                            the] (1973)
           DAY,D.J.
           London Transport Executive. Planning Research Divisio
           Operational Research Memorandum M.277. 1973.

8.3.16   Minibus Research Programme. [*On-bus Phase of the]
                                            (1973)
           DAY,D.J.
           London Transport Executive. Planning Research
           Division. Operational Research Memorandum M.261. 197

8.3.17   Minibus Study. [*L.T.] (1974)
           SMITH,D.
           Social and Community Planning Research. January 1974

8.3.18   Model of Vehicle Comfort and a Method for its
                             Assessment. [*A] (1973)
           MANENICA, I. and CORLETT, E.N.
           Ergonomics. Vol.16. No.6. November 1973. (pp. 849-
                                                          854).

           The methods of a questionnaire survey of bus and
           hovercraft passengers are described. The paired
           comparison technique was used to assess preferences
           for various modes of transport and qualities of the
           passenger environment in these modes.

8.3.19. Perception and Cognition [*The Structural Analysis
         of Environmental]: a multidimensional scaling
         approach. (1976)
         GARLING,T.
         Environment and Behavior. Vol.8.No.3.September 1976.
                                            (pp.385-416)

8.3.20. Perceptions of the Neighbourhood and the Desire to
         Move Out. (1972)
         KASL,S,V. and HARBURG,E.
         Journal of the American Institute of Planners.Vol.38.
                  No.5.September 1972.(pp.318-324)

8.3.21. Program Background.(1972)
         URBAN MASS TRANSPORTATION ADMINISTRATION. 1972.

8.3.22. Route Choice Criteria. [*Research into] (1974)
         BOTTOM,C.G. and SMITH,R.S.
         London Transport Executive. Planning Research
         Division. Operational Research Memorandum M. 320.
                  April 1974. (9pp. plus Appendix).

         The study was conducted as part of general research
         into factors affecting passengers' choice of route
         through the Underground network. Regression tech-
         niques were used to examine approximately forty
         journeys involving real choice of route, from the
         1972 origin and destination survey.

8.3.23. Rural Public Transport-A Study in Bedfordshire. (1974)
         HOLLINGS,D. and WARMAN,P. (AMV Ltd.)
         Paper read at a Rural Transport Seminar held at the
         Polytechnic of Central London. November 1974. (pp.41-
                  52 of Seminar Proceedings)

         The paper outlines an approach to the study of public
         transport for the requirements of a local authority,
         using for illustration some results from a study of
         public transport in Bedfordshire. (see ref.4.5.9. above).
         The methods outlined and discussed include statistical
         analyses of transport needs and public transport
         provision in the county, and qualitative sociological
         investigations into community attitudes to public
         transport provision.

8.3.24. Rural Travel Survey. [*West Midlands] (1972)
(Regional Model Study/Birmingham West Orbital
Route Study). Methodological Report.

BERTHOUD,R.
Social and Community Planning Research. Report
           P.235. August 1972.(24pp. plus appendices).

This document describes the survey methods used in
a home interview survey of travel behaviour in the
area to the west of the West Midlands Conurbation.
The brief for the survey was to establish an inventory of weekday travel undertaken by public and private
transport by persons resident in the survey area.
Descriptions are given of the sampling selection,
interviewing and fieldwork, and data preparation
procedures. Appendices provide further details of the
coding, editing and computer edit check specifications
and also include copies of the questionnaires and
other survey documents.

8.3.25. SELNEC Transport Model. [* Calibration and Testing
                                      of the] (1969)
WILSON,A.G., et al.
Regional Studies. Vol.3. No.3. December 1969.(pp.337-
                                                  350)

This paper describes the mathematical model used in
the South East Lancashire North East Cheshire Transportation Study. The description concentrates on the
innovations which have been introduced in this particular model, with particular reference to the distribution and modal split submodels. The process of
calibrating and testing the model is described and some
preliminary results are presented. A number of conclusions are drawn and some directions for further
research are noted.

8.3.26. Socio-Psychological Models of Travel Choice-the T.S.U.
                                              approach.(1977)
HEGGIE,I.G.
Traffic Engineering and Control. Vol.18. No.12.
             December 1977.(pp.583-585)

Recent developments in Oxford University Transport
Studies Unit's approach to the study of travel choice,
using a combination of qualitative and quantitative
investigations, are outlined in this article.

8.3.27.   Spatial Orientation in a Subway System. (1976)
          BRONZAFT, A.L., DOBROW, S.B. and O'HANLON, T.J.
          Environment and Behavior. Vol.8. No.4. December 1976.
                                            (pp. 575-594)

          The psychological impact of travel information and
          its effect on travel behaviour are evaluated in this
          account of a study of the orientational problems
          of users of the New York City Subway and of their
          usage of the Subway Guide as an aid in this orien-
          tation.

8.3.28.   Transept Computing Manual. (1976)
          DALY, A.J. and TOWNSEND, R.
          Local Government Operational Research Unit (LGORU).
          Report No.T58. 1976 (130 pp.)
          Royal Institute of Public Administration.

8.3.29.   Transit Surveying Process. [*Successive Overlays -
                            a Small City] (1974)
          CORRADINO, J.C., COOMER, B.D. and UPSHAW, W.S.
          Traffic Engineering. Vol.44.No.15. 1974. (pp. 9-15)

          The method identifies potential markets for public
          transport using passenger cars per dwelling unit,
          average income, the numbers of females of 16 to 24
          years and of persons aged 62 years or over, and the
          number of dwelling units per acre. The method is
          recommended as a first stage for low-cost studies
          in smaller towns.

8.3.30.   Transit Validation for City Centres. (1971)
          SEGELHORST, S.W.
          Journal of Transport Economics and Policy. Vol.5.
                            No.1. January 1971. (pp. 28-39)

8.3.31   Travel Decision - Making Behaviour. [*Report on
          Investigations of Household] (1977)
          DIX, M.C.
          Oxford University Transport Studies Unit. Working
          Paper No.27. April 1977. (43pp.)

          The paper was prepared in collaboration with
          I.G. Heggie and P.M. Jones for presentation at the
          World Conference on Transport Research, Rotterdam,
          April 1977.

8.3.32.   Trip Generation Techniques.(1971)
          DOUGLAS, A. and LEWIS, R.
          Printerhall, London. 1971.

8.3.33.   Urban and Regional Models in Geography and Planning.
                                                        (1974)
          WILSON, A.G.
          John Wiley. London. 1974. (432 pp.)

8.3.34.   **User Response to a Foot Street.** (1975)
          BISHOP, D.
          Town Planning Review. Vol.46. No.1. January 1975.
                                                (pp. 31-46)

8.3   Subsidiary References.

1.1   New Towns - Transport and Mobility.

1.1.6   *Demand Bus for a New Town.* (1971)
1.1.17   *Transport and New Towns. Volume One.* (1976)
1.1.21   *Transportation for a New Town.* (1971)
1.1.24   *Transportation Inputs in New Town Planning.* (1969)

1.2   New Towns - Non-Transport Aspects.

1.2.9   *Criteria for Evaluating New Towns.* (1975)
1.2.34   *New Towns: The data bank, its construction and organisation.*
                                                      (1972)
1.2.46   *The Programming of Social Provision in New Communities.* (1976)

2.1.   Runcorn.

2.1.6   *Runcorn Busway Study.* (1976)
2.1.10 *Runcorn Travel Survey.* (1973)

2.3   Telford.

2.3.6   *Telford Transportation Study.* (1976/7)

2.4   Other New Towns.

2.4.1   *Aycliffe Housing Survey: A Study of Housing in a New Town.*
                                                      (1970)
2.4.8   *East Kilbride Housing Survey: A Study of Housing in a New*
                                                Town. (1970)
2.4.16   *A Category Analysis Approach to Estimating the Influence of*
         Dial-a-Ride on the Community of Old Harlow. (1976)
2.4.17   *Dial-a-Bus Demand Modelling and Evaluation: Predictions for*
         the Harlow Experiment. (1975)
2.4.18   *Dial-a-Bus Planning Survey of Old Harlow.* (1973)
2.4.19   *The Harlow Dial-a-Bus Experiment: Comparison of predicted*
         and observed patronage. (1977)
2.4.22   *How was the Harlow Dial-a-Ride Service Planned?* (1974)
2.4.53   *The New Town Goal of Self-Containment.* (1974) [Stevenage]

3.1   Studies of Modal Choice Behaviour and Value of Travel Time.

3.1.8   *A Behavioural Explanation of the Association Between Bus and*
         Passenger Arrivals at a Bus Stop. (1974)
3.1.14   *A Theoretical Estimate of the effect of London Car Commuters*
         Transferring to Bus Travel. (1968)
3.1.21   *Generalised Cost Time and the Problem of Equity in Transport*
                                                Studies. (1973)
3.1.22   *Generalising and Generalised Cost Function.* (1974)
3.1.23   *A Study of Individual Journey Series: an integrated*
         interpretation of the transportation process. (1972)
3.1.24   *Journey Times by Bus and Car in Central London in 1972.* (1973)
3.1.30   *Planning for the Work Journey; a generalised explanation of*
                                                modal choice. (1970)
3.1.31   *Choice of Travel Mode for Journey to Work: Some Findings.* (1967)
3.1.43   *Modal Choice in Greater London.* (1969)
3.1.44   *Demand and Choice Models of Modal Split.* (1970)
3.1.45   *Urban Structure and Modal Split in the Journey to Work.* (1977)

4.4.45   Skokie Swift - the Commuters' Friend.   (1968)
4.4.47   Zonal Taxi Systems: An Improvement in Local Mobility.   (1976)
4.4.48   Alternative Taxicab Systems: A London Case Study.   (1976)
4.4.52   Symposium on Unconventional Bus Services.   (1977)

4.5 Public Transport - General and Miscellaneous.

4.5.11   Research and Public Transport.   (1974)
4.5.12   Survey of Public Transport.   (1972)
4.5.13   Public Transport for Rural Communities.   (1977)
4.5.18   Urban Passenger Transport: Some trends and prospects.   (1977)
4.5.19   Mobility Evaluation for Urban Public Transportation.   (1976)
4.5.23   Study of Rural Transport in Devon.   (1971)

5.1 Private Motor Transport.

5.1.2   Forecasting Car Ownership: a new approach.   (1977)
5.1.10   A Theory of Household Automobile Allocation Decisions.   (1976)
5.1.11   Theory of Urban Household Automobile Ownership Decisions.
                                                                   (1976)
5.1.12   The Distribution of Household Car Ownership.   (1977)
5.1.13   The Future Proportions of Non-Car Owning and Multi-Car
                                           Owning Households.   (1970)
5.1.14   Characteristics of Households with and without Cars in 1970.
                                                                   (1974)

6.1 Non-Motorised Travel.

6.1.7   Pedestrian Planning and Design.   (1971)
6.1.10   Two Experiments on Methods of Training Children in Road Safety.
                                                                   (1971)
6.1.11   Towards Effective Segregation.   (1975)
6.1.12   The Characteristics of the Walk Trip.   (1973)

7.1 Transport Policy.

7.1.23   Optimal Subsidies for Public Transit.   (1975)
7.1.25   The Use of Survey Research in Policy Analysis.   (1975)
7.1.28   Study of Traffic Restraints in Singapore.   (1975)
7.1.37   The Comparative Study of Transport Systems: Swedish Urban
         Transport Policy and its Application in Britain.   (1974)
7.1.38   Transportation Planning, Policy and Analysis.   (1976)
7.1.39   Transportation Studies: a critical assessment.   (1968)
7.1.40   Transportation Studies: a review of results to date from
                                           typical areas.   (1968)
7.1.41   Transportation Studies: a review of results to date from
         typical areas - West Midlands Conurbation.   (1968)
7.1.54   Merseyside Area Land - Use Transportation Study.   Technical
                                           Report No.24.   (1969)

9.2 Bibliographies.

9.2.3   Buses in Urban Areas.   1970 - 1976.   (1976)
         [Includes a section on theoretical models used in the
                             planning of bus services.]

9. Information Sources.

9.1   Journals.

A short list of general reference works precedes the detailed lists of relevant journals This includes three specialised indexes to articles in transport journals (9.1.1-3), and three general press and periodicals directories (9.1.4-6).

The detailed lists of journals (9.1.7 -55) do not provide a comprehensive catalogue of all periodicals which contain material relevant to transport or to new towns: articles listed in this bibliography have been derived from over one hundred separate periodicals and many more journals from time to time include relevant articles. ULRICH's International Periodicals Directory (9.1.5) which gives a full listing of international periodicals, classified by subject, is a useful guide to the full range of potentially useful source journals.   The lists presented in this subsection are intended as a preliminary guide to the principal sources of relevant articles.   They comprise all journals from which two or more articles have been included in this bibliography, together with a small number of additional journals which are known to be potentially useful sources of material.   The following are the ten journals with the greatest numbers of articles included in the bibliography, and this list gives some indication of the leading sources of journal articles for researchers investigating aspects of transport in new towns:-

Transportation Research Record (formerly Highway Research Record)

Traffic Engineering and Control

Journal of Transport Economics and Policy

Town and Country Planning

Town Planning Review

Transportation Research

Chartered Institute of Transport Journal

Ergonomics

Transportation

Urban Studies

For convenience the journals have been arranged alphabetically by title (followed by frequency of publication in brackets) within three groups according to the main focus of their subject material, as follows:-

1.   Transport Journals (9.1.7-25),

including the U.S. TRANSPORTATION RESEARCH BOARD'S

Transportation Research Record (9.1.23), formerly entitled Highway Research Record, which is not a regularly published journal. Nine of the transport journals listed are U.K. publications, five are U.S. publications, three are international, and two are joint U.K. and U.S. publications.

2. Planning, Environment and Architecture Journals (9.1.26-39), including the New Towns Bulletin (9.1.32) which is a newsheet rather than a journal, but which is a useful source of up-to-date information on developments in individual new towns and on the background to official policy on new towns. Town and Country Planning (9.1.37 and 1.2.48) regularly contains articles on new towns and presents an annual record of progress in British new towns in the February issue each year.

3. Other Journals (9.1.40-55)
This group covers a fairly wide range of subjects including sociology (9.1.40, 9.1.51, 9.1.53), economics (9.1.42 and 9.1.51), and ergonomics (9.1.41, 9.1.43, 9.1.45). The journals relating to marketing and advertising (9.1.44, 9.1.46 9.1.48-49, 9.1.55) include articles relevant to the marketing aspects of public transport, and together with the publications relating to psychology (9.1.47, 9.1.54) and statistics (9.1.50) are a valuable source of material on survey techniques.

(i)   GENERAL REFERENCE   WORKS

Specialised bibliographical references to transport journals.

9.1.1   Traffic and Transportation: a permuted title index
          and research guide. (1976)
          HAIGHT, F.A. and TUNG, J.S.N.
          Pennsylvania Technical Publications. Boalsburg. 1976.
          (341 pp.)

          The index covers articles contained in the journals
          Journal of Transport Economics and Policy, Traffic
          Engineering and Control, Traffic Quarterly,
          Transportation, Transportation Research, and Transport-
          ation Science.

9.1.2   Transport in Current Periodicals. [* Bibliography of]
                                                        (1976)
          OTTLEY, G.
          Journal of Transport History. N.S. Vol.3. No.4.
          September 1976. (pp. 286-293).

          An earlier list, for 1974, is contained in the same
          journal, Vol.3. No.2. 1976.(pp. 119-126).

9.1.3   Transport Journals 1965-1976. [* A Bibliography of
          the Major] (1976)
          WATERS II, W.G. and TSE, A.
          The Logistics and Transportation Review. Vol.12.No.2.
          1976.

          Articles contained in the major transport journals are
          listed chronologically by journal, and an authors'
          index is included.   The journals covered include the
          Chartered Institute of Transport Journal, Journal of
          Transport Economics and Policy, Traffic Engineering
          and Control, Transportation Planning and Technology,
          and Transportation Research.

General Press and Periodicals Directories.

9.1.4   Newspaper Press Directory. (Annual).
          BENN. London.

          Details are given of a large number of periodical
          publications in the U.K. and abroad, including news-
          papers, periodicals, directories, annuals and yearbooks.
          A classified index of periodicals is included.

9.1.5   Ulrich's   International Periodicals Directory.
          (Every two years)
          R.R.BOWKER COMPANY. New York and London

          A classified guide to current international periodicals,
          which also includes details of periodicals which have

been discontinued since the previous issue. **The**
Directory covers periodicals which are issued more
frequently than once a year and usually published at
regular intervals over an indefinite period of time.
Supplements are published in alternate years in
Bowker Serials Bibliography, which also contains
lists of annuals, directories and yearbooks.

9.1.6   Willing's Press Guide (Annual)
         WILLING, London. (ed. J.A.A.Boag)
         A Comprehensive Index and Handbook of the Press of the
         United Kingdom, Northern Ireland and the Republic
         of Ireland together with the Principal European and
         U.S.A. Publications.

         The Guide contains a fairly full list of periodicals,
         magazines, newspapers and annuals, and includes
         a classified index of publications in subject groups.

(ii)   SELECTED LIST OF JOURNALS

Transport Journals

9.1.7   BUSES. (Monthly)
         Ian Allan Ltd.
         Terminal House, Shepperton, Middlesex.

9.1.8   CHARTERED INSTITUTE OF TRANSPORT JOURNAL.(Six times a
         year)
         (Formerly Institute of Transport Journal, up to 1971)
         Chartered Institute of Transport
         80, Portland Place, London. W1N 4DP

         The Journal includes the Transport Research Bulletin
         twice a year.

9.1.9   HIGH SPEED GROUND TRANSPORTATION JOURNAL. (Three times
         a year).
         Planning Transport Associates Inc.
         Box 4824, Duke Sta., Durham, NC 27706, U.S.A.

9.1.10   HIGHWAY ENGINEER. [*THE] (Monthly)
         (Formerly Journal of the Institution of Highway
         Engineers)
         Institution of Highway Engineers
         14,Queen Anne's Gate, London SW1H 9AF

         HIGHWAY RESEARCH RECORD - See Transportation Research
         Record: ref. 9.1.23 below

         INSTITUTE OF ROAD TRANSPORT ENGINEERS: JOURNAL AND
         PROCEEDINGS - see Transport Engineer: ref.9.1.18 below.

         INSTITUTE OF TRANSPORT JOURNAL - See Chartered
         Institute of Transport Journal: ref. 9.1.8 above.

9.1.11   INTERNATIONAL JOURNAL OF TRANSPORT ECONOMICS. (Three
          times a year)
          Rivista Internazionale di Economia dei Transporti
          Via G.A. Guattani, 00161, Rome, Italy.

          JOURNAL OF THE INSTITUTION OF HIGHWAY ENGINEERS
          - see The Highway Engineer: ref. 9.1.10 above.

9.1.12   JOURNAL OF TRANSPORT ECONOMICS AND POLICY. (Three
          times a year)
          London School of Economics and Political Science
          Houghton Street, London WC2A 2AE

9.1.13   MOTOR TRANSPORT. (Weekly)
          IPC Transport Press Ltd.
          Dorset House, Stamford Street, London SE1 9LU.

          Incorporates Bus and Coach supplement.

          PROCEEDINGS OF THE AMERICAN SOCIETY OF CIVIL
          ENGINEERS - see Transportation Engineering Journal:
          ref. 9.1.20 below.

9.1.14   TAXI.(Fortnightly)
          Licensed Taxi Drivers' Association
          9, Woodfield Road, London W9.

          The technical newspaper of the taxi trade.

9.1.15   TAXINEWS.(Monthly)
          Owner Drivers' Society
          1, Buckingham Gate, London SW1.

9.1.16   TRAFFIC ENGINEERING AND CONTROL. (Monthly)
          Printerhall Ltd.
          29, Newman Street, London W1P 3PE

          The journal includes regular summaries of current
          research activities and reports of relevant conferences
          as well as articles relating to aspects of traffic and
          transport.

9.1.17   TRAFFIC QUARTERLY. (Quarterly)
          Eno Foundation for Transportation
          P.O. Box 55, Saugatuck Station, Westport, Connecticut,
          06880. U.S.A.

9.1.18   TRANSPORT ENGINEER. (Monthly)
          Institute of Road Transport Engineers
          1, Cromwell Place, London SW7 2JF

          Formerly Institute of Road Transport Engineers:
          Journal and Proceedings.

9.1.19   TRANSPORTATION. (Quarterly)
          Elsevier Scientific Publishing Co.
          P.O. Box 211, Amsterdam, Netherlands.

          An international transport journal with text in
          English.

9.1.20   TRANSPORTATION ENGINEERING JOURNAL [Proceedings of the
          American Society of Civil Engineers]. (Quarterly)
          American Society of Civil Engineers
          345, East 47th. Street, New York, 10017, U.S.A.

9.1.21   TRANSPORTATION PLANNING AND TECHNOLOGY. (Quarterly)
          (Formerly Transportation Technology)
          Gordon and Breach Science Publishers Ltd.
          42, William IV Street, London WC2, and:
          1, Park Avenue, New York, 10016, U.S.A.

9.1.22   TRANSPORTATION RESEARCH (Six times a year)
          Pergamon Press
          Headington Hill Hall, Oxford OX3 OBW, and:
          Maxwell House, Fairview Park, Elmsford, New York,
          10523, U.S.A.

9.1.23   TRANSPORTATION RESEARCH RECORD. (Irregular)
          (Formerly Highway Research Record)
          Transportation Research Board
          National Academy of Sciences, 2101 Constitution
          Avenue, N.W., Washington D.C., 20418, U.S.A.

9.1.24   TRANSPORTATION SCIENCE (Quarterly)
          U.S. Operations Research Society
          428, East Preston Street, Baltimore, Maryland
          21202, U.S.A.

          TRANSPORTATION TECHNOLOGY - See Transportation
          Planning and Technology: ref. 9.1.21 above.

9.1.25   U.I.T.P. REVUE. (Quarterly)
          International Union of Public Transport
          (Union Internationale des Transports Publics)
          19, Avenue de l'Uruguay, Brussels 5, Belgium.

Planning, Environment and Architecture Journals.

9.1.26   ARCHITECTS' JOURNAL. [*THE] (Weekly)
          Architectural Press Ltd.
          9, Queen Anne's Gate, London SW1H 9BY

9.1.27   ARCHITECTURAL DESIGN. (Monthly)
          Standard Catalogue Co. Ltd.
          26, Bloomsbury Way, London WC1A 2SS

9.1.28   BUILT ENVIRONMENT. (Monthly to March 1975; Quarterly
thereafter).
(Formerly Official Architecture and Planning)
George Godwin Ltd.
Builder House, 4 Catherine Street, London WC2B 5JN

9.1.29   ENVIRONMENT AND BEHAVIOR. (Quarterly)
Sage Publications Inc.
275,South Beverly Drive, Beverly Hills, California
20036, U.S.A.

An interdisciplinary journal which includes articles
on aspects of environmental perception, psychological
aspects of spatial analysis and measurement of
environmental images.

9.1.30   GREATER LONDON INTELLIGENCE QUARTERLY. (Quarterly)
(Formerly Quarterly Bulletin of the Intelligence
Unit)
Greater London Council
County Hall, London SE1 7PB.

9.1.31   JOURNAL OF THE AMERICAN INSTITUTE OF PLANNERS (Six times
a year to 1975; Quarterly thereafter)
American Institute of Planners
1776,Massachussetts Avenue, N.W. Wasinghton D.C.
20036, U.S.A.

JOURNAL OF THE REGIONAL STUDIES ASSOCIATION - see
Regional Studies: ref 9.1.34 below.

JOURNAL OF THE ROYAL TOWN PLANNING INSTITUTE - see
The Planner: ref. 9.1.33 below.

9.1.32   NEW TOWNS BULLETIN. (Monthly)
New Towns Association
Glen House, Stag Place, London SW1E 5AJ

A monthly newsheet containing current references to
new town planning and developments. Items relevant
to new towns are summarised from Hansard and other
official publications, from DOE press notices, from
several journals and from national and local newspapers.

OFFICIAL ARCHITECTURE AND PLANNING - see Built
Environment: ref 9.1.28 above.

9.1.33   PLANNER. [*THE] (Ten times a year to 1975; seven   times
a year thereafter)
(Formerly Journal of the [Royal] Town Planning
Institute)
Royal Town Planning Institute
26,Portland Place, London W1N 4BE

QUARTERLY BULLETIN OF THE INTELLIGENCE UNIT - see
Greater London Intelligence Quarterly: ref. 9.1.30
above.

9.1.34   REGIONAL STUDIES.(Quarterly)
          (Journal of the Regional Studies Association)
          Pergamon Press
          Headington Hill Hall, Oxford OX3 OBW, and:
          Maxwell House, Fairview Park, Elmsford, New York,
          10523, U.S.A.

9.1.35   SOCIO-ECONOMIC PLANNING SCIENCES (Six times a year)
          Pergamon Press
          Headington Hill Hall, Oxford OX3 OBW, and:
          Maxwell House, Fairview Park, Elmsford, New York,
          10523, U.S.A.

          SURVEYOR AND MUNICIPAL ENGINEER - see Surveyor -
          Public Authority Technology: ref. 9.1.36 below.

          SURVEYOR - LOCAL GOVERNMENT TECHNOLOGY - see Surveyor-
          Public Authority Technology: ref. 9.1.36 below.

9.1.36   SURVEYOR - PUBLIC AUTHORITY TECHNOLOGY. (Weekly)
          (Formerly Surveyor and Municipal Engineer, and:
          Surveyor - Local Government Technology)
          IPC Building and Contract Journals Ltd.
          Surrey House, 1 Throwley Way, Sutton, Surrey.

9.1.37   TOWN AND COUNTRY PLANNING. (Monthly)
          Town and Country Planning Association
          28,King Street, London WC2E 8JG

          The February issue each year (January issue before
          1975) is concerned wholly with new towns and includes
          topical articles, a factual record of the activities
          of individual new towns, a new town directory and
          statistical summaries of the progress of each new town.
          (see ref. 1.2.48 above).

9.1.38   TOWN PLANNING REVIEW. (Quarterly)
          Liverpool University Press
          123,Grove Street, Liverpool L7 7AF
          (Produced by the Department of Civic Design, Town
          and Regional Planning and Transport Studies, University
          of Liverpool.)

9.1.39   URBAN STUDIES. (Three times a year)
          Longman Group Ltd.
          43-45 Annandale Street, Edinburgh   EH7 4AT

Other Journals

9.1.40   AMERICAN SOCIOLOGICAL REVIEW. (Six times a year)
          American Sociological Association
          1722,North Street, N.W., Washington D.C. 20036, U.S.A.

9.1.41   APPLIED ERGONOMICS.(Quarterly)
             IPC Science and Technology Press Ltd.
             IPC House, 32,High Street, Guildford, Surrey.

             Contains articles relating to the technology of man's
             relations with machines, environment and work systems.

             BRITISH JOURNAL OF MARKETING - See European Journal
             of Marketing: ref. 9.1.44 below.

9.1.42   ECONOMIC JOURNAL (Quarterly)
             Royal Economic Society
             Cambridge University Press, 200,Euston Road,London NW1

9.1.43   ERGONOMICS(Six times a year)
             Taylor and Francis Ltd.
             10-14, Macklin Street, London WC2B 5NF

             This international journal is concerned with the
             scientific study of human factors in relation to
             working environments and equipment design, and is the
             official publication of the Ergonomics Society,
             Nederlandse Vereniging Voor Ergonomie, and the
             International Ergonomics Association. An abstracting
             service is included three times a year. (see ref.
             9.3.8 below).

9.1.44   EUROPEAN JOURNAL OF MARKETING. (Quarterly)
             (Formerly British Journal of Marketing)
             M.C.B. (European Marketing and Consumer Studies) Ltd.
             200, Keighley Road, Bradford BD9 4JZ, West Yorkshire.

9.1.45   HUMAN FACTORS. (Six times a year)
             Human Factors Society
             John Hopkins University Press, Baltimore, Maryland,
             21218, U.S.A.

9.1.46   JOURNAL OF ADVERTISING RESEARCH (Six times a year)
             Advertising Research Foundation
             3, East 54th Street, New York, 10022, U.S.A.

9.1.47   JOURNAL OF APPLIED PSYCHOLOGY. (Six times a year)
             American Psychological Association, Inc.
             1200, 17th Street, N.W., Washington D.C. 20036, U.S.A.

9.1.48   JOURNAL OF MARKETING.(Quarterly)
             American Marketing Association
             222,South Riverside Plaza, Chicago, Illinois, 60606,
             U.S.A.

             This is primarily an abstracting journal.

9.1.49   JOURNAL OF MARKETING RESEARCH. (Quarterly)
             American Marketing Association
             222,South Riverside Plaza, Chicago, Illinois,
             60606, U.S.A.

9.1.50 JOURNAL OF THE ROYAL STATISTICAL SOCIETY:
        SERIES A - GENERAL   (Quarterly)
        SERIES B - METHODOLOGICAL (Three times a year)
        SERIES C - APPLIED STATISTICS. (Three times a year)
        Royal Statistical Society
        21, Bentinck Street, London W1M 6AR

9.1.51 MANCHESTER SCHOOL OF ECONOMICS AND SOCIAL STUDIES
                                              (Quarterly)
        Department of Economics, Manchester University.
        Dover Street, Manchester M13 9P1

9.1.52 NEW SCIENTIST (Weekly)
        Bernard Dixon
        128, Long Acre, London WC2E 9QM

9.1.53 NEW SOCIETY. (Weekly)
        New Science Publications
        128, Long Acre, London WC2E 9QM

9.1.54 PSYCHOLOGICAL REVIEW. (Six times a year)
        American Psychological Association, Inc.
        1200, 17th Street, N.W. Washington D.C. 20036
        U.S.A.

9.1.55 PUBLIC OPINION QUARTERLY.(Quarterly)
        American Association for Public Opinion Research
        Columbia University, New York NY 10027

9.2 Bibliographies.

The bibliographies listed in this subsection have been arranged in the following order:-

1. <u>Transport Bibliographies</u> (9.2.1-18)

2. <u>New Towns Bibliographies</u> (9.2.19-30)

3. <u>Other Bibliographies</u> (9.2.31-40), covering other aspects of planning and the environment (9.2.33-34, 9.2.36-37, 9.2.39-40) and survey methodology (9.2.35, 9.2.38). This list includes the photocopied <u>Catalogues of the U.K. Department of the Environment Library</u> (9.2.40), published in fifteen volumes, which comprises journal articles, with abstracts, as well as books, papers, reports and other official material. The Catalogues, which are more comprehensive than a normal bibliography, are useful both as an initial guide to references, using the detailed subject index, and for checking details of references obtained from other sources.

The subsidiary references appended to this subsection include items entered elsewhere in the bibliography which provide substantial lists of additional references on individual topics.

Bibliographical sources on specific subjects are discussed in greater detail in the introductions to the relevant subsections.

.2.1   Application of behavior and attitude research to
        transportation system planning and design. [*Annotated
                            bibliography of the] (1976)
        SHEPARD, M.E.
        Council of Planning Librarians, Exchange Bibliography
                            No. 1066. June 1976.
        Also published by the Transportation and Urban Analysis
        Department, General Motors Corporation Research
        Laboratories, Warren, Michigan. GMR-2089. (28 pp.)

        The bibliography provides 130 annotated references
        to material on psychological aspects of transportation
        planning. It is divided into four sections:- psychometric
        techniques, behavior modification, environmental
        psychology, and marketing. The section on psychometric
        techniques forms the greater part of the bibliography
        (over one hundred references) and is subdivided into
        sections on scaling techniques, non-scaling techniques,
        attitude surveys, behavioral modal choice models, and
        miscellaneous behavioral models. Most of the references
        are to material of United States origin.

.2.2   Bicycle Transportation. [*Bibliography of] (1977)
        POLYTECHNIC OF CENTRAL LONDON. TRANSPORT STUDIES GROUP.
        Bibliography No.3. January 1977.

        Covers geographical networks, planning, design standards
        and safety.

.2.3   Buses in Urban Areas. 1970-1976. (1976)
        DEPARTMENTS OF THE ENVIRONMENT and TRANSPORT.
        Headquarters Library, Bibliography Series No. 17c.
                            December 1976. (60 pp.)
        Compiled by J. Collins and edited by C.M. Lambert.

        This bibliography contains 360 references to literature
        relating to buses in urban areas available in the
        Headquarters Library of the Departments of Environment
        and Transport. The emphasis is on material published
        since 1974. The bibliography is arranged in seven
        main sections and further subdivided into:- (i) Books;
        pamphlets and conference reports; (ii) Articles;
        (iii) Other countries. The main sections are:-
        A. DOE Publications.
        B. Urban Transport: Policy and Research - subdivided
           into general works and those on choice of modes.
        C. Management and Operation of Bus Services - this
           section comprises over half of the references in the
           bibliography and is subdivided into eleven parts.
           Part (i) relates to overall bus operation and
           management and Part (xi) includes miscellaneous
           references. Parts (ii) to (x) deal with specific
           aspects:-

Bus Priority Schemes; Bus Lanes; Busways; Rapid
Transport; Demand-Actuated Travel and Minibuses;
One-Man Operation; Monitoring and Control; Passenger
Facilities; and Fares and Tickets.
D. Theoretical Models - used in the planning of bus
   services.
E. Design and New Technology.
F. Background Reading - historical references.
G. Research in Progress.
The majority of the references are annotated.

9.2.4 Control and Communication. [*Bibliography]: (1976)
WARWICK UNIVERSITY. URBAN TRANSPORT RESEARCH GROUP/
LANCHESTER POLYTECHNIC.
Working Paper 30. 1976.

Section S.3 contains references on control systems
relating to automated transport systems, and a subsection on human tolerance research is also included.

9.2.5 Control and Organisation of Transport. (2nd. ed. 1975).
CHARTERED INSTITUTE OF TRANSPORT.
Library Bibliographies. 1975. (35 pp.)

9.2.6 Environmental Effects and Transport. (1975)
STANLEY, J.
Southampton University. Department of Economics.
Environmental Economics Study Group. Bibliography
                    Series 12. 1975. (5 pp.)

9.2.7 Environmental effects of urban road traffic - an
                    annotated bibliography. (1972)
CHU, CHEN.
Centre for Environmental Studies. London. CES 1P 26.
                                April 1972. (77 pp.)

References to literature relating to research and
other studies on the environmental effects of urban
road traffic are included in this bibliography.
These effects include traffic noise, exhaust fumes,
delay and risks to pedestrians crossing roads, visual
intrusion and community severance. Literature relating to relevant survey techniques and evaluation
methodology is also included. Entries are presented
under six headings, with additional sections listing
current and proposed research projects, bibliographies
and journals.

9.2.8 Land Use/Transportation Studies: A Select Bibliography.
                                                (1977)
HUGHES, N.J.
The National Institute for Physical Planning and
Construction Research. Dublin. July 1977. (5 pp.)

Contains 29 references to British and U.S. material,
mainly to items published since 1970.

9.2.9 Passenger Transport Interchange Between Inland Surface
        Modes - a bibliography for 1968-1973. (1974)
        SMARE, A.D. and BRUCE, S.
        University of Newcastle Upon Tyne. Transport Operations
                            Group. April 1974. (67 pp.)

        This bibliography is classified into four main sections,
        covering:- Research Results and Techniques; Operating
        Experience; Architecture and Construction; and General
        Assessments. An introduction to each section gives a
        brief review of the items contained therein. A secondary
        classification identifies references according to mode
        and, in the case of rail and bus, to function (inter-
        city, suburban or urban). Abstracts are provided for
        the more extensive references. Information detailing
        addresses of publishers and authors of the articles
        follows the bibliography. Reference journals and other
        sources of information are also listed, and a cross-
        index to geographical locations referred to in the entries
        is provided. The final section reviews the work reported
        in the bibliography and outlines areas in which further
        research could usefully be undertaken.

9.2.10 Pedestrian [*The]: Planning and Research. (1976)
        ELKINGTON, J., McGLYNN, R. and ROBERTS, J.
        Transport and Environment Studies (TEST). London. 1976.
                                            (235 pp.)

        This literature review and annotated bibliography
        represents part of a study carried out by Transport
        and Environment Studies for the U.K. Department of the
        Environment between 1974 and 1976, entitled: "Improving
        the Pedestrian's Environment". The literature review
        is presented under the headings:- Pedestrian Activity;
        Accidents and Road Crossing Behaviour; Pedestrian
        Perception; The Walking Environment; Trip Suppresion
        and Severance; Improvement Schemes for Pedestrians; and
        U.K. Legislation and the Pedestrian. The annotated
        bibliography is arranged in alphabetical order of
        authors, and an index is included.

9.2.11 Rapid Transit: a select reading list. (1970)
        DEPARTMENTS OF THE ENVIRONMENT and TRANSPORT .
        Headquarters Library, Bibliography Series No.12. 1970.
                                (contains 213 entries).

9.2.12 Road Passenger Transport. (1976)
        CHARTERED INSTITUTE OF TRANSPORT.
        Library Bibliographies. 1976. (41 pp.)

9.2.13　Transport Policies and Planning.　(1977)
DEPARTMENTS OF THE ENVIRONMENT and TRANSPORT.
Headquarters Library, Bibliography Series No.17A. 1977.
(82 pp.)
Compiled by C.M. Lambert.

This general bibliography brings together a selection
of recent (mainly British) literature on all aspects
of transport policies and planning, particularly that
published between 1974 and 1977.　The list contains
four hundred references arranged in ten main sections,
each subdivided into: (i) Books, pamphlets and conference reports; (ii) Articles; (iii) Other Countries.
An authors' index is included. The main sections
comprise:-
A. DOE/DTp.　Publications, since 1974.　Some references
   relating to the setting up of the DTp., as a
   separate government department in September 1976
   are also included.
B. Transport Planning: General Works.
C. Local Government Transport Policies and Planning-
   particularly literature relating to Transport
   Policies and Programmes.　Details of structure
   plan documents relating specifically to transport
   are also included.
D. Urban Transport, with a separate section on London
   and a select list of Transportation Surveys.
E. Planning Techniques used for transport planning.
F. Environmental Impact.
G. Energy Conservation.
H. Background Reading.
I. Bibliographies.
J. Research - lists some general items relating to
   transport research and a selection of current
   research projects.

9.2.14　Transport Policy Consultation Document 1976.　(1977)
DEPARTMENTS OF THE ENVIRONMENT and TRANSPORT.
Headquarters Library, Bibliography Series No. 17D. 1977.
(27 pp.)
Compiled by C.M. Lambert.

A selection of replies by numerous organisations to
the Government's document:- Transport Policy: a
Consultation Document (see ref. 7.1.77 above) is listed.
Most of the 114 entries are annotated and the material
is arranged in three sections:-
A. Documents issued by associations and/or specific
   references to the documents in published articles,
   listed alphabetically by organisation.
B. Material produced by University and Polytechnic
   departments, listed alphabetically by name of the
   University or Polytechnic.
C. General review articles and articles discussing the
   reactions of several of the associations listed in
   Section A.

9.2.15   **Transport: sources of information together with a
          short bibliography.** (1973).
          DEPARTMENTS OF THE ENVIRONMENT and TRANSPORT
          Headquarters Library, Information Series.   January 1973.
          Compiled by H.A. Pugh.   (36 pp.)

          217 items are listed, arranged in two sections. The
          first section gives the names and addresses of relevant
          British and International organisations. The second
          section lists some important bibliographies, directories,
          reports, manuals, histories, legal and statistical works.
          Lists of periodicals and abstracting journals are also
          included. The lists do not include descriptive and
          theoretical studies on transport.

9.2.16   **Transportation: a select bibliography.**   (1973)
          ROYAL TOWN PLANNING INSTITUTE.
          New Series. No.3. January 1973.(38 pp.)

          A list of material relating to transport held in the
          RTPI Library, arranged under eighteen headings.

9.2.17   **Transportation Systems Bibliography.**   (1974)
          BIERMAN, D.E.
          Council of Planning Librarians.Exchange Bibliography.
          Monticello, Illinois. 1974. (100 pp.)

9.2.18   **Trip Generation.**   (1967)
          DEPARTMENTS OF THE ENVIRONMENT and TRANSPORT.
          Headquarters Library, Bibliography Series No.7. 1967.
                                                (83 entries)

New Towns Bibliographies.

9.2.19   **Environmental New Town** [*Towards an]: a selected
                                        bibliography. (1976)
          BAINBRIDGE, D. A.
          Council of Planning Librarians. Exchange Bibliography
          No. 967. Monticello, Illinois. 1976. (14 pp.)

9.2.20   **New Communities in the U.K.: a Classified Bibliography.**
                                                           (1973)
          VEAL, A.J.
          University of Birmingham. Centre for Urban and Regional
          Studies. Research Memorandum No. 21. October 1973.
                                                (127 pp.)

          This document contains a series of bibliographies
          containing some 850 references to literature on new
          towns, expanded towns and housing estates. An
          introductory section outlines the development of new
          communities in the U.K., with particular emphasis on
          social planning aspects. The new towns content is
          divided into two sections, dealing with Master Plans
          and related planning documents, and with research –
          the main emphasis being on substantive social research
          references. Other sections cover the history and

development of new communities in the U.K.,town
development and town expansion and housing estates.
The sections on new and expanded towns are further
subdivided into general references and those dealing
with individual towns, arranged alphabetically. The
bibliography also contains an annotated list of the
Centre for Urban and Regional Studies' publications
up to 1973.

9.2.21   New Communities in the U.K: Supplementary bibliography.
                                                               (1975)
VEAL, A. J.
University of Birmingham. Centre for Urban and
Regional Studies. Working Paper No.35. 1975. (33 pp.)

This bibliography, containing over 300 references, is
a supplement to Birmingham University's : New Communities
in the U.K: a Classified Bibliography. 1973. (see ref.
9.2.20 above). It lists material published since 1973
and items omitted from the earlier bibliography.

9.2.22   New town planning and development. [*Selected
                                     bibliography on] (1973)
BRANCH, M.C.
Council of Planning Librarians. Exchange Bibliography
Nos. 363-364. Monticello, Illinois. 1973. (88 pp.)

This list of some 550 annotated references provides
material for background reading for a study of new
town development.

9.2.23   New Towns. [*Annotated Exploratory Bibliography on]
                                         (1976)
KEMPER, R.V., OSGOOD, S., and SCHOUTEN, R.M.
Council of Planning Librarians. Exchange Bibliography
                                No. 956. 1976. (57 pp.)

This bibliography contains 67 annotated references
to literature relating to new towns' socio-cultural
dimensions, residents' characteristics, and planners'
ideologies. The emphasis is on new towns in the U.S.A.,
but literature relating to new towns in other countries
is also included. A topical index card and geographical
index are provided.

9.2.24   New Towns: a select bibliography. (3rd. ed. 1975).
ROYAL INSTITUTE OF PUBLIC ADMINISTRATION. 1975. (4 pp.)

Contains selected items mainly published in the 1960's
and early 1970's.

9.2.25   New Towns Bibliography. 1977 (1977)
NEW TOWNS ASSOCIATION. (21 pp.)

An up-to-date list of references to current literature
on new towns, divided into official and non-official
publications on new towns in general, followed by
separate sections for individual new towns, arranged
alphabetically by town. The bibliography is periodically
updated.

9.2.26   New Towns in Britain: A Short List of Publications.
                                                      (1974)
         DEPARTMENTS OF THE ENVIRONMENT and TRANSPORT.
         Headquarters Library, Bibliography Series No.134.
                                   December 1974. (4 pp.)
         Compiled by R. da Souza.

         A short list of 22 publications on new towns divided
         into three sections:- legislation in force; other
         official reports and publications; and non-official
         publications.

9.2.27   New Towns. (1976)
         DEPARTMENTS OF THE ENVIRONMENT and TRANSPORT.
         Headquarters Library, Bibliography Series No.65.
                                   July 1976. (406 pp.)

         This substantial bibliography is regularly updated,
         the most recent edition covering the period April
         1973 to July 1976. Many of the 2,635 items are
         annotated. The material is arranged by year of
         publication up to 1955, and thereafter in nine sections
         according to date, the final section covering the
         period April 1973 to July 1976. Within each section
         the references are placed alphabetically by author
         under the headings:-(i) General, (ii) British New
         Towns, with a separate subsection for each new town,
         in alphabetical order, and (iii) New Towns Overseas.
         An author and subject index is included.

9.2.28   New Towns Planning and Development: A Worldwide
                                      Bibliography.(1973)
         GOLANY, G.
         Urban Land Institute. ULI Research Report 20.
                                   Washington D.C. 1973. (256 pp.)

         Contains over 4,500 references covering virtually all
         aspects of new towns in the U.S. and other countries.

9.2.29   Sociology of new towns and cities   [*The]: a classified
                                      bibliography.(1974)
         ALLEN, I.L.
         Council of Planning Librarians. Exchange Bibliography
         No.518. Monticello, Illinois. 1974. (19 pp.)

9.2.30   Urban environment and residential satisfaction with an
         emphasis on new towns [*The]: an annotated bibliography.
                                                      (1973)
         GLANCE, R. and FREUND, E.C.
         Council of Planning Librarians, Exchange Bibliography
         No. 429. Monticello, Illinois. 1973. (72 pp.)

         This bibliography contains 241 annotated items relating
         to new town environment evaluation, arranged in five
         sections:- Bibliographic Section; General Readings;
         Cognitive Structuring of Social Settings; Social Inter-
         actions in Social Settings; and Design of Social Settings.
         An authors' index is included.

Other Bibliographies.

9.2.31   Economics and Statistics. (1966)
          DEPARTMENTS OF THE ENVIRONMENT and TRANSPORT.
          Headquarters Library, Bibliography Series No.6. 1966.
                                                (168 entries).

9.2.32   List of Titles. (1977)
          DEPARTMENTS OF THE ENVIRONMENT and TRANSPORT.
          Headquarters Library, Bibliography Series. March 1977.
                                                (11 pp.)

          A list of the 197 titles available in the Department
          of the Environment/Department of Transport Bibliography
          Series, with subject index.

9.2.33   Regional and Town Expansion Studies 1962-1968. (1968)
          DEPARTMENTS OF THE ENVIRONMENT and TRANSPORT.
          Headquarters Library, Bibliography Series No. 138. 1968.
                                                (87 entries).

9.2.34   Regional Studies and Reports of the Economic Planning
                                          Councils. (1976)
          DEPARTMENTS OF THE ENVIRONMENT and TRANSPORT.
          Headquarters Library, Bibliography Series No. 195. 1976.
                                                (68 entries).

9.2.35   Social and Business Research. [*Bibliography on Methods of]
                                                (1973)
          BELSON, W.A. and THOMPSON, B.A.
          Crosby Lockwood. London. 1973.

9.2.36   Social Aspects of Planning: a select list of references.
                                          (1972)
          DEPARTMENTS OF THE ENVIRONMENT and TRANSPORT.
          Headquarters Library, Bibliography Series No.155. 1972.
                                                (39 entries).

9.2.37   Structure Plans :
          A. Structure Plan documents. (1976) : 290 entries.
          B. The literature and debate on structure plans and
                  structure planning. (1976): 186 entries.
          DEPARTMENTS OF THE ENVIRONMENT and TRANSPORT.
          Headquarters Library, Bibliography Series No.152. 1976.

9.2.38   Survey Methodology Literature. [*Indexes to] (1974)
          U.S. BUREAU OF THE CENSUS.
          Technical Paper No.34. U.S. Government Printing Office.
          Washington D.C. 1974.

9.2.39   Town and Country Planning: select list of publications.
                                          (1974)
          DEPARTMENTS OF THE ENVIRONMENT and TRANSPORT.
          Headquarters Library, Bibliography Series No. 70. 1974.
                                                (294 entries).

9.2.40   U.K. Department of the Environment Library. [*Catalogues
of the] (1977)
G. K. HALL & Co., Boston, Massachussetts. 1977.

These volumes contain photocopies of the centralised
catalogues of the Department of the Environment Library,
covering the main Headquarters Library, two major sub-
libraries and six regional libraries. The libraries
of the DOE specialised research establishments (including
the Building Research Station and Transport and Road
Research Laboratory) are not included. The catalogues
shown contain some 250,000 items, including books,
pamphlets, reports, conference proceedings, acts, bills,
House of Commons papers, Command Papers, House of
Commons and House of Lords debates,Hansard and Statutory
Instruments. They also include all Census volumes,
development plans and structure plans of planning
authorities in England and Wales, European Community
documentation, and local and private acts of Parliament.
Relevant journal articles are also included and abstracts
are presented for these. The catalogues are presented
in five parts, contained in fifteen volumes:-
(1) Author catalogue of books, pamphlets and monographs
    including government publications, reports and
    published and semi-published material (5 volumes).
(ii) Classified catalogue of books and other material
    (4 volumes).
(iii) Author catalogue of periodical articles (2 volumes).
(iv) Classified catalogue of periodical articles, including
    abstracts. (4 volumes).
(v) Subject index (one part-volume).

9.2 Subsidiary References.

1.2 New Towns - Non-Transport Aspects

1.2.26   New-Town Planning: principles and practice. (1976)
1.2.27   The New Town Story. (1970)
1.2.33   New Towns: the British Experience. (1972)
1.2.39   Recreational Planning in New Communities: A Review of British
Experience. (1975)
1.2.43   Social Development Work in the New Communities. (1974)
1.2.48   Town and Country Planning. (February 1978)

3.1 Studies of Modal Choice Behaviour and Value of Travel Time.

3.1.32   Journey to Work: Modal Split. (1967)
3.1.59   Assessment of Preferences and Perceptions toward Attributes of
Transportation Alternatives. (197?
3.1.102 Value of Time. (1976)
3.1.108 Human Effort and the Value of Travel Time. (1976)

3.3 Interaction Between Land Use and Travel.

3.3.3   The Rôle of Accessibility in Basic Transportation Choice
Behaviour. (1976)

3.4 Transport and Mobility - General and Miscellaneous.

3.4.1   Environment and Behavior: planning and everyday life. (1977)
3.4.2   Environmental Psychology: Man and his Physical Setting. (1970)

4.1 Public Transport - Operational Aspects.

4.1.71   The Design and Location of Urban Public Transport Interchanges.
(1973)

4.2 Public Transport - Marketing Approach.

4.2.25   The Management of Urban Public Transport: a marketing
perspective. (1975)
4.2.44   The Rôle of Psychological Needs in Mass Transit. (1972)

4.3 Public Transport - Ergonomic Aspects.

4.3.8   Literature Survey of Passenger Comfort Limitations of High-Speed
Ground Transportation. (1965)
4.3.14   Programming Environmental Improvements in Public Transportation.
(1974)
4.3.26   Human Factors in Engineering and Design. (1974 edition)
4.3.44   Passenger Psychological Dynamics. (1968)
4.3.62   A Critical Assessment of Studies Relating Whole-Body Vibration
and Passenger Comfort. (1976)
4.3.66   Passengers' Reaction to Vibration. (1972)

9.3   Abstracting and Indexing Services.

This subsection lists regular abstracting and indexing publications, together with a few which are available on request. The abstracting and indexing services listed below have been arranged alphabetically by name of publication, followed by frequency of publication in brackets. Since several of these cover a wide range of subject material no attempt has been made to categorise them. The following paragraphs give some indication of the most useful services for obtaining information on literature relating to transport, survey techniques and new towns.

The TRANSPORT AND ROAD RESEARCH LABORATORY's Technical Information and Library Services provide a computerised data retrieval system from their information storage base which covers worldwide published material on roads and transport, and details of transportation research projects. The service provides a list of references with detailed abstracts on requested topics which is an extremely useful starting point for transport researchers. A number of the references on transport in new towns contained in subsection 1.1 of this bibliography have been derived from this source.

Regularly published indexes and lists of abstracts speci-fically relating to transport include the following:-
Current Literature in Traffic and Transportation (9.3.5),
HRIS Abstracts (9.3.10), MIRA Abstracts (9.3.12),Transportation Research Abstracts (9.3.19), and U.I.T.P. Biblio-Index:
Verkehr(9.3.20). The UNIVERSITIES TRANSPORT STUDIES GROUP provides for its members a computerised list of published and unpublished literature produced by members of the Group (9.3.22).

A number of more comprehensive regular indexing and abstracting services also contain details of transportation literature. Among these, the fortnightly Library Bulletin produced by the Headquarters Library of the DEPARTMENTS OF ENVIRONMENT AND TRANSPORT (9.3.6), and Geo Abstracts, published every two months at the UNIVERSITY OF EAST ANGLIA (9.3.9) include a substantial volume of transport - related material. Other sources which contain relevant literature include the GLC's monthly Urban Abstracts (9.3.21), Sage Urban Studies Abstracts (9.3.14), the Architectural Periodicals Index (9.3.1), British Humanities Index (9.3.2), British Technology Index (9.3.3), and the U.S. publication Environmental Periodicals Bibliography (9.3.7). Material relating to the ergonomic aspects of transport can be found in Ergonomics Abstracts (9.3.8), produced quarterly at the UNIVERSITY OF BIRMINGHAM, and the U.S. publication Psychological Abstracts (9.3.13). Abstracts of literature relevant to research into the marketing aspects of transport and to survey methodology are presented in the British Market Research Abstracts (9.3.11), and in the U.S. publications Psychological Abstracts (9.3.13), Sociological Abstracts (9.3.17), and the Journal of Marketing (9.1.48), which is primarily an abstracting journal. The indexing publications Social Sciences Citation Index (9.3.15) and Social Sciences Index (9.3.16) also contain references to literature in these subject areas.

There are no abstracting or indexing services which relate specifically to new towns, but Geo Abstracts (9.3.9), the DEPARTMENTS OF THE ENVIRONMENT AND TRANSPORT Library Bulletin (9.3.6) and the GLC's Urban Abstracts (9.3.21) each include subsections on new towns. Items on British new towns are also included in the Architectural Periodicals Index (9.3.1), the British Humanities Index (9.3.2) and the British Technology Index (9.3.3.), and abstracts of literature on new towns are sometimes included in Sage Urban Studies Abstracts (9.3.14).

9.3.1   Architectural Periodicals Index. (AP1) (Quarterly
                                with annual cumulation.)
        THE BRITISH ARCHITECTURAL LIBRARY, Royal Institute
                                of British Architects.

The Index, issued quarterly since August 1972, covers more than 450 British and foreign journals concerned with architecture, planning and the environment. The emphasis is on British material, and items on new towns and some on transport are included. The Index is arranged alphabetically by subject under headings derived from the RIBA Periodicals Subject Index, and brief abstracts are presented for some entries. The fourth issue each year contains an annual cumulation, and an index to the names of authors, architects and planners in the cumulation.

9.3.2   British Humanities Index. (Quarterly with annual
                                        cumulation).
        LIBRARY ASSOCIATION, London.

The Index, which replaced the Subject Index to Periodicals from 1915, covers some 350 periodicals (almost entirely British). Subjects indexed include planning, geography and architecture.

9.3.3   British Technology Index. (Monthly with annual
                                        cumulation).
        LIBRARY ASSOCIATION, London.

The Index is a current subject guide to articles in over 360 British technical journals. An author index has also been included from 1972. Subjects covered include town and traffic planning, architecture and engineering.

9.3.4   Building Science Abstracts. (Twice a year up to
                                        December 1976)
        BUILDING RESEARCH ESTABLISHMENT, Garston, Watford.

The Abstracts, now discontinued, were arranged in four main subject groups:- Materials; Engineering; Construction; Design and Environment. The latter heading covered the environmental aspects of transport.

9.3.5   Current Literature in Traffic and Transportation.
                                        (Monthly)
        TRANSPORTATION CENTER LIBRARY, NORTHWESTERN UNIVERSITY,
        Evanston, Illinois, U.S.A.

9.3.6 Departments of the Environment and Transport Library
                                    Bulletin. (Fortnightly)
       DEPARTMENTS OF ENVIRONMENT AND TRANSPORT.
       Headquarters Library.

       The Bulletin provides abstracts of current literature
       on subjects relevant to the two Departments under the
       following headings:- Housing and Construction;
       Planning and Land Use (including a subsection on New
       and Expanded Towns); Environmental Conservation and
       Pollution; Water and Sewerage; Waste Management;
       Transport (including a subsection on Passenger Trans-
       port); Government and Administration; Social Sciences;
       and Science and Technology. A supplement of legisla-
       tion, circulars and technical memoranda issued or
       sponsored by the two Departments is issued with the
       Bulletin once a month.

9.3.7 Environmental Periodicals Bibliography. (Six times a
                                                    year).
       INTERNATIONAL LIBRARY, Santa Barbara, California.

       Part I of the Index, General Human Ecology, includes
       some relevant material on transportation. A cumula-
       tive Annual Index is also published.

9.3.8 Ergonomics Abstracts. (Quarterly)
       ERGONOMICS INFORMATION ANALYSIS CENTRE, Department of
       Engineering Production, University of Birmingham.

       A comprehensive list, with abstracts, of current
       ergonomics publications. A selection of the abstracts,
       usually amounting to approximately 75 items under forty
       headings, is presented in the Abstracting Service of
       the journal Ergonomics three times a year. (see
       ref. 9.1.43 above.) This Birmingham University
       publication replaces the Ergonomics Abstracts formerly
       compiled by the Warren Spring Laboratories of the
       Department of Scientific and Industrial Research.

9.3.9 Geo Abstracts. (Six times a year).
       GEO ABSTRACTS LTD., University of East Anglia, Norwich.

       Section F of the seven-part abstracting service, headed
       'Regional and Community Planning,' includes relevant
       items on transportation and on new towns. Subsection
       headings include:- Planning Problems; Planning Theory
       and Techniques; National Planning; Regional and
       Economic Planning; Sub-Regional Planning; Urban
       Development; Transportation [(1) Process; (2) Techniques;
       (3) Planned Projects]; Rural Planning; Environmental
       Planning; Social Planning and Housing; Planning Law
       and Administration.

9.3.10　HRIS Abstracts.　(Quarterly).
HIGHWAY RESEARCH INFORMATION SERVICE. Transportation
Research Board. Washington D.C.

The publication contains selected abstracts of research
reports, technical papers in conference proceedings,
and journal articles stored on the magnetic computer
tape records of the Highway Research Information Service.

9.3.11　Market Research Abstracts. (Twice a year)
MARKET RESEARCH SOCIETY, London.

These Abstracts cover British and United States
journals and other sources relating to market,
psychological, statistical and sociological research.
Publications covered include the Journal of the Market
Research Society, Journal of Advertising Research (U.S.),
Journal of Marketing Research (U.S.), Operational
Research Quarterly (U.S.), Operations Research (U.S.),
Journal of Consumer Research (U.S.), Journal of the
American Statistical Association (U.S.), and Journal
of the Royal Statistical Society - Series A and C.
Relevant sections include those on Survey Techniques;
Statistics, Models and Forecasting; Attitude and
Behaviour Research; and Applications of Research.

9.3.12　MIRA Abstracts.　(Monthly)
MOTOR INDUSTRY RESEARCH ASSOCIATION, Nuneaton.

9.3.13　Psychological Abstracts. (Monthly)
AMERICAN PSYCHOLOGICAL ASSOCIATION, Washington D.C.
20036.
The Abstracts cover international literature in
psychology and related disciplines. Relevant sections
include: Psychometrics and Applied Psychology (with
subsections on Human Factors Engineering, Environmental Psychology and Environmental Issues); Marketing
and Advertising.

9.3.14　Sage Urban Studies Abstracts. (Quarterly)
SAGE PUBLICATIONS, London and Beverly Hills.

Each issue contains some 250 abstracts of recent
literature covering books, articles, pamphlets,
government publications, significant speeches and
legislative research studies. Author and subject
indexes are included. The material covered is international, but the emphasis is on literature of United
States origin. The detailed subject headings vary
from issue to issue, but normally include Urbanism,
Urban History, Architecture and Design, Planning
Growth Management, Urban Finance, Economic Development
and Location Theory, Land Use, Environment and Energy,

Transportation, Housing, Education, Urban Crime,
Social Services, Socioeconomic Conditions, Government
and Politics.

9.3.15   Social Sciences Citation Index. (Annually)
         INSTITUTE FOR SCIENTIFIC INFORMATION, Philadelphia,
                                                    U.S.A.

         An international multidisciplinary Index to the
         literature of the social, behavioural and related
         sciences. Journals covered include those concerned
         with area studies, economics, geography, psychology,
         sociology, statistics, and urban planning and develop-
         ment.

9.3.16   Social Sciences Index. (Quarterly)
         THE H.W. WILSON CO., New York.

         This Index, which before April 1974 was known as the
         Social Sciences and Humanities Index, contains author
         and subject lists of periodical articles in fields
         which include anthropology, area studies, economics,
         environmental science, geography, psychology, public
         administration and sociology.

9.3.17   Sociological Abstracts. (Five times a year).
         SOCIOLOGICAL ABSTRACTS, INC., San Diego, U.S.A.

         Relevant sections include Methodology and Research
         Technology; Market Structures and Consumer Behaviour;
         Urban Structures and Ecology; Community Development;
         and Environmental Interactions.

9.3.18   TRRL Information Storage and Retrieval System. (On
                                         request, from 1965.)
         TRRL TECHNICAL INFORMATION AND LIBRARY SERVICES,
                                         Crowthorne, Berkshire.
         The Transport and Road Research Laboratory Technical
         Information and Library Services have maintained a
         computerised information storage and retrieval system
         since 1965. Searches of the data base are made on
         request free of charge. The data base includes
         abstracts of worldwide published material in the
         fields of roads and related transport acquired
         through the International Road Research Documentation
         (IRRD) scheme; details of U.K. research projects; and
         summaries of similar projects in progress in a number
         of other countries.

9.3.19   Transportation Research Abstracts. (Six times a year)
         TRANSPORTATION RESEARCH BOARD, Washington D.C.

         The Abstracts, published in Transportation Research
         News, cover current transportation literature,

Transportation Research Board publications, and
the latest research activity of the Transportation
Research Board and of government and industry in the
U.S. and elsewhere. The abstracts were known as
Highway Research Abstracts up to 1974.

9.3.20 U.I.T.P. Biblio-Index: Verkehr. (Quarterly)
INTERNATIONAL UNION OF PUBLIC TRANSPORT, Belgium.

Summaries of the indexed literature are presented in
English, French and German.

9.3.21 Urban Abstracts. (Monthly with annual cumulation)
GREATER LONDON COUNCIL, Research Library. (GLC
                              Intelligence Unit).

The Abstracts are compiled from journal articles and
selected reports, books and pamphlets received in
the Research Library. Major topics covered include
environment and pollution, housing, planning and
land use (including a subsection on new towns and
town development), social planning, and transport.
A list of Statutory Instruments and Circulars in
these fields is also included.

9.3.22 U.T.S.G. Famulus References. (On request to members
                              of U.T.S.G.)
UNIVERSITIES TRANSPORT STUDIES GROUP.

A computerised reference system available to members
of U.T.S.G., listing published and unpublished reports,
articles, conference papers and other literature
produced by the Group's members.

9.3 Subsidiary References.

9.1 Journals.

*9.1.1   Traffic and Transportation: a permuted title index and
                              research guide. (1976)*
9.1.2   Bibliography of Transport in Current Periodicals.   (1976)
9.1.3   A Bibliography of the Major Transport Journals 1965 - 1976.   (1976)
9.1.48   Journal of Marketing.   (Quarterly)

9.2 Bibliographies

9.2.38   Indexes to Survey Methodology Literature.   (1974)

9.4   Research Registers .

This subsection draws together a number of publications
which list ongoing or recent research in the fields of
transport and of new towns, arranged in two groups:-

1. <u>General Research Registers</u> (9.4.1-8)offering fairly
comprehensive compilations
of research projects.

2. <u>Research Registers Issued by Specific Research
Institutions and Departments</u> (9.4.9-23)

These are often published as part of an Annual Report,
and give details of current research conducted by
the particular establishment, or lists of publications
arising from its research activities.

The DEPARTMENTS OF THE ENVIRONMENT AND TRANSPORT'S annual
<u>Register of Research Part III: Roads and Transport</u> (9.4.2)
is a comprehensive source of information on current and
recently completed transport research projects in the U.K.
<u>Part II of the Register of Research</u> (9.4.1) which covers
<u>Environmental Planning</u>, also includes a subsection on public
transport. The DEPARTMENTS OF THE ENVIRONMENT AND TRANSPORT
also publish an annual <u>Register of Surveys</u> (9.4.3) which gives
details of U.K. research projects involving surveys in the
fields of transport and other environment-related subjects.
At the time of writing the BRITISH LIBRARY is compiling a
new national register of research in academic institutions,
to be published in several volumes at the end of 1978 as:
<u>Research in British Universities , Polytechnics and Colleges</u>
(RBUPC). The information will also be available as an on-line
computer service through the British Library Automated
Information Service (BLAISE). This register,which will cover th
physical, biological and social sciences, will replace
<u>Scientific Research in British Universities and Colleges</u>
(SRBUC), published jointly by the Department of Education
and Science and the British Council up to 1975. Several
other sources of general information on transport research
projects are listed in the subsidiary references at the end
of this subsection. These include the journals <u>Traffic
Engineering and Control</u> (9.1.16) and the <u>Chartered Institute
of Transport Journal</u> (9.1.8) which regularly publish details
of current research projects; the TRANSPORT AND ROAD RESEARCH
LABORATORY'S <u>Information Storage and Retrieval System</u> (9.3.18),
the data base for which includes details of U.K. and U.S.
transportation research projects; and the U.S. TRANSPORTATION
RESEARCH BOARD'S <u>Transportation Research Abstracts</u> (9.3.19),
published six times a year, which gives details of current
transport research projects in the United States and elsewhere.

The most comprehensive available source of information on
international research projects on roads and road transport
is the 1977 World Survey of Current Research and Development
on Roads and Road Transport (9.4.5). The bulletin produced
twice yearly by the EUROPEAN CONFERENCE OF MINISTERS
OF TRANSPORT: Research on Transport Economics (9.4.4)
gives details of research relating to transport economics
in ECMT member countries and some other countries.

Specific institutions issuing lists of current research
projects or of publications arising from their research
on transport or transport-related topics include the European
Conference of Ministers of Transport (9.4.11), General Motors
Research Laboratories (9.4.12), the Institute for Consumer
Ergonomics (9.4.13), London Transport Executive (9.4.14),
the National Bus Company (9.4.16), the Transport and Road
Research Laboratory (9.4.19) the Polytechnic of Central
London (9.4.18), and the Universities of Cambridge (9.4.15),
Birmingham (9.4.21) Leeds (9.4.22), and Oxford (9.4.23).

Details of current research projects on new towns are provided
by the NEW TOWNS ASSOCIATION'S Summary of Research being
Undertaken in New Towns (9.4.6), and by the subsection on
new towns in the DEPARTMENT OF THE ENVIRONMENT'S annual
Register of Research Part II: Environmental Planning.
Research projects including surveys in new towns are included
in the DEPARTMENTS OF THE ENVIRONMENT AND TRANSPORT'S annual
Register of Surveys (9.4.3): the Register does not contain
a separate subsection on new towns, but a number of items
included in the 1977 edition are listed in the index under
the names of individual new towns, or under the general
index entry for new towns. The Building Research Establishment (9.4.9), Cambridge University's Martin Centre for
Architectural and Urban Studies (9.4.15), the Open University
New Towns Study Unit (9.4.17) and Birmingham University's
Centre for Urban and Regional Studies (9.4.20) all regularly
publish details of, or lists of publications arising from,
their research concerning British new towns. Research
reports published by staff at the Centre for Urban and
Regional Studies also include details of other publications
resulting from the Centre's research programme on social
development in new communities.

9.4   Research Registers

(i)   General Research Registers

9.4.1   Register of Research, 1977. Part II: Environmental Planning.
                                                              (1977)
         DEPARTMENT OF THE ENVIRONMENT.
         Headquarters Library. 1977. (390pp.)

         (published annually from 1974)

         Details are given of environmental planning projects in
         the U.K., based on data collected during the early part
         of 1976.   The information is presented under the
         headings:- Land and Land Use; Physical and Economic
         Planning and Development; Demography; Sociology;
         Housing; New Towns; Central Government; Local
         Government; Public Services and Needs (including a
         subsection on public transport); Industry and Labour;
         Conservation; Landscape and Environment; Sport,
         Recreation and Countryside; Natural Resources; Water
         and Water Supply.   Indexes of research sponsors,
         workers and organisations are included and a list of
         research organisations' addresses is provided.

9.4.2   Register of Research, 1977. Part III: Roads and Transport.
                                                              (1977)
         DEPARTMENTS OF ENVIRONMENT and TRANSPORT.
         Headquarters Library. 1977. (362pp.)

         (published annually from 1974)

         This volume gives descriptions of current and recently
         completed road and transport projects in the U.K. in
         the following fields:- Transport Economics and Administra-
         tion; Transport and Land Use; Traffic Engineering and
         Control; Design of Transport Structures; Construction
         and Supervision of Construction Work; Materials;
         Foundations; Maintenance of Roads and Structures;
         Accident Studies and Road Safety; and Vehicles.
         Indexes of research workers, sponsors and organisations
         are appended, as is a list of addresses of research
         organisations.

9.4.3   Register of Surveys. (1977)

         DEPARTMENTS OF ENVIRONMENT and TRANSPORT.
         Headquarters Library. Information Series No.29. 1977
                                                           (244pp.)
         (published annually from 1974)

         This register describes current and recently completed
         surveys, plans, studies, operations, practice and
         development projects in the fields of building, planning,
         transport and pollution.   Details are given of the
         scope of each project, the research or survey workers
         involved, sponsorship and finance, dates of the project,
         and reports and publications.   The main text is
         supported by indexes of subjects, workers, organisations
         and sponsors, and a list of addresses of organisations
         is provided.

9.4.4   <u>Research on Transport Economics.</u> (twice a year from 1968)

EUROPEAN CONFERENCE OF MINISTERS OF TRANSPORT.
ECMT   Documentation Centre. Paris.

This ECMT information bulletin presents a survey of
current research projects in transport economics in
ECMT member countries and in certain other industrial-
ised countries.   The May issue each year lists the
new projects for the year and the November issue gives
a general review of research activities planned,
under way and recently completed.

9.4.5   <u>1977 World Survey of Current Research and Development</u>
<u>on Roads and Road Transport</u>. (1977)

INTERNATIONAL ROAD FEDERATION, in co-operation with the
ORGANISATION FOR ECONOMIC CO-OPERATION AND DEVELOPMENT
(OECD) and the TRANSPORTATION RESEARCH BOARD.

International Road Federation. Washington DC. December 1977
(744pp.)

(published annually from 1966)

This report covers an inventory of 51 countries, and
since the U.S. Transportation Board ceased publication
of its Highway Research in Progress in 1975, (see ref.
9.4.8 below) is the only world-wide inventory of road
and road transport research in progress.   The material
is arranged under country headings, listed alphabetically,
and brief abstracts of the projects are given.   An
index of the research projects by 'subject area' is
included.

9.4.6   <u>1977 Summary of Research being Undertaken in New Towns.</u>
(1977)
NEW TOWNS ASSOCIATION.   June 1977.   (39pp.)

A regularly updated list of research currently being
undertaken in British new towns, with separate sections
for projects being carried out by Development Corporations
and those conducted by other bodies or organisations.
A descriptive summary of each research project is given,
with details as to investigators, sponsors, cost, dates,
and - where applicable - publications.

9.4.7   <u>Register of Research - North West Region</u>.(1975)

NORTH WEST ECONOMIC PLANNING BOARD.   (Research Section)
Projects relevant to regional planning.   No.10. May 1975.
(39pp.)
This booklet lists research projects being undertaken
in the North West in 1975 which were relevant to
regional planning.   At the time of writing no subsequent edition of the list has been issued.

9.4.8 **Highway Research in Progress**. (annually up to 1975)
HIGHWAY RESEARCH BOARD up to 1974.
TRANSPORTATION RESEARCH BOARD after 1974.

The final volume in the Highway Research in Progress
(HRIP) series was issued in 1975. Subsequent Highway
Research in Progress information is included in the
International Road Federation's World Survey of Current
Research and Development on Roads and Road Transport.
(see ref. 9.4.5 above).

(ii) Research Registers Issued by Specific Research Institutions
and Departments.

9.4.9 BUILDING RESEARCH ESTABLISHMENT.
The Annual Report,
published by H.M.S.O. gives details of the progress of
the Establishment's research relating to new towns
under the general section heading:- 'Planning'.

B.R.E. News (Quarterly)
describes research projects currently under way at the
Building Research Establishment and lists all the
Establishment's new publications.

9.4.10 CENTRE FOR ENVIRONMENTAL STUDIES,
The Annual Report gives general information on the
Centre for Environmental Studies' research strategy and
specific details of current research projects under the
headings (in 1976):- Industry and Employment, Land Use
and Local Planning, Planning Research Applications
Group, Local Government Finance, General Studies, and
Modernisation in Non-Industrial Areas. The Centre's
publications are listed and a summary of research projects
is appended. Publications lists are also issued
regularly.

9.4.11 EUROPEAN CONFERENCE OF MINISTERS OF TRANSPORT.
Reports of ongoing research are included in the Annual
Report and Resolutions of the Council of Ministers,
and the organisation also publishes abstracts of
transport research in: Research on Transport Economics,
issued twice a year. (see ref. 9.4.4 above)

9.4.12 GENERAL MOTORS RESEARCH LABORATORIES, Warren, Michigan.
A list of research seminars, publications, presentations
and symposia arising from the Laboratories' research
activities is issued annually. Research relating to
transport planning is covered in the section headed:
'Transportation and Urban Analysis'.

9.4.13 INSTITUTE FOR CONSUMER ERGONOMICS, Loughborough
        University of Technology.
        A regularly updated list of reports and publications
        produced by or under the supervision of staff of the
        Institute for Consumer Ergonomics is issued.   The
        1977 list includes several reports relating to aspects
        of transportation and passenger behaviour, and some
        relevant methodological reports.

9.4.14 LONDON TRANSPORT EXECUTIVE: PLANNING RESEARCH DIVISION.
        Lists of Research Reports, Research Memoranda and
        Technical Notes are regularly issued.   The main findings
        of the research described in the listed reports are
        summarised.

9.4.15 THE MARTIN CENTRE FOR ARCHITECTURAL AND URBAN STUDIES,
        University of Cambridge.
        The Annual Report 1976-77 gives details of completed
        and current research, publications and graduate studies.
        The work of the Centre is characterised by the use of
        quantitative methods, mathematical and logical models
        and computer aids in a variety of subjects relating to
        urban and regional planning.   Specific projects have
        included aspects of transportation and of new towns,
        a number of working papers on the latter arising from
        an SSRC sponsored project concerned with the establish-
        ment of a new towns data bank in the early 1970's.
        This research was carried out by the Centre for Land
        Use and Built Form Studies, which was amalgamated into
        the Martin Centre in 1974.

9.4.16 NATIONAL BUS COMPANY.
        The National Bus Company's Research Office produces
        a twice-yearly Research Bulletin which outlines its
        research projects in the marketing and operational
        fields.   The National Bus Company also produces an
        Annual Report and Accounts, published by H.M.S.O.

9.4.17 OPEN UNIVERSITY: New Towns Study Unit.
        The Unit, which was established in 1970, conducts
        evaluative new towns research and operates an
        enquiry service.   It produces a catalogue of pub-
        lications which have resulted from the findings
        of the Unit's new towns research projects.

9.4.18 POLYTECHNIC OF CENTRAL LONDON: TRANSPORT STUDIES GROUP.
        The Reports and Publications List (1973-1977) lists
        the Group's research reports, discussion papers,
        bibliographies, and external publications.   It also
        includes a list of Rural Transport Seminar papers
        presented at annual one-day seminars on Rural Trans-
        port held at the Polytechnic of Central London

        and these include an annual review of rural transport
        research which has some relevance to transport studies
        in the broader context.

9.4.19 **TRANSPORT AND ROAD RESEARCH LABORATORY. (TRRL)**
The Annual Research Report, published by H.M.S.O., gives
details of research undertaken by or sponsored by TRRL
during the course of each year.

9.4.20 **UNIVERSITY OF BIRMINGHAM: CENTRE FOR URBAN AND REGIONAL
STUDIES.**
The Centre has been carrying out research into the
social development of new communities since 1967 and
has also conducted research relating to environmental
perception. The Annual Report gives details of
projects currently being undertaken and lists CURS
Research Memoranda, Occasional Papers and Working
Papers.

9.4.21 **UNIVERSITY OF BIRMINGHAM: DEPARTMENT OF TRANSPORTATION
AND ENVIRONMENTAL PLANNING.**
A register of research carried out in the Department
between 1971 and 1973 has been produced ('Research,
1971/73'), and a new edition covering subsequent
projects is to be issued during 1978.

9.4.22 **UNIVERSITY OF LEEDS: INSTITUTE FOR TRANSPORT STUDIES.**
Working Paper 81: List of Abstracts (1972-1976)
presents abstracts of all currently available
Working Papers produced by the Institute for Transport
Studies between 1972 and 1976.

9.4.23 **UNIVERSITY OF OXFORD: TRANSPORT STUDIES UNIT.**

A list of publications arising from the Unit's transport
research activities is available.

9.4 Subsidiary References.

1.2 New Towns - Non-Transport Aspects.

*1.2.39   Recreational Planning in New Communities: A Review of British
Experience. (1975)*

9.1 Journals.

*9.1.8   Chartered Institute of Transport Journal. (Six times a year)
[Includes the Transport Research Bulletin twice a year.]*
*9.1.16   Traffic Engineering and Control. (Monthly)
[Included regular summaries of current research activities.]*

9.2 Bibliographies.

*9.2.13   Transport Policies and Planning. (1977)
[Section J lists some general items relating to transport research
and a selection of current research projects.]*

9.3 Abstracting and Indexing Services.

*9.3.18   TRRL Information Storage and Retrieval System. (On request)
[The data base includes details of U.K. and international
transportation research projects.]*
9.3.19   Transportation Research Abstracts. (Six times a year.)

The statistical sources listed below have been arranged in the following groups:-

1. Specific Sources of Transport Statistics (9.5.1-14)

2. Other Statistical Sources (9.5.15-23)

Other useful sources of statistics are listed in the subsidiary references at the end of this subsection. Sources of statistical information on new towns are discussed in the introductions to subsections 1.1, 1.2, and 2.1-4.

Subsection 9.6 lists a number of useful guides to sources of transport information (9.6.1-7) and other relevant information guides (9.6.8-20). The CENTRAL STATISTICAL OFFICE'S Guide to Official Statistics (9.6.10) is a particularly valuable aid to the location of statistical material, identifying both published and unpublished sources for the subject areas covered in the Guide. In the 1976 volume Section 3, on Population and Vital Statistics, gives a detailed description of material available from the 1966 and 1971 Censuses of Population. Section 8 deals with transport statistics, which are discussed by mode (subsection 8.3 covering road transport), with a preliminary subsection on general sources of transport statistics (8.1). An introductory passage identifies other parts of the Guide which deal with particular aspects of transport statistics, such as employment figures for the transport industry, and means of transport to work enumerated in the 1971 Census. The Open University publication Transport and Communications by RUBRA (9.6.6) also outlines the location and content of British published transport data and includes a critical examination of their potential uses.

The most comprehensive collection of statistical series on transport in Britain is contained in Transport Statistics Great Britain (9.5.14), published annually since 1976 by the DEPARTMENT OF TRANSPORT, the SCOTTISH DEVELOPMENT DEPARTMENT and the WELSH OFFICE. The 1978 report includes analyses from the 1975/76 National Travel Survey as well as detailed tables covering private and passenger transport, road traffic, accident figures and trends, and household expenditure on transport. Many of the tables show trends over the period 1966-76. The Monthly Digest of Statistics includes monthly statistics on new registrations of road vehicles, vehicles currently licensed and vehicle miles travelled. Passenger journeys and receipts are given for the latest four years and for each quarter of the latest three years. The two papers delivered by WHITE to the Annual Seminars on Public Transport Operational Research held at Leeds University (4.1.36-37) examine available statistics on bus operation and discuss limitations of these as sources of information on passenger demand. Details of personal and household car availability by administrative areas, including new towns, are given in the 1971 Census volume on Availability of Cars (9.5.16). The County volumes of the 1971 Census provide journey to work data for administrative areas, again including new towns, and this data is also included in the volume England and Wales: Economic Activity New Towns.

Specific Sources of Transport Statistics

9.5.1 Basic Road Statistics.(Annually)
BRITISH ROAD FEDERATION.

Basic Road Statistics presents statistics covering most
aspects of roads and road traffic in Britain. The
majority of the tables refer to Great Britain as a whole,
but those for household car ownership are broken down
by region. Figures are included for motor vehicles in
use and new registrations; growth and forecast growth
of road traffic; estimated annual mileage by class of
vehicle; road accidents; consumers' expenditure on
transport; passenger mileages and expenditure; household car ownership; and road mileage. An appendix
summarises legislative measures which have affected
road users since 1930.

9.5.2 British Railways Board Annual Report and Accounts.(Annually)
BRITISH RAILWAYS BOARD.

The statistical section includes figures, for the
latest two years, of passenger receipts, average fare
per passenger journey and average fare per passenger
mile, each analysed by type of fare and class of travel.
The report also gives an alphabetical list of unremun-
erative passenger stations receiving grants during the
year, and shows for each station the amount and source
of grant.

**9.5.3 Business Monitor M1: Number of Road Vehicles,
New Registrations.(Monthly)**
DEPARTMENT OF INDUSTRY.(Business Statistics Office,
Newport)
H.M.S.O.

Figures are given of private car and motor cycle registrations in the United Kingdom for the current month
and year to date, with corresponding figures for the
previous year. In the last month of each quarter
private and public transport vehicle registration
figures are given for each licensing authority area.
Figures are also given of public transport vehicles
registered by fuel type in the current month and for
the year to date, with corresponding figures for the
previous year. Public transport registrations are
also broken down by seating capacity of vehicle.

9.5.4 Motor Transport: Bus and Coach Supplement.
IPC TRANSPORT PRESS LTD.

The results of an annual survey of municipal bus operators,PTEs and London Transport are published in the
Bus and Coach supplement to the weekly paper Motor
Transport. These include figures for passenger trips,
receipts, vehicle miles, fleet size and working expenses.

[For a discussion and some analysis of these and other available data on bus operators see: P.R.White: 'Analysis of Recent Trends in Demand, Cost and Efficiency in Urban Bus Operation' (1976) - ref. 4.1.36 above; and: 'Further Analysis of Trends in Demand, Cost and Efficiency in Urban Public Transport' - ref. 4.1.37 above.]

9.5.5   National Bus Company Annual Report and Accounts.
(Annually)
NATIONAL BUS CO.

Details are included of receipts and expenditure, capital, capital expenditure, and operations. Annual estimates of the number of passengers carried are given.

9.5.6   National Travel Survey 1972/73:   Cross-sectional analysis of passenger travel in Great Britain.(1975)
DEPARTMENT OF THE ENVIRONMENT.
H.M.S.O. 1975. (24pp.)

Detailed results from the National Travel Survey, based on the records of 7,113 households between April 1972 and March 1973, are presented in forty-three tables.   Figures are included for vehicle availability;   weekly expenditure on public transport by household income;   number of journeys per week by age and sex;   purpose of journeys;   parking at work;   car ownership by make and age of car. [Preliminary data from the 1975/76 National Travel Survey are presented in Transport Statistics Great Britain 1966-1976 (1978 edition) - ref. 9.5.14 below; in Regional Statistics 1977 - No.13, which includes regional details - ref. 9.5.22 below;   and in the British Road Federation's Road Talk No.4, January 1978 - ref. 3.1.80 above.   Unpublished tables can also be purchased from the Department of Transport]

9.5.7   National Travel Survey 1972/73:   Number of journeys per week by different types of households, individuals and vehicles.(1976)
DEPARTMENT OF THE ENVIRONMENT.
H.M.S.O. 1976.(23pp.)

9.5.8   National Travel Survey 1972/73:   A comparison of the 1965 and 1972/73 Surveys.(1976)
DEPARTMENT OF THE ENVIRONMENT.
H.M.S.O. 1976.(42pp.)

Data from the 1965 and 1972/73 National Travel Surveys are compared for the use made of each mode of transport by households living in different types of area and by different socio-economic groups, journey purpose and type of ticket used.   Figures of car ownership, occupancy rates and usage are given for each type of area.

9.5.9   Policy for Roads: England, 1978. (Annually)
        DEPARTMENT OF TRANSPORT.
        Cmnd. 7132
        H.M.S.O.

        This annual White Paper supersedes 'Roads in England:
        Report by the Secretary of State for the Environment
        for the Year' (see ref. 9.5.12 below).

9.5.10 Proposed Increase in London Taxicab Fares. (1968)
        NATIONAL BOARD OF PRICES AND INCOMES.
        Cmnd. 3796. NBPI Report No. 87. 1968.

        Details are given of fleet sizes, systems of operation,
        trends in ownership, journey characteristics, length
        of jobs, availability of cabs by time of day, and
        other statistics relating to taxicab operation.

9.5.11 Road Accidents in Great Britain. (Annually)
        DEPARTMENT OF THE ENVIRONMENT.
        H.M.S.O.

        Detailed tables for the year show accidents by month,
        road surface condition, class of road, number of
        vehicles involved, and lighting conditions.   Casual-
        ties are shown by class of road user, month, day of
        week, hour of day, age, region and county.   Casualty
        rates per 100,000 population are given by age and sex.
        The report also includes a review of the road traffic
        accidents in the year and comparative figures for
        previous years and for other countries.

9.5.12 Roads in England: Report by the Secretary of State
        for the Environment for the Year. (Annually up to
                                                    1975/76)
        DEPARTMENT OF THE ENVIRONMENT.
        H.M.S.O. 1976 (59pp.)

        The report described how the Secretary of State's
        responsibilities for the improvement, operation and
        maintenance of the trunk road system were carried
        out and what policies affected the development of
        the system during the year.   It also covered the
        effects of Government policies on local authority
        roads.   Details were given of road building and
        improvement during the year for economic planning
        regions and for Greater London.   This report has
        now been superseded by the annual White Paper:
        'Policy for Roads' (see ref. 9.5.9 above).

9.5.13 Traffic Commissioners' Annual Reports. (Annually)
        TRAFFIC COMMISSIONERS.
        Departments of the Environment and Transport.

        The reports, published by each area Traffic Commis-
        sioner, give details of applications, decisions and
        appeals regarding PSV licences ; vehicle inspections,
        suspension and revocations of vehicle licences;
        PSV driving tests, refusals, suspension and revocations

of PSV driving and conductor licensing; and con-
victions under Acts and Regulations governing the
industry.

9.5.14   Transport Statistics Great Britain.(Annually, from
                                                    1976)
         DEPARTMENT OF TRANSPORT, SCOTTISH DEVELOPMENT DEPART-
         MENT and WELSH OFFICE.
         H.M.S.O.

         This publication replaced the Department of the En-
         vironment's 'Passenger Transport in Great Britain' and
         'Highway Statistics' in 1976, and also presents addit-
         ional data.   It is the most comprehensive source of
         statistical information relating to inland surface
         transport in Great Britain.   Transport Statistics
         Great Britain 1966-1976 (1978-198pp.) includes anal-
         yses from the 1975/76 National Travel Survey and
         comparisons with the results of earlier surveys, and
         the first published results from the Department of
         Transport's Long-Distance Travel Surveys.   Many of
         the tables cover the eleven years 1966-1976, and
         some contain forecasts for years ahead.   Detailed
         analyses include figures of passenger kilometres,
         journeys and receipts by rail and by public and
         private road transport;   vehicle registrations; car
         ownership;   details of road passenger vehicles by
         type, type of operator, seating capacity and operating
         kilometres;   accidents and casualties from 1926;
         road traffic figures and trends;   and household
         expenditure on transport.

Other Statistical Sources.

9.5.15   Annual Abstract of Statistics.(Annually)
         CENTRAL STATISTICAL OFFICE.
         H.M.S.O.

         Relevant sections are those on Population and Vital
         Statistics (Ch.II);   Social Conditions (Ch.III);
         Labour (Ch.VI);   Transport and Communications (Ch.X)
         and Personal Income, Expenditure and Wealth (Ch.XV).
         In the 1977 volume (517pp.) most tables give annual
         figures for each of the years 1966 to 1976, and some
         include figures for the early months of 1977.   Most
         statistics relate to the United Kingdom of Great
         Britain and Northern Ireland, some to Great Britain,
         and some to England and Wales.   Further information
         on regional details is published in 'Regional Statis-
         tics', also published annually by the Central Statis-
         tical Office.   (see ref. 9.5.22 below).

9.5.16   Census of Population.(Full censuses every ten years;
         1966 - 10% sample census)
         OFFICE OF POPULATION CENSUSES AND SURVEYS.

         The most detailed statistics available relating to
         population and households are those collected in the
         periodic censuses, the last two being for 1966
         (10% sample census) and 1971.

The following volumes from the 1971 Census contain particularly useful material for studies of transport in new towns :-

Census 1971: England and Wales: County Reports. (H.M.S.O.) For each county the first group of tables gives figures of population according to age, sex, marital status, country of birth, and economic activity. Figures of population density are also included. The second and third groups give statistics about households. The figures in each group are broken down by local authority areas (as constituted at 1971), wards, new towns and conurbation centres. A second series of County Reports is available for England and Wales, analysing the data by the new local government areas as constituted at 1st. April, 1974. (not published by H.M.S.O.)

Census 1971: England and Wales: Economic Activity New Towns. (10% sample)(H.M.S.O.) This volume provides figures relating to new towns on employment, industry, socio-economic class, workplace of resident population, area of residence of working population, and method of transport to work.

Census 1971: England and Wales: Availability of Cars. (H.M.S.O.) This volume gives an analysis of enumerated households and persons by numbers of cars available to households for England and Wales, regions, conurbations, sub-divisions of regions, counties, local authority areas, conurbation centres and new towns.

SPECIAL AND UNPUBLISHED CENSUS STATISTICS. Unpublished data from the Census can be purchased from the Customer Services Section of the Office of Population Censuses and Surveys, at Titchfield, Hants. (see ref. 9.6.31 below), from whom Information Papers giving details of the services available, including charges, can also be obtained. In general, the following types of tabulation are available :-

(i) Many tabulations can be obtained for smaller local authority areas than those given in the published volumes.

(ii) Where figures relating to specific new towns are not given in the published tables these can often be supplied in unpublished form.

(iii) Key statistics can be obtained for smaller enumeration districts than the smallest local authority units, and for the 1971 Census (for the first time) for 100 metre squares within the national grid system.

(iv) Special analyses can be produced on particular subjects. Notes on the material available are included in relevant subject reports.

9.5.17   Family Expenditure Survey. (Annually)
         DEPARTMENT OF EMPLOYMENT.
         H.M.S.O

         The annual report on the Family Expenditure Survey
         includes figures of average weekly household ex-
         penditure on various forms of transport.   The data
         is analysed by size, composition and average weekly
         income of households;   by occupation of head of
         household;   and by type of administrative area.
         Some regional analyses are included.

9.5.18   General Household Survey.
         OFFICE OF POPULATIONS CENSUSES AND SURVEYS.
         Social Survey Division.
         H.M.S.O.

         The General Household Survey is an inter-departmental
         continuous sample survey of households sponsored by
         the Central Statistical Office.   The most recent
         report available as at mid-1978 is for 1974.   A wide
         range of social and socio-economic topics is covered,
         including demographic details, housing, employment,
         leisure, education and health.

9.5.19   Local Government Trends.(Annually)
         CHARTERED INSTITUTE OF PUBLIC FINANCE AND ACCOUNTANCY.

         The report includes statistics on British new towns,
         including figures on population, employment, housing,
         industry, offices, shops and financial results.

9.5.20   Monthly Digest of Statistics.(Monthly)
         CENTRAL STATISTICAL OFFICE.
         H.M.S.O.

         The Monthly Digest is a collection of the main statis-
         tical series from all Government departments.   A Sup-
         plement of Definitions and Explanatory Notes is
         published annually with the January issue.

9.5.21   Progress on Land Sold or Leased by Development
         Corporations/Commission for the New Towns.
         ["The Publicity Sheet"] (Quarterly)
         NEW TOWNS DIRECTORATE.(Department of the Environment)

         The 'Publicity Sheet' gives statistics for each new
         town in England, Wales and Scotland, covering population;
         new houses and flats completed and under construction;
         new schools and the number of children provided for;
         the number of firms;   new shops completed; and office
         space.

9.5.22   Regional Statistics.(Annually)
         CENTRAL STATISTICAL OFFICE.
         H.M.S.O.

         The annual report presents a selection of the main
         official statistics that are available on a regional
         basis, covering a broad range of social, economic
         and demographic topics.   Relevant chapters from

421

the 1977 report (No.13 -212pp.) include those on
Population and Vital Statistics (Ch.2); Social
Characteristics (Ch.3); Social Services (Ch.4);
Health (Ch.5); Housing (Ch.6); Employment (Ch.8);
Transport (Ch.12 - including regional details from
the National Travel Survey 1975/6); Personal Incomes
(Ch.13); and Household Expenditure (Ch.14).

9.5.23   Social Trends. (Annually from 1970)
          CENTRAL STATISTICAL OFFICE.
          H.M.S.O.

          'Social Trends' brings together key social and demogra-
          phic data from other offical statistical sources.
          Trends and distributions are recorded on topics
          including population, households, education, employ-
          ment, personal income and wealth, personal expenditure,
          health, housing, environment, leisure, public safety
          and social participation. An introductory social
          commentary is also included (for example, see ref.
          8.1.117 above). Detailed figures in the 1977 volume
          (No.8 - 264pp.) include an analysis of passenger
          transport use, resources by type of transport, and
          prices of fares and running costs in Britain over the
          latest five years and earlier two years.

9.5 Subsidiary References.

1.2 New Towns - Non-Transport Aspects.

1.2.27   The New Town Story. (1970)
1.2.33   New Towns: the British Experience. (1972)
1.2.34   New Towns: the data bank, its construction and organisation.
*   (1972)*
1.2.48   Town and Country Planning. (February 1978)
1.2.50   Commission for the New Towns: Annual Reports. (Annually)
1.2.51   Annual Reports of the Development Corporations in England and
*   Wales. (Annually)*

2.1 Runcorn.

2.1.17   Home Interview Social Survey. (1966)
2.1.20   1976 Runcorn Household Census (1976)
2.1.21   1969 Social Survey: the first 500 Families. (1969)
2.1.22   Statistical Profile of Runcorn New Town. (1964)
2.1.24   Creating a Community: A Study of Runcorn New Town. (1973)

2.2 Skelmersdale.

2.2.6   New Town Progress. (1973)
2.2.7   Report on Recreation and Leisure Facilities in Skelmersdale
*   New Town. (1969)*
2.2.8   Skelmersdale New Town Population and Social Surveys. (Annually)

2.3 Telford.

2.3.1   Bus Services for Telford: Report of the short term bus study.
*   (1976)*

2.3.6	*Telford Transportation Study. (1976/7)*
2.3.13	*Executive Housing Survey: a study of attitudes in the medium to upper private housing market. (1976)*
2.3.14	*A Facility Survey of Telford Development Corporation Industrial Estates. (1974)*
2.3.15	*"Help": A report on the needs of and services for the elderly in Telford. (1975)*
2.3.17	*Leisure and Recreation Study. (1972)*
2.3.18	*Progress Report. (1974)*
2.3.19	*Progress Report. (1976)*
2.3.20	*Shopping Patterns in a New Town - Madeley District. (Undated)*
2.3.21	*Social Survey. (1973)*
2.3.22	*Telford Survey Report - Shopping Patterns in New Towns. (Undated)*

2.4 Other New Towns.

2.4.1	*Aycliffe Housing Survey: A Study of Housing in a New Town. (1970)*
2.4.3	*Basildon - Shopping; Work for Women; Leisure. (1967)*
2.4.4	*Reports on research carried out by Bracknell Development Corporation.*
2.4.5	*Crawley: A Study of Amenities in a New Town. (1967)*
2.4.7	*Cumbernauld '67: A Household Survey and Report. (1968)*
2.4.8	*East Kilbride Housing Survey: A Study of Housing in a New Town. (1970)*
2.4.9	*East Kilbride '70. A Social and Economic Survey. (1970)*
2.4.11	*Glenrothes Area Public Transport Study: Final Report. (1977)*
2.4.13	*Harlow 1976 Household Survey. (1977)*
2.4.15	*Harlow Bus Study. Final Report. (1976)*
2.4.16-23	*[Statistics relating to the Harlow Dial-a-Bus Service]*
2.4.40	*"Seven Years On". Milton Keynes Household Survey. 1976. (1977)*
2.4.56	*Stevenage Household Survey. March 1976. (1976)*
2.4.59	*Stevenage Superbus Experiment. Summary Report. (1974)*
2.4.61	*Stevenage Traffic Accident Survey 1957-1966. (1967)*

3.1 Studies of Modal Choice Behaviour and Value of Travel Time .

3.1.80	*Road Talk: Travel in Britain. (1978)*

4.1 Public Transport - Operational Aspects.

4.1.36	*Analysis of Recent Trends in Demand, Cost and Efficiency in Urban Bus Operation. (1976)*
4.1.37	*Further Analysis of Trends in Demand, Cost and Efficiency in Urban Public Transport. (1977)*
4.1.39	*Variations in the Demand for Bus and Rail Travel in London up to 1974. (1975)*

4.4 Public Transport - Demonstration Projects and Innovatory Systems.

4.4.48	*Alternative Taxicab Systems: A London Case Study. (1976)*

9.6 Other Sources.

The lists of other sources of information have been arranged in the following order:-

1. Guides to Sources of Transport Information. (9.6.1 -7)

2. Other Information Guides. (9.6.8-20)

3. Directory of Relevant Departments and Organisations.
(9.6.21-134)

   (a) Central Government Departments and Establishments.
   (9.6.21-34)

   (b) Relevant New Town Development Corporations,
   County and District Councils. (9.6.35-43)

   This list is restricted to those authorities
   directly connected with Runcorn, Skelmersdale
   and Telford. For each new town the Development
   Corporation is listed first, followed by the
   relevant County Council and then the District
   Council.

   (c) Passenger Transport Operators. (9.6.44-47)

   The bus operators listed are principally those
   concerned with bus operation in Runcorn,
   Skelmersdale and Telford. London Transport
   Executive and the Eastern Counties Omnibus
   Company have also been listed since reports
   published by these bodies have been included
   in this bibliography.

   (d) University and Polytechnic Departments. (9.6.48-64)

   Only those departments known to be involved
   either currently or in the recent past with
   research on transport or new towns have been
   included.

   (e) Consultants. (9.6.65-78)

   The list consists of firms of consultants whose
   activities are known to include transportation
   planning.

   (f) Other Organisations. (9.6.79-134)

   The list includes a wide range of organisations
   whose work or interests are relevant to various
   aspects of transport and mobility, new towns, or
   research techniques.

9.6   Other Sources.

Guides to Sources of Transport Information.

9.6.1   Little Red Book. [*The] (Annually)
IAN ALLAN LTD., Shepperton, Middlesex.

The directory includes details of all major and most
independent bus operators in Britain; other organisations related to the bus and coach industry; and
major operators in other countries in Western Europe.

9.6.2   National Index of Traffic and Transportation Surveys.
(1975)
DEPARTMENTS OF THE ENVIRONMENT AND TRANSPORT.
Headquarters Library, Information Series No.LIB/INF/
21. October 1975. (98pp.)

The Index was started by the Department of the
Environment Statistics Directorate in 1967, and
updated in 1973, as a reference source for people or
organisations interested in various aspects of
transport policy or research. The Department holds
a detailed record on microfiche of the objectives,
methodology and scope of each survey listed, and these
details are available on application to the Department.
Most of the surveys contained in the Index are local
or regional studies, and the main lists are organised
on a geographical basis by country (England, Scotland,
Wales) and then alphabetically by county according to
six main survey types:- Origin and Destination surveys;
Parking Surveys; Land Use Surveys; Traffic Generation
Surveys; Comprehensive Travel Surveys; and Other Types
of Survey. Within each survey group the studies are
also divided into three time periods:- Pre-1966; 1966-
1969; 1970 and later. DOE sponsored surveys which do
not fall into the regional/local category are listed
separately at the end of the Index. Lists can also
be obtained, on application to the DOE Headquarters
Library Research Section, of all studies within the
Index which cover specific aspects (for instance, all
those in which information on public transport fares
was recorded), or using particular methodologies of
data collection or analysis.

9.6.3   New Directions in Transport: Sources of Information.
(1975)
ASLIB.
London. 1975. (122pp.)

Proceedings of a one-day conference held at the
Library Association, London, 30th October 1973, by
the ASLIB Planning and Transportation Group and the
Reference, Special and Information Section of the
Library Assocation.

9.6.4   Road Safety. (1973)
        DEPARTMENTS OF THE ENVIRONMENT AND TRANSPORT.
        Headquarters Library, Information Series No. LIB/INF/
                                    9. 1973. (15pp.)

9.6.5   Road Traffic Engineering and Control. (1973)
        DEPARTMENTS OF THE ENVIRONMENT AND TRANSPORT.
        Headquarters Library, Information Series No. LIB/INF/
                                    11. 1973. (38pp.)

9.6.6   Transport and Communications. (1975)
        Unit 13 of Social Sciences: A Second Level Course.
                                    Statistical Sources.
        RUBRA,N.
        The Open University. 1975. (152pp.)

        This volume presents a guide to the location and
        content of British published transport data, identi-
        fying their inadequacies and to what extent they can
        be interpolated and disaggregated. It also outlines
        some trends in transport and communications during
        recent decades and considers how far they have been
        influenced, and might be in the future, by economic
        circumstances and planning.Appendices give details
        of fuel consumption by mode and of users of transport
        by industry, and a chronological outline of the major
        Parliamentary measures affecting road transport
        between 1909 and 1973.

9.6.7   U.K. Transport Organisations. (1976)
        DEPARTMENTS OF THE ENVIRONMENT AND TRANSPORT.
        Headquarters Library, Information Series No. LIB/INF/
                                    14A. November 1976. (49pp.)
        Compiled by H.A. PUGH.

        The names, addresses and telephone numbers of U.K.
        organisations concerned with land transport, inland
        waterways and ports are listed by type of transport,
        with separate sections for Government departments and
        for general transport organisations.

Other Information Guides.

9.6.8   Annual List of Publications. (Annually)
        DEPARTMENT OF THE ENVIRONMENT.

        The list gives details of all publications issued by
        the Department each year, and publications of the
        Department of the Environment/Department of Transport
        research establishments. It includes H.M.S.O. and
        Departmental Circulars, Acts and Statutory Instruments.

9.6.9   British Official Publications. (2nd Revised Edition:
                                                     1973)
        PEMBERTON, J.E.
        Pergamon Press. Oxford. 1973. (328pp.)

9.6.10   Guide to Official Statistics. (1976 and 1978)
          CENTRAL STATISTICAL OFFICE.
          H.M.S.O. 1976 and 1978.

          The Guide covers all official and some important non-
          official sources of statistics for the United Kingdom
          and Isle of Man. It includes broad content descrip-
          tions of all relevant publications, regular and ad hoc,
          containing a significant amount of statistical infor-
          mation. The availability of non-published information
          is indicated where this is considered to be of relev-
          ance. The contents are arranged by subject, each
          subject subsection identifying the main sources and
          describing the relevant statistics contained in them.
          A list of Government Department contact points gives
          sources for obtaining additional information. The
          Guide also includes an Alphabetical Keyword Index,
          which includes an entry on new towns, and a
          Bibliography which gives further details of published
          sources (e.g. publisher, frequency of publication,
          price). The Central Statistical Office intends to
          update the Guide at approximately annual intervals.

9.6.11   Hansard. (Daily, Weekly, and Sessional)
          HOUSE OF COMMONS.

          Hansard provides an almost verbatim record of
          Parliamentary debates and of written and oral questions
          and answers in the House of Commons. It is an authori-
          tative and useful source of background material for
          studies of official policy on a wide range of subjects,
          including transport matters and new towns. The answers
          to Parliamentary questions, for example, often include
          specific statistical information provided by relevant
          Government departments which is not always readily
          available through the usual published channels. They
          may also contain references to further sources of
          information. Hansard is indexed by speaker and by
          subject. A consolidated sessional index is published
          as a bound volume which accompanies the final bound
          reprints of the daily and weekly parts, and a weekly
          index is also produced. A separate Hansard reports
          House of Lords debates. This is also published in
          daily and weekly parts and bound sessional volumes,
          with weekly and sessional indexes. A cumulative index
          is also produced.

9.6.12   Information for Planning: Studies Towards the Collection,
          Organisation, and Dissemination of Information for
                                        Planners . (1974)
          UNIVERSITY OF EDINBURGH. DEPARTMENT OF URBAN DESIGN AND
          REGIONAL PLANNING.
          Final Report for the period April 1971 - June 1974.
          OSTI Report No.5198. June 1974. (138pp. plus Appendices.)

9.6.13   Information Series: List of Titles. (1977)
         DEPARTMENTS OF THE ENVIRONMENT AND TRANSPORT.
         Headquarters Library. March 1977. (4pp.)

         Eighteen titles available in the Series as at March
         1977 are listed, with dates of publication.   The
         Information Series consists of lists of the main
         organisations and sources of published information
         on various topics relevant to the Departments of the
         Environment and Transport, prepared by the staff of
         the DOE/DTP. Library Service.

         (see refs. 9.2.15, 9.4.3, 9.6.2, 9.6.4, 9.6.5, 9.6.7
         above, and 9.6.14, 9.6.15 and 9.6.20 below.)

9.6.14   New Towns in the U.K. (1977)
         DEPARTMENTS OF THE ENVIRONMENT AND TRANSPORT.
         Headquarters Library, Information Series. No. LIB/INF/
                          12. September 1977. (124pp.)
         Compiled by S.KIDD.

         The guide lists and outlines the work of the main
         departments and organisations concerned with new
         town planning and research, and describes the most
         important relevant statistical and other published
         information sources.   Indexes of titles and of
         organisations are included.   An Appendix provides a
         table showing the local authority area(s) in which
         each new town in England, Wales and Scotland is
         situated (both pre - and post - local government
         reorganisation in April 1974 in England and Wales,
         and May 1975 in Scotland).

9.6.15   Quality of Life in Urban Settlements. (1974)
         DEPARTMENTS OF THE ENVIRONMENT AND TRANSPORT.
         Headquarters Library. Information Series No. LIB/INF/
                          16. 1974.   (28pp.)

9.6.16   Sourcebook of Planning Information: a discussion of
         sources of information for use in urban and regional
         planning and in allied fields. (1971)
         WHITE, B.
         Clive Bingley. London. 1971. (632pp.)

         A chapter on Development Plans and Reports (Ch.9)
         contains a discussion of a number of new town master
         plans and other new town plans and studies, including
         those for Skelmersdale (pp.197-8), Runcorn (pp.198-
         9) Telford (pp.195-6), and Dawley (pp.194-5). Chapter
         11, on Documentary Sources, includes a useful subsec-
         tion on Traffic and Transportation Planning (pp.489-
         512).   Other chapters of particular relevance are
         those on Statistical Sources (Ch.10); Journals (Ch.12)-
         which includes journals in related subjects such as
         economics, sociology and politics as well as those
         directly concerned with planning; and Guides to
         Sources of Information (Ch.13.)

9.6.17　Sources of Economic and Business Statistics. (1972)
EDWARDS, B.
Heinemann. London. 1972. (272pp.)

The book covers the main economic and business
statistics available in this country (at 1972),
describing their origin, possible uses, and mode of
publication.　An introductory chapter on Government
statistical sources discusses where the statistics
are, how they have been obtained, and some limitations
and pitfalls in their use.　Other relevant sections
include ch.7. on Transport Statistics (pp.140-163)
and ch.10 on the Government's Family Expenditure
Survey. (pp.220-224).

9.6.18　Sources of Social Statistics. (1974)
EDWARDS, B.
Heinemann. London. (276pp.)

The second chapter discusses some of the main class-
ification systems used in economic and social statis-
tical series, including the Standard Industrial
Classification; Classification of Occupations;
Registrar-General's Socio-economic Groups; and the
Registrar-General's Economic Planning Regions.
Population and vital statistics and housing statis-
tics are among the other statistical sources examined.

9.6.19　Sources of Statistics [*General] (1976)
LOCK, G.F.
Vol.V of: Reviews of United Kingdom Statistical Sources.
(ed. W.F. Maunder).
Published for the Royal Statistical Society and the
Social Science Research Council by Heinemann
Educational Books Ltd: London. 1976. (61pp.)

The volume provides an overview of the whole field of
economic and social statistical sources.

9.6.20　Town and Country Planning. (1974)
DEPARTMENTS OF THE ENVIRONMENT AND TRANSPORT.
Headquarters Library. Information Series No. LIB/INF/
6. 1974. (38pp.)

Directory of Relevant Departments and Organisations.

(a) CENTRAL GOVERNMENT DEPARTMENTS AND ESTABLISHMENTS

9.6.21　BUILDING RESEARCH ESTABLISHMENT. (Department of the
Environment)
Bucknall's Lane, Garston, Watford WD2 7JR.
Hertfordshire. (Garston) 09273-74040

9.6.22　CENTRAL STATISTICAL OFFICE.
Great George Street, London SW1P 3AQ.
01-233-3000

9.6.23   COMMISSION FOR THE NEW TOWNS.
          Glen House, Stag Place, London SW1E 5AJ
          01-834-8034

9.6.24   DEPARTMENT OF THE ENVIRONMENT.
          2, Marsham Street, London SW1P 3EB
          01-212-3434
          (See also refs. 9.6.21 above, and 9.6.25, 9.6.29
                              and 9.6.32-4 below.)

9.6.25   DEPARTMENTS OF THE ENVIRONMENT AND TRANSPORT: Library
                                                        Services.
          2, Marsham Street, London SW1P 3EB
          01-212-4847. (General Enquiries).
          01-212-4657 and 4328 (Research Section).

9.6.26   DEPARTMENT OF TRANSPORT.
          2, Marsham Street, London SW1P 3EB
          01-212-3434
          (See also refs. 9.6.25 above, and 9.6.27 and 9.6.32-
                                                      4 below.)

9.6.27   DEPARTMENT OF TRANSPORT: NORTH WEST REGIONAL OFFICE.
          Sunley Building, Piccadilly Plaza, Manchester M1 4BE
          061-832-9111

9.6.28   NATIONAL ECONOMIC DEVELOPMENT OFFICE. (NEDO)
          Millbank Tower, 21-24 Millbank, London SW1P 4QX
          01-211-7074 and 5582.

9.6.29   NEW TOWNS DIRECTORATE. (Department of the Environment)
          Becket House, 1 Lambeth Palace Road, London SE1 7ER
          01-928-7855

9.6.30   NORTH WEST ECONOMIC PLANNING BOARD.
          Sunley Building, Piccadilly Plaza, Manchester M1 4BE
          061-832-9111   (Research Section x. 346)

9.6.31   OFFICE OF POPULATION CENSUSES AND SURVEYS.
          St.Catherine's House, Kingsway, London WC2B 6JP
          01-242-0262

          Census Division, Customer Services Section.
          Segensworth Road, Titchfield, Fareham, Hampshire
          PO 15 5RR.(Titchfield) 032-94-42511 (Supply of special
                      and unpublished statistics: x. 231 and 296)

          ROAD RESEARCH LABORATORY (RRL): see TRANSPORT AND ROAD
          RESEARCH LABORATORY - ref. 9.6.34 below.

9.6.32   TRAFFIC COMMISSIONERS FOR THE NORTH WESTERN TRAFFIC
          AREA. (Departments of the Environment and Transport.)
          Arkwright House, Parsonage Gardens, Deansgate,
          Manchester M60 9AN
          061.832-8644

9.6.33   TRAFFIC COMMISSIONERS FOR THE WEST MIDLAND TRAFFIC
          AREA. (Departments of the Environment and Transport)
          Cumberland House, 200 Broad Street, Birmingham B15 1TD
          021-643-5011

9.6.34   TRANSPORT AND ROAD RESEARCH LABORATORY (TRRL)
          (Departments of the Environment and Transport)
          Old Wokingham Road, Crowthorne, Berkshire RG11 6AU
          (Crowthorne) 034-46-3131.

          Known as the ROAD RESEARCH LABORATORY (RRL) up to 1972

    (b)   RELEVANT NEW TOWN DEVELOPMENT CORPORATIONS, COUNTY
          AND DISTRICT AUTHORITIES.

9.6.35   RUNCORN DEVELOPMENT CORPORATION.
          Chapel Street, Runcorn WA7 5AR, Cheshire
          (Runcorn) 092-85-73477

9.6.36   CHESHIRE COUNTY COUNCIL.
          County Hall, Chester CH1 1SF
          (Chester) 0244-602424

          Highways and Transportation Department.
          Backford Hall, near Chester CH1 6EA
          (Chester) 0244-59446

          Planning Department.
          Commerce House, Hunter Street, Chester CH1 1SN
          (Chester) 0244-603133

9.6.37   HALTON DISTRICT COUNCIL.
          Municipal Buildings, Kingsway, Widnes WA8 7QF
          051-424-2061

9.6.38   SKELMERSDALE DEVELOPMENT CORPORATION.
          Pennylands, Skelmersdale, Lancs. WN8 8AR
          (Skelmersdale) 0695-24242

9.6.39   LANCASHIRE COUNTY COUNCIL.
          P.O. Box 78, County Hall, Preston PR1 8XJ
          (Preston) 0772-54868

          County Surveyor's Department, Transportation Section.
          P.O. Box 9, Guild House, Cross Street, Preston PR1 8RD
          (Preston) 0772-54733

9.6.40   WEST LANCASHIRE DISTRICT COUNCIL.
          Council Offices, 52 Derby Street, Ormskirk L39 2OF
          0695-72444

9.6.41   TELFORD DEVELOPMENT CORPORATION
          Department of Engineering Services.
          Priorslee Hall, Telford TF2 9NT, Salop.
          (Telford) 0952-613131

          Social Development and Planning Departments.
          Malinslee House, Telford TF3 4LQ, Salop.
          (Telford) 0952-501000

9.6.42   SALOP COUNTY COUNCIL.
          Shirehall, Abbey Foregate, Shrewsbury SY2 6NII
          (Shrewsbury) 0743-222374

9.6.43   THE WREKIN DISTRICT COUNCIL.
          Malinslee House, Telford TF3 4LQ, Salop.
          (Telford) 0952-505051

   (c)   PASSENGER TRANSPORT OPERATORS.

9.6.44   BRITISH RAILWAYS BOARD.
          222 Marylebone Road, London NW1 6JJ
          01-262-3232

          British Railways Board Research Department.
          The Railway Technical Centre, London Road, Derby
          DE2 8UP. (Derby) 0332-49203

          CROSVILLE MOTOR SERVICES LTD: See NATIONAL BUS COMPANY-
                                            ref. 9.6.47 below.

          EASTERN COUNTIES OMNIBUS COMPANY: See NATIONAL BUS
                                   COMPANY - ref. 9.6.47 below.

9.6.45   LONDON TRANSPORT EXECUTIVE.
          55 Broadway, London SW1
          01-222-5600

9.6.46   MERSEYSIDE PASSENGER TRANSPORT EXECUTIVE.
          24 Hatton Garden, Liverpool 3
          051-236-7411

          MIDLAND RED BUS COMPANY: see NATIONAL BUS COMPANY -
                                            ref. 9.6.47 below.

9.6.47   NATIONAL BUS COMPANY.
          25 New Street Square, London EC4A 3AP
          01-583-9177

          Marketing and Operational Research.
          Deanery Mews, Minster Precincts, Peterborough PE1 1XX
          (Peterborough)   0733-54994

          RELEVANT NBC SUBSIDARIES.
          Crosville Motor Services Ltd.,
          Crane Wharf, Chester CH1 3SQ
          (Chester) 0244-315400

          Eastern Counties Omnibus Company.
          P.O. Box No.10, 79 Thorpe Road, Norwich NR1 1UB
          (Norwich) 0603-60421

          Midland Red Bus Company.
          Midland House, 1 Vernon Road, Edgbaston, Birmingham
          B16 9SJ. 021-454-4808

Ribble Motor Services Ltd.
Frenchwood Avenue, Preston, Lancs. PR1 4LU
(Preston) 0772-54754

(d)   UNIVERSITY AND POLYTECHNIC DEPARTMENTS.

9.6.48   BIRMINGHAM UNIVERSITY.
Centre for Urban and Regional Studies
Selly Wick House, Selly Wick Road, Birmingham B29 7JF
021-472-4281

Department of Transportation and Environmental
                                    Planning.
P.O. Box 363, Birmingham B15 2TT
021-472-1301

9.6.49   CAMBRIDGE UNIVERSITY.
Martin Centre for Architectural and Urban Studies
6   Chaucer Road, Cambridge CB2 2EB
(Cambridge) 0223-69501

(Formerly the Centre for Land Use and Built Form
                                    Studies)

CENTRAL LONDON POLYTECHNIC: see POLYTECHNIC OF
CENTRAL LONDON - ref. 9.6.61 below.

9.6.50   CRANFIELD INSTITUTE OF TECHNOLOGY.
Centre for Transport Studies
Cranfield, Bedford MK43 OAL
(Bedford) 0234-750111

9.6.51   DURHAM UNIVERSITY.
North East Area Study
44-45, Old Elvet, Durham DH1 3HY
0385-64466

9.6.52   LEEDS POLYTECHNIC.
School of Town Planning
14 St. Paul's Street, Leeds 1
0532-458481

9.6.53   LEEDS UNIVERSITY.
Institute for Transport Studies
Woodhouse Lane, Leeds LS2 9JT
0532-31751

9.6.54   LIVERPOOL POLYTECHNIC.
Business Research Centre
Byrom Street,
Liverpool L3 3AF
051-207-3581

Department of Town and Country Planning
53 Victoria Street
Liverpool L1 6EY
051-709-0571

434

9.6.55   LONDON UNIVERSITY.
          Imperial College of Science and Technology
          South Kensington, London SW7 2BX
          01-589-5111

          University College.
          Gower Street, London WC1E 6BT
          01-387-7050

          University College: Traffic Studies Group.
          20 Flaxman Terrace, London WC1
          01-387-7050

9.6.56   LOUGHBOROUGH UNIVERSITY OF TECHNOLOGY.
          Institute for Consumer Ergonomics
          Loughborough, Leicestershire. LE11 3TU
          (Loughborough)   0509-67812

9.6.57   NEWCASTLE UPON TYNE UNIVERSITY.
          Department of Civil Engineering: Transport Operations
          Research Group. Claremont Road, Newcastle Upon Tyne
          NE1 7RU.   0632-28511

9.6.58   OPEN UNIVERSITY.
          New Towns Study Unit
          Walton Hall, Milton Keynes, Bucks. MK7 6AA
          0908-63335

9.6.59   OXFORD POLYTECHNIC.
          Headington, Oxford OX3 OBP
          (Oxford) 0865-64777

9.6.60   OXFORD UNIVERSITY.
          Transport Studies Unit
          11 Bevington Road, Oxford OX2 6NB
          (Oxford) 0865-511038

9.6.61   POLYTECHNIC OF CENTRAL LONDON.
          Transport Studies Group
          35 Marylebone Road, London NW1 5LS
          01-486-5811

9.6.62   READING UNIVERSITY.
          Department of Geography
          Whiteknights Park, Reading RG6 2AH
          (Reading) 0734-85123

9.6.63   STRATHCLYDE UNIVERSITY.
          Department of Operational Research
          Livingstone Tower, 26 Richmond Street, Glasgow G1 1XH
          041-552-4400

          Strathclyde Area Survey.
          McCance Building, Glasgow G1 1XQ
          041-552-4400

          UNIVERSITIES TRANSPORT STUDIES GROUP: See ref. 9.6.134
                                                      below.

9.6.64 **WARWICK UNIVERSITY.**
Urban Transport Research Group
Gibbet Hill Road, Coventry CV4 7AL, West Midlands.
(Coventry) 0203-24011

(e) CONSULTANTS

9.6.65 **ALASTAIR DICK AND ASSOCIATES.**
24 Gravel Hill, Leatherhead KT22 7HG, Surrey
Leatherhead 79399
and:
23 Lower Belgrave Street, London SW1W ONS
01-730-4976/6731

9.6.66 **ARTHUR ANDERSEN AND COMPANY.**
1 Surrey Street, London WC2R 2PS
01-836-1200

9.6.67 **C.A.M.** (Computer Aided Marketing)
Ebury Gate, 23 Lower Belgrave Street, London SW1W ONS
01-730-4544

9.6.68 **COLIN BUCHANAN AND PARTNERS.**
47 Princes Gate, London SW7
01-589-8841

9.6.69 **FREEMAN FOX AND ASSOCIATES.**
28-30 Grosvenor Gardens, London SW1W ODY
01-730-4500

9.6.70 **JAMIESON MACKAY AND PARTNERS.**
3 Mandeville Place, Wigmore Street, London W1M 5LB
01-487-5331

Queen Anne House, Queen Square, Bristol.
0272-299044

20 Royal Terrace, Glasgow G3 7NY
041-332-3868

9.6.71 **LOGICA LTD.**
64 Newman Street, London W1P 3PG
01-580-8361

9.6.72 **MARTIN AND VOORHEES ASSOCIATES.**
112 Strand, London WC2R OAA
01-836-0871

9.6.73 **METRA CONSULTING GROUP.**
Ebury Gate, 23 Lower Belgrave Street, London SW1W ONS
01-730-0855

9.6.74 **NATHANIEL LICHFIELD AND PARTNERS.**
The Old Brewery, 2 Old Brewery Mews, Hampstead High
Street, London NW3 1PZ
01-794-7751/4

9.6.75   PEAT, MARWICK, MITCHELL, AND COMPANY.
          80 Goswell Road, London EC1V 7DB
          01-253-8505

9.6.76   SCOTT WILSON KIRKPATRICK AND PARTNERS.
          Scott House, Basing View, Basingstoke RG21 2JG
          (Basingstoke) 0256-61161

9.6.77   S.I.A.
          Ebury Gate, 23 Lower Belgrave Street; London SW1W ONS
          01-730-4544

9.6.78   R.TRAVERS MORGAN AND PARTNERS.
          Wellington House, 125 Strand, London WC2R OAR
          01-836-5474

   (f)   OTHER ORGANISATIONS

9.6.79   AGE CONCERN (National Old People's Welfare Council)
          Bernard Sunley House, 60 Pitcairn Road, Mitcham,
                                        Surrey CR4 3LL
          01-640-5431

9.6.80   AMERICAN SOCIETY OF CIVIL ENGINEERS. (A.S.C.E.)
          345 East 47th Street, New York 10017, U.S.A.

9.6.81   ARCHITECTURAL ASSOCIATION.
          34-36, Bedford Square, London WC1B 3ES
          01-636-0974

9.6.82   ASSOCIATION OF PUBLIC PASSENGER TRANSPORT OPERATORS.(Inc.)
          (Formerly Municipal Passenger Transport Association)
          6 Parkway, Chelmsford, Essex CM2 ONN
          (Chelmsford) 0245-58191

9.6.83   ASSOCIATION OF SPECIAL LIBRARIES AND INFORMATION
                                        BUREAUX (ASLIB)
          Planning and Transportation Group
          3 Belgrave Square, London SW1X 8PL
          01-235-5050

9.6.84   BRITISH CYCLING BUREAU.
          Greater London House, Hampstead Road, London NW1 7QX
          01-387-6868

9.6.85   BRITISH LEYLAND U.K. LTD.
          Passenger Service Vehicles.
          Southall, Middlesex
          01-574-2424

          Truck and Bus Division.
          Hough Lane, Leyland, Preston, Lancs.
          (Leyland) 077-44-21400

9.6.86   BRITISH ROAD FEDERATION LTD.
          26 Manchester Square, London W1M 5RF
          01-935-0221

9.6.87   BRITISH STANDARDS INSTITUTION.(BSI)
          2 Park Street, London W1A 2BS
          01-629-9000

9.6.88   CENTRAL COUNCIL FOR THE DISABLED.
          34 Eccleston Square, London SW1V 1PE
          01-0834-0747

9.6.89   CENTRE FOR ENVIRONMENTAL STUDIES.(CES)
          62 Chandos Place, London WC2N 4HH
          01-240-3424

9.6.90   CHARTERED INSTITUTE OF PUBLIC FINANCE AND ACCOUNTANCY.
          (Formerly the Institute of Municipal Treasurers and
                                                  Accountants)
          1 Buckingham Place, London SW1E 6HS
          01-834-6433

9.6.91   CHARTERED INSTITUTE OF TRANSPORT.
          (Formerly the Institute of Transport)
          80 Portland Place, London W1N 4DP
          01-580-5216

9.6.92   CHICAGO TRANSIT AUTHORITY.
          Merchandise Mart Plaza, P.O. Box 3555, Chicago,
                                    Illinois 60654, U.S.A.
          312-664-7200

9.6.93   CONFEDERATION OF BRITISH ROAD PASSENGER TRANSPORT LTD.
          Sardinia House, Lincoln's Inn Fields, London WC2
          01-831-7546

9.6.94   CONSUMERS' ASSOCIATION.
          14 Buckingham Street, London WC2N 6DS
          01-839-1222

9.6.95   EUROPEAN CONFERENCE OF MINISTERS OF TRANSPORT.(ECMT)
          3 Rue Andre Pascal, Paris 16e, France.

9.6.96   FRIENDS OF THE EARTH LTD.
          9 Poland Street, London W1V 3DG
          01-434-1648

9.6.97   GENERAL MOTORS RESEARCH LABORATORIES.
          Technical Information Department
          Warren, Michigan 48090, U.S.A

9.6.98   GREATER LONDON COUNCIL.
          County Hall, London SE1 7PB
          01-633-6884

          HIGHWAY RESEARCH BOARD. (HRB): See TRANSPORTATION
          RESEARCH BOARD - ref. 9.6.132 below.

          INSTITUTE OF MUNICIPAL TREASURERS AND ACCOUNTANTS: See
          CHARTERED INSTITUTE OF PUBLIC FINANCE AND ACCOUNTANCY-
                                        ref. 9.6.90 above.

9.6.99   INSTITUTE OF ROAD TRANSPORT ENGINEERS.
            1 Cromwell Place, London SW7 2JF
            01-589-3744

            INSTITUTE OF TRANSPORT: See CHARTERED INSTITUTE OF
                                    TRANSPORT 9.6.91 above.

9.6.100   INSTITUTION OF CIVIL ENGINEERS.
            1-7 Great George Street, London SW1P 3AA
            01-839-3611

9.6.101   INSTITUTION OF HIGHWAY ENGINEERS.
            14 Queen Anne's Gate, London SW1H 9AF
            01-839-3582

9.6.102   INSTITUTION OF MECHANICAL ENGINEERS.
            1 Birdcage Walk, London SW1
            01-839-1211

9.6.103   INSTITUTION OF MUNICIPAL ENGINEERS.
            25 Eccleston Square, London SW1V 1NX
            01-834-5082

9.6.104   LICENSED TAXI DRIVERS ASSOCIATION.
            9 Woodfield Road, London W9
            01-286-1046

9.6.105   LOCAL GOVERNMENT OPERATIONAL RESEARCH UNIT.(LGORU)
            (a branch of the Royal Institute of Public
                                        Administration)
            201 King's Road, Reading RG1 4LH
            (Reading) 0734-661234

            Northern Group.
            Quay House, Quay Street, Manchester M3 3JH
            061-834-7253

9.6.106   MARKET RESEARCH SOCIETY.
            51 Charles Street, London W1
            01-499-1913

9.6.107   MEDICAL COMMISSION ON ACCIDENT PREVENTION.(MCAP)
            50 Old Brompton Road, London SW7 3EA
            01-584-9240

9.6.108   MOTOR INDUSTRY RESEARCH ASSOCIATION. (MIRA)
            Watling Street, Nuneaton, CV10 OTU, Warwickshire
            (Nuneaton) 0682-68541

            MUNICIPAL PASSENGER TRANSPORT ASSOCIATION:See
            ASSOCIATION OF PUBLIC PASSENGER TRANSPORT OPERATORS.
                                    (Inc.)-ref. 9.6.82 above.

9.6.109   NATIONAL CONSUMER COUNCIL.
            18 Queen Anne's Gate, London SW1H 9AA
            01-930-5752

9.6.110 NATIONAL COUNCIL FOR THE OMNIBUS INDUSTRY.
         c/o National Bus Company
         25 New Street Square, London EC4A 3AP
         01-583-9177

         NATIONAL OLD PEOPLE'S WELFARE COUNCIL: See AGE
         CONCERN - ref. 9.6.79 above.

9.6.111 NEW TOWNS ASSOCIATION.
         Glen House, Stag Place, London SW1E 5AJ
         01-828-1104

9.6.112 NOP MARKET RESEARCH LTD.
         76-86 Strand, London WC2R ODZ
         01-836-1511

9.6.113 OMNIBUS SOCIETY.
         216 Hastings Road, Bromley Common, Kent BR2 8QH.
                                            (Publications)
         and:
         78 Nightingale Road, Petts Wood West, Orpington,
                              Kent BR5 1BQ (Membership)

9.6.114 OPINION RESEARCH CENTRE. (ORC)
         30 Welbeck Street, London W1M 8AB
         01-486-5151

9.6.115 ORGANISATION FOR ECONOMIC CO-OPERATION AND DEVELOPMENT.
         3 Rue Andre Pascal, Paris 16e, France   (OECD)

9.6.116 OWNER DRIVERS' SOCIETY. (Taxi trade)
         1 Buckingham Gate, London SW1
         01-834-3976

9.6.117 PEDESTRIANS' ASSOCIATION FOR ROAD SAFETY.
         166 Shaftesbury Avenue, London WC2H 8JH
         01-836-7220

9.6.118 PLANNING AND TRANSPORT RESEARCH COMPUTATION CO., LTD.
                                            (PTRC)
         109, Bedford Chambers, King Street, London WC2
         01-836-2208

9.6.119 POLITICAL AND ECONOMIC PLANNING. (PEP)
         12 Upper Belgrave Street, London SW1X 8BB
         01-235-5271

         [Now called POLICY STUDIES INSTITUTE (PSI).]

9.6.120 REGIONAL STUDIES ASSOCIATION.
         62 Chandos Place, London WC2N 4HH
         01-240-3424

9.6.121 RESEARCH SERVICES LTD.
         Station House, Harrow Road, Stonebridge Park,
         Wembley HA9 6DE
         01-240-2450

9.6.122   ROYAL INSTITUTE OF BRITISH ARCHITECTS. (RIBA)
          66 Portland Place, London W1N 4AD
          01-580-5533

9.6.123   ROYAL INSTITUTE OF CHARTERED SURVEYORS.(RICS)
          12 Great George Street, London SW1P 3AD
          01-839-5600

          ROYAL INSTITUTE OF PUBLIC ADMINISTRATION: See LOCAL
          GOVERNMENT OPERATIONAL RESEARCH UNIT (LEORU) - ref.
                                          9.6.105 above.

9.6.124   ROYAL SOCIETY   FOR THE PREVENTION OF ACCIDENTS.
                                              (ROSPA)
          Royal Oak Centre, Brighton Road, Purley, Surrey
          CR2 2UR
          01-668-4272

9.6.125   ROYAL TOWN PLANNING INSTITUTE. (RTPI)
          (Formerly the Town Planning Institute)
          26 Portland Place, London W1N 4BE
          01-636-9107

9.6.126   SOCIAL AND COMMUNITY PLANNING RESEARCH. (SCPR)
          10, Duncan Terrace, London N1 8BE
          01-278-6943

9.6.127   TOWN AND COUNTRY PLANNING ASSOCIATION.   (TCPA)
          17 Carlton House Terrace, London SW1Y 5AH
          01-930-8903/4/5

          TOWN PLANNING INSTITUTE: See ROYAL TOWN PLANNING
                              INSTITUTE - ref. 9.6.125 above.

9.6.128   TRANSPORT AND ENVIRONMENT STUDIES. (TEST)
          24 Floral Street, London WC2E 9DS
          01-240-1307

9.6.129   TRANSPORT AND GENERAL WORKERS UNION.(TGWU)
          Transport House, Smith Square, London SW1
          01-828-7788

9.6.130   TRANSPORT SALARIED STAFFS ASSOCIATION.
          10 Melton Street, London NW1
          01-387-2101

9.6.131   TRANSPORT 2000.
          40 James Street, London W1 5HS
          01-486-8523

9.6.132   TRANSPORTATION RESEARCH BOARD. (TRB)
          (Formerly Highway Research Board)
          National Academy of Sciences
          2101 Constitution Avenue, N.W., Washington D.C.,
          20418, U.S.A.

9.6.133   UNION INTERNATIONALE DES TRANSPORTS PUBLICS.(UITP)
          (International Union of Public Transport)
          19 Avenue de l'Uruguay, Brussels 5, Belgium.

9.6.134   UNIVERSITIES TRANSPORT STUDIES GROUP. (UTSG)

          University College London: Traffic Studies Group
          20 Flaxman Terrace, London WC 1
          01-387-7050

9.6   Subsidiary References.

1.2   New Towns - Non-Transport Aspects.

1.2.33   New Towns: the British Experience. (1972)
1.2.39   Recreational Planning in New Communities: A Review of British
*   Experience. (1975)*
1.2.48   Town and Country Planning. (February 1978)
1.2.50   Commission for the New Towns: Annual Reports. (Annually)
1.2.51   Annual Reports of the Development Corporations in England and
*   Wales. (Annually from 1947).*

3.4   Transport and Mobility - General and Miscellaneous.

3.4.1   Environment and Behavior: planning and everyday life. (1977)

9.2   Bibliographies.

9.2.15   Transport: Sources of information together with a short
*   bibliography. (1973)*

Index of Authors.

INDEX OF AUTHORS.

Bacalis, G.J. (Stevens, R.D. and) 1.1.21
Bainbridge, D.A. 9.2.19
Bains, M.A. 7.1.19
Baker, R.C. 4.4.24
Balachandra, M. (Dais, J.L. and) 4.3.31
Balkus, K. 4.2.7
Bamford, T.J.G. (and Wigan, M.R.) 3.1.99
Banaka, W.H. 8.1.44
Barber, J. (and Searle, G.) 3.1.111
Bardagjy, J.C. (Diffrient, N., Tilley, A.R. and) 4.3.28
Bardsley, M. (Vincent, R.A., Layfield, R.E. and) 2.1.6
Barnett, D.C. 4.1.80
Barry, W.S. 4.2.26
Bartwell, F.T. (and Clarke, M.J.) 4.3.66
Basildon Development Corporation 2.4.3
Bass, F.M. et al 8.1.56
Batchelor, G.H. 4.3.59
Bates, J.J. (Collins, P.H. and) 4.1.92
Bauer, H.J. 4.1.67, 4.3.25
Baum, H.J. 4.1.62
Baumann, D. et al 1.2.22
Baxter, R.S. (and Lenzi,G.) 3.3.7
Beaumont Lewis, C. 4.4.46
Beck, R.J. (and Wood, D) 8.3.3
Beckmann, M.J. (and Burns, L.) 5.1.10
Beeching, Lord 7.1.63
Beesley, M.E. 3.1.107; (and Kain, J.F.) 3.3.44; (Foster, C.D.
                                     and) 8.2.17
Beetham, A. 4.1.33
Beier, F.J. 4.2.35
Belkin, M. (and Liberman, S.) 8.1.79
Bell, C.R. (Provins, K.A. and) 4.3.18
Bell, M.C. 4.3.40
Belson, W.A. 8.1.87, 8.1.91, 8.1.113; (and Thompson, B.A.)
                                     9.2.35
Bendixson,T. 2.4.32, 4.4.2, 6.1.2, 6.1.13
Bennet, R.F. 4.2.3, 4.4.43; (and McCorquodale,D.) 4.5.16
Bent, D. (Nie, N.H., - , and Hull, C.) 8.1.106
Bentley, G.A. (-, Bruce, A.J. and Jones, D.R.) 3.1.36
Benwell, M. 3.2.11, 3.2.12
Beranek, L.L. (and Miller, L.N.) 4.3.41
Berent, P.H. 8.1.37
Bermingham, T.P. (Maw, J.R., Bradley, J. and) 4.1.85
Berrett, B. 1.1.11
Berthoud, R. 2.1.10, 8.3.24; (and Jowell,R.) 2.1.24
Best, R. 1.2.33
Betts, T.J. (and Holmes, K.) 4.5.13
Bierman, D.E. 9.2.17
Birmingham University [see: University of Birmingham]
Bishop, D. 8.3.34
Black, I. (Smith, M.G., McIntosh, P.T. and) 4.1.55
Black, S. 4.3.30
Blackman, John, Associates 7.1.56
Blumenfeld , H. 3.3.20

Buchanan, C.D. 3.3.19
Buchanan, C.M. et.al 2.3.5
Buchanan Report 7.1.73
Bucher, R. (-, Fritz, C.E. and Quarantelli, E.L.) 8.1.111
Buck, T. 4.4.45
Buckinghamshire County Council 4.4.31
Buckles, P.A. 2.4.55, 2.4.58, 3.1.24
Building Research Establishment/Station 1.2.11, 1.2.41,
        3.1.36, 3.2.33, 3.2.46, 3.2.48, 8.1.63, 9.3.4, 9.4.9
Buisson, C. 2.4.54
Bull, H.C. (Archer, P.R., -, and Lucarotti, P.S.K.) 5.1.1;
        (Knight, D., Slevin, R. and) 4.2.27; (Thomas, K. and)
                                    4.5.1
Bullock, N. (-, Dickens, P., Shapcott, M., and Steadman, P.)
                                    3.1.116
Bunker, R.C. 2.4.62
Burby, III, R. (and Weiss, S.F.) 1.2.24
Burckardt, J.E. (and Eby, C.L.) 3.1.68
Burns, L. (and Golob, T.F.) 3.3.3; (-, Golob, T.F. and
        Nicolaidis, G.) 5.1.11; (Beckmann, M.J. and) 5.1.10
Burns, T. (and Stalker, G.M.) 4.2.24
Bursey, N.C. (Mullen,P., -, and White, M.T.) 2.3.7
Burt, M.E. 3.3.33
Burton, T.L. (and Cherry, G.E.) 8.1.104
Butler, J. (Morton-Williams, J. and) 2.4.14
Butt, K.U. (Kirby, R.F., -, Kemp, M.A., McGillivray, R.G.
        and Wohl, M.) 4.4.35
Byron, C.H. 2.4.3

Calouste Gulbenkian Foundation [see: Gulbenkian Foundation]
Cambridge University [see: University of Cambridge]
Campbell, D.T. 8.1.18
Camden, London Borough of 4.1.27
Camps, F.E. (and Lawrence, D.R.) 5.1.15
Cannell, C.F. (Kahn, R.L. and) 8.1.43
Canter, D. (and Tagg, S.K.) 8.3.11
Cantilli. E.J. 4.3.14
Canty, E.T. 4.4.27; (and Sobey, A.J.) 4.4.32; (Constantino,
                D.P., Dobson, R. and) 3.1.42;
                (Golob, T.F., -, and Gustafson, R.L.)
                3.1.18
Carnegie-Mellon University [see: University, Carnegie-Mellon]
Carp, F.M. 3.2.3, 3.2.39
Carstens, J. P. et al 4.3.8
Cartwright, D.P. 8.1.74
Casper, U. 1.2.29
Central Council for the Disabled 3.2.8
Central Housing Advisory Committee 1.2.53
Central London Polytechnic [see: Polytechnic of Central
                                    London]
Central Statistical Office 3.1.116, 8.1.117, 9.5.15,
                9.5.20, 9.5.22, 9.5.23, 9.6.10
Centre for Environmental Studies (C.E.S.) 1.2.9, 1.2.15,
                3.1.46, 3.3.51, 7.1.25, 9.2.7, 9.4.10
Centre for Land Use and Built Form Studies [see: University
                                of Cambridge]
C.E.S. [see: Centre for Environmental Studies]

447

Chamberlin , Powell & Bon (-, Shankland, G. and Jones, D.G.)
3.2.26
Champion, A.G.   1.2.25
Channon, C. (Joyce, T. and) 8.1.57
Chapanis, A. (Morgan, C.T., Cook, J.S., -, and Lund, M.W.)
4.3.23
Chapin, S. (Brail, R.K. and) 3.3.9
Chapman, H. (Lichfield, N. and) 2.4.64, 3.3.12
Charles River Associates 3.1.78
Chartered Institute of Public Finance and Accountancy 4.1.88,
9.5.19
Chartered Institute of Transport 9.2.5, 9.2.12
Chave, E.J. (Thurstone, L.L. and) 8.1.13
Chave, S.P.W. (Lord Taylor and) 1.2.19
Cheesman, R. (-, Lindsay, W. and de Porzecanski, M.) 1.2.34;
(de Porzecanski, M., -, and Lindsay, W.) 1.2.35;
(Lindsay, W., -, and de Porzecanski, M.) 1.2.28
Cherry, G.E. (Burton, T.L. and) 8.1.104
Cheslow, M.D. 3.1.77
Chicago Transit Authority 4.4.45
Chidsey, K.D. (Shackel, B., -, and Shipley,P.) 4.3.9
Chisholm, M.et al (eds.) 3.2.57
Chu, C. 9.2.7
Churchill, J.D.C. 1.1.3, 7.1.26
Civic Trust for the North West 2.2.9
Clapp, R.G. (-, Holligan, P.E.,Jain, S.C., and Lippke, B.R.)
8.1.53
Clark, J.M. (Ashford, N.J. and) 8.2.20
Clarke, M.J. 4.3.10; (Bartwell, F.T.and) 4.3.66; (Oborne,
D.J. and) 8.1.84, 8.1.85
Claxton, E.C. 6.1.3, 6.1.11
Clayton, D.G.E. 4.2.5
Clyde, C. (Rees, F.J., Dix, M. and) 8.1.10
Cobbe, R. 4.1.44
Coe, G.A. (and Jackson, R.L.) 4.1.22; (Jackson, R.L., -,
and Finnamore, A.J.) 4.1.20
Colborne, H.V. 6.1.10
Cole, W.S. (and Tyson, W.J.) 7.1.7
Coleman, A.H. (Millward,C. -, and Dunford, J.E.) 4.1.70
Coleman, S.D. 2.4.10
Coles, O.B. (Wabe, J.S. and) 4.1.32
Colin Buchanan. [see: Buchanan, Colin]
College of General Practioners 1.2.14
Collier, J.C. 7.1.32
Collins, J. 9.2.3
Collins, L. (and Montgomery, C.) 8.1.66
Collins, M.F. (and Pharoah, T.M.) 7.1.30
Collins, P.H. (and Bates, J.J.) 4.1.92; (and Flower, S.P.)
5.1.16; (and Lindsay, J.F.) 4.1.59; (Wagon, D.J.
and) 4.1.71
Commission for the New Towns 1.2.50
Commonwealth Bureau of Roads [Australia] 3.1.19, 4.2.48
Conover, D.W. (Woodson, W.E. and) 4.3.22

Constantine, T.   3.4.4
Constantino, D.P. (-, Dobson, R. and Canty, E.T.) 3.1.42
Consumers' Association   4.1.82
Cook, J.S. (Morgan, C.T., -, Chapanis, A. and Lund, M.W.)
                                                    4.3.23
Cook, S.W. (Selltiz, C., Jahoda, M., Deutsch, M. and -)
                                                    8.1.101
Coomer, B.D. (Corradino, J.C., -, and Upshaw, W.S.) 8.3.29
Cooper, J.B. 7.1.31
Cooper, P. (-, Lindsay, W. and Taylor, E.) 1.2.30, 1.2.31
Corlett, E.N. (Manenica, I. and) 8.3.18
Corradino, J.C. (-,Coomer, B.D. and Upshaw, W.S.) 8.3.29
Council of Planning Librarians 9.2.1, 9.2.17, 9.2.19,
                   9.2.22,   9.2.23,   9.2.29,   9.2.30
Cousins, S. 5.1.5; (Nankivell, C. and) 2.4.34
Cowan, P. 2.4.41; (ed.) 3.3.51
Cox, E. (Harris, A.I., -, and Smith, C.R.W.) 3.2.70
Cox, O. 1.2.57
Cox, R. 8.1.31; (Fisher, G.H. and) 8.1.30
Cracknell, J.A. (Ridley, G., Rushton, P. and) 4.1.11
Craik, K.H. 4.3.55
Cranfield Institute of Technology: Centre for Transport
       Studies 2.4.16, 2.4.18, 2.4.22, 3.1.86, 3.2.12,
       4.1.99,   4.1.100, 4.2.27, 4.4.14, 4.4.17, 4.4.18
       4.4.20,   4.5.1,   5.1.1
Crawley Planning Group 2.4.6
Cresswell, R. 1.2.9, 1.2.15, 2.4.35, 2.4.53
Cronbach, L.J. 8.1.71
Cross, R.B. (ed.) 3.1.60
Crosville Motor Services Ltd.   2.1.8
Crowther Report   7.1.73
Crumlish, J.D.   8.2.1
Cullen, G. 1.2.38
Cullingworth, J.B. 1.2.53, 3.2.54; (Orr, S. and) (eds.)
                                                    8.2.8
Culpin & Partners, Clifford 7.1.55
Cumbernauld Development Corporation 2.4.7
Cundill, M.A. (and Watts, P.F.) 4.1.7
Curd, H.V. (Gustafson, R.L., -, and Golob, T.F.) 8.1.114
Curtin, J.F. 4.1.56

Dais, J.L. (and Balachandra, M.) 4.3.31
Dale, P. (Eversley, D. and) 2.4.32
Dalkey, N.C.(-, Rourke, D.O., Lewis, R. and Snyder, D.)
                                                    8.1.59
Dalton, M. 4.1.76
Dalvi, M.Q. 7.1.11; (Bonsall, P., -, and Hills, P.J.) (eds.)
            3.4.5,   8.1.4; (Lee, N. and) 3.1.109, 3.1.110
Daly, A.J. 3.2.36; (and Gale,H.S.) 4.1.40; (-, Phillips,
     G.W., Rogers, K.G. and Smith, P.J.) 4.1.96; (and Rogers,
     K.G.) 4.1.21; (and Townsend, R.) 8.3.28

Damodoran, L. (Mitchelson, D.L. and) 8.1.35
Damon, A. (-, Stoudt, W. and McFarland, R.A.) 4.3.19
Daniels, P.W. 1.2.36
Davidson, K.B. 3.3.5
Davies, A.L. (and Rogers, K.G.) 3.1.40
Davis, E.W. 4.3.35
Daws, L.F. 3.2.46; (and Bruce, A.J.) 3.2.48
Davison, R.F.F. 5.1.18, 5.1.19; (and Vass, P.) 4.1.34
Day, D.J. 4.2.10, 8.3.15, 8.3.16; (Heraty, M.J. and)
           4.4.37; (Symonds, A.A.S. and) 4.4.11
Day, M.P. (Seddon, P.A. and) 3.1.115
Day, N.D. (Bryce, C.E., -, and McDonald,C.) 8.2.16
Daykin, P. 4.4.4
Dean, R.D. (and McGothlen, C.L.) 4.3.17
Deming, W.E. 8.1.33
Department of Education and Science 3.2.75, 3.2.76
Department of Employment 3.2.80, 9.5.17
Department of the Environment 1.1.29, 1.2.56, 1.2.57, 1.2.58,
           2.4.38, 2.4.59, 3.2.74, 3.3.54, 4.1.69,
           4.1.102, 4.4.53, 4.4.54, 4.5.23, 7.1.68,
           7.1.77, 8.2.21, 9.5.6, 9.5.7, 9.5.8,
           9.5.11, 9.5.12, 9.6.8
Departments of the Environment and Transport 9.5.13
Departments of the Environment/Transport Headquarters Library
      9.2.3, 9.2.11, 9.2.13, 9.2.14, 9.2.15, 9.2.18, 9.2.26,
      9.2.27, 9.2.31, 9.2.32, 9.2.33, 9.2.34, 9.2.36,
      9.2.37, 9.2.39, 9.3.6, 9.4.1, 9.4.2, 9.4.3, 9.6.2,
      9.6.4, 9.6.5, 9.6.7, 9.6.13, 9.6.14, 9.6.15, 9.6.20
Department of Health and Social Security 3.2.71
Department of Health for Scotland 1.2.55
Department of Industry 9.5.3
Department of Scientific and Industrial Research 3.3.53
Department of Transport 4.1.101, 4.4.55, 4.4.56, 7.1.76,
           7.1.78, 9.5.9, 9.5.14
Departmental Committee on the London Taxicab Trade 4.5.21
Deutsch, M. (Selltiz, C., Jahoda, M., -, and Cook, S.W.)
                                         8.1.101
Development Corporations (Annual Reports) 1.2.51
Dick & Associates, Alastair 2.4.15
Dickens, P. (Bullock, N., -, Shapcott, M. and Steadman,P.)
                                         3.1.116
Dickey, J.W. (Morgan, K.R. and) 1.1.4
Dieckmann, D. 4.3.65
Diffrient, N. (-, Tilley, A.R. and Bardagjy, J.C.) 4.3.28
Dix, M.C. 8.1.42, 8.3.31; (Rees, F.J., -, and Clyde,C.)
                                         8.1.10
Dixon, M.G. 2.4.47
Dobrow, S.B. (Bronzaft, A.L., -, and O'Hanlon, T.J.) 8.3.27
Dobson, R. 3.1.4, 8.1.70, 8.1.86; (-, Golob, T.F. and
           Gustafson, R.L.) 8.1.94; (and Kehoe, J.F.) 3.1.12;
           (and Nicolaidis, G.) 3.1.60; (Constantino, D.P.,
           -, and Canty, E.T.) 3.1.42; (Golob,T.F. and)
           3.1.59; (Golob, T.F., -, and Sheth, J.N.) 8.1.19

Gibberd, F. 2.4.12
Gillan, J. (and Wachs, M.) 3.2.14
Gillespie & Associates, William (Hugh Wilson and Lewis
        Womersley, Jamieson, Mackay and) 2.4.24
Ginzberg. E. (and Reilly, E.W.) 4.1.48
Glance, R. (and Freund, E.C.) 9.2.30
Glasgow University [see: University of Glasgow]
Glenrothes Development Corporation 1.1.27
Glock, C.V. (ed.) 8.1.105
Goddard & Smith (-, Sir F. Snow & Partners, R. Seifert
                    & Partners) 2.1.13
Golany, G. 1.2.26, 9.2.28
Goldman, A.E. 8.1.39
Golob, T.F. 3.1.5; (-, Canty, E.T. and Gustafson, R.L.)
            3.1.18; (and Dobson, R.) 3.1.59; (-, Dobson,R.
            and Sheth, J.N.) 8.1.19; (-, Hepper, S.J. and
            Pershing, J.J.) 8.3.10; (and Recker, W.W.)
            8.1.2; (Burns, L. and) 3.3.3; (Burns,L., -,
            and Nicolaidis, G.) 5.1.11; (Dobson,R., -,
            and Gustafson, R.L.) 8.1.94; (Gensch, D.H. and)
            8.1.20; (Gustafson, R.L., Curd, H.V. and)
            8.1.114
Good, G.E. 8.3.13
Goode, W.J. (and Hatt, P.K.) 8.1.103
Goodwin, P.B. 3.1.21, 3.1.37, 3.1.102, 3.1.108, 3.3.23,
                                                4.1.63
Goss, A. 1.2.22; (Tetlow, J. and) 3.3.35
Government Social Survey 3.2.73, 3.2.79
Grayson, G. (Branton, P. and) 4.3.53
Greater London Council [GLC] 3.1.27, 3.1.34, 3.1.54, 3.1.90,
        3.3.5, 3.3.34, 4.1.9, 4.1.49, 4.1.74, 5.1.3,
        7.1.24, 7.1.49, 7.1.50, 9.1.30, 9.3.21
Greater Manchester P.T.E. 7.1.51
Greco, W.L. (Nakkash, T. Z. and) 3.1.92
Green B.F. 8.1.3
Gregerman, A.S. 2.4.36
Gregory, P. (and Young,M.) 3.2.15
Grey, A. 4.1.57, 4.1.58
Griffiths, E. 4.5.15
Grigg, A.O. (and Smith, P.G.) 4.2.41
Guilford, J.P. 8.1.72
Gulbenkian Foundation, Calouste 2.4.52
Gustafson, R.L. (-, Curd, H.V. and Golob, T.F.) 8.1.114;
                (Dobson, R., Golob, T.F. and) 8.1.94;
                (Golob, T.F., Canty, E.T.and) 3.1.18
Gutnecht, R. 4.1.61
Guttman, L. 8.1.95, 8.1.97
Guy, C. 1.2.21
Gwilliam, K.M. 7.1.43; (and Judge, E.J.) 3.3.40

Hudson, D.M. 1.2.17, 3.2. 35
Hudson, R. (and Johnson, M.R.D.) 1.1.16, 1.2.1
Hughes, N.J. 9.2.8
Hull, C. (Nie, N.H., Bent, D. and) 8.1.106
Human Factors Society 4.3.43, 9.1.45
Hunt, A. 3.2.69, 3.2.79
Hutchinson, T.P. (Jolliffe, J.K. and) 3.1.8
Hyde, D.L. 4.1.78
Hyde, P.J. (Rigby, J.P. and) 3.2.41
Hyman, G.M.(and Wilson, A.G.) 3.1.46
Hyman, H.H. 8.1.41

Illich, I.D. 7.1.5
Illinois University. [see: University of Illinois]

Independent Operators [Telford] (Colin Buchanan & Partners,
        Salop County Council, Telford Development Corporation,
        Midland Red Omnibus Co., District of the Wrekin
        Council and) 2.3.1
Independent Commission on Transport, The 7.1.3
Insko, C.A. (and Schopler, J.) 8.3.1
Institute d'Amenagement et d'Urbanisme de la Region Parisienne
                                3.1.55
Institute for Consumer Ergonomics [Loughborough University
                        of Technology.] 9.4.13
Institute for Scientific Information. [Philadelphia] 9.3.15
Institute of Biology 4.3.1
Institute of British Geographers 4.1.93, 4.5.14, 8.3.4
Institute of Community Studies 3.2.21, 3.2.22, 3.2.34
Institute of Economic Affairs 7.1.29
Institute of Environmental Sciences 4.3.17
Institute of Municipal Treasurers and Accountants [see:
        Chartered Institute of Public Finance and Accountancy.]
Institute of Public Administration, New York. 1.1.22
Institute of Transport [see: Chartered Institute of Transport.]
Institution of Civil Engineers 2.1.7, 3.2.55, 4.2.4, 4.4.33,
                        7.1.39, 7.1.40, 7.1.41
Institution of Mechanical Engineers 4.3.12, 4.3.66
Instituto de Estudios de Administration Local-Centro de
                        Documentation, Madrid. 4.4.34
International Bank for Reconstruction and Development (IBRD)
                        7.1.28, 8.3.14

International Federation of Pedestrian Associations 6.1.6,
                                6.1.11
International Library (Santa Barbara) 9.3.7
International Organisation for Standardization (ISO) 4.3.63
International Road Federation 3.1.97; (-, Organisation for
        Economic Co-operation and Development and the
        Transportation Research Board) 9.4.5
International Study Week in Traffic and Safety Engineering
                                4.1.28

International Union of Public Transport (see UITP)
IPC Transport Press Ltd. 9.5.4
Ireland, J.V. 3.3.2
Irvine Development Corporation 2.4.25
Ittelson. W.H. (Proshansky, H.M., -, and Rivlin, L.G.)
                                    (eds.) 3.4.2

Jack, Professor D.T. 4.1.103
Jackson, M.W. 4.4.1
Jackson, P. (and Palmer, R.W.) 3.1.81
Jackson, R. 7.1.23
Jackson, R.L. (-, Coe, G.A. and Finnamore, A.J.) 4.1.20;
                          (Coe, G.A. and) 4.1.22
Jacobs, O. 8.1.82
Jahoda, M. (Selltiz, C., -, Deutsch, M. and Cook, S.W.) 8.1.101
Jain, S.C. (Clapp, R.G, Holligan, P.E., -, and Lippke, B.R.)
                                              8.1.53
James, J.R. 1.2.57
Jamieson, G.B. (-, Mackay, W.K., and Latchford, J.C.R.)
                                              3.3.17
Jamieson Mackay & Partners 2.4.11
Jamieson & Mackay (Hugh Wilson & Lewis Womersley, -, and
                   William Gillespie Associates) 2.4.24
Jenkins, E. 2.1.1
Jenkins, H. 4.1.75
Jenkins, I.A. (and Skelton, N.G.) 3.2.17
Jenkins, J.J. (-, Russell, W.A. and Suci, J.) 8.1.99
Jessiman, W. et al 8.2.6
Johns, E. 1.2.5
Johnson, E. (Hoinville, G. and) 3.1.13, 3.1.63
Johnson, J. 8.1.32
Johnson, M.R.D. (Hudson, R. and) 1.1.16, 1.2.1
Jolliffe, J.K. (and Hutchinson, T.P.) 3.1.8
Jones, D.G. (Chamberlin, Powell and Bon; Shankland, G. and)
                                              3.2.26
Jones, D.R. (Bentley, G.A., Bruce, A. and) 3.1.36
Jones, P.M. 3.1.95, 8.3.12
Jones, W.H. 4.4.23; (Hovell, P.J. and) 4.4.21, 4.4.22;
            (Hovell, P.J. -, and Moran, A.J.) 4.2.25
Jowell, R. (Berthoud, R. and) 2.1.24; (Hoinville, G. and)
            8.1.36; (Hoinville,G., and Associates)
                                              8.1.109
Joyce, T. (and Channon,C.) 8.1.57
Judge, E.J. (Gwilliam, K.M. and) 3.3.40

Kahn, R.L. (and Cannell, C.F.) 8.1.43
Kain, J.F. (Beesley, M.E. and) 3.3.44; (Meyer, J.R. -, and
                        Wohl, M.) 3.4.6
Kalton, G. (Moser, C.A. and) 8.1.100
Kannel, E.J. (and Heathington, K.W.) 3.1.94
Kanwit . E.L. (and Eckartt, A.F.) 3.3.41
Karn, V. 2.4.1, 2.4.8

Kasl, S.V. (and Harburg, E.) 8.3.20
Katz, D.K. (Festinger, L.F. and) 8.1.23, 8.1.74
Keane, J.G. 8.1.49
Keck, C.A. (Hartgen, D.T. and) 4.4.12
Kehoe, J.F. (Dobson, R. and) 3.1.12
Keith, R.A. (Voorhees, A.M. and) 4.5.20
Kemp, M.A. 4.1.38, 4.1.50; (Kirby, R.F. Butt, K.U., -,
    McGillivray,R.G. and Wohl, M.) 4.4.35
Kemper, R.V. (-, Osgood, S. and Schouten, R.M.) 9.2.23
Kendall, M.G. 8.1.90
Kendall, P. (Merton, R.K., Fiske, M. and) 8.1.38
Kenney, K.C. (Edwards, A.L. and) 8.1.8
Kent County Council Planning Department 3.1.62
Kerensky, O.A. 3.3.48
Kerridge, M.S.P. 7.1.2
Kettle, P.(Lichfield, N., -, and Whitbread, M.) 8.2.12
Kidd, S. 9.6.14
Kimber, R. (-, Richardson, J.J., Brookes, S.K.) 7.1.36
Kimberley, C. 2.3.8
Kirby, R.F. (-, Butt, K., Kemp, M.A., McGillivray,R.G. and
                            Wohl, M.) 4.4.35
Kirk, N.S. (Ashford, N.J. and) 4.3.24; (Ashford, N.J.,
        Feeney, R.J., -, Richardson, J. and Stroud, P.G.)
                            4.3.7

Kirkpatrick, M. (ed.) 4.3.43
Kirwan, R.M. 8.2.8
Knight, D. (-, Slevin, R. and Bull, H.C.) 4.2.27
Koboyashi, K. (-, Aoki, Y.and Tani, A.) 8.2.11
Koons, E.R. 6.1.6
Koschade, J.B. 1.1.26
Kotler, P. 4.2.32
Kraft, G. (Domencich, T.A. and) 4.1.64
Krishnan, K.S. (Nicolaidis, G. and) 4.1.19
Kuang, H.P. 8.1.29
Kuenstler, P. (ed.) 1.2.7
Kulash, D.J. 4.2.40

Lambden, W. 4.1.5
Lambert, C.M. 9.2.3, 9.2.13, 9.2.14
Lancaster, K. 8.1.26
Lanchester Polytechnic [see: Polytechnic, Lanchester]
Landsberger, H.A. 4.1.65
Lane, R. (-, Powell, T.J., and Prestwood Smith, P.) 4.1.1
Langley Research Centre 4.3.20
Lansing, J.B. (and Hendricks, G.) 3.3.25; (et al) 3.3.26
Latchford, J.C.R. (Jamieson, G.B., Mackay, W.K. and) 3.3.17
Latscha, W. 4.1.46
Laurence, D.R. (Camps, F.E. and) 5.1.15
Laurent, A. 8.1.78
Lave, C.A. 3.1.6
Layfield, R.E. (Vincent, R.E., -, and Bardsley, M.) 2.1.6
Lee, N. (and Dalvi, M.Q.) 3.1.109, 3.1.110; (and Stedman,I.)
                            4.1.47

London University [see: University of London.]
Long, J. (and Norton, A.) 7.1.18
Loomba, J.K. (Holsti, O.R., -, and North, R.C.) 8.1.28
Louvierè, J.J. (and Norman, K.L.) 8.3.7
Lovelock, C.H. 4.2.38
Low, N. 3.3.24
Lowe, S.R. 4.4.7; (Doganis, R.S. and) 4.4.48
Lucarotti, P.S.K. (Archer, P.R., Bull, H.C. and) 5.1.1
Lund, M.W. (Morgan, C.T., Cook, J.S., Chapanis, A. and) 4.3.23
Lynam, D.A. (and Everall, P.F.) 3.1.28, 3.1.29
Lynn, R. 4.3.2
Lyons, D.J. 4.5.2

MacBriar, I.D. (Ochojna, A.D. and) 8.1.24
McCallum, E.P. 3.1.97
McCallum, I.R.M. (ed.) 3.3.22
McCarthy, P.S. 3.1.33
McCormick, E.J. 4.3.26
McCorquodale, D. (Bennett, R. F. and) 4.5.16
McDonald, C. (Boyce, C.E., Day, N.D. and) 8.2.16
McFadden, D. (Domencich, T.A. and) 3.1.78
McFadgen, D.G. 3.1.50
McFarland, R.A. et al. 3.2.4; (Damon, A., Stoudt, W. and)
                                         4.3.19
McGillivray, R.G. 3.1.44; (Kirby, R.F., Butt, K.U., Kemp, M.A.,
           -, and Wohl, M.) 4.4.35
McGlynn, R. (Elkington, J., -, and Roberts, J.) 9.2.10;
           (Roberts, J. and) 4.4.25
McGothlen, C.L. (Denn, R.D. and) 4.3.17
McGowan, J. (Webster, A.T. and) 4.1.13
McIntosh, P.T.(Smith, M.G. and) 4.1.51; (Smith, M.G., -, and
           Black, I.) 4.1.55
Mackay, W.K. (Jamieson, G.B., -, and Latchford, J.C.R.) 3.3.17
McKee, W. (May, P. and) 6.1.5
McKenzie, J. (Fry, J. and) (eds.) 1.2.14
McLeod, P.B. (Hensher, D.A., -, and Stanley, J.K.) 3.1.2
McMillan, R.K. (and Assael, H.) 3.1.1
Macourt, M.P.A. 8.1.98
Madin and Partners, J.H.D. 2.3.9
Madin Design Group, John 2.3.10
Maloney & Associates, J.F. 7.1.52
Manchester University [see: University of Manchester]
Manenica, I. (and Corlett, E.N.) 8.3.18
Mangan, D.O. (O'Flaherty, C.A. and) 3.1.114
Marcadal, G. 3.1.52
Market Research Society [London] 8.1.76, 9.3.11
Martin, B.V. 7.1.40
Martin, P.H. 2.4.17, 2.4.19; (Mitchell, C.G.B. and) 2.4.23
Martin and Voorhees Associates (Freeman,Fox & Associates, -,
           and West Yorkshire Metropolitan County Council) 4.5.4
           [see also AMV Ltd., and Voorhees, A.M.]
Maryland Metropolitan Transit Authority 4.4.26

Maryland, University of [see: University of Maryland]
Maunder, W.F. (ed.) 9.6.19
Maw, J.R. 4.2.22; (and Bradley, J.) 4.2.42; (-, Bradley, J.
    and Bermingham, T.P.) 4.1.85; (Bradley, J. and)
    4.1.8, 4.1.23, 4.2.21; (Bradley, J., -, and
    Muir, R.M.) 4.2.47
Maxwell, A.E. 8.1.73
Maxwell Stamp, A. (Chairman) 4.5.21
May, P. (and McKee,W.) 6.1.5
Meads, R.H. 1.1.14
Medical Commission on Accident Prevention (MCAP) 5.1.15
Mercer, J. 2.1.2, 2.1.7, 2.1.9
Merseyside PTE 7.1.53; (Peat, Marwick, Mitchell & Co. with
    DOE and) 4.1.69
Merton, R.K. (-, Fiske, M. and Kendall, P.) 8.1.38
Metcalfe, A.E. (Rogers, K.G., Townsend, G.M. and) 3.1.30
Meyburg, A.H. (Stopher, P.R. and) 3.1.74; (Stopher, P.R. and)
    (eds.) 3.1.3, 3.1.4, 3.1.10, 3.1.69, 3.1.77
Meyer, J.R. (-, Kain, J.F. and Wohl, M.) 3.4.6
Meyers, A.W. (Everett, P.B., Hayward, S.C. and) 4.2.45
Michelson, W. (ed.) 8.1.22
Michigan, University of [see: University of Michigan]
Midland Red Omnibus Co. (Colin Buchanan & Partners, Salop
    County Council, Telford Development Corporation, -,
    District of the Wrekin Council, The Independent
    Operators) 2.3.1
Millar, A.E. (ed.) 4.3.20
Miller, G.A. 8.1.46
Miller, L.N. (Beranek, L.L. and) 4.3.41
Millward, C. (-, Coleman, A.H., and Dunford, J.E.) 4.1.70
Millward, S. (ed.) 3.4.4
Milne, R. 2.4.42
Milton Keynes Community Services Association 2.4.32
Milton Keynes Development Corporation 2.4.29, 2.4.30, 2.4.31,
    2.4.37, 2.4.40 (-, National Bus Company, and DOE) 2.4.38
Ministry of Health 3.2.72
Ministry of Housing and Local Government 1.2.53, 3.3.52,
    7.1.65, 7.1.69
Ministry of Labour 3.2.79
Ministry of Town and Country Planning 1.2.55
Ministry of Transport 3.1.117, 4.1.103, 4.5.22, 7.1.64,
    7.1.65, 7.1.69, 7.1.72, 7.1.73, 7.1.74, 7.1.75
Mishan, E.J. 7.1.4
Mitchell, C.G.B. 3.2.49, 4.4.33, 6.1.12; (and Martin, P.H.)
    2.4.23; (and Slevin,R.) 4.4.16; (and Speller, B.E.)
    2.4.21; (and Town, S.W.) 3.3.4; (Tunbridge,
    R.J. and) 4.4.13
Mitchelson, D.L. (and Damodaran, L.) 8.1.35
Møller, A. 4.3.39
Monroe, R.E. 4.1.77
Montgomery, C. (Collins, L. and) 8.1.66
Moore, V. 7.1.13
Moorhead, R. (and Lepper, R.) 4.3.58

Moran, A.J. (Hovell, P.J., Jones, W.H. and) 4.2.25
Morgan, C.T. 4.3.42; (-, Cook, J.S., Chapanis, A. and Lund,
                  M.W.) 4.3.23
Morgan, K.R. (and Dickey, J.W.) 1.1.4
Morris, D. (and Levine, S.) 4.3.48
Morris, P.J. (Fairhurst, M.H. and) 4.1.39
Morris, R.L. 1.1.25
Morrison, D.F. 8.1.68
Morton, N. 7.1.59
Morton-Williams, J. (and Butler,J.) 2.4.14
Moser, C.A. (and Kalton, G.) 8.1.100
Motor Industry Research Association (MIRA) 9.3.12
Moyes, A. (and Willis, E.) 4.1.93
Muir, R.M. (Bradley, J., Maw, J.R. and) 4.2.47
Muldrew, V. 4.1.99, 4.1.100
Mullen, P. 4.1.42;   (-, Bursey, N.C. and White, M.T.) 2.3.7;
                  (and Lewis, R.M.) 4.1.43;   (and White,
                  M.T.) 5.1.2
Mumford, L. (Intro.) 1.2.32
Munby, D. (Williams, T.E.H. and) 3.3.39
Munden, J.M. 5.1.17
Municipal Passenger Transport Association 4.1.78 [see also:
      Association of Public Passenger Transport Operators
      (Incorporated).]
Munt, P.W. (and Woodhall, R.) 3.1.90
Murchison, C. (ed.) 8.1.15
Murphy, C. 7.1.16
Murrell, J.F. 8.1.93
Murrell, K.F.H. 4.3.16

Nakkash, T.Z. (and Greco, W.L.) 3.1.92
Nankivell,C. (and Cousins , S.) 2.4.34
Nash, A.N. (Paine, F.T., -, Hille, S.J. and Brunner,G.A)3.1.15, 3.1.16.
Nash, C.A. (Brown, R.H. and) 4.1.84
Nathaniel Lichfield & Associates/Partners [see: Lichfield, N.]
National Analysts Inc. 4.2.6
National Board for Prices and Incomes 9.5.10
National Bus Company 9.4.15, 9.5.5; (Milton Keynes
            Development Corporation, -, and DOE) 2.4.38
National Capital Transportation Agency 4.2.6, 4.3.35, 4.3.54
National Confederation of Parent-Teacher Associations 3.2.42
National Consumer Council 7.1.20
National Corporation for the Care of Old People 3.2.19
National Council of Social Service 1.2.23. 3.2.27, 3.2.38
National Council of Women 4.5.12
National Economic Development Office (NEDO) 3.2.78, 7.1.67
National Innovations Centre 3.2.15
National Institute for Physical Planning and Construction
                  Research, Dublin 9.2.8
National Institute of Economic and Social Research 3.3.43,
                                          3.3.49
National Old People's Welfare Council (Age Concern) 3.2.1,
            3.2.2, 3.2.10, 3.2.47

National Technical Information Servce, Springfield, Virginia.
8.1.82
NATO   4.3.24,   8.1.35
Newberry, G.M.   3.3.50
Newcastle Transit Authority, Pennsylvania   7.1.56
Newcastle Upon Tyne University [see: University of Newcastle
Upon Tyne]
Newell, G.F. (ed.)   3.1.23
Newman, J.W.   4.2.33
New Towns Association   9.2.25,   9.4.6
New Towns Commission   2.4.5
New Towns Committee   1.2.55
New Towns Directorate   (DOE)   9.5.21
New Towns Study Unit [see: University, Open]
New Towns Technical Officers Committee   1.1.13
New York State Department of Transportation   4.4.12
Nicholl, J.P.   3.1.26
Nicholson, J.H.   1.2.23
Nicolaidis, G.   8.1.77,   8.1.96;   (and Krishnan, K.S.)   4.1.19;
(Burns, L., Golob, T.F. and)   5.1.11; (Dobson,
R. and)   3.1.60
Nie, N.H. (-, Bent, D. and Hull, C.)   8.1.106
Noise Advisory Council   4.3.68
Norman, A.   3.2.19
Norman, K.L. (Louviere, J.J. and)   8.3.7
Norman, L.G. (ed.)   5.1.15
North, R.C. (Holsti, O.R., Loomba, J.K. and)   8.1.28
North West Economic Planning Board (Research Section)   9.4.7
North West Economic Planning Council   1.2.45
North West Sports Council
Northwestern University, Illinois [see: University: Northwestern,
Illinois]
Norton, A. (Long, J. and)   7.1.18
Nuckols, R.C.   8.1.48

Oborne, D.J.   4.3.61,   4.3.62,   8.1.92;   (and Clarke, M.J.)
8.1.84,   8.1.85
Ochojna, A.D.   2.4.16,   4.4.17;   (and MacBriar, I.D.)   8.1.24;
(and Ward, V.)   2.4.18; (Slevin,R. and)   4.4.18
OECD [see: Organisation for Economic Co-operation and
Development]
Office of Health Economics   1.2.14,   3.2.30
Office of Population Censuses and Surveys   3.2.69,   3.2.70
3.2.77,   8.1.115,   8.1.116,   9.5.16,   9.5.18.
O'Flaherty, C.A. (and Mangan, D.O.)   3.1.114
Ogilvy, A.A.   1.2.11,   1.2.41
Ognibene, P.   8.1.83
O'Hanlon, T.J.   (Bronzaft, A.L., Dobrow, S.B. and)   8.3.27
Oi, W. (and Schuldiner, P.)   3.1.79
Old Dominion Research Foundation   4.3.20
Oldfield, R.H. (Webster, F.V. and)   3.1.82
Omnibus Society   1.1.9,   7.1.17
Open University [see: University, Open]

Operations Research Inc. 4.3.35, 4.3.54
Operations Research Society of America 4.1.31
Opinion Research Centre (ORC) 3.1.86
Oppenheim, A.N. 8.1.80
Organisation for Economic Co-operation and Development 1.2.3,
        3.3.47, 7.1.28; (International Road Federation, -,
        and the Transportation Research Board 9.4.5
Orr, S. (and Cullingworth, J.B.) (eds.) 8.2.8
Osborn, Sir F.J. (and Whittick, A.) 1.2.32
Osborn, S.E. 4.2.19
Osgood, C.E. (-, Suci, G.J. and Tannenbaum. P.H.) 8.1.61
Osgood, S. (Kemper, R.V., -, and Schouten, R.M.) 9.2.23
Ottley, G. 9.1.2
Oxford University [see: University of Oxford]

Paaswell, R.E. 3.2.7; (and Edelstein, P.) 3.2.9
Pailing, K.B. (and Solesbury, W.) 5.1.13
Paine, F.T. (-, Nash, A.N., Hille, S.J., and Brunner, G.A.)

                                3.1.15, 3.1.16
Palmer, R.W. (Jackson, P. and) 3.1.81
Parker, G.B. 4.1.95, 4.2.4
Parker Morris Report 3.3.52
Payne, S.L. 8.1.88
Peak, J. 1.2.18
Peat, Marwick, Mitchell & Co. (with DOE and Merseyside PTE)
                                                4.1.69

Peddle, J. 4.4.44
Pemberton, J.E. 9.6.9
PEP [see: Political and Economic Planning]
Perraton, J.K. 6.1.4, 8.2.15
Pershing, J.J. (Golob, T.F., Hepper, S.J. and) 8.3.10
Peterborough Development Corporation 2.4.45
Peterson, G.L. (and Worrall, R.D.) 3.3.8
Pettigrew, A.M. 4.2.18
Pharoah, T.M. (Collins, M.F. and) 7.1.30
Phelps, R. 2.2.13
Phillips, G.W. (Daly, A.J., -, Rogers, K.G. and Smith, P.J.)
                                                4.1.96

Phillips, I. (Ellen, E.R. and) 7.1.8
Pike, D.H. (-, Fuller, P.I. and White, M.T.) 2.3.7
Pinder, P. 3.2.68
Planning and Transport Research and Computation Co. Ltd.
        (PTRC) 2.3.5,   2.4.23,   2.4.55,   2.4.60,   3.1.95,
        3.2.17,   3.3.23,   4.1.12,   4.1.14,   4.1.15,   4.1.18
        4.1.41,   4.1.63,   4.1.71,   4.1.73,   4.1.75, 4.1.77,
        4.1.80,   4.1.91,   4.1.92,   4.2.31,   4.4.4,   4.4.11
        4.4.16,   4.4.37,   4.4.39,   6.1.12,   7.1.31,   7.1.32,
        7.1.43,   8.2.7
Planning Research Unit 3.2.8
Plowden, S.P.C. 3.3.38

Policy Studies Institute (PSI) [see: Political and Economic Planning]
Political and Economic Planning (PEP) 1.2.2, 1.2.16, 2.1.23,
       3.1.35, 3.2.18, 3.2.29, 3.2.37, 3.2.45, 3.2.63,
       3.2.68, 3.3.14 [Now called Policy Studies Institute]
Polytechnic, Lanchester 3.1.58, 9.2.4
Polytechnic, Liverpool 1.2.12
Polytechnic of Central London 4.1.33, 4.1.87, 4.4.36,
       4.4.40, 4.4.44, 4.4.48, 4.5.13, 8.3.9, 8.3.23,
       9.2.2, 9.4.18
Popper, R.J. (and Hoel, L.A.) 4.5.19
Port Authority of Allegheny County 4.2.1
Porteous, J. Douglas 3.4.1
de Porzecanski,M.(-, Cheesman, R. and Lindsay, W.) 1.2.35;
                      (Cheesman, R., Lindsay, W. and) 1.2.34;
                      (Lindsay, W., Cheesman R. and) 1.2.28
Potter, S. 1.1.17, 1.1.18, 1.1.19; (Hillman, M. and) 1.1.1
Pountney, M.T. (Adderson, I.M., -, and Hole, W.V.) 8.1.63
Powell, T.J. (Lane, R., -, and Prestwood Smith, P.) 4.1.1
Prescott Clarke, P. 4.4.30; (and Stowell, R.) 2.1.25;
                      (Hedges, B. and) 4.1.54
Prest, A.R. (and Turvey, R.) 8.2.2
Prestwood Smith, P.(Lane, R., Powell, T.J. and) 4.1.1
Price, Sir F. 1.2.33
Prince, E.J. 2.4.26, 2.4.27
Pritchard, N. 2.2.14
Proshansky, H.M. (-, Ittelson, W.H. and Rivlin, L.G.) (eds.)
                      3.4.2
Proudlove, J.A. 1.1.20
Provins, K.A. (and Bell, C.R.) 4.3.18
PTRC [see: Planning and Transport Research and Computation Co,Ltd.]
Pugh, H.A. 9.2.15, 9.6.7
Pugh, J.V. (Chairman) 7.1.65
Pushkarev, B.S. (and Zupan, J.M.) 6.1.8

Quandt, R.E. (ed.) 3.1.87
Quarantelli, E.L. (Bucher, R., Fritz, C.E. and) 8.1.111
Quarmby, D.A. 3.1.31, 4.1.60; (Harrison, A.J. and) 3.1.104
Quinby, H.D. 4.4.6

Radcliffe, D.R. 2.2.1
Raj, D. 8.1.110
Rapoport, R. (Fogarty, M., -, and Rapoport, R.N.) 3.2.45
Rapoport, R.N. (Fogarty, M., Rapoport, R. and) 3.2.45
Rapson, G.H. 4.1.15
Rawes, G.R. (and Wren, K.) 1.2.57
Reason, L. 1.2.12
Recker, W.W. (Golob, T.F. and) 8.1.2
Redditch Development Corporation (and Hugh Wilson & Lewis
                      Womersley) 2.4.48
Rees, F.J. 8.1.112; (-, Dix, M. and Clyd, C.) 8.1.10
Reeves, T. (Wedderburn, D., Holder, A. and) 4.1.91
Regional Science Association 3.3.46
Regional Science Research Institute 8.2.16

465

Regional Studies Association 1.1.1, 1.2.17, 1.2.37, 3.3.40
Reichman, S. 3.1.69
Reilly, E.W. (Ginzberg, E. and) 4.1.48
Reith, Lord 1.2.55
Research Projects Ltd. 3.1.43, 4.2.14
Rhys, D.G. 4.1.45
Richards, B. 4.4.19
Richardson, J. (Ashford, N.J., Feeney, R.J., Kirk, N.S., -,
                and Stroud, P.G.) 4.3.7
Richardson, J.J. (Kimber, R., -, and Brookes, S.K.) 7.1.36
Ridley, G. (-, Rushton, P. and Cracknell, J.A.) 4.1.11
Rigby, J.P. (and Hyde, P.J.) 3.2.41
Rivlin, L.G. (Proshansky, H.M.,Ittelson, W.H. and) (eds.) 3.4.2
Road Research Laboratory (RRL) [see: Transport and Road
                                Research Laboratory]
Roark, J.J. (Turner, C.G. and) 3.3.42
Roberts, J. (and McGlynn, R.) 4.4.25; (Elkington, J., McGlynn,
                R. and) 9.2.10
Robinson, J.F.F. 2.4.46
Robinson, J.P. (and Shauer, P.K.) 8.1.6
Rogers, K.G. (-, Townsend, G.M. and Metcalf, A.E.) 3.1.30;
              (Daly, A.J. and) 4.1.21; (Daly, A.J., -, and
              Whitbread, A.W.) 3.2.23; (Daly, A.J., Phillips,
              G.W., -, and Smith, P.J. 4.1.96; (Davies, A.L.
              and) 3.1.40
Roos, D. 4.4.10
Rourke, D.O. (Dalkey, N.L., -, Lewis, R. and Snyder, D.)
                                8.1.59
Royal College of Surgeons 5.1.15
Royal Institute of British Architects (RIBA) 9.3.1
Royal Institute of Public Administration 3.1.30, 3.1.40
        3.2.23, 3.2.40, 4.1.21, 4.1.96, 8.3.28, 9.2.24
Royal Society of Arts 7.1.6
Royal Statistical Society 9.6.19.
Royal Town Planning Institute (RTPI) 3.3.45, 3.3.48, 9.2.16
Rubra, N.9.6.6
Ruffell-Smith, H.P. (Brooks, B.M., -, and Ward, J.S.) 4.3.11
Runcorn Development Corporation 2.1.3, 2.1.12, 2.1.14 - 2.1.22
Runcorn U.D.C. 2.1.13
Rural District Councils Association 4.5.15
Rushton, P. (Ridley, G., -, and Cracknell, J.A.) 4.1.11
Russell, W.A. (Jenkins, J.J., -, and Suci, G.J.) 8.1.99

Sacramento Transit Authority 4.3.46
S. A. E. 4.3.60
Saenger, E.L. (ed.) 4.3.43
Sage Publications Inc. 9.3.14
Salford University [see: University of Salford.]
Salley, M.A. 1.1.15
Salmon, V. 4.3.36
Salop County Council (Colin Buchanan & Partners,-, Telford
    Development Corporation, Midland Red Omnibus Co., District
    of the Wrekin Council, and the Independent Operators) 2.3.1

Sammons, R. (and Hall, P.) 3.1.45
Sampson, P. 8.1.34, 8.1.76
Satterley, G. (Brogan, J.D., Heathington, K.W. and) 4.1.29
Schaeffer, K.H. (and Sclar, E.) 3.3.1
Scaffer, F. 1.2.27
Schiller, R.K. 3.3.18
Schleyfman, F.M. (Shakhbazyan, G. Kh. and) 4.3.50
Schneider, L.M. 4.2.37
Schnore, L.E. 4.5.17
Schopler, J. (Insko, C.A. and) 8.3.1
Schouten, R.M. (Kemper, R.V., Osgood, S. and) 9.2.23
Schuldiner, P. (Oi, W. and) 3.1.79
Schumacher, E.F. 7.1.21
Sclar, E. (Schaeffer, K.H. and) 3.3.1
Scott, C. 8.1.52
Scottish Development Department 2.4.24, 3.3.54, 7.1.47, 7.1.65, 7.1.76, 9.5.14

SCPR [see: Social and Community Planning Research]
Scraggs, D.A. (Holroyd, E.M. and) 3.1.25, 3.1.113
Searle, G. (Barber, J. and) 3.1.111
Seddon, P.A. (and Day, M.P.) 3.1.115
Segelhorst, S.W. 8.3.30
Seifert, R. & Partners (Goddard & Smith, Sir Frederick Snow & Partners, and) 2.1.13
Self, P. [Introduction] 1.2.33
Selltiz, C. (-, Jahoda, M., Deutsch, M., and Cook, S.W.) 8.1.101
Shackel, B. (-, Chidsey, K.D. and Shipley, P.) 4.3.9
Shaffer, M.T. 8.1.12
Shakhbazyan, G. Kh. (and Schleyfman, F.M.) 4.3.50
Shanas, P. (-, Townsend, P. et al) 3.2.32
Shankland, G. (Chamberlin, Powell and Bon, -, and Jones, D.G.) 3.2.26
Shapcott, M. (Bullock, N., Dickens, P., -, and Steadman, P.) 3.1.116

Sharp, C. 4.1.98
Sharp, Lady E. 7.1.75
Shauer, P.K. (Robinson, J.P. and) 8.1.6
Shaw, G.K. (Hare, E.H. and) 1.2.20
Sheehan, J.K. 4.3.54
Sheffield City Council 7.1.55
Sheldon, N.W. (and Brandwein, R.)7.1.12
Shenfield, B. (and Allen, I.) 3.2.18
Shepard, M.E. 9.2.1
Sherif, M. (Hovland, C.I. and) 8.1.5
Sherrett, A. (and Wallace, J.P. III) 8.1.21
Sheth, J.N. (Golob, T.F., Dobson, R. and) 8.1.19
Shipley, P. (Shackel, B., Chidsey, K.D. and) 4.3.9
Shipman, W.D. 7.1.22
Shoenburger, R.W. (and Harris, C.S.) 4.3.38
Shostak, L.A. (and Fuller, S.F.) 7.1.25
Sidney Hollander Associates (Washington Metropolitan Area Transit Commission and) 4.2.15

Spence, R.   7.1.39
Spencer, J.   3.2.62
Spiller, C.J.   (Eyles, D. and)   3.1.39
Spreiregen, P.D. (ed.)   3.3.20
Spring, M.   2.3.26
SSRC [see: Social Science Research Council.]
Stalker, G.M. (Burns, T. and)   4.2.24
Standing Conference on London and S.E. Regional Planning
7.1.58
Stanford University, California [see: University, Stanford]
Stanley, J.   9.2.6
Stanley, J.K.   3.1.9;   (Hensher, D.A., McLeod, P.B. and)
3.1.2; (Hensher, D.A., Smith, R.A., Hooper, P.G. and)
4.2.48
Stanley,P.A.   8.3.4
Stark, S.   3.1.58
Starkie, D.N.M.   7.1.38
Steadman, P. (Bullock, N., Dickens, P., Shapcott, M. and)
3.1.116
Stedman, I.   (Lee, N. and)   4.1.47
Stein, M.M.   8.1.11
Stevenage Development Corporation   2.4.50 - 51,   2.4.56 - 57,
2.4.59 - 61,   2.4.63
Stevens, R.D. (and Smith, R.L.)   1.1.6;   (and Bacalis, G.J.)
1.1.21
Stevens, S.S.   8.1.58
Stone, P.A.   3.3.43,   3.3.49
Stopher, P.R.   3.1.34,   3.1.48,   8.1.69;   (and Meyburg, A.H.)
3.1.74; (and Meyburg, A.H.) (eds.)   3.1.3,   3.1.4,
3.1.10,   3.1.69,   3.1.77; (Hensher, D.A. and)   3.1.11
Stoudt, W.   (Damon, A., -, and McFarland, R.A.)   4.3.19
Stouffer, S.A. (ed.)   8.1.1,   8.1.97
Stowell, R.   (Prescott-Clarke, P. and)   2.1.25
Stranz, W.   1.2.10,   2.4.49
Strathclyde University [see: University of Strathclyde]
Stringer and Wenzel (eds.)   3.2.60
Stroud, P.G. (Ashford, N.J., Feeney, R.J., Kirk, N.S.,
Richardson, J., and)   4.3.7
Studer, R.G.   4.3.5
Suchman, E.A.   8.1.1
Suci, G.J. (Jenkins, J.J., Russell, W.A. and) 8.1.99;
(Osgood, C.E.,-, and Tannenbaum, P.H.)   8.1.61
Sunderland Corporation   3.2.24,   7.1.59
Symonds, A.A.S. (and Day, D.J.)   4.4.11

Tagg, S.K. (Canter, D. and)   8.3.11
Tani, A. (Koboyashi, K., Aoki, Y., and)   8.2.11
Tanner, J.C. 5.1.4,   5.1.20
Taylor, Lord (and Chave, S.P.W.)   1.2.19
Taylor, M.A.   3.1.83
Tebb, R.G.P.   4.1.68
Tehan, C. (and Wachs, M.)   4.2.44

Telecommunications Consultancy Service 4.4.20
Telford Development Corporation 2.3.2 -3, 2.3.10 -2 4;
    (and Colin Buchanan & Partners) 2.3.4: (Colin Buchanan
    & Partners, Salop County Council, -, Midland Red Omnibus
    Co., District of the Wrekin Council, the Independent
    Operators) 2.3.1
TEST [see: Transport and Environment Studies]
Tetlow, J. (and Goss, A.) 3.3.25
Thomas, K. 8.1.4; (and Bull, H.C.) 4.5.1
Thomas, R. 1.1.5, 1.2.2, 1.2.16, 2.4.32, 3.1.35; 2.2.37
    (ed.)
Thomas, T.C. (and Thompson, G.I.) 3.1.103, 3.1.106
Thomas, W. 1.2.3
Thompson, B.A. (Belson, W.A. and) 9.2.35
Thompson, G.I. (Thomas, T.C. and) 3.1.103, 3.1.106
Thomson, J.M. 3.4.3, 7.1.27
Thorns, D.C. 1.2.8
Thurstone, L.L. 8.1.17, 8.1.62, 8.1.67; (and Chave, E.J.)
                                              8.1.13
Tilley, A.R. (Diffrient, N., -, and Bardagjy, J.C.) 4.3.28
Tinker, J. 4.1.66
Tipping, D.G. 3.1.64
Tolley, R.S. 2.3.2 5
Tomlinson, G. 4.3.46
Town, S.W. (Mitchell, C.G.B. and) 3.3.4
Town and Country Planning Association 1.2.33, 1.2.48
Townroe, P.M. (ed.) 7.1.42
Townsend, G.M. (Rogers, K.G., -, and Metcalf, A.E.) 3.1.30
Townsend, P. 3.2.34; (Shanas, E.,-, et al) 3.2.32
Townsend, R. (Daly, A.J. and) 8.3.28
Traffic Commissioners 9.5.13
Traffic Research Corporation 7.1.54
Transport and Environment Studies [TEST] 9.2.10
Transport and Road Research Laboratory [TRRL] 2.1.6, 2.1.8,
    2.4.17, 2.4.19, - 23, 3.1.14, 3.1.28 - 29, 3.1.82 - 84,
    3.1.99, 3.2.16, 3.2.41, 3.2.49, 3.2.64, 3.3.4, 3.3.33,
    3.3.53, 4.1.7, 4.1.13, 4.1.16, 4.1.20, 4.1.22, 4.1.34,
    4.1.40, 4.1.50 - 52, 4.1.55, 4.1.57, 4.1.60, 4.1.68,
    4.1.94, 4.2.41, 4.3.11, 4.3.33, 4.4.3, 4.4.13 - 14,
    4.4.18, 4.4.46, 4.4.52, 4.5.11, 4.5.18, 5.1.4, 5.1.12,
    5.1.14, 5.1.17 - 20, 6.1.10, 9.3.18, 9.4.19
Transportation Center Library, [Northwestern University,
                                      Illinois] 9.3.5
Transportation Commonwealth of Massachussetts 7.1.52
Transportation Research Board [TRB] 3.1.5, 3.1.7, 3.1.12,
    3.1.59, 3.1.112, 3.2.67, 3.3.42, 4.1.25, 4.2.36,
    4.3.7, 4.4.9, 5.1.11, 8.3.10, 9.3.10, 9.3.19,
    9.4.8; (International Road Federation, Organisation
    for Economic Co-operation and Development and) 9.4.5
Travers Morgan and Partners, R. 4.1.2, 7.1.45 - 46; (and
                West Yorkshire Metropolitan County) 4.1.3
TRB [see: Transportation Research Board]

Treasury , The 7.1.66, 7.1.71
Trench, S. (and Slack, J.A.) 7.1.57
Trenchard, M.R. 4.2.16
Trevelyan, P. 6.1.12; (and Wright, L.) 4.1.73
Tripp, H. Alker 3.3.32
Trodden, C.W. 4.4.39
TRRL [see: Transport and Road Research Laboratory]
Tse, A. (Waters II, W.G. and) 9.1.3
Tulpule, A.H. 5.1.14, 5.1.20
Tunbridge, R.J. 4.4.3; (and Mitchell, C.G.B.) 4.4.13
Tung, J.S.N. (Haight, F.A. and) 9.1.1
Tunstall, J. 3.2.31
Turner, C.G. (and Roark, J.J.) 3.3.42
Turnock, D. 4.4.38
Turns, K.L. 4.1.24
Turvey, R. (Prest, A.R. and) 8.2.2
Tyson, W.J. 4.1.30, 4.1.41, 4.1.86 - 7, 7.1.9;(Coles,
                                       W.S. and) 7.1.7

Uhl, K.P. 4.2.28
UITP [see: Union Internationale des Transports Publics]
Union Internationale des Transports Publics [UITP] 4.1.46,
      4.1.61, 4.1.97, 4.2.3, 7.1.8, 9.3.20
United Aircraft Corporation 4.3.8
United Nations 1.2.44, 1.2.49, 1.2.57 - 58
Universities Transport Studies Group [UTSG] 4.1.35, 4.3.10,
                                                       9.3.22
University of Birmingham : Centre for Urban and Regional
      Studies 1.2.39, 1.2.43, 2.4.1, 2.4.8, 3.1.105,
      3.2.54, 9.2.20 - 21, 9.4.20; Department of
      Engineering Production [Ergonomics Information Analysis
      Centre] 9.3.8 ; Department of Transportation and
      Environmental Planning 2.4.62, 4.3.21, 8.3.4, 9.4.21
University of California: Berkeley 3.1.50
                        - Los Angeles 4.2.44
University of Cambridge: Centre for Land Use and Built Form
                          Studies 1.2.28, 1.2.30 -31,
                          1.2.34 -35, 8.2.15, 9.4.15
                        - Martin Centre for Architectural and
                          Urban Studies 3.2.61, 9.4.15
University, Carnegie-Mellon [Pittsburgh] 4.2.1
University of Durham 1.1.16, 1.2.1, 2.4.46, 8.1.98
University of East Anglia 4.1.93, 4.5.14
                        - Geo Abstracts Ltd., 9.3.9
University of Edinburgh 3.2.8, 9.6.12
University of Essex 1.2.17
University, Florida State 4.3.45
University of Glasgow 2.4.10
University of Illinois, Urbana 8.1.19
University of Leeds 3.4.5, 4.1.36 - 37, 7.1.11, 8.1.10,
                     8.1.112, 9.4.22
University of Liverpool 4.4.21 - 23

University of London: London School of Economics and Political
                     Science-Survey Research Centre   8.1.87,
                     8.1.91
                   - University College - School of
                     Environmental Studies   8.2.13
                   - Traffic Studies Group   2.4.59
University of Loughborough [see: University of Technology,
                                      Loughborough]
University of Maryland   3.1.16,   4.2.9
University of Michigan: Survey Research Center, Ann Arbor
                     3.3.25 -26,   8.1.6
University of Newcastle Upon Tyne : Department of Civil
           Engineering - Transport Operations Research Group
           2.1.9,   2.4.58,   4.1.95,   4.2.2,   4.2.13,   4.2.16,
           4.2.20,   4.2.34,   4.3.40,   9.2.9
University, Northwestern [Illinois] 2.4.36,   9.3.5
University, Open   9.6.6
                   - New Towns Study Unit   1.1.1,   1.1.5,   1.1.17-
                     19,   1.2.9,   1.2.15,   1.2.37,   2.4.35,
                     2.4.53,   3.2.35,   5.1.7,   9.4.17
University of Oxford : Transport Studies Unit   3.1.20,   8.1.42,
                     8.3.12,   8.3.31,   9.4.23
University of Salford: Department of Civil Engineering   3.4.4
University of Southampton : Department of Civil Engineering
                     1.1.8,   3.1.111,   6.1.13
                   - Department of Economics   9.2.6
University, Stanford [California]   4.2.38
University of Strathclyde   2.4.9
University of Technology, Loughborough : Institute for
                     Consumer Ergonomics   9.4.13
University of Virginia :   Transportation Study Group   1.1.4
University of Warwick :   Urban Transport Research Group   9.2.4
University of York   3.3.21,   3.3.50,   4.3.57,   4.4.1,   4.4.24,
                                                              4.5.7
Upshaw, W.S. (Corradino, J.C., Coomer, B.D. and)   8.3.29
Urban Institute, Washington D.C.   4.2.40,   4.4.35
Urban Land Institute [ULI] , Washington D.C.   9.2.28
Urban Mass Transportation Administration   8.3.21,   4.2.44,
                                                    4.3.44 - 45

U.S. Bureau of the Census   9.2.38
U.S. Department of Commerce   4.3.8,   8.2.1
U.S. Department of Housing and Urban Development [HUD] 1.1.23,
                                                    4.4.5,   4.4.49
U.S. Department of Transportation   3.1.88,   4.2.44,   4.3.44,
                                                    4.3.56,   8.1.25
U.S.S.R. Academy of Medical Sciences 4.3.50
UTSG [see: Universities Transport Studies Group]

Valero, J.   4.4.34
Vanier, D.J.   (and Wotruba, T.R.)   4.2.39
Vass, P. (Dawson, R.F.F. and)   4.1.34
Veal, A.J. 1.2.39,   3.1.105,   9.2.20,   9.2.21
Vickerman, R.   3.1.56

Vidakovic, V. 3.1.23
Vincent, R.A. (-, Layfield, R.E. and Bardsley, M.) 2.1.6
Virginia University [see: University of Virginia]
Voorhees, A.M., & Associates Ltd., 3.3.36, 4.5.9 [see also:
          AMV Ltd. and Martin & Voorhees Associates]
Voorhees, A.M. (and Keith, R.A.) 4.5.20

Wabe, J.S. 3.1.101; (and Coles, O.B. 4.1.32)
Wachs, M. 3.2.20, 8.1.60; (Gillan, J. and) 3.2.14;
          (Tehan, C. and) 4.2.44
Wagon, D.J. (and Collins, P.H.) 4.1.71

Wallace, J.P. III (Sherret, A. and) 8.1.21
Ward, J.S. (Brooks, B.M., Ruffell-Smith, H.P., and) 4.3.11
Ward, V. (Ochojna, A.D. and) 2.4.18
Wardrop, J.G. (Smeed, R.J. and) 3.1.85
Warman, P. (Hollings, D. and) 8.3.23
Warner, S.L. 3.1.51
Warwick University [see: University of Warwick]
Wasey, E. 3.1.53
Washington Development Corporation 2.4.65
Washington Metropolitan Area Rapid Transit Authority/
                    Commission 4.2.6, 4.4.28;
                    (and Sidney Hollander Assoc.)
                                        4.2.15
Waters II, W.G. (and Tse, A.) 9.1.3
Watson, P.L. (Geok, L.L., -, and Holland, E.P.) 7.1.28
Watts, P.F. 2.4.20; (Cundill, M.A. and) 4.1.7
Webster, A.T. (and McGowan, J.) 4.1.13
Webster, F.V. 3.1.14, 4.1.26, 4.5.11, 4.5.18; (and
          Oldfield, R.H.) 3.1.82
Wedderburn, D. (-, Holder, A. and Reeves, T.) 4.1.91
Weinberger, M. 8.1.89
Weiss, S.F. (Burby III, R. and) 1.2.24
Welford, A.T. 3.2.44
Wells, W.D. 8.1.40
Welsh Office 3.2.71, 3.2.75, 3.3.54, 7.1.76, 9.5.14
Wenzel (Stringer and) (eds.) 3.2.60
West Midlands P.T.E. 7.1.60
West Yorkshire Metropolitan County Council (and West Yorkshire
          P.T.E.) 7.1.61; (Freeman Fox & Associates, Martin
          & Voorhees Assoc., and) 4.5.4; (R. Travers Morgan
          & Partners and) 4.1.3
West Yorkshire P.T.E. (West Yorkshire Metroploitan County
                            Council and) 7.1.61
Whalley, A. (Hillman, M. and) 2.4.33, 3.3.14-15; (Hillman,
          M., Henderson, I. and) 3.2.28-29, 3.2.37 3.2.63
Whitbread, A.W. (Daly, A.J., Rogers, K.G. and) 3.2.23
Whitbread, M. 8.2.13; (Lichfield, N., Kettle, P. and) 8.2.12
White, L.E. 1.2.44
White, M.J. 3.3.27
White, M.T. (Mullen, P. and) 5.1.2; (Mullen, P., Bursey,
          N.C. and) 2.3.7; (Pike, D.H., Fuller, P.I. and)
          2.3.7

White, P.R.   3.3.11,   4.1.35-37,   4.1.89,   4.5.10,   7.1.37;
          (and Holmes, R.W.)   4,1.18
Whittick, A.   2.4.2,   2.4.28,   2.4.43;   (Osborn, Sir F.J. and)
                                                          1.2.32
Wilbur Smith & Associates   4.4.5,   7.1.47
William Gillespie [see: Gillespie, William]
Williams, P.M.   4.1.53
Williams, T.E.H.   1.1.28; (and Munby, D.) (eds.) 3.3.39
Willing 9.1.6
Willis, E. (Moyes, A. and) 4.1.93
Willmott, P.   3.2.58,   5.1.3,   8.1.102; (Young, M. and)
                                              3.2.21-22
Wilson, A.G. 8.3.33; (et al) 8.3.25; (Hyman, G.M. and)
                                              3.1.46
Wilson, F.R.   3.1.32
Wilson, L. Hugh & Womersley, L.   2.2.2; (-, Jamieson &
          Mackay and William Gillespie & Associates) 2.4.24:
          (Redditch Development Corporation and)   2.4.48
Wilson Co., H.W.   9.3.16
Wing, R.F.   4.3.51
Wirz, H.M.   1.2.42
Wohl, M. (Kirby, R.F., Butt, K.U., Kemp, M.A., McGillivray,
          R.G. and)   4.4.35; (Meyer, J.R., Kain, J.F. and)
                                              3.4.6
Womersley, L. [see: Wilson, L. Hugh & Womersley, L.]
Wood, D. (Beck, R.J. and) 8.3.3
Woodhall, R. (Munt, P.W. and) 3.1.90
Woodson, W.E. (and Conover, D.W.) 4.3.22
Worcester, R.M.   4.2.11,   8.1.27   (ed.)
Working Group of Local Authority Associations 7.1.19
Working Group on Research into Road Traffic Noise 4.3.33
Working Party on Public Transport in Milton Keynes 2.4.37
World Health Organisation [WHO]4.3.49
Worrall, R.D. (Peterson, R.L. and) 3.3.8
Wotruba, T.R. (Vanier, D.J. and) 4.2.39
Wren, K. (Rawes, G.R. and) 1.2.57
Wren, M.B.   4.2.23
Wrekin Council, District of the (Colin Buchanan & Partners,
          Salop County Council, Telford Development Corporation,
          Midland Red Omnibus Co., -, The Independent Operators)
                                              2.3.1
Wright, L. (Trevelyan, R. and) 4.1.73
Wroot, R. (Downes, J.D. and) 3.1.84
Wytconsult 4.5.4

Yates, L.B.   4.1.9; (and Howerd, T.J.) 3.1.27
York University [see: University of York]
Young, M. (ed.) 3.2.53; (and Willmott, P.) 3.2.21-22;
                      (Gregory, P. and) 3.2.15
Young, T.D. (Hamilton, T.D. and) 4.1.90

Zahavi, Y.   3.1.88-89
Zehner, R.B.   1.1.2
Zupan, J.M. (Pushkarev, B.S. and) 6.1.8

Acknowledgements.

We gratefully acknowledge the financial and technical support
of Liverpool Polytechnic in the production of this bibliography. In particular we would like to thank Mr. S. Bruffell
and his department for the printing; Mrs. Shelagh Bruce for
supervising the typing; Denise Argent and Joan Stewart for so
ably and patiently typing the draft material; and Paul Holding
for his draughtsmanship.

The front cover was designed by students of Liverpool
Polytechnic's Graphic Design Department under the supervision
of Bruce Sabine, to whom particular thanks are due. Special
acknowledgement should also be made of the substantial
assistance provided by Reg Triplett and his staff at Liverpool
Polytechnic's Victoria Street Library.

The three new town Development Corporations have provided us
with much useful information and material and we would
particularly like to thank the following officials:-

Runcorn Development Corporation: Mr. J.F. Connell, Chief
Engineer, and his Department.

Skelmersdale Development Corporation: Mr. A.D. Hall,
Engineering Director;
Mr. A. Choraffa of the
Engineer's Department and Mr. P. Roberts of the Planning
Department.

Telford Development Corporation: Mr. T. Stevenson and Mr. T.
Wastling of the Department of
Engineering Services;

Mr. P. Fuller of the Planning Department and Dr. J. Maguire
of the Social Development Department.

We would also like to express our gratitude to the many other
individuals and organisations who assisted in supplying,
suggesting or discussing material to be included in the
bibliography. These include John Bradley and Malcolm Fairhurst
(London Transport Executive); Malcolm Buchanan (Colin Buchanan
and Partners); Jennifer Butler (Social and Community Planning
Research); Robin Carruthers (J. Travers Morgan and Partners);
M . J. Clarke and D.J. Oborne (University College, Swansea;)
Professor M. Cordey-Hayes, M. Benwell, P. Lucarotti and
V. Muldrew (Cranfield Institute of Technology Centre for
Transport Studies); Martin Dix (Oxford University Transport
Studies Unit); Christopher Doubleday (University of Cambridge:
the Martin Centre for Architectural and Urban Studies);
Richard Gillian (Computer Aided Marketing);Mr. K. Hanson
(Transport Librarian at Imperial College of Science and
Technology, London University); Dr. Mayer Hillman and Anne
Whalley (Political and Economic Planning);David Hollings and
Sheila Stark (Martin and Voorhees Associates);

Drs. Howard Kirby and John Murchland (University College, London: Traffic Research Group); John Madgett (Eastern Counties Omnibus Company, Norwich); Rex Medley (National Bus Company: Marketing and Operational Research Division, Peterborough); Paul Mullen (Department of the Environment); Jenny Potter (National Consumer Council); Dr. Stephen Potter (The Open University, New Towns Study Unit); Nicola Skelton and Mary Strain (University of Newcastle Upon Tyne: Transport Operations Research Group); Christopher Turner (Nathaniel Lichfield and Partners); Peter White (Polytechnic of Central London: Transport Studies Group); John Wood (Jamieson Mackay and Partners).

Help is also acknowledged from the following research establishments, consultants and other organisations: Alastair Dick and Associates; Age Concern; Birmingham University Department of Transportation and Environmental Planning; the Chicago Transit Authority; The Departments of the Environment and Transport Headquarters Library; General Motors Research Laboratories, Warren, Michigan; the Institute of Consumer Ergonomics, Loughborough University of Technology; Leeds University Institute for Transport Studies; the New Towns Association; Opinion Research Centre, London; the Transport and Road Research Laboratory's Technical Information and Library Services; Warwick University Urban Transport Group.

Finally, we should like to thank Dr. Brian Newton of the Department of Town and Country Planning, Liverpool Polytechnic, for his helpful comments on section 1·2 of the bibliography.